Purification of the Soul

Concept, Process and Means

By

Jamaal al-Din M. Zarabozo

2002

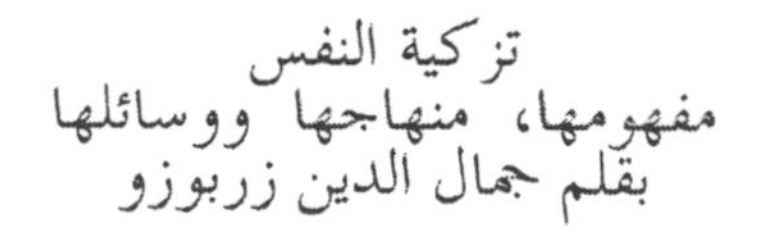
تزكية النفس
مفهومها، منهاجها ووسائلها
بقلم جمال الدين زربوزو

Purification of the Soul: Concept, Process and Means
By Jamaal al-Din M. Zarabozo

Published by:
Al-Basheer Company for Publications and Translations
10515 E. 40th Avenue, Suite 108
Denver, CO 80239-3264
U.S.A.
www.al-basheer.com

(Note: Not affiliated with Basheer Publications)

ISBN 1-891540-16-5

Preface

In the name of Allah, Most Compassionate, Most Merciful

All praises are due to Allah; we praise Him; we seek His help; we seek His forgiveness; and we seek His guidance. We seek refuge in Allah from the evil in our souls and the badness of our deeds. For whomever Allah guides, there is none to lead him astray. And for whomever He allows to go astray, there is none to guide him. I bear witness that there is none worthy of worship except Allah, for whom there is no partner. And I bear witness that Muhammad is His servant and Messenger. O believers, have *taqwa* [fear] of Allah according to His right and die not save as Muslims. O mankind, have *taqwa* of your Lord, the One who created you from one soul and created from it its mate and from them spread forth many men and women. And fear Allah from whom you demand your mutual rights and [do not cut] familial ties. Surely, Allah is ever an All-Watcher over you. O believers, have *taqwa* of Allah and always speak the truth. He will direct you to do righteous deeds and will forgive you your sins. And whosoever obeys Allah and His Messenger has indeed achieved a great achievement.

To proceed: Verily, the truest speech is the Book of Allah. The best guidance is the guidance of Muhammad. The worst affairs are the innovated ones. Every innovated matter is a heresy. And every heresy is a going astray. And every astray act is in the Hell-fire.

I praise and thank Allah for giving me the ability to complete this book. I pray that He accepts this work from me and forgives me for any mistakes and errors that have occurred herein.

As always, there are many people whom I would like to thank for their help in this particular work. First, I would like to express my thanks to sister Iman who edited and reviewed the work. I must also express my appreciation to Nahar al-Rashid, Humaidan al-Turki, Muhammad al-Osimi and Fahd al-Yahya. Of course, as always, my beloved wife's contribution and patience are greatly appreciated.

There are a couple of other points that need to be made in this preface. First, the translations of Quranic verses appearing in this work are a combination of the translations of Yusuf Ali, Khan and al-Hilaali and Saheeh International. Second, there are a few portions of this work that were taken verbatim or near-verbatim from this author's *Commentary on the Forty Hadith of al-Nawawi* or from this author's *IbnTaimiyyah: Mujtahid, Mujaahid and Mujaddid* (from the old *al-Basheer* magazine). I would like to express my appreciation for the permission to reproduce those portions in this work.

Finally, I pray that this work is beneficial to those who read it. If anyone has any comments, corrections or suggestions for this work, they should feel free to contact me through the publisher.

Jamaal Zarabozo
Boulder, CO
U.S.A.
Nov. 29, 2001
Ramadhaan 14, 1422

Table of Contents

Introduction

For a number of reasons, this is a very important time to be writing a book of this nature. First, the concept of purification of the soul as a whole is and always will be central to the message of Islam and to the welfare of humans, both in this life and in the Hereafter. Indeed, it was a main mission of the messengers and prophets themselves.

Second, there is a very strong need to shed light on the correct path of purification as delineated by the Quran and Sunnah—free of the foreign influence[1], deviations and heresies that have found their way into this realm of the religion and have caused a great deal of harm. The path described by the Quran and Sunnah is the only path that can result in a true purification of the soul. Indeed, it is the only path that is truly consistent with the purpose for which humans were created. Hence, any discussion of purification of the soul must rely heavily and exclusively on the Quran and the Sunnah and what can be correctly derived from those two sources.

Third, as Karzoon noted, many Muslims themselves are today being influenced by secular, materialistic psychology, leading them to neglect the spiritual side of humans and to ignore the guidance that Islam offers for the purification of the soul.[2] This influence often occurs at a level wherein the person himself may not be completely aware that it is occurring. For example,

---

[1] In the many books written throughout the history related to the soul and its purification, one can note the clear influence of Greek philosophy, Hindu beliefs and Christian monasticism. For a discussion of this point, see Abdul Hameed al-Bilaali, *Manhaj al-Taabieen fi Tarbiyah al-Nufoos* (Kuwait: Maktabah al-Manaar al-Islaamiyyah, 1997), p. 18.

[2] Anas Karzoon, *Manhaj al-Islaam fi Tazkiyah al-Nafs* (Jeddah: Daar Noor al-Maktabaat, 1997), vol. 1, p. 4. Kazrzoon gives the example of one Ahmad Ameen who, in a book entitled *al-Akhlaaq* ("Ethics"), claimed that Islam does not offer a complete methodology for dealing with the soul, only giving some words of ethical advice that are not of any practical importance.

many Muslims today, especially those who grew up or are studying in the West, read articles and books coming from non-Muslim writers. The concepts or suggestions offered in those works may seem very beneficial, benign or not contrary to Islamic teachings. However, upon closer inspection one may then realize that the philosophy behind those works and their goals are not consistent with those of Islam. For example, this author has met some Muslims who upon reading about Yoga and meditation found these acts quite attractive without realizing that the manner and goal of those acts are different from those of Islam and, furthermore, those acts were taking them away from the correct forms of prayer, contemplation and remembrance found in the Quran and Sunnah.[1]

Fourth, for some time now, there has been an Islamic revival spreading throughout the Muslim world. Upon closer inspection, it seems that this revival is somewhat tenuous and delicate, in the sense that for many Muslims it is more of an "emotional" phenomenon. In order for this revival to be truly successful and lead to what it needs to lead to, it must be guided by the comprehensive teachings of Islam. First and foremost among those teachings is what is related to the purification of the soul. Without the purification of the souls, the revival will only be on the outer shell and will, in fact, be a "deceptive" revival, in the sense that the inner consciousness will not have been reformed and the lapse back to pre-revival times may be very close at hand. Indeed, without the purification of the souls, the very goals of the revival from the outset may be wrong. Thus, the revival may be used simply as a tool to remove an oppressive regime, for

---

[1] Badri comments on the difference between Islamic contemplation and that of Eastern religions, "Contemplation as a form of worship may, at first, be viewed within the sphere of recent interest of Western psychology in meditation procedures and their ability to bring altered states of consciousness. However, although Islamic contemplation can achieve the relaxing benefits of meditation... it differs from all the other forms of meditative procedures which are derived from Eastern religions in that its main objective is more cognitive and intellectual. In Islamic contemplation, altered states of consciousness are not an end in themselves, as the goal is a deeper insightful knowledge of God as the Creator and Sustainer of the Universe." Malik Badri, *Contemplation: An Islamic Psychospiritual Study* (Herndon, VA: IIIT, 2000), pp. 1-2.

example, followed by a return to a new secular, materialistic way of life instead of a truly Islamic society.[1]

Fifth, as noted by al-Abdul Lateef, in this day and age, one can easily become preoccupied with many things of this world. This preoccupation can be so great that one can forget that his soul is in need of constant watching and purification. When this occurs, the hearts become hard, it becomes difficult to perform righteous deeds and one is overcome by the allure of this world and its attractions.[2] Hence, today one needs to be reminded of the concept and means of purification so that the heart may remain alive and not drowned in the godlessness of contemporary cultures. Otherwise, the heart can become so engulfed in materialism and consumerism that it fails to listen to the reminders in its own soul and in the revelation that has come from Allah.[3]

Sixth, those who should know and understand the complete guidance of Islam best are the people known as the *Ahl al-Sunnah wa al-Jamaah,* those who are dedicated to following the way of the Prophet (peace and blessings of Allah be upon him), his Companions and those who followed along their path. These are the people who rely upon the true sources that delineate the correct path to follow. However, even though the purification of the soul was stressed by the Prophet (peace and blessings of Allah be upon him) and his Companions, al-Abdul Lateef notes that when one considers the members of the *Ahl al-Sunnah wa al-Jamaah* today, one finds them divided, fighting, bickering, following their desires and so forth.[4] Hence, the members of the *Ahl al-Sunnah wa*

---

[1] This might even explain why some Muslims resort to extremist or terrorist acts, going beyond the limits set by the Shareeah. When the Muslim purifies his soul, he will readily and willingly remain within the commands set by Allah, having full trust in Allah that the proper ends will result.

[2] Abdul Azeez al-Abdul Lateef, *Maalim fi al-Sulook wa Tazkiyah al-Nufoos* (Riyadh: Daar al-Watan, 1414 A.H.), p. 56.

[3] In Yassine's words, "It seems impossible to make a modern man listen to reason when he himself has little reason to live beyond the fearsome desire to enjoy the 'good' things of consumerism." Abdessalam Yassine, *Winning the Modern World for Islam* (Iowa City, IA: Justice and Spirituality Publishing, Inc., 2000), p. xv. Modern man not only fails to listen to reason but he also fails to listen to the clear signs from his own soul that recognizes the disastrous path he is following.

[4] Al-Abdul Lateef, p. 11.

al-Jamaah themselves are sorely in need of a reminder concerning the purification of the soul and the true way to achieve that purification. In this sense, one could think of this work as echoing or reminding one of Allah's words,

أَلَمْ يَأْنِ لِلَّذِينَ ءَامَنُوٓا۟ أَن تَخْشَعَ قُلُوبُهُمْ لِذِكْرِ ٱللَّهِ وَمَا نَزَلَ مِنَ
ٱلْحَقِّ وَلَا يَكُونُوا۟ كَٱلَّذِينَ أُوتُوا۟ ٱلْكِتَٰبَ مِن قَبْلُ فَطَالَ عَلَيْهِمُ
ٱلْأَمَدُ فَقَسَتْ قُلُوبُهُمْ ۖ وَكَثِيرٌ مِّنْهُمْ فَٰسِقُونَ

"Has not the time arrived for the believers that their hearts be humbly affected by Allah's reminder and the truth which has been revealed (to them), and that they should not become like those to whom was given revelation aforetime, but long ages passed over them and their hearts grew hard? In fact, many among them are rebellious transgressors" (*al-Hadeed* 16).

Seventh, the Muslim world is once again experiencing a period of clear trials and tribulations. As this author writes these words, non-Muslim forces are bombing yet another Muslim country. Even more confusing is the fact that Muslims themselves are supporting and participating in this semi-genocide. These kinds of trials drive many people to all sorts of extremism while many others are driven to confusion, anxiety or despair. The purified soul understands and handles everything in the proper manner. He is able to see things in a very different light and, hence, Allah willing, he is guided to make the correct decisions concerning such situations.

Eighth, some of the *Ahl al-Sunnah* have a tendency to concentrate on other essential matters (such as academic matters of belief, fiqh, the grading of hadith and so forth) while failing to also concentrate on the question of purification of the soul. The problem with this approach, as al-Bilaali noted, is that the issues of purification of the soul are almost completely non-apparent among those who have some knowledge of the Quran and Sunnah. This has left the door open for the charlatans and mystics to spread their teachings although they have no sound source in the Quran and Sunnah.[1]

Indeed, some of the *ahl al-Sunnah* intentionally may have a tendency to shy away from this topic since it has become the domain of the Sufs and much of what has been written on this topic has definitely been influenced by the thoughts of the Sufis. It is sometimes difficult to read about this topic and determine what is correct according to the Quran and Sunnah and what is beyond the correct and true path of the Prophet Muhammad (peace and blessings of Allah be upon him).

A complete, scholarly, balanced, fair and just critique of the entire concept and structure of Sufism is beyond the realm of this work. Indeed, that is deserving of a complete volume in itself and it was not the goal or purpose of this present work. However, whenever discussing purification of the soul, one is forced to deal with the question of Sufism or mysticism in Islam. In many ways, the adherents of Sufism have claimed "the purification of the soul" to be their specialty. Many times they give the impression that they alone hold the secret to it. They imply that their path is some special, exclusive path that alone can achieve it. Therefore, any comprehensive work on the purification of the soul must deal with their claims head on. Indeed, Islahi eloquently expressed this author's thoughts some forty years earlier when he wrote in his work on self-purification,

> Since the subject of discussion of this book is the same as that of mysticism [that is, Sufism], it has been my unpleasant duty to criticise the mysticism generally in vogue. It is possible to hurt the feelings of those who cannot tolerate criticism of the system adopted by them, but I am sure no impartial reader will find my criticism devoid of the spirit of inquiry (of the Truth) and that of upholding the teachings of the Quran and the Sunnah.[2]

---

[1] Al-Bilaali, p. 15.

[2] Amin Ahsan Islahi, *Self-Purification and Development* (Delhi: Adam Publishers and Distributors, 2000), p. viii. He then goes on to write (p. viii), "I have carefully gone through the objections raised by some people on some issues discussed in this book and have found nothing

Another point that should be made in this introduction is that this author, to the best of his ability, has used only authentic or acceptable hadith and narrations in this work. In this author's view, this is an approach that should be followed no matter what the topic is. However, on this particular topic it is of extreme importance to point this out because this is a topic concerning which many liberties were taken when it came to the hadith and reports quoted as evidence.[1] Numerous fabricated and very weak hadith can be found in works directly or indirectly related to purification of the soul. Although purification of the soul is an issue that is central to the overall message of Islam, Karzoon notes that the reason behind this haphazard use of hadith and lack of authenticity was that these topics were considered matters of *fadhaail* (virtuous deeds) and a strict verification of the hadith used was not required.[2] Even given the difference of opinion concerning the use of weak hadith while discussing the merits of deeds,[3] there is no excuse for the types of hadith and reports that one can find in books related to purification of the soul. It is only by avoiding those types of reports that one can find the true and pure Islamic methodology of purification of the soul. Therefore, again, this author has done his best to avoid any hadith that is

---

noteworthy in them. Some people are very active in the support of mysticism but they neither know its good points nor its faults. Such empty shells of criticism do not at all help the cause of the Truth." Incidentally, this same work was published years earlier as: Amin Ahsan Islahi, *How to Attain True Piety and Righteousness* (Safat, Kuwait: Islamic Book Publishers, 1982). The above quote may be found on pp. 1-2 of the earlier edition. (Note that it is the publication from Adam Publishers that will be referred to in the remainder of this work.)

[1] A secondary problem concerning many works concerning more "spiritual" topics exists with respect to the reports from many of the early scholars. Abdul Malik al-Qasim noted this problem concerning the many works on *zuhd* (living a simple life). He wrote, "Some of these books contain exaggerations and unduly elevate some of creation above their deserved status. Also, these books contain fake tales and superstitious accounts conveyed from the Sufis and other deviant sects." Abdul Malik al-Qasim, *Silent Moments: The Description of Before & After Death Aspects* (Riyadh: Darussalam, 1999), p. 7.

[2] Karzoon, p. 5.

[3] This author has discussed in detail the question of the use of weak hadith in Jamaal Zarabozo, *Commentary on the Forty Hadith of al-Nawawi* (Boulder, CO: al-Basheer Company for Publications and Translations, 1998), vol. 1, pp. 80-101.

clearly unauthentic according to the principles of the sciences of hadith.[1]

Finally, a work of this nature is very difficult and compelling for thc author as well as, perhaps, for many readers. Upon studying the examples and lives of the prophets, the Companions and later scholars, as well as some of their beautiful insights, it is easy to get the feeling of being on the outside looking in. Sometimes, it is truly difficult to compare oneself with those noble people. However, such does not remove the obligation of learning about these important issues and of conveying them to others. At the very least, this knowledge should alert the person to what he should aspire to or what he can, Allah willing, become. When a person falls short of the mark, as many inevitably do, this knowledge should help him realize his shortcoming. This realization, in turn, should drive him to seek Allah's forgiveness, Allah's help and Allah's guidance. Such may further help him along the path of improving himself, purifying his soul and drawing himself closer to Allah.

The approach to be followed in this work is as follows:

Chapter 1 is a discussion of the importance of purification of the soul for all of mankind, Muslims as well as non-Muslims. In

---

[1] This author has personally done an in-depth study of the hadith quoted by Abu Haamid al-Ghazaali in his very influential work *Ihyaa Uloom al-Deeen* ("Revival of the Religious Sciences"), in the section entitled "The Book of Knowledge." Al-Ghazaali's use of hadith is not atypical of the hadith used in works related to the purification of the soul. In fact, in some respects his work is actually better because the hadith he quotes are, for the most part, at least traceable to some of the books of hadith. In "The Book of Knowledge," al-Ghazaali quoted approximately 218 hadith. Relying mostly on the works of al-Iraaaqi, ibn al-Subki and al-Zabeedi, this author found that of those 218 hadith, 67 were acceptable (meaning either *sahih* or *hasan*), 64 were weak and 86 were completely rejected (meaning very weak, fabricated or false). It is very disheartening to find well over one-third or approximately 39% are completely unacceptable while only approximately 31% are acceptable hadith. Indeed, the weak and the completely rejected combined for approximately 69% of the hadith that al-Ghazaali (may Allah forgive him) used in that work. This work is the basis for many works and concepts that came after al-Ghazaali. (The above numbers are considered approximations because there were a small number of hadith concerning which this author made no final conclusion concerning their status and there were a few other hadith that were borderline, easily falling into one of two categories.)

that chapter, there is a brief review and critique of other approaches to this issue.

Chapter 2 offers a definition of the terms *tazkiyah* or purification and *nafs* or soul. The chapter then attempts to offer a comprehensive and unique definition of the compound term "purification of the soul."

Chapter 3 discusses the importance of self-purification in the light of the Quran and Sunnah. In particular, that chapter discusses the relevance of this topic to the plight of the Muslim world today.

Chapter 4 presents the goal and scope of the correct Islamic vision of purification of the soul. Historically speaking, there has been a great deal of misunderstanding concerning both of these central issues, that is, the goal and the scope of spiritual purification.

Chapter 5 discusses the process of purification as outlined in a very important *qudsi* hadith. Each of the steps of the process are clearly spelled out and discussed in detail.

Chapter 6 is entitled "Means and Measures to Help One Along the Path of Purification" and offers practical steps that assist the individual move towards his goal of spiritual purification.

Chapter 7 covers the impediments and dangers to spiritual purification. It is usually not sufficient to know what one should do but one also needs to know what are the important matters that one must avoid.

Chapter 8 is a comparison of the path of purification as outlined in Chapter 6 with the path espoused by the Sufis. As noted, Sufis seem to proclaim themselves as the masters of spiritual purification. In this chapter, some of their major claims concerning this topic are critiqued in the light of the pure teachings of the Quran and Sunnah.

The next chapter, Chapter 9, is a brief and succinct review of the major benefits and results that accrue from following the correct path of purification as found in the Quran and authentic hadith of the Prophet (peace and blessings of Allah be upon him). This chapter covers the benefits and results for the individual as well as for the Muslim Nation as a whole. It also covers the benefits that accrue in both this world and the Hereafter.

Chapter 1
Mankind and the Purification of the Soul

A Concern for Virtually All of Mankind

In reality, the question of the soul and its proper treatment is not a central issue for Muslims alone. Much of mankind has been concerned with this question for ages. It seems natural for an individual to wonder about his soul.[1] He may ask himself questions like the following: "What is the soul?" "Is there anything special about my soul or is it just like any other animal crawling on this earth?" "What is my soul's potential?" "What is the way that I am supposed to behave?" "Is there some way to improve my soul?" "What are the ways and means to follow that will improve my soul and allow it to reach its full potential?" "Is my soul in need of purification? If yes, what are the means by which I may purify my soul?"

Furthermore—and this is a phenomenon that has been seen over and over again in the secular and agnostic West—when one proclaims, "I know the way to purify your soul and the secret to life," he will immediately attract listeners and followers, even if his message has no truth or value to it at all. This is a sign of how desperate humans are when it comes to knowing the secrets of their souls, finding the way to purify the soul, finding the way to true contentment and eternal happiness. It is difficult for a human to live with this unknown factor in his life. Furthermore, it must be considered normal to have a great deal of concern over what is

---

[1] Indeed, as shall be discussed later, Allah has created humans with a natural disposition towards wanting to know the truth and recognizing the truth. There is a natural tendency to accept or recognize that there must be something beyond the physical world that one sees around him.

going to happen to oneself in the future. What, for example, is the reality after death and how can one prepare his soul for that inevitable occurrence? Ibn Hazm once noted, "I have tried to find one goal which everyone would agree to be excellent and worthy of being striven after. I have found one only: to be free from anxiety... Dispelling anxiety is a goal upon which all nations agree... In the case of every other objective there will always be some people who do not desire it. For example... there are some who have no interest in amassing a fortune, preferring abstinence to ownership..."[1]

Almost every human recognizes that there is something more to this life than the physical world around them, although some may never wish to face that fact. Most recognize that the matters of the mind and the heart are something beyond the mere physical presence that humans witness. Those who recognize this fact often seek the answers to those questions that are troubling their soul. They seek that path that they believe is out there: the path that purifies their souls and brings them to their full potential.

However, a study of the plethora of answers to the above and similar other questions shows that most of mankind is simply confused when it comes to answering them. Indeed, their contradictory views show that they are at a complete loss. For example, Karzoon notes that modern psychology has distorted the concept of the soul and nature of mankind in the greatest possible fashion. Man, to many modern day thinkers and psychologists, is no more than a mere animal driven by natural instincts. Values and morals have become virtually meaningless—with some psychologists proclaiming that there is no such thing as sin or a

---

[1] Ali ibn Hazm al-Andalusi, *Al-Akhlaaq wa al-Seer fi Mudaawaah al-Nufoos* (Shariqah, UAE: Daar al-Fath, 1993), pp. 23-24. The above English translation came from Ibn Hazm al-Andalusi, *In Pursuit of Virtue* (London: Ta Ha Publishers, 1998), pp. 121-122. The word ibn Hazm used, which was translated as "anxiety," was *hamm,* which does not translate well into just one English word. Lane has translated it as, "Anxiety; or disquietude, or trouble, of mind; solicitude; care; or grief or sorrow; distress or disquietude, affecting the heart of mind, by reason of some harm, or annoyance, that is expected to happen; differing from غم [*ghamm*] which signifies distress, or disquietude, affecting the heart of mind, by reason of what has happened..." E. W. Lane, *Arabic-English Lexicon* (Cambridge, England: The Islamic Texts Society, 1984), vol. 2, p. 3045.

morally wrong act. The human has become a physical body without a soul.[1]

Before discussing the Islamic definition and means of purification of the soul, it is appropriate at this time to offer a brief review of some of the other approaches that attempt to answer some of the fundamental questions concerning the soul, its existence, purpose and path of purification or happiness. This short overview and critique will allow the Muslim to be even more appreciative of the guidance that Allah has bestowed upon him. Out of gratitude and thankfulness for Allah's guidance, the Muslim should then, in turn, take this guidance more seriously and intend to abide by it to the best of his ability.

A Brief Review of Other Approaches and Conceptions

A comprehensive review of other beliefs and ideologies concerning the soul and its health, although very important and possibly extremely enlightening, is well beyond the scope of this work. However, at least a brief review of some other approaches is definitely called for.[2] (The following critiques may seem one-sided. That is just for the sake of brevity. It does not mean to imply that there is nothing positive or good about any of the approaches or faiths covered. Indeed, Judaism and Christianity may have some remnants of the true teachings that have come down from their prophets that are extremely beneficial and enlightening. However, this critique is simply meant to demonstrate that in their totality they are incapable of leading to the true purification—and hence true happiness—of the soul.)

The "Eastern Faiths"

In the West today, particularly since the time of the musical group the Beatles, many are looking towards the "East" to find answers to their troubling questions related to the soul.

---

[1] Cf., Karzoon, vol. 1, p. 2.

[2] Obviously, there are other religions and belief systems. "Completeness" in this regard is beyond the scope of this work. What has been presented is meant to be representative of what exists.

Hence, a discussion of Hinduism and Buddhism is particularly warranted at this point.

Hinduism

Hinduism could be aptly described as a philosophical and mythological system of belief rooted in Indian history. It is difficult to determine what it has to offer with respect to the purification of the soul, especially since it is open to virtually any belief system and way of life. *The Encyclopedia Britannica* explains,

> In principle, Hinduism incorporates all forms of belief and worship without necessitating the selection or elimination of any. It is axiomatic that no religious idea in India ever dies or is superseded--it is merely combined with the new ideas that arise in response to it. Hindus are inclined to revere the divine in every manifestation, whatever it may be, and are doctrinally tolerant, allowing others--including both Hindus and non-Hindus--whatever beliefs suit them best. A Hindu may embrace a non-Hindu religion without ceasing to be a Hindu, and because Hindus are disposed to think synthetically and to regard other forms of worship, strange gods, and divergent doctrines as inadequate rather than wrong or objectionable, they tend to believe that the highest divine powers complement one another. Few religious ideas are considered to be irreconcilable. The core of religion does not depend on the existence or nonexistence of God or on whether there is one god or many. Because religious truth is said to transcend all verbal definition, it is not conceived in dogmatic terms. Moreover, the tendency of Hindus to distinguish themselves from others on the basis of practice (orthopraxy) rather than doctrine (orthodoxy) further de-emphasizes doctrinal differences.[1]

[1] Copyright 1994-1999 Encyclopædia Britannica.

Therefore, one finds that Hinduism is actually a massive collection of different and sometimes contradicting beliefs. For example, Hindus are famous for revering the cow and considering it the mother of humans while, in reality, this is true only for some Hindus. Other Hindus see nothing wrong in even eating cows.

Hinduism is a strange combination of seeking to please a number of gods while at the same time believing that there is actually only one reality called Brahman. Again, *The Encyclopedia Britannica* states,

> The pervasive force lying within all being, Brahman is conceived as the "self," or *atman*, of all forms of life, and many Hindu traditions portray the conscious realization of the identity between the individual self and the cosmic principle as the final religious goal.[1]

In sum, as the *Upanishad* state, "Whoever thus knows 'I am Brahman!' becomes this All."[2] It is by this means that one escapes the endless transmigration of the souls.

This belief is essentially the same belief as that of *wahdah al-wujood* or monism that is found among many Sufi groups. What this means is that everything that occurs and all creatures—the evil, the despicable and the devilish—are nothing but part and parcel of that one entity that Hindus are trying to discover they are all part of. In sum, the whole of the experienced existence is nothing but illusion without any real substance save being a

---

[1] Copyright 1994-1999 Encyclopædia Britannica. The Britannica also states, "Hindus believe in an uncreated, eternal, infinite, transcendent, and all-embracing principle, which, 'comprising in itself being and non-being,' is the sole reality, the ultimate cause and foundation, source, and goal of all existence. This ultimate reality is called *brahman.* As the All, *brahman* causes the universe and all beings to emanate from itself, transforms itself into the universe, or assumes its appearance. *Brahman* is in all things and is the Self (*atman*) of all living beings. *Brahman* is the creator, preserver, or transformer and reabsorber of everything. Although it is Being in itself, without attributes and qualities and hence impersonal, it may also be conceived of as a personal high God, usually as Vishnu (Visnu) or Shiva. This fundamental belief in and the essentially religious search for ultimate reality--*i.e.,* the One that is the All--have continued almost unaltered for more than 30 centuries and have been the central focus of India's spiritual life." Ludwig also states that "to know Brahman as the ultimate is the goal" [Theodore Ludwig, *The Sacred Paths of the East* (Upper Saddle River, NJ: Prentice-Hall, 2001), p. 54].

[2] Quoted from Ludwig, p. 63.

"projection superimposed on the one Reality, the Brahman."[1] In the history of Sufism, this belief system, not surprisingly, had a horrendous effect as, when one truly claims to believe in this, all things become permissible to the person. There is no distinction between good and evil. There is no distinction between what is lawful and what is not lawful. There is not even any distinction between the object of one's worship and adoration and the most vile part of the universe. In fact, all of those things become meaningless since everything is one and the same in the ultimate reality.

In practice, though, the claimed belief in the ultimate realization that all form part of one Brahman does not deny the fact that in worldly life, the Hindu is, in reality, trying to appease and please all different types of gods.[2] Furthermore, these are gods that are often times depicted in their scriptures as warring against each other and hating each other.[3] Allah has described the plight of the person that has put himself into this belief system and situation,

ضَرَبَ ٱللَّهُ مَثَلًا رَّجُلًا فِيهِ شُرَكَآءُ مُتَشَٰكِسُونَ وَرَجُلًا سَلَمًا

لِّرَجُلٍ هَلْ يَسْتَوِيَانِ مَثَلًا ٱلْحَمْدُ لِلَّهِ بَلْ أَكْثَرُهُمْ لَا يَعْلَمُونَ

"Allah puts forth a similitude: a [slave] man belong to many partners disputing with one another [like those who worship more than one god] and a [slave] man belonging to only one man [like those who worship only Allah]. Are those two equal in comparison? All the praises are to Allah. Yet most of them know not" (*al-Zumar* 29). From an Islamic perspective, there is no way for a person to please more than one god as, by the Islamic definition of the word "God", God must be the thing that is

---

[1] Ludwig, p. 55.

[2] Indeed, phallic symbols are used to represent some of their gods. One can only imagine the effect that this must have on one's soul as he takes this part of the anatomy to represent his god. Other gods are depicted in a manner that is unbecoming even most Hindus themselves, with sexual adventures and so forth. See, for example, the story of Krishna in Ludwig, pp. 66-67.

[3] For example, Brahma (the creator god) argued with Vishnu over who was greater only to discover that Shiva (a third god) was the supposed greatest, supremely powerful god—even though Shiva is not the creator god. Cf., Ludwig, p. 57.

foremost in one's heart. But what must be even more frustrating is the attempt to please various gods with different needs while claiming to believe that those gods and oneself are actually all one and the same reality.

The Vedas, a collection of Hindu writings, stress the torture of the body and the denial of anything that the soul may be inclined to. They present the belief in the transmigration of the soul. Thus, Hindus put their bodies through extreme challenges and tests to remove what they have done in the past and what they may do in the future life. Actually, they have very little hope of rescue from this circle of transmigration. Even death is not a rescue or an escape as it simply implies the moving to another body and going through the same type of process over again. The Hindus are also known for their class system. The lowest class, "the untouchables" have been eternally created to serve the priestly class and others. They are the slaves of the other classes and there is no escape for them from that plight.

Buddhism

In the midst of the Hindu (Brahman) religious thought was born the prince Siddhartha Gautama, who later became known as the Buddha ("the awakened one"), due to his self-professed claim of discovering the truth behind this existence. Displeased with what he found as the source of enlightenment, he presented his own views on many issues—never claiming to be inspired by God, indeed even refusing to delve into those many and natural metaphysical questions whose answers the vast majority of humans seek.[1]

The Encyclopedia Britannica gives the basic teachings of virtually all Buddhists[2] as,

---

[1] Cf., Ludwig, pp. 110-111.

[2] Buddhism broke up into three main divisions (Theravada, Mahayana and Tantrism), in part due to external influences. Some of these groups saw Buddha as a god who came to rid the world of its evils, others worshipped him as a holy saint and so forth. The Mahayana dates from about the First Century CE and seems to be the furthest away from the original teachings of Buddha.

> The essence of the Buddha's early preaching was said to be the Four Noble Truths: (1) life is fundamentally disappointment and suffering; (2) suffering is a result of one's desires for pleasure, power, and continued existence; (3) in order to stop disappointment and suffering one must stop desiring; and (4) the way to stop desiring and thus suffering is the Noble Eightfold Path--right views, right intention, right speech, right action, right livelihood, right effort, right awareness, and right concentration. The realization of the truth of anatman (no eternal self) and *pratitya-samutpada* (the law of dependent origination[1]) was taught as essential for the indescribable state of release called nirvana ("blowing out").[2]

Hence, Buddhists view this world as being filled with pain and afflictions. The source of that pain and affliction is one's pleasures and hopes. Pleasures result in pain. If the soul cannot achieve those hopes, it once again feels pain. Therefore, the pleasures and hopes need to be removed for true peace. Hence, Buddhists view the soul, with its natural urges and needs, as being evil and one must free itself from it. Anything that the soul longs for must be cut off and overridden. This is in order to attain nirvana ("transcendent freedom"), which is described as being like the blowing out of a candle. This is where one realizes the truth of eternal nothingness and that everything is simply an illusion.[3]

---

[1] Taken to its logical conclusion, this belief in "the law of dependent origination" or "dependent co-arising" is a very pessimistic view of the world in which everything is predetermined by what has gone before without the existence of a god or creator. Ludwig (p. 103) describes this belief in this manner, "Dependent co-arising is essentially a doctrine of causality, showing the interconnectedness of everything. There is no god who causes everything; but it is also false to assert that everything happens randomly by chance. Rather, the truth is that everything and every event are caused by something prior in an interrelated process. Every condition contributes to the next, but is itself conditioned by countless other determining conditions."

[2] Copyright 1994-1999 Encyclopædia Britannica.

[3] Karzoon, vol. 1, pp. 85-86. Yoga is used as a means to achieve nirvana. The word means "union" in the sense that the person becomes united with his soul. Some claim that there is a great deal of health benefits to Yoga, even for those who do not believe in the philosophy of Buddhism. Karzoon noted that there is a book available in Arabic, *al-Yoogha fi Meezaan al-Naqd al-Ilmi* that demonstrates the falseness of such claims. See Karzoon, vol. 1, pp. 87-88.

The end result of this fleeing from the requirements of this worldly life and the fact that only monks can achieve true nirvana in a future life leads to the fact that, as Nadwi describes it, "The Buddhist religion has instructed virtuous people to abandon the world and has advised them to get rid of all wealth and, when they feel hungry, to take their begging bowls and stand at people's doors."[1] The result is that they, supposedly the pious, have to rely and depend on those who are not pious and who earn money wrongfully to give them if they want to or not give them if they do not want to. This will definitely have its effect on one's heart, as one's heart is usually attached to the person who provides for him. Hence, they are going to end up having a need and love for others and that must go against their claim of giving up all attachments and need in this world.[2]

Furthermore, in Buddhist thought, one is put under complete control of another human, who, in reality, may or may not possess true piety. This is explained in *The Encyclopedia Britannica*,

> Adherents of the Vajrayana tradition believe that as all things are in truth of one nature--the void--the physical-mental processes can be used as a vehicle for enlightenment. In the *Kalacakra Tantra* it is written that the Buddha taught that in this age of degeneration enlightenment must be achieved through one's own body, which contains the whole cosmos. This doctrine is taught in all the tantras. Vajrayana specialists warn, however, that in order to use correctly the body's

---

[1] Sulaiman Nadwi, *Worship in Islam* (Karachi: Darul Ishaat, 1994), p. 183.

[2] From the Islamic perspective: "The important point for the Muslim is to realize that Allah and Allah alone is able to truly grant his needs. Therefore, he should turn only to Allah and realize that, even if Allah uses other humans to meet his needs, the one who truly fulfilled his needs is Allah. Beyond that understanding, a Muslim should do his best never to rely on others but to work for himself and, by the help of Allah, accomplish every deed without the help of any other human. In fact, it is recorded in *Sahih Muslim* that the Prophet (peace be upon him) took an oath from a number of Companions, such as Abu Bakr, Abu Dharr and Thaubaan, that they would never ask for anything from anyone. If any of these Companions dropped their stick or their camel reins, they would never ask anyone to pick it up for them but would get it themselves." Quoted from the author's *Commentary on the Forty Hadith of al-Nawawi*, vol. 2, p. 749.

> processes to achieve an identification of the void with compassion, the aspirant must follow absolutely the instructions of a master or teacher who has been initiated into the mysteries. Such a master alone can direct every step so that the pupil learns to control mental and physical processes instead of being dominated by them. Therefore, the first step toward enlightenment in Vajrayana practice is the undergoing of initiation by a master.[1]

The process toward the ultimate goal of "enlightenment" is further described in the same encyclopedia,

> This process of advancement toward enlightenment involves the identification of the initiate with gods or goddesses that represent various cosmic forces... After this visualization, the initiate identifies with the divinities and finds that each in turn is *shunyata,* or voidness. The culmination of this process, called *vajrasattva yoga,* gives the initiate a diamondlike body beyond all duality. Four stages in the process are described in four different groups of tantras, the *Kriya-tantra, Carya-tantra, Yoga-tantra,* and *Anuttarayoga-tantra.* These four stages are likened to the fourfold phases of courtship: the exchange of glances, a pleasing or encouraging smile, the holding of hands, and consummation in the sexual act. The first stage involves external ritual acts, whereas the second combines these outward acts with contemplation. The third stage involves only contemplation, and the fourth is the unification of all dualities in the sexual act, symbolically or effectively. This last stage, however, is divided into two phases. The first involves the use by the initiate of controlled imagination, which allows him to experience the union on an ideational level. The second phase is the *maithuna,* or sexual coupling. This act, however, cannot be construed as an ordinary

---

[1] Copyright 1994-1999 Encyclopædia Britannica. The reader familiar with Sufism will readily note the clear influence or overlap of Buddhist thought on Sufi teachings on this point.

> physical mating, because the initiate has already realized the voidness of all things, allowing him to act with perfect control over his emotions and without attachment. Whereas the ordinary sexual act gives rise to only momentary pleasure, this *maithuna* is considered to be an appropriate technique for attaining enlightenment and eternal bliss. It is quite easy to misinterpret the *Guhyasamaja-tantra* when it states that adultery and eating of human flesh are actions of the bodhisattva if one does not realize that this imagery points to the belief that voidness alone exists, beyond good or evil, or that the initiate must act only with compassion for the benefit of the salvation of the world.[1]

In his Master's thesis, being a study of Buddhism and its relationship to Sufism, Naumsook makes the following noteworthy conclusions concerning Buddhism,

> Buddhism nullified the divine and its worship. [This fact] constitutes a big lacuna in this religion for belief in God is instinctual or natural to human nature. Overlooking this creates much difficulty. This is why the followers of Buddha filled this deficiency by worshipping the Buddha [himself].
>
> There are also many contradictions, doubts, misunderstandings and difficulties in the teaching of Buddha...
>
> Buddha's teachings call for the curbing of sexual desire... It advocates this by adopting a monastic form of life through deserting of society, family, property and so on... [This] brings in egoism and neglect of duties towards friends and society.[2]

---

[1] Copyright 1994-1999 Encyclopædia Britannica. This author does not feel that this passage needs further comment except it should be noted once again that many Sufis come to the same conclusion.

[2] Abdullah Mustafa Naumsook, *Al-Boodhiyyah: Tareekhuhaa wa Aqaaiduhaa wa Alaaqah al-Soofiyyah biha* (Riyadh: Adhwa al-Salaf, 1999), modified from its abstract in English, pp. 2-3.

The Jewish and Christian Traditions

Moving now to those faiths which, from an Islamic perspective, were definitely originally rooted in revelation from God, Judaism and Christianity need to be discussed. One would expect such faiths to have a better concept of the soul and its purification. Unfortunately, though, the original teachings of the prophets were not kept pure of adulteration and distortion. This adulteration and distortion has so perverted the teachings of the prophets that much of what is found in the Bible is actually very damaging with respect to purification of the soul, as shall be demonstrated shortly.

As shall be discussed later in an Islamic perspective, one of the most important facets in purifying the soul is the correct and proper belief about God, the Lord and Creator. A distorted view of God, especially one where God Himself is pictured as having traits that noble humans would not want to possess, will definitely negatively impact the soul and the feeling of any need to purify the soul. If God Himself is not perfect, pure and righteous, why should any human creature of God feel that he must try to purify himself? The obvious distortions of the Bible[1] concerning God and His attributes are plentiful and can supply anyone with an excuse to also behave in an evil manner. For the sake of brevity, only a few examples illustrating this point shall be given.

The *New International Version* of Genesis 3:8-11, reads,

> 8 Then the man and his wife heard the sound of the LORD God as he was walking in the garden in the cool of the day, and they hid from the LORD God among the trees of the garden. 9 But the LORD God called to the man, "Where are you?" 10 He answered, "I heard you in the garden, and I was afraid because I was naked; so I hid." 11 And he said, "Who told you that you were naked? Have you eaten from the tree that I commanded you not to eat from?"

---

[1] For an excellent discussion of how and why the Old Testament and the New Testament were not preserved properly and a comparison with how the Quran was preserved, see M. Mustafa Azami, *Quranic Text—Recording and Collection: A Comparative Study with the Old and New Testaments* (forthcoming), *passim*.

Here, God is pictured as walking in the garden in the cool of the day. What is even more astonishing is that Adam and Eve were able to hide from God and he had to ask, "Where are you?" If a human is able to hide from Him in the garden, how is it that this Lord is going to have knowledge of the sins that people commit? It would be difficult for any human to gender in his heart the kind of love and fear of God that he should have when he believes that his God is so faulty and weak that an event like this could occur to him.

In Genesis 32:24-28,[1] there is the story and literal description of Jacob wrestling with and defeating God. In verse 28, it says, "You [Jacob] have wrestled with God and with men, and you have won." In other words, the creator of the universe whom mankind is expected to worship and submit to was defeated by a mere mortal in a wrestling match.

The Old Testament even pictures God as one who intended to do evil but then repented. Exodus 32:14 states, "And the Lord repented of the evil which he thought to do unto his people" (*King James Version*). It would not be surprising for anyone to turn away from God and not consider Him worthy of worship if He himself has to repent from His own evil.[2]

Furthermore, in the Talmud[3] it states that there was a dispute between God and the Jewish scholars. After a lengthy debate with no resolution, they decided to refer the matter to one of the rabbis. After his decision, God was forced to admit that He was mistaken.[4] Thus, God is not even perfect with respect to His knowledge. If Jews believe this, it would not be surprising to find

---

[1] The *New King James Version* reads: 24 Then Jacob was left alone; and a Man wrestled with him until the breaking of day. 25 Now when He saw that He did not prevail against him, He touched the socket of his hip; and the socket of Jacob's hip was out of joint as He wrestled with him. 26 And He said, "Let Me go, for the day breaks." But he said, "I will not let You go unless You bless me!" 27 So He said to him, "What is your name?" And he said, "Jacob." 28 And He said, "Your name shall no longer be called Jacob, but Israel; for you have struggled with God and with men, and have prevailed."

[2] Of course, this begs the question of to whom is it that God must or should repent ?

[3] The Talmud is, "An authoritative, influential compilation of rabbinic traditions and discussions about Jewish life and law." *Larousse Dictionary of Beliefs and Religions* (Edinburgh: Larousse, 1995), p. 513.

[4] Cf., Karzoon, vol. 1, p. 97.

Jews turning away from the revelation from God for perhaps "better sources of knowledge".

One vital role of the messengers of God, which has profound effects upon the purification of the soul, is to be an excellent example for all others who wish to follow the Straight Path. If the character of the messengers, these prime examples, are blemished and their souls cannot be considered pure, this opens the door for all others to use the messengers' shortcomings as an excuse for their own shortcomings. Indeed, if the messengers themselves did not truly purify their souls, how could purification be expected from others? Once again, upon turning to the distorted Old Testament, one finds the prophets and righteous people depicted with horrific characters, performing acts that no noble person would wish to perform.[1]

For example, Exodus 32:1-6 has the story of Aaron, the brother of Moses and one of the religious leaders for the tribe of Israel, making a golden calf as an idol for worship.[2] In 2 Samuel, chapter 11, verses 1-17, the leader of the Jewish people David, whom the Muslims consider a prophet, is shamelessly pictured as committing adultery, doing his best to conceal it and then doing his best to have the woman's husband killed.[3] Solomon is also

---

[1] It would not surprise this author if these distortions were intentionally done by some mischievous folk in order to encourage or allow people to do evil in the same way that the supposedly righteous people did sinful acts.

[2] The *King James Version* reads: 1 And when the people saw that Moses delayed to come down out of the mount, the people gathered themselves together unto Aaron, and said unto him, Up, make us gods, which shall go before us; for as for this Moses, the man that brought us up out of the land of Egypt, we wot not what is become of him. 2 And Aaron said unto them, Break off the golden earrings, which are in the ears of your wives, of your sons, and of your daughters, and bring them unto me. 3 And all the people brake off the golden earrings which were in their ears, and brought them unto Aaron. 4 And he received them at their hand, and fashioned it with a graving tool, after he had made it a molten calf: and they said, These be thy gods, O Israel, which brought thee up out of the land of Egypt. 5 And when Aaron saw it, he built an altar before it; and Aaron made proclamation, and said, To morrow is a feast to the LORD. 6And they rose up early on the morrow, and offered burnt offerings, and brought peace offerings; and the people sat down to eat and to drink, and rose up to play.

[3] The *New International Version* reads: 1 In the spring, at the time when kings go off to war, David sent Joab out with the king's men and the whole Israelite army. They destroyed the Ammonites and besieged Rabbah. But David remained in Jerusalem. 2 One evening David got up from his bed and walked around on the roof of the palace. From the roof he saw a woman bathing. The woman was very beautiful, 3 and David sent someone to find out about her. The

accused of committing idolatry simply out of love for his many wives.[1]

Karzoon also notes, based on the teachings of the Talmud, that it is part of Jewish belief that the soul is inherently evil. They considered the attainment of virtue to be something very difficult since it goes against the nature of mankind. It was God's plan to make humans inherently evil while obliging them to follow a law

---

man said, "Isn't this Bathsheba, the daughter of Eliam and the wife of Uriah the Hittite?" 4 Then David sent messengers to get her. She came to him, and he slept with her. (She had purified herself from her uncleanness.) Then she went back home. 5 The woman conceived and sent word to David, saying, "I am pregnant." 6 So David sent this word to Joab: "Send me Uriah the Hittite." And Joab sent him to David. 7 When Uriah came to him, David asked him how Joab was, how the soldiers were and how the war was going. 8 Then David said to Uriah, "Go down to your house and wash your feet." So Uriah left the palace, and a gift from the king was sent after him. 9 But Uriah slept at the entrance to the palace with all his master's servants and did not go down to his house. 10 When David was told, "Uriah did not go home," he asked him, "Haven't you just come from a distance? Why didn't you go home?" 11 Uriah said to David, "The ark and Israel and Judah are staying in tents, and my master Joab and my lord's men are camped in the open fields. How could I go to my house to eat and drink and lie with my wife? As surely as you live, I will not do such a thing!" 12 Then David said to him, "Stay here one more day, and tomorrow I will send you back." So Uriah remained in Jerusalem that day and the next. 13 At David's invitation, he ate and drank with him, and David made him drunk. But in the evening Uriah went out to sleep on his mat among his master's servants; he did not go home. 14 In the morning David wrote a letter to Joab and sent it with Uriah. 15 In it he wrote, "Put Uriah in the front line where the fighting is fiercest. Then withdraw from him so he will be struck down and die." 16 So while Joab had the city under siege, he put Uriah at a place where he knew the strongest defenders were. 17 When the men of the city came out and fought against Joab, some of the men in David's army fell; moreover, Uriah the Hittite died.

[1] I Kings, chapter 11, verses 1-10 of the *New International Version* reads: 1 King Solomon, however, loved many foreign women besides Pharaoh's daughter-- Moabites, Ammonites, Edomites, Sidonians and Hittites. 2 They were from nations about which the LORD had told the Israelites, "You must not intermarry with them, because they will surely turn your hearts after their gods." Nevertheless, Solomon held fast to them in love. 3 He had seven hundred wives of royal birth and three hundred concubines, and his wives led him astray. 4 As Solomon grew old, his wives turned his heart after other gods, and his heart was not fully devoted to the LORD his God, as the heart of David his father had been. 5 He followed Ashtoreth the goddess of the Sidonians, and Molech the detestable god of the Ammonites. 6 So Solomon did evil in the eyes of the LORD; he did not follow the LORD completely, as David his father had done. 7 On a hill east of Jerusalem, Solomon built a high place for Chemosh the detestable god of Moab, and for Molech the detestable god of the Ammonites. 8 He did the same for all his foreign wives, who burned incense and offered sacrifices to their gods. 9 The LORD became angry with Solomon because his heart had turned away from the LORD, the God of Israel, who had appeared to him twice. 10 Although he had forbidden Solomon to follow other gods, Solomon did not keep the LORD's command.

that would be beyond their ability. Hence, man is in a loss between following his natural, evil inclinations or following the law from God. For that reason, they claim that David was not sinful when he murdered and committed adultery because the real cause for his plight was God Himself.[1] If this is a person's perception of the human soul, it must become very easy to allow one's soul to be completely denigrated and abased.

The Prophet Jesus (peace and blessings of Allah be upon him) was the last prophet sent from the Tribes of Israel. In the light of the Gospels as they are now, as the Jews became completely engrossed in this world and materialistic desires, Jesus' message of reform concentrated upon "the Kingdom of God" and renouncing this world. Jesus' followers met with much persecution after him and they did not have public forums to openly spread their message. This opened the door for a new "convert," Paul, to spread a very distorted and untrue picture of Jesus (peace and blessings of Allah be upon him) and his message. It was this false depiction of Jesus that gained strength and

---

[1] Karzoon, vol. 1, pp. 99-100. Also see the respective references that he refers to in that work. There are two more points about Judaism that provide further obstacles to the purification of the soul. First, Judaism has a very scanty view of the Hereafter, with its reckoning and eternal rewards or punishments. Indeed, their books mostly stress worldly results of their deeds only. Hence, they have no strong feeling of being held accountable for their deeds. Second, the Jews, being the supposed chosen people, look upon the Gentiles as some kind of lower being. Hence, they are not expected to behave toward the Gentiles in any dignified, noble manner. Indeed, the current actions of the Zionist and right-wing Jews towards the non-Jew is probably closest related to the teachings one find in Deuteronomy 20:10-18, which reads in the King James Version, "10 When thou comest nigh unto a city to fight against it, then proclaim peace unto it. 11 And it shall be, if it make thee answer of peace, and open unto thee, then it shall be, that all the people that is found therein shall be tributaries unto thee, and they shall serve thee. 12 And if it will make no peace with thee, but will make war against thee, then thou shalt besiege it: 13 And when the LORD thy God hath delivered it into thine hands, thou shalt smite every male thereof with the edge of the sword: 14 But the women, and the little ones, and the cattle, and all that is in the city, even all the spoil thereof, shalt thou take unto thyself; and thou shalt eat the spoil of thine enemies, which the LORD thy God hath given thee. 15 Thus shalt thou do unto all the cities which are very far off from thee, which are not of the cities of these nations. 16 But of the cities of these people, which the LORD thy God doth give thee for an inheritance, thou shalt save alive nothing that breatheth: 17 But thou shalt utterly destroy them; namely, the Hittites, and the Amorites, the Canaanites, and the Perizzites, the Hivites, and the Jebusites; as the LORD thy God hath commanded thee: 18 That they teach you not to do after all their abominations, which they have done unto their gods; so should ye sin against the LORD your God."

constituted the major source of deviation in the history of Christianity. This and other factors led to Christianity not being a true or correct source of guidance for the purification of the soul.

The Christian conception of God and God having a son is, of course, completely blasphemous from an Islamic perspective. What it must convey to the soul, especially in its Christian perspective, can be quite detrimental and confusing. For example, if this were god's son, as he is pictured, there is nothing special about him. He lived like a human being, eating and drinking. He suffered like a human and even prayed out to God. If the Romans and Jews[1] defeated God's own son and he could not save himself, even crying out to his father, then what can one expect of oneself, a mortal human and not a son of God? Indeed, it seems as though there was nothing special about the son of God. If that is so, maybe there is nothing special or worth worshipping about God Himself.

Among the sad deviations that occurred in the history of Christianity were the concepts of monasticism and celibacy. It was sad in the sense that it was perceived as a way of purifying the soul while, in reality, it was something that the soul could never accept or apply. It was not consistent with the nature of the soul and, hence, it could never actually rectify the soul. This is, of course, one of the explanations for all of the outrages and exploits that went on historically in the monasteries (being so well known that there is no need to document them here). This way of life, inconsistent with man's nature, was never ordained by Allah. Instead, they invented it and it was not within their means to abide by it. Allah says in the Quran,

---

[1] So that this author may not somehow perversely be accused of anti-Semitism, the following quote should be noted. Israel Shahak writes, "According to the Talmud, Jesus was executed by a proper rabbinical court for idolatry, inciting other Jews to idolatry and contempt of rabbinical authority. All classical Jewish sources which mention his execution are quite happy to take responsibility for it: in the Talmudic account the Romans are not even mentioned." Israel Shahak, *Jewish History, Jewish Religion: The Weight of Three Thousand Years* (London: Pluto Press, 1997), pp. 97-98. He also wrote (pp. 20-21) about Jesus' fate, "the Talmud states that his punishment in hell is to be immersed in boiling excrement."

ثُمَّ قَفَّيْنَا عَلَىٰٓ ءَاثَـٰرِهِم بِرُسُلِنَا وَقَفَّيْنَا بِعِيسَى ٱبْنِ مَرْيَمَ
وَءَاتَيْنَـٰهُ ٱلْإِنجِيلَ وَجَعَلْنَا فِى قُلُوبِ ٱلَّذِينَ ٱتَّبَعُوهُ رَأْفَةً وَرَحْمَةً
وَرَهْبَانِيَّةً ٱبْتَدَعُوهَا مَا كَتَبْنَـٰهَا عَلَيْهِمْ إِلَّا ٱبْتِغَآءَ رِضْوَٰنِ ٱللَّهِ فَمَا
رَعَوْهَا حَقَّ رِعَايَتِهَا ۖ فَـَٔاتَيْنَا ٱلَّذِينَ ءَامَنُوا۟ مِنْهُمْ أَجْرَهُمْ ۖ وَكَثِيرٌ
مِّنْهُمْ فَـٰسِقُونَ

"Then, in their wake, We followed them up with (others of) Our Messengers. We sent after them Jesus the son of Mary, and bestowed on him the Gospel. We ordained in the hearts of those who followed him compassion and mercy. But the monasticism that they invented for themselves, We did not prescribe for them. (We commanded) only the seeking for the good pleasure of Allah; but that they did not foster as they should have done. Yet We bestowed, on those among them who believed, their (due) reward, but many of them are rebellious transgressors" (*al-Hadeed* 27).

A study of the New Testament demonstrates that there are teachings attributed to Jesus (peace and blessings of Allah be upon him) which are completely impractical, to the point that one cannot even claim that Jesus or his immediate followers even practiced those teachings—not to speak of those Christians who came later. Their impracticality is a sign that they are not consistent with the nature of humans. (This is also a sign that they must not have come from God as a message for the purification of the soul.) For example, one finds in the New Testament:

> 21 Jesus answered, "If you want to be perfect, go, sell your possessions and give to the poor, and you will have treasure in heaven. Then come, follow me" (Matthew 19:21, *New International Version*).

> 39 But I tell you, Do not resist an evil person. If someone strikes you on the right cheek, turn to him the other also. 40 And if someone wants to sue you and take your tunic, let him have your cloak as well. 41 If someone forces you to go one mile, go with him two miles. 42 Give to the one who asks you, and do not turn away from the one who wants to borrow from you. 43 "You have heard that it was said, 'Love your neighbor and hate your enemy.' 44 But I tell you: Love your enemies and pray for those who persecute you" (Matthew 5:39-44, *New International Version*).

> 7 When they kept on questioning him, he straightened up and said to them, "If any one of you is without sin, let him be the first to throw a stone at her" (John 8:7, *New International Version*).

This last quote, although accepted by numerous Christian commentators as not part of the original versions of John[1], would put an end to any form of ordering good and eradicating evil in society. Indeed, taken to its logical conclusion, since all humans are sure to sin, it means that no one should ever be punished for any crime or sin they commit in this world.

In addition, in particular for Catholics, another impediment to the true purification of the soul is the concept of the confessional. Here, one turns to another human being who concocts some simple formula to efface the effects of one's sins. It is not expected that a person would appreciate the gravity of a sin if, for example, a few "hail Marys" obliterates any negative ramification of that sin. Such an easy way to remove any blemish

---

[1] The fellows of "The Jesus Seminar," stated about this passage, "It is almost certainly not a part of the original text of John, but it is a noteworthy tradition nonetheless... While the Fellows agreed that the words did not originate in their present form with Jesus, they nevertheless assigned the words and story to a special category of things they wish Jesus had said and done." [Robert W. Funk, Roy W. Hoover and the Jesus Seminar, *The Five Gospels: What did Jesus Really Say?* (New York: MacMillan Publishing Company, 1993), p. 426.] This quote needs no further comment and simply displays the sad state of the Christian faith due to how distorted their scriptures became.

from a sin leaves the door to sinning open, removing any fear due from the eternal consequences of one's sins.

Protestants, in particular "Born again," Christians have a belief that they are (in essence, automatically) forgiven for their sins simply due to their belief in "Jesus as Lord." It is expected that this would have a profound negative effect on the purification and reformation of the soul. With this belief, one loses a very important aspect of belief in God: the fear of God. The fear of God is not simply a fear of His punishment but it is also includes the fear that God has not accepted one's repentance or that God is not pleased with one's work (due to, for example, ulterior motives interfering with the purity of the deed). This feeling of fear is a driving force in the soul, perpetually driving it to improve itself and further purification.[1] If this feeling is missing, the effects of sins are belittled and one succumbs to their influence while all along believing that he has been saved.[2]

Beyond all of that, Christianity has a fundamental problem that can be very disturbing to the soul. This problem is related to its central belief in the trinity and the fact that God has a son that is somehow half-human. This is something repugnant to the soul and incomprehensible to the mind. In fact, many Christian leaders themselves describe the trinity as a "mystery." It is in a mystery that one is supposed to base his entire life and

---

[1] It is also detrimental for the purification of the soul when the feeling of fear is too dominant and the feeling of hope is missing from the heart. At that point, the person despairs and sees no point to his acts of purification. Both extremes—the complete dominance of fear or the complete dominance of hope—must be avoided in order for the soul to be truly and adequately purified. Another feeling that must be present in the heart is that of love for God. This is the third component that provides the proper balance for the purification of the soul. If this component is too dominant, one once again strays from the proper course of purification. This manner of deviation is also found among many Christians. For most or many Christians, love is greatly stressed, to the point that some even say, "God is love."

[2] There are a number of other aspects related to Christianity that could be questioned with respect to purification of the soul; one is their current form of worship. Unfortunately, a detailed critique of those issues is beyond the scope of this work. For example, in many cases, church services are not much more than singing and dancing—although this was not the case with Jesus or the early church fathers. The question that needs to be asked is: How are practices like these supposed to draw one closer to the one true God and reform one's life? Another example is related to the holidays that the Christians celebrate. Many of these holidays are admittedly pagan rituals. Again, how is it that pagan rituals are going to help a person draw closer to the one true God?

hopes. He is required to have a "leap of faith." If not exposed to any other truths, a person may be satisfied with a belief of that nature. However, if he is ever exposed to beliefs that are understandable and acceptable to his soul, such as the pure and true beliefs of Islam, he will be forced to doubt or question his own beliefs—or just ignore that central question and accept the matter at some abstract level and leave the matter at that. This is hardly the basis for true contentment and purification of the soul.

Modern "Science" and Psychology and the Treatment of the Soul

With respect to modern science and, in particular, psychology, one cannot really speak about the goal of "purification of the soul." That is much too "normative" or "other worldly" for the secularist, positive scientists.[1] Instead, attention has turned to

---

[1] It is interesting to note how some psychologists try to claim that they are studying something other than the "soul." For example, one researcher wrote, "It is strange that, although everyone speaks glibly of 'psychology,' which means the science of the psyche, many people are confused as to the meaning of the word 'psyche' or vaguely equate it with the word 'soul.' Yet 'psyche' has a much wider meaning than the 'soul,' the latter used, as it generally is, in the Christian sense of the word. Roughly, 'psyche' refers to everything *inside*, in contradistinction to the *outside* world. Formerly the inner human being was always equated with the conscious ego, but research during the last seventy or eighty years has predicated the existence of the unconscious, i.e., that a great deal exist *in us* that the ego does not know..." Barbara Hannah, *Jung: His Life and Work* (Wilmette, IL: Chiron Publications, 1999), p. 68. It seems that Hannah herself could possibly be accused of using the word "soul" rather glibly in the quote above. It is unknown to this author on what basis one can claim that something that exists "in us" is not part of or related to the soul, especially from an Islamic perspective on the soul. In fact, it is interesting to note that in the *Larousse Dictionary of Beliefs and Religions* [(Edinburgh: Larousse, 1995), p. 496] under "Islamic view of soul," one finds, "The word for the independent soul is *nafs*, which is equivalent to the Greek word *psyche*." The psychiatrist and physician M. Scott Peck shows that it is more than coincidence that the word "soul" is missing from the vocabulary of many researchers today. In *Denial of the Soul*, he wrote, "The word 'soul' is probably in the vocabulary of every second-grader... Then why is it that [it] is not in the professional lexicon of psychiatrists, other mental health workers, students of the mind, and physicians in general? There are two reasons. One is that the concept of God is inherent in the concept of soul, and 'God talk' is virtually off-limits within these relatively secular professions. Religious though individuals in these professions might be personally, they would not want to offend their secular colleagues. Nor, for that matter, would they care to lose their jobs. The fact is that to speak of God or the soul in their professional gatherings would be politically incorrect. The other reason is that these professionals properly have a test for intellectual rigor, and the soul is something

what can be described as an attempt at making the soul (or person or psyche) content with itself, regardless of what state that soul may be in. Furthermore, attention has been turned to only those matters that can be "quantified." In reality, although proponents of modern psychology may not see it in this light, it is merely an attempt to overcome the physiological and medical maladies, such as depression, worthlessness and anxiety that are in themselves a result of a lack of spiritual purification. Therefore, it is important to give at least a brief overview of some relevant psychological and scientific theories because their possible influence in one's everyday life is very great. Indeed, they greatly influence the philosophies behind science, politics, media and other realms of life today.

When the Church lost its control over Europe, life began to be perceived in a very different fashion. Many scientists and philosophers turned away from the church and renewed interest in the ancient Greek and Roman works, which contained pagan philosophies emphasizing the joys of this world. Monasticism and abstinence lost all appeal. The Protestant revolution opened the door for individual interpretation of the Bible and salvation being a mere matter of faith, not deeds.

Science and human reasoning became the new gods. Obviously, with respect to the understanding of the soul, this was a great setback. In reality, the link to the one source—God—that could shed some light on the nature of the soul and its purification was broken. Although the scriptures and teachings of the Jews and Christians are badly distorted, at least they conveyed the message that humans are God's creatures, having a morally responsible soul and destined for a meeting with the Lord. These concepts were, for the most part, lost in Europe after the Renaissance and, to this day, they have very little influence on Western people's lives. Now, a new secular philosophy and

---

that cannot be completely defined... Yet this impossibility of adequate definition is not the primary stumbling block. Psychiatrists have no difficulty including 'light,' 'love,' and 'consciousness' in their professional vocabulary. Their primary problem with the 'soul word' is the blatancy of its connection to God." M. Scott Peck, *Denial of the Soul: Spiritual and Medical Perspectives on Euthanasia and Morality* (New York: Harmony Books, 1997), pp. 129-130.

modern science (and its new science of psychology) were the only disciplines that could respectably reflect on life and its meaning.

Maryam Jameelah has aptly described the process that Western thought and science next went through,

> The tragedy of Western science lay not in its specific discoveries which were of such tremendous benefit to the human race, but rather the dogmatic, narrow, materialistic outlook of the scientists themselves. After Copernicus, the Western astronomer saw man as only a puny speck on a tiny planet revolving around a tenth-rate star, drifting aimlessly in an endless cosmic ocean. Since God, the angels and Satan were not to be seen through their telescopes they concluded that man was absolutely alone in a cold, complex cosmic machine, his creation perhaps only an accident or a mistake. Feeling like a stranger in the universe without tangible proof of any God who cherished his welfare, Western man thus abandoned as futile the search for the ultimate meaning and purpose of life and began to regard Nature as he does today—as an enemy to be conquered, possessed and then manipulated by mechanical means to advance his material well-being.
>
> To Western scientists like Descartes, Nature was nothing more than a machine which had no spiritual significance. All living beings, including man, were a mere matter of automatic chemical reactions. "Give me the elements," boasted Descartes, "and I will construct the universe!"
>
> Intoxicated by the theory advanced by Newton that the entire universe was regulated by immutable mathematical laws, the protagonists of the so-called Age of Enlightenment taught that all beliefs contrary to human experience and observation must be discarded. Miracles, prophecy, revelation as well as religious rites and ceremonies were ridiculed as superstition. Voltaire taught that God created the universe exactly as a watchmaker assembles a watch, afterwards having no further concern with it. Hume rejected all religious

> beliefs on the ground that they could not be proved either by scientific experiments or human reason.[1]

The effects of these kinds of belief—as can be witnessed in the history and contemporary situation of mankind—are devastating. In essence, man has no purpose and no reason for being. If that is the case, on what real basis can one even make a plea for morality, ethical behavior and spiritual purification?[2] Years ago, Bertrand Russell wrote,

> That man is the product of causes which had no provision of the end they were achieving; that his origin, his growth, his hopes and fears, his loves and beliefs are but the outcome of accidental collocations of atoms; that no amount of heroism, no intensity of thought and feeling can preserve an individual life beyond the grave, that all the labour of the ages, all the devotion, all the inspiration of human genius are destined for extinction in the vast death of the solar system and that the whole temple of man's achievement must inevitably be buried beneath the debris of a universe in ruins—all these things are so nearly certain that no philosophy which rejects them can hope to stand.[3] Only within the scaffold of these

---

[1] Maryam Jameelah, *Islam Versus the West* (Lahore, Pakistan: Muhammad Yusuf Khan, 1971), pp. 12-13. In a work entitled *People of the Lie: The Hope for Healing Evil*, American psychiatrist Scott Peck also noted, "The major reason for this strange state of affairs is that the scientific and religious models have hitherto been considered totally immiscible—like oil and water, mutually incompatible and rejecting. In the late seventeenth century, after the Galileo affair proved hurtful to both, science and religion worked out an unwritten social contract of nonrelationship. The world was quite arbitrarily divided into the 'natural' and the 'supernatural'. Religion agreed that the 'natural world' was the sole province of the scientists. And science agreed, in turn, to keep its nose out of the spiritual—or for that matter, anything to do with values. Indeed, science defined itself as 'value free.'" M. Scott Peck, *People of the Lie: The Hope for Healing Evil* (New York: Touchstone Books, 1983), p. 40.

[2] This author has personally worked in a prison system in the United States and a common response given by inmates as to why they committed their crimes was, "Why not?" People of that nature are, in reality, putting into practice the thoughts reproduced above of Bertrand Russell, respected by many in the West as a great philosopher.

[3] This same approach appeared and dominated one school of psychology. Hunt notes, "Behaviorists had swept them [that is, freedom and will] aside as mentalist illusions, and even cognitive psychologists had avoided them because a freely willed act seems an uncaused act—a

> truths, only on the firm foundation of unyielding despair, can man's habitation be safely built.[1]

The continued secularism of life since Russell's time accompanied with a science that has virtually no real purpose to it led Jacques Monod, Noble Prize winning physician who died in 1976, to state,

> Man knows, at last, that he is alone in the indifferent immensity of the universe in which he emerged by chance. He knows now that, like a gypsy, he is marginal to the universe in which he lives: a universe that is deaf to his music and indifferent to his hopes, his suffering, and his crimes.[2]

Steven Weiberg, also a Nobel Prize-winner, stated, "The more we know the universe, the more it appears pointless and strange to us."[3]

Incidentally, from an Islamic perspective this simply demonstrates the extreme to which modern day *jaahiliyyah* (ignorance of God) has gone. From a Quranic perspective, there is more than one branch of knowledge. One such branch is related to the outward aspects of this physical creation. However, even that knowledge should, in turn, lead the person to the true, metaphysical knowledge concerning the reality of this creation. It should lead a person to recognize the existence of the Creator and the greatness of that Creator. In fact, if this knowledge does not lead one to accepting God, there is something definitely wrong with the mindset of the person who has attained that knowledge. Allah has said,

---

concept anathema to science." [Morton Hunt, *The Story of Psychology* (New York: Anchor Books, 1994, p.652.]

[1] Quoted in Jameelah, p. 17. It is amazing how religious adherents are sometimes criticized for believing in predestination or *qadar*. (In reality, as shall be discussed later, the Islamic belief in *qadar* is a very positive belief leading to positive results.) Is there anything more pessimistic and despairing than the belief that all humans are merely part of some cosmic order that goes along on its own and cannot truly be affected by humans? Humans become no more than atoms following some scientific laws and having no effect or meaning to their actions.

[2] Quoted in Yassine, p. 74.

[3] Quoted in Yassine, p. 75.

سَنُرِيهِمْ ءَايَـٰتِنَا فِى ٱلْـَٔافَاقِ وَفِىٓ أَنفُسِهِمْ حَتَّىٰ يَتَبَيَّنَ لَهُمْ أَنَّهُ ٱلْحَقُّ ۗ

"Soon will We show them Our Signs in the (furthest) regions (of the earth), and in their own souls, until it becomes manifest to them that this is the Truth" (*Fussilat* 53). Certainly, Allah has fulfilled this promise. Allah has definitely showed mankind all sorts of clear signs and evidence—even deep within their own body and souls.

Secular scientists may have some knowledge of the external aspects of this world but that is the extent of their knowledge. They cannot understand the real meaning behind everything they see around them in this universe. Hence, the knowledge that they have does not really benefit them at all. Allah says about them,

لَا يُخْلِفُ ٱللَّهُ وَعْدَهُۥ وَلَـٰكِنَّ أَكْثَرَ ٱلنَّاسِ لَا يَعْلَمُونَ ﴿٦﴾ يَعْلَمُونَ
ظَـٰهِرًا مِّنَ ٱلْحَيَوٰةِ ٱلدُّنْيَا وَهُمْ عَنِ ٱلْـَٔاخِرَةِ هُمْ غَـٰفِلُونَ ﴿٧﴾ أَوَلَمْ
يَتَفَكَّرُوا۟ فِىٓ أَنفُسِهِم ۗ مَّا خَلَقَ ٱللَّهُ ٱلسَّمَـٰوَٰتِ وَٱلْأَرْضَ وَمَا بَيْنَهُمَآ
إِلَّا بِٱلْحَقِّ وَأَجَلٍ مُّسَمًّى ۗ وَإِنَّ كَثِيرًا مِّنَ ٱلنَّاسِ بِلِقَآئِ رَبِّهِمْ
لَكَـٰفِرُونَ

"Allah does not violate His promise. But most of mankind simply do not know. They know what is apparent of the worldly life but they, of the Hereafter, are heedless. Do not contemplate concerning themselves? Allah has not created the heavens and the earth and what is between them except in truth and for a specified term. And, indeed, many of the people are disbelievers in the meeting with their Lord" (*al-Room* 7-8).

Psychology

Among modern sciences, psychology is the one discipline that truly claims to study what goes on within a person. Regardless of how psychologists may try to hide the fact, they are actually dealing with the soul. Save for some religious folk, they are the people who claim to be able to help others achieve internal happiness or some semblance of peace. Hence, a discussion of their views is essential to understanding how modern science treats the soul, in order to discover if they truly have something that is beneficial for the purification of the soul.

According to Karzoon, most of contemporary psychology is based on the premise that humans are completely subservient to their physical make-up and being.[1] Although psychology went through historical stages (stressing the psyche, the intellect and the conscience), now it greatly concentrates on only outward behavior and how such behavior can be explained. Hence, psychology has never truly studied humans as a complete whole. In fact, as a whole, psychologists have always tried to concentrate on one particular aspect that they believe dominates the whole. This faulty methodology has led to faulty conclusions and conceptions. Freud, for example, stated that the subconscious is the true human. In the subconscious lie the sexual motives driving the person. In the end, a human is pictured as a pure animal, nothing more.[2]

The empirical school of psychology is also completely restricted by the physical world and is not able to get in touch with the spiritual side, even though they do not theoretically deny

---

[1] Karzoon, vol. 1, p. 65.

[2] Freud developed the concepts of the id, ego and superego. Not surprisingly, a Muslim writer claimed that all three of those were discovered centuries ago in Islam, as the Quran speaks about the three phases of the soul (to be discussed later). This is typical of what many Muslim writers try to do as they attempt to incorporate all forms of "modern science" under some "Quranic teachings." Karzoon, vol. 1, pp. 67-68 refutes the notion that the Quran supports Freud's theory. This is definitely not the place to enter into a detailed critique of Freud, nor does this author feel comfortable even reproducing some of his thoughts. However, this author would venture to say that there is no question that anyone today who has such a preoccupation with perverted sexual attractions would be considered not a genius but, instead, mentally unbalanced.

the role of God or the soul.[1] However, by definition, this school is restricting itself to certain sources of knowledge (human experience) and ignoring all others (revelation from God, for example). Logically speaking, there is a problem with this approach. This is like having one hundred references available to find an answer but restricting oneself to just one of those resources without any demonstrative proof that the other sources are not reliable.

The behaviorists' school developed attempting to remove all issues related to the nature of the mind and soul. The basic premise of this school, which had notable proponents like Thorndike, Pavlov, Watson and the neo-behaviorists Hull and Skinner, may be summarized as:

> Mind is an illusion; there is no incorporeal self within us; our mental experiences, including consciousness, awareness of self, and thinking, are only physiological events taking place in the nervous system in response to stimuli.[2]

In fact, J. B. Watson even wrote, "[As a psychologist, you] must describe the behavior of man in no other terms than those you would use in describing the behavior of the ox you slaughter."[3] He also stated,

> Human beings do not want to class themselves with other animals. They are willing to admit that they are animals but "something else in addition." It is the "something else" that causes the trouble. In this "something else" is bound up everything that is classed as religion, the hereafter, morals, love of children, parents, country, and the like.[4]

Hence, as Badri noted,

---

[1] Hunt (p. 72) says of the original empiricists, "while dutifully mentioning God and the soul, [they] proposed earthly explanations of human mental activities and behavior."
[2] Hunt, p. 244.
[3] Quoted in Badri, p. 3.
[4] Quoted in Badri, p. 3.

> It is obvious that behaviorism adamantly denies that humans have an innate good or evil nature, and that what they believe in is neither true nor false. Like a dry leaf on a windy day, their nature, values and beliefs are completely determined by environmental stimuli; there is no place in the behavioristic conception for any global ethical truths or moral standards. It also excludes any notion of human freedom of choice and any conscious moral or spiritual decision-making.[1]

A great flaw in most, if not all, of these approaches is that they have to take the human himself as he exists in contemporary society as the subject of study.[2] However, how can it be determined whether the humans who are being studied are "normal" or "abnormal"? Psychologists are forced to assume that the common characteristics among the subjects make up the "normal" human. While writing about Freud, the *Encyclopedia Britannica* noted,

> To be fully universal, psychoanalysis--a term Freud coined in 1896--would also have to examine the male psyche in a condition of what might be called normality. It would have to become more than a psychotherapy and develop into a complete theory of the mind. To this end Freud accepted the enormous

---

[1] Badri, pp. 3-4. It is important to note that those who have gone to an extreme concerning the Islamic belief in *Qadar* (Divine preordainment) as well as the Sufis who went to the extreme of *wahdah al-wujood* or monism necessarily come to the same conclusions.

[2] The problem with this approach is not that human nature has changed over time. In essence, human nature never changes with respect to its leaning toward the fundamental belief in Allah. However, the person's environment can negatively influence a person and turn him away from recognizing or following that truth that his soul recognizes. The Prophet (peace and blessings of Allah be upon him) stated in a hadith to be discussed later, "Every child is born in the *fitrah* [the natural disposition in which humans are created]. Then his parents convert him to Judaism, Christianity or Magianism. Just like an animal giving birth to a perfect baby animal, do you find it mutilated at all?" Then Abu Hurairah read the verse, "Allah's *fitrah* upon which He has created mankind. [Let there be no change in the creation or religion of Allah, that is the straight religion]" (*al-Room* 30). (Recorded by al-Bukhari and Muslim.)

> risk of generalizing from the experience he knew best: his own.[1]

But in the Western world of the past few centuries, there has been a strong movement away from belief in God, revelation and religion. The subjects who are studied reflect that tendency. Although that tendency is very common among those people, that tendency in itself may be something abnormal for humans. The entire study group has been influenced by this abnormal behavior that has not been characteristic of humans throughout their entire history.[2] Given this fact, it would not be surprising to find that the conclusions reached by many psychologists and others is very distant from the way "normal" humans are supposed to be.[3]

It would not be a logical conclusion, then, to put one's trust or hope in such a science. In fact, about a century ago, William James, a pioneer in psychology, characterized "the science of psychology" in the following manner,

> A string of raw facts; a little gossip and wrangle about opinions; a little classification and generalization on the mere descriptive level; a strong prejudice that we *have* states of mind, and that our brain conditions them; but not a single law in the sense in which physics shows us laws, not a single proposition from which any consequence can causally be deduced.[4]

---

[1] Copyright 1994-1999 Encyclopædia Britannica.

[2] In addition, there can also be a type of "self-fulfilling prophecy" with respect to what or who is normal. Hoffman noted this point back in 1951. He wrote about his experiences while studying sociology at Union College in New York, while critiquing modern secular science, "We [supposedly] discovered the 'laws' governing all human activity and society. However, we are not yet aware of the normative impact of sociological research: the more people read about what is 'normal' according to statistical data, the more they tend to adapt to this norm. Sociology is a self-fulfilling prophecy! Indeed, my fellow students at Psi Upsilon Fraternity are virtually obsessed with an urge to appear normal..." Murad Wilfried Hofmann, *Journay to Islam: Diary of a German Diplomat 1951-2000* (Leicester, United Kingdom: The Islamic Foundation, 2001), pp. 3-4.

[3] Cf., Muhammad Qutb, *Diraasaat fi Nafs al-Isnaaniyyah* (Beirut: Dar al-Shurooq, 1983), p. 14.

[4] Quoted from Hunt, p. 640.

Hunt notes that in all of these areas psychology has improved since the time of James.[1] The truth remains, though, that psychology is not able to offer the soul, the least empirically and physically testable or touchable part of the human, what it needs to know its true course in life.

In sum, secular scientists and psychologists are mostly concerned with the physiological needs of humans. They have completely neglected, intentionally or out of necessity, the spiritual side, which is what raises mankind above being an animal. (Yet at the same time they try to tackle issues like depression that are directly related to the state of the soul.) This fact is recognized by many of the Western scholars themselves. For example, Erich Fromm stated that modern psychology stresses, for the most part, issues that are trivial and insignificant dealing with the behavior of humans. At the same time, it ignores the important human problems and values.[2] In fact, the Nobel Prize-winning Carrel concludes in his classic work *Man the Unknown* that everything related to actual make-up and needs of the soul cannot be determined by mere material and physical observations. He wrote, "We are only able to understand specific aspects concerning our souls but we cannot understand the human as a complete whole."[3]

Freud himself was forced to admit that science in itself is not going to bring about what the soul truly requires. He wrote,

> Science, apart from the emphasis on the real world, has essentially negative characteristics in that it limits itself to tangible material truth[4] and rejects illusions. Some of our fellow men who are dissatisfied with this state of affairs and desire something more for their momentary

---

[1] Hunt, p. 640.

[2] Quoted from Karzoon vol. 1, pp. 69-70, who, in turn, was quoting from the Arabic translation of Fromm's work *Religion and Psychoanalysis.* Alexis Carrel has similar important statements as quoted in Karzoon, vol. 1, p. 70.

[3] See the long quote from Carrel's work in Qutb, pp. 15-18.

[4] This in itself is not entirely true. Science relies on hypotheses and not merely on truth. The scientific hypotheses may eventually be proven to be false, at which time the "scientific truths" need to be rediscovered and restated.

> piece of mind, may look for it where they can find it, but we cannot help them.[1]

Badri, a trained psychologist himself and an Islamic critic of the science, stated,

> It is not surprising, therefore, that these psychological schools [behaviorism, Freudian psychology and neuropsychiatry] and their artificial oversimplification of complex cognitive activities and feelings, in spite of securing respect for many years by providing scientific explanations of human behavior, have failed to provide satisfactory results. The optimism of fifty years ago has not dissipated, and the social and psychological problems of Western societies are probably the only variables that have surpassed economic inflation in their sharp increase. Their failure is not surprising since the psychology of humankind, with all its complex variables and spiritual aspects, could never be reduced to the chemical and physical data of laboratory experiments.[2]

Conclusions Concerning Other Conceptions of the Soul and Its Possible Purification

In this author's view, an unbiased evaluation of all of these other approaches[3] leads to one very important conclusion: None of these other approaches and conceptions seems to be consistent with the true nature of human beings. Indeed, they intentionally avoid some of the fundamental questions upon which their premises should be built.[4] Hence, their initial starting

---

[1] Quoted in Jameelah, p. 18.

[2] Badri, p. 5.

[3] That is, Hinduism, Buddhism, Judaism, Christianity, secular modern science and psychiatry.

[4] Muhammad Qutb makes the point that the following questions must be answered first and then one may proceed to study the nature of the soul: What is a human? What is his responsibility? What is his role in life? What is his capabilities and limits? Psychologists avoid these questions, claiming that they do not fall under the realm of psychology. However, it is because they avoid these questions that those same psychologists will never be able to develop a

points are wrong and, therefore, it is not surprising that they should end up going into directions that are simply unacceptable to a sound mind and soul. The fact is that, sooner or later, in one way or another, the essential question of life has to be addressed and the assumption that all is for naught cannot be accepted by human nature.[1]

There are a number of reasons for the confusion and loss among the adherents of the varied approaches to dealing with the soul. Additionally, there are a number of reasons why they can never lead to any true happiness or purification of the soul.

First, many of them, in particular the secular psychologists and scientists, fail to recognize humans as a most noble creation of an all-wise, all-powerful God. Indeed, they refuse to admit that God has any influence over life. Indeed, in their studies, human actions are completely determined by sexual drive, economic influences, conditioned reflexes and so forth.[2] They see humans as being independent of God, the Creator and Lord of the Universe. They speak or theorize about humans as if humans came to this world on their own and that they are simply another physical being like all of the other physical beings, living under the same laws of nature that they claim to have comprehended. They completely neglect or cannot deal with properly the obvious spiritual, non-physical side that is part of every human.[3] This

---

complete picture of humans. Instead, what they have done is study some aspect of man's behavior and tried to conclude that that is what man is all about. See Muhammad Qutb, pp. 13-14.

[1] As Yassine (p. 62) noted, "Even if the noise of modern culture is terribly invasive and agitating, nature—our primary nature—the conscience that lies at the base of our innermost being, will never be totally convinced that we are here for no reason. At the base of human conscience there is also a straining toward what is above, toward the spirit. This tension may swoon and faint, but it can never die. It may be deafened during childhood and disabled from hearing the external call, or it may be blinded to the light of day by a certain kind of education and an uncertain culture, but it does not die. It retires to some dungeon of modern man's conscience, duped by the hype that science may one day be able to revive the dead. A victim of his illusions, modern man have himself frozen in some cryogenic morgue for millionaires. Science may one day offer everyone the elixir of an extended youth that ancient alchemists dreamed of—but will it answer the question that dwells in us?"

[2] Muhammad Qutb, pp. 23-25.

[3] William James once said, "The greatest cure for anxiety, without a doubt, is faith." (Quoted in Karzoon, vol. 1, p. 73. On p. 74, he has similar quotes from Dale Carnegie, Dr. Brill and Carl Jung. Karzoon (vol. 1, pp. 74-75) notes that it is very unfortunate that many psychologists still

fundamental approach obviously clouds their views and, therefore, makes their conclusions far-fetched. These far-fetched conclusions include picturing humans as if human himself is God who has made and makes his own world, he is a completely dependent slave to those forces acting upon him (thus belittling the role and potential of humans) or he is completely an animal with no difference between him and any other animal in this creation.[1]

Second, as a corollary to the above, many have turned their backs on basing their theories on revelation from God. Hence, they are ignoring the Creator of humans who is, without a doubt, the greatest source of knowledge concerning humans. Allah says,

أَلَا يَعْلَمُ مَنْ خَلَقَ وَهُوَ ٱللَّطِيفُ ٱلْخَبِيرُ

"Should not He who has created know [about His creation] while He is the Most Kind and Courteous, the All-Aware" (*al-Mulk* 14). Indeed, He not only created them in the first place but He is well aware of what their own souls conjure at this moment. Allah says,

وَلَقَدْ خَلَقْنَا ٱلْإِنسَٰنَ وَنَعْلَمُ مَا تُوَسْوِسُ بِهِۦ نَفْسُهُۥ وَنَحْنُ أَقْرَبُ إِلَيْهِ مِنْ حَبْلِ ٱلْوَرِيدِ

"And indeed We have created man and We know what his own self whispers to him. And We are nearer to him than his jugular vein [by Our knowledge]" (*Qaaf* 16). (As noted earlier, the major problem with those faiths that were originally revealed from God is that they lost their authentic texts and allowed their texts and their beliefs to be sullied by external sources and beliefs.) All humans must realize how faulty an approach to self-awareness is one that rejects revelation from God. Humans should admit—and many do save for the most arrogant among them—that they have never been able to discover the secrets behind the soul, the secrets of the giving of life and the secrets of death and what lies beyond it. The only one with true knowledge of the soul is God.

---

insist on the fact that "knowledge" alone will bring about happiness and that there is some type of essential conflict between "knowledge" and faith.

[1] Cf., Muhammad Qutb, p. 26.

Therefore, it is not logical for a person to ignore the only true source of knowledge on this topic. The only correct approach, then, is to turn to that source of knowledge and try, with one's limited capabilities, to comprehensively understand what has come from Him via revelation.

Third, by necessity, humans must concentrate their secular studies and research on the physical, tangible aspects of humans. But this is not all that there is to mankind. In one brief but clear verse, Allah informs mankind that there is a physical component to man as well as another component that is of a different realm. Allah says,

إِذْ قَالَ رَبُّكَ لِلْمَلَـٰٓئِكَةِ إِنِّى خَـٰلِقٌۢ بَشَرًا مِّن طِينٍ ﴿٧١﴾ فَإِذَا سَوَّيْتُهُۥ وَنَفَخْتُ فِيهِ مِن رُّوحِى فَقَعُوا۟ لَهُۥ سَـٰجِدِينَ

"Behold, the Lord said to the angels, 'I am about to create man from clay. When I have fashioned him (in due proportion) and breathed into him of My spirit, fall down in obeisance unto him'" (*Saad* 71-72). At the same time, Allah has stated that He has granted mankind a very little amount of knowledge when it comes to the human spirit or *rooh*. Allah says,

وَيَسْـَٔلُونَكَ عَنِ ٱلرُّوحِ ۖ قُلِ ٱلرُّوحُ مِنْ أَمْرِ رَبِّى وَمَآ أُوتِيتُم مِّنَ ٱلْعِلْمِ إِلَّا قَلِيلًا

"And they ask you [O Muhammad] concerning the *rooh* (the spirit). Say, 'As for the *rooh*, its knowledge is with my Lord.' And of knowledge, you [mankind] have been given but only a little" (*al-Israa* 85).[1] Mankind, though, has either not recognized or

[1] It should be noted that there is a difference of opinion as to what the *rooh* ("spirit") refers to in this verse. The Quranic commentators have mentioned six different opinions, including: (1) the spirit that is breathed into humans; (2) a special angel; (3) a special creation of Allah that has angel-like characteristics but human-like appearance; (4) the angel Gabriel; (5) the Quran itself; and (6) the Prophet Jesus (peace be upon him). The second opinion was narrated in the form of a hadith and as a statement of Ali ibn Abu Taalib (may Allah be pleased with him). Ibn Katheer rejects both the hadith and statement as strange and objectionable. Ibn al-Qayyim claims that the majority of the early scholars stated that this *rooh* mentioned is not the spirit of

refuses to recognize its limited ability to conquer this realm of reality. Hence, humans continue to make proclamations about the soul and some may even claim that they have found the key to the soul's happiness and purification. Those proclamations, though, are not based on true knowledge but only on conjecture and speculation. It is not surprising that they are very confusing and not convincing; thus, it is also not surprising that they cannot aid humans in achieving true happiness.

Fourth, man-made theories or distorted scriptures can indeed be very dangerous for one's spiritual well-being. These theories or scriptures may set a person on a path that is very far from the straight path to leads to spiritual purification. When these theories are supported by false but cleverly stated arguments or when these scriptures are propped up by religious bodies, their harms become even greater as they are believed in wholeheartedly by those who have been duped into thinking they are true and beneficial. The end result is that people can become blind to their

---

human beings. Instead, it is in reference to the angel that will come with Allah on the Day of Judgment, as referred to in *al-Naba* 38. He supports his contention by stating that the verse is in reference to something unknown except through revelation. However, the "spirit" of humans is not something unseen and it is something that has been talked about by many people throughout the generations. Al-Qaasimi concluded from the context of the verse that the *rooh* here is in reference to the Quran, the fifth opinion expressed above. The majority of the scholars of *tafseer* support the view that the *rooh* is in reference to the "spirit" of humans. This is the conclusion of al-Tabari, al-Baghawi, ibn al-Jauzi, ibn Atiyya, Abu Hayaan, ibn Katheer, ibn Hajar (as quoted by Abdul Raheem) and al-Aloosi. This seems to be the correct interpretation, Allah knows best. Cf., Muhammad ibn al-Qayyim, *al-Rooh fi al-Kalaam ala Arwaah al-Amwaat wa al-Ahyaa* (Riyadh: Daar ibn Taimiyyah, 1992), vol. 2, pp. 517-518; Jamaal al-Deen al-Qaasimi, *Mahaasin al-Taweel* (Cairo: Dar Ihyaa al-Kutub al-Arabi, n.d.), vol. 10, p. 3994; Muhammad ibn Jareer al-Tabari, *Jaami al-Bayaan an Taweel Aayi al-Quraan* (Beirut: Daar al-Fikr, 1988), vol. 9, p. 15, pp. 156-157; al-Husain al-Baghawi, *Tafseer al-Baghawi: Maalim al-Tanzeel* (Riyadh: Daar Taiba, 1409 A.H.), vol. 5, pp. 125-126; Abdul Rahmaan ibn al-Jauzi, *Zaad al-Maseer fi Ilm al-Tafseer* (Beirut: Daar al-Fikr, 1987), vol. 5, p. 58; Abdul Haqq ibn Atiyyah, *al-Muharrar al-Wajeez fi Tafseer al-Kitaab al-Azeez* (Beirut: Daar al-Kutub al-Ilmiyyah, 1993), vol. 3, pp. 481-482; Muhammad ibn Yoosuf Abu Hayyaan, *Al-Bahr al-Muheet fi al-Tafseer* (Makkah: al-Maktabah al-Tijaariyyah, n.d.), vol. 7, p. 106; Ismaaeel ibn Katheer, *Tafseer al-Quran al-Adheem* (Kuwait: Jamiyyah Ihyaa al-Turaath al-Islaami, 1991), vol. 3, pp. 68-69; Al-Sayyid Abdul Raheem, footnotes to Ali al-Maawardi, *al-Nukat wa al-Uyoon Tafseer al-Maawardi* (Beirut: Daar al-Kutub al-Ilmiyah, 1992), vol. 3, p. 270; Mahmood al-Aloosi, *Rooh al-Maani fi Tafseer al-Quran wa al-Saba al-Mathaani* (Cairo: Maktabah Daar al-Turaath, n.d.), vol, 15, p. 151. This footnote was taken from the author's *Commentary on the Forty Hadith of al-Nawawi*, vol. 1, p. 403.

misguidance, although an outsider can clearly see the falsehood that their beliefs and lives are based on. They may believe that they are doing some good—at least they have tried to convince themselves of that fact while not allowing themselves to see the truth of the matter. In the end, though, their deeds will be fruitless. Such people have turned away from the truth and the clear signs that Allah has sent in favor of their own theories or clearly distorted scriptures. They are either among those or akin to those described in the verses,

قُلْ هَلْ نُنَبِّئُكُم بِٱلْأَخْسَرِينَ أَعْمَٰلًا ﴿١٠٣﴾ ٱلَّذِينَ ضَلَّ سَعْيُهُمْ فِى
ٱلْحَيَوٰةِ ٱلدُّنْيَا وَهُمْ يَحْسَبُونَ أَنَّهُمْ يُحْسِنُونَ صُنْعًا ﴿١٠٤﴾ أُو۟لَٰٓئِكَ
ٱلَّذِينَ كَفَرُوا۟ بِـَٔايَٰتِ رَبِّهِمْ وَلِقَآئِهِۦ فَحَبِطَتْ أَعْمَٰلُهُمْ فَلَا نُقِيمُ
لَهُمْ يَوْمَ ٱلْقِيَٰمَةِ وَزْنًا ﴿١٠٥﴾ ذَٰلِكَ جَزَآؤُهُمْ جَهَنَّمُ بِمَا كَفَرُوا۟
وَٱتَّخَذُوٓا۟ ءَايَٰتِى وَرُسُلِى هُزُوًا

"Say: Shall we tell you of those who lose most in respect of their deeds? Those whose efforts have been wasted in this life while they thought that they were acquiring good by their works? They are those who deny the Signs of their Lord and the fact of their having to meet Him (in the Hereafter): vain will be their works, nor shall We, on the Day of Judgment, give them any weight. That is their reward, Hell—because they rejected faith, and took My Signs and My Messengers by way of jest" (*al-Kahf* 103-106).

In sum, it is, therefore, inconceivable that these views could truly offer a means for a person to purify his soul or find true happiness.

Perhaps one main reason behind the potential and definite failure for all of these other views should be discussed in more detail. As noted earlier, the essence of the problem is really quite simple. None of those approaches is compatible with the true nature of human beings and with the reality of the existence—the presence of only one true God—in which they are living. Hence, it is not surprising that none of those approaches can lead to the true purification of a human. Indeed, it is not surprising that none of those approaches can even lead to a semblance of true happiness in either this life or the Hereafter. This is because humans have been endowed with a natural disposition that recognizes the truth or the reality of there being only one true God and that humans should worship that one true God.[1] This fact may lie deep within a person's soul, hidden or covered but it is still there. Nowadays, many people believe in the effect of the subconscious and even of subliminal messages influencing a person's behavior. Regardless of the truth of those theories, there is deep within the soul the knowledge and inclination to recognize the truth.[2]

Allah says in the Quran,

وَإِذْ أَخَذَ رَبُّكَ مِنۢ بَنِىٓ ءَادَمَ مِن ظُهُورِهِمْ ذُرِّيَّتَهُمْ وَأَشْهَدَهُمْ عَلَىٰٓ أَنفُسِهِمْ أَلَسْتُ بِرَبِّكُمْ ۖ قَالُوا۟ بَلَىٰ ۛ شَهِدْنَآ ۛ أَن تَقُولُوا۟ يَوْمَ ٱلْقِيَٰمَةِ إِنَّا كُنَّا عَنْ هَٰذَا غَٰفِلِينَ

"When your Lord drew forth from the Children of Adam from their loins, their descendants, and made them testify concerning themselves, (saying), 'Am I not your Lord (Who cherishes and

---

[1] Ibn Taimiyyah wrote, "The heart can only become sound, achieve success, take pleasure, be satisfied, experience enjoyment, become pleased, attain serenity and calmness through the *'ibaadah* [worship] of its Lord, having love of Him and turning to Him (in repentance). Even if it were to attain every type of pleasure from creation, it will not acquire serenity and tranquillity. This is because the heart possesses an intrinsic need for its Lord, since He is its diety, love and pursuit and with Allah the heart achieves joy, pleasure, delight, amenity, serenity and tranquillity." [Ahmad ibn Taimiyyah,] *Ibn Taymiyyah's Essay on Servitude* (Birmingham, United Kingdom: al-Hidaayah Publishing and Distribution, 1999), p. 121. Ahmad Fareed notes that in the same way that the heavens and the earth would be destroyed if there were any God other than Allah, also the heart is destroyed by such. There is no hope for its reform or goodness until it recognizes its lord and worships Him alone. See Ahmad Fareed, *Al-Tazkiyah bain Ahl al-Sunnah wa al-Soofiyyah* (no publication information given), p. 15.

[2] This natural disposition, recognizing the existence of only one true God and Lord, is seen most prominently when humans are facing great danger. It is at that time that they cry out to their Lord, the one they know in their soul that can help them. Allah has mentioned this behavior in a number of verses in the Quran. See, for example, *Yoonus* 12 and *Yoonus* 22-23.

sustains you)?' They said, 'Yes! We do testify!' (This was) lest you should say on the Day of Judgment, 'Of this we were never aware'" (*al-Araaf* 172). Al-Bukhari and Muslim also record,

مَا مِنْ مَوْلُودٍ إِلاَّ يُولَدُ عَلَى الْفِطْرَةِ فَأَبَوَاهُ يُهَوِّدَانِهِ أَوْ يُنَصِّرَانِهِ أَوْ يُمَجِّسَانِهِ كَمَا تُنْتَجُ الْبَهِيمَةُ بَهِيمَةً جَمْعَاءَ هَلْ تُحِسُّونَ فِيهَا مِنْ جَدْعَاءَ ثُمَّ يَقُولُ أَبُو هُرَيْرَةَ رَضِي اللَّهم عَنْهم (فِطْرَةَ اللَّهِ الَّتِي فَطَرَ النَّاسَ عَلَيْهَا) الآيَةَ

"Every child is born in the *fitrah* [the natural disposition in which humans are created]. Then his parents convert him to Judaism, Christianity or Magianism. Just like an animal giving birth to a perfect baby animal, do you find it mutilated at all?" Then Abu Hurairah read the verse, "Allah's *fitrah* upon which He has created mankind. [Let there be no change in the creation or religion of Allah, that is the straight religion]" (*al-Room* 30). (Recorded by al-Bukhari and Muslim.) The Prophet (peace and blessings of Allah be upon him) also said,

أَلا إِنَّ رَبِّي أَمَرَنِي أَنْ أُعَلِّمَكُمْ مَا جَهِلْتُمْ مِمَّا عَلَّمَنِي يَوْمِي هَذَا كُلُّ مَالٍ نَحَلْتُهُ عَبْدًا حَلالٌ وَإِنِّي خَلَقْتُ عِبَادِي حُنَفَاءَ كُلَّهُمْ وَإِنَّهُمْ أَتَتْهُمُ الشَّيَاطِينُ فَاجْتَالَتْهُمْ عَنْ دِينِهِمْ وَحَرَّمَتْ عَلَيْهِمْ مَا أَحْلَلْتُ لَهُمْ وَأَمَرَتْهُمْ أَنْ يُشْرِكُوا بِي مَا لَمْ أُنْزِلْ بِهِ سُلْطَانًا

"Behold, my Lord commanded me that I should teach you that which you do not know and which He has taught me today. [He has stated that] the property which I [Allah] have conferred upon them is lawful for them. I have created My servants all having a natural inclination to the worship of Allah. But the devils come to them and turn them away from their [true] religion. And he makes unlawful what I declared lawful for them and he commands them to ascribe partners with Me for which no authority has been sent down." (Recorded by Muslim.)

However, Allah did not leave humans with only their natural disposition to help them find the truth. Instead, He reinforced the foundation that was already within their own souls by sending messengers and revealing books. Indeed, in Allah's mercy, the punishment in the Hereafter is related not to the natural disposition but to the response to the messengers who were merely reinforcing and developing what the soul was already prepared for. Allah says,

رُّسُلًا مُّبَشِّرِينَ وَمُنذِرِينَ لِئَلَّا يَكُونَ لِلنَّاسِ عَلَى ٱللَّهِ حُجَّةٌۢ بَعْدَ ٱلرُّسُلِ ۚ وَكَانَ ٱللَّهُ عَزِيزًا حَكِيمًا

"Messengers who gave good news as well as warning, that mankind, after (the coming) of the Messengers, should have no plea against Allah. And Allah is Exalted in Power, Wise" (*al-Nisaa* 165). And Allah clearly states that He does not punish any people until He has sent unto them a messenger and they refuse to follow his teachings. Allah says,

مَّنِ ٱهْتَدَىٰ فَإِنَّمَا يَهْتَدِى لِنَفْسِهِۦ ۖ وَمَن ضَلَّ فَإِنَّمَا يَضِلُّ عَلَيْهَا ۚ وَلَا تَزِرُ وَازِرَةٌ وِزْرَ أُخْرَىٰ ۗ وَمَا كُنَّا مُعَذِّبِينَ حَتَّىٰ نَبْعَثَ رَسُولًا

"Who receives guidance, receives it for his own benefit: who goes astray does so to his own loss: no bearer of burdens can bear the burden of another: nor would We visit with Our Wrath until We had sent a messenger (to give warning)" (*al-Israa* 15).

The conclusion from all of the preceding is quite clear: The only true way of understanding the soul and finding what will purify and rectify the soul is by turning to the One who created that soul and who knows its innermost workings. This means that one must turn to the revelation from Allah to understand how to deal with the soul and what is the proper direction for the soul. There is no other possible or acceptable source of guidance in this matter. Hence, if a person sincerely desires to purify his soul and develop his soul to its fullest potential, he must turn to the Quran and Sunnah, submitting to these two sources and following them to the best of his ability, as they are the only true and unadulterated revelations from God meant for mankind today. It is only these sources that can give him the true, comprehensive knowledge of the soul and it is only these two sources that can inspire his soul to the correct path of purification.

Furthermore, as noted earlier and as shall be discussed later in more detail, the first true step in the process of purification of the soul is the garnering and holding of correct beliefs and faith, in particular the belief about God. Without this correct belief, numerous evils and mistakes result, like those found in the beliefs of the Jews and Christians. If one does not start off with the right kind of awe and admiration for God—which could not result from the incorrect beliefs and scriptures of those two groups—it is not expected that God would occupy His proper place in an individual's heart. God should be the main object of love and admiration in a person's heart and this results from knowing the truth about God and His perfect and exalted attributes, far above what the Jews and Christians attribute to Him. This belief can be called the true foundation for the purification of the soul.

One Passage from the Quran

Before concluding this chapter which discussed many of the non-Islamic concepts concerning the human, the soul and means of purification and before discussing the concept of the soul itself, this author would like to draw the reader's attention to one passage of the Quran that uniquely resolves many of philosophical dilemmas that many humans are facing.[1] This set of verses takes one back to the true incident of the creation of Adam, the first human—an incident that is beyond the realm of scientific theories and guesswork, no matter how much humans may speculate about it. Allah says,

[1] Muhammad Qutb discussed these verses and some of these issues in Qutb, *Diraasaat*, ppp. 28-34. The following discussion is partially based on his discussion.

وَإِذْ قَالَ رَبُّكَ لِلْمَلَٰٓئِكَةِ إِنِّى جَاعِلٌ فِى ٱلْأَرْضِ خَلِيفَةً ۖ قَالُوٓا۟ أَتَجْعَلُ
فِيهَا مَن يُفْسِدُ فِيهَا وَيَسْفِكُ ٱلدِّمَآءَ وَنَحْنُ نُسَبِّحُ بِحَمْدِكَ
وَنُقَدِّسُ لَكَ ۖ قَالَ إِنِّىٓ أَعْلَمُ مَا لَا تَعْلَمُونَ ﴿٣٠﴾ وَعَلَّمَ ءَادَمَ ٱلْأَسْمَآءَ
كُلَّهَا ثُمَّ عَرَضَهُمْ عَلَى ٱلْمَلَٰٓئِكَةِ فَقَالَ أَنۢبِـُٔونِى بِأَسْمَآءِ هَٰٓؤُلَآءِ إِن
كُنتُمْ صَٰدِقِينَ ﴿٣١﴾ قَالُوا۟ سُبْحَٰنَكَ لَا عِلْمَ لَنَآ إِلَّا مَا عَلَّمْتَنَآ ۖ إِنَّكَ
أَنتَ ٱلْعَلِيمُ ٱلْحَكِيمُ ﴿٣٢﴾ قَالَ يَٰٓـَٔادَمُ أَنۢبِئْهُم بِأَسْمَآئِهِمْ ۖ فَلَمَّآ
أَنۢبَأَهُم بِأَسْمَآئِهِمْ قَالَ أَلَمْ أَقُل لَّكُمْ إِنِّىٓ أَعْلَمُ غَيْبَ ٱلسَّمَٰوَٰتِ
وَٱلْأَرْضِ وَأَعْلَمُ مَا تُبْدُونَ وَمَا كُنتُمْ تَكْتُمُونَ ﴿٣٣﴾ وَإِذْ قُلْنَا
لِلْمَلَٰٓئِكَةِ ٱسْجُدُوا۟ لِءَادَمَ فَسَجَدُوٓا۟ إِلَّآ إِبْلِيسَ أَبَىٰ وَٱسْتَكْبَرَ وَكَانَ
مِنَ ٱلْكَٰفِرِينَ ﴿٣٤﴾ وَقُلْنَا يَٰٓـَٔادَمُ ٱسْكُنْ أَنتَ وَزَوْجُكَ ٱلْجَنَّةَ
وَكُلَا مِنْهَا رَغَدًا حَيْثُ شِئْتُمَا وَلَا تَقْرَبَا هَٰذِهِ ٱلشَّجَرَةَ فَتَكُونَا
مِنَ ٱلظَّٰلِمِينَ ﴿٣٥﴾ فَأَزَلَّهُمَا ٱلشَّيْطَٰنُ عَنْهَا فَأَخْرَجَهُمَا مِمَّا كَانَا
فِيهِ ۖ وَقُلْنَا ٱهْبِطُوا۟ بَعْضُكُمْ لِبَعْضٍ عَدُوٌّ ۖ وَلَكُمْ فِى ٱلْأَرْضِ مُسْتَقَرٌّ
وَمَتَٰعٌ إِلَىٰ حِينٍ ﴿٣٦﴾ فَتَلَقَّىٰٓ ءَادَمُ مِن رَّبِّهِۦ كَلِمَٰتٍ فَتَابَ عَلَيْهِ ۚ إِنَّهُۥ
هُوَ ٱلتَّوَّابُ ٱلرَّحِيمُ ﴿٣٧﴾ قُلْنَا ٱهْبِطُوا۟ مِنْهَا جَمِيعًا ۖ فَإِمَّا يَأْتِيَنَّكُم

مِّنِّى هُدًى فَمَن تَبِعَ هُدَاىَ فَلَا خَوْفٌ عَلَيْهِمْ وَلَا هُمْ يَحْزَنُونَ ﴿٣٨﴾ وَٱلَّذِينَ كَفَرُوا۟ وَكَذَّبُوا۟ بِـَٔايَـٰتِنَآ أُو۟لَـٰٓئِكَ أَصْحَـٰبُ ٱلنَّارِ ۖ هُمْ فِيهَا خَـٰلِدُونَ

"Behold, your Lord said to the angels, 'I will create a successor on the earth.' They said, 'Will You place therein those who will make mischief therein and shed blood while we do celebrate Your praise and glorify Your holy (name)?' He said, 'I know what you know not.' And He taught Adam the names of all things; then He placed them before the angels, and said, 'Tell Me the names of these if you are right.' They said, 'Be You exalted. Of knowledge we have none but what You have taught us. In truth, it is You who is perfect in knowledge and wisdom.' He said, 'O Adam! Tell them their names.' When he had told them, Allah said, 'Did I not tell you that I know the secrets of heavens and earth, and I know what you reveal and what you conceal?' And behold, We said to the angels, 'Bow down to Adam.' And they bowed down, but not so Iblis. He refused and was haughty. He was of those who reject faith. We said, 'O Adam! Dwell you and your wife in the Garden; and eat of the bountiful things therein as (where and when) you will but approach not this tree, or you will run into harm and transgression.' Then did Satan make them slip from the (Garden), and get them out of the state (of felicity) in which they had been. We said, 'Get down all with enmity between yourselves. On earth will be your dwelling place and your means of livelihood for a time.' Then Adam learned from his Lord words of inspiration, and his Lord turned towards him, for He is Oft-Returning, Most Merciful. We said, 'All of you get down from here: and if, as is sure, there comes to you guidance from Me, whosoever follows My guidance, on them shall be no fear, nor shall they grieve. But those who reject faith and belie Our signs, they shall be companions of the Fire; they shall abide therein'" (*al-Baqarah* 30-39).

In this passage, Allah has explained to mankind the following fundamental points, which can be considered the embarking points or the necessary background for the proper conceptualization of the purification of the soul:

(1) The human is a unique and distinct creature. It is created by God and placed on this earth, in this creation, for a purpose. The human is not part of God in any way. Any claim that it is somehow related, descended or evolved from any other animal or creature (even the angels or of God Himself) is definitely false. Therefore, any theories or belief system directly based on such a premise is also, by definition, false.

(2) This creation, the human, has a very important role in this world. Its importance and nobility can be seen in the fact that the angels were ordered to bow down to Adam, the forefather of all humans. Furthermore, Allah has placed this creature on this earth to be its successors and inhabitants and He has made available all of the earth's resources, to be used in the proper manner. Therefore, it must be a creature that is distinct in its characteristics, above and beyond the other animals and creatures placed on this earth.

(3) This creation, the human, has also been granted certain important capabilities. These include the ability to understand, intend or will something, struggle, direct oneself towards Allah, receive His words, follow His guidance and repent to Him whenever the individual fails to submit to Him properly. It also has the ability to sustain itself and has means of livelihood for itself.

(4) This creature also has some weakness to it. Furthermore, he has an eternal enemy with a band of followers in wait for him, ready to pounce on him at any moment to take him away from the path of God. Unless he controls himself and struggles against all opposing forces, he can be prone to loving desires, forgetting his covenant with God, forgetting the guidance and disbelieving in Allah.

(5) Finally, this creature is a creature with more than one possible potential. It has the potential to raise itself to a great existence by submitting to the guidance that comes to it from Allah. At the same time, though, it has the potential to drag itself down to the lowest of lows by disregarding the guidance of Allah and befriending its archenemy Satan.

(6) The key to salvation, purification and happiness is in following the guidance that comes from Allah. The worth of this life and one's status in the eternal abode is determined by one's faith, acceptance and following that which Allah has, via His indescribable mercy, revealed for the guidance of mankind.

Summary

For many people today, life has become simply pointless living and satisfactionless consumerism. This is true for those in the "advanced, capitalist" countries of the West as well as for many in the Third World countries who are eagerly striving to imitate the leaders in the developed countries. Values, purpose, goals and even purification of the soul have been forgotten by or lost to many. Shames writes,

> Consumption without excuses and without the need of justification—the beauty part was that it finessed the irksome question of values and of purpose. During the past decade [the 1980's], many people came to believe there didn't have to *be* a purpose. The mechanism didn't require it. Consumption kept the workers working, which kept the paychecks coming, which kept the people spending, which kept investors investing, which meant there was more to consume. The system, properly understood, was independent of values and needed no philosophy to prop it up. It was a perfect circle, complete in itself—and empty in the middle.[1]

Many people may even try to ignore the essential questions concerning the very meaning and purpose of their existence.[2] But can any human truly escape such questions? Isn't

---

[1] Laurence Shames, *The Hunger for More: Searching for Values in an Age of Greed* (New York: Times Books, 1989), back cover.

[2] In fact, the Arabic word *kaafir* that means an unbeliever also lexically means the one who covers something. Hence, a farmer is called a *kaafir* becomes he plants the seed and then covers it with topsoil. In reality, the unbeliever—who is shown Islam and obstinately chooses to reject it—is one who recognizes at some level within his being something in his soul that is telling him that his way of life is wrong. Instead of responding to that sign, he tries to cover it up

it necessary that these questions will pose themselves in the person's mind sooner or later? Yassine has expressed this struggle and dilemma eloquently when he wrote,

> What is life for? This is the central and vital question, the question no one can suppress or muffle, the question no one dares consider foolish.
> But it is a question that is not to be asked publicly in an age deprived of sense and occupied with other problems that have more to do with "how" than "what for." Curious about everything, open to the universe of space as well as the universe of molecules, meddlesome, punctilious, inquisitive into the least detail about every subject, our technical and scientific era remains, for all that, tragically irrelevant to this question...
> Modern man clings to the desire of prolonging his life and enjoying a better life thanks to material progress and better health, but he takes great pains to elude the essential question. He escapes his anxiety by amusing himself, so as to forget the inevitable and to avoid facing the fact of his own death. Why life at all if life is nothing but an absurd coincidence, and if after life there is nothing but death and the foulness of the grave? Might as well commit suicide now!
> In post-modern societies, comforts may repress the essential question, even as misery can make us forget it; but nothing can manage to suppress it altogether, since it lives in the very heart of every human, whether he can formulate it or not. It always returns, like a shooting pain, urgently, demanding an answer...[1]

This continual drive for some answers can be seen in the different movements that pop up every now and then—the new age movement, revival of fundamentalist Christianity, the interest

---

and ignore it. Due to this insistence to cover that truth and his intention to continue to do so for as long as he lives, his destiny will be punishment in the Hell-fire forever.

[1] Yassine, pp. 61-62.

in Eastern religions. This is because the soul itself, in a sense, demands its rights. Yassine notes,

> Even if the noise of modern culture is terribly invasive and agitating, nature—our primary nature—the conscience that lies at the base of our innermost being, will never be totally convinced that we are here for no reason.
>
> At the base of human conscience there is also a straining toward what is above, toward the spirit. This tension may swoon and faint, but it can never die...
>
> Modernity is relentless in driving out the spiritual; yet the latter is so much a part of human nature, that it cannot be banished. Instead it returns in fatal forms: the industry of charlatanism flourishes in the nooks and crannies of modern societies that combat the true nature of humankind.
>
> The outlet of sectarian spiritualism runs counter to true spirituality. How many are those who fall into its macabre clutches: the sects that devour live human flesh, the collective suicide cults, are always lurking around the edges of modern societies...[1]

Given the contemporary status of many of the religions and faiths of the world and also the state of modern science, it is not surprising that many do not even try to delve into questions related to the soul and its purification because the answers they have been presented with in the past are not satisfying. Undoubtedly, most of the answers that are available today cannot possibly satisfy the soul. The crass materialism, scientism and failure to find answers in "rational" religions has led many to seek some sort of a-rational or mystical answers in their lives.[2] One

---

[1] Yassine, p. 62.

[2] Of course, a number of factors have led to such development. Hoffman notes, "Eugen Biser sees another mechanism behind this [move to the mystical and a-rational]: modern man's abolition of sin, among other things, through 'structural exculpation.' One useful method of such exculpation is the adoption of personal convictions as a moral standard (*Gesinnungsethik*), as if good intentions could sanctify the methods and results of actions. But despite this modern man still fails to achieve his 'salvation.' In fact, as it turns out, he has only replaced his earlier problem of guilt with his new problem of suffering from the

could argue that this is natural since those mystical ways claim to quench the dire needs of the soul. Unfortunately, those mystical paths, such as the path of the Sufis to be discussed in detail in Chapter 8, offer no more reliable or satisfactory answers than any of the other paths described earlier.

However, as has already been pointed out, not all is lost. There still exists a revelation, preserved and unadulterated, that has come from the Creator. There still exists the pure teachings of a man who was directly inspired by the Lord of all creation. It is in this revelation and these teachings that the correct and true answers to the most fundamental questions are to be found. In the Quran and the Sunnah lies the salvation for the soul, the only true way for its purification. This way must be understood correctly and followed properly, as no other way will suffice for mankind. The explanation of the Islamic concept of the purification of the soul and its means is the burden of the remainder of this book.

---

meaninglessness of his existence. In turn, this has led to the current 'religious proliferation' with its anti-intellectual attitude, i.e., a tendency towards [Christian] fundamentalism and/or mysticism. According to Karl Rahner, we may extrapolate from all this that 'the Christian of the future will be a mystic or not at all.'" Murad Hofmann, *Islam the Alternative* (Beltsville, MD: Amana Publications, 1992), p. 48.

Chapter 2
Definition and Discussion of Terms

"Purification of the soul" is an English translation for the Islamic concept of *tazkiyah al-nafs* (تزكية النفس). It is a phrase made up of two distinct terms. As is true for many compound phrases, an in-depth understanding of each term will assist in understanding the concept that is sought by the phrase itself. Since the discussion of the meaning of *tazkiyah* will be relatively brief, the term *nafs* will be dealt with first.

The Definition of *al-Nafs*

There are a number of questions surrounding the concept of the soul itself. For example, is it a part of the body or one of its accidents (non-essential properties)? Or is it a body placed in another body where it resides? Or is it a pure substance? Is it the same as spirit (*rooh*) or different from it? With respect to the word "human", does "human" refer to the spirit only, or the spirit and the body, or both of them together or either one of them? Are there three souls, namely the one inciting to evil (*al-ammarah bi-l-su'*), the second admonishing (*al-lawwamah*), and the third tranquil (*al-mutma'innah*), or just one soul? Does the spirit (*al-rooh*) die, or is it the body alone that dies?[1]

---

[1] Obviously, the discussion of the concept of *nafs* itself could take many pages. The discussion here will be restricted to topics that are essential to the question of *tazkiyah al-nafs* or topics that are misunderstood and abused in the context of *tazkiyah al-nafs*. Two books are available in English that discuss the concept of the soul in greater detail. The interested reader may consult: Abu Bilal Mustafa al-Kanadi, *Mysteries of the Soul Expounded* (Jeddah: Abul-Qasim Publishing House, 1994); Suhaib Hasan, *The Journey of the Soul* (London: Al-Quran Society, 1995).

As for the essential nature of the soul, in *Sharh al-Aqeedah al-Tahaawiyyah,* ibn Abi al-Izz wrote,

> There is a difference of opinion about the essential nature of the spirit. Some say it is a body. Some say it is an accident. Others say that they do not know what it is, either a physical entity or an accident. Some say that the spirit is nothing but the four natural components.[1] Some say that it is the pure blood free of any odor or odorous impurities. Some say that it is the natural heat, which is life itself. Some say that it is a non-composite physical entity that is spread throughout the animal world that drives that world and that it is not divided into essence and body, and that all in the animal world possess the same kind of spirit. Others say it is the breath that is breathed in and out. And there are still other opinions...
>
> The Quran, Sunnah, consensus of the Companions and rational thought prove that the soul is a body of a different essence than the physical body that is seen. It is a body from light and a higher source. It is very light, living and moving. It is implemented through the physical limbs. It spreads through them like water spreads through a watering place, or olive oil spreads through an olive tree or like fire in a coal. As long as the limbs are healthy to accept the effects of that light body (the soul), the soul remains in that body and drives that physical body's feelings, movements and volition. But if it becomes bad, the mixture of the compounds becomes bad, and it no longer accepts that effect, the spirit leaves the body and goes to the world of the spirits.
>
> The evidence for that is Allah's statement, "Allah receives (humans') souls at the time of their death" (*al-Zumar* 42). This states that the souls are given death, kept and sent. Allah also says, "If you could see, when

---

[1] In Greek and Arabic medicine, the human body was considered to be composed of four natural components, earth, air, fire and water. When they were out of sync, the body did not function properly.

> the wrongdoers reach the pangs of death and the angels stretch out their hands, saying: Deliver up your souls" (*al-Anaam* 93). This states that the angels stretch out their hands to grasp the souls. It describes the soul as coming out. It also shows that the soul is punished on that day and it goes to its Lord. Furthermore, Allah says, "He it is Who gathers your soul at night and knows that which you commit by day. Then He raises you again to life therein" (*al-Anaam* 60). This states that the souls are taken by night and then returned to their bodies during the day. And the angels take them at death. Allah also says, "But ah! Thou soul at peace! Return unto your Lord, content in His good pleasure. Enter among My bondmen. Enter My garden" (*al-Fajr* 27-30). Here the soul is described as returning, entering and being pleased.
> The Prophet (peace be on him) said, "When the soul is seized, the eyes watch it." [Recorded by Muslim.] This describes the soul as being seized and the eyesight seeing it...[1]

Ibn Abi al-Izz also deals with the question of the difference between the *nafs* ("the soul") and the closely related term *rooh* ("the spirit"), noting,

> As for the question whether soul (*nafs*) and spirit (*rooh*) are two different things or the same thing, the correct view is that the words mean different things, some of which are the same and some that differ. Take, for instance, *nafs*. Sometimes it refers to *rooh* (spirit); sometimes it refers to something that is associated

---

[1] Ibn Abi al-Izz, *Commentary on the Creed of At-Tahawi by ibn Abi al-Izz* (Riyadh: Al-Imam Muhammad ibn Saud Islamic University, 2000), pp. 349-353. One of the views that has been expounded is that the soul is eternal in nature. Ibn Abi al-Izz also deals with this question in some detail. He begins his discussion by noting (p. 354), "Some people say that the spirit is eternal. However, the prophets of Allah are agreed that it is a contingent being, created, fashioned, controlled and nourished by Allah. One of the basic principles of all prophetic religions is that the world is contingent. This is also the belief of the Companions and their Successors. After them, some people who had little knowledge of the Quran and the Sunnah began to claim that the spirit is eternal."

> with the body. Hence when we want to refer to something isolated from the body, we use the term *rooh*. Thirdly, *nafs* may mean blood... As for *rooh*, it does not refer to the body, neither by itself nor in combination with *nafs*.[1]

Karzoon has offered the following definition for *nafs*, which is very relevant to the discussion of the purification of the soul, "It is something internal in the entity of a human whose exact nature is not perceived. It is ready to accept direction towards good or evil. It combines together a number of human attributes and characteristics that have a clear effect on human behavior."[2]

Karzoon has highlighted what is of central interest here concerning the human soul: Allah, in His infinite wisdom, has created humans in such a way that they are capable of accepting and following a direction to what is good as well as a direction to what is evil. Indeed, perhaps every human has within him characteristics that are good and characteristics that are evil. The issue before him is which of these characteristics is he going to support and develop and which of them is he going to control or virtually eradicate. If he develops his noble qualities and lives according to them, he will be following the correct path. If he follows and obeys the lowly desires of his self, he will lead himself to his own destruction. In reality, therefore, the only salvation for

---

[1] Ibn Abi al-Izz, p. 353. Ibn Abi al-Izz (p. 354) also discusses the intriguing question of the immortality of the soul. He wrote, "As to the question whether the spirit (*al-rooh*) is mortal or not, people have different views. Some say that it is mortal, for it is a soul (*nafs*) and every soul is to die. Allah has said, 'All that is on earth will perish, but will abide (forever) the Face of your Lord, Full of Majesty, Bounty and Honor' (*al-Rahmaan* 26-27), and 'Everything (that exists) will perish except His own Face' (*al-Qasas* 88). These people say that when even angels will perish, the souls of men will certainly also perish. Others say that the spirits do not perish, because they have been created to abide forever; only the bodies perish. In support, they cite those hadith which talk of the pleasure and pain which spirits will suffer after they leave their bodies till Allah gives them new bodies. The correct view on the issue may be stated like this: One may understand the death of the soul to mean its departure from the body, not its destruction. In this sense, the soul is mortal. But if one means that it perishes and disappears completely, then it is not mortal in that sense. It continues to live after death, and has pleasure or pain."

[2] Karzoon, vol. 1, p. 16. Also see Abdul Rahman Habankah al-Meedaani, *al-Akhlaaq al-Islaamiyyah* (Beirut: Daar al-Qalam, n.d.), vol. 1, p. 215.

him lies in purifying his soul, to bring about what is best in it and eradicate or minimize its evils. This fact is very clearly indicated in Allah's words,

وَنَفْسٍ وَمَا سَوَّىٰهَا ﴿٧﴾ فَأَلْهَمَهَا فُجُورَهَا وَتَقْوَىٰهَا ﴿٨﴾ قَدْ أَفْلَحَ مَن زَكَّىٰهَا ﴿٩﴾ وَقَدْ خَابَ مَن دَسَّىٰهَا

"By the soul, and the proportion and order given to it, and its enlightenment as to its wrong and its right, truly he succeeds who purifies it, and he fails who corrupts it" (*al-Shams* 7-10).

When giving a speech, the Prophet (peace and blessings of Allah be upon him) would often begin with a preamble that included the words,

وَنَعُوذُ بِاللَّهِ مِنْ شُرُورِ أَنْفُسِنَا وَسَيِّئَاتِ أَعْمَالِنَا

"We seek refuge in Allah from the evil in our souls and from the sinfulness of our deeds."[1] Al-Qaari explains this as seeking refuge in Allah from the appearance of the lowly, base and natural characteristics of the soul.[2]

The important point is that these words demonstrate that there is a potential for evil within the souls of humans. The guidance of truth has come from Allah in the form of revelation reaffirming what is already found within the natural disposition of humans (the *fitrah*) but, at the same time, humans must be aware that within the soul there is a potential for evil and straying from the truth. However, this does not mean that the soul is inherently evil. When the scholars discuss the importance of overcoming the soul and its evil, they are, in reality, simply emphasizing the fact that the soul has a potential for evil and that said potential must be stopped or overcome. This does not mean that the soul is in

---

[1] These words form part of the preamble by which the Prophet (peace and blessings of Allah be upon him) would begin his speeches. It is recorded by Ahmad, al-Nasaa`ee, al-Tirmidhi, Abu Dawood and ibn Maajah. For a complete discussion of the sources and authenticity of these words, see Muhammad Nasir al-Din al-Albani, *Khutbah al-Haajah* (Damascus: al-Maktab al-Islaami, 1400 A.H.), *passim*.

[2] Ali ibn al-Sultaan al-Qaari, *Mirqaat al-Mafaateeh Sharh Mishkaat al-Masaabeeh* (Multaan, Pakistan: Maktabah Hapaaniyah, n.d.), vol. 6, pp. 214-215.

and of itself evil and something that humans must free themselves from to become truly spiritually pure. Although some may seem to espouse such a view, there is no evidence for it in either the Quran or Sunnah.

Allah also says,

وَأُحْضِرَتِ ٱلْأَنفُسُ ٱلشُّحَّ ۚ وَإِن تُحْسِنُوا۟ وَتَتَّقُوا۟ فَإِنَّ ٱللَّهَ كَانَ

بِمَا تَعْمَلُونَ خَبِيرًا

"And human selves are swayed by greed. But if you do good and stay away from evil, verily, Allah is ever well-acquainted with what you do" (*al-Nisaa* 128).

Hence, the gamut is very wide. The soul may accept the guidance from Allah and be among the most noble of creations and very pleasing to Allah. On the other hand, the individual may stunt the inherently good qualities in his soul—including the recognition of *tauheed* or the true oneness of Allah—and, thereby, deliberately allow his evil potential to blossom. Every individual should be aware of the possibility of either of these two scenarios. The person should or must work to overcome any evil tendency in his soul while giving full support to all of the good potential in his soul.

Although the human has these potentialities within him, his soul can be volatile. There are times when his soul builds upon its evil inclinations and encourages him to do evil, dragging him into deeds that are definitely wrong. This is the state of the soul described in the verse, in the words of Yoosuf,

وَمَآ أُبَرِّئُ نَفْسِىٓ ۚ إِنَّ ٱلنَّفْسَ لَأَمَّارَةٌۢ بِٱلسُّوٓءِ إِلَّا مَا رَحِمَ رَبِّىٓ ۚ إِنَّ

رَبِّى غَفُورٌ رَّحِيمٌ

"Nor do I absolve my own self (of blame). The (human) soul is certainly prone to evil, unless my Lord does bestow His Mercy. But surely my Lord is Oft-Forgiving, Most Merciful" (*Yoosuf* 53).[1]

[1] Similarly, Allah says while quoting the Samirite who set up the calf for worship among the Tribe of Israel, "I saw what they saw not, so I took a handful (of dust) from the footprint of the

This is a reference to what is known as *al-nafs al-ammaratu bi-l-soo`* (the soul that is inclined to evil). According to al-Jurjaani, this is the soul that is inclined to the physical world and seeks after the bodily and physical pleasures and desires. It debases the heart, dragging it down to the lowest abyss. It is the seat of evil and the spring for evil character.[1]

If a person allows his lowly or earthly characteristics to rule his life, he then feels no remorse for the wrong or sin that he has done. He is not at that level of moral consciousness where he can truly appreciate his evil. Such a person has turned his back on the guidance from Allah and His remembrance. When the person refuses to take Allah as his patron, Allah then gives him another companion:

وَمَن يَعْشُ عَن ذِكْرِ ٱلرَّحْمَـٰنِ نُقَيِّضْ لَهُۥ شَيْطَـٰنًا فَهُوَ لَهُۥ قَرِينٌ

"If anyone withdraws himself from remembrance of (Allah) Most Gracious, We appoint for him a devil to be an intimate companion to him" (*al-Zukhruf* 36). At this point, Satan easily whispers to him and encourages him to do evil, while his soul, inclined to those acts, willfully obeys.

Indeed, there is an aspect that is mentioned by Allah that is truly unbelievable upon reflection. This is the fact that the soul wrongs and harms itself. One can imagine someone, for example, wronging someone else for the sake of some worldly benefit—this is imaginable and witnessed, although it is obviously not proper. However, it does not make any sense for a person to harm and wrong his own soul. This means that he is working against his own good; he is doing something that is of direct harm and no true benefit to his soul. Is it conceivable that a supposedly "sane" person would willingly and consciously do that to himself? However, this is what happens over and over again to the majority of mankind. This demonstrates the depths of misguidance that

---

Messenger, and threw it (into the calf): thus did my soul suggest to me" (*Taha* 96). One of the early grave sins performed by mankind is described as an act made alluring and good by the person's own soul, leading, however, to his own loss. Allah says about the son of Adam who killed his brother, "The (selfish) soul of the other led him to the murder of his brother: he murdered him, and became (himself) one of the lost ones" (*al-Maaidah* 30).

[1] Quoted in Karzoon, vol. 1, p. 50.

mankind can reach.[1] This is something that Allah points to on a number of occasions. In fact, Allah even describes humans as "losing their own selves," meaning causing their own ruin and loss. Allah says,

وَمَنْ خَفَّتْ مَوَٰزِينُهُۥ فَأُو۟لَـٰٓئِكَ ٱلَّذِينَ خَسِرُوٓا۟ أَنفُسَهُم بِمَا كَانُوا۟

بِـَٔايَـٰتِنَا يَظْلِمُونَ

"Those whose scale will be light will put their souls in perdition, for that they wrongfully treated Our Signs" (*al-Araaf* 9). Allah also says,

مَّنْ عَمِلَ صَـٰلِحًا فَلِنَفْسِهِۦ ۖ وَمَنْ أَسَآءَ فَعَلَيْهَا ۗ وَمَا رَبُّكَ بِظَلَّـٰمٍ

لِّلْعَبِيدِ

"Whoever works righteousness benefits his own soul; whoever works evil, it is against his own soul. And your Lord is never unjust (in the least) to His servants" (*Fussilat* 46).

The main way that a person harms his own soul is by disobeying Allah, His creator, who, out of His mercy, sent him guidance to lead him to the path of true bliss and happiness. When a human disobeys Allah and ignores His wonderful guidance, he is, in reality, doing no more than simply harming himself. Allah says, for example,

وَمَن يَتَعَدَّ حُدُودَ ٱللَّهِ فَقَدْ ظَلَمَ نَفْسَهُۥ ۚ

"Any who transgresses the limits of Allah, does verily wrong his (own) soul" (*al-Talaaq* 1).[2]

---

[1] These depths are highlighted in the verse, *al-Araaf* 179, where Allah describes those humans who do not use the means given to them of intelligence, sight and hearing as being more misguided than the cattle.

[2] See also *al-Baqarah* 231 wherein the one who holds on to his marriage ties simply to harm his wife is described as harming his own soul. Also see *al-Baqarah* 54 wherein Moses tells the Tribe of Israel that they had wronged their own souls by worshipping the calf. Also see *al-Kahf* 35 where the owner of the prosperous garden who was not remindful of Allah and His bounties is described as wronging his own soul. See *Faatir* 32 where the believers who committed a great

When one considers what a person does to his own soul and the concept of punishment in the Hereafter, it is only fitting—even from the soul's point of view when viewed objectively—that the person be punished. The person has wronged himself and he should be required to pay the consequences for his deed. After describing the punishment of some peoples in the Hell-fire, Allah says,

وَمَا ظَلَمْنَٰهُمْ وَلَٰكِن ظَلَمُوٓا۟ أَنفُسَهُمْ

It was not We that wronged them: they wronged their own souls" (*Hood* 101).

In reality, a human has no right to wrong himself.[1] Hence, one of the first steps along the road to repentance and purifying one's soul is the recognition that one has done wrong to his soul. He must repent to Allah for the wrong that he has done to his own self as it is only Allah who can forgive him for what he has done. Adam and Eve, the parents of mankind, were taught the following words of repentance:

قَالَا رَبَّنَا ظَلَمْنَآ أَنفُسَنَا وَإِن لَّمْ تَغْفِرْ لَنَا وَتَرْحَمْنَا لَنَكُونَنَّ مِنَ ٱلْخَٰسِرِينَ

"They said, 'Our Lord! We have wronged our own souls. If You forgive us not and bestow not upon us Your mercy, we shall certainly be lost'" (*al-Araaf* 23). Allah also says,

---

deal of evil are described as wronging their own souls. *Al-Nisaa* 97 and *al-Nahl* 28 described those whom the angels bring death to while they are wronging their own souls.

[1] The slogan, for example, "It's my body and I have the right to do with it what I want," is based on the false premise that this body has come into existence on its own without anybody else having any right over it. The fact is that the body has come into creation by the command of God who still is its rightful owner and guardian. Hence, if God has defined something as harmful or wrong for the body, no individual has the right to do that act.

وَٱلَّذِينَ إِذَا فَعَلُواْ فَٰحِشَةً أَوْ ظَلَمُوٓاْ أَنفُسَهُمْ ذَكَرُواْ ٱللَّهَ فَٱسْتَغْفَرُواْ لِذُنُوبِهِمْ وَمَن يَغْفِرُ ٱلذُّنُوبَ إِلَّا ٱللَّهُ وَلَمْ يُصِرُّواْ عَلَىٰ مَا فَعَلُواْ وَهُمْ يَعْلَمُونَ

"And those who, having done some shameful act or wronged their own souls, earnestly bring Allah to mind and ask for forgiveness for their sins—and who can forgive sins except Allah—and are never obstinate in persisting knowingly in (the wrong) they have done [their reward is forgiveness]" (*ali-Imraan* 135). In fact, in the verse quoted above referring to the soul inclined to evil, Allah says while quoting Yoosuf,

وَمَآ أُبَرِّئُ نَفْسِيٓ ۚ إِنَّ ٱلنَّفْسَ لَأَمَّارَةٌۢ بِٱلسُّوٓءِ إِلَّا مَا رَحِمَ رَبِّيٓ ۚ إِنَّ رَبِّي غَفُورٌ رَّحِيمٌ

"Nor do I absolve my own self (of blame). The (human) soul is certainly prone to evil, except when My Lord bestows His Mercy: surely my Lord is Oft-Forgiving, Most Merciful" (*Yoosuf* 53). The words of Yoosuf end by noting that Allah is oft-forgiving, most merciful. Al-Aloosi notes that this implies that Allah's mercy is great for the one who repents and leaves what his soul has been leading him towards. Furthermore, Allah is also merciful in that He helps and keeps the soul from always being in that state of driving the person to do evil.[1]

Indeed, it is part of Allah's mercy upon mankind that for individuals who have some faith and true belief in God[2], even after the soul drives the person to commit a sin, there is a feeling of

---

[1] Mahmood Al-Aloosi, *Rooh al-Maani fi Tafseer al-Quraan al-Adheem wa al-Saba al-Mathaani* (Cairo: Maktabah Daar al-Turaath, n.d.), vol. 13, p. 3.

[2] Indeed, such may even be true for some who claim not to believe in God but still have some remnants of their natural disposition such that they can still feel some remorse when performing something they feel is morally wrong. Others, though, have gone to such an extreme that their moral conscience is completely dead and they cannot even recognize any wrong from any right.

remorse and anxiety. The soul bounces back from being overcome by the desire to commit a sin and recognizes the wrong that it has done. At this time, the sinner blames himself for the sin that he has committed, asking himself why he continues to do acts like that when he knows that they are wrong. In this state, the soul is described as a "self-reproaching soul." Allah says in the Quran,

وَلَآ أُقْسِمُ بِٱلنَّفْسِ ٱللَّوَّامَةِ

"And I swear by the reproaching soul" (*al-Qiyaamah* 2). Many of the early scholars noted that this refers to the soul of the believer. Mujaahid said, "This is the soul which blames itself for what it has done and it feels remorse. It blames itself for doing wrong, as to why he did it, and for doing good, as to why he did not do more of it."[1] When al-Hasan al-Basri was asked about the above verse, he replied, "By Allah, we do not see a believer except that he blames himself. [Asking himself,] 'What did I intend by my speech? What did I intend by my eating? What did I intend by my internal thoughts?' As for the sinner, he just continues along without blaming himself."[2]

Many people swing between those two states of the soul: being driven to performing evil and then feeling remorse afterwards. However, when the true faith becomes strong in a person's heart, the inclinations to evil within his soul become very weak. They are virtually completely dominated by the inclinations to piety. Thus, the inclinations to commit evil are rarely ever responded to or complied with.[3]

---

[1] Quoted in Abu Abdillaah Muhammad al-Qurtubi, *Al-Jaami li-Ahkaam al-Quraan* (Beirut: Daar Ihyaa al-Turaath al-Arabi, 1966), vol. 19, p. 92. Also see Karzoon, vol. 1, p. 53.

[2] Ismaaeel ibn Katheer, *Tafseer al-Quraan al-Adheem* (Riyadh: Dar Taibah, 1999), vol. 8, p. 275.

[3] Karzoon (vol. 1, p. 57) points out one of the main differences between the self-reproaching soul and the soul of rest and tranquility. He states that the soul of rest and tranquility is in such a state of piety that it does not take a great effort on its part to repel the evil inclinations in the soul. When evil inclinations come to it, they are quickly dispelled, to such an extent that they can be described as completely under control. On the other hand, the self-reproaching soul has to struggle mightily to defeat the evil inclinations. Due to its own weakness, the evil inclinations are often time the victors and even when they are not the victors, the struggle is a lengthy, difficult battle for the soul.

Here the soul reaches a new level. It is a level that is not completely free of sin but it so dominated by goodness that the soul feels a tranquility and rest that cannot be imagined or known by those who have never experienced it. It is a soul that is obedient to Allah, pleased with what He has decreed and relying on Him alone. It is a soul that has tasted the sweetness of faith and does not seek any substitute or replacement for that faith. This is the sought-after state of the soul that feels tranquility and is at peace. It is the state referred to in the verses,

يَٰٓأَيَّتُهَا ٱلنَّفْسُ ٱلْمُطْمَئِنَّةُ ﴿٢٧﴾ ٱرْجِعِىٓ إِلَىٰ رَبِّكِ رَاضِيَةً مَّرْضِيَّةً ﴿٢٨﴾ فَٱدْخُلِى فِى عِبَٰدِى ﴿٢٩﴾ وَٱدْخُلِى جَنَّتِى

"(To the righteous soul will be said:) 'O soul in (complete) rest and satisfaction! Come back to your Lord, well pleased and well-pleasing unto Him! Enter, then, among My Devotees! Yea, enter My Heaven!'" (*al-Fajr* 27-30).

The soul that is at rest is not a result that is reached without effort. If the person allows his soul to run uncontrollably and undisciplined—destroying its potential for good rather than increasing it—it will drive him to do evil. But if he controls his soul—that is, he forces himself to actually control himself—then his soul can reach this potential state. Indeed, this state is reached through the process of the purification of the soul.

In sum, the soul is a non-physical entity whose precise study is beyond the realm of secular science. However, through revelation from its Creator much can be known about it. Among the most important facts is its potential for either good or evil. In essence, Allah has provided guidance for the soul such that there is no excuse for anyone to allow his soul to be devoured by evil or evil forces. If an individual does that, he is simply wronging his own soul and thereby deserving of a hapless life in both this world and the Hereafter.

The Definition of *Tazkiyah*

The word *tazkiyah* is derived from the three-letter root of *za*, *kaf* and *waw* (زكو). The definition for this root is given by Lane as, "It increased, or augmented; it received increase and blessing from God; it throve by the blessing of God; and produced fruit."[1] In addition, it also implies "purification" or *al-tahaarah*, goodness and lauditory praise.[2] Al-Raaghib al-Asfahaani notes that this definition applies to both matters of this world as well as of the Hereafter.[3] In other words, Allah could increase, purify and bless something of this world as well as of the Hereafter.

The word *zakaat* (the obligatory alms) comes from this same root. Al-Asfahaani states that it is called *zakaat* because the person who gives it hopes for blessings or he gives it to purify his soul or for both of these aspects.[4]

The word *tazkiyah* (تزكية) itself[5] is the transitive verbal noun (*masdar*) of *zakkaa* (زكا), which is commonly referred to as Form II of the above verb. In that form, it means, "to purify something or somebody," as in "He purified it."[6] It also means to increase something or to give it praise. Islahi defines it as,

---

[1] Lane, *Arabic-English Lexicon*, vol. 1, p. 1240.

[2] Muhammad ibn al-Mandhoor, *Lisaan al-Arab* (Beirut: Daar Saadir, n.d.), vol. 14, p. 358.

[3] Al-Raaghib al-Asfahaani, *Mufradaat Alfaadh al-Quraan* (Damascus: Daar al-Qalam, 1997), p. 380. It should be noted that in his famous work *Basaair Dhawi al-Tamyeez fi Lataaif al-Kitaab al-Azeez*, al-Fairoozabaadi wrote four pages under the heading *al-zakaat*. The first two pages he took verbatim from al-Asfahaani's work and then he added about two pages of extra material, quotes from poetry and so forth. Cf., Muhammad al-Fairoozabaadi, *Basaair Dhawi al-Tamyeez fi Lataaif al-Kitaab al-Azeez* (Beirut: al-Maktabah al-Ilmiyyah, n.d.), vol. 3, pp. 132-135.

[4] Al-Asfahaani, p. 381.

[5] The word *tazkiyah* itself is not found in the Quran. However, conjugations of its source, the Form II verb *zakkaa*, abound in the Quran. The interested reader may research the following found in the Quran: زكاها is found once (*al-Shams* 9); تزكوا is found once (*al-Najm* 53); تزكيهم occurs once (*al-Taubah* 103); يزكون also occurs once (*al-Nisaa* 49); يزكى is found twice (*al-Nisaa* 49, *al-Noor* 21); يزكيكم is found once (*al-Baqarah* 151); يزكيهم occurs five times (*al-Baqarah* 129, *al-Baqarah* 174, *ali-Imraan* 77, *ali-Imraan* 164, *al-Jumuah* 2); تزكى is found three times (*Taha* 76, *Faatir* 18, *al-Ala* 13); تزكى occurs once (*al-Naaziaat* 18); and يزكى occurs once (Abasa 3).

[6] Cf., Lane, vol. 1, p. 1240.

"purification of something from adulterants, its growth and development and to bring it to the height of its perfection."[1]

Al-Asfahaani notes that this act of purification is attributed in the Quran at times to the human himself, since it is via his intention, faith, deeds, efforts, sacrifice and grace from Allah that he achieves the purification. Hence, for example, Allah says,

قَدۡ أَفۡلَحَ مَن زَكَّىٰهَا

"Indeed, he succeeds who purifies it [that is, his own self]" (*al-Shams* 9). At other times, the act of purification is attributed to Allah, as Allah is, in fact, its real source. It is only by Allah's grace and guidance that one can truly attain purification. Allah, therefore, says,

بَلِ ٱللَّهُ يُزَكِّى مَن يَشَآءُ وَلَا يُظۡلَمُونَ فَتِيلًا

"Allah does purify whom He wills. And never will they fail to receive justice in the least little thing" (*al-Nisaa* 49). Sometimes the act is attributed to the Prophet (peace and blessings of Allah be upon him) since he is the medium via which the path of purification is recognizable, witnessed and known. Indeed, as shall be discussed later, he was the first and the best guide to the path of purification. Allah, for example, says,

كَمَآ أَرۡسَلۡنَا فِيكُمۡ رَسُولًا مِّنكُمۡ يَتۡلُواْ عَلَيۡكُمۡ ءَايَٰتِنَا وَيُزَكِّيكُمۡ

"As We have sent among you a Messenger of your own, rehearsing to you Our Signs, and purifying you" (*al-Baqarah* 151).[2]

Al-Asfahaani also notes that in the Quran there are two forms of *tazkiyah*. One is by action. This is praiseworthy and is found in the verse quoted above,

---

[1] Islahi, p. 19. Probably, "the height of its perfection," should be changed to, "the height of its potential" in order to avoid the claim of perfection for anything other than Allah Himself and His attributes.

[2] Al-Asfahaani, p. 381.

قَدْ أَفْلَحَ مَن زَكَّىٰهَا

"Truly he succeeds who purifies it" (*al-Shams* 9). The second form is by a statement, wherein, for example, one testifies to the righteousness of another person.[1] However, this second form is blameworthy if a person does it for himself. In fact, Allah has prohibited a person from claiming about himself that he is pious and purified. Allah says,

فَلَا تُزَكُّوٓا۟ أَنفُسَكُمْ ۖ هُوَ أَعْلَمُ بِمَنِ ٱتَّقَىٰٓ

"So do not claim for yourselves purity. He [Allah] is most knowing of who fears Him" (*al-Najm* 32).[2]

Finally, *tazkiyah* is the opposite of *al-tadsiyah*. This is clear in the Quranic verses,

قَدْ أَفْلَحَ مَن زَكَّىٰهَا ۝٩ وَقَدْ خَابَ مَن دَسَّىٰهَا

"He who purifies it [that is, the soul] has succeeded and he who corrupts it has failed" (*al-Shams* 9-10). The root meaning of *dassaahaa* and *tadsiyah* is to bury something, hide it in something else[3] or make it obscure. The person who decides to debase his soul rather than purify it must, in general, hide himself from others due to the wrongs and sins he is committing—at least such is true in any society that has retained a minimum level of moral consciousness.[4] Hence, the sinner buries his soul and, in essence, loses it in sins and acts of disobedience. He thereby makes it vile and obscured, of no good reputation. Definitely, with Allah, who has the true measures of a person's worth, his soul becomes

---

[1] For example, what would usually be termed a letter of recommendation in English is commonly described as a letter of *tazkiyah* in Arabic. Another term used by the jurists for this concept is *al-tadeel* (التعديل). That concept is not of great relevance here but the interested reader may consult Wizaarah al-Auqaaf wa al-Shuoon al-Islaamiyyah, *al-Mausooah al-Fiqhiyyah* (Kuwait: Wizaarah al-Auqaaf wa al-Shuoon al-Islaamiyyah, 1988), vol. 11, pp. 238-251.

[2] Al-Asfahaani, p. 381.

[3] Cf., Sideeq ibn Hasan al-Bukhaari, *Fath al-Bayaan fi Maqaasid al-Quraan* (Beirut: al-Maktabah al-Ariyyah, 1992), vol. 15, p. 256.

[4] Muhammad ibn al-Qayyim, *Al-Jawaab al-Kaafi liman Sa`ala an al-Dawaa al-Shaafi* (Beirut: Daar al-Nadwah al-Hadeethah, 1405 A.H.), p. 95.

despised and disgraced.[1] Thus, al-Zajjaaj explained this verse by saying that the person makes his soul lowly, despicable, contemptible, vile and wretched.[2] Another implication of his burying or concealing his soul is that the person neglects what it needs to grow properly, since it is no longer in his sight and he is no longer conscience of what is best for it. Hence, he does not allow his soul to receive its needed guidance.[3]

The *Shareeah* Definition of *Tazkiyah al-Nafs*

Now that the two terms by themselves have been discussed, the meaning of the compound phrase may be determined. Many of the authors who have written on this topic have offered a definition of this compound term. However, at times the definitions are somewhat general and technically not very precise. Here, only some of the more precise or accurate definitions shall be discussed.

Islahi gives the following as the Shareeah definition, "It [purification of the soul] conveys the sense of checking ourselves from erroneous tendencies and leanings and turning them to the path of virtue and piety (fear of God's displeasure) and developing it [the soul] to attain the stage of perfection... [In other words,] with rightly guided consciousness the extreme struggle to help the good prevail and to vanquish the evil is *tazkiah* in the Quranic sense of the term."[4]

Karzoon has offered the following definition of *tazkiyah al-nafs*, "It is the purification of the soul from inclination towards evils and sins[5], and the development of its natural disposition

---

[1] Ibid., p. 95.

[2] Ibraaheem al-Zajjaaj, *Maani Al-Quran wa Iraabuhu* (Beirut: Aalim al-Kitaab, 1988), vol. 5, p. 332. The text above is based on ibn Taimiyyah's quote from al-Zajjaaj in *Majmooah*, vol. 10, p. 353.

[3] Cf., Ismaaeel ibn Katheer, *Tafseer al-Quraan al-Adheem* (Riyadh: Dar Taibah, 1999), vol. 8, p. 412,

[4] Islahi, pp. 20-21.

[5] Karzoon (vol. 1, p. 12) goes on to stress that the goal of purification of the soul does not imply removing the blameworthy characteristics and attributes from a person. He argues that such would go against his nature by which he was created by Allah. Instead, its goal is to make the praiseworthy qualities dominant and to control and direct the negative qualities to matters that

toward goodness, which leads to its uprightness and its reaching the level of *ihsaan*."[1]

Karzoon supports his definition by quoting the following hadith:

ثلاثٌ من فعَلَهُنَّ فقَد ذاق طعم الإيمان مَنْ عَبَدَ الله عزّ وجلّ وحده بأنّه لا إله إلا هو وأعطى زكاة ماله طيِّبة بها نفسُه في كُلّ عام و لم يُعطِ الهَرِمَةَ ولا الدرنة ولا المريضة ولكن من أوسط أموالكم فإن الله عز وجل لم يسألكم خيرها و لم يأمركم بشرِّها وزكّى نفسه فقال رجل وما تزكية النفس فقال أن يعلم أنّ الله عزّ وجلّ معه حيث كان

"There are three acts that whoever does them has tasted the sweetness of faith. [They are found in:] he who worships Allah alone as none is worthy of worship save Him; he who gives his zakat yearly on his wealth pleasingly from his soul, not giving [for example] a weak, old animal, a mangy animal or a sick animal. Instead, he gives from the median qualify of his wealth as Allah does not ask for the best of it and He does not order for the worst of it [to be given]; and he who purifies his soul." A man asked, "What is the purification of the soul?" He replied, "That he knows that Allah is with him wherever he may be."[2]

---

are pleasing to Allah. Hence, one purifies the soul from leaning toward evil and frees it from blameworthy aspects. In this author's view, the negative character traits that Allah naturally endows a person with may be changed or may be made so dormant that they are virtually non-existent. Allah knows best. (This author has discussed the changing of a person's innate character traits in *Commentary on the Forty Hadith*, vol. 2, pp. 1036-1039.)

[1] Karzoon, vol. 1, p. 12. The term *ihsaan* shall be defined shortly.

[2] Although some scholars have graded the chain of this hadith as *sahih* or *hasan*, upon closer inspection this author noted that some of them failed to discuss the complete chain in detail. This hadith is recorded by al-Tabaraani in *al-Mujam al-Sagheer,* al-Baihaqi in *al-Sunan. al-Tareekh al-Kabeer* by al-Bukhari (vol. 5, p. 31), *al-Ahaad wa al-Muthaani* by ibn Amr al-Shaibaani (vol. 2, p. 300), *Mujam al-Sahaabah* by ibn Qaani (vol. 2, p. 102) and *Tahdheeb al-Kamaal* by al-Mizi (vol. 16, p. 164). All of their chains are the same, being from Abdullah ibn Saalim back to the Prophet (peace and blessings of Allah be upon him). However, after Abdullah comes either Abdul Hameed ibn Ibraaheem on the authority of Abdullah or Ishaaq ibn Ibraaheem from Amr ibn al-Haarith on the authority of Abdullah. It is this link after Abdullah where the chain becomes questionable. Ibn Hajar said about Abdul Hameed ibn Ibraaheem,

This hadith, which is one of the few if not the only hadith to explicitly mention terms related to "purification of the soul," describes the one who has purified his soul as being the one who knows that Allah is with him wherever he may be.[1] In other

---

"He is honest except that his books were lost to him and his memory was very bad." However, al-Arnaaoot and Maroof then note, "In fact, he is weak. Al-Nasaa'ee said, 'He is nothing.' On another occasion, he said, 'He is not trustworthy.'" They also quote Abu Haatim as saying that he had heard the hadith of Saalim from al-Zubaidi but he lost his book and did not memorize those hadith. Abu Haatim said he came thirty years later and the people were still narrating that book (which he had lost years prior) from him. They said that the book of ibn Zibreeq, which contained the hadith of Saalim, was simply read to al-Zubaidi and he simply approved of them and narrated those hadith to them even though his memory was not such that he could have known those hadith precisely and certified their correctness. Abu Haatim then noted that kind of narration is not worth anything. (Cf., al-Arnaaoot and Maroof, vol. 2, pp. 295-296.) What is very significant about this report is that ibn Zibreeq is the same Ishaaq ibn Ibraaheem of the other chain of this hadith. In sum, the chain going through Abdul Hameed ibn Ibraaheem is definitely weak. As for the other chain, Amr ibn al-Haarith is not a well-known narrator. Although ibn Hajar calls him *maqbool* (meaning, acceptable if there is supporting evidence for his report) and al-Arnaaoot and Maroof did not comment on that grading, only two people have been known to narrate from him, Ishaaq ibn Ibraaheem and his ex-slave Ulwah. In *al-Meezaan*, al-Dhahabi concludes that he is a person whose acceptability as a narrator is not known. Ishaaq ibn Ibraaheem is a narrator who has had some complementary words said about him as well as some very disparaging remarks. Yahya ibn Maeen thought highly of him and Abu Haatim gave him a passing mark. On the other hand, Muhammad ibn Auf said, "I do not doubt that Ishaaq ibn Zibreeq is a liar." Finally, al-Nasaa`ee stated that he is not trustworthy when he narrates from Amr ibn al-Haarith. Unfortunately, the hadith under discussion here is one of his narrations from Amr ibn al-Haarith. Therefore, this chain is also weak. This author's conclusion is that this hadith is weak and in need of supporting evidence to be accepted. The narration via Abdul Hameed cannot be used as supporting evidence in this case because it may actually have the same source: the book of ibn Zibreeq. Allah knows best. Finally, it should also be noted that ibn Katheer mentions this hadith in his commentary on the Quran (vol. 8, p. 9), stating that it was recorded by Abu Nuaim. Unfortunately, this author was not able to find this hadith in the works by Abu Nuaim available to him. However, on at least one other occasion, Abu Nuaim did use the chain of Ishaaq from Amr above. Hence, until proven otherwise, this author is forced to assume that Abu Nuaim had this hadith from one of the chains discussed and criticized above. Cf., the relevant biographical entries in Yusuf al-Mizi, *Tahdheeb al-Kamaal fi Asmaa al-Rijaal* (Beirut: Muassasah al-Risaalah, 1992); Ahmad ibn Hajar, *Tahdheeb al-Tahdheeb* (Beirut: Muassasah al-Risaalah, 1996); Bashaar Maroof and Shuaib al-Arnaaoot, *Tahreer Taqreeb al-Tahdheeb li-l-Haafidh Ahmad ibn Ali ibn Hajar al-Asqalaani* (Beirut: Muassasah al-Risaalah, 1997); Muhammad al-Dhahabi, *Meezaan al-Itidaal fi Naqd al-Rijaal* (Beirut: Daar al-Marifah, n.d.).

[1] This is in reference to Allah's knowledge. It does not mean that Allah is physically with all people or in all places, as many believe. Allah is above the Throne and above and beyond all of

words, the individual is aware of Allah's presence and he is not unmindful of the fact that Allah sees and hears everything that he does. This knowledge on his part—as is true with all knowledge—is of no benefit unless it influences his behavior and actions. The result of that knowledge should be that he reforms himself, both outwardly and inwardly, and he obeys Allah in all aspects of his life. Hence, what the Prophet (peace and blessings of Allah be upon him) described in this hadith is very close to what the Prophet (peace and blessings of Allah be upon him) gave as a definition for *ihsaan* in the famous hadith of the Angel Gabriel. In that hadith, the Angel asked him, "What is *ihsaan*?" and he replied,

أَنْ تَعْبُدَ اللّٰهَ كَأَنَّكَ تَرَاهُ فَإِنْ لَمْ تَكُنْ تَرَاهُ فَإِنَّهُ يَرَاكَ

"[It is] to worship Allah as if you see Him, and if you cannot achieve [this state of devotion] as if you are seeing Him, then [you must know that] He is seeing you." (Recorded by Muslim.)

Ibn Taimiyyah made a very important point whose concept should be covered in the definition of *tazkiyah al-nafs*. He stated that the root of *zakaah* means an increase in goodness. However, he notes, goodness does not increase unless evil is abandoned and avoided, in the same way that a crop does not grow unless the silt is removed from it. Similarly, a soul and deeds cannot be purified until what negates that purification is removed.[1]

Furthermore, as shall be discussed in the fourth chapter, the goal of the process of purification of the soul should also be captured within the definition of *tazkiyah al-nafs* because it is a necessity for the soul that yearns for this goal that it has naturally been created with. This goal is to be a complete and true *abd* or servant of Allah.

In sum, therefore, this author has derived the following definition of "purification of the soul":

His creation. For more on this point, see *Commentary on the Creed of at-Tahawi by ibn Abi al-Izz* (Riyadh: Al-Imam Muhammad ibn Saud Islamic University, 2000), pp 227-241.

[1] Ahmad ibn Taimiyyah, *Majmooah al-Fataawa* (Riyadh: Maktabah al-Ubaikaan, 1997), vol. 10, p. 353.

Purification of the soul equals the process in which the healthy elements found in the soul are fostered, built upon and added to while any invading contaminants are removed or controlled such that the person worships Allah properly and fulfills his purpose in life, which can culminate in the ultimate expression of true *ihsaan*.

The definition can be further explained thusly:

"Process": Purification of the soul is a "process." In other words, it is not something static. It is, in fact, dynamic and it can be volatile. A person may be moving closer and closer to his absolute potential with respect to purification of his soul or he may move further away from it. As noted earlier, for most people, they will be moving closer to their potential at some times while at other times they may be moving away from that desired goal. In addition, using the term "process" in the definition is also an allusion to the fact that there is a certain way or path that one must follow in order for the soul to be properly or correctly purified. That essential path will be discussed in detail in Chapter 5.

"Soul": The concept of the soul has been discussed in detail. It includes many components, most importantly the heart and the ability to decide on a path of goodness or a path of evil.

"Healthy elements": The healthy elements in the soul are those that Allah has inherently blessed the soul with, such as the instinctive belief in the oneness of God, the yearning to know one's purpose in life and the yearning to please that one God. In addition to the inherent healthy elements, one also strives to add other healthy elements that further assist one along the path of purification.

"Contaminants": These include the diseases and passions that overcome the heart and soul due to weakness in one's will to obey Allah, doubts and negligence. External forces, such as Satan and his troops, can spur them on. These will be discussed in more detail in Chapter 7.

"Worships": This is the goal and purpose of one's life, as shall be discussed in detail in Chapter 4. In essence the soul becomes more purified as it becomes more and more a true servant of Allah.

"Ihsaan": As quoted earlier, the Messenger of Allah (peace and blessings of Allah be upon him) explained this concept when he said, "It is that you worship Allah as if you see Him. And even though you do not see Him, He sees you." In reality, this is the ultimate level that a person can reach in this worldly life. A person who has the quality of *ihsaan* is described as a *muhsin*. He is different from the one who is described as a believer or *mu`min*. He is, in essence, at one level beyond being simply a believer. Every *muhsin* must meet all of the conditions of a Muslim and a believer. Hence, every *muhsin* is a Muslim and a believer. However, not every believer deserves to be called a *muhsin*. Being a *muhsin* is a stage higher than that of being a believer or a Muslim.[1]

Summary

In this chapter, the basic terms of *tazkiyah* and *nafs* as well as the compound term *tazkiyah al-nafs* have been dealt with in detail. The important conclusion is the final definition of *tazkiyah al-nafs* or purification of the soul, which has been defined thusly: the process in which the healthy elements found in the soul are fostered, built upon and added to while any invading contaminants are removed or controlled such that the person worships Allah properly and fulfills his purpose in life, which can culminate in the ultimate expression of true *ihsaan*.

[1] The author has dealt with this topic in more detail in *Commentary on the Forty Hadith of al-Nawawi*, vol. 1, pp. 312ff. Note that Karzoon states (vol. 1, p. 13), "When Islam and *imaan* are sincerely fulfilled, *ihsaan* comes as a necessary result." This may be true in a very general sense of the word *ihsaan*. However, this is not how the concept is understood and explained by the scholars concerning the specific characteristic of *ihsaan*. As explained above, a person could be a believer having true *imaan* but he may not meet the characteristics of those who are deserving of the title *muhsin*.

Chapter 3
The Importance of Purification of the Soul in the Quran and Sunnah

The subject matter of this book is perhaps the most important of all obligations upon an individual. It deals with the purification of the soul. The purification of the soul means purifying the soul from *kufr*, *shirk*, hypocrisy, sins and all evil or foul characteristics—and filling the soul with proper belief, purity, sincerity, good deeds and all good characteristics. Although some among mankind may not be willing to recognize this fact; in reality, there cannot possibly be anything more important in one's life than these aspects. Indeed, purification of the soul is one of the goals of the Shareeah. In fact, the entire religion revolves around the purification of the soul whose goal is the correct and proper worship of Allah.[1]

The importance of self-purification can be seen in numerous verses of the Quran. Allah says,

قَدْ أَفْلَحَ مَن تَزَكَّىٰ

"But those will prosper who purify themselves" (*al-Ala* 14). Allah also says, after swearing by a number of aspects of His miraculous creation,

وَٱلشَّمْسِ وَضُحَىٰهَا ۝١ وَٱلْقَمَرِ إِذَا تَلَىٰهَا ۝٢ وَٱلنَّهَارِ إِذَا جَلَّىٰهَا ۝٣ وَٱلَّيْلِ إِذَا يَغْشَىٰهَا ۝٤ وَٱلسَّمَآءِ وَمَا بَنَىٰهَا ۝٥ وَٱلْأَرْضِ وَمَا

---

[1] Cf., Muhammad ibn Saeed al-Qahtaani, introduction to Ahmad ibn Taimiyyah, *Tazkiyah al-Nafs* (Riyadh: Daar al-Muslim, 1994), p. 3.

طَحَىٰهَا ﴿٦﴾ وَنَفْسٍ وَمَا سَوَّىٰهَا ﴿٧﴾ فَأَلْهَمَهَا فُجُورَهَا وَتَقْوَىٰهَا ﴿٨﴾ قَدْ أَفْلَحَ مَن زَكَّىٰهَا ﴿٩﴾ وَقَدْ خَابَ مَن دَسَّىٰهَا

"By the sun and its (glorious) splendor; By the moon as it follows (the sun); By the day as it shows (the sun's) glory; By the night as it conceals it; By the firmament and its (wonderful) structure; By the earth and its (wide) expanse; By the soul, and the proportion and order given to it; And its enlightenment as to its wrong and its right; Truly he who purifies it succeeds, And he fails that corrupts it" (*al-Shams* 1-10).[1] One should ponder over these beautiful verses and their significance. Allah swears by many of the great and magnificent parts of His creation in order to emphasize something related to the soul of each and every individual. After all of these statements, all of this amazing creation boils down to one reality for the soul: There are truly just two choices facing the soul, either to purify this soul or to corrupt it.

It is by purification of one's soul and heart that one becomes close to Allah and becomes truly successful. As Allah says,

يَوْمَ لَا يَنفَعُ مَالٌ وَلَا بَنُونَ ﴿٨٨﴾ إِلَّا مَنْ أَتَى ٱللَّهَ بِقَلْبٍ سَلِيمٍ

"The Day [of Judgment] whereon neither wealth nor sons will avail, except him who comes to Allah with a clean, sound heart" (*al-Shuaraa* 88-89).

However, Allah Himself is not in need of the person's purification nor is He in need of anybody's worship. When the person purifies his soul, he is doing so for his own benefit only. Allah has said,

وَمَن تَزَكَّىٰ فَإِنَّمَا يَتَزَكَّىٰ لِنَفْسِهِۦ ۚ وَإِلَى ٱللَّهِ ٱلْمَصِيرُ

---

[1] Ibn Taimiyyah argues that in these sets of verses from *al-Ala* and *al-Shams*, Allah is not simply informing that those who purify themselves are successful. Instead, the purport of these verses is that they are a direct command from Allah: everyone must work to purify the soul. Cf., Ahmad ibn Taimiyyah, *Tazkiyah al-Nafs* (Riyadh: Daar al-Muslim, 1994), pp. 40-41.

"And whoever purifies himself does so for the benefit of his own soul; and the destination (of all) is to Allah" (*Faatir* 18). The latter portion of that verse implies that whether one purifies his soul or not he is, in the end, going to have to meet Allah. If he does not purify his soul, he himself has sentenced his soul to eternal damnation. On the other hand, if he did purify his soul, he has fulfilled his obligations to his Lord and to his soul and his reward when he returns to Allah will be eternal happiness.

When Allah sent His Prophet Moses (peace and blessings of Allah be upon him) to one of the greatest tyrants in the history of mankind, the Pharaoh, Allah told Moses,

ٱذْهَبْ إِلَىٰ فِرْعَوْنَ إِنَّهُۥ طَغَىٰ ﴿١٧﴾ فَقُلْ هَل لَّكَ إِلَىٰٓ أَن تَزَكَّىٰ ﴿١٨﴾
وَأَهْدِيَكَ إِلَىٰ رَبِّكَ فَتَخْشَىٰ

"Go to Pharaoh, for he has indeed transgressed all bounds. And say to him, 'Would you like to be purified (from sin) and that I guide you to your Lord, so you then fear Him?'" (*al-Naaziaat* 17-19).

Furthermore, a fact that is clearly highlighted in the Quran itself is that it was one of the roles of the Prophet (peace and blessings of Allah be upon him) to aid in purification—this was one of his most important roles as stressed in the Quran:

كَمَآ أَرْسَلْنَا فِيكُمْ رَسُولًا مِّنكُمْ يَتْلُواْ عَلَيْكُمْ ءَايَـٰتِنَا
وَيُزَكِّيكُمْ وَيُعَلِّمُكُمُ ٱلْكِتَـٰبَ وَٱلْحِكْمَةَ وَيُعَلِّمُكُم مَّا لَمْ
تَكُونُواْ تَعْلَمُونَ

"A similar (favor have you already received) in that We have sent among you a messenger of your own, rehearsing to you Our signs, and purifying you, and instructing you in the Book and the

Wisdom, and in new knowledge that beforehand you did not know" (*al-Baqarah* 151).[1]

Allah also says,

لَقَدْ مَنَّ ٱللَّهُ عَلَى ٱلْمُؤْمِنِينَ إِذْ بَعَثَ فِيهِمْ رَسُولًا مِّنْ أَنفُسِهِمْ يَتْلُوا۟ عَلَيْهِمْ ءَايَـٰتِهِۦ وَيُزَكِّيهِمْ وَيُعَلِّمُهُمُ ٱلْكِتَـٰبَ وَٱلْحِكْمَةَ وَإِن كَانُوا۟ مِن قَبْلُ لَفِى ضَلَـٰلٍ مُّبِينٍ

"Allah did confer a great favor on the Believers when He sent among them a Messenger from among themselves, rehearsing unto them the Signs of Allah, sanctifying them, and instructing them in Scripture and Wisdom, while before that, they had been in manifest error" (*ali-Imraan* 164).

After analyzing a number of verses in the Quran related to the concept of purification of the soul, in particular those quoted above, Islahi makes the following concise and accurate conclusions:

> (1) That the only object of the faith and the Shari'ah and the supreme end in view in raising the prophets has ever been *tazkiah*. The importance attached to it in

[1] In *al-Baqarah* 129, Allah also mentions the prayer of the Prophet Abraham (peace and blessings of Allah be upon him), "Our Lord! Send among them a messenger of their own, who shall recite Your signs to them and instruct them in the Book and Wisdom, and purify them. Verily, You are the Exalted in Might, the Wise." In an interesting argument, Islāhi (pp. 2-3) writes, "The style of expression of the Quran itself has elucidated the fact that in the verse stating the purpose of raising the prophet the issue at stake is the reformation of man. The other two mentioned along with it, the rehearsal of the Signs and instruction in Scripture and Wisdom have been narrated not as the real object but as means in the attainment of the real object. In support of our argument we would like to invite the attention of the reader once again to the verses quoted above. In the verse [*al-Baqarah*] 129 the word *tazkiah* or purification occurs at the close of the verse, whereas in the verse [*al-Baqarah*] 151 it occurs in the beginning. Now any one given to deep thought cannot but conclude that this variation of expression in stating the same thing must have some pertinent reason behind it. Giving a little further thought to it we can see for ourselves that *tazkiah* or purification and development were intended to be the be-all and end-all of all the activities and striving of the prophet, since it is the importance of the supreme object that is to be kept in view in the beginning of one's mission and also at the close of it. It is the starting point as well as the goal of all his activities. It is the point where he starts his journey and also his destination."

the programme of the faith is exclusive to it and all other things have a secondary importance only, being the means of attaining this object. The activities of the prophets, however diverse and multi-faceted on the surface, their real target was man and the *tazkiah* of human society.

(2) The other point that has been brought to light is the fact that the source of *tazkiah* is the Book revealed by God—Al-Quran. The *tazkiah* starts with the instruction in the Book and later on, it is the truths and the mysteries derived from this fountain head that the prophet reveals to the people and perfects their *tazkiah*. It is this underlying reason behind coupling *tazkiah* with the rehearsing of the Signs in the verses quoted earlier, and makes it clear that *tazkiah* follows in the wake of such rehearsal and is naturally the outcome of it...

(3) The third thing that it elucidates is that *tazkiah* is not limited to any particular section of the human society but concerns the whole of humanity, there being no course left for anybody's redemption save through *tazkiah* or self-culture. It is not any specialization for some in the faith but an indispensable, individual need for everyone without exception and without it entry to heaven is barred.[1]

The Importance of Purification of the Soul for the Individual and Society

The long-run importance of purification of the soul for the individual and for society actually lies in the benefits and results of purifying the soul. A discussion of those results and benefits will be presented in a separate chapter after the process and means are discussed.

At this point in the book, however, the author would like to comment upon a number of points, in particular the

[1] Islahi, pp. 5-6.

relationship between the purification of the soul and the plight of the Muslim world today. That discussion will be followed by a few words on the importance of purification of the soul for the various sectors of the Muslim nation.

Purification of the Soul and the Plight of the Muslim Nation Today

Currently, one may hear a great deal of discussion concerning the plight of the Muslims and what needs to be done to resolve the many problems in today's Muslim world and elsewhere. Many Muslims cannot figure out why they, given that the Muslims have the true religion, are facing the difficulties that they are currently facing. Muslims are, indeed, facing grave difficulties today. Many times, it seems as though the blood and honor of a Muslim is worth absolutely nothing today—even to those people who make a great show of claiming to believe in and stand for human rights. This seems to be a very dire plight that contemporary Muslims are experiencing. Unfortunately, though, the solutions for those problems are sometimes not understood by many Muslims.

In trying to solve the problems of the Muslim *Ummah*, some Muslims have emphasized the material aspect while others emphasize some kind of "democratic" political approach.[1] The first group sees the entire problem as a result of the military-caliphate weakness of the Muslims. Once this problem can be resolved, the Muslims will have the physical strength to defeat their worldly enemies and establish the caliphate and so forth. Indeed, establishing the caliphate is the overall goal in life for many of these people, virtually ignoring the more general concept

---

[1] There are some who advocate a spiritual reformation as the key. Unfortunately, for many who advocate this, they fail to view Islam and the purification of the soul in its entirety, restricting the reformation to some acts of worship without reforming the entire worldview and goals of the individual Muslims themselves. Islam is not simply a matter of the ritual acts of worship but it must also extend to all the actions of the heart as well as, for example, the business practices, marriage laws and rules of government. Until all of these are part and parcel of an individual's and community's reform, the true purification of the soul and victory from Allah may never come about.

of purification of the soul in the meantime. On the other hand, the others see the plight of the Muslim *Ummah* as a result of the Muslims estranging themselves from contemporary civilization. If the Muslims would simply compromise with the other ideologies of the world and accept some of what they request, the differing parties or ideologies would be able to live in peace, with the Muslims having their own states to run their own internal affairs. Others attempt to combine these two approaches and emphasize Muslim unity wherein the different Muslims countries as they are today should come together to forge a militarily and politically strong entity. This should then resolve the current plight of the Muslims of today.

In the light of the teachings of the Quran, however, it seems very clear that the problems faced by the Muslims are the result of the actions that they themselves are performing. Every believer must realize and believe with certainty that victory and support come only from Allah. Allah has said,

وَمَا ٱلنَّصْرُ إِلَّا مِنْ عِندِ ٱللَّهِ ٱلْعَزِيزِ ٱلْحَكِيمِ

"There is no help [or victory] except from Allah, the Exalted, the Wise" (*ali-Imraan* 126). Allah also says,

إِن يَنصُرْكُمُ ٱللَّهُ فَلَا غَالِبَ لَكُمْ وَإِن يَخْذُلْكُمْ فَمَن ذَا ٱلَّذِى يَنصُرُكُم مِّنۢ بَعْدِهِۦ

"If Allah helps you none can overcome you: if He forsakes you, who is there, after that, that can help you?" (*ali-Imraan* 160).

In other words, Muslims will only be living in a situation where the Muslims and Islam are dominant and where the blood and honor of a Muslim is respected when Allah blesses them with such a situation. No one can defeat or frustrate Allah's plan. Thus, no one can defeat or subjugate Muslims unless Allah allows for that to occur. Allah, though, does not give victory to the Muslims simply because they carry the name "Muslim" or "Islam". And, if Allah does not give the Muslims victory, then no one else will ever be able to bring victory to the Muslims.

Allah also says,

إِنَّا لَنَنصُرُ رُسُلَنَا وَٱلَّذِينَ ءَامَنُوا۟ فِى ٱلْحَيَوٰةِ ٱلدُّنْيَا وَيَوْمَ يَقُومُ ٱلْأَشْهَـٰدُ

"We will, without doubt, help Our Messengers and those who believe, (both) in this world's life and on the Day when the witnesses will stand forth" (*Ghaafir* 51). Ibn al-Qayyim noted that this verse means that whoever has a shortcoming in his faith will, thereby, receive a correspondingly lesser amount of help and victory from Allah. If a believer suffers any form of affliction from his enemy, it is due to his own sins, either leaving an obligatory act or performing a forbidden act, which represents his weakness in his faith.[1]

Hence, the current plight of the Muslims will not change until Allah wills for them to have victory and dominance. However, Allah will not give them that victory, peace and tranquility unless and until they meet the criterion or fulfill the causes of such Divine support. In fact, Allah has actually promised the true believers that He will establish them in the land when they meet the proper criteria. Allah says,

وَعَدَ ٱللَّهُ ٱلَّذِينَ ءَامَنُوا۟ مِنكُمْ وَعَمِلُوا۟ ٱلصَّـٰلِحَـٰتِ لَيَسْتَخْلِفَنَّهُمْ فِى ٱلْأَرْضِ كَمَا ٱسْتَخْلَفَ ٱلَّذِينَ مِن قَبْلِهِمْ وَلَيُمَكِّنَنَّ لَهُمْ دِينَهُمُ ٱلَّذِى ٱرْتَضَىٰ لَهُمْ وَلَيُبَدِّلَنَّهُم مِّنۢ بَعْدِ خَوْفِهِمْ أَمْنًا ۚ يَعْبُدُونَنِى لَا يُشْرِكُونَ بِى شَيْـًٔا ۚ وَمَن كَفَرَ بَعْدَ ذَٰلِكَ فَأُو۟لَـٰٓئِكَ هُمُ ٱلْفَـٰسِقُونَ

"Allah has promised to those among you who believe and work righteous deeds that He will, of a surety, grant them in the land inheritance (of power) as He granted it to those before them. [He also promises] that He will establish in authority their religion, the one which He has chosen for them. And [He promises] that

---

[1] Muhammad ibn al-Qayyim, *Ighaathah al-Luhfaan min Masaayid al-Shaitaan* (Beirut: Daar al-Fikr), vol. 2, p. 182.

He will change (their state) after the fear in which they (lived) to one of security and peace. 'They will worship Me (alone) and do not associate anything with Me.' If any do reject faith after this, they are rebellious and wicked" (*al-Noor* 55). There is something more to this promise then having some minimum allegiance to Islam. Indeed, as can be seen in the world today, simply carrying the name "Muslim" is not sufficient to earn the great Divine favor of being established in the land.

The key to attaining Allah's favor and grace in this life and in the Hereafter is in the purification of the soul. Allah has given all believers a very moving example in the case of the people around the Prophet (peace and blessings of Allah be upon him) himself. Even though the Prophet (peace and blessings of Allah be upon him) was in their midst, when they failed to obey Allah properly, Allah did not bless them with victory and support.

One can study the examples of the Battle of Badr and the Battle of Uhud to see when Allah gave the believers a clear victory and support and when Allah did not do so. In the Battle of Badr, the Muslims were greatly outnumbered and their weaponry was limited. Even with their inferior or weak position, Allah gave them a stunning victory over the disbelievers due to their strong faith and obedience to Allah. They did make the necessary material or physical preparations to meet their enemy but that was not the main cause of their stunning victory. Instead, it was their *taqwa,* their fear of Allah and their lack of sins that made this small band pleasing to Allah and, hence, Allah would not allow any great harm to come to them. Allah refers to that battle in these words,

وَلَقَدْ نَصَرَكُمُ ٱللَّهُ بِبَدْرٍ وَأَنتُمْ أَذِلَّةٌ فَٱتَّقُوا۟ ٱللَّهَ لَعَلَّكُمْ تَشْكُرُونَ

"Allah had helped you at Badr, when you were a contemptible little force; then fear Allah; thus may you show your gratitude" (*ali-Imraan* 123).

In the Battle of Uhud, on the other hand, one sees the result of disobeying Allah or His Messenger (peace and blessings of Allah be upon him). In the Battle of Uhud, the Prophet (peace and blessings of Allah be upon him) gave a clear command to the archers to remain in their positions no matter how they saw the tide of the battle turning. But when some of the archers saw the Muslims getting the upper hand, they neglected their sincerity to Allah and fighting solely for His sake. They began to fear that they would lose out on the war booties. Therefore, they disobeyed the direct command from the Prophet—they sinned in their actions. It was due to their sin that the disbelievers were able to attack the Muslims from the outpost of the archers and keep the Muslims from another stunning defeat of the Quraish. The Muslims suffered from that partial defeat, with many of them being killed during the battle. Concerning such events, Allah has said,

وَلَقَدْ صَدَقَكُمُ ٱللَّهُ وَعْدَهُۥٓ إِذْ تَحُسُّونَهُم بِإِذْنِهِۦ ۖ حَتَّىٰٓ إِذَا فَشِلْتُمْ
وَتَنَٰزَعْتُمْ فِى ٱلْأَمْرِ وَعَصَيْتُم مِّنۢ بَعْدِ مَآ أَرَىٰكُم مَّا تُحِبُّونَ ۚ
مِنكُم مَّن يُرِيدُ ٱلدُّنْيَا وَمِنكُم مَّن يُرِيدُ ٱلْءَاخِرَةَ ۚ ثُمَّ صَرَفَكُمْ
عَنْهُمْ لِيَبْتَلِيَكُمْ ۖ وَلَقَدْ عَفَا عَنكُمْ ۗ وَٱللَّهُ ذُو فَضْلٍ عَلَى ٱلْمُؤْمِنِينَ

"Allah did indeed fulfil His promise to you when by His permission you were about to annihilate your enemy, until you flinched and fell to disputing about the order, and disobeyed it after He brought you in sight (of the booty) which you covet. Among you are some that hanker after this world and some that desire the Hereafter. Then did He divert you from your foes in order to test you. But He forgave you: for Allah is full of grace to those who believe" (*ali-Imraan* 152). Shortly afterwards, Allah says,

إِنَّ ٱلَّذِينَ تَوَلَّوْا۟ مِنكُمْ يَوْمَ ٱلْتَقَى ٱلْجَمْعَانِ إِنَّمَا ٱسْتَزَلَّهُمُ
ٱلشَّيْطَٰنُ بِبَعْضِ مَا كَسَبُوا۟ ۖ

"Those of you who turned back on the day the two hosts met, it was Satan who caused them to fail, because of some (evil) they had done" (*ali-Imraan* 154); that is, they succumbed to Satan due to some of their sins.

Finally, Allah says,

لَقَدْ مَنَّ ٱللَّهُ عَلَى ٱلْمُؤْمِنِينَ إِذْ بَعَثَ فِيهِمْ رَسُولًا مِّنْ أَنفُسِهِمْ يَتْلُوا۟
عَلَيْهِمْ ءَايَـٰتِهِۦ وَيُزَكِّيهِمْ وَيُعَلِّمُهُمُ ٱلْكِتَـٰبَ وَٱلْحِكْمَةَ وَإِن
كَانُوا۟ مِن قَبْلُ لَفِى ضَلَـٰلٍ مُّبِينٍ ﴿١٦٤﴾ أَوَلَمَّآ أَصَـٰبَتْكُم مُّصِيبَةٌ قَدْ
أَصَبْتُم مِّثْلَيْهَا قُلْتُمْ أَنَّىٰ هَـٰذَا ۖ قُلْ هُوَ مِنْ عِندِ أَنفُسِكُمْ ۗ إِنَّ ٱللَّهَ عَلَىٰ
كُلِّ شَىْءٍ قَدِيرٌ

"Allah did confer a great favor on the believers when He sent among them a messenger from among themselves, reciting to them the Signs of Allah, sanctifying them, and instructing them in the Book and Wisdom, while before that, they had been in manifest error. What! When a single disaster smites you, although you smote (your enemies) with one twice as great, do you say? 'From where is this?' Say (to them): 'It is from yourselves: for Allah has power over all things" (*ali-Imraan* 164-165). Here, Allah reminds the believers of the blessing that He has bestowed upon them. He sent to them such a guidance that there was no reason for them to sway from the straight path; indeed, they even had the Messenger (peace and blessings of Allah be upon him) alive among themselves. Hence, before mentioning why Allah afflicts the Muslims with hardships and difficulties, He first reminded them of guidance that He had given them, the key to the purification of their souls. If they ignore that guidance and path, even if only to a partial extent, the result will be evil for them. Hence Allah afflicted them with hardship due to their own misdeed. After the clear guidance, once they strayed they had no real right to ask from whence did their misfortune come. It should have been clear to them. It was the result of what their own hands wrought.

Allah also reminds the believers,

مَّآ أَصَابَكَ مِنْ حَسَنَةٍ فَمِنَ ٱللَّهِ ۖ وَمَآ أَصَابَكَ مِن سَيِّئَةٍ فَمِن نَّفْسِكَ ۚ

"Whatever good happens to you is from Allah; but whatever evil happens to you, is from your (own) soul" (*al-Nisaa* 79).

There are many examples of this nature that one could cite. It is indeed notable that whenever the Prophet (peace and blessings of Allah be upon him) would send out an expedition, the first thing that he would remind them of is that they are going out for the sake of Allah and that they should have *taqwa* or fear of Allah. Al-Tirmidhi records:

سُلَيْمَانَ بْنِ بُرَيْدَةَ عَنْ أَبِيهِ قَالَ كَانَ رَسُولُ اللَّهِ صَلَّى اللَّهم عَلَيْهِ وَسَلَّمَ إِذَا بَعَثَ أَمِيرًا عَلَى جَيْشٍ أَوْصَاهُ فِي خَاصَّةِ نَفْسِهِ بِتَقْوَى اللَّهِ وَمَنْ مَعَهُ مِنَ الْمُسْلِمِينَ خَيْرًا وَقَالَ اغْزُوا بِسْمِ اللَّهِ وَفِي سَبِيلِ اللَّهِ قَاتِلُوا مَنْ كَفَرَ بِاللَّهِ

Sulaiman ibn Buraidah narrated from his father that whenever the Messenger of Allah (peace and blessings of Allah be upon him) would send a general over an army he would advise him about himself to have fear (*taqwa*) of Allah and to treat those of the Muslims with him well. Then he would say, "Fight in the name of Allah for the sake of Allah and fight whoever disbelieves in Allah."[1] In the famous letter that the second caliph Umar ibn al-Khattaab wrote to Saad ibn Abi Waqaas, Umar stated,

> I order you and the soldiers who are with you to be aware of Allah under all circumstances as *taqwa* [fear and awareness] of Allah is a better weapon against your enemy and a stronger strategy in battle. And I order you and those with you to be very much on the defensive against any sins, more than your enemies are, for the sins of an army are more feared than their enemies. Verily, Allah helps the Muslims due to the sins of their enemies; if it were not for that we would not be able to overcome them for our numbers are not like theirs and our power is not like theirs. If we are equal in sins to them, they will be able to overtake us due to their

[1] Recorded by al-Tirmidhi and others. According to al-Albaani, it is *sahih*. See Muhammad Naasir al-Deen al-Albaani, *Saheeh Sunan al-Tirmidhi* (Riyadh: Maktab al-Tarbiyyah al-Arabi li-Duwal al-Khaleej, 1988), vol. 2, p. 59.

> (military) power. If we were not aided by our virtue we would not be able to overcome them due solely to our power.... And ask Allah to help yourselves in the same way that you ask for help against your enemies.[1]

In other words, Allah brings about defeat and humiliation to the Muslims due to the sins committed by the Muslims themselves. It is the Muslims' own hands that are responsible for their plight. It is their lack of *taqwa* and purification that lands them in the situation that they are in. Without the purification of the soul, the individual is dragged down to clinging onto this world and avoiding anything that may risk the things that he loves in this world. He fears dying, he becomes cowardly, he compromises his faith and he surrenders to the strength of others all so that he can protect the little that he has of this world. He then becomes an open prey to all his enemies, as with the case with many parts of the Muslim world today. Indeed, the Prophet (peace and blessings of Allah be upon him) made this point very clear when he stated,

يُوشِكُ الأُمَمُ أَنْ تَدَاعَى عَلَيْكُمْ كَمَا تَدَاعَى الْأَكَلَةُ إِلَى قَصْعَتِهَا فَقَالَ قَائِلٌ وَمِنْ قِلَّةٍ نَحْنُ يَوْمَئِذٍ قَالَ بَلْ أَنْتُمْ يَوْمَئِذٍ كَثِيرٌ وَلَكِنَّكُمْ غُثَاءٌ كَغُثَاءِ السَّيْلِ وَلَيَنْزَعَنَّ اللَّهُ مِنْ صُدُورِ عَدُوِّكُمْ الْمَهَابَةَ مِنْكُمْ وَلَيَقْذِفَنَّ اللَّهُ فِي قُلُوبِكُمُ الْوَهْنَ فَقَالَ قَائِلٌ يَا رَسُولَ اللَّهِ وَمَا الْوَهْنُ قَالَ حُبُّ الدُّنْيَا وَكَرَاهِيَةُ الْمَوْتِ

"The Nations shall soon summon one another to attack you as people when eating invite others to share their dish." Someone asked, "Will that be because we will be small in numbers at that time?" He [the Messenger of Allah (peace and blessings of Allah be upon him)] replied, "No, you will be numerous but you will be like the froth on the sea. Allah will remove fear of you from the hearts of our enemies and Allah will cast *wahn* into your hearts."

---

[1] Quoted in Abdullah Ghaushah, *Al-Jihaad Tareeq al-Nasr* (Wizaarah al-Auqaaf, 1976), p. 172.

A person asked, "What is *wahn?*" He replied, "Love of the world and hatred of death."[1]

Therefore, from the current state of affairs of the Muslim *Ummah* it can be concluded that the Muslims are greatly in need of purifying their souls. Allah willing, this purification of the souls will lead them to putting Allah first, sacrificing for His cause and bearing with patience any and all forms of hardship that they may have to face along the path of returning the Muslim Nation to its proper state.

A Misconception Concerning the Means and Results of Purification of the Soul

It is important at this point to clarify a misconception concerning purification of the soul. When some Muslims hear that the plight of the Muslim *Ummah* will not change until the Muslims purify their own souls, they become disgruntled because they believe that this means that simply by people returning to the mosque and praying and perhaps doing a few other things that somehow the world will change and the Muslims will gain the upper hand. They think that such a miraculous change is not going to occur and it is unreasonable to even expect something of that nature from Allah.

However, this attitude is built upon an incorrect understanding of purification of the soul. Indeed, it reflects a misunderstanding of Islam as a whole and it is a sign that purification of the soul is indeed greatly needed. Purification of the soul implies a complete reformation of the person, his conception of life, his goals, his aspirations, his deeds and so forth. The difference between the purified soul and one who is not so purified is not simply a difference between one attending the mosque, fasting Ramadhan and performing some other acts of worship while the other fails to do so.

---

[1] Recorded by Abu Dawood. According to al-Albaani, it is *sahih*. See Muhammad Naasir al-Deen al-Albaani, *Saheeh Sunan Abi Dawood* (Riyadh Maktab al-Tarbiyah al-Arabi li-Duwal al-Khaleej, 1989), vol. 3, p. 810.

When the soul is purified, like the souls of the Companions were purified, the change is a complete change in the person. The person leaves behind all of the major remnants of *kufr* (disbelief), ignorance, innovation and lusts and becomes filled with faith, knowledge and guidance. The person's perception and idea of what his life is all about completely changes. His purpose and goal becomes clear in front of him and he tries to put all of his energy and time into fulfilling that purpose and goal. He now has very different answers to questions like: What should he do with his life? What should he do with his time? What should he do with his wealth?

One can take some examples from the situation of the Muslim *Ummah* today.[1] One should think about how much wealth Allah has given the Muslim *Ummah* of today. The Muslim *Ummah* of today and Muslim individuals of today are perhaps richer than at any time in the history of Islam. Yet how is that wealth spent? How much of that wealth is spent on items that are purely expensive, luxury items, not to speak of how much of that wealth is spent on forbidden products?

A simple example can be cited. If one were to go to Orlando, Florida in the summertime and visit Disney World and other attractions, one can see a large number of Muslim visitors that have come from around the world with the sole intent of visiting Disney World and similar other places.[2] Ignoring the question of what one finds there and whether or not it is permissible for a Muslim to visit such a place filled with music,

---

[1] Al-Qahtaani highlights the following as signs that this *Ummah* is in need of purification of the souls: the true religion is missing in many parts of this *Ummah*, this *Ummah* is being defeated by the onslaught of the thoughts and beliefs of the disbelievers, the members of this *Ummah* are taking on the manners and behavior of those with whom Allah is displeased and angered, this *Ummah* is filled with disgrace because its members are chasing after the tails of cattle (that is, worldly matters) leading to cowardice and a hatred for death, this *Ummah* has forgotten that Allah is greater and more powerful than everything and has come to believe that power rests in the Western disbelieving countries (the "superpowers") and it is an *Ummah* that has forgotten its past and its real source of honor and glory. Cf., al-Qahtaani, (Riyadh: Daar al-Muslim, 1994), p. 4.

[2] Unfortunately, the above is not simply hypothetical. This author has personally known of a large number of Muslim families who have traveled from parts of the Muslim world to Florida or California solely with the purpose of visiting these types of locations for the sake of their children.

magic, dancing, women not properly dressed and so on, it literally takes a family of five thousands of dollars to travel from, for example, the Middle East to Florida. Yet all of that money is spent, supposedly, just so a child or two can have a good time and enjoyment. The question is: Is that really the purpose for which such money should be spent, especially when so many Muslims are living in difficult circumstances in this day and age? Can one imagine anyone among the Companions of the Prophet (peace and blessings of Allah be upon him), for example, spending a comparable amount of money during their time on such an excursion? It is inconceivable to imagine that the Companions would ever do anything of that nature. At the same time, though, Muslims nowadays cannot conceive of behaving like the Companions and they will claim that "times have changed" and "we are living in a different reality today." It is definitely true that the standard of living has changed over the years. That, though, does not seem to be the root cause of the difference. It is inconceivable to think of the Companions behaving in such a fashion not because "times have changed" but because the people and their priorities and goals have changed. So many Muslims have changed to such an extent that they have difficulty even conceiving of living with the same goals and priorities as those of the Companions.

One can take another example, less dramatic than the first but perhaps touching more people. This example deals with how one spends the free time that Allah has blessed him with. In particular, one should consider how much time he spends on activities that are not truly beneficial in any meaningful way (such as watching sports, television, movies and so forth). In fact, on this issue of how one benefits from one's free time, the Messenger of Allah (peace and blessings of Allah be upon him) said,

نِعْمَتَانِ مَغْبُونٌ فِيهِمَا كَثِيرٌ مِنَ النَّاسِ الصِّحَّةُ وَالْفَرَاغُ

"There are two blessings whose profit [or reward] many people lose: good health and free time." (Recorded by al-Bukhari.)

Whenever giving an example of this nature, one is inevitably asked, "What, from the Shareeah point of view, is the problem with, for example, watching a football game for three hours?" The question in itself shows that the questioner is missing the point that is trying to be made.[1] It is not just a question of "what is the problem with it?" The issue for a Muslim is: does he really have that time to spend wherein he is not benefiting himself at all? Can he afford to lose that time which he will never get back again? When he stands in front of Allah, can he really feel that he has used that free time, which is a bounty from Allah, in an acceptable fashion?

Of course, there is nothing wrong with rest and relaxation when needed.[2] Indeed, it is a necessity. However, it could be argued that there are some ways that are simply non-beneficial or perhaps even harmful. As shall be discussed in more detail in the following chapter, the point is that the person's goal and purpose must be very clear in his mind. All of his activities should be focused on the idea of helping him achieve his goal and purpose. If the goal and purpose of his life is very clear in his mind, he will not waste a lot of time in doing things that do not benefit him in achieving that goal and purpose. As the goal and purpose becomes even clearer in his mind, the more he concentrates his efforts on ensuring that what he is doing is actually beneficial, moving him toward his goal—neither away from it nor in a static position with respect to it.

Another inevitable question that one receives when discussing an issue of this nature is: "Do you mean to imply that there is no such thing as fun and enjoyment in Islam[3]?" Once

---

[1] In this work, the author is in no way intending to give religious verdict concerning the watching of sports live or on television.

[2] There is also probably a difference between one who is tired and needs to relax so he does something relaxing and someone going out of his way to, for example, watch a football game at 1:00 on a Sunday afternoon. In the latter case, it is no longer a matter of being tired and just getting some rest and relaxation. It has now become a goal and a purpose in itself that at that time and for the following three hours the person is going to be engaged in that activity of watching football. The matter obviously becomes much worse when the person cannot make it to the mosque because he is preoccupied watching sports or something of that nature. This demonstrates that his priorities need to be adjusted.

[3] In reality, there are numerous forms of relaxation and enjoyment in Islam that are permissible as well as beneficial, not involving a waste of money nor a waste of one's valuable time. For a complete discussion from a Shareeah perspective on relaxation, amusement and enjoyment, see Maadoon Rasheed, *Qadhaayaa al-Lahu wa al-Tarfeeh bain al-Haajah al-Nafsiyyah wa al-Dhawaabit al-Shariyyah* (Riyadh: Dar Taibah, 1998), *passim*.

again, this question[1] demonstrates how far our perceptions are from the proper ones. Actually, the question should be turned around to: "What should I as a Muslim consider enjoyable, relaxing or even fun?" This is a matter of priority and perspective. To take an extreme example that may help clarify the issue, many non-Muslims turn to alcohol or drugs and claim that they do that because they enjoy it. A Muslim looks at that—especially many converts who experienced that in the past and are now at a completely different level of understanding—and he cannot understand how they find that to be fun and entertainment. The same type of argument can be made with respect to today's Muslims vis-à-vis the Companions. One cannot imagine the Companions wasting their time in some of the pursuits that many Muslims spend a great deal of their quality hours in. This is because their purpose and goal was very different and much loftier.

The purified soul gets rest, enjoyment and pleasure by doing acts that are pleasing to Allah or, at the very least, doing acts that he knows will not harm him with respect to Allah. This was the way of the Prophet (peace and blessings of Allah be upon him) and his Companions. As the Prophet (peace and blessings of Allah be upon him) would say to Bilal,

يَا بِلالُ أَقِمِ الصَّلاةَ أَرِحْنَا بِهَا

"O Bilaal, make the *iqaamah* for the prayer, giving us rest by it."[2]

The things that they really enjoyed and felt pleasure with were the acts that when performed would bring Allah's pleasure to them. That is the greatest joy that anyone can achieve. Consider the fact that Muslims have only two Eids or celebrations during the year. Both of those celebrations come after completing a very important act of worship or drawing oneself closer to Allah (the fast of Ramadhaan and the pilgrimage to Makkah). The fact that these are the only two Eids sanctioned is a clear indication to

---

[1] Which this author has in fact received virtually every time he lectured on this topic.

[2] Recorded by Ahmad and Abu Dawood. According to al-Albaani, it is *sahih*. See Muhammad Naasir al-Deen al-Albaani, *Saheeh al-Jaami al-Sagheer* (Beirut: al-Maktab al-Islaami, 1986), vol. 2, p. 1307.

all believers that the real source of joy and happiness must be in completing those acts that are pleasing to Allah. It is upon performing these acts that one attains a true happiness well beyond the material means of pleasure found in this world.

It should be clear by now that the things in which one finds true enjoyment and pleasure are closely related to one's concept of what he wants to get out of this life. Again, if his true goal is that of pleasing Allah, he will find pleasure when he performs those acts that are pleasing to Allah. Indeed, he will consider himself successful and in a good state only when he is able to perform acts of that nature. The ultimate, of course, is when he sacrifices his life for that goal. When Haraam ibn Milhaan was stabbed at the Battle of Bir Maoonah and was about to die, he said, "I swear by the Lord of the Kaabah that I have succeeded and prospered." (Recorded by al-Bukhari.)

Although that is the reality, some Muslims have strayed so far from these concepts that they cannot even fathom such an existence or even understand what many of the scholars stated in the past. One devout Muslim stated, "The people of the night [who perform the voluntary late night prayers] get more pleasure from their nights than the people of entertainment get from their entertainment. If it were not for the nights, I would not wish to remain in this world."[1] Another stated, "There is nothing left of the pleasures of this world save three: the late night voluntary prayers, meeting with the brethren and congregational prayers."[2]

Hence, what Muslims, as individuals and as societies, will do with their time, wealth and energy will be completely different when their souls have become purified. The vast majority of the Muslim youth, for example, will not be spending hours and hours to perfect their soccer shot or basketball shots simply so that they can win the World Cup or be in the Olympics. Instead, many, if not most, of them will be studying their religion; their exercise will be fasting and the late night prayers; and their goal will be the

[1] Quoted in Ahmad Fareed, *Al-Tazkiyah bain Ahl al-Sunnah wa al-Soofiyyah*, p. 13.
[2] Ibid., p. 13.

spreading of Islam and working for the sake of Allah in jihad, dawah, good deeds and so forth.[1]

In sum, there is a very strong correlation between the question of purification of the soul and the state of the Muslim Nation. Purification of the souls implies a change in the people themselves. This is an all-inclusive type of change that even demands a change in the way people use their time, energy and wealth. They will become dedicated and strong for the sake of Allah such that perhaps even a small band of them can defeat a much larger band of disbelievers to their belief, fear of Allah, *taqwa* and purification. In their hearts they want Islam. They want to establish what Allah orders from them concerning this world. There is no desire for *jaahiliyyah,* the ways of the West, consumerism and hedonism. In their hearts there is no desire to fight simply for such mundane matters as higher wages or nationalism. They will have no desire to live like disbelievers while simply being under the banner of Islam. In fact, until Muslims are willing to go out for the sake of Allah alone and not for some sort of worldly gain, they would not have yet completely purified their souls, which means Allah may not grant them victory. As for those whose souls are purified, Allah may grant them victory even if they are few in number as He granted victory to the Muslims at Badr. At that time, the attacks on the Muslims will come to an end. They will be free of the diseases that leave them an open target for their enemies. They will have dignity, honor and respect because all dignity, honor and respect is actually rooted with Allah, as Allah says,

فَإِنَّ ٱلْعِزَّةَ لِلَّهِ جَمِيعًا

"All honor belongs to Allah alone" (*al-Nisaa* 139).

---

[1] In the past century or so, Muslims have also allowed themselves to believe that through getting doctorates, becoming engineers and so forth, they are serving the Muslim Ummah in the best possible way. Yes, such studies and disciplines may be important. But the Muslim Nation has been having people of that nature and caliber for the past century while there has been very little resultant change in the Muslim Nation. Those degrees have helped very little in improving the relationship with Allah for the masses as a whole. Perhaps Muslims are emphasizing something that is definitely important but at the same time they are sorely neglecting something that is even more important. Thus they are being snared by one of the traps of Satan.

Purification of the Soul and the Scholars, Reformers and Callers to Islam

The importance of purification of the soul for the reform and change in the state of the Muslim Nation was touched upon in the previous section. In essence, Allah does not grant victory to the believers until they have purified their souls of disbelief, idolatry and committing many sins. However, there are a few other points that should be highlighted concerning specific sectors of the Muslim population who are working for the triumph and spread of Islam. In particular, the scholars, reformers and callers to the religion of Islam have to consider purification of their own souls a top priority.

Particularly in non-Muslim lands, there are many sincere brothers and sisters who are very much attracted to and enthusiastic concerning the field of *dawah* or calling others to the path of Allah. Those who are truly sincere in their intentions to work for the sake of Islam must especially first consider themselves and their own souls' purification. Working for the sake of Allah is not a matter of glory or fame in this world and it certainly is not some type of popularity contest. Instead, this work is one of trials and perseverance.[1] Those who take on this work are taking upon themselves a great responsibility and like all great responsibilities, one should work hard to make sure that he meets the requirements needed for such a job. One can take the example of the Prophet (peace and blessings of Allah be upon him) himself. Shortly after receiving his first revelations and as he was about to carry this message to his people, Allah instructed him,

---

[1] In fact, patience and perseverance in themselves are usually only the result of some purification and spiritual growth on the part of the individual. In the Quran, Allah says, "Therefore be patient with what they say, and exalt (constantly) the praises of your Lord, before the rising of the sun, and before its setting; yea, celebrate them for part of the hours of the night, and at the ends of the day: that you may be satisfied" (*Taha* 130). Al-Qaradhaawi noted, "Allah follows the order to have patience with the order to extol Him in a number of verses. Perhaps the secret behind that is that the extolling of Allah's greatness gives the individual a spiritual weight by which he can taste the sweetness of patience and by which the tightness in his chest [that is, his stress] may be relaxed." Yoosuf al-Qaradhaawi, *al-Sabr fi al-Quraan* (Beirut: Muassasah al-Risaalah, 1985), p. 28.

يَـٰٓأَيُّهَا ٱلْمُزَّمِّلُ ۝١ قُمِ ٱلَّيْلَ إِلَّا قَلِيلًا ۝٢ نِّصْفَهُۥٓ أَوِ ٱنقُصْ مِنْهُ قَلِيلًا ۝٣ أَوْ زِدْ عَلَيْهِ وَرَتِّلِ ٱلْقُرْءَانَ تَرْتِيلًا ۝٤ إِنَّا سَنُلْقِى عَلَيْكَ قَوْلًا ثَقِيلًا

"O you folded in garments! Stand (to prayer) by night save a little of it, half of it, or a little less or a little more; and recite the Quran in slow, measured rhythmic tones. Soon shall We send down to you a weighty message" (*al-Muzzammil* 1-5). In order for the Messenger of Allah (peace and blessings of Allah be upon him) and the early Muslims to be able to carry this weighty message of Islam or the Quran, they must be spiritually qualified and pure. Hence, Allah first instructed them to spend long hours in prayer during the late night so that they would be ready to bear the great responsibilities related to carrying and spreading Allah's message.

Allah also describes those who were the true leaders in matters of faith,

وَجَعَلْنَـٰهُمْ أَئِمَّةً يَهْدُونَ بِأَمْرِنَا وَأَوْحَيْنَآ إِلَيْهِمْ فِعْلَ ٱلْخَيْرَٰتِ وَإِقَامَ ٱلصَّلَوٰةِ وَإِيتَآءَ ٱلزَّكَوٰةِ ۖ وَكَانُوا۟ لَنَا عَـٰبِدِينَ

"And We made them leaders, guiding (men) by Our command, and We sent them inspiration to do good deeds, to establish regular prayers, and to practice regular charity; and they constantly served Us (and Us alone)" (*al-Anbiyaa* 73).

In order to be a true and effective worker for Islam, one must have a good understanding and knowledge of the religion itself. Although there are many factors affecting one's knowledge of Islam, many scholars note that one of the first steps to be blessed by knowledge of the faith is the act of repenting and turning unto Allah. Allah says,

تَبْصِرَةً وَذِكْرَىٰ لِكُلِّ عَبْدٍ مُّنِيبٍ

"An insight and reminder for every slave who turns [to Allah] in repentance" (*Qaaf* 8). Allah also says,

وَمَا يَتَذَكَّرُ إِلَّا مَن يُنِيبُ

"And none remembers except those who turn [to Allah] in repentance" (*Ghaafir* 13). Commenting on these verses, both al-Ghazaali and ibn al-Qayyim noted that it is only the one who overcomes the allures of this world and turns to Allah who is given the vision and understanding.[1] Indeed, the realization that one must turn and repent to Allah is a first step in the path of purification. It is also a very important first step for anyone sincerely interested in working for Islam. Once that step is taken in a serious and continual fashion, the person should turn his attention more and more to learning the faith. This is a second step that must also be considered a prerequisite for serious acts of spreading the faith. Via this process, Allah blesses him, Allah willing, with more and more knowledge of the faith and a proper understanding of Allah's blessed religion and this in turn makes his efforts in calling others more accepted and successful.

Besides being a matter of trials and perseverance, calling people to the way of Allah also requires being accepted by the people themselves, such that one's teaching and advice is listened to. In this respect, two matters are of great importance. First, love for the caller must be planted in the hearts of the listeners. Second, the caller himself must be setting the proper example so that the others do not see him simply as a hypocrite. He must be of strong faith such that when he is tried or tempted, he does not buckle under the pressure and compromise his faith—thus causing himself ruin as well as causing harm to the overall message of Islam. On all of these counts, obviously, purification of the soul is a must for the caller himself.

Regarding the first point, having love in the hearts of others, the hearts are between the fingers of the Merciful. It is Allah alone who brings the hearts together and who places love in the hearts of the other believers. Allah gives this blessing to those who truly believe and perform the righteous deeds. Allah says,

---

[1] Cf., Nabeel Haamid al-Maaz, *Al-Tazkiyah: Dharooratuhaa, Wasaailuhaa, Mawaaniuhaa* (Cairo: Daar al-Tauzee wa al-Nashr al-Islaami, 1998), p. 37. Al-Maaz (p. 38) also recounts the renowned practice of ibn Taimiyyah who, whenever he was bothered by an issue or question, would seek Allah's forgiveness until Allah made the issue clear to him.

إِنَّ ٱلَّذِينَ ءَامَنُوا۟ وَعَمِلُوا۟ ٱلصَّٰلِحَٰتِ سَيَجْعَلُ لَهُمُ ٱلرَّحْمَٰنُ وُدًّا

"Indeed, [for] those who have believed and done righteous deeds, the Most Merciful will appoint for them affection" (*Maryam* 96). Ibn Abbaas explained this verse as meaning that Allah will place love for them in the hearts of the believers. Al-Shaukaani further notes that people will have love for those true believers without them seeking that from them, due to the natural consequences that occur.[1]

Furthermore, the Messenger of Allah (peace and blessings of Allah be upon him) stated that love and acceptance is a result of being beloved to Allah, which is a result of purifying one's soul. The Messenger of Allah (peace and blessings of Allah be upon him) said,

إِذَا أَحَبَّ اللَّهُ عَبْدًا نَادَى جِبْرِيلَ إِنَّ اللَّهَ يُحِبُّ فُلاَنًا فَأَحِبَّهُ فَيُحِبُّهُ جِبْرِيلُ فَيُنَادِي جِبْرِيلُ فِي أَهْلِ السَّمَاءِ إِنَّ اللَّهَ يُحِبُّ فُلاَنًا فَأَحِبُّوهُ فَيُحِبُّهُ أَهْلُ السَّمَاءِ ثُمَّ يُوضَعُ لَهُ الْقَبُولُ فِي أَهْلِ الأَرْضِ

"If Allah loves a person, He calls Gabriel saying, 'Allah loves so and so. So, love him.' Gabriel will then love him. He [Gabriel] then makes an announcement among the inhabitants of the heaven, 'Allah loves so and so; therefore, love him also.' So all the inhabitants of the heaven then love him and he is then granted acceptance among the people of the earth."[2] (Recorded by al-Bukhari.)

The second point, setting the proper example and living according to what one is preaching, is also of extreme importance for the worker calling to Islam. To say one thing and then to do another is a behavior that is very distasteful to others, even

---

[1] Muhammad ibn Ali al-Shaukaani, *Fath al-Qadeer al-Jaami bain Fanna al-Riwaayah wa al-Diraayah min Ilm al-Tafseer* (Egypt: Mustafa al-Baabi and sons, 1964), vol. 3, p. 353.

[2] This is a truly special kind of acceptance, love, respect and support. The others love and support such a person even though he does not give them things of this world, which is one of the main ways by which people attain others' love. Similarly, there is no blood relationship between them upon which this love is based. This is yet another miraculous gift that Allah gives to His devoted servants. Cf., al-Bilaali, pp. 131-132.

disbelievers, and can quickly lead to the non-acceptance of one's teachings. Allah has warned against such behavior in a number of places in the Quran. For example, Allah says,

يَٰٓأَيُّهَا ٱلَّذِينَ ءَامَنُوا۟ لِمَ تَقُولُونَ مَا لَا تَفْعَلُونَ ﴿٢﴾ كَبُرَ مَقْتًا

عِندَ ٱللَّهِ أَن تَقُولُوا۟ مَا لَا تَفْعَلُونَ

"O you who believe! Why do you say that which you do not? Grievously odious is it in the sight of Allah that you say that which you do not" (*al-Saff* 2-3). Allah also says,

أَتَأْمُرُونَ ٱلنَّاسَ بِٱلْبِرِّ وَتَنسَوْنَ أَنفُسَكُمْ وَأَنتُمْ تَتْلُونَ ٱلْكِتَٰبَ ۚ أَفَلَا

تَعْقِلُونَ

"Do you enjoin right conduct on the people, and forget (to practice it) yourselves. And yet you study the Scripture? Will you not understand" (*al-Baqarah* 44). It must be noted that one will not truly be able to live up to his call and preaching to Islam unless he himself has or is purifying his own soul.

The above does not mean to imply that the caller to Islam must be perfect or some type of angel. Indeed, even if someone is a sinner, it is still obligatory upon him to stop sins when he is able to and encourage others to do what is right. At the same time, though, in order for him to be truly effective and pleasing to Allah, he should be, in his practice, manners, knowledge and behavior, above and beyond those whom he is calling to the path of Allah. In other words, he himself must first take the question of purification of the soul very seriously and work to improve himself to the best of his ability. Hence, if the callers to Islam today are not having much success in their missions and are not being responded to positively and with love, it may be yet another sign that they also are in need of the means and process of purification.

Summary

The importance of the concept of purification of the soul can clearly be established in the light of numerous verses of the Quran. However, this chapter went beyond the mere presentation of the clear and explicit verses of the Quran. It also discussed the monumental changes resulting from purifying the souls. The change is such that the entire being and persona changes. The changes are such that it leads to Allah blessing the Nation with victory and support. This is exactly what the Muslim Nation as a whole as well as the Muslim workers are in dire need of given today's current state of affairs.

Chapter 4
The Goal and Scope of Purification According to the Quran and Sunnah

Before saying any word about the process of purification, the goal of purification according to the Quran and Sunnah needs to be clearly spelled out. Before setting out on any path, it is very important for the person to understood the goal of that path. When he does that, it sometimes becomes very easy for him to recognize the things that may lead him off of the correct path and away from that goal. He may see things that he recognizes not to be helpful to him in achieving his goal—even though others may claim that they lead to the same goal. On the other hand, if a person starts along a "noble path" without a clear conception of his goal, he may easily be misled. Furthermore, when a person is seeking a path of purification, it is important that he recognize what is the goal of his purification. An incorrect goal can be very dangerous to his process of purification.

One's only purpose and long-run goal in this life is to worship Allah. This fact that perhaps every Muslim admits to must move from the theoretical, abstract level to the real, applied level. In essence, everything else must be sacrificed for this goal. This is the behavior of any human when he has a goal that is of utmost importance in his heart or when he has a love that is more important to him than anything else imaginable. He will be relentless in his pursuit of that goal. One can consider the example of Olympic athletes who practice up to 18 hours a day for ten or fifteen years or the example of those studying for the bar exam and so forth. In the same way, a Muslim must be "relentless" in the pursuit of his goal. Furthermore, though, the goal of the Muslim is much loftier and significant than all of the goals that the non-Muslims pursue so vigorously in their lives.

Hence, anything and everything else must be sacrificed for that goal. Or, in other terms, anything else is secondary and can never take precedence over the person's long-term, utmost important and ultimate goal. In addition, any other subgoal or temporary goal must be consistent with the overall goal in one's life. Otherwise, it is not permissible to pursue those other goals that contradict one's overall purpose and goal in life.

Once a person is, by the grace of Allah, able to identify the one true and worthy goal of his purification, everything else should be made subservient to that one goal. Again, nothing else will be allowed to interfere with that goal or take precedence over it. This is like the example of the Prophet Abraham (peace and blessings of Allah be upon him) when he was asked to sacrifice his only son, a son that he had anxiously awaited for many years. His willingness to sacrifice his son and his son's willingness to be sacrificed was due to the fact that they realized what their purpose and goal in life was. Life together would mean nothing to them if they knew that by so living they were interfering with their entire purpose. Hence, they had the will and the courage to perform the sacrifice commanded by Allah. They had the willingness to sacrifice for the sake of the ultimate goal.

Furthermore, this goal should be something consciously on a person's mind, ruling his behavior and actions on a day-to-day—even minute-to-minute—basis, above and beyond any of the short-term and intermediate goals of this life. Indeed, all of the short-term intermediate goals of this life must be subservient to that long-run goal and purpose of a person's entire being. Indeed, they are not only subservient to that long-run goal, but they must be serving that long-run goal.

It is saddening to think that a person could realize the true and lofty purpose of his creation and then allow other insignificant goals to deviate him from his ever-important goal and purpose. Sometimes, this swerving from the right course is very short-term, such as fulfilling a quickly satisfied desire. However, sometimes such may be extremely time- and energy-consuming and inconsistent with his final goal, such as putting in hours and hours of practice to become something which is not pleasing to Allah or which is simply not beneficial.

In reality, the more that one can focus on his goal, the more he will be able to overcome obstacles and difficulties. This is because his focus will allow him never to lose sight of the "bigger picture." By constant reminders, such as daily prayers and reading the Quran, a believer should be able to be constantly on guard with respect to his actions and their relationship with his ultimate goal and purpose in life.

In fact, the identification of the goal leads to the very important aspect of intention. It is intention that accompanies every single act. Intention is, in fact, the true driving force behind every conscious act that a person performs. The Prophet (peace and blessings of Allah be upon him) made this fact clear when he stated,

إِنَّمَا الأَعْمَالُ بِالنِّيَّاتِ وَإِنَّمَا لِكُلِّ امْرِئٍ مَا نَوَى

"Surely, all actions are but driven by intentions and, verily, every man shall have but that which he intended." (Recorded by al-Bukhari and Muslim.) Intention is the key. If that intention springs from a clear understanding of one's goal in life, the resultant actions will be sound and proper, leading to his prosperity and goodness in both this life and the Hereafter. If that intention springs from a muddled understanding of one's goal in life or of an undesirable goal in life, it is not surprising that the resultant deeds are evil in themselves and evil for the person himself.

The Creation and Role of Humans

One of the first things that every human should realize is that this creation as a whole and humans in particular have not been created in vain and without a noble purpose. Allah says in the Quran,

وَمَا خَلَقْنَا ٱلسَّمَآءَ وَٱلْأَرْضَ وَمَا بَيْنَهُمَا بَٰطِلًا ۚ ذَٰلِكَ ظَنُّ ٱلَّذِينَ
كَفَرُوا۟ ۚ فَوَيْلٌ لِّلَّذِينَ كَفَرُوا۟ مِنَ ٱلنَّارِ ﴿٢٧﴾ أَمْ نَجْعَلُ ٱلَّذِينَ ءَامَنُوا۟

وَعَمِلُوا۟ ٱلصَّـٰلِحَـٰتِ كَٱلْمُفْسِدِينَ فِى ٱلْأَرْضِ أَمْ نَجْعَلُ ٱلْمُتَّقِينَ
كَٱلْفُجَّارِ

"Not without purpose did We create the heaven and earth and all between! Such is the thought of unbelievers! But woe to the unbelievers because of the fire (of Hell)! Shall We treat those who believe and work deeds of righteousness the same as those who do mischief on earth? Shall We treat those who guard against evil, the same as those who turn aside from the right?" (*Saad* 27-28). There is a purpose to this creation and, hence, those who do righteous deeds are not the same as those who spread evil. Allah has also said,

أَيَحْسَبُ ٱلْإِنسَـٰنُ أَن يُتْرَكَ سُدًى

"Does man think that he will be left uncontrolled, (without purpose)?" (*al-Qiyaamah* 36).

In reality, the original, physical creation of the first human was not greatly different from the creation of the other creatures of this world. The physical make-up was from clay and water. This fact is noted in numerous places in the Quran. For example, Allah says,

وَهُوَ ٱلَّذِى خَلَقَ مِنَ ٱلْمَآءِ بَشَرًا فَجَعَلَهُۥ نَسَبًا وَصِهْرًا ۗ وَكَانَ رَبُّكَ
قَدِيرًا

"It is He Who has created man from water. Then has He established relationships of lineage and marriage, for your Lord has power (over all things)" (*al-Furqaan* 54). Allah also says,

وَلَقَدْ خَلَقْنَا ٱلْإِنسَـٰنَ مِن صَلْصَـٰلٍ مِّنْ حَمَإٍ مَّسْنُونٍ

"We created man from sounding clay, from mud molded into shape" (*al-Hijr* 26).

It is in the next stage of the creation of the first human, Adam, in which the real distinction occurred. At this point, humans are made a very separate and unique creature, combining a physical aspect and a special spiritual aspect that God bestowed on them. In fact, this is what makes them very different from the other living creatures on this same planet. This stage is described in the verse,

ثُمَّ سَوَّىٰهُ وَنَفَخَ فِيهِ مِن رُّوحِهِۦ ۖ وَجَعَلَ لَكُمُ ٱلسَّمْعَ وَٱلْأَبْصَـٰرَ وَٱلْأَفْـِٔدَةَ ۚ قَلِيلًا مَّا تَشْكُرُونَ

"But He fashioned him in due proportion, and breathed into him the soul from Him. And He gave you (the faculties of) hearing and sight and feeling (and understanding). Yet little thanks do you give" (*al-Sajdah* 9).

Even before Allah created this creation, He informed the angels that this creation was to have a special purpose on this earth, succeeding the creations before him. Allah says,

وَإِذْ قَالَ رَبُّكَ لِلْمَلَـٰٓئِكَةِ إِنِّى جَاعِلٌ فِى ٱلْأَرْضِ خَلِيفَةً ۖ

"Behold, your Lord said to the angels, 'I will create upon the earth a successive authority'" (*al-Baqarah* 30). After Allah breathed into this creation with a spirit from Him and after He had bestowed knowledge upon him, the angels, Allah's noble creation, were ordered to prostrate to this new creation. Allah says, for example,

فَإِذَا سَوَّيْتُهُۥ وَنَفَخْتُ فِيهِ مِن رُّوحِى فَقَعُوا۟ لَهُۥ سَـٰجِدِينَ

"When I have fashioned him (in due proportion) and breathed into him of a spirit from Me, fall down in obeisance unto him" (*al-Hijr* 29).

Furthermore, Allah states that humans on their own opted to accept the responsibility of the trust. Other creations were offered this heavy responsibility but they all refused. It was only humans who took this job on. Allah describes this occurrence in the following verse. Allah says

إِنَّا عَرَضْنَا ٱلْأَمَانَةَ عَلَى ٱلسَّمَـٰوَٰتِ وَٱلْأَرْضِ وَٱلْجِبَالِ فَأَبَيْنَ أَن يَحْمِلْنَهَا وَأَشْفَقْنَ مِنْهَا وَحَمَلَهَا ٱلْإِنسَـٰنُ ۖ إِنَّهُۥ كَانَ ظَلُومًا جَهُولًا

"We did indeed offer the trust to the heavens and the earth and the mountains; but they refused to undertake it, being afraid thereof. But man undertook it. He was indeed unjust and foolish" (*al-Ahzaab* 72). Although mankind took on a heavy responsibility, Allah then helped mankind in many ways to fulfill this trust. (Furthermore, Allah will also reward mankind in a special fashion when they fulfill this trust.)

That is, along with this came some distinguishing characteristics that set this creation apart from the animals on this earth. Among the most prominent distinguishing features of a human being are the following:

(1) A sound, natural disposition that is ready and capable to be directed to the belief in Allah alone as the object of worship;

(2) An ability to comprehend and understand matters via the intelligence and mind that Allah has bestowed on humans;

(3) A free will to decide between the path of goodness or the path of evil, as well as a limited free will to enact that choice that he has made;

(4) A responsibility for the choices he has made, which is a necessary result of being given free will and ability.[1]

Another important characteristic related to humans is that Allah has put at their disposal all that is created in the heavens and the earth. In reality, humans have been created solely to serve Allah and, to help them to do so, Allah has made all things of the physical cosmos under their potential control. Allah says,

ٱللَّهُ ٱلَّذِى سَخَّرَ لَكُمُ ٱلْبَحْرَ لِتَجْرِىَ ٱلْفُلْكُ فِيهِ بِأَمْرِهِۦ وَلِتَبْتَغُوا۟

مِن فَضْلِهِۦ وَلَعَلَّكُمْ تَشْكُرُونَ ﴿١٢﴾ وَسَخَّرَ لَكُم مَّا فِى ٱلسَّمَٰوَٰتِ

وَمَا فِى ٱلْأَرْضِ جَمِيعًا مِّنْهُ ۚ إِنَّ فِى ذَٰلِكَ لَءَايَٰتٍ لِّقَوْمٍ يَتَفَكَّرُونَ

"It is Allah Who has subjected the sea to you, that ships may sail through it by His command, that you may seek of His bounty, and that you may be grateful. And He has subjected to you, as from

---

[1] Cf., Karzoon, vol. 1, pp. 20-21.

Him, all that is in the heavens and on earth: behold, in that are signs indeed for those who reflect" (*al-Jaathiyah* 12-13). This opens up for humans a great potential to achieve a tremendous amount of good.[1]

Given all of these special characteristics, as was mentioned earlier, the human should realize that he has a special and noble purpose and goal in this life. He should realize that his Creator is too wise and lofty to create him simply for sport.

أَفَحَسِبْتُمْ أَنَّمَا خَلَقْنَـٰكُمْ عَبَثًا وَأَنَّكُمْ إِلَيْنَا لَا تُرْجَعُونَ

"Did you then think that We had created you in jest, and that you would not be brought back to Us (for account)?" (*al-Muminoon* 115).

Hence, he should realize that his actions in this life have a real ramification to them. In this sense, *nothing* that he does is meaningless or without consequences. All of his deeds and his choices are like a trial wherein he demonstrates whether he is desirous of what is good and proper or not. Indeed, Allah has made this point very clear,

تَبَـٰرَكَ ٱلَّذِى بِيَدِهِ ٱلْمُلْكُ وَهُوَ عَلَىٰ كُلِّ شَىْءٍ قَدِيرٌ ﴿١﴾ ٱلَّذِى خَلَقَ ٱلْمَوْتَ وَٱلْحَيَوٰةَ لِيَبْلُوَكُمْ أَيُّكُمْ أَحْسَنُ عَمَلًا ۚ وَهُوَ ٱلْعَزِيزُ ٱلْغَفُورُ

"Blessed be He in Whose hands is Dominion; and He has power over all things; He Who created death and life, that He may try which of you is best in deed; and He is the Exalted in Might, Oft-Forgiving" (*al-Mulk* 1-2).

It is extremely important for the human to realize this point, that he has a purpose in this life. He must realize that he is not simply an animal that has evolved through benign material processes nor is he a sexually-inhibited driven creature, like Darwin, Freud and others have led so many people to believe. Indeed, this realization may be the first step along the path of

---

[1] At the same time, though, when used improperly it can be used to bring about a great deal of evil. Allah says, "Mischief has appeared on land and sea because of what the hands of men have earned. That (Allah) may give them a taste of some of their deeds: in order that they may turn back (from Evil)" (*al-Room* 41).

purification of the soul. Without realizing this fact, there may be no need, meaning or purpose to purifying one's soul—if one is just an animal, then it is expected for him to behave like an animal; if nothing is morally wrong or right since there is no God or real purpose to existence, it is expected for people to behave in any fashion they wish. When a person's eyes are open to the reality of this creation, his purpose and role in it, theoretically speaking, there should be a great and profound effect on his life.

Islahi notes that the "first condition [in the process of purification] is the sincere firm resolve to change and reform."[1] However, that first step may never come about if the person does not realize that he has a very important and noble purpose in this life. Hence, this realization must come first. Once this realization occurs, then there should be an immediate leap to that resolve to change and reform.[2]

Karzoon noted,

> When a person becomes heedless of his goal for which he was created and the role that he has been given, he becomes busy with other goals... This changes them [that is, such people] from their essential human nature and position by which Allah honored them. Due to this, contradiction and confusion occurs in the make-up of the human. The human is then dragged into two different directions: the direction of the spirit (*rooh*) and the direction of the body.[3]

Karzoon then notes that the only way to make those two aspects compatible is via the teachings of Islam. It is these

---

[1] Islahi, p. ix.

[2] Incidentally, this author has personally noted that when many people convert to Islam the radical change in their direction and purpose sometimes does not occur. In many cases, this is because the information that they were given about Islam was not sufficient. It may have presented the convert with the basic beliefs and teachings of Islam but it failed to stress the fact that being a Muslim means that he now has a definite and resolute goal in his life. All aspects of his life must now become subservient to his new goal and purpose. Islam is not a religion that one can marginalize in one's life like many or most contemporary Jews and Christians do with their faiths. This is a fundamental point that every convert must understand before converting. If this point is not understood, it would not be surprising to see the individual revert back to his earlier faith or simply become a non-committed Muslim. Allah knows best.

[3] Karzoon, vol. 1, p. 24.

teachings alone that can properly and in a balanced manner fulfil the needs of both the *rooh* and the body. Indeed, he continues, this demonstrates the relationship between the purification of the soul and the responsibility to "maintain and rule" this world. The latter is done by righteous deeds upon the path of Allah and it is not done through individual purification while leaving aside the society and the surrounding people. On the other hand, ignoring that path is what leads to the kind of society that exists today, wherein a primary goal is the meeting of the bodily desires while greater and more important ethical and moral issues and needs are being ignored.[1]

The Goal of Purification of the Soul

The goal of Islamic purification is clear from the definition given earlier of "purification of the soul": the goal is to become as complete and truthful a servant of Allah as one can be. Allah explains that purpose in life in the verse,

وَمَا خَلَقْتُ ٱلْجِنَّ وَٱلْإِنسَ إِلَّا لِيَعْبُدُونِ

"I have only created jinn and men that they may worship Me" (*al-Dhaariyaat* 56).

The goal of life is to worship and please Allah—thus, to receive His pleasure in return. As shall be discussed in the next chapter, this is accomplished by strengthening one's faith and humbly submitting to Allah through the obligatory and voluntary deeds. This submission includes the outward submission as well as a submission of the acts of the heart.

Some people seem not attracted by this goal. They seem to think that there is something more that they can forge for themselves (such as somehow uniting with Allah in this worldly existence). However, such could not be further from the truth. In fact, Allah has described the most noble of creation as His slaves and servants, demonstrating that there is no way of life or being that is more noble and elevated than that of being a true servant

[1] Karzoon, vol. 1, p. 25.

of Allah. This is the foremost praise that Allah has bestowed on any of the creation. Allah has said about the angels, for example,

وَلَهُۥ مَن فِى ٱلسَّمَٰوَٰتِ وَٱلْأَرْضِ ۚ وَمَنْ عِندَهُۥ لَا يَسْتَكْبِرُونَ عَنْ عِبَادَتِهِۦ وَلَا يَسْتَحْسِرُونَ ﴿١٩﴾ يُسَبِّحُونَ ٱلَّيْلَ وَٱلنَّهَارَ لَا يَفْتُرُونَ

"To Him belongs whosoever is in the heavens and on earth. And those who are near Him (the angels) are not too proud to worship Him, nor are they weary (of His worship). They celebrate His praises night and day, nor do they ever flag or intermit" (*al-Anbiyaa* 19-20). Allah also says,

لَّن يَسْتَنكِفَ ٱلْمَسِيحُ أَن يَكُونَ عَبْدًا لِّلَّهِ وَلَا ٱلْمَلَٰٓئِكَةُ ٱلْمُقَرَّبُونَ ۚ وَمَن يَسْتَنكِفْ عَنْ عِبَادَتِهِۦ وَيَسْتَكْبِرْ فَسَيَحْشُرُهُمْ إِلَيْهِ جَمِيعًا

"The Messiah [Jesus] will never be so proud to reject being a slave to Allah, nor the angels who are near (to Allah). And whosoever rejects worshipping Him and is proud, then He will gather them all together unto Himself" (*al-Nisaa* 172).

Allah has described the Messenger of Allah Muhammad (peace be upon him) as His slave and servant in numerous places in the Quran. For example, on the most momentous occasion of Allah taking the Prophet (peace and blessings of Allah be upon him) from Makkah to Jerusalem (which further led to the Prophet being taken to the heavens and Allah speaking directly to Him), Allah said,

سُبْحَٰنَ ٱلَّذِىٓ أَسْرَىٰ بِعَبْدِهِۦ لَيْلًا مِّنَ ٱلْمَسْجِدِ ٱلْحَرَامِ إِلَى ٱلْمَسْجِدِ ٱلْأَقْصَا ٱلَّذِى بَٰرَكْنَا حَوْلَهُۥ لِنُرِيَهُۥ مِنْ ءَايَٰتِنَآ ۚ إِنَّهُۥ هُوَ ٱلسَّمِيعُ ٱلْبَصِيرُ

"Exalted be He who took His slave [Muhammad (peace be upon him)] for a journey by night from *al-Masjid al-Haraam* (in Makkah) to the farthest mosque (in Jerusalem), the area of which We have blessed, in order that We might show him some of Our signs. Verily, He is the All-Hearer, the All-Seer" (*al-Israa* 1).

The Messenger of Allah (peace be upon him) said,

لا تُطْرُونِي كَمَا أَطْرَتِ النَّصَارَى ابْنَ مَرْيَمَ فَإِنَّمَا أَنَا عَبْدُهُ فَقُولُوا عَبْدُ اللَّهِ وَرَسُولُهُ

"Do not extol me like the Christians extolled the son of Mary. I am His slave-servant, so say, 'Slave of Allah and His Messenger.'" (Recorded by al-Bukhari.)

Furthermore, all of the messengers sent by Allah were sent specifically to teach this principle and bring all of mankind to the worship of Allah alone. Allah says,

وَلَقَدْ بَعَثْنَا فِي كُلِّ أُمَّةٍ رَّسُولًا أَنِ ٱعْبُدُوا۟ ٱللَّهَ وَٱجْتَنِبُوا۟ ٱلطَّـٰغُوتَ

"For We assuredly sent among every people a messenger, (with the Command), 'Worship Allah, and eschew all false gods'" (*al-Nahl* 36).

This is the ultimate goal for mankind. There can be no greater goal. In fact, this is the only goal that can be true solace to the soul of humans because this is the goal that is recognized deep within the person's soul. As noted earlier, this wanting to know and worship one's Lord is something deep within the natural make-up of mankind. Without finding this reality, man can never find true happiness.

Furthermore, the most exalted, noble, and honored a human can be is by worshipping Allah. In reality, there is nothing greater or nobler than that. That is the maximum potential. This is something that should be clear on every Muslim's mind. The more he moves to that goal, the happier he should become and the more honor he should feel by submitting himself to the only true God and Lord. When he realizes this fact, his efforts should be exerted to maximize this potential.

Actually, when a person realizes that he has only one, clear goal, the effects upon his soul are profound. He need not chase after an endless array of goals, never being able to satisfy or achieve any of them completely. (Indeed, many times people's goals are contradictory and they can never achieve all of them.) His energies need not be exhausted trying to serve a myriad of goals. When he has one goal and one goal alone, he can easily gauge whether he is moving towards achieving that goal or not. He can put all of his energy and thought into working towards that one ultimate goal. He can be certain about his goal and his path will be clear. Hence, he has no reason to be filled with doubt or confusion. As he moves closer and closer to that one ultimate goal, he can experience true joy and contentment. Allah has described the state of he who recognizes and seeks the true *tauheed* in the verse as opposed to those who seek after many goals and gods,

ضَرَبَ ٱللَّهُ مَثَلًا رَّجُلًا فِيهِ شُرَكَآءُ مُتَشَـٰكِسُونَ وَرَجُلًا سَلَـمًا لِّرَجُلٍ هَلْ يَسْتَوِيَانِ مَثَلًا ۚ ٱلْحَمْدُ لِلَّهِ ۚ بَلْ أَكْثَرُهُمْ لَا يَعْلَمُونَ

"Allah puts forth a parable: a man belonging to many partners at variance with each other, and a man belonging entirely to one master. Are those two equal in comparison? Praise be to Allah! But most of them have no knowledge" (*al-Zumar* 29).

It cannot be overemphasized that the goal must always be to worship Allah completely and properly. The goal can never be, for example, as many have wrongly thought, to become part of God or one with God. Indeed, the Messenger of Allah (peace be upon him) was the most purified of mankind. He was the most complete servant and slave of Allah. Through his teachings, he also purified his noble Companions. In his teachings, the Creator and the creation always remained distinct. There was never any merging of the two of them. The Messenger of Allah (peace be upon him) was always the slave and Allah was always the Lord. The two never became united into one. Also, the Prophet (peace and blessings of Allah be upon him) never tried to "lose his self-identify" in Allah. Such "unification" is not the purpose or goal of mankind. The purpose or goal, again, is to recognize Allah as the Lord and to worship Him alone.

Ibaadah ("Worship") and *Uboodiyyah* ("Servitude")—The Goal of Purification of the Soul and the Purpose of One's Creation

As noted above, the purpose behind the creation of humans was for them to worship Allah properly. Allah has said,

وَمَا خَلَقْتُ ٱلْجِنَّ وَٱلْإِنسَ إِلَّا لِيَعْبُدُونِ

"I have only created jinn and men, that they may worship Me" (*al-Dhaariyaat* 56). Indeed, all of the messengers of Allah were sent with this very clear message: humans must worship Allah alone and negate and refrain from all other objects of worship. This indeed is the dividing line between being rightly guided and being astray. Allah says,

وَلَقَدْ بَعَثْنَا فِى كُلِّ أُمَّةٍ رَّسُولًا أَنِ ٱعْبُدُوا۟ ٱللَّهَ وَٱجْتَنِبُوا۟ ٱلطَّٰغُوتَ

فَمِنْهُم مَّنْ هَدَى ٱللَّهُ وَمِنْهُم مَّنْ حَقَّتْ عَلَيْهِ ٱلضَّلَٰلَةُ

"Certainly We sent among every nation a messenger [proclaiming], 'Worship Allah [alone] and avoid all false gods. Of them were some that Allah guided. And of them were those upon whom misguidance was [deservedly] decreed" (*al-Nahl* 36). Allah also says,

وَمَآ أَرْسَلْنَا مِن قَبْلِكَ مِن رَّسُولٍ إِلَّا نُوحِىٓ إِلَيْهِ أَنَّهُۥ لَآ إِلَٰهَ إِلَّآ أَنَا۠

فَٱعْبُدُونِ

"We never sent any messenger before you [Muhammad] save that We revealed unto him that there is none deserving of worship except Allah, so worship Me alone" (*al-Anbiyaa* 25).

The goal of a person's life is the true worship or *ibaadah* of Allah. Al-Miqreezee notes that this proper form of worship entails four aspects:

(1) Determining what Allah and His Messenger (peace and blessings of Allah be upon him) love and are pleased with;

(2) The embodying of and enacting upon those beloved aspects in one's own heart;

(3) Enacting upon those aspects in one's speech;

(4) Further enacting upon those aspects in one's actions.[1]

Each one of these aspects is necessary if a person desires to fulfill his goal of being a true worshipper and servant of Allah. The individual first recognizes that the manner that he is to worship Allah is not based on his own individual inclinations, logic or whims. Instead, it must be based on what comes from Allah Himself. Allah is the only one who can state how He is to be worshipped. Hence, the first step is to determine what Allah wants from the individual and what is pleasing to Him. This is achieved by getting knowledge of the Quran and Sunnah. This knowledge must then be transformed into an acceptance and desire for those things in one's heart. One must recognize those things as the true good things and one, hence, must have a feeling of love for those things in one's heart. When this is accomplished, the proclamation of one's acceptance and belief as well as the application of this acceptance via one's deeds should automatically accompany it.

In general, these four aspects are usually summarized in two very important points. For anyone's worship to be proper it must be (1) performed sincerely and purely for the sake of Allah and it must be (2) in accordance with what Allah has revealed in the Quran and Sunnah. Allah has said,

فَمَن كَانَ يَرْجُواْ لِقَآءَ رَبِّهِۦ فَلْيَعْمَلْ عَمَلًا صَـٰلِحًا وَلَا يُشْرِكْ بِعِبَادَةِ رَبِّهِۦٓ أَحَدًۢا

"Whoever hopes in meeting his Lord, let him work righteousness, and, in the worship of his Lord, admit no one as partner" (*al-Kahf* 110).

It is this behavior or way that humans must exhibit in their lives. It is for this purpose that they have been created and Allah has placed them in this world to try them so that they may

[1] Quoted by the translator of ibn Taimiyyah, *Servitude*, from Al-Maqreezi, *Tajreed al-Tauheed al-Mufeed*, p. 29, fn. 54.

demonstrate their sincerity and submissiveness to Allah. Allah says,

ٱلَّذِى خَلَقَ ٱلْمَوْتَ وَٱلْحَيَوٰةَ لِيَبْلُوَكُمْ أَيُّكُمْ أَحْسَنُ عَمَلًا

"[Blessed is] He Who created death and life, that He may try which of you is best in deed; and He is the Exalted in Might, Oft-Forgiving" (*al-Mulk* 2). In this verse, Allah has stated that He is looking to see who is the best in deeds. In explaining this verse, al-Fudhail ibn Iyaadh said, "[It means] the most sincere and the most correct." The people ask him, "How does it become the most sincere and the most correct?" He replied, "Indeed, the action, if it is done sincerely but not correctly, is not accepted and if it is done correctly but not sincerely, it is also not accepted. [It is not accepted by Allah] until it is done sincerely and correctly. The pure and sincere deed is that which is for Allah alone and the correct deed is that which conforms to the Sunnah."[1]

Finally, Ibn Taimiyyah has expounded further on the true meaning of *ibaadah* ("worship, service"). He wrote,

> As for *'Ibaadah,* its original meaning also denotes lowliness and submission. One says, "a pathway that is *mu'abbad*" i.e., it has become smoothed out because of being treaded upon.
> However, the *'Ibaadah* that has been enjoined (upon us) encompasses the meaning of submission along with the meaning of love. It embodies the utmost degree of submission to Allah through the utmost degree of love of Him...
> One who submits to a person whilst possessing hatred for him is not an *'aabid* (i.e., worshipper) of him and (in contrast) if he was to love someone and at the same time does not submit to him, he is likewise not an *'aabid* of him, as is the case of a man who loves his child and friend.
> Consequently, only one of the two (qualities) is not sufficient as far as the *'ibaadah* of Allah is concerned. Rather, it is necessary that Allah be the most beloved

[1] Quoted from *Ibn Taymiyyah's Essay*, p. 80.

above all else to the *'abd* and that he holds Allah to be the greatest of all. Indeed, none other than Allah deserves total love and submission.[1]

The Scope of the Purification of the Soul

It is important to realize that purification of the soul does not imply some kind of abstract purification wherein a person's heart becomes pure yet that "purification" is not reflected in the person's deeds. This fallacious thinking is often found among those who stress the purification of the "inner soul." Indeed, it is not uncommon, especially in the West under the influence of some new form of "Sufism," to find people engaged in what they call "purification of the soul," while they do not pray the five daily prayers, fast the month of Ramadhaan and so forth. In essence, such people cannot truly claim to love what Allah loves or dislike what Allah dislikes. If they did, their purified souls would insist upon their performing, at the very least, the ritual acts of worship that form the foundation of the faith.[2]

One argument that is heard to justify the above way of living is that the ritual acts of worship, such as prayers, fasting and so forth, are only meant to help in purifying one's soul. Once one has actually purified one's soul, he is no longer in need of performing those types of acts. In other words, those acts are simply for some type of common folk who have not reached the enlightened and purified stage of those who do not pray or fast.

This is a fallacious argument for many reasons. First, those ritual acts of worship are not simply means to achieve a better end but they are also goals in and of themselves. In other words, in themselves they are acts of worship and good deeds that

---

[1] [Ahmad ibn Taimiyyah,] *Ibn Taymiyyah's Essay on Servitude*, pp. 37-38.

[2] The Messenger of Allah (peace and blessings of Allah be upon him) said, "Islam is built upon five [pillars]: testifying that there is none worthy of worship except Allah and that Muhammad is the Messenger of Allah, establishing the prayers, giving the zakat, making the pilgrimage to the House and fasting the month of Ramadhaan." Recorded by al-Bukhari and Muslim. Given the emphasis that the Prophet (peace and blessings of Allah be upon him) has given these acts in this hadith, it is inconceivable that any serious Muslim would be complacent concerning them.

every human must perform.[1] Second, the Prophet (peace and blessings of Allah be upon him) was the most noble of all humans and he never stopped performing those ritual acts nor did he ever hint that he or anyone else would ever be excused from performing them. In fact, Allah tells him in the Quran,

وَٱعۡبُدۡ رَبَّكَ حَتَّىٰ يَأۡتِيَكَ ٱلۡيَقِينُ

"And worship your Lord until there comes unto you [the hour that is] certain (*al-yaqeen*)" (*al-Hijr* 99). *Al-yaqeen* or "the certain thing" in this verse is a reference to death.[2] Even if one were to argue that the Prophet (peace and blessings of Allah be upon him) continued performing those acts simply as an example for the common, non-enlightened folk, his closest Companions, for whom Allah in the Quran has declared His pleasure, never stopped performing the ritual acts of worship and were never informed by the Prophet (peace and blessings of Allah be upon him) that they were no longer required to perform those acts. Third, the soul passes through different stages and is always volatile. A person's faith is susceptible to increasing or decreasing. There is no evidence that there is a certain plateau that one may reach that ensures that he will never go back again to a lower level. There is also no evidence that there is a certain plateau beyond which one cannot improve himself further. Hence, the soul is always and forever in need of the acts of worship and other facets that keep it purified and along the Straight Path or that move it even closer to Allah and His pleasure.

In sum, the process of purification of the soul is a process that is never ending with respect to this worldly life. Until a person's death, he must always be aware of this goal and working to improve himself or, at the very least, ensure that he does not slip back to a lesser level of self-purification. This is a continuous process and actually requires an arduous struggle. This process continues until a person reaches his worldly end and his deeds are sealed. Hence, the person is always in need of performing the ritual acts of worship and other purifying acts, as they are keys in

---

[1] Cf., Ibraaheem al-Shaatibi, *Al-Muwaafaqaat fi Usool al-Shareeah* (Beirut: Daar al-Marafah, n.d.), vol. 1, pp. 162ff.
[2] Cf., ibn Katheer, *Tafseer* (Dar Taibah), vol. 4, p. 553.

bringing him closer to Allah and, at the very least, maintaining him at the point that he has been blessed to reach.

Furthermore, one cannot claim that there is somehow some level or point beyond which the purifying soul neither seeks nor should seek. As Islahi noted,

> [*Tazkiah*] does not rest contented with somehow bringing the soul to the right path, but over and above that it strives to take it to ever-increasing heights of superiority. *Tazkiah* does not stop at the stage where we learn a little about God and the Shariah conferred by Him on man, but it is its endeavour that we may attain a true and firm knowledge of God and His attributes. *Tazkiah* does not keep before it as its goal that our habits be reformed to a certain degree but strives after the goal of making ourselves the embodiment of all the beautiful traits of man's character... *Tazkiah* does not demand only that our soul may somehow be subordinated to the Commandments of the Shariah, but its real demand lies in breaking this unruly steed of our soul in such a way that it carries out the orders of God and His apostle in the best possible manner...[1]

Indeed, if that inner soul is purified, it should be the driving force behind the person's acts. The Prophet (peace and blessings of Allah be upon him) said,

وَإِنَّ فِي الْجَسَدِ مُضْغَةً إِذَا صَلَحَتْ صَلَحَ الْجَسَدُ كُلُّهُ وَإِذَا فَسَدَتْ فَسَدَ الْجَسَدُ كُلُّهُ أَلا وَهِيَ الْقَلْبُ

"In the body there is a morsel of flesh which, if it be sound, all the body is sound and which, if it be diseased, all of the body is diseased. This part of the body is the heart." (Recorded by al-Bukhari and Muslim.)

Finally, Allah has left no room for anyone to step outside of the commands of the Shareeah or texts of the Quran and

[1] Islahi, pp. 22-23.

Sunnah. Such contrary behavior is nothing but following in the footsteps of the hated enemy Satan. Allah has made this point very clear when He said,

يَـٰٓأَيُّهَا ٱلَّذِينَ ءَامَنُوا۟ ٱدْخُلُوا۟ فِى ٱلسِّلْمِ كَآفَّةً وَلَا تَتَّبِعُوا۟ خُطُوَٰتِ ٱلشَّيْطَـٰنِ ۚ إِنَّهُۥ لَكُمْ عَدُوٌّ مُّبِينٌ

"O you who believe! Enter into Islam completely [by submitting to all of its laws] and follow not the footsteps of Satan, for he is to you an avowed enemy" (*al-Baqarah* 208).

Another very important to keep in mind is that purification of the soul is not simply related to the ritual acts of worship or acts that one may consider "religious" or "spiritual."[1] As noted earlier, the goal of purification is to become as complete a servant of Allah as one can. The correct concept of servitude or *ibaadah* is very comprehensive. *Ibaadah* is, as ibn Taimiyyah stated in his well-known and widely accepted definition of the term,

> a noun comprising every word or deed, internal or manifest, that Allah loves and approves. This includes prayer, zakat, fasting, pilgrimage, speaking the truth, fulfilling trusts, doing good to parents and relatives, keeping promises, enjoining good, forbidding evil, jihad against the disbelievers and hypocrites, good behavior towards neighbors, orphans, the poor, travelers, slaves and animals, prayer and supplication,

---

[1] Historically speaking, some pious folk made the error of going to an opposite extreme when they noted the masses indulging in the comforts of this world. They decided to denounce everything of this world as being against the concept of purification of the soul, even working within society to make it a more religious environment. However, their opposite extreme is also an incorrect approach. The correct approach is that of the proper balance in one's life. This is where one neither over-indulges in or is overly-attached to the comforts of this world nor does he neglect his lawful needs and responsibilities in this world. As always, the guiding principles to find this balance are found in the Quran, the Sunnah and the way of the Companions of the Prophet (peace and blessings of Allah be upon him). As a starting point, one may study and reflect upon the following verse of the Quran: "But seek, with the (wealth) which Allah has bestowed on you the Home of the Hereafter, but do not forget your portion in this world. But do good, as Allah has been good to you, and seek not (occasions for) mischief in the land: for Allah loves not those who do mischief." (*al-Qasas* 77).

> remembering God and reading the Quran and so on; similarly it includes to love Allah and His Prophet (peace and blessings of Allah be upon him), to fear Him and turn to Him in repentance, to be patient in adversity and thankful in prosperity, to resign oneself to Allah's decrees, to put one's trust in His help, to hope for His mercy, and to fear His punishment. All of these form part of *ibaadah* (worship and servitude) to God.[1]

Hence, the purification of the soul permeates every part of a person. It touches upon his internal characteristics as well as his outward actions. As Islahi noted, "*Tazkiah* deals with all the apparent and hidden aspects of ourselves... Our thoughts, our apprehensions, our inclinations, our movements, our eating and drinking, our engagements, hobbies, and interests, the daily routines in our lives, in short, no department and nothing that touches our lives is outside the pale of *tazkiah*."[2]

When the soul becomes purified, every conceivable form of interaction will be influenced by that purification. In fact, one even has to be wary of going to extremes with respect to the acts of worship, even though such acts in themselves are definitely means of self-purification. However, even with respect to those types of acts, they will only have their proper overall beneficial effect when they are performed within the limits set forth by the Shareeah. This fact is beautifully taught in the following hadith recorded by al-Bukhari: Abu Juhaifah narrated from his father who said, "The Prophet (peace and blessings of Allah be upon him) forged a brotherhood between Salmaan and Abu al-Dardaa. Salmaan visited Abu al-Dardaa and found his wife Umm al-Dardaa dressed in shabby attire. He asked her, "What is going on

---

[1] Ibn Taimiyyah, *Majmoo*, vol. 10, p. 449. The word *ibaadah* is used by scholars in two different ways, thus occasionally being a source of confusion. In one usage, it is the general meaning as given above by ibn Taimiyyah. However, it is also sometimes used to refer to the particular ritual acts of worship only. Hence, one finds in the works of *fiqh*, for example, a chapter on *ibaadaat* (meaning the ritual acts, such as ritual cleanliness, prayer, zakat) and then a chapter on *muaamalaat* (acts of social interaction, such as business dealings and so forth). Again, in the general sense of the word, though, all of these deeds fall under the realm of *ibaadah* or the correct worship and servitude to Allah.

[2] Islahi, p. 21.

with you?" She replied, "Your brother Abu al-Dardaa has no need for this worldly life." Abu al-Dardaa then came and he prepared some food for him. He told him, "Eat." He replied, "I am fasting." Salmaan replied, "I will not eat until you eat," so he then ate. At night, Abu al-Dardaa went to perform late night prayers. Salmaan told him, "Sleep," so he slept. He then went again to perform late night prayers and Salmaan told him again, "Sleep," so he slept. It was the last portion of the night, Salmaan told him, "Now get up." They then both prayed. Salmaan then told him, "Your Lord has a right over you, your own self has a right over you and your wife has a right over you. And give everyone who has a right its proper due." The Prophet (peace and blessings of Allah be upon him) then came and he mentioned what Salmaan had said and the Prophet (peace and blessings of Allah be upon him) told him [Abu al-Dardaa], "Salmaan has spoken the truth."[1]

In sum, purification of the soul is inclusive of:

(a) One's relationship with the Lord,

(b) One's relationship with his own soul and its rights upon him,

(c) One's relationship with society as a whole,

(d) One's relationship with one's relatives, spouse, children and others who have special rights upon a person,

(e) One's relationship with the animals that Allah has placed in this creation,

(f) One's relationship with the environment and all the resources that Allah has created which are supposed to be used in a responsible and ethical manner.

One's soul is only truly purified when all of these realms fall within the one goal and purpose of his purification. In other words, when they are all guided by the guidance found in the Quran and Sunnah.

Murad has noted a very important point that is actually one of the benefits of this proper understanding of purification of the soul, reflecting once again the importance of having one single comprehensive goal in one's life. He noted,

---

[1] Extremism with respect to acts of worship is dealt with in detail in Abdul Rahmaan al-Mutairi, *Religious Extremism in the Lives of Contemporary Muslims* (Denver, CO: Al-Basheer Company for Publications and Translations, 2001), pp. 419-435.

> Unless you approach *tazkiya* as an all-embracing process, you will find that your life is compartmentalised, certain parts impeding the development of others. This can only result in a life of disharmony and unhappiness. Approached as a comprehensive and all-embracing process, however, you will find that each part of your life will complement some other part. This should, God willing, make your struggle on the path to God and *Janna* [Paradise] easier and full of grace.[1]

Summary

This chapter has set forth a fundamental component of the process of purification of the soul. For the most part, it has been concerned with the goal of that process. The conclusion of this chapter is that, first, the goal must be understood properly and, second, the goal must be clearly in one's mind as he goes about his daily activities. Not understanding the goal properly and not keeping it in mind are two pitfalls that have in the past kept and continue to keep people from fulfilling the requirements needed to purify one's soul. Another pitfall is not realizing the entire scope of the process of purification. The process must reach to every realm of one's life as every realm is touched upon with guidance from the Quran or Sunnah.

---

[1] Khurram Murad, *In the Early Hours: Reflections on Spiritual and Self Development* (Markfield, United Kingdom: Revival Publications, 2000), p. 16.

Chapter 5
The Process of Purification

In this work, it has been claimed that perhaps the most important goal in life is *tazkiya*. An obvious question that then flows from that thesis is: Does Islam have its own unique way or process of *tazkiya*? If the answer to that question is yes, one then has the right to ask another question: Can anyone claim that there is any other way that will also result in the purification of one's soul? The fact is that the Messenger of Allah (peace and blessings of Allah be upon him) was sent by Allah. One of his main purposes was to purify mankind and, in particular, his followers. Given this pure guidance from Allah, there is no need for anyone to turn to any other source of information to find a path of purification.

On this point, Islahi made the following important comments,

> [Given its importance and the fact that it was one of the goals of the Prophet's mission, it must be taken as a given that] the Prophet could not have left the world leaving the mission of *tazkiah* incomplete... Its importance demands that the principles of *tazkiah* must have been laid down carefully with as much precision and detail as were the principles and rules and regulations of the Islamic Shariah, leaving no loopholes for any transgression or corruption in either of them. Just as a *Mujtahid* in the sphere of the Islamic Shariah is strictly bound to judge his *ijtehad* in the light of the Shariah and its spirit in general, and also present it to be judged and criticized if necessary according to the same criteria, anybody who puts up anything in the field of *tazkiah* according to his own *ijtehad* must bring the pointers from the Quran and the Sunnah or the practice of the Prophet and his companions in support of his opinion; otherwise *ijtehad* on the basis of his

personal opinion and tastes or his intuition will carry no weight.[1]

It is also just as important to realize that any path of purification, any belief or practice that is not consistent with that which the Prophet (peace and blessings of Allah be upon him) brought cannot possibly be a better way of purification than that which is known to be approved by Allah. The most that any human can reasonably argue is that Allah approved of the Prophet's way and declared him as being one who is purifying the people. If someone wanted to seek another path of purification, the most that that person could claim is that the Prophet's way is one way and some other way is also a good way. However, that is a very dangerous statement. There could not possibly be any sound proof that a particular way other than that of the Prophet (peace and blessings of Allah be upon him) is pleasing to Allah and will purify the soul. Any other path will be derived either from human reasoning or human desires. Neither of these sources can claim that what they come up is pleasing to Allah. This is because only Allah knows what is pleasing to Him. Therefore, if one is serious about trying to purify his soul, one has no recourse but to follow as exactly as possible the guidance and example of the Prophet Muhammad (peace and blessings of Allah be upon him).

Allah says,

وَكَذَٰلِكَ أَوْحَيْنَآ إِلَيْكَ رُوحًا مِّنْ أَمْرِنَا ۚ مَا كُنتَ تَدْرِى مَا

ٱلْكِتَٰبُ وَلَا ٱلْإِيمَٰنُ وَلَٰكِن جَعَلْنَٰهُ نُورًا نَّهْدِى بِهِۦ مَن نَّشَآءُ مِنْ

عِبَادِنَا ۚ وَإِنَّكَ لَتَهْدِىٓ إِلَىٰ صِرَٰطٍ مُّسْتَقِيمٍ

"And thus have We, by Our command, sent inspiration to you. You knew not (before) what was revelation or what was faith. But We have made the (Quran) a light wherewith We guide such of Our servants as We will; and verily you do guide (men) to the straight path" (*al-Shoora* 52). Commenting on this verse, al-Ashqar notes that Allah mentioned two attributes for what He

---

[1] Islahi, pp. 6-7.

revealed. First, it is a *rooh* and it is the *rooh* that first gives true life. Second, it is a light and it is the light that uncovers the darkness. Before having this *rooh*, the soul of the human was truly dead in a spiritual sense. Once Allah brings life to a person, He has also provided him with the light that he must use and rely on to distinguish truth from falsehood and good from evil.[1] It is this *rooh* and light which Allah revealed to the Prophet (peace and blessings of Allah be upon him) that is the source of being guided to the Straight Path, the path of purification, as Allah makes clear at the end of the above verse.

In addition, there is ample evidence from the Quran and Sunnah demonstrating that the path of Islam, the Straight Path, the path of purification is indeed one path and only one path. Anything not consistent with the guidance of the Quran and Sunnah will take one away from the Straight Path and will not be accepted by Allah. Allah says, for example,

وَمَن يَبْتَغِ غَيْرَ ٱلْإِسْلَـٰمِ دِينًا فَلَن يُقْبَلَ مِنْهُ وَهُوَ فِى ٱلْـَٔاخِرَةِ مِنَ ٱلْخَـٰسِرِينَ

"And whoever seeks a religion other than Islam, it will never be accepted from him and in the Hereafter he will be one of the losers" (*ali-Imraan* 85). Allah also says,

إِنَّ ٱلدِّينَ عِندَ ٱللَّهِ ٱلْإِسْلَـٰمُ

"Verily, the true religion with Allah is Islam" (*ali-Imraan* 19). Indeed, there is no Islam today other than that path which the Messenger of Allah (peace and blessings of Allah be upon him) brought.

Allah also says,

[1] Umar al-Ashqar, *Minhaaj Tazkiyah al-Nafs fi al-Islaam* (Amman, Jordan: Daar al-Nafaais, 1992), pp. 21-22.

وَأَنَّ هَٰذَا صِرَٰطِى مُسْتَقِيمًا فَٱتَّبِعُوهُ وَلَا تَتَّبِعُوا۟ ٱلسُّبُلَ فَتَفَرَّقَ بِكُمْ عَن سَبِيلِهِۦ ذَٰلِكُمْ وَصَّىٰكُم بِهِۦ لَعَلَّكُمْ تَتَّقُونَ

"This is My Straight Path, so follow it. Follow not other ways, as you will then stray from His Way" (*al-Anaam* 153). Note the Prophet's explanation of this verse,

عَنْ عَبْدِ اللَّهِ بْنِ مَسْعُودٍ قَالَ خَطَّ لَنَا رَسُولُ اللَّهِ صَلَّى اللَّهم عَلَيْهِ وَسَلَّمَ خَطًّا ثُمَّ قَالَ هَذَا سَبِيلُ اللَّهِ ثُمَّ خَطَّ خُطُوطًا عَنْ يَمِينِهِ وَعَنْ شِمَالِهِ ثُمَّ قَالَ هَذِهِ سُبُلٌ قَالَ يَزِيدُ مُتَفَرِّقَةٌ عَلَى كُلِّ سَبِيلٍ مِنْهَا شَيْطَانٌ يَدْعُو إِلَيْهِ ثُمَّ قَرَأَ (إِنَّ هَذَا صِرَاطِي مُسْتَقِيمًا فَاتَّبِعُوهُ وَلَا تَتَّبِعُوا السُّبُلَ فَتَفَرَّقَ بِكُمْ عَنْ سَبِيلِهِ)

Abdullah ibn Masood said, "The Prophet (peace and blessings of Allah be upon him) drew for us a line and then he said, 'That is the path of Allah.' Then he drew lines to the right and to the left of it and he said, 'These are—Yazeed the subnarrator said various—paths. Upon each such path is a devil calling towards it. Then he recited the verse, 'This is My Straight Path, so follow it. Follow not other ways, as you will then stray from His Way' [*al-Anaam* 153]."[1]

In order for any act to be accepted by Allah, it must be performed with the correct intention and it must be in accordance with the guidance that has come via the Prophet (peace be upon him). Allah alludes to this fact in many verses in the Quran and has shown beyond any doubt that the way of the Prophet Muhammad (peace and blessings of Allah be upon him) is, in fact, the only acceptable way of life and the only means of purification. Allah has said, for example,

---

[1] Recorded by Ahmad. Its chain is *hasan*. See the discussion in Shuaib al-Arnaaoot, et al., *Musnad al-Imaam Ahmad* (Beirut: Muassasat al-Risaalah, 1996), vol. 7, pp. 207-209.

لَّقَدْ كَانَ لَكُمْ فِي رَسُولِ ٱللَّهِ أُسْوَةٌ حَسَنَةٌ لِّمَن كَانَ يَرْجُواْ ٱللَّهَ وَٱلْيَوْمَ ٱلْأَخِرَ وَذَكَرَ ٱللَّهَ كَثِيرًا

"Verily you have in the Messenger of Allah the best example for whoever desires Allah and the Hereafter and who remembers Allah often" (*al-Ahzaab* 21);

قُلْ إِن كُنتُمْ تُحِبُّونَ ٱللَّهَ فَٱتَّبِعُونِي يُحْبِبْكُمُ ٱللَّهُ وَيَغْفِرْ لَكُمْ ذُنُوبَكُمْ ۗ وَٱللَّهُ غَفُورٌ رَّحِيمٌ ۝ قُلْ أَطِيعُواْ ٱللَّهَ وَٱلرَّسُولَ ۖ فَإِن تَوَلَّوْاْ فَإِنَّ ٱللَّهَ لَا يُحِبُّ ٱلْكَٰفِرِينَ

"Say [O Muhammad]: If you truly love Allah, then follow me and Allah will love you and forgive your sins. And Allah is Oft-Forgiving, Ever Merciful. Say [to them O Muhammad]: [You must] obey Allah and the Messenger. If they then turn away, then verily Allah loves not the disbelievers" (*ali-Imraan* 31-32).

The Messenger of Allah (peace and blessings of Allah be upon him) also said,

مَنْ عَمِلَ عَمَلاً لَيْسَ عَلَيْهِ أَمْرُنَا فَهُوَ رَدٌّ

"Whoever does an act that is not in accord with our matter will have it rejected." (Recorded by Muslim.)

Therefore, purification of the soul or becoming a complete believer comes about through the knowledge and application of the teachings of the Quran and Sunnah. Any other mode of purification, such as special types of physical exercises (such as breathing exercises) or special types of *dhikr* that are not found in the Quran or Sunnah cannot bring the person closer to Allah; nay, those actions will only make the person closer to Satan.

Now that it has been established that the way of the Prophet (peace and blessings of Allah be upon him) is but one way and it is the only way of purification and of pleasing Allah, the next issue is that of the clarity of its path as presented in the Quran and Sunnah. On this point, Islahi notes,

> The knowledge of *tazkiah* can never be a mystery, shared by the selected few and transmitted by them mysteriously from father to son or the teacher to the disciple. *Tazkiah* is universally needed by men for their redemption and prosperity in the Hereafter. The prophets are raised for the purification of individuals... How could it be possible that [for] the thing essential like air and water for every person, the Prophet would have kept a top secret and transmitted to one or two persons only before departing from the world?... Where *tazkiah* or purification of human souls is concerned, which is undeniably a thing of universal need, secrecy about it is neither feasible nor advisable.[1]

The Path of Purification According to Islam/Quran/Sunnah

Since the Prophet (peace be upon him) was sent to purify the souls of the people, there can be no question that his method of purification of the soul is the method that is approved by Allah and that is pleasing to Allah.

Indeed, the path of purification in Islam is a complete, balanced way. It develops the souls of humans and refines their character—but all in a way that is consistent with their natural disposition and form of creation. It purifies the human of evil attributes and characters. It removes diseases and afflictions from

---

[1] Islahi, pp. 7-8. Islahi continues (pp. 8-9), "The *ulama* (erudite in learning) of the Hanafi School do not attach any importance to the traditions reported by one or two persons only [note that this is an exaggeration on Islahi's part], reasoning that things of such universal need could not have been reported so sparingly. But these very people when they step into the field of mysticism feel much elated in their attempts at proving the knowledge of *tazkiah* as a mystery, saying how can the uninitiated be introduced to the knowledge of these things which is all mysteries and intuitions? Intoxicated with this pride they seem to forget that if mysticism aims at and deals with *tazkiah* or self-culture, which is in general demand, how could a secret buried in a few hearts meet this universal demand?" Islahi (pp. 9-18) goes on to refute the supposed evidence found in two hadith that the Sufis present for the mysterious or secret passing on of such knowledge.

the heart and soul. It results in a person who understands his purpose in this creation, who understands what his goal is and understands how he is supposed to live his life. It, therefore, leads to the real source of happiness in both this life and the Hereafter.

The path espoused by the Quran and Sunnah is amazingly very clear and actually easy to follow for all those whose intentions are pure. Indeed, it is a path that is open for every human to follow. It basically is comprised of three components: (1) purification of one's beliefs; (2) drawing closer to Allah by performing the obligatory deeds and (3) drawing even closer to Allah by the voluntary deeds.

A Paradox Resolved

When studying the process of purification, one may conclude that there is something of a paradox: The steps of the very process are, in essence, only performed by those who have achieved the means of purification. However, the process works like this: intention, then the first step. As a person takes the initial baby steps, Allah comes running, supporting and guiding him. This fact is found in the hadith,

يَقُولُ اللَّهُ تَعَالَى أَنَا عِنْدَ ظَنِّ عَبْدِي بِي وَأَنَا مَعَهُ إِذَا ذَكَرَنِي فَإِنْ ذَكَرَنِي فِي نَفْسِهِ ذَكَرْتُهُ فِي نَفْسِي وَإِنْ ذَكَرَنِي فِي مَلَإٍ ذَكَرْتُهُ فِي مَلَإٍ خَيْرٍ مِنْهُمْ وَإِنْ تَقَرَّبَ إِلَيَّ بِشِبْرٍ تَقَرَّبْتُ إِلَيْهِ ذِرَاعًا وَإِنْ تَقَرَّبَ إِلَيَّ ذِرَاعًا تَقَرَّبْتُ إِلَيْهِ بَاعًا وَإِنْ أَتَانِي يَمْشِي أَتَيْتُهُ هَرْوَلَةً

"Allah has said, 'I am as My servant expects of Me. I am with him when he mentions [or remembers] Me. If he remembers Me to himself, I mention him to Myself. If he mentions Me to a gathering, I mention him to a gathering that is better than his. And if he draws near to Me a hand's span, I draw near to him a forearm's length. And if he draws near to Me a forearm's length, I draw near to him an arm's length. And if he comes to Me walking, I go to him at speed." (Recorded by al-Bukhari and Muslim.)

It is when the person himself stops or decides to retreat that the process comes to an end. Then the individual, due to his own decision, such as laziness or succumbing to desires, remains at a specific point or begins to retreat to a weaker state. He can only bounce back from that state by having the resolve to change his ways. He will then take the first step in that renewed direction and once again Allah will come to his aid, help him, bless him and guide him once again to more good deeds.

Purification of One's Beliefs

A person's beliefs are the most important aspect of his being. They are, in general, the driving forces behind his way of life and personal choices.[1] The true and effective beliefs never remain at an abstract level but their influence is manifested on a day-to-day practical level. To take a simple example, the question of cheating and stealing is directly related to one's overall belief system. If a person believes that these acts are morally wrong and that there is an all-knowing, just God who will hold him accountable for his deeds, he will most likely refrain from such acts. But if a person does not believe in any eternal ramifications or any day of judgment, his deciding factor may only be the chances of being caught and the severity of the punishment for those acts.

One's faith and beliefs are also the first criteria by which a person and his acts will be judged on the Day of Judgement. Without the proper belief, especially the essential belief about God and *tauheed,* all of a person's deeds will be in vain. In a very instructive passage in the Quran, Allah has stated what amounts to a warning to those who refuse to correct their beliefs while they claim to be performing good deeds. Allah says,

---

[1] The Prophet (peace and blessings of Allah be upon him) said, "Surely, all actions are but driven by intentions and, verily, every man shall have but that which he intended." (Recorded by al-Bukhari and Muslim.) This means that for every consciously chosen act, there is an intention and belief system behind the act that has led the person to do that act. This is true for "inconsequential deeds" as well as the major life choices a person makes. Hence, all of his important deeds revolve around his beliefs about himself, his purpose, his goal and the world around him.

قُلْ هَلْ نُنَبِّئُكُم بِالْأَخْسَرِينَ أَعْمَالًا ﴿١٠٣﴾ الَّذِينَ ضَلَّ سَعْيُهُمْ فِي الْحَيَاةِ الدُّنْيَا وَهُمْ يَحْسَبُونَ أَنَّهُمْ يُحْسِنُونَ صُنْعًا ﴿١٠٤﴾ أُولَٰئِكَ الَّذِينَ كَفَرُوا بِآيَاتِ رَبِّهِمْ وَلِقَائِهِ فَحَبِطَتْ أَعْمَالُهُمْ فَلَا نُقِيمُ لَهُمْ يَوْمَ الْقِيَامَةِ وَزْنًا ﴿١٠٥﴾ ذَٰلِكَ جَزَاؤُهُمْ جَهَنَّمُ بِمَا كَفَرُوا وَاتَّخَذُوا آيَاتِي وَرُسُلِي هُزُوًا ﴿١٠٦﴾ إِنَّ الَّذِينَ آمَنُوا وَعَمِلُوا الصَّالِحَاتِ كَانَتْ لَهُمْ جَنَّاتُ الْفِرْدَوْسِ نُزُلًا ﴿١٠٧﴾ خَالِدِينَ فِيهَا لَا يَبْغُونَ عَنْهَا حِوَلًا

"Say: Shall we tell you of those who lose most in respect of their deeds? Those whose efforts have been wasted in this life while they thought that they were acquiring good by their works? They are those who deny the signs of their Lord and the fact of their having to meet Him (in the Hereafter). Vain will be their works, nor shall We, on the Day of Judgment, give them any weight. That is their reward, Hell, because they rejected faith, and took My Signs and My Messengers by way of jest. As to those who believe [correctly] and work righteous deeds, they have for their entertainment the Gardens of Paradise wherein they shall dwell (forever). No change will they wish for themselves" (*al-Kahf* 103-108).

In another very moving passage in the Quran, Allah forcefully describes how fruitless the deeds of the non-believers are and how, in reality, they are a people enveloped in darkness, misguidance and loss. The great grandeur of all their deeds and accomplishments will mean nothing because the driving force behind them was not pure and worthy of reward. Allah says,

وَٱلَّذِينَ كَفَرُوٓاْ أَعۡمَٰلُهُمۡ كَسَرَابِۭ بِقِيعَةٖ يَحۡسَبُهُ ٱلظَّمۡـَٔانُ مَآءً حَتَّىٰٓ
إِذَا جَآءَهُۥ لَمۡ يَجِدۡهُ شَيۡـٔٗا وَوَجَدَ ٱللَّهَ عِندَهُۥ فَوَفَّىٰهُ حِسَابَهُۥۗ وَٱللَّهُ سَرِيعُ
ٱلۡحِسَابِ ﴿٣٩﴾ أَوۡ كَظُلُمَٰتٖ فِي بَحۡرٖ لُّجِّيّٖ يَغۡشَىٰهُ مَوۡجٞ مِّن فَوۡقِهِۦ
مَوۡجٞ مِّن فَوۡقِهِۦ سَحَابٞۚ ظُلُمَٰتُۢ بَعۡضُهَا فَوۡقَ بَعۡضٍ إِذَآ أَخۡرَجَ يَدَهُۥ
لَمۡ يَكَدۡ يَرَىٰهَاۗ وَمَن لَّمۡ يَجۡعَلِ ٱللَّهُ لَهُۥ نُورٗا فَمَا لَهُۥ مِن نُّورٍ

"As for the Unbelievers, their deeds are like a mirage in sandy deserts, which the man parched with thirst mistakes for water. When he comes up to it, he finds it to be nothing. But he finds Allah (ever) with him, and Allah will pay him his account. And Allah is swift in taking account. Or (the unbelievers' state) is like the depths of darkness in a vast deep ocean, overwhelmed with billow topped by billow, topped by (dark) clouds: depths of darkness, one above another. If a man stretches out his hand, he can hardly see it! For any to whom Allah gives not light, there is no light" (*al-Noor* 39-40).[1]

---

[1] The commentators note that in these verses two sets of disbelievers are being described. The first group is those disbelievers who call others to their way of life, reckoning that they have some sound deeds and beliefs. In reality, it is nothing but a mirage and a false hope. The person follows that for a long time and, only after such an arduous journey through life, discovers that it was all only a deception. What he finds instead at the end is Allah and Allah's reckoning. This is the similitude of those disbelievers who think that they are going to find true happiness by following their false creeds. The second group covers the followers and masses who simply accept and blindly follow what the leaders of misguidance proclaim, until Allah seals their heart and leaves them in complete darkness due to their own decision not to use their hearts and minds to recognize the falsehood of what they nonchalantly accepted. Allah describes them as being in such darkness that they cannot even see their hands in front of them. This is the case with the blind disbeliever who has no idea of where he is going and to where he is being led. Allah even describes the skies as being covered with clouds, such that the person has perhaps lost his last chance for guidance, the stars in the sky by which one can find direction. These two groups are in complete ignorance, doubt, loss and confusion. Indeed, true and complete darkness. Cf., al-Qurtubi, vol. 12, pp. 283-286; Sayyid Qutb, *Fi Dhilaal al-Quraan* (Beirut: Daar al-Shurroq, 1981), vol. 4, pp. 2521f; Karzoon, vol. 1, p. 130.

Furthermore, if a person consciously chooses a belief system that is wrong and based on false perceptions, his entire goal in life will be wrong. This will have a profound effect on his soul. His soul has been created with a natural inclination to worship and serve the only one true God. Any other way of life will be a type of perversion that will corrupt and ruin the soul, whether the person is willing to recognize or admit that fact or not.

Therefore, without any question, the first step in the process of purification of the soul is purification and correction of one's beliefs. First and foremost is one's beliefs concerning Allah. Another very important point is one's beliefs about and attitude towards the Messenger of Allah (peace and blessings of Allah be upon him). One's beliefs about the Hereafter or what occurs after death also have a prominent role in the purification of the soul. Indeed, even one's beliefs about *qadar* (pre-ordainment) play an essential and distinctive role in one's purification.

The Proper Belief in Allah

The proper belief in Allah or *tauheed*[1] is without a doubt the first aspect on the road to self-purification and the key to real success and happiness in this life and in the Hereafter. Allah says,

قَدْ أَفْلَحَ مَن تَزَكَّىٰ

"He has certainly succeeded who has purified himself" (*al-Ala* 14). The Quranic commentators note that this is referring first to

---

[1] *Tauheed* is the pure and true "Islamic monotheism." It is free of any form of associating of partners with Allah, of likening Allah to any of His creatures or of likening any of Allah's creatures to Him. Hence, it is free of all of the distortions that one finds among the other commonly referred to "monotheistic religions," such as Judaism and Christianity. Note that this author has discussed the articles of faith as well as the pillars in Islam in *Commentary on the Forty Hadith of al-Nawawi* (as well as in *He Came to Teach You Your Religion*, which is taken from the *Commentary*). However, the emphasis in those works was in explaining the meanings of the articles of faith and the importance of the pillars. In this work, the emphasis is strictly on the ramifications of the articles of faith and the pillars of Islam on the purification of the soul. Therefore, for an explanation of the beliefs and a discussion of the importance of the pillars, the interested reader is referred to those works.

purifying oneself from *shirk* (associating partners with Allah) and *kufr* (disbelief).[1] It has been narrated that ibn Abbaas explained this verse by saying, "Whoever purifies himself from *shirk*."[2]

Indeed, it has been deviations from the correct belief in God that has misled most of mankind.[3] In other words, for much of mankind today, it is not the case that they do not believe in God but it is the case that their belief, based on their own whims and desires or their choice to blindly follow others, is distorted and not based on any true source of knowledge concerning God. For example, many people today believe that as long as a person is a "nice" person and does not do harm to others, God would never be displeased with such a person and they will enter Paradise or achieve some kind of bliss.[4] Thus, having the proper belief about God does not even enter into the equation, as long as the person is a "nice" person. Actually, a person could be a devil worshipper or a believer in one hundred idols yet all of that does not seem to matter. Although one may commonly hear such ideas expressed, all such thoughts are simply the people's own suppositions about God. They are false and have no proof to support them.

Although much of mankind has turned a deaf ear to the revelations from Allah, it was part of the great mercy of Allah that He had sent to every people a messenger calling them to the first

---

[1] For the explanation of this verse and why it must be in reference to disbelief and idolatry, see al-Fakhar al-Raazi, *Al-Tafseer al-Kabeer* (Beirut: Daar Ihyaa al-Turaath al-Arabi, n.d.), vol. 31, pp. 146-147; al-Aloosi, vol. 15, p. 109. Cf., also, Jalaal al-Deen al-Suyooti, *al-Durr fi al-Tafseer al-Mathoor* (Beirut: Daar al-Kutub al-Ilmiyyah, 1990), vol. 6, p. 567-568. Note that there is the following hadith: The Messenger of Allah (peace and blessings of Allah be upon him) said about the verse, "He has certainly succeeded who has purified himself," "[That is,] the one who testifies that there is none worthy of worship except Allah, abandons the idols and bears witness that I am the Messenger of Allah." This hadith was recorded by al-Bazzaar from the Companion Jaabir. Al-Bazaar said, "We do not know of it from Jaabir save through this chain." Commenting on this chain, al-Haithami said, "Recorded by al-Bazaar from his teacher Ibaad ibn Ahmad al-Arazami and he is rejected." Cf., Noor al-Deen Ali al-Haithami, *Kashf al-Astaar an Zawaaid al-Bazzaar ala al-Kutub al-Sittah* (Beirut: Muassasah al-Risaalah, 1984), vol. 3, p. 80; Noor al-Deen Ali al-Haithami, *[Bughyah al-Raaid fi Tahqeeq] Majma al-Zawaaid wa Manba al-Fawaaid* (Beirut: Daar al-Fikr, 1992), vol. 7, p. 289.

[2] Quoted in al-Tabari, vol. 15, p. 156.

[3] Examples and ramifications were given earlier concerning the incorrect beliefs of the Hindus, Buddhists, Jews and Christians.

[4] This author has heard this statement from numerous people who are adherents of Christianity, Judaism and, amazingly, Islam.

fundamental truth of life: there is none worthy of worship except Allah. Allah says,

وَلَقَدْ بَعَثْنَا فِي كُلِّ أُمَّةٍ رَّسُولًا أَنِ ٱعْبُدُوا۟ ٱللَّهَ وَٱجْتَنِبُوا۟ ٱلطَّٰغُوتَ ۖ فَمِنْهُم مَّنْ هَدَى ٱللَّهُ وَمِنْهُم مَّنْ حَقَّتْ عَلَيْهِ ٱلضَّلَٰلَةُ ۚ فَسِيرُوا۟ فِي ٱلْأَرْضِ فَٱنظُرُوا۟ كَيْفَ كَانَ عَٰقِبَةُ ٱلْمُكَذِّبِينَ

"For We assuredly sent among every people a messenger, (with the command), 'Worship Allah, and eschew all false gods.' Of the people were some whom Allah guided, and some on whom error became inevitably (established). So travel through the earth, and see what was the end of those who denied (the truth)" (*al-Nahl* 36).

In reality, the acceptance of this fact—that there is none worthy of worship except Allah, the first statement of the testimony of faith—is the first step on the road to purification of the soul, purifying one's beliefs and one's heart from any form of *shirk* or associating partners with Allah. One's heart must possess the minimum of *tauheed*. Ibn al-Qayyim noted, "*Tauheed* is the first call of the messengers, it is the first stage along the path and the first rank that the person who is heading towards Allah must take."[1]

Associating partners with Allah is a great form of wrongdoing. In particular, one is completely wronging one's own soul and dignity by submitting to and worshipping beings that do not deserve a human's worship whatsoever. Allah has stated in the Quran, while quoting Luqmaan,

إِنَّ ٱلشِّرْكَ لَظُلْمٌ عَظِيمٌ

"Indeed associating [partners with Allah] is a great wrongdoing" (*Luqmaan* 13).

Allah has said in the Quran,

---

[1] Muhammad ibn al-Qayyim, *Mudaarij al-Saalikeen bain Manaazil Iyyaaka Nabudu wa Iyyaaka Nastaeen* (Beirut: Daar al-Kitaab al-Arabi, n.d.), vol. 3, p. 443.

يَـٰٓأَيُّهَا ٱلَّذِينَ ءَامَنُوٓاْ إِنَّمَا ٱلْمُشْرِكُونَ نَجَسٌ

"O believers! Verily, the polytheists are impure" (*al-Tauba* 28). This is a spiritual impurity—which is the opposite of the purification of the soul.

Allah also says,

وَوَيْلٌ لِّلْمُشْرِكِينَ ۝٦ ٱلَّذِينَ لَا يُؤْتُونَ ٱلزَّكَوٰةَ وَهُم بِٱلْـَٔاخِرَةِ هُمْ كَـٰفِرُونَ

"Woe to those who associate others with Allah—those who do not come with the pure testimony of faith (*zakaat*) and who disbelieve in the Hereafter" (*Fussilat* 6-7). Ibn al-Qayyim noted,

> The majority of the early Quranic commentators and of those who came afterwards say that the word *zakaat* in this verse means *tauheed,* the testimony that there is none worthy of worship save Allah. Belief in it is that by which the heart is purified. This includes denying in one's heart any other god save the true God. This is its [the heart's] purification and the confirmation of Allah being the one and only God. This is the foundation of every form of purification and growth.[1]

In a number of places in the Quran, Allah juxtaposes the ramifications and effects of the correct belief in Allah with the effects of different incorrect beliefs. For example, Allah says,

فَمَن يُرِدِ ٱللَّهُ أَن يَهْدِيَهُۥ يَشْرَحْ صَدْرَهُۥ لِلْإِسْلَـٰمِ ۖ وَمَن يُرِدْ أَن يُضِلَّهُۥ يَجْعَلْ صَدْرَهُۥ ضَيِّقًا حَرَجًا كَأَنَّمَا يَصَّعَّدُ فِى ٱلسَّمَآءِ ۚ كَذَٰلِكَ يَجْعَلُ ٱللَّهُ ٱلرِّجْسَ عَلَى ٱلَّذِينَ لَا يُؤْمِنُونَ

[1] Ibn al-Qayyim, *Ighaathah*, vol. 1, p. 81; Also see al-Qurtubi, vol. 19, p. 199, ibn Katheer, *Tafseer* (Daar Taibah), vol. 4, p. 94 and al-Abdul Lateef, p. 60.

"Those whom Allah wills to guide, He opens their breast to Islam; those whom He wills to leave straying, He makes their breast close and constricted, as if they had to climb up to the skies. Thus does Allah (heap) wrath on those who refuse to believe" (*al-Anaam* 125).

In the following passage, Allah has beautifully described the fruits of the correct belief as well as the results of all false beliefs. Allah says,

أَلَمْ تَرَ كَيْفَ ضَرَبَ ٱللَّهُ مَثَلًا كَلِمَةً طَيِّبَةً كَشَجَرَةٍ طَيِّبَةٍ أَصْلُهَا
ثَابِتٌ وَفَرْعُهَا فِى ٱلسَّمَآءِ ﴿٢٤﴾ تُؤْتِىٓ أُكُلَهَا كُلَّ حِينٍۭ بِإِذْنِ رَبِّهَا ۗ
وَيَضْرِبُ ٱللَّهُ ٱلْأَمْثَالَ لِلنَّاسِ لَعَلَّهُمْ يَتَذَكَّرُونَ ﴿٢٥﴾ وَمَثَلُ
كَلِمَةٍ خَبِيثَةٍ كَشَجَرَةٍ خَبِيثَةٍ ٱجْتُثَّتْ مِن فَوْقِ ٱلْأَرْضِ مَا لَهَا مِن
قَرَارٍ ﴿٢٦﴾ يُثَبِّتُ ٱللَّهُ ٱلَّذِينَ ءَامَنُوا۟ بِٱلْقَوْلِ ٱلثَّابِتِ فِى ٱلْحَيَوٰةِ
ٱلدُّنْيَا وَفِى ٱلْءَاخِرَةِ ۖ وَيُضِلُّ ٱللَّهُ ٱلظَّٰلِمِينَ ۚ وَيَفْعَلُ ٱللَّهُ مَا يَشَآءُ

"Don't you see how Allah sets forth a parable? A goodly word is like a goodly tree, whose root is firmly fixed, and its branches (reach) to the heavens, it brings forth its fruit at all times, by the leave of its Lord. So Allah sets forth parables for men, in order that they may receive admonition. And the parable of an evil word is that of any evil tree. It is torn up by the root from the surface of the earth. It has no stability. Allah will establish in strength those who believe, with the word that stands firm, in this world and in the Hereafter; but Allah will leave to stray those who do wrong. Allah does what He wills" (*Ibraaheem* 24-27). It is narrated that ibn Abbaas said, "The goodly word is the testimony that there is none worthy of worship except Allah."[1] This verse shows that *tauheed* or proper belief is the foundation upon which all other good is built. It is a foundation that continues to give and give,

[1] Quoted in ibn Katheer, *Tafseer* (Daar Taibah), vol. 4, p. 491.

with its proceeds reaching the highest limits. Such is the way with the true faith; it continually and perpetually benefits the person in this life and eternally in the Hereafter. It also follows that the stronger and better supported the foundation or roots, the greater will be the fruits. On the other hand, the false beliefs, such as *shirk,* have no solid ground to them. Indeed, they are not much more than an illusion in the sense that they can never bear the produce that its followers claim or believe in.

Allah also says,

فَٱجْتَنِبُوا۟ ٱلرِّجْسَ مِنَ ٱلْأَوْثَـٰنِ وَٱجْتَنِبُوا۟ قَوْلَ ٱلزُّورِ ﴿٣٠﴾ حُنَفَآءَ لِلَّهِ غَيْرَ مُشْرِكِينَ بِهِۦ ۚ وَمَن يُشْرِكْ بِٱللَّهِ فَكَأَنَّمَا خَرَّ مِنَ ٱلسَّمَآءِ فَتَخْطَفُهُ ٱلطَّيْرُ أَوْ تَهْوِى بِهِ ٱلرِّيحُ فِى مَكَانٍ سَحِيقٍ

"Shun the filth [and abomination][1] from idols, and shun the word that is false, being true in faith to Allah, and never assigning partners to Him. If anyone assigns partners to Allah, he is as if he had fallen from heaven and been snatched up by birds, or the wind had swooped (like a bird on its prey) and thrown him into a far-distant place" (*al-Hajj* 30-31). In his explanation of this verse, Maudoodi wrote,

> In this parable "heaven" means the original human nature. Man by nature is the servant of none else but Allah and inherently accepts the doctrine of *tauheed.* That is why the one who follows the guidance of the Prophets becomes firm in these dictates of his nature and soars higher and higher. On the other hand, the one who rejects Allah or associates a partner with Him

---

[1] Note that both Abdullah Yusuf Ali and Muhammad Taqi-ud-Din al-Hilali with Muhammad Muhsin Khan translated the word *al-rijs* as "abomination." "Abomination" is defined as, "anything greatly disliked or abhorred...a vile, shameful, or detestable action, condition, habit, etc." [*Webster's Encyclopedic Unabridged Dictionary of the English Language* (New York: Portland House, 1989), p. 4.] That perhaps does not completely capture the essence of the word *al-rijs*. *Al-Rijs* is defined as, "Uncleanness, dirt, or filth: or an unclean, a dirty, or a filthy thing... anything that is disliked, or hated, for its uncleanness, dirtiness, or filthiness..." Lane, vol. 1, p. 1037.

> falls down from the "heaven" of his nature. Then he either becomes a victim of satans and evil leaders like the birds of the parable, which snatch away the fallen man, or he becomes a slave of his lusts, passions, whims, etc., which have been likened to the wind in the parable. They lower him down from one wrong position to the other till he falls into the deepest abyss of degradation.[1]

It is no secret and no wonder that the first portion of the Prophet's mission, as demonstrated by the revelations that he received in Makkah, concentrated on purification of belief. It was dedicated to removing all forms of ignorance, superstition and false creeds. Once this process is completed and one has a true grasp of the concept of *tauheed,* it becomes very difficult to be misled from the path—unless one consciously and intentionally desires to do so. This is because the concept of *tauheed* can become so clear and beautiful in the eyes of the person that all beliefs that are clearly incompatible with this *tauheed* become repugnant to him. He will be disgusted with the idea of worshipping a human, or he himself becoming equal to god or uniting with god and so forth. He will quickly and clearly understand that all of these are nothing but the plots and plans of Satan, the arch-enemy of humans.

The effects on the soul of the true monotheism or *tauheed* that was brought by the Prophet (peace and blessings of Allah be upon him) are profound. Once this concept is truly understood and embodied in a person, there is a certain type of nobility (for lack of a better word) and feeling of purpose that accompanies the soul. The person realizes that he is not to submit to, physically bow down or prostrate to anything or anyone other than Allah. He does not turn in his prayers to anyone other than Allah, nor can anyone grant him forgiveness save Allah. He does not turn to dead humans who, in reality, were no more than humans themselves. He does not sit at the base of wooden or metal idols that other humans themselves actually created. He does not fear any form of

---

[1] Abul Ala Maudoodi, *The Meaning of the Quran* (Lahore, Pakistan: Islamic Publications, Ltd., 1981), vol. VII, pp. 201-202.

spirits such that he has to appease them by offering sacrifices to them. Furthermore, such a person will base his life on his belief in there being only one true God.

All of these things are forbidden to him by the concept of *tauheed*. But they are more than simply forbidden for him. He understands fully well that all of these acts are not becoming a human being that Allah has created for a very special and noble purpose. All of these acts are beneath a human and, in fact, it is inconceivable that a person who has a sane understanding of reality would ever take part in those types of acts. Why should a human bow down and pray to another human who has to eat and drink to survive just like himself? How could anyone claim that another being has any share in the divinity with Allah and therefore is deserving of having others humble and prostrate themselves before him?

On the other end of the spectrum there is the committing of *shirk*, which includes all of the other beliefs prevalent in the world today. This includes the other "monotheistic" faiths of Judaism and Christianity. Those who commit *shirk* go to an extreme for which, in truth, there is no excuse. Their own souls and beings know that their *shirk* is completely repugnant and that they are following it only to satisfy some lowly desires. Hence, Allah will forgive any sin except *shirk*. Allah says,

إِنَّ ٱللَّهَ لَا يَغۡفِرُ أَن يُشۡرَكَ بِهِۦ وَيَغۡفِرُ مَا دُونَ ذَٰلِكَ لِمَن

يُشۡرِكۡ وَمَن يَشَآءُۚ بِٱللَّهِ فَقَدِ ٱفۡتَرَىٰٓ إِثۡمًا عَظِيمًا

"Allah does not forgive that partners should be set up with Him; but He forgives whatever is less than that for whom He pleases; to set up partners with Allah is to devise a sin most heinous indeed" (*al-Nisaa* 48; see also *al-Nisaa* 116).

Those who commit *shirk* are deserving of an eternal damnation as it was their intention to forever remain along the path of their false beliefs. Hence, Allah has forbidden His pleasure and paradise for them, saying,

إِنَّهُۥ مَن يُشۡرِكۡ بِٱللَّهِ فَقَدۡ حَرَّمَ ٱللَّهُ عَلَيۡهِ ٱلۡجَنَّةَ وَمَأۡوَىٰهُ ٱلنَّارُۖ وَمَا لِلظَّٰلِمِينَ مِنۡ أَنصَارٖ

"Whoever joins others with Allah, Allah will forbid him the Garden, and the Fire will be his abode. There will for the wrongdoers be no one to help" (*al-Maaidah* 72).

Once again, therefore, without this first step of purification—the purification of one's beliefs at least to the extent of removing all forms of *shirk*—nothing else will be of any avail. The heart must be purified first with *tauheed* before one can truly move on to anything else. If that is not done first, then all of the following steps will be in vain. Any deed that is not done purely and solely for the sake of Allah will be in vain and rejected by Allah. A hadith *qudsi* states,

أَنَا أَغْنَى الشُّرَكَاءِ عَنِ الشِّرْكِ مَنْ عَمِلَ عَمَلاً أَشْرَكَ فِيهِ مَعِي غَيْرِي تَرَكْتُهُ وَشِرْكَهُ

"I am the most self-sufficient and am in no need of having a partner. Whoever does a deed for My sake as well as for someone [or something] else will have that action rejected by Me with the one he associates [with Allah]." (Recorded by Muslim.)

Allah's Names and Attributes

A hadith in *Musnad Ahmad* states,

عَنْ أُبَيٍّ أَنَّ النَّبِيَّ صَلَّى اللَّهم عَلَيْهِ وَسَلَّمَ سَأَلَهُ أَيُّ آيَةٍ فِي كِتَابِ اللَّهِ أَعْظَمُ قَالَ اللَّهُ وَرَسُولُهُ أَعْلَمُ فَرَدَّدَهَا مِرَارًا ثُمَّ قَالَ أُبَيٌّ آيَةُ الْكُرْسِيِّ

Ubayy narrated that the Prophet (peace and blessings of Allah be upon him) had asked him, "Which verse in the Book of Allah is the greatest?" He replied, "Allah and His Messenger know best." The Prophet (peace and blessings of Allah be upon him) repeated the question a number of times and then said, "Ubayy, it is the verse of the Throne."[1] "The verse of the Throne" is the 255th verse of *soorah al-Baqarah*.[2] It is completely related to the names, attributes and greatness of Allah. This is the greatest verse in the Quran. It supplies humans with the greatest form of knowledge and a form of knowledge that can only be known from its direct source Allah Himself.[3]

---

[1] Muslim has something similar but with different wording.

[2] The verse's translation is: "Allah—there is no deity except Him, the Ever-Living, the Sustainer of [all] existence. Neither drowsiness overtakes Him nor sleep. To Him belongs whatever is in the heavens and whatever is on earth. Who is it that can intercede with Him except by His permission? He knows what is [presently] before them and what will be after them, and they encompass not a thing of His knowledge except what He wills. His footstool extends over the heavens and the earth, and their preservation does not tire Him. And He is the Most High, the Most Great."

[3] Those Muslims who were influenced by attempts at human reasoning in the form of man-made philosophies and theologies barred themselves from this very important positive knowledge concerning the names and attributes of Allah. Since man cannot have a correct conception of God except through means that He has revealed and since these people ignored those means, the best that they could come up with is a description of what Allah is not. In fact, Muhammad Asad explicitly wrote in his commentary on the Quran, "Far from being able to imagine Him, we can only realize what He is *not*." [Muhammad Asad, *The Message of the Quran* (Gibraltar: Dar al-Andalus, 1980), p. 990.] This incorrect approach affecting one's conception of Allah is a great travesty. Abdul Azeez al-Qaari commented on this approach by saying, "We know that the first obligation is to know and recognize Allah. Are we supposed to know Allah through the path of the scholastic theologians? If that were the case, then we would say, 'He does not have a form nor anyone resembling Him nor body nor shape nor meat nor blood nor personality nor appearance nor mass nor color nor taste nor smell nor feel nor experience of heat or cold or dryness nor wetness nor length nor width nor depth nor togetherness nor separateness nor movement nor stationariness nor can He be divided and He cannot be put into different parts and limbs and He does not face a direction and He does not have a right side or left or front or back or above or below and He is not part of this world and He is not outside of this world.' [Al-Qaari quoted that passage from *Sharh al-Aqaid al-Nasafiya* by Saad al-Taftazani (Damascus: Wazarat al-Thiqafa, 1974), p. 36.] Some even go to another extreme and say, 'He is not an existence nor is He not not an existence.' That way of knowing Allah is called by some ignorant people as being the wiser and more intelligent way of knowing Allah! Or should we instead know Allah through the way of the Quran and the manner of the Prophet (peace be upon him) and we describe Allah in the manner that He described Himself and in the manner that the Prophet (peace be upon him) described Him. And we then say: 'There is nothing similar to Him and He is the Hearer, the Seer. Vision comprehends Him not but He comprehends all vision. He is the Subtle, the Aware.' [In fact, we must] not go beyond the style of the Quran or the style of the Prophet (peace be upon him). But we describe Allah in the manner that He described Himself in His Quran and in the manner that His Messenger described Him without any denial of His attributes or any comparison between the Divine and non-Divine nor do we make any unacceptable interpretation and we do not say that anything is similar to Him or His attributes. We recognize the meanings of those attributes and we

Without a doubt, one of the greatest blessings that Allah has bestowed upon the Islamic nation is a revelation giving a detailed knowledge of Allah's names and attributes. When one reads the Bible, for example, one does not find the true names and attributes presented in such a way and so often that one's attention is directly drawn to them. This great knowledge has been preserved via Allah's revelation to the Prophet Muhammad (peace and blessings of Allah be upon him)—thus being another great blessing for this Muslim Nation.

Unfortunately, upon reading these names at the ends of Quranic verses, for example, many people have a tendency to read over them quickly without giving them much thought, especially within their context in the relevant verses.[1] They should be a cause for understanding—in themselves and in the context of the verses in which they are mentioned. This will drive the human to want to come even closer to his Lord.

Every Muslim should realize the following: Allah is the giver of all sustenance, above His Throne above the heavens administering the affairs of His creation, commanding, forbidding, sending messengers, revealing books, being pleased, being angered, rewarding, punishing, giving, withholding, honoring, debasing. He sees and hears all things from above the heavens and earth. He knows what is made manifest and what is kept hidden.

---

confirm them." [Abdul Azeez al-Qaari, "*Aqeeda* First... If they but Knew," *Al-Basheer* (March-April 1989, Vol. 2, No. 6), p. 18.] Incidentally, the same incorrect approach can be found in the man-made Hindu beliefs and their concept of the ultimate reality Brahman. In the *Upanishad*, one finds: "It is not coarse, not fine, not short, not long, not glowing, not adhesive, without shadow and without darkness, without air and without space, without stickiness, odorless, tasteless, without eye, without ear, without voice, without mouth, without measure, without inside and without outside." Quoted from Ludwig, p. 54.

[1] A very cold, abstract belief in God may be one of the greatest reasons why God can be believed in yet that belief has virtually no effect on the person's life. Such is the case with "deism," which is the belief in a "God who created the world but has since remained indifferent to his creation" [*Webster's Encyclopedic Unabridged Dictionary of the English Language* (New York: Portland House, 1989), p. 381]. In fact, this approach to belief in God seems to be very prevalent today. There is no question that the hearts may not be attracted to a being that cannot hear his plea or see his plight. Similarly, a God that is not loved nor loves in return will not have a strong response in the heart. Again, if God cannot be approached nor does God come close to His servant, the heart will not be naturally inclined to God. If there is no belief in God's mercy, compassion, wisdom and purpose to His creation, it would be natural for the heart to turn away from Him.

He does whatever He wills. He is attributed with every attribute of perfection and free of even the tiniest amount of imperfection or shortcoming. Not even an atom moves save by His will and permission. A leaf does not fall from a tree except that He is fully aware of it. None can ever intercede with Him or have any right with Him except by His own permission and will.[1]

When a person keeps these facts in mind and ponders over them, the results should be very positive. These attributes of Allah should drive the person to want to know Allah even more. In fact, it is actually the recognition of these facts that makes the person realize in a very complete sense that he must worship Allah alone and that there is no meaning or sense in worshipping anyone other than Allah. Allah says in the Quran,

رَّبُّ ٱلسَّمَٰوَٰتِ وَٱلْأَرْضِ وَمَا بَيْنَهُمَا فَٱعْبُدْهُ وَٱصْطَبِرْ لِعِبَٰدَتِهِۦ ۚ هَلْ تَعْلَمُ لَهُۥ سَمِيًّا

"Lord of the heavens and the earth and all that is between them, so worship Him and abide patiently in His worship. Do you know of any who is similar to Him?" (*Maryam* 65). In this verse, Allah shows that there is none similar to Allah at all. The clear inference is that He alone is the one with His attributes, among them being the Lord of the heavens and the earth, and, hence, how can anyone reasonably argue for worshipping anyone other than Him? Similarly, how could anyone turn away from worshipping Him even if His worship requires patience and perseverance?

As shall be discussed shortly, the Prophet (peace and blessings of Allah be upon him) was the most purified of souls and the best example to follow. On one occasion, he alluded to his way of life as being the best way of life. In this hadith, he indicated why his way of life is definitely the best and why none can do better than he did when it comes to worshipping Allah and getting close to Him. When the Prophet (peace and blessings of Allah be upon him) performed an act which was a type of *rukhsah* or less strict practice, some people avoided what he himself did.

---

[1] Cf., quote from ibn al-Qayyim, *al-Fawaaid* in Fauz bint Abdul Lateef al-Kurdi, *Tahqeeq al-Uboodiyyah bi-Marifah al-Asmaa wa al-Sifaat* (Riyadh: Daar Taibah, 1421 A.H.), p. 168.

Upon hearing of that, the Prophet (peace and blessings of Allah be upon him) said,

مَا بَالُ أَقْوَامٍ يَتَنَزَّهُونَ عَنِ الشَّيْءِ أَصْنَعُهُ فَوَاللَّهِ إِنِّي لَأَعْلَمُهُمْ بِاللَّهِ وَأَشَدُّهُمْ لَهُ خَشْيَةً

"What is wrong with a people who avoid something that I have done. By Allah, I am more knowledgeable of Allah than them and I have greater fear of Him than them." (Recorded by al-Bukhari.)

The knowledge and understanding of the names and attributes should then play a profound role in the development and purification of the soul. Every one of Allah's names should lead a person to greater love of Allah as well as greater fear of Him, accompanied by attempting to get closer to Him with those great attributes by performing righteous deeds.[1]

Ibn Taimiyyah noted, "Whoever knows the names of Allah and their meanings, believing in them, will have a more complete faith than the one who does not know them but just believes in them in general."[2] Ibn Saadi also noted, "Whenever a person's knowledge of Allah's beautiful names and attributes increases, his faith also increases and his certainty is further strengthened."[3] If one has a good knowledge of Allah's names and attributes, one will then have an opening to understanding what takes place in this creation. This fact was beautifully expressed by ibn al-Qayyim when he said, "Whoever knows Allah, knows everything other than Him. Whoever is ignorant of his Lord is even more ignorant of everything other than Him."[4]

Indeed, the effect of this knowledge should be so great that a true understanding of those names and living according to

---

[1] A detailed discussion of these aspects is beyond the scope of this work. The interested reader may consult al-Kurdi, pp. 247-400. Ibn al-Qayyim noted that every one of Allah's names obligates a specific form of worship from the human in response to that name and attribute of Allah. See Muhammad ibn al-Qayyim, *Miftaah Daar al-Saadah* (Beirut: Daar al-Fikr, n.d.), vol. 2, p. 90.

[2] Ahmad ibn Taimiyyah, *Majmoo Fatawaa Shaikh al-Islaam ibn Taimiya* (Collected by Abdul Rahmaan Qaasim and his son Muhammad, no publication information given), vol. 7, p. 234. Also see al-Kurdi p. 163.

[3] Quoted in al-Kurdi, p. 164.

[4] Ibn al-Qayyim, *Mudaaraj*, vol. 3, p. 351.

their implications should lead one directly to Allah's pleasure and paradise. In fact, the Messenger of Allah (peace and blessings of Allah be upon him) clearly told this Muslim nation,

إِنَّ لِلَّهِ تِسْعَةً وَتِسْعِينَ اسْمًا مِائَةً إِلاَّ وَاحِدًا مَنْ أَحْصَاهَا دَخَلَ الْجَنَّةَ

"Allah has ninety-nine names, one hundred less one. Whoever memorized them all by heart will enter Paradise."[1] (Recorded by al-Bukhari and Muslim.)

The Development and Growth of One's Faith and Its Ramification for the Purification of the Soul

When one first makes the *shahaadah,* he has started on the road to self-purification. The first step is to cleanse oneself of the clear, major, encompassing form of *shirk,* wherein one recognizes an actual partner with Allah. This is the first and absolutely necessary step, such that no other act or step will be of benefit or use without it. However, this does not mean that it is a once and for all step or a constant with no room for growth and improvement.

Murad perceptively noted,

> You now have a mission: to become a *mumin* [true believer] and *mujahid* [one who strives for the sake of Allah]. As you embark upon this mission you may come to feel that your knowledge of Islam is somewhat limited or perhaps that you are unable to attain those heights of submission and purification that you desire or others expect of you. This is only natural. You must not, however, allow these feelings of personal shortcomings to undermine your efforts to practise

[1] The above is Muhammad Muhsin Khan's translation of the hadith. He also added the following footnote, "Memorizing Allah's Names means to believe in those Qualities of Allah derived from those Names and should be accompanied by good deeds which Allah's Names inspire us to do. Just knowing Allah's Names by heart will not make a vicious man enter Paradise. Therefore, the word 'memorized' in the Hadith means to behave in accordance with the implications of Allah's Names." Muhammad Muhsin Khan, *The Translation of the Meanings of Sahih al-Bukhari* (Riyadh: Darussalam Publishers and Distributors, 1997), vol. 9, p. 296.

> Islam. Remember that Islam is a state of becoming not a state of being. Each day you must strive to improve and better yourself—and you will improve [Allah willing]...
> Once you have committed yourself to Allah, all that you have must be spent in His way. This is the ideal. Ideals, however, are always difficult to achieve—and this you must understand and accept. Ideals are always to be pursued; if they are easily and always achievable, they can hardly remain as ideals. Keeping to your side of the bargain [mentioned in *al-Taubah* 111[1]] then is an ideal that you must always seek to maintain. It is this seeking and this striving to spend all that we have in the way of Allah that is known as *jihad* and alternatively, in this instance, as *tazkiya*.[2]

When a person first embraces Islam—or when a born Muslim first makes a commitment to Islam—his heart may be free of the great *shirk* and disbelief, but that does not mean that he understands all of the concepts of *tauheed* or that in his heart there is not some minor remnants of shirk and disbelief. Allah says about the Bedouins,

---

[1] The verse reads: "Allah has purchased from the believers their souls and their wealth. For theirs (in return) is the Garden (of Paradise). They fight for His Cause, and slay and are slain. [This reward is] a promise binding on Him in truth, through the Torah, the Gospel, and the Quran. And who is more faithful to his covenant than Allah? Then rejoice in the bargain which you have concluded. That is the achievement supreme."

[2] Murad, pp. 6-7. Elsewhere (p. 13), he wrote, "Likewise, hope is central to your efforts and your success. You must sincerely hope and believe that everything you do to earn the pleasure of Allah will lead you to fulfillment. A superiority complex negates the task of self development. An inferiority complex is derived from a lack of confidence in Allah and oneself. You should never allow yourself to believe that you cannot fulfil your obligations nor should you despair of the mercy of Allah. Confidence, hope and determination are all important ingredients for your success."

قَالَتِ ٱلْأَعْرَابُ ءَامَنَّا قُل لَّمْ تُؤْمِنُوا۟ وَلَٰكِن قُولُوٓا۟ أَسْلَمْنَا وَلَمَّا يَدْخُلِ ٱلْإِيمَٰنُ فِى قُلُوبِكُمْ وَإِن تُطِيعُوا۟ ٱللَّهَ وَرَسُولَهُۥ لَا يَلِتْكُم مِّنْ أَعْمَٰلِكُمْ شَيْـًٔا إِنَّ ٱللَّهَ غَفُورٌ رَّحِيمٌ

"The Bedouins say, 'We have believed.' Say [to them], 'You have not yet [truly believed] but instead you should say, "We have submitted" for faith has yet to [completely] penetrate your hearts. But if you obey Allah and His Messenger, He will not deprive you [of the rewards for] your deeds. Verily, Allah is Forgiving, Merciful" (*al-Hujuraat* 14). Indeed, some shortcomings with respect to the complete concept of *tauheed* even occurred among new Muslims at the time of the Prophet (peace and blessings of Allah be upon him), although they were fluent in Arabic, thus having an understanding of the basic meanings of the Quran, and they also lived during the time of the revelation itself. Note the following report:

عَنْ أَبِي وَاقِدٍ اللَّيْثِيِّ أَنَّ رَسُولَ اللَّهِ صَلَّى اللَّهم عَلَيْهِ وَسَلَّمَ لَمَّا خَرَجَ إِلَى حُنَيْنٍ مَرَّ بِشَجَرَةٍ لِلْمُشْرِكِينَ يُقَالُ لَهَا ذَاتُ أَنْوَاطٍ يُعَلِّقُونَ عَلَيْهَا أَسْلِحَتَهُمْ فَقَالُوا يَا رَسُولَ اللَّهِ اجْعَلْ لَنَا ذَاتَ أَنْوَاطٍ كَمَا لَهُمْ ذَاتُ أَنْوَاطٍ فَقَالَ النَّبِيُّ صَلَّى اللَّهم عَلَيْهِ وَسَلَّمَ سُبْحَانَ اللَّهِ هَذَا كَمَا قَالَ قَوْمُ مُوسَى اجْعَلْ لَنَا إِلَهًا كَمَا لَهُمْ آلِهَةٌ وَالَّذِي نَفْسِي بِيَدِهِ لَتَرْكَبُنَّ سُنَّةَ مَنْ كَانَ قَبْلَكُمْ

Abu Waaqid al-Laithi narrated that when the Messenger of Allah (peace and blessings of Allah be upon him) was going out to the Hunain [before its battle] they passed by a tree of the polytheists known as *dhaat anwaat* on which they would hang their weapons. They [some Companions] said, "O Messenger of Allah (peace and blessings of Allah be upon him), make for us a *dhaat anwaat* like they have a *dhaat anwaat*." The Prophet (peace and blessings of Allah be upon him) said, "Exalted by Allah. This is like when the people of Moses said, 'Make for us an idol like they have an idol.'

By the One in whose Hand is my soul, you shall certainly follow the practices of the people who came before you."[1]

However, as one grows in faith, new horizons become clear to him—they may actually be related to things that he already admitted to knowing but he had never really experienced or tasted them in the past. These new understandings related to his faith purify him even further and allow him to grow spiritually in matters that have been difficult for people to describe.

The quote below from ibn al-Qayyim highlights some aspects of faith that may not necessarily be in the person's heart when he first becomes Muslim or when he is practicing Islam. However, as he grows in the faith, these aspects become stronger and stronger and they begin to develop in him more and more of their desired effects. For example, a new Muslim may see the rain come down from the sky and then recall the forecast on the news the previous night, simply thinking that all of the factors were there for the rain to come and hence it rained. On the other hand, the believer whose knowledge and realization of Allah is at a different level, realizes that Allah has brought about that rain not haphazardly. Perhaps, it was an act of mercy from Allah or the first moments of some punishment from Allah.

Ibn al-Qayyim wrote,

> When the servant knows that Allah alone is in charge of harming and benefiting, giving and withholding, creating and providing, giving life and bringing about death, it produces the acts of worship of completely putting one's trust and reliance in Him in one's heart, and what such reliance necessitates of trust and outward deeds. The servant's knowledge about Allah's hearing, seeing and knowledge—not even the smallest of physical particles in the heavens and earth is unseen to Him—and that He knows the secret and hidden and the deception of the eyes as well as what is hidden in the breasts produces in the person a keen guarding over his tongue, physical limbs and thoughts in the

[1] Recorded by Ahmad and al-Tirmidhi. According to al-Albaani, it is *sahih*. See al-Albaani, *Saheeh Sunan al-Tirmidhi*, vol. 2, p. 235.

> heart to keep them away from everything that is displeasing to Allah. Furthermore, it makes him involve those bodily parts in acts that are beloved and pleasing to Allah. This in turn produces an inward shyness. It also produces a shyness that makes the person avoid the forbidden and evil acts. [The servant's] knowledge of Allah's self-sufficiency, generosity, graciousness, kindness and mercy makes the person become very hopeful in Allah. Furthermore, it produces in him similar acts of external and inward forms of worship in accord with his level of understanding and knowledge. Similarly, his recognition of Allah's grandeur, greatness and magnificence produces in him humility, submission and love. It also produces in him internal emotions and feelings of worship as well as the external acts that these require. Similar, his knowledge of Allah's perfection, beauty and exalted attributes manifests itself in a special kind of love found in the different levels of worship.[1]

Finally, every believer must keep in mind the fact that faith increases and decreases. Hence, the believer should always be on the lookout for any sign that his faith is decreasing. Indeed, he should take positive steps to increase his faith. One can find an example in the Companions of the Prophet (peace and blessings of Allah be upon him). One Companion took another by the hand and said, "Come let us [increase our] faith for a period of time." (Recorded by al-Bukhari.) Thus was in reference to reading the Quran, remembering Allah and so forth, actions which will help one revive and increase one's faith.

---

[1] Ibn al-Qayyim, *Miftaah Daar al-Saadah*, vol. 2, p. 90.

The Ramification of the Proper Belief in Allah on the Soul and Its Purification

As demonstrated above, the effects and ramifications of the proper belief in Allah on the soul and its purification are numerous and far-reaching. However, this author would like to especially highlight one aspect in particular: Allah's help and support. When a person is sincerely turning to Allah by trying to worship Him in the proper manner—that is, do exactly what his soul is naturally inclined to and what truly purifies the soul—Allah supports him and helps him in those acts. The Prophet (peace and blessings of Allah be upon him) said, in a hadith quoted earlier,

يَقُولُ اللَّهُ تَعَالَى أَنَا عِنْدَ ظَنِّ عَبْدِي بِي وَأَنَا مَعَهُ إِذَا ذَكَرَنِي فَإِنْ ذَكَرَنِي فِي نَفْسِهِ ذَكَرْتُهُ فِي نَفْسِي وَإِنْ ذَكَرَنِي فِي مَلَإٍ ذَكَرْتُهُ فِي مَلَإٍ خَيْرٍ مِنْهُمْ وَإِنْ تَقَرَّبَ إِلَيَّ بِشِبْرٍ تَقَرَّبْتُ إِلَيْهِ ذِرَاعًا وَإِنْ تَقَرَّبَ إِلَيَّ ذِرَاعًا تَقَرَّبْتُ إِلَيْهِ بَاعًا وَإِنْ أَتَانِي يَمْشِي أَتَيْتُهُ هَرْوَلَةً

"Allah has said, 'I am as My servant expects of Me. I am with him when he mentions [or remembers] Me. If he remembers Me to himself, I mention him to Myself. If he mentions Me to a gathering, I mention him to a gathering that is better than his. And if he draws near to Me a hand's span, I draw near to him a forearm's length. And if he draws near to Me a forearm's length, I draw near to him an arm's length. And if he comes to Me walking, I go to him at speed." (Recorded by al-Bukhari and Muslim.)

Furthermore, the individual knows that none of his deeds will ever go to waste. Allah knows about any efforts he makes and Allah will not wrong him in any way. Allah says,

إِنَّ ٱلَّذِينَ ءَامَنُواْ وَعَمِلُواْ ٱلصَّـٰلِحَـٰتِ إِنَّا لَا نُضِيعُ أَجْرَ مَنْ أَحْسَنَ عَمَلًا

"As to those who believe and work righteousness, verily We shall not suffer to perish the reward of any who do a (single) righteous deed" (*al-Kahf* 30). The believer simply has to move forward, doing the righteous acts, and he knows that those acts will not be in vain. Furthermore, he knows that Allah is with him whenever he acts righteously and justly. Ultimately, regardless of how bleak things may look at any given time in this world, it is only those who align themselves with Allah and take him as their God who will be successful. Allah says,

وَمَن يَتَوَلَّ ٱللَّهَ وَرَسُولَهُۥ وَٱلَّذِينَ ءَامَنُوا۟ فَإِنَّ حِزْبَ ٱللَّهِ هُمُ ٱلْغَٰلِبُونَ

"As to those who turn (for friendship) to Allah, His Messenger, and the (fellowship of) believers, it is the party of Allah that must certainly triumph" (*al-Maaidah* 56). Allah also says,

إِنَّا لَنَنصُرُ رُسُلَنَا وَٱلَّذِينَ ءَامَنُوا۟ فِى ٱلْحَيَوٰةِ ٱلدُّنْيَا وَيَوْمَ يَقُومُ ٱلْأَشْهَٰدُ ﴿٥١﴾ يَوْمَ لَا يَنفَعُ ٱلظَّٰلِمِينَ مَعْذِرَتُهُمْ ۖ وَلَهُمُ ٱللَّعْنَةُ وَلَهُمْ سُوٓءُ ٱلدَّارِ

"Verily, We do help our messengers and the believers in the life of this world and We shall help them on the Day when the witnesses shall stand. The Day when no profit will it be to wrongdoers to present their excuses, but they will (only) have the curse and the home of misery" (*Ghaafir* 51-52).

Hence, in the end it is those who align themselves with Allah who will be the successful ones. Thus, the true believer is able to face anything and everything in this life. He knows that this world is not some form of automatically, law-driven, evolutionary existence that does not have an all-powerful, all-wise, compassionate force behind it. At no time does his soul have to despair or enter into a state of depression. Allah is ever watching and ever aware. Indeed, he can concentrate on purifying his soul and he can be certain that everything else he needs will be there for him.

The Attitude Toward the Messenger of Allah (peace and blessings of Allah be upon him)[1]

Directly related to the belief in *tauheed* and directly related to the question of purification of the soul is one's attitude toward the Messenger of Allah (peace and blessings of Allah be upon him). One does not become a Muslim and one does not begin on the path of purification until he makes the testimony of faith. This testimony is composed of two very different but essential components: "I bear witness that there is none worthy of worship except Allah and I bear witness that Muhammad is the Messenger of Allah." By making this testimony, the person is affirming his intent to worship none other than Allah as well as to worship Allah in the manner set forth by the Prophet Muhammad (peace and blessings of Allah be upon him). With respect to both matters, the individual dedicates himself to Allah via the teachings that have come through the Messenger of Allah (peace and blessings of Allah be upon him).

Unfortunately, among Muslims today there are some incorrect attitudes toward the Messenger of Allah (peace and blessings of Allah be upon him).[2] These attitudes may be summarized as:

(1) There are some people who look upon the Prophet (peace and blessings of Allah be upon him) as his only role was to receive the revelation from Allah and pass it on to others. Once he conveyed that revelation, his role was finished and there was nothing more to his person or being. These people, obviously, downplay the role of the Prophet's Sunnah and teachings. Indeed, they may ignore it completely. The mistake that these people make is that they fail to realize that the Prophet (peace and blessings of

---

[1] For the sake of emphasis, this section has been entitled, "The attitude toward the Messenger of Allah (peace and blessings of Allah be upon him)," rather than simply, "Belief in the Messenger of Allah (peace and blessings of Allah be upon him)." This is because among those who state their belief in the Prophet, especially in the past couple of centuries, there is a grave misunderstanding concerning their attitude towards him. For example, as discussed in the text above, some do not take him as the example *par excellence* for all aspects of life while others do not consider his teachings valid for all times and so forth.

[2] Cf., Islahi, pp. 81-88. Islahi's approach and discussion is different from that found here but there is a great deal of commonality between the two discussions.

Allah be upon him) did not simply convey the wording of the text of the Quran. Instead, it was also his job to teach that text and to explain it to others. Furthermore, it was also his job to implement that revelation in the best of all possible ways, to be an example for all who come afterwards. Hence, he himself was a light or source of guidance and someone who purified others. All of that he did under the inspiration and guidance of Allah. Finally, it was necessary for the Prophet (peace and blessings of Allah be upon him) to accompany the revelation in order to give the revelation its concrete, practical and correct form. As one author aptly put it, "The Message remains uninterpreted, mystical and non-practical without the Messenger, and the Messenger, without the Message, may be deified by those to whom he is sent."[1]

(2) There are among Muslims today many who have some respect for the Prophet (peace and blessings of Allah be upon him) as a "great man" and they do believe in the Quran as a revelation from Allah. However, at the same time, they do not consider the Prophet's Sunnah to be anything more than the thoughts of a very perceptive man who lived at a certain time and place. In other words, they do not accept the fact that the Prophet's Sunnah was also a form of inspiration and guidance that is also true for all times until the Day of Judgment. Hence, these people will easily and with few qualms reject any statement of the Prophet (peace and blessings of Allah be upon him) if they feel that times have changed, scientific knowledge has increased or human civilization has advanced such that the Prophet's words are no longer valid. Obviously, these people have established their own intellect or likings as a barrier between them and the complete guidance that the Prophet (peace and blessings of Allah be upon him) brought as the key to the purification of the soul.

(3) There is another group among the Muslims of today who also completely misunderstand the proper attitude and relationship with the Prophet (peace and blessings of Allah be upon him). In reality, these people do not follow the Prophet's teachings and take him as the ultimate example. At the same time, though, they claim to have the greatest amount of love and

[1] Qazi Ashfaq Ahmad, *Words that Moved the World: How to Study the Quran* (Leicester, United Kingdom: The Islamic Foundation, 1999), p. 8.

affection for the Prophet (peace and blessings of Allah be upon him). These people demonstrate their love of the Prophet (peace and blessings of Allah be upon him) only by praying to the Prophet (peace and blessings of Allah be upon him) or by celebrating his birthday (*maulid*). Both of these acts are completely inconsistent with the Prophet's teachings. In reality, these people ignore the Prophet's teachings in general. Furthermore, they will not benefit at all from the love that they claim to have for the Prophet (peace and blessings of Allah be upon him). The true love of the Prophet (peace and blessings of Allah be upon him) requires one to believe in everything that he has said, follows what he has commanded and take him as the example *par excellence*.

(4) Many of the Sufis also have a very distorted impression of the Prophet (peace and blessings of Allah be upon him) and the teachings that have been passed down from him. These people make a distinction between what they term the Shareeah and the *tareeqah*, the former being the plain teachings that lack the mysteries and hidden truths while the latter contains the real truths and keys to the mysteries of this creation. They claim that the *tareeqah* was only passed on secretly by the Prophet (peace and blessings of Allah be upon him) while the Shareeah he gave to everyone. They claim that they are the only ones who have those secret teachings which are passed on through their "saints." These Sufis many times ridicule those who follow the Shareeah—the path that the Prophet Muhammad (peace and blessings of Allah be upon him) was clearly and undeniably upon—as people who follow "empty shells" and who are "worshippers of the apparent." Although many of these Sufis claim that the Prophet (peace and blessings of Allah be upon him) passed on both forms of knowledge, in essence, this view is a means of turning away from the Sunnah of the Prophet (peace and blessings of Allah be upon him) by the claim that the Sunnah is, in essence, something the Prophet (peace and blessings of Allah be upon him) did to benefit the masses and it was not meant to convey the true hidden mysteries. Therefore, these people are forced to rely more on the

teachings of their "saints,"[1] even if those teachings clearly contradict what has been definitively passed on from the Prophet (peace and blessings of Allah be upon him). [Their argument would have been valid if they somehow could prove that their secret teachings also originated with the Prophet (peace and blessings of Allah be upon him). However, this is something that they cannot prove in any way whatsoever.] Hence, these people are almost completely lost to the true means of purification taught by the Prophet (peace and blessings of Allah be upon him).

All of these incorrect attitudes toward the Prophet (peace and blessings of Allah be upon him) greatly harm one's journey to purify the soul. The Prophet (peace and blessings of Allah be upon him) was sent to a society in ignorance—which had no concept of how to purify the soul except by the guesses of humans (no matter how elaborately they may be presented they were still guesswork), much like what most people follow in today's society. Allah says,

كَمَآ أَرْسَلْنَا فِيكُمْ رَسُولًا مِّنكُمْ يَتْلُوا۟ عَلَيْكُمْ ءَايَـٰتِنَا وَيُزَكِّيكُمْ وَيُعَلِّمُكُمُ ٱلْكِتَـٰبَ وَٱلْحِكْمَةَ وَيُعَلِّمُكُم مَّا لَمْ تَكُونُوا۟ تَعْلَمُونَ

"A similar (favor have you already received) in that We have sent among you a Messenger of your own, reciting to you Our Signs, and purifying you, and instructing you in the Book and Wisdom, and he teaches you that which you knew not" (*al-Baqarah* 151).

In another set of verses, Allah gives the Prophet (peace and blessings of Allah be upon him) a teaching that demonstrates that his main purpose was certainly the purification and reformation of mankind.[2] The Prophet (peace and blessings of

[1] In fact, as Islahi (p. 85) points out, many of them claim that "the position enjoyed by Shaikh Mohiyuddin ibn-Arabi is higher (I seek refuge in God from such blasphemy) than that of any prophet."

[2] Al-Ashqar notes that since the purification of the soul was one of the most important roles of the Prophet (peace and blessings of Allah be upon him), it should be of extreme importance to every individual Muslim. However, in particular, it must of great importance to the teachers,

Allah be upon him) himself had to be careful never to lose sight of that goal of his mission. Allah reminds the Prophet (peace and blessings of Allah be upon him) in the following verses which were revealed after the Prophet (peace and blessings of Allah be upon him) turned away from a blind man while he was busy in conversation with some other men,

عَبَسَ وَتَوَلَّىٰٓ ﴿١﴾ أَن جَآءَهُ ٱلْأَعْمَىٰ ﴿٢﴾ وَمَا يُدْرِيكَ لَعَلَّهُۥ يَزَّكَّىٰٓ ﴿٣﴾ أَوْ يَذَّكَّرُ فَتَنفَعَهُ ٱلذِّكْرَىٰٓ

"(The Prophet) frowned and turned away because there came to him the blind man (interrupting). But what could tell you that perchance he might grow (in spiritual understanding) or that he might receive admonition, and the teaching might profit him?" (*Abasa* 1-4).

Hence, everyone has to understand who the Prophet (peace and blessings of Allah be upon him) was and what is his role in purifying one's soul. His role is simple: His is the human example that every Muslim must aspire to as his way was based on guidance from Allah. His life and behavior is the one showing all Muslims the proper way to purify their souls. This is true whether one is speaking about how to pray, fast, fight, order good, become patient, earn Allah's love, become a devout worshipper, deal with friends, associates, family, orphans and so forth. This point cannot be overemphasized because in some of the works on *tazkiyah* one can actually find no mention of this basic and fundamental step of purification of the soul or, if this principle is actually mentioned, it is rarely put into practice in the teachings of the work by directly quoting the statements or example of the Prophet (peace and blessings of Allah be upon him).[1]

---

those calling to Islam and those working to raise the Muslims from their plight as they are supposed to fulfill this role in the absence of the Messenger of Allah (peace and blessings of Allah be upon him). Al-Ashqar, *Minhaaj*, p. 9.

[1] This author randomly chose two of the many works of "non-extreme" Sufism available in English to demonstrate this point. In Kashaani's *Misbah al-Hidaayah* (being an abridgement of *The Awarif ul Maarif* by Shahab-ud-Din Suhrawardi), the author states (p. 22), "After the rank of being a prophet, no rank is higher than being a deputy for a prophet to call me, by the path of Muhammad, to God." This is an excellent starting point. However, on pages 22-198 (simply

Commenting on the phenomenon of failing to recognize or turn to the Prophet (peace and blessings of Allah be upon him) as the teacher of purification of the soul, ibn al-Qayyim wrote,

> The concept of purification of the souls must be submitted to the way of the messengers. Allah has sent them alone for the purpose of this purification and has put them in charge of it. He has placed in their hands the call, teachings and clarification. They have been sent to cure the souls of the nations. Allah says, "It is He Who has sent among the Unlettered a messenger from among themselves, to rehearse to them His Signs,

---

taken as an example wherein many important topics are discussed), the Prophet (peace and blessings of Allah be upon him) is alluded to or quoted on only twenty-two pages (pp. 22, 28, 30, 32, 34, 35, 42, 45, 46, 47, 48, 49, 63, 64, 70, 71, 77, 90, 91, 95, 104 and 113) and most of those were simply in passing without any true substance to the passage. Perhaps even more amazing is that in those 177 pages, not one verse of the Quran was quoted. In those same 177 pages, numerous other Sufi shaikhs, such as al-Junaid and others, were quoted verbatim (often times supporting actions or beliefs that have no strong support in the Sunnah). The author did not seem to find any need to quote the Prophet's statements verbatim. [Cf., Shahab-ud-Din Suhrawardi, *The Awarif-ul-Maarif* (Lahore, Pakistan: Sh. Muhammad Ashraf, 1991, pp. 22-198.] A second work comes from the Shadhili Sufi order, which has a number of followers in the West, entitled *The Mystical Teachings of al-Shadhili*. A chapter entitled, "His [that is, al-Shadhili's] Opinions, Injunctions, Doctrine on Sufism and Other Sciences," deals with the essential teachings of the order and covers pages 107-202. These pages at least contain a number of Quranic quotations. The Prophet (peace and blessings of Allah be upon him) is referred to, directly or indirectly, on thirty-five pages (pp. 110, 114, 123, 125, 126, 127, 128, 130, 131, 135, 136, 142, 143, 146, 147f, 148, 149, 150, 153f, 154, 155, 156, 157, 158, 159, 160, 167, 172, 174, 178, 187, 191, 193, 200, 201). On many of these pages, the Prophet (peace and blessings of Allah be upon him) is mentioned only as part of a supplication, such as asking Allah to bless the Prophet (peace and blessings of Allah be upon him). However, in these thirty-five pages, only seven hadith (pp. 125, 127, 136, 167, 178, 187) are actually quoted, and even some of them are of doubtful authenticity. On the other hand, on seven pages (pp. 131, 135, 147f, 150, 153f, 158, 160), the Prophet (peace and blessings of Allah be upon him) is reported to have been supposedly seen and quoted by some "saint" via a dream, vision or what is akin to a séance (which they refer to as a *sama* session). Cf., Elmer H. Douglas (translator) and Ibrahim M. Abu-Rabi (editor), *The Mystical Teachings of al-Shadhili Including His Life, Prayers, Letters and Followers: A Translation from the Arabic of ibn al-Sabbagh's* Durrat al-Asrar wa Tuhfat al-Abrar (Albany, NY: State University of New York Press, 1993), pp. 107-202. For a discussion of dreams, visions, mystical trances and spiritual trips and why they cannot be used as a source of guidance, beliefs, law or ethics, see Uthmaan ibn Ali ibn Hasan, *Manhaj al-Istidlaal ala Masaail al-Itiqaad ind Ahl al-Sunnah wa al-Jamaah* (Riyadh: Maktabah al-Rushd, 1992), vol. 2, pp. 635-688.

> to purify them, and to instruct them in the Book and Wisdom, although they had been before in manifest error" (*al-Jumuah* 2). Purification of the soul is more difficult and harder than curing one's physical body. Whoever [tries to] purify his soul via spiritual exercises, striving and seclusion which the messengers never taught is like a sick person who tries to cure himself based on his own personal opinion. What is the place of his opinion with respect to the knowledge of the physician? The messengers are the physicians of the hearts. There is no way to purify the hearts or make them sound except via their paths and at their hands, with a complete submission and obedience to them.[1]

Furthermore, Allah makes it clear that the Prophet (peace and blessings of Allah be upon him) was sent to these people to be an example *par excellence* for anyone who wants to come closer to Allah and be successful in the Hereafter. Allah says,

لَّقَدْ كَانَ لَكُمْ فِي رَسُولِ ٱللَّهِ أُسْوَةٌ حَسَنَةٌ لِّمَن كَانَ يَرْجُوا۟ ٱللَّهَ وَٱلْيَوْمَ ٱلْءَاخِرَ وَذَكَرَ ٱللَّهَ كَثِيرًا

"You have indeed in the Messenger of Allah a beautiful pattern (of conduct) for any one whose hope is in Allah and the Final Day, and who engages much in the remembrance of Allah" (*al-Ahzaab* 21). Hence, the true believer would do his best to emulate the Prophet (peace and blessings of Allah be upon him) in all matters of his life as sanctioned by the Shareeah.[2]

This desire to emulate is called "pursuance" by Islahi and he explains it thusly,

> The scope of pursuance is much wider than that of obedience. Under obedience fall only those things which are in the nature of Commandments, highly

---

[1] Ibn al-Qayyim, *Madaarij*, vol. 2, p. 315.

[2] There are some matters that are specific to the Prophet (peace and blessings of Allah be upon him) only and there are some acts of the Prophet (peace and blessings of Allah be upon him) that were due to custom, for example, and not necessarily meant as exemplary for all peoples.

> stressed duties and the do's and don'ts, but in the ambit of pursuance fall even the commendatory and non-obligatory acts... Man may obey something without the least tinge of sincerity and love in it. But in pursuance the sentiments of reverence and regard for the pursued in one's life is an essential condition... The reason behind the zest of the Companions in the pursuance of the Prophet was the love of God, and to become a beloved of His could not be attained only through obedience to the Prophet, but in fact through following him sincerely in all walks of life. The Prophet is the embodiment of the cognition of God and every air and style of his is the sign of such cognition. That is why those who love God love every iota in the life of the Prophet. In the life of the Prophet they observe the knowledge that is acquired through the cognition of God; they notice actions that result from such cognition and they watch habits that God is pleased with... And since they do it all for the love of God, they are rewarded by Him and become His beloved. It is this fact brought out in the following verse of the Quran: "Say (O Mohammad), 'If you love God, follow me: God will love you'" [*ali-Imraan* 31].[1]

There is another important fact that definitively needs to be emphasized concerning the belief in the Prophet (peace and blessings of Allah be upon him). He is not just an example, but he is *the* example. There is no manner of living and no belief system that is superior to that of the Prophet Muhammad (peace and blessings of Allah be upon him). Furthermore, there is no individual who was closer and more beloved to Allah than the Prophet Muhammad (peace and blessings of Allah be upon him).[2]

---

[1] Islahi, pp. 92-93.

[2] The Messenger of Allah (peace and blessings of Allah be upon him) said, "Allah took me as His most intimate friend (*khaleel*) as He had earlier taken Abraham as His most intimate friend." (Recorded by Muslim.) The Messenger of Allah (peace and blessings of Allah be upon him) also said, "If I were to take an inhabitant of the Earth as my most intimate friend, I would choose Abu Bakr. But Allah, the Most Gracious, has taken your companion [that is, the Prophet] as His most intimate friend." (Recorded by Muslim.)

This point is being emphasized here because, particularly with respect to the steps to purify one's soul, some Muslims have a tendency to turn to examples other than the Prophet Muhammad (peace and blessings of Allah be upon him). They read the lives and teachings of their so-called "saints," shaikhs and "holy men," and are more dedicated to these people and their way of lives than they are to the life of the Prophet (peace and blessings of Allah be upon him). This is a very serious mistake. As noted earlier, one of the primary roles of the Prophet (peace and blessings of Allah be upon him) was to purify mankind. He is the one who demonstrated the proper method of purification. The way of life or the teachings of anyone else must be judged in the light of the Prophet's way of life and teachings. If they are consistent with the Prophet's way of life and teachings, they are accepted and believed in although they always remain secondary to the prime example of the Prophet Muhammad (peace and blessings of Allah be upon him). If they are inconsistent with the Prophet's way of life and teachings, they are to be rejected and ignored no matter how "holy" it is believed the person was.[1]

Everyone on the road to spiritual purification must appreciate the role of the Prophet (peace and blessings of Allah be upon him) and his efforts on behalf of mankind. The Prophet (peace and blessings of Allah be upon him), via the inspiration from Allah, has given a beautiful parable demonstrating his efforts and man's unfortunate heedlessness. The Prophet (peace and blessings of Allah be upon him) said,

مَثَلِي وَمَثَلُكُمْ كَمَثَلِ رَجُلٍ أَوْقَدَ نَارًا فَجَعَلَ الْجَنَادِبُ وَالْفَرَاشُ يَقَعْنَ فِيهَا وَهُوَ
يَذُبُّهُنَّ عَنْهَا وَأَنَا آخِذٌ بِحُجَزِكُمْ عَنِ النَّارِ وَأَنْتُمْ تَفَلَّتُونَ مِنْ يَدِي

"The similitude of me and you is like that of a man who lit a fire. The insects and moths started to fall into it while he is trying to keep them from it. [Similarly,] I am trying to keep you from the

---

[1] In reality, unless one has exhausted everything that Prophet (peace and blessings of Allah be upon him) has given concerning this manner, why would one look to anyone other than the one whom Allah has specifically mentioned as being sent to purify mankind?

Fire but you are plunging into it [by getting] out of my hands." (Recorded by Muslim.)

A person will not be able to completely internalize this and act upon this concept until he has a strong love and appreciation for the Prophet (peace and blessings of Allah be upon him). In fact, this love for Prophet (peace and blessings of Allah be upon him) is a requirement of the faith itself. In other words, one's faith cannot be proper without it and one cannot purify himself without it. The Messenger of Allah (peace and blessings of Allah be upon him) himself said,

لا يُؤْمِنُ أَحَدُكُمْ حَتَّى أَكُونَ أَحَبَّ إِلَيْهِ مِنْ وَالِدِهِ ووَلَدِهِ وَالنَّاسِ أَجْمَعِينَ

"None of you are true believers until I am more beloved to him than his father, his children and all of mankind." (Recorded by al-Bukhari and Muslim.) In fact, the words of Allah are also very strong on this issue. Allah has declared,

قُلْ إِن كَانَ ءَابَآؤُكُمْ وَأَبْنَآؤُكُمْ وَإِخْوَٰنُكُمْ وَأَزْوَٰجُكُمْ وَعَشِيرَتُكُمْ وَأَمْوَٰلٌ ٱقْتَرَفْتُمُوهَا وَتِجَٰرَةٌ تَخْشَوْنَ كَسَادَهَا وَمَسَٰكِنُ تَرْضَوْنَهَآ أَحَبَّ إِلَيْكُم مِّنَ ٱللَّهِ وَرَسُولِهِۦ وَجِهَادٍ فِى سَبِيلِهِۦ فَتَرَبَّصُوا۟ حَتَّىٰ يَأْتِىَ ٱللَّهُ بِأَمْرِهِۦ ۗ وَٱللَّهُ لَا يَهْدِى ٱلْقَوْمَ ٱلْفَٰسِقِينَ

"Say: If your fathers, your sons, your brethren, your wives, your tribe, the wealth you have acquired, merchandise for which you fear that there will be no sale, or dwellings you desire are dearer to you than Allah and His Messenger and striving in His way: then wait till Allah brings His command to pass. Allah guides not wrongdoing folk" (*al-Tauba* 24).

On this point, also, Islahi has made an excellent comment, noting that the love for the Prophet (peace and blessings of Allah be upon him) is a love

> based on intellect and principles which a person comes to foster with a principle or an ideology,[1] and because of which he keeps that principle and that particular ideology predominant everywhere in his life, and sacrifices every other principle, way of life or desire to that cherished principle or way of life, but not vice versa. For the promotion and upliftment of this principle and ideology he can see everything else degraded but cannot tolerate the degradation of his cherished ideology. If his own self is in the way of his ideology he gives it a fight, and if others stand in the way to block it he fights them, so much so that even if the demands of his own wife and children and relatives collide with the demands of this ideology, he stands on the side of his ideology to support it and without any pangs of love and regards, spurns the wishes of his wife and children and the demands of his tribe and nation.[2]

When a love of this nature is truly internalized, it becomes natural for the person to emulate and imitate his object of admiration. One see this phenomenon in all walks of life. This explains why fans, for example, want to know so many details about the actors, athletes or stars that they idolize. Part of the

---

[1] Islahi began this passage by writing (p. 95), "But it should be noted that the love for the Prophet mentioned here is not that sentimental love which every person naturally has for his family and his relations..." However, this is not correct. The love for the Prophet (peace and blessings of Allah be upon him) must encompass both types of love (the sentimental and the intellectual). This is true because when one studies the Prophet's sacrifices, mercy, compassion for the believers and other characteristics, one will definitely develop that natural and sentimental love that one has for his closest relatives. Indeed, even this love for the Prophet (peace and blessings of Allah be upon him) should be greater than for anyone else as what the Prophet (peace and blessings of Allah be upon him) has done for the believers in sacrificing and conveying the message is of more importance than what one's parents have done for him. Actually, Islahi himself (p. 98) writes, supporting this comment on the quote from him above, "The love of the companions for the Prophet was not merely based on principle and intellect but sentiment also. But the sentiments never crossed the limits of the Book of God and the Prophet's Sunnah. On the other hand, they put up with the greatest troubles but could not tolerate a thorn-prick to the Prophet; in protecting and shielding him (in battles) their own bodies became badly wounded with arrows and sword cuts but they did not let him receive the least injury while they lived..."

[2] Islahi, pp. 95-96.

goal is to know about them and part of the goal is to try to emulate them as much as possible. This feeling of devotion and willingness to emulate must be even greater for the person who realizes that via emulation and following of the Prophet (peace and blessings of Allah be upon him) he can conquer the true way to spiritual purification.

In sum, in order to truly purify one's soul, one must make sure that one's attitude toward the Messenger of Allah (peace and blessings of Allah be upon him) is correct. One must have belief in the Messenger of Allah (peace and blessings of Allah be upon him) and that belief must be correct. One must also obey the Prophet (peace and blessings of Allah be upon him), seek to emulate him and love him and his way.[1] When all of these matters are fulfilled, one is on the firmest path leading to the purification of the soul, which in itself was one of the main purposes for the sending of the Prophet Muhammad (peace and blessings of Allah be upon him).

Murad offers one more interesting point concerning the Messenger of Allah (peace and blessings of Allah be upon him) and his role in the purification of one's soul. After discussing the materialism of Western societies, how such societies are even creeping upon the Muslim world and how the West's ultimate emphasis upon what can be materially measured and denial of the unseen is the antithesis of Islam, he noted,

> Once you have chosen to live in a "Western type" society, the only source of light for you is the Messenger of Allah. He was also faced with an almost similar situation. As he came down from the cave of Hira, after his experience of receiving the light of Divine guidance, he re-entered a culture and society which were quite "alien" to his Message. His Message began by linking the whole of life to the name of Allah. That was the starting point. All knowledge, all culture, all civilisation and all human action must be centred on one pivot and that is the name of Allah. This was a

---

[1] Islahi (p. 96) noted, "Obedience without love is hypocrisy and love without obedience and pursuance [that is, emulation] is innovation."

> totally strange Message for the society in which he had to operate. So, we need to look at the Prophet's Sunna in the context of operating in an "alien" society and see how we can practise a genuine Islamic culture...
> Secondly, while living in an "alien" culture, you have to preserve your Islamic identity—not only through rational arguments, but through emotional, cultural and civilisational symbols. It is only the Sunna that can provide these emotional and civilisational symbols through which you will not only preserve your identity but strengthen and advance it.[1]

Belief in the Angels

Another fundamental belief that forms a cornerstone for the purification of the soul is the belief in the angels. When the Messenger of Allah (peace and blessings of Allah be upon him) was asked by the Angel Gabriel, "What is faith?" he replied,

أَنْ تُؤْمِنَ بِاللَّهِ وَمَلَائِكَتِهِ وَكُتُبِهِ وَرُسُلِهِ وَالْيَوْمِ الآخِرِ وَتُؤْمِنَ بِالْقَدَرِ خَيْرِهِ وَشَرِّهِ

"It is to believe in Allah, His angels, His books, His messengers, the Last Day and to believe in the divine decree, [both] the good and the evil thereof." (Recorded by Muslim.)

The believer knows that there are angels with him at all times, recording every one of his deeds. The believer already knows that Allah is aware of everything that he does. But that belief about Allah may be somewhat abstract or theoretical to have any strong effect on the individual. When he further knows that there are noble creatures that are specifically meant to be in his company alone and recording his deeds alone, this has a further reinforcing effect on him. This also reinforces the fact that there is some weight or ramification to every deed, good or bad, that he performs.

However, a believer's belief in the angels goes much beyond that. The believer knows that the angels are noble

---

[1] Murad, pp. 91-93.

creatures who support and aid whatever is true and just. Therefore, whenever the believer decides to perform a good deed, stand up for the truth and sacrifice for what is right, he knows that there are creatures in this world who are going to support him and help him in his cause, like the angels supported and helped the believers in the time of the Prophet (peace and blessings of Allah be upon him). In fact, such is promised from Allah, as the following verses from *soorah ali-Imraan* indicate:

وَلَقَدْ نَصَرَكُمُ ٱللَّهُ بِبَدْرٍ وَأَنتُمْ أَذِلَّةٌ ۖ فَٱتَّقُوا۟ ٱللَّهَ لَعَلَّكُمْ تَشْكُرُونَ ﴿١٢٣﴾ إِذْ تَقُولُ لِلْمُؤْمِنِينَ أَلَن يَكْفِيَكُمْ أَن يُمِدَّكُمْ رَبُّكُم بِثَلَٰثَةِ ءَالَٰفٍ مِّنَ ٱلْمَلَٰٓئِكَةِ مُنزَلِينَ ﴿١٢٤﴾ بَلَىٰٓ ۚ إِن تَصْبِرُوا۟ وَتَتَّقُوا۟ وَيَأْتُوكُم مِّن فَوْرِهِمْ هَٰذَا يُمْدِدْكُمْ رَبُّكُم بِخَمْسَةِ ءَالَٰفٍ مِّنَ ٱلْمَلَٰٓئِكَةِ مُسَوِّمِينَ ﴿١٢٥﴾

"Allah had helped you at Badr, when you were a contemptible little force; then fear Allah. Thus may you show your gratitude. Remember when you said to the believers, 'Is it not enough for you that Allah should help you with three thousand angels (specially) sent down? Indeed, if ye remain firm, and act aright, even if the enemy should rush here on you in hot haste, your Lord would help you with five thousand angels making a terrific onslaught' (*ali-Imraan* 123-125).

Allah also says,

إِذْ يُوحِى رَبُّكَ إِلَى ٱلْمَلَٰٓئِكَةِ أَنِّى مَعَكُمْ فَثَبِّتُوا۟ ٱلَّذِينَ ءَامَنُوا۟ ۚ

"Remember your Lord inspired the angels (with the message), 'I am with you: give firmness to the believers" (*al-Anfaal* 12).

The angels even ask for the believer's forgiveness and pray on behalf of the believer. Allah says in the Quran,

هُوَ ٱلَّذِى يُصَلِّى عَلَيْكُمْ وَمَلَٰٓئِكَتُهُۥ لِيُخْرِجَكُم مِّنَ ٱلظُّلُمَٰتِ إِلَى ٱلنُّورِ ۚ وَكَانَ بِٱلْمُؤْمِنِينَ رَحِيمًا

"He it is Who sends blessings on you, as do His angels, that He may bring you out from the depths of darkness into light: and He is full of mercy to the believers" (*al-Ahzaab* 43). In particular, the believers know that the angels are praying for them and supporting them when they do righteous acts pleasing to Allah. For example, among many hadith of this nature, the Messenger of Allah (peace and blessings of Allah be upon him) said,

إِنَّ اللَّهَ وَمَلَائِكَتَهُ وَأَهْلَ السَّمَوَاتِ وَالْأَرَضِينَ حَتَّى النَّمْلَةَ فِي جُحْرِهَا وَحَتَّى الْحُوتَ لَيُصَلُّونَ عَلَى مُعَلِّمِ النَّاسِ الْخَيْرَ

"Allah, the angels and the inhabitants of the heavens and earths, even the ant in its hole and the fish, pray for the one who teaches people good."[1]

Their prayers for the person can continue for a long time, even after the person has completed his act. In another hadith, the Messenger of Allah (peace and blessings of Allah be upon him) said,

مَا مِنْ رَجُلٍ يَعُودُ مَرِيضًا مُمْسِيًا إِلاَّ خَرَجَ مَعَهُ سَبْعُونَ أَلْفَ مَلَكٍ يَسْتَغْفِرُونَ لَهُ حَتَّى يُصْبِحَ وَكَانَ لَهُ خَرِيفٌ فِي الْجَنَّةِ وَمَنْ أَتَاهُ مُصْبِحًا خَرَجَ مَعَهُ سَبْعُونَ أَلْفَ مَلَكٍ يَسْتَغْفِرُونَ لَهُ حَتَّى يُمْسِيَ وَكَانَ لَهُ خَرِيفٌ فِي الْجَنَّةِ

"No man goes to visit an ill person in the late afternoon save that seventy thousand angels go with him and [continue] to seek forgiveness for him until the morning and he shall have a garden in Paradise. And if one goes to him in the morning, seventy

---

[1] Recorded by al-Tabaraani. According to al-Albaani, it is *sahih*. See al-Albaani, *Saheeh al-Jaami*, vol. 1, p. 376.

thousand angels go with him and seek his forgiveness until the evening and he shall have a garden in Paradise."[1]

In fact, a believer knows that he can potentially reach the point where all the angels love him and spread love for him in this world. The Messenger of Allah (peace and blessings of Allah be upon him) said,

إِذَا أَحَبَّ اللَّهُ الْعَبْدَ نَادَى جِبْرِيلَ إِنَّ اللَّهَ يُحِبُّ فُلَانًا فَأَحْبِبْهُ فَيُحِبُّهُ جِبْرِيلُ فَيُنَادِي جِبْرِيلُ فِي أَهْلِ السَّمَاءِ إِنَّ اللَّهَ يُحِبُّ فُلانًا فَأَحِبُّوهُ فَيُحِبُّهُ أَهْلُ السَّمَاءِ ثُمَّ يُوضَعُ لَهُ الْقَبُولُ فِي الأَرْضِ

"If Allah loves a person, He calls Gabriel saying, 'Allah loves so and so. So, love him.' Gabriel will then love him. He then makes an announcement among the inhabitants of the heaven, 'Allah loves so and so; therefore, love him also.' So all the inhabitants of the heaven then love him and he is then granted acceptance among the people of the earth." (Recorded by al-Bukhari and Muslim.)

Indeed, the believer can be the recipient of a most beautiful prayer expressed by the angels on his behalf. Note the following passage from the Quran expressing the prayers said by those angels very close to Allah,

ٱلَّذِينَ يَحْمِلُونَ ٱلْعَرْشَ وَمَنْ حَوْلَهُۥ يُسَبِّحُونَ بِحَمْدِ رَبِّهِمْ وَيُؤْمِنُونَ بِهِۦ وَيَسْتَغْفِرُونَ لِلَّذِينَ ءَامَنُوا۟ رَبَّنَا وَسِعْتَ كُلَّ شَىْءٍ رَّحْمَةً وَعِلْمًا فَٱغْفِرْ لِلَّذِينَ تَابُوا۟ وَٱتَّبَعُوا۟ سَبِيلَكَ وَقِهِمْ عَذَابَ ٱلْجَحِيمِ ۝٧ رَبَّنَا وَأَدْخِلْهُمْ جَنَّـٰتِ عَدْنٍ ٱلَّتِى وَعَدتَّهُمْ وَمَن صَلَحَ مِنْ ءَابَآئِهِمْ وَأَزْوَٰجِهِمْ وَذُرِّيَّـٰتِهِمْ ۚ إِنَّكَ أَنتَ ٱلْعَزِيزُ ٱلْحَكِيمُ ۝٨ وَقِهِمُ

[1] Recorded by Ahmad, Abu Dawood and al-Tirmidhi. According to al-Albaani, it is *sahih*. Cf., al-Albaani, *Saheeh al-Jaami al-Sagheer*, vol. 2, p. 996.

ٱلسَّيِّـَٔاتِ ۚ وَمَن تَقِ ٱلسَّيِّـَٔاتِ يَوْمَئِذٍ فَقَدْ رَحِمْتَهُۥ ۚ وَذَٰلِكَ هُوَ ٱلْفَوْزُ ٱلْعَظِيمُ

"Those [angels] who sustain the Throne (of Allah) and those around it sing glory and praise to their Lord, believe in Him, and implore forgiveness for those who believe: 'Our Lord! Your reach is over all things, in mercy and knowledge. Forgive, then, those who turn in repentance, and follow Your path; and preserve them from the penalty of the blazing fire! And grant, our Lord, that they enter the gardens of eternity which You have promised to them, and to the righteous among their fathers, their wives, and their posterity! You art (He), the Exalted in Might, Full of Wisdom. And preserve them from (all) ills; and any whom You do preserve from ills that Day, on them will You have bestowed mercy indeed: and that will be truly (for them) the highest achievement'" (*Ghaafir* 7-9). One can only imagine how great the effect on the person if he knows that by faith and good deeds these noble creatures will be making this beautiful prayer for him.

There is no question that these different aspects of belief can be a very strong force in the soul.[1] In essence, when the person sincerely seeks to purify his soul and perform only good deeds, he, in reality, has all of creation—save for the devils and weak-willed ones of mankind and jinn—supporting him and ready and willing to help him fulfill that goal.[2] Even the Creator is ready to help him. This can give the believer a strength that will allow him to overcome, in a spiritual sense, the greatest obstacles of this worldly existence.

---

[1] In the West, there has been something of a fad concerning the belief in the angels. There has been a strong belief in "guardian angels" that have profoundly affected many non-Muslims. If these people knew the reality and the details concerning the angels that are known by Muslims, the effect on their lives could be even greater. Unfortunately for these people who hold some beliefs about angels, their belief in the angels without the proper belief in God may be of no benefit whatsoever.

[2] Indeed, even inanimate objects of nature have a love for the true believers. The Messenger of Allah (peace and blessings of Allah be upon him) once said, "Uhud is a mountain which loves us and we love it." (Recorded by al-Bukhari and Muslim.)

In addition to the above, the proper and firm belief in the angels should assist the believer in his process of purification due to the following:

(1) The believer recognizes that the angels are a very great and magnificent creation. For example, in one hadith, the Prophet (peace and blessings of Allah be upon him) described the angel Gabriel as having six hundred wings. (Recorded by al-Bukhari.) Another hadith in *Sahih Muslim* describes the angel Gabriel as sometimes filling the entire horizon. The greatness and magnificence of this type of creature points to the greatness and magnificence of its Creator. It is this kind of knowledge that develops a person's love, awe and admiration for Allah. This knowledge that leads to these feelings and understanding can greatly help and influence person in his path of purification.[1]

(2) When the believer realizes how Allah has created these great creatures to be at the service of man and to support the believers in their attempts to do good deeds, it makes the person very grateful and humble towards Allah. It is a great blessing that Allah has given so much concern to the plight of this creature, the human, that He has created these great beings to help humans achieve their ultimate success. Anyone who becomes aware of this fact should turn toward Allah with sincere thankfulness and gratitude—the type of gratitude that is exhibited by worshipping Allah alone.

(3) When one learns about the angels—their purity, constant worship of Allah, support of the believers and striving against evil—one develops a strong love for them. This love is a special type of love, it is not simply built upon emotion and feelings. Instead, it is built upon recognizing what is good and beloved to Allah and recognizing the importance of loving what is good. It is of extreme importance that the believer learn to develop this type of love. It is through this type of process that one begins to truly love for the sake of Allah and hate for His sake. This manner of feeling love is, in reality, one of the cornerstones of this religion of Islam.

---

[1] Cf., Ahmad Fareed, *al-Thamaraat al-Zakiyyah fi al-Aqaaid al-Salafiyyah* (Maktabah al-Tauiyyah al-Islaamiyyah, 1409 A.H.), pp. 174.

(4) Although the essential nature of humans and angels differs, when a believer hears about the perpetual and beautiful worship of Allah that the angels perform, this should make him strive to "compete," in a sense, with this noble creature. In other words, when the believer realizes that there is a creature that is beloved to Allah and that is worshipping Allah at all times, he will be very shy to have any other creature outperform him in his worship of Allah, even if their natures differ and one cannot truly compare the different forms of worship. In any case, the believer will not rest easy until he believes he has done what he can to compete with the noble angels and also attain the love of Allah.

(5) As noted above, the believer must realize that the angels are recording each and every one of his deeds. Beyond that, he has to realize that the angels are always in his presence. However, even beyond that, the believer must be aware of how he behaves with respect to these noble and beloved creatures of Allah. The Prophet (peace and blessings of Allah be upon him) stated,

مَنْ أَكَلَ مِنْ هَذِهِ الشَّجَرَةِ الْمُنْتِنَةِ فَلا يَقْرَبَنَّ مَسْجِدَنَا فَإِنَّ الْمَلائِكَةَ تَأَذَّى مِمَّا يَتَأَذَّى مِنْهُ الإِنْسُ

"Whoever eats from this stinky plant [such as garlic and onions] should not come close to our mosques. Verily, the angels are bothered by that which also bothers humans." (Recorded by Muslim.) Thus, bad smells and things of that nature also harm the angels and may keep these blessed creatures and their prayers of mercy away from the believer. In fact, the Prophet (peace and blessings of Allah be upon him) said,

إِنَّ الملائكةَ لا تَدْخُلُ بيتاً فيهِ بولٌ مُنْتَقِعٌ

"The angels do not enter a house in which there is stale, smelly urine [that has not been cleaned or removed]."[1] Hence, even if no other humans are around, the believer is aware that the angels are

---

[1] Recorded by al-Tabaraani in *al-Ausat* and al-Haithami said its chain is *hasan*. Cf., Noor al-Deen al-Haithami, *Kitaab Majma al-Bahrain fi Zawaaid al-Mujamain* (Riyadh: Maktabah al-Rushd, 2000), vol. 1, p. 303.

always present. Thus, he is always shy and careful in their presence, avoiding anything that may cause harm to these beloved and noble creatures.

Belief in the Divine Decree (*al-Qadar*)

Although the belief in the divine decree or "preordainment" has been at times greatly maligned and misunderstood, leading to inactivity and excuses for committing sins[1], the correct concept can and should have a very positive influence on the soul and its purification.

The belief in the Divine Decree is once again related to the fact that this creation is not a "soulless," mechanical, lifeless creation. This belief is something dominant in the lives of Western disbelievers today, partially under the influence of Voltaire who likened God to a person who makes a watch and then has nothing to do with the working of the watch afterwards. On the contrary, the reality is that Allah is living and watching this creation and He alone has complete control over life, death, sustenance, harm and benefits. Everyday, He is creating, giving life, taking life, giving sustenance, guiding people and so on. Allah says,

كُلَّ يَوْمٍ هُوَ فِي شَأْنٍ

"Every day He is [bringing about] a matter" (*al-Rahmaan* 29).

The importance of the belief in Divine Decree can be seen in a number of ways, including the following points:

(1) The believer understands that the outward laws of nature are to be respected and used but he also knows that behind them is the all-Powerful, all-Wise God who still has ultimate power over all things and still invokes laws that are greater than

---

[1] For example, there developed the belief that one should accept everything that occurs as a type of submission to Allah and, therefore, one should not work to remove poverty, disease or ignorance since they have all been decreed by Allah. There also developed the idea that everything is decreed and, therefore, man has no free will and no role to play. This is also incorrect as Allah has given humans a limited free will. However, Allah knows in advance, by virtue of His infinite knowledge, what they are going to decide and going to do. This knowledge is different from causation.

what mankind witnesses in his life. One simple example can demonstrate the great ramifications of this belief on the actions of the individual. From a purely worldly point of view, when a person gives in charity or is generous, he loses part of his wealth, so he can see the immediate effects on his bank balance, for example. However, the believer knows that that is not completely how this creation works. He knows that from a strictly materialistic, secular point of view, it looks like his wealth may have decreased but he also knows that there is God working in this creation that will not let that charity go for naught. In fact, he knows that any charity that he gives for the sake of Allah will have a positive result in the end.[1] Hence, the Prophet (peace and blessings of Allah be upon him) said,

مَا نَقَصَتْ صَدَقَةٌ مِنْ مَالٍ وَمَا زَادَ اللَّهُ عَبْدًا بِعَفْوٍ إِلاَّ عِزًّا وَمَا تَوَاضَعَ أَحَدٌ لِلَّهِ إِلاَّ رَفَعَهُ اللَّهُ

"Charity does not decrease wealth in any way. Allah adds to the respect of the servant who is forgiving. And Allah elevates in the estimation of the people the one who is humble."[2] (Recorded by Muslim.) Allah also says,

وَمَآ أَنفَقْتُم مِّن شَىْءٍ فَهُوَ يُخْلِفُهُۥ وَهُوَ خَيْرُ ٱلرَّٰزِقِينَ

"Nothing do you spend in the least (in His Cause) but He replaces it, for He is the best of those who grant sustenance" (*Saba* 39).[3]

---

[1] Sometimes people fail to give charity because their belief in this fact is wavering and their soul and Satan make them doubt, believing that once they give up a portion of their wealth they will never see it or its replacement again.

[2] There may be many factors at work that a person cannot perceive related to the giving of zakat and charity for the sake of Allah. The person may not necessarily see any actual increase in the amount of wealth that he possesses but Allah may be protecting him from situations that would be very costly to him. For example, Allah may keep him and his family healthy, may keep their possessions free from destruction and so forth. Hence, he is facing fewer costs while another person with more wealth but not willing to give charity may be inflicted with great medical or business costs that will cause him financial ruin. All of these aspects are decreed and determined by Allah and Allah alone and may be directed related to a person's good deeds and acts of charity.

[3] Note that the "opposite" law works for *riba* or interest. Unfortunately, some Muslims insist on taking interest, arguing that they may lose a percentage of their wealth due to inflation while

(2) Furthermore, the believer must be fully certain that Allah has foreknowledge of everything that is going to occur and He has already recorded all that shall take place. Nothing can take place without His will and permission. Everything, including, or especially, life and death, is completely under His control. Until a person completely accepts and understands these facts, he can never truly look toward Allah as the only Lord and only one worthy of worship. If, for example, someone can do something that goes against what Allah had willed and decreed, it shows that that person is stronger than Allah and, hence, is deserving of some form of worship instead of Allah. This means that there is some other power other than Allah. If that were the case, it would not be Allah alone who should be submitted to. Instead, it would be the greater of those two powers in a particular situation.[1] Instead, though, once a person believes in God, he should immediately recognize that no other source can harm or help him other than Allah. Allah says,

وَلَئِن سَأَلْتَهُم مَّنْ خَلَقَ ٱلسَّمَٰوَٰتِ وَٱلْأَرْضَ لَيَقُولُنَّ ٱللَّهُ ۚ قُلْ
أَفَرَءَيْتُم مَّا تَدْعُونَ مِن دُونِ ٱللَّهِ إِنْ أَرَادَنِىَ ٱللَّهُ بِضُرٍّ هَلْ هُنَّ
كَٰشِفَٰتُ ضُرِّهِۦٓ أَوْ أَرَادَنِى بِرَحْمَةٍ هَلْ هُنَّ مُمْسِكَٰتُ رَحْمَتِهِۦ ۚ
قُلْ حَسْبِىَ ٱللَّهُ ۖ عَلَيْهِ يَتَوَكَّلُ ٱلْمُتَوَكِّلُونَ

---

seeing no reason to leave that money to the banks, for example. However, Allah has clearly said, "Allah will deprive interest of all blessing, but will give increase for deeds of charity. He loves not creatures ungrateful and wicked" (*al-Baqarah* 276). Hence, one may believe that he is getting some form of increase in wealth through *riba* but, in reality, that wealth has no blessings in it and will just lead to evil results for whoever decides to take it. Thus even if this money (which was actually a creation of the banks in the first place) was left to the banks and disbelievers, it will not benefit them in the long-run. In fact, it may definitely harm them.

[1] Those who believe in a multitude of gods, a god of rain, crops, air and so forth, are faced with this dilemma and forced to try to appease and worship all of those gods in a number of different ways. By the grace and mercy of Allah, the true believers have been saved from such misconceptions and confusions in their lives.

"If indeed you ask them who it is that created the heavens and the earth, they would be sure to say, 'Allah.' Say: 'See you then the things that you invoke besides Allah. Can they, if Allah wills some harm for me, remove His penalty? Or if He wills some grace for me, can they keep back His grace?' Say: 'Sufficient is Allah for me, in Him trust those who put their trust'" (*al-Zumar* 38).

If a person believed, even to the slightest extent, in the false concept that there are some forces other than Allah who can act independently of Allah or who can frustrate Allah's plan, his heart will never become free to completely worship Allah alone. This is one reason why the early companions did not even like to ask others for favors that were within their means. Hence, all of these facets must be understood and internalized by the believer before he can truly worship Allah in a "complete" manner and in a manner that Allah is supposed to be worshipped.

(3) When a person understands these facts, he puts his trust in Allah and Allah alone. There is no need to fear anyone or anything other than Allah. Indeed, there is no need to seek any kind of ultimate benefit or help except in Allah. This frees the human from any kind of servitude to anything else—all things which are not deserving of such servitude, such as other humans, rulers and priests, the stars and zodiacal signs, idols and so forth.

Hence, the person turns for prayer, guidance and help to Allah and Allah alone. He knows that Allah alone can help and he is confident that if he is true to Allah, Allah will indeed help him. In other words, it is through the proper belief in the Divine Decree that these important acts of worship in the heart are freed from all forms of diseases and made strong and healthy.

The Prophet (peace and blessings of Allah be upon him) eloquently taught these truths to the young but precocious ibn Abbaas, saying,

يَا غُلاَمُ إِنِّي أُعَلِّمُكَ كَلِمَاتٍ احْفَظِ اللَّهَ يَحْفَظْكَ احْفَظِ اللَّهَ تَجِدْهُ تُجَاهَكَ إِذَا سَأَلْتَ فَاسْأَلِ اللَّهَ وَإِذَا اسْتَعَنْتَ فَاسْتَعِنْ بِاللَّهِ وَاعْلَمْ أَنَّ الأُمَّةَ لَوِ اجْتَمَعَتْ عَلَى أَنْ يَنْفَعُوكَ بِشَيْءٍ لَمْ يَنْفَعُوكَ إِلاَّ بِشَيْءٍ قَدْ كَتَبَهُ اللَّهُ لَكَ وَإِنِ اجْتَمَعُوا عَلَى أَنْ

يَضُرُّوكَ بِشَيْءٍ لَمْ يَضُرُّوكَ إِلاَّ بِشَيْءٍ قَدْ كَتَبَهُ اللَّهُ عَلَيْكَ رُفِعَتِ الأَقْلاَمُ وَجَفَّتِ الصُّحُفُ

"O young man, I shall teach you some words [of advice]. Be mindful of Allah and Allah will protect you. Be mindful of Allah, and you will find Him in front of you. If you ask, ask of Allah. If you seek help, seek help in Allah. Know that if the nation were to gather together to benefit you with something, they would not benefit you with anything except that which Allah has already recorded for you. If they gather to harm you by something, they would not be able to harm you by anything except what Allah has already recorded against you. The pens have been lifted and the pages have dried."[1]

(4) When the person understands the belief in the Divine Decree, there is a beautiful balance that is created in his life. It is a Shareeah obligation upon the believer to follow the outward or external causes that he witnesses in this world. However, at the same time, he does not put all of his trust in these outward causes by believing that they are forces and causes in themselves independent of the will of Allah. That would actually be a type of *shirk* or associating partners with Allah.

On the other hand, the believer does not ignore these worldly causes and simply claim that he is putting his trust in Allah to achieve his goals. In this way, he would be disobeying Allah and the commands of the Shareeah to work toward his desired goal. The Prophet (peace and blessings of Allah be upon him) has expressed his concept in a beautiful statement in which he said,

الْمُؤْمِنُ الْقَوِيُّ خَيْرٌ وَأَحَبُّ إِلَى اللَّهِ مِنَ الْمُؤْمِنِ الضَّعِيفِ وَفِي كُلٍّ خَيْرٌ احْرِصْ عَلَى مَا يَنْفَعُكَ وَاسْتَعِنْ بِاللَّهِ وَلَا تَعْجَزْ وَإِنْ أَصَابَكَ شَيْءٌ فَلا تَقُلْ لَوْ أَنِّي فَعَلْتُ كَانَ كَذَا وَكَذَا وَلَكِنْ قُلْ قَدَرُ اللَّهِ وَمَا شَاءَ فَعَلَ فَإِنَّ لَوْ تَفْتَحُ عَمَلَ الشَّيْطَانِ

[1] Recorded by al-Tirmidhi and others. It has been graded *sahih* by al-Albaani, Ahmad Shaakir and many others. Cf., Al-Albaani, *Saheeh al-Jaami*, vol. 2, pp. 1317-1318; Ahmad Shaakir's footnotes to Ahmad ibn Hanbal, *al-Musnad* (Cairo: Daar al-Hadeeth, 1995), vol. 4, p. 286.

"A strong[1] believer is better and more beloved to Allah than a weak believer—however, there is goodness in every [believer]. Be eager for [and strive after] what benefits you and seek help in Allah. And do not be too weak or lazy to do so. If something afflicts you, do not say, 'If only I had done such and such.' But instead say, 'The decree of Allah and whatever He wills, He does.' If you say, 'If,' it opens the door for deeds of Satan." (Recorded by Muslim.)

(5) Furthermore, the hadith just quoted also highlights that a person should not despair by questioning himself after performing an act. It is obligatory upon him only to do what is correct and permissible according to the Shareeah. Once he does that, he does not commit any sin.[2] That is the important matter. If he achieves his goal or not, that is in the hand and decree of Allah. He actually has no control over that. Whatever was going to occur to him would have occurred and he can do nothing to change what has already happened. He can take comfort in the fact that he did what he needed to do and the rest Allah decrees according to His wisdom and rule. In other words, he has acted without disobeying Allah and regardless of what occurs in this life, he need not fear that what has occurred may harm him in his eternal life.

(6) The firm believer in *al-qadar* knows that everything is according to Allah's will. This includes military victories in this life as well as the time of one's death. When these aspects are joined together and clear in the believer's mind, he realizes that he has no reason to fear anyone other than Allah. On the contrary, he should strive and sacrifice for the sake of Allah as, in reality, there

---

[1] Al-Nawawi notes that the meaning of "strong" in this hadith is, "of strong resolve, one whose mind is intent on the affairs of the Hereafter. The person of this quality is more forthcoming in opposing the enemy in jihad, he is quicker to go after the enemy and to chase after them... He is also more anxious and prompt in the prayers, fasting, remembrance..." See Yahya al-Nawawi, *Sharh Saheeh Muslim* (Beirut: Daar al-Fikr, n.d.), vol. 16, p. 214.

[2] This is especially true and even more comforting to the soul if the person had prayed the *salaat al-istikhaarah* before commencing his action. In this prayer, the person asks Allah for guidance concerning what decision he should make on a specific matter. After performing that prayer, he can feel at rest, knowing that whatever decision he was guided to was the best. Even if the results seem not that good, the person knows that, if he was sincere, his current situation is better than the alternatives that would have resulted had he not performed that prayer and been guided to that choice.

is no rational reason not to strive for the sake of Allah. The only result of striving for the sake of Allah could be victory in this life, hardships decreed by Allah alone for which he will earn Allah's pleasure or the final end of this life through martyrdom. This belief was something that the Companions clearly understood as they spread the message of Islam to the different areas of the world. It was a belief that was a direct implementation of, for example, the following verses of the Quran:

إِن تُصِبْكَ حَسَنَةٌ تَسُؤْهُمْ وَإِن تُصِبْكَ مُصِيبَةٌ يَقُولُوا۟ قَدْ أَخَذْنَآ
أَمْرَنَا مِن قَبْلُ وَيَتَوَلَّوا۟ وَّهُمْ فَرِحُونَ ﴿٥٠﴾ قُل لَّن يُصِيبَنَآ إِلَّا مَا
كَتَبَ ٱللَّهُ لَنَا هُوَ مَوْلَىٰنَا وَعَلَى ٱللَّهِ فَلْيَتَوَكَّلِ ٱلْمُؤْمِنُونَ ﴿٥١﴾
قُلْ هَلْ تَرَبَّصُونَ بِنَآ إِلَّآ إِحْدَى ٱلْحُسْنَيَيْنِ وَنَحْنُ نَتَرَبَّصُ بِكُمْ
أَن يُصِيبَكُمُ ٱللَّهُ بِعَذَابٍ مِّنْ عِندِهِۦٓ أَوْ بِأَيْدِينَا فَتَرَبَّصُوٓا۟ إِنَّا
مَعَكُم مُّتَرَبِّصُونَ

"If good befalls you, it grieves them. But if a misfortune befalls you, they say, 'We indeed took our precautions beforehand,' and they turn away rejoicing. Say: 'Nothing will happen to us except what Allah has decreed for us. He is our Protector.' And in Allah let the believers put their trust. Say: 'Can you expect for us (any fate) other than one of two glorious things (martyrdom or victory)? But we can expect for you that either Allah will send His punishment from Himself or by our hands. So wait; we too will wait with you'" (*al-Taubah* 50-52).

Allah says to those who think that they can extend their lives by being niggardly or cowardly, thinking that they control their own destiny while forgetting that Allah has determined all things,

ثُمَّ أَنزَلَ عَلَيْكُم مِّنۢ بَعْدِ ٱلْغَمِّ أَمَنَةً نُّعَاسًا يَغْشَىٰ طَآئِفَةً مِّنكُمْ ۖ
وَطَآئِفَةٌ قَدْ أَهَمَّتْهُمْ أَنفُسُهُمْ يَظُنُّونَ بِٱللَّهِ غَيْرَ ٱلْحَقِّ ظَنَّ
ٱلْجَٰهِلِيَّةِ ۖ يَقُولُونَ هَل لَّنَا مِنَ ٱلْأَمْرِ مِن شَىْءٍ ۗ قُلْ إِنَّ ٱلْأَمْرَ كُلَّهُۥ
لِلَّهِ ۗ يُخْفُونَ فِىٓ أَنفُسِهِم مَّا لَا يُبْدُونَ لَكَ ۖ يَقُولُونَ لَوْ كَانَ لَنَا مِنَ
ٱلْأَمْرِ شَىْءٌ مَّا قُتِلْنَا هَٰهُنَا ۗ قُل لَّوْ كُنتُمْ فِى بُيُوتِكُمْ لَبَرَزَ ٱلَّذِينَ
كُتِبَ عَلَيْهِمُ ٱلْقَتْلُ إِلَىٰ مَضَاجِعِهِمْ ۖ وَلِيَبْتَلِىَ ٱللَّهُ مَا فِى صُدُورِكُمْ
وَلِيُمَحِّصَ مَا فِى قُلُوبِكُمْ ۗ وَٱللَّهُ عَلِيمٌۢ بِذَاتِ ٱلصُّدُورِ

"After (the excitement) of the distress, He sent down calm on a band of you overcome with slumber, while another band was stirred to anxiety by their own feelings, moved by wrong suspicions of Allah, suspicions due to ignorance, They said, 'What affair is this of ours?' Say [to them,] 'Indeed, this affair is wholly Allah's.' They hide in their minds what they dare not reveal to you. They say (to themselves), 'If we had had anything to do with this affair, we would not have been in the slaughter here.' Say: 'Even if you had remained in your homes, those for whom death was decreed would certainly have gone forth to the place of their death.' (All this was) that Allah might test what is in your breasts and purge what is in your hearts: For Allah knows well the secrets of your hearts" (*ali-Imraan* 154).

(7) Karzoon highlights one of the important corollaries to the belief in *al-Qadar*.[1] It is another aspect that can have a very positive effect on a person's spiritual progress. It is the recognition that no evil is to be attributed to Allah; evil is only to be attributed to humans and the creation. In fact, the Messenger of Allah (peace and blessings of Allah be upon him) said,

---

[1] Karzoon, vol. 1, pp. 152-153.

وَالْخَيْرُ كُلُّهُ فِي يَدَيْكَ وَالشَّرُّ لَيْسَ إِلَيْكَ والشر ليس عليك

"All the good is in Your Hand and evil is not to be attributed to You." (Recorded by Muslim.)

What Allah has decreed is good throughout, based on wisdom, justice and mercy. This is true even though humans may incorrectly view things in a different light and perceive them as very bad and evil, thereby becoming confused or even "mad at God".[1] The "negative" things that happen to a person may be in

---

[1] Although it is difficult to take an event of this nature as an example, the horrific and tragic events of September 11, 2001 demonstrated the weak understanding of God and His decree on the part of many "learned" Christians. In fact, no less a Christian preacher than Billy Graham stated to the audience at the National Cathedral, "You may even be mad at God," and he has also admitted that he has never satisfactorily understood why God allows evil. Indeed, after that event, this author heard many Christians asking how can God who is supposed to be merciful and just allow such acts. Their confusion and psychological crisis can be directly related to their incorrect beliefs about God and their lack of understanding their purpose in this life. They only recognize God as loving while they also claim that He is just. At the same time, though, these same people have, in reality, turned their backs on God, virtually removing His guidance from every realm of life. Furthermore, they have allowed all forms of immorality to spread throughout their land. Yet they cannot fathom that they are deserving of punishment and deserving of acts, whether natural disasters or man-made catastrophes, that may lead them to reflection and repentance. They also cannot fathom that they have been created for a purpose yet they live their lives completely heedless and intentionally unaware of any responsibility to God. Indeed, Allah explains to all of mankind, "Mischief has appeared on land and sea because of what the hands of men have earned. That (Allah) may give them a taste of some of their deeds: in order that they may turn back (from Evil)" (*al-Room* 41). It is amazing that instead of awaking and repenting, their attitude is to question what God allows to occur. Indeed, their attitude is such that no matter how many signs or warnings Allah gives them, they will not change. (*Soorah al-Jaathiyah* 27-37 seems to be a very true picture of these types of people.) Hence, in their arrogance and chosen ignorance, it is not expected that they should ever achieve any form of spiritual reformation or purification. They are neither fulfilling their purpose in life nor allowing such events to cause any change in their ways. If this is the case, they have no argument in front of Allah if Allah should punish them both in this life and in the Hereafter. Thus, such punishments are not evil at all but merely Divine justice as they deny the role of God day in and day out of their lives. (The voices that tried to awaken the masses were either few and far between or were drowned about the masses who simply do not want to hear that type of reminder. On September 16, 2001, ABC News (radio) reported that a preacher did actually preach that the great tragedy should show America, with all of its power and global dominance, that it must stop its arrogance and repent to God. The ultraconservative Jerry Falwell was even more explicit, blaming the event on the liberals, feminists and homosexuals. This author can only assume that enormous political pressure was put on him to retract his statements so that the political power of the religious right would not be greatly damaged by expressing such

the form of a trial from Allah or an act that reforms or disciplines the person. Allah has decreed that He shall try all human beings, especially those who say that they believe. It is through these trials that a person definitively demonstrates his faith and his willingness to submit to Allah,[1] such that these trials will be a source of Allah's love for him in this life and the Hereafter.

Sometimes, humans are deserving of punishment or retribution for their actions when they disobey Allah. Allah says,

وَمَآ أَصَٰبَكُم مِّن مُّصِيبَةٍ فَبِمَا كَسَبَتْ أَيْدِيكُمْ وَيَعْفُواْ عَن كَثِيرٍ

"Whatever misfortune happens to you is because of the things your hands have wrought, and for many (of them) He grants forgiveness" (*al-Shoora* 30). By the wonderful grace and mercy of Allah, this worldly punishment serves as both a type of training or reform as well as a means of removing sins—and every human has to admit that he commits sins. The Messenger of Allah (peace and blessings of Allah be upon him) said,

إِذَا أَرَادَ اللَّهُ بِعَبْدِهِ الْخَيْرَ عَجَّلَ لَهُ الْعُقُوبَةَ فِي الدُّنْيَا وَإِذَا أَرَادَ اللَّهُ بِعَبْدِهِ الشَّرَّ أَمْسَكَ عَنْهُ بِذَنْبِهِ حَتَّى يُوَافِيَ بِهِ يَوْمَ الْقِيَامَةِ

"When Allah wants good for His servant, He hastens his punishment in this world. When Allah wants evil for His servant, He withholds from him [the punishment] due to his sins until he recompenses him for it on the Day of Resurrection."[2]

(8) When a person realizes this fact, he realizes that everything that Allah does with respect to him can be a source of great good, there is no need for despair or sorrow as all can be

---

unpopular views concerning this horrific tragedy. It seems that people do not want to hear speech of this nature at all.) Incidentally, for a good discussion on the wisdom behind the creation of Satan, the leader of evil, the interested reader should consult Umar al-Ashqar, *The World of the Jinn and Devils* (Boulder: Al-Basheer Company for Publications and Translations, 1998), pp. 225-243.

[1] Allah says in the Quran, "Does mankind think that they will be left alone on saying, 'We believe,' and that they will not be put to trials? We did try those before them, and Allah will certainly know [and show] those who are true from those who are false" (*al-Ankaboot* 2-3).

[2] Recorded by al-Tirmidhi and others. According to al-Albaani, it is *sahih*. See al-Albaani, *Saheeh al-Jaami*, vol. 1, p. 118.

good. The Prophet (peace and blessings of Allah be upon him) indicated this fact when he said,

عَجَبًا لِأَمْرِ الْمُؤْمِنِ إِنَّ أَمْرَهُ كُلَّهُ خَيْرٌ وَلَيْسَ ذَاكَ لِأَحَدٍ إِلاَّ لِلْمُؤْمِنِ إِنْ أَصَابَتْهُ سَرَّاءُ شَكَرَ فَكَانَ خَيْرًا لَهُ وَإِنْ أَصَابَتْهُ ضَرَّاءُ صَبَرَ فَكَانَ خَيْرًا لَهُ

"The affair of the believer is amazing, as all of it is good. This is not true save for the believer. If happiness comes to him, he is thankful and that is good for him. If he is afflicted with evil, he is patient and that is good for him." (Recorded by Muslim.)

This fact is another blessing from Allah for which Allah, in turn, is once again deserving of praise, thanks and getting closer to Him. When these matters are truly realized, the soul is always at peace, with only one preoccupation, the true worship of Allah—knowing that everything is occurring by the will of Allah and according to His wisdom.

(9) A direct relationship between belief in Divine Decree and purification of the soul is that those who do not believe in or understand this concept are susceptible to major diseases of the soul, such as *kibr* (arrogance and pride[1]) and anguish or depression. When a person who believes that God has nothing to do with what actually takes place in this world accomplishes something, he thinks it is all his own doing and greatness. When he fails, he must, if he is consistent in his own logic, admit his own failure. If he fails often, it can bring about feelings of uselessness, anguish, dissatisfaction and depression. In reality, though, his accomplishments and failures are all trials from Allah. The believer must realize this fact and not go to the extremes described above. He should realize that he cannot accomplish

---

[1] Some among mankind have become very haughty due to scientific advancements, some even more so since cloning has been "conquered." Their arrogance leads them to deny the very existence or importance of God. In reality, though, all that they did in cloning was to take a material that Allah created for them and then they harnessed it according to the laws that Allah set forth in order to produce a result that Allah had already decreed for them. Instead of becoming arrogant and vain, perhaps these people should consider how long Allah had kept that knowledge from them and how much toil and trouble, time and dollars they had to exhaust to come up with this knowledge and process—and even then they have not perfected it. When considered by this perspective, for humans as a whole, this "magnificent scientific achievement" was a very humbling experience indeed.

anything save by the grace and will of Allah who has the ability to confound any of his efforts. Similarly, he should realize when he does not achieve his goal that such was by Allah's decree and that there is some good in that, whether he knows it or not, as long as he remains patient. Allah says,

مَآ أَصَابَ مِن مُّصِيبَةٍ فِى ٱلْأَرْضِ وَلَا فِىٓ أَنفُسِكُمْ إِلَّا فِى كِتَٰبٍ مِّن قَبْلِ أَن نَّبْرَأَهَآ ۚ إِنَّ ذَٰلِكَ عَلَى ٱللَّهِ يَسِيرٌ ﴿٢٢﴾ لِّكَيْلَا تَأْسَوْا۟ عَلَىٰ مَا فَاتَكُمْ وَلَا تَفْرَحُوا۟ بِمَآ ءَاتَىٰكُمْ ۗ وَٱللَّهُ لَا يُحِبُّ كُلَّ مُخْتَالٍ فَخُورٍ

"No misfortune can happen on earth or in your souls but is recorded in a decree before We bring it into existence. That is truly easy for Allah, in order that you may not despair over matters that pass you by, nor exult over favors bestowed upon you. Allah loves not any vainglorious boaster" (*al-Hadeed* 22-23).

(10) Another disease of the soul that is removed by a complete and correct belief in divine decree is the disease of envy.[1] When a person realizes that everything is in the control of Allah, there is no room to envy anyone else. Indeed, envy implies that the person is unhappy with the way Allah has distributed something in this world. Even if someone achieves something by

---

[1] Some Muslims, unfortunately, go beyond even envy and declare that Allah's distribution of wealth, children and so forth in this world is unfair. They obviously do not realize that all of these aspects are trials. Allah says, "Your wealth and your children may be but a trial: but in the presence of Allah is the highest reward" (*al-Taghaabun* 15). Furthermore, Allah gives according to His will, plan and wisdom. Mankind does not even have the right to question Allah concerning His division. When making statements of this complaining nature, these people are saying something very serious indeed. They should realize that Allah is much more honorable, perfect and majestic than to do something that is unfair. Some go beyond that and claim that they have not received what they deserve from Allah. In fact, this author has heard this from Muslims who are quite well off. They should realize that everything that they receive from Allah is nothing but a blessing from Him that He has decreed. No one can force Allah to give anything to anyone. Secondly, in the face of all the sins mankind commits, none among humans should honestly claim any right upon Allah to give him any good or blessing—except by humbly appealing to His great mercy and compassion. Finally, given that Allah has given most of mankind the blessing of life, intelligence, sight, hearing and so forth, how can they claim that Allah has not been fair to them by claiming that they are deserving of many more blessings than those great blessings?

unethical means, there is no need or room for envy. Allah has allowed that person to achieve that ends by unethical means but Allah is not unaware of what that person did. Allah may punish him in this life or in the Hereafter. Indeed, Allah may even use that person or that achievement for some good in this life for others while it will be a source of punishment and evil for the person himself.

All of these factors make belief in *al-Qadar* (preordainment) one of the most important beliefs for the purification of the soul. Hence, it is not surprising that anyone who does not believe in it is a disbeliever. Note the following important incident recorded by Muslim in his *Sahih*,

> It is narrated on the authority of Yahya ibn Yamur that the first man who discussed *Qadar* in Basra was Ma'bad al-Juhani. I [Yahya] along with Humaid ibn Abdul Rahman al-Himyari set out for pilgrimage or *Umrah* and said, "If it should so happen that we come into contact with anyone of the Companions of the Messenger of Allah (peace be upon him), we shall ask him about what is being talked about concerning *Qadar*." Unexpectedly, we came across 'Abdullah ibn 'Umar ibn al-Khattab while he was entering the mosque. My friend and I surrounded him. One of us was on his right side and the other stood on his left. I expected that my friend would authorize me to speak [for both of us]. Therefore, I said, "O Abu Abdul Rahman [Abdullah ibn Umar], there have appeared some persons in our land who recite the Quran and pursue knowledge." Then, after explaining their affairs, I said, "They claim that there is no such thing as Divine Decree and all events are new [to everyone, including Allah]." [Abdullah ibn Umar] then said, "When you happen to meet such persons, tell them that I have nothing to do with them and they have nothing to do with me. And, verily, they are in no way responsible for my belief." Abdullah ibn Umar then swore by Allah and said, "If any of them [who does not believe in Divine Decree] had with him gold equal to the bulk of

> the Mountain of Uhud and then he should spend it [in the way of Allah], Allah would not accept that from him unless he affirms his faith in Divine Decree."[1] He then said, "My father Umar ibn al-Khattaab told me..." [He then went on to narrate the famous hadith of Jibreel.]

Belief in the Hereafter

Another one of the articles of faith in Islam is belief in the Hereafter. Like the other aspects of faith discussed so far, the proper and correct belief in this article is both essential as well as extremely beneficial to the purification of the soul. It is this belief and knowledge that informs the soul that there is a purpose to this creation and that, in the end, he will meet his Lord. In forceful words, Allah clearly shows that there could be no other way for His creation to be, given His majesty and greatness. Allah says,

أَفَحَسِبْتُمْ أَنَّمَا خَلَقْنَـٰكُمْ عَبَثًا وَأَنَّكُمْ إِلَيْنَا لَا تُرْجَعُونَ ﴿١١٥﴾

فَتَعَـٰلَى ٱللَّهُ ٱلْمَلِكُ ٱلْحَقُّ لَآ إِلَـٰهَ إِلَّا هُوَ رَبُّ ٱلْعَرْشِ ٱلْكَرِيمِ

"Did you then think that We had created you in jest, and that you would not be brought back to Us (for account)? Therefore exalted be Allah, the King, the Truth; there is no god but He, the Lord of the Throne of Honor" (*al-Muminoon* 115-116).

Allah is just, wise and compassionate. He will not allow the deeds that are performed in this world, after He sent clear guidance, to go without reward or punishment. Allah makes it abundantly clear that those who do righteous deeds will definitely

[1] Ibn Hubairah points out that this hadith demonstrates that though some people may read the Quran and study a great deal, they have a deficiency in their beliefs and they follow heresies. Therefore, their deeds will not be raised to Allah whatsoever and their studying of the religion will not be accepted by Allah. Their evil or false beliefs will prevent their deeds from being accepted. This is because the beliefs are the foundations of one's religion and only a practice that has the proper foundation is pleasing to Allah. See al-Wazeer ibn Hubairah, *Al-Ifsaah an Maana al-Sihaah* (Riyadh: Daar al-Want, 1996), vol. 1, p. 299.

be dealt with differently from those who intentionally performed and propagated evil. Allah says,

أَمْ حَسِبَ ٱلَّذِينَ ٱجْتَرَحُوا۟ ٱلسَّيِّـَٔاتِ أَن نَّجْعَلَهُمْ كَٱلَّذِينَ ءَامَنُوا۟
وَعَمِلُوا۟ ٱلصَّٰلِحَٰتِ سَوَآءً مَّحْيَاهُمْ وَمَمَاتُهُمْ ۚ سَآءَ مَا يَحْكُمُونَ
﴿٢١﴾ وَخَلَقَ ٱللَّهُ ٱلسَّمَٰوَٰتِ وَٱلْأَرْضَ بِٱلْحَقِّ وَلِتُجْزَىٰ كُلُّ نَفْسٍۭ
بِمَا كَسَبَتْ وَهُمْ لَا يُظْلَمُونَ ﴿٢٢﴾ أَفَرَءَيْتَ مَنِ ٱتَّخَذَ إِلَٰهَهُۥ هَوَىٰهُ
وَأَضَلَّهُ ٱللَّهُ عَلَىٰ عِلْمٍ وَخَتَمَ عَلَىٰ سَمْعِهِۦ وَقَلْبِهِۦ وَجَعَلَ عَلَىٰ
بَصَرِهِۦ غِشَٰوَةً فَمَن يَهْدِيهِ مِنۢ بَعْدِ ٱللَّهِ ۚ أَفَلَا تَذَكَّرُونَ ﴿٢٣﴾ وَقَالُوا۟
مَا هِىَ إِلَّا حَيَاتُنَا ٱلدُّنْيَا نَمُوتُ وَنَحْيَا وَمَا يُهْلِكُنَآ إِلَّا ٱلدَّهْرُ ۚ
وَمَا لَهُم بِذَٰلِكَ مِنْ عِلْمٍ ۖ إِنْ هُمْ إِلَّا يَظُنُّونَ

"What! Do those who seek after evil ways think that We shall hold them equal with those who believe and do righteous deeds, that equal will be their life and their death? Ill is the judgment that they make. Allah created the heavens and the earth for just ends, and in order that each soul may find the recompense of what it has earned, and none of them be wronged. Do you see such a one as takes as his god his own vain desire? Allah has, knowing (him as such), left him astray, and sealed his hearing and his heart (and understanding), and put a cover on his sight: Who, then, will guide him after Allah (has withdrawn guidance)? Will you not then receive admonition? And they say, 'What is there but our life in this world? We shall die and we live, and nothing but time can destroy us.' But of that they have no knowledge; they have merely conjecture" (*al-Jaathiyah* 21-24).[1]

---

[1] These verses remind this author of a passage from Freud. In this passage, like so many others from other secular scientists, Freud bases his premise on what he sees around him in this

The positive effects on the soul and its purification due to the correct belief in the Hereafter include the following:

(1) A strong belief in the Hereafter develops a strong moral consciousness, keeping the person from committing sins and giving him a strong internal force to help him keep his desires in check. The believer not only knows that Allah sees what is in his heart but he also knows that Allah will hold him accountable for his deeds and intentions. Allah says,

لِّلَّهِ مَا فِي ٱلسَّمَٰوَٰتِ وَمَا فِي ٱلْأَرْضِ ۗ وَإِن تُبْدُوا۟ مَا فِىٓ أَنفُسِكُمْ أَوْ تُخْفُوهُ يُحَاسِبْكُم بِهِ ٱللَّهُ ۖ فَيَغْفِرُ لِمَن يَشَآءُ وَيُعَذِّبُ مَن يَشَآءُ ۗ وَٱللَّهُ عَلَىٰ كُلِّ شَىْءٍ قَدِيرٌ

"To Allah belongs all that is in the heavens and on earth. Whether you show what is in your minds or conceal it, Allah calls you to account for it. He forgives whom He wills, and punishes whom He wills. For Allah has power over all things" (*al-Baqarah* 284).

(2) The belief in the great rewards in the Hereafter—and the greatest of all of them, being able to see Allah in the Hereafter—is a strong incentive driving the believer to perform the best deeds he can perform. Allah has promised the pious the reward of Paradise in numerous places in the Quran. This promise is not an illusion or meaningless words. Instead, it is a fact of the

---

world without realizing that there are other forces at work and that there is more to this creation than what meets the eye in this short worldly existence. Indeed, in this passage Freud has made the classical mistake made by so many: judging or denying matters that humans have not yet experienced simply on the basis that those matters are not known to humans now. The flaw in that logic is so clear that it is amazing that so many philosophers commit such errors. Freud wrote, "It seems not to be true that there is a power in the universe which watches over the well-being of every individual with parental care, bringing all within His fold to a happy ending. On the contrary, the destinies of men are incompatible with any universal principle of justice. Earthquakes, floods and fires do not distinguish between the good and devout man and the sinner and unbeliever... it is no means the rule that virtue is rewarded and wickedness punished. It often happens that the violent, crafty and unprincipled seize the desirable goods of this world while the pious go away empty. Dark, unfeeling and unloving powers determine human destiny. The concept of divine justice, which according to religion governs the world, seems to have no existence." Quoted in Jameelah, p. 16.

life after death in this world. A person will either be granted the blessings of Paradise or the torment of the Hell-fire. A person's final abode will be determined by his faith, his sincerity to Allah, his submission to Allah and his seeking of Allah's pleasure and forgiveness. In essence, it will be determined by the efforts that he put forth to purify his soul and make himself worthy of being entered into Allah's paradise and receiving Allah's approval.

(3) The correct and strong belief in the Hereafter removes greed and continual desire for the goods and pleasures of this world. Such pleasures and goods are fleeting and non-eternal, but the rewards with Allah are permanent. Hence, worldly pleasures are not worth pursuing if they require giving up something of the Hereafter and Allah's pleasure. Hence, Allah reminds the believers not to be overcome with this world as this is not their real goal and purpose. The Hereafter is better and everlasting. Allah says,

بَلْ تُؤْثِرُونَ ٱلْحَيَوٰةَ ٱلدُّنْيَا ﴿١٦﴾ وَٱلْأَخِرَةُ خَيْرٌ وَأَبْقَىٰٓ

"Nay (behold), you prefer the life of this world but the Hereafter is better and more enduring" (*al-Ala* 16-17).

This belief allows the person to sacrifice anything of this worldly life for the sake of truth and justice. There is no room for compromise if Allah's pleasure and paradise is at stake. Hence, the true believer in the Hereafter will always stand for truth and will be willing to sacrifice his wealth and life for that noble goal. In fact, Allah has described the believers in the following manner,

إِنَّ ٱللَّهَ ٱشْتَرَىٰ مِنَ ٱلْمُؤْمِنِينَ أَنفُسَهُمْ وَأَمْوَٰلَهُم بِأَنَّ لَهُمُ
ٱلْجَنَّةَ ۚ يُقَٰتِلُونَ فِى سَبِيلِ ٱللَّهِ فَيَقْتُلُونَ وَيُقْتَلُونَ ۖ وَعْدًا عَلَيْهِ
حَقًّا فِى ٱلتَّوْرَىٰةِ وَٱلْإِنجِيلِ وَٱلْقُرْءَانِ ۚ وَمَنْ أَوْفَىٰ بِعَهْدِهِۦ مِنَ ٱللَّهِ ۚ
فَٱسْتَبْشِرُوا۟ بِبَيْعِكُمُ ٱلَّذِى بَايَعْتُم بِهِۦ ۚ وَذَٰلِكَ هُوَ ٱلْفَوْزُ ٱلْعَظِيمُ

"Allah has purchased from the believers their souls and their wealth. For them (in return) is the Garden (of Paradise). They fight in His Cause, and slay and are slain. [This reward is] a promise binding on Him in truth, through the Torah, the Gospel, and the Quran: and who is more faithful to his covenant than Allah? Then rejoice in the bargain which you have concluded. That is the achievement supreme" (*al-Taubah* 111).

(4) A strong belief in the Hereafter helps the believer to have patience in the face of the trials and tribulations of this worldly existence. The soul remains at rest regardless of what occurs in this life because the true ramifications of all deeds are not witnessed in this life but in the Hereafter. Indeed, this understanding will give him the moral fortitude that is needed to meet one's responsibilities and obligations towards oneself and towards others in this life, even if they require sacrifice and struggle. On this point, a passage from Badri is enlightening,

> If a person's worldview does not include belief in the soul or in the hereafter, it is only natural for him (or her) to be a hedonistic animal trying to enjoy his material life and avoid any painful experiences as much as possible. But when this craving is hampered by life's problems or mere sickness and old age, such individuals will inevitably feel dejected, anxious or depressed, succumb to neurotic and psychotic reactions, or try to deny their deprivation through alcohol, drugs or suicide. Consequently, if human beings are not believed to have been bestowed with a God-given soul [and face the Hereafter], why should women be expected to bear babies of unwanted pregnancies...[1]

---

[1] Badri, p. 107. In addition to what Badri stated, one can also note strong and drastic reactions from those who do not have a belief in the Hereafter when it comes to anything that may put their lives and material well-being at risk. In other words, panic and overreaction can become commonplace. Since this worldly life is all such people have and all they can possibly have, they fear losing any part of it or any form of its pleasures. Hence, they go to extremes to ensure that their precious lives and wealth are not afflicted by anything harmful.

Conclusions Concerning the Purification of One's Beliefs

In sum, the purification of one's beliefs and faith is the first step along the path of purification and, in reality, it forms the final step in one's process—as one grows in faith and increases one's knowledge and certainty. As a person understands these articles of faith better, he internalizes them more. They become the foundation for his understanding of reality. In this way, he then has the correct understanding of his reality and surroundings as these articles of faith are the only true beliefs, consistent with reality, found among humans.

In turn, the correct beliefs and the true faith have a strong, positive impact upon all aspects of one's life, thus contributing to the overall goal of purification of the soul. His beliefs become the basis for his actions and deeds. They are the source of his ethics and morals. They are the reason he does what he does and refrains from what he does not do.

In other words, when the beliefs are correct and the faith is true, the person's understanding of this creation becomes true. He then turns his complete attention to the real purpose of his creation and his real goal in life. Hence, he ends up dedicating himself to worshipping Allah in the proper manner. His beliefs are proper, his acts become proper and his heart is cleansed of all the sources of disease and illness.

Distortions and heresies in belief can be devastating for the purification of the soul.[1] Mention has been made of some of the beliefs of the Jews, Christians, psychiatrists and so forth. To briefly cite one example here, Allah speaks about one of the beliefs that developed among the Jews and how that belief deceived them and, hence, misled them from the true path. Allah says, while commenting on the Jewish belief that they are the chosen people and that, at the most, they will only be punished for the same number of days in which they worshipped the calf,

---

[1] A discussion of the negative effects of innovations and heresies is found in Chapter 7.

أَلَمْ تَرَ إِلَى ٱلَّذِينَ أُوتُوا۟ نَصِيبًا مِّنَ ٱلْكِتَـٰبِ يُدْعَوْنَ إِلَىٰ
كِتَـٰبِ ٱللَّهِ لِيَحْكُمَ بَيْنَهُمْ ثُمَّ يَتَوَلَّىٰ فَرِيقٌ مِّنْهُمْ وَهُم مُّعْرِضُونَ ﴿٢٣﴾
ذَٰلِكَ بِأَنَّهُمْ قَالُوا۟ لَن تَمَسَّنَا ٱلنَّارُ إِلَّآ أَيَّامًا مَّعْدُودَٰتٍ ۖ وَغَرَّهُمْ
فِى دِينِهِم مَّا كَانُوا۟ يَفْتَرُونَ

"Have you not turned your sight to those who have been given a portion of the Book? They are invited to the Book of Allah, to settle their dispute, but a party of them turn back and decline (the arbitration). This is because they say, 'The Fire shall not touch us but for a few numbered days.' Their own forgeries deceive them as to their own religion" (*ali-Imraan* 23-24). They arrogantly refused to submit to the judgment because they believed that they were destined only to spend a few days in the Hell-fire regardless of the deeds that they performed. In so doing, they were only damaging and destroying their own souls.

A belief similar to this and to the born-again faith among Christians developed among the Muslims. This was the belief of the Murjiah, which as it spread among the people led to the understanding that as long as a person is a Muslim (states the testimony of faith), no deeds can harm him and he cannot fall outside of the fold of Islam. The ramifications of a belief of this nature are quite obvious and, unfortunately, can be seen throughout the Muslim world today. Due to this heretical belief, one finds numerous Muslims today who never pray, fast and so on, but they swear to the authenticity of their belief and affirm that they will be in Paradise. Their lack of practice—and thus failure to take the proper steps to purify their souls—is directly related to their false belief that they are Muslims and are pure regardless of their deeds. Indeed, some of them even perform deeds that take them out of the fold of Islam but their false beliefs have made them completely oblivious to this fact. Due to their false belief, they are actually perfectly satisfied that they are true and pious Mulsims.

Purifying One's Soul and Getting Closer to Allah by Performing the Obligatory Deeds

In numerous places in the Quran, Allah makes it clear that the key to salvation is not a mere declaration of one's faith or a false faith that has no righteous deeds as its fruits.[1] Instead, the key is a true faith that combines with and is the driving force behind performing righteous deeds. In fact, the scholars note that faith is actually comprised of the belief in the heart, the statement of the tongue and the deeds of the physical body. Hence, a person's faith cannot be complete without performing the proper deeds.

Allah clearly relates the performance of good deeds with having faith. For example, He says,

فَمَن يَعْمَلْ مِنَ ٱلصَّٰلِحَٰتِ وَهُوَ مُؤْمِنٌ فَلَا كُفْرَانَ لِسَعْيِهِۦ وَإِنَّا لَهُۥ كَٰتِبُونَ

"Whoever works any act of righteousness and has faith, his endeavor will not be rejected: We shall record it in his favor" (*al-Anbiyaa* 94). Indeed, the only way to be saved from perdition is through faith and good deeds, as Allah says,

وَٱلْعَصْرِ ﴿١﴾ إِنَّ ٱلْإِنسَٰنَ لَفِى خُسْرٍ ﴿٢﴾ إِلَّا ٱلَّذِينَ ءَامَنُوا۟ وَعَمِلُوا۟ ٱلصَّٰلِحَٰتِ وَتَوَاصَوْا۟ بِٱلْحَقِّ وَتَوَاصَوْا۟ بِٱلصَّبْرِ

"By (the token of) Time (through the ages), verily man is in loss, except those who have faith, do righteous deeds, (join together) in the mutual teaching of truth, and of patience and constancy" (*al-Asr* 1-3). In another verse, Allah clearly shows that it is faith and deeds that lead one to Paradise or the Hell-fire. Allah says,

---

[1] In addition to the verses to be quoted above, one may also take note of *al-Maaidah* 72, *al-Kahf* 107, *Maryam* 59-60, *al-Hajj* 56, *al-Noor* 55, *al-Shoora* 22-23 and *al-Fath* 29. These verses are in addition to those verses that give a general description of the believers. Those verses describe the believers by the deeds that they perform. See, for example, *al-Muminoon* 1-10.

بَلَىٰ مَن كَسَبَ سَيِّئَةً وَأَحَٰطَتْ بِهِۦ خَطِيٓـَٔتُهُۥ فَأُو۟لَٰٓئِكَ أَصْحَٰبُ ٱلنَّارِ ۖ هُمْ فِيهَا خَٰلِدُونَ ﴿٨١﴾ وَٱلَّذِينَ ءَامَنُوا۟ وَعَمِلُوا۟ ٱلصَّٰلِحَٰتِ أُو۟لَٰٓئِكَ أَصْحَٰبُ ٱلْجَنَّةِ ۖ هُمْ فِيهَا خَٰلِدُونَ

"Nay, whoever earns evil and his sin has surrounded him, they are Companions of the Fire: therein shall they abide (forever). But those who have faith and work righteousness, they are companions of the garden: therein shall they abide (forever)" (*al-Baqarah* 81-82).

Indeed, it is the faith in combination with good deeds that distinguishes the servants of Allah from those who failed to fulfil their potential as humans, falling instead to the lowest abyss. Allah says,

لَقَدْ خَلَقْنَا ٱلْإِنسَٰنَ فِىٓ أَحْسَنِ تَقْوِيمٍ ﴿٤﴾ ثُمَّ رَدَدْنَٰهُ أَسْفَلَ سَٰفِلِينَ ﴿٥﴾ إِلَّا ٱلَّذِينَ ءَامَنُوا۟ وَعَمِلُوا۟ ٱلصَّٰلِحَٰتِ فَلَهُمْ أَجْرٌ غَيْرُ مَمْنُونٍ

"We have indeed created man in the best of moulds. Then do We abase him (to be) the lowest of the low, except those who believe and do righteous deeds: for they shall have a reward unfailing" (*al-Teen* 4-6).

Allah also relates entry into Paradise or Hell with the deeds that one performs. In one verse, Allah states,

ٱلَّذِينَ تَتَوَفَّىٰهُمُ ٱلْمَلَٰٓئِكَةُ طَيِّبِينَ ۙ يَقُولُونَ سَلَٰمٌ عَلَيْكُمُ ٱدْخُلُوا۟ ٱلْجَنَّةَ بِمَا كُنتُمْ تَعْمَلُونَ

"(Namely) those whose lives the angels take in a state of purity, saying (to them), 'Peace be on you; enter the Garden because of (the good) which you did (in the world).'" (*al-Nahl* 32); on the other hand, Allah states two verses later about those who performed evil deeds,

فَأَصَابَهُمْ سَيِّـَٔاتُ مَا عَمِلُوا۟ وَحَاقَ بِهِم مَّا كَانُوا۟ بِهِۦ يَسْتَهْزِءُونَ

"But the evil results of their deeds overtook them, and that very (wrath) at which they had scoffed hemmed them in" (*al-Nahl* 34).

This does not mean to imply that it is by deeds alone that one is entered into Paradise. Indeed, the greatest deeds that one can perform are not such that they would deserve Paradise in return. However, via the performance of good deeds, Allah showers the person with His grace and mercy. It is this grace and mercy that allows the person to be entered into Paradise. If a person does not have faith followed up with righteous deeds, he is not deserving of Allah's mercy and, hence, he will not receive this great reward from Allah. This is the meaning of the Prophet's words,

لَنْ يُدْخِلَ أَحَدًا عَمَلُهُ الْجَنَّةَ قَالُوا وَلا أَنْتَ يَا رَسُولَ اللَّهِ قَالَ لا وَلا أَنَا إِلاَّ أَنْ يَتَغَمَّدَنِي اللَّهُ بِفَضْلٍ وَرَحْمَةٍ

"One's deeds will not enter anyone into Paradise." They said, "Not even you, O Messenger of Allah?" he replied, "No, not even me unless Allah covers me with His grace and mercy." (Recorded by al-Bukhari with this wording.)

Finally, as if addressed to all who claim to be on the path of purification, Allah gives a very clear command and directive:

فَمَن كَانَ يَرْجُوا۟ لِقَآءَ رَبِّهِۦ فَلْيَعْمَلْ عَمَلًا صَـٰلِحًا وَلَا يُشْرِكْ بِعِبَادَةِ رَبِّهِۦٓ أَحَدًۢا

"Whoever hopes to meet his Lord, let him work righteousness, and, in the worship of his Lord, admit no one as partner" (*al-Kahf* 110).

The importance of righteous deeds, first and foremost the obligatory deeds among them, is also highlighted in a very important and well-known hadith *qudsi*. In fact, in this hadith *qudsi*, Allah has succinctly described the path of purification of the "servant of Allah," that is, the person who is already a believer. The hadith from *al-Bukhari* states:

قَالَ رَسُولُ اللَّهِ صَلَّى اللَّهم عَلَيْهِ وَسَلَّمَ إِنَّ اللَّهَ قَالَ مَنْ عَادَى لِي وَلِيًّا فَقَدْ آذَنْتُهُ بِالْحَرْبِ وَمَا تَقَرَّبَ إِلَيَّ عَبْدِي بِشَيْءٍ أَحَبَّ إِلَيَّ مِمَّا افْتَرَضْتُ عَلَيْهِ وَمَا يَزَالُ عَبْدِي يَتَقَرَّبُ إِلَيَّ بِالنَّوَافِلِ حَتَّى أُحِبَّهُ فَإِذَا أَحْبَبْتُهُ كُنْتُ سَمْعَهُ الَّذِي يَسْمَعُ بِهِ وَبَصَرَهُ الَّذِي يُبْصِرُ بِهِ وَيَدَهُ الَّتِي يَبْطِشُ بِهَا وَرِجْلَهُ الَّتِي يَمْشِي بِهَا وَإِنْ سَأَلَنِي لَأُعْطِيَنَّهُ وَلَئِنِ اسْتَعَاذَنِي لَأُعِيذَنَّهُ

"Allah the Almighty has said, 'For whoever has mutual animosity with a friend (*wali*) of Mine, I declare war upon him. My servant does not draw near to Me with anything more beloved to Me than the religious duties that I have imposed upon him; and My servant continues to draw near to Me with supererogatory works such that I love him. And when I love him, I am his hearing with which he hears, his seeing with which he sees, his hand with which he strikes, and his leg with which he walks. Were he to ask of Me, I would surely give him; and were he to ask Me for refuge, I would surely grant him it.'" (Recorded by al-Bukhari.)

In a verse quoted earlier, Allah says,

قَدْ أَفْلَحَ مَن زَكَّىٰهَا ﴿٩﴾ وَقَدْ خَابَ مَن دَسَّىٰهَا

"Truly he succeeds who purifies it, and he fails who corrupts it" (*al-Shams* 9-10). According to early scholars of the Quran such as Sufyaan ibn Uyainah, Qataadah and others, the meaning of this verse is, "Successful is the one who purifies his soul by obeying Allah and performing righteous deeds."[1]

Allah has also said,

[1] Quoted in ibn Taimiyyah, *Tazkiyah*, pp. 37-38.

وَءَاخَرُونَ ٱعْتَرَفُوا۟ بِذُنُوبِهِمْ خَلَطُوا۟ عَمَلًا صَٰلِحًا وَءَاخَرَ سَيِّئًا عَسَى ٱللَّهُ أَن يَتُوبَ عَلَيْهِمْ ۚ إِنَّ ٱللَّهَ غَفُورٌ رَّحِيمٌ ﴿١٠٢﴾ خُذْ مِنْ أَمْوَٰلِهِمْ صَدَقَةً تُطَهِّرُهُمْ وَتُزَكِّيهِم بِهَا

"Others (there are who) have acknowledged their wrong doings: they have mixed an act that was good with another that was evil. Perhaps Allah will turn unto them (in mercy): for Allah is Oft-Forgiving, Most Merciful. Of their goods take alms, that so you may purify and sanctify them by it" (*al-Taubah* 102-part of103). This passage is referring to the obligatory zakat. Ibn Taimiyyah states that this passage is a proof that the good deeds are a means and step in the cleansing and purification of the soul from previous sins.[1]

Hence, the second obligatory step in purifying the soul and becoming beloved to Allah is the performance of the deeds that Allah has made obligatory upon the believers. (This goes hand in hand with the increase in *imaan* and *tauheed* and there is a very important dynamic relationship between the two that is difficult sometimes to fathom but which is very clear to the person who experiences it.) Again, this point is made very clearly in the *qudsi* hadith just quoted above. In that hadith, Allah has said,

وَمَا تَقَرَّبَ إِلَيَّ عَبْدِي بِشَيْءٍ أَحَبَّ إِلَيَّ مِمَّا افْتَرَضْتُ عَلَيْهِ

"My servant does not draw near to Me with anything more loved by Me than the religious duties I have imposed upon him."

After mentioning that no one should oppose the devoted servants of Allah, Allah then gives a description of those devoted servants or *auliyaa*. The root of the word *al-mawaala* (from which the word *auliyaa* is derived) is "to come closer".[2] Therefore, the true "devoted servants" or *auliyaa* of Allah are those who work to get closer to Allah by performing the deeds that take them closer

---

[1] Ibn Taimiyyah, *Tazkiyah*, p. 52.
[2] While the opposite of that, *al-muaadat*, means to "go farther away".

to Him, thereby purifying their own souls. The true enemies of Allah are those who go farther away from Allah by performing those deeds that take them farther away from Him, thereby debasing their own souls.

It is clear from this hadith that those who claim to love Allah and claim to get closer to Allah but at the same time do not follow the commands of Allah as stated by His Messenger are actually lying—either to themselves out of ignorance or knowingly to everyone. This was the case with the polytheists who claimed to be getting closer to Allah by worshipping the intercessors that they invented. Allah says,

أَلَا لِلَّهِ ٱلدِّينُ ٱلْخَالِصُ ۚ وَٱلَّذِينَ ٱتَّخَذُوا۟ مِن دُونِهِۦٓ أَوْلِيَآءَ مَا نَعْبُدُهُمْ إِلَّا لِيُقَرِّبُونَآ إِلَى ٱللَّهِ زُلْفَىٰٓ إِنَّ ٱللَّهَ يَحْكُمُ بَيْنَهُمْ فِى مَا هُمْ فِيهِ يَخْتَلِفُونَ ۗ إِنَّ ٱللَّهَ لَا يَهْدِى مَنْ هُوَ كَـٰذِبٌ كَفَّارٌ

"Surely pure religion is for Allah only. And those who choose protecting friends beside Him (say): We worship them only that they may bring us near unto Allah. Lo, Allah will judge between them concerning that wherein they differ. Lo, Allah guides not him who is a liar, an ingrate" (*al-Zumar* 3).

Note that the stress here has been on the obligatory deeds. This is due to their extreme importance. Indeed, everyone should dedicate himself to performing those deeds first. In other words, one has to tend to the obligatory deeds before preoccupying oneself with voluntary deeds. As al-Toofi stated,

> The order to perform the obligatory duties is a strict one. The one who does not perform them falls into punishment. On both of these matters, the case of the voluntary deeds is different. They are similar to the obligatory deeds in that in both of them one earns a reward. However, the obligatory deeds are more complete. For that reason, they are more beloved to Allah and take one closer to Him. The obligatory deeds are like the foundation while the voluntary deeds are like the branches and the building. If a person fulfills

> the obligatory deeds in the way that they are commanded to be fulfilled, with proper respect and esteem by submitting to Him and demonstrating the greatness of His Lordship and submission of His worship, one gets closer to Him in the greatest way.[1]

The obligatory deeds are like the foundation or roots while the voluntary deeds are like the branches. If a person first fulfills those foundations, he is demonstrating his foundation of being willing to submit to Allah. Hence, that is the best way that he earns his Lord's approval.[2] However, if one does not first fulfill those deeds that Allah has made obligatory, one does not demonstrate his willingness to submit and obey whatever Allah has ordered. In other words, he fails to fulfill one of the greatest steps in the process of purification. Therefore, the first step must be the fulfillment of the obligatory duties.

The Importance of Obligatory Deeds

The *qudsi* hadith quoted above makes it clear that the most important deeds that a person can perform to take himself closer to Allah are the deeds that Allah Himself has made obligatory upon His servants. The true believer gets closer and closest to Allah by fulfilling the obligatory duties. Again, Allah said, as just quoted,

وَمَا تَقَرَّبَ إِلَيَّ عَبْدِي بِشَيْءٍ أَحَبَّ إِلَيَّ مِمَّا افْتَرَضْتُ عَلَيْهِ

"My servant does not draw near to Me with anything more loved by Me than the religious duties I have imposed upon him." Allah is the One who determined that His slaves must perform these deeds. The determination of these deeds is His right and His right

---

[1] Quoted in Ahmad Fareed, *Al-Tazkiyah baina Ahl al-Sunnah wa al-Soofiyah* (no publication information given), p. 22.

[2] Cf., Ahmad ibn Hajar, *Fath al-Baari bi-Sharh Saheeh al-Bukhaari* (Makkah: al-Maktaba al-Tijaariyyah, 1993), vol. 13, p. 145.

alone. In addition, He has also made it clear that He is most pleased by those obligatory deeds.[1]

The obligatory deeds may be divided into the following four categories:

(1) The obligatory deeds (feelings and emotions) of the heart:

The obligatory deeds first and foremost include the obligatory deeds of the heart. These are the most important of all obligations and they draw one closest to Allah. The actions of the heart are obligatory under all circumstances.[2] These include having a pure intention, being sincere in one's faith, having love for Allah and His Messenger (peace and blessings of Allah be upon him), putting one's trust and reliance in Allah, having fear of Allah and so forth. In addition, like the avoidance of forbidden deeds discussed below, fulfilling what is obligatory with respect to the heart also includes freeing the heart of such evils and sins as pride, arrogance, envy, unjustified hatred, greed and so forth.

The aspects of the heart need to be concentrated upon and reformed to the best of one's ability. This is because the rest of one's acts actually follow what flows or is directed from the

---

[1] The obligatory deeds referred to here, according to ibn Hajar, include both the deeds that are obligatory on the individuals as well as those deeds that are obligatory on the community as a whole. Ibn Hajar, *Fath* (al-Maktaba al-Tijaariyyah), vol. 13, p. 145.

[2] Sometimes the physical obligations are dropped due to certain circumstances while the obligations of the heart are still obligatory. For example, Allah says in the Quran, "[For not participating in the jihad] there is no blame on those who are infirm, or ill, or who find no resources to spend (on the cause), if they are sincere (in duty) to Allah and His Messenger: no ground (of complaint) can there be against such as do right: and Allah is Oft-Forgiving, Most Merciful" (*al-Taubah* 91). Such people can be excused from taking part in the jihad but they can never be excused from being sincere to Allah, which is an essential deed of the heart. Ibn Taimiyyah noted, "According to the agreement of the people of faith, all of these deeds of the heart are obligations upon each individual. Whoever leaves them is either a disbeliever or a hypocrite. However, people differ [in their level of fulfillment of these deeds] like they differ with respect to the outward acts..." (Quoted in al-Abdul Lateef, p. 68.) Ibn al-Qayyim stated, "The actions of the heart are more of an obligation upon the individual than the actions of the body. The servitude of the heart [to Allah] is greater, more and longer lasting than the servitude of the physical body. In fact, it is obligatory under all circumstances." Quoted from al-Abdul Lateef, p. 69.

heart.[1] The Messenger of Allah (peace and blessings of Allah be upon him) said,

أَلا وَإِنَّ فِي الْجَسَدِ مُضْغَةً إِذَا صَلَحَتْ صَلَحَ الْجَسَدُ كُلُّهُ وَإِذَا فَسَدَتْ فَسَدَ الْجَسَدُ كُلُّهُ أَلا وَهِيَ الْقَلْبُ

"In the body there is certainly a morsel of flesh which, if it be sound, all the body is sound and which, if it be spoiled, all of the body is spoiled. This part of the body is the heart." (Recorded by al-Bukhari and Muslim.) Furthermore, no matter how excellent one's outward deeds may seemingly appear, if they are not driven and backed by the proper deeds of the heart, those outward deeds will be meaningless and fruitless. A person could fast every day and pray all night long but if his heart is not filled with belief in Allah, purity towards Him, love for Him and fear of Him, those supposed acts of worship will have no weight on the Day of Judgment.[2]

Therefore, a number of these types of "deeds" of the heart are discussed below. It is important to note that these actions are also goals in themselves, being great acts of worship in themselves as well as means to further one's purification of the soul. Furthermore, it is when these acts are "perfected" or completed that one in fact purifies his soul. This, though, does not mean that a circular argument is being presented here (that is, one purifies one's heart by purifying one's heart). Instead, there are different degrees or levels of excellence with respect to all of these deeds. In general, for all of these deeds, there is a minimum level without which one cannot truly be considered a believer. For many of these deeds, there is a great distance between the minimum level and the level one reaches when one's soul is truly or greatly purified. Hence, the one who wishes to truly purify his soul must continually work on these aspects of the heart to further improve himself and bring himself even closer to Allah.

---

[1] Because the feelings and beliefs in the heart are the driving force behind all of one's deeds, ibn al-Qayyim considers the purification of the heart and its deeds as the real goal. The actions of the body are simply complementary and a necessary consequence of the purification of the heart. Cf., Ibn al-Qayyim, *Madaarij*, vol. 1, p. 101.

[2] Cf., Ali Ahmad Uthmaan, *Tazkiyah al-Nafs wa Makaanatuhaa fi al-Islaam* (1416 A.H.), p. 6.

(2) The ritual pillars of Islam:

The second category of obligatory deeds is made up of the ritual pillars of Islam. This is a reference to the daily prayers, zakat, fasting Ramadhaan and the pilgrimage. These acts of worship play a vital role in purifying and reforming the soul. Hence, they or their equivalents can be found in the messages of all of the previous prophets as well. Due to their extreme importance, they shall be discussed separately below. They shall also be discussed in detail below because many do not seem to appreciate or understand the great ramifications of these essential deeds for the purification of the soul. Because these pillars are underestimated, not applied properly or not understood well, people turn to other deeds, such as heretical forms of remembrance of Allah, as ways of purifying their souls. The results of that incorrect approach are grave. Once again, there are no deeds that can take a person closer to Allah that are more important or more beneficial than the deeds that Allah Himself has obligated upon His servants.

(3) The other obligatory acts:

There are many obligatory acts in Islam, such as fulfilling one's trust, being dutiful to one's parents, observing the rights of neighbors and others in society, taking part in the obligatory jihad and so forth. These various acts span virtually every aspect of a person's life. One should keep in mind that even those acts that seem "minor" and very simple can also be a great source of purification of the soul since they are acts in obedience to the commands of Allah. Note, for example, what Allah states in the following verse about not entering houses until one has received permission to do so,

وَإِن قِيلَ لَكُمُ ٱرْجِعُوا۟ فَٱرْجِعُوا۟ ۖ هُوَ أَزْكَىٰ لَكُمْ ۚ

"If you are asked to go back, go back: that makes for greater purity for yourselves" (*al-Noor* 28).[1]

---

[1] Cf., al-Maaz, p. 118.

(4) Abstaining from the forbidden acts:

Avoiding the forbidden deeds is a type of obligation from Allah, a type of "negative command".[1] Avoiding such acts should go hand in hand with the performance of the obligatory duties and the purification of the soul.[2]

The effect of repeated sinful acts can be seen in the following hadith. The Messenger of Allah (peace and blessings of Allah be upon him) said,

إِنَّ الْعَبْدَ إِذَا أَخْطَأَ خَطِيئَةً نُكِتَتْ فِي قَلْبِهِ نُكْتَةٌ سَوْدَاءُ فَإِذَا هُوَ نَزَعَ وَاسْتَغْفَرَ وَتَابَ صُقِلَ قَلْبُهُ وَإِنْ عَادَ زِيدَ فِيهَا حَتَّى تَعْلُوَ قَلْبَهُ وَهُوَ الرَّانُ الَّذِي ذَكَرَ اللَّهُ (كَلَّا بَلْ رَانَ عَلَى قُلُوبِهِمْ مَا كَانُوا يَكْسِبُونَ)

"When the human commits a sin, in his heart is written a black mark. When he leaves [that sin], seeks forgiveness and repents, his heart is polished [and cleaned]. If he returns to it, [the black mark] increases in it [the heart] until it dominates his heart. That is the stain which Allah has mentioned [in the verse,] 'By no means! But on their hearts is the stain of the (ill) which they do' [*al-Mutaffifeen* 14].'"[3]

Umar ibn al-Khattaab said, "The most virtuous deed is to perform the deeds Allah has made obligatory and remain away from what Allah has forbidden accompanied with a pure intention in Allah's sight."[4] Umar ibn Abdul Azeez also said, "The best act of worship is the fulfilling of what is obligatory and the abstaining from what is forbidden."[5] Ibn Taimiyyah wrote,

---

[1] The prohibition of adultery, for example, is actually an *obligation* to avoid adultery.

[2] In fact, some scholars argue that avoiding the forbidden can even take precedence over fulfilling the obligatory. This view is based on the following hadith that leaves no room for ever indulging in what is forbidden while accepting that one may not fulfill all that is required. The Messenger of Allah (peace and blessings of Allah be upon him) said, "What I have forbidden you, stay away from. What I have ordered you [to do], do as much of it as you can." (Recorded by al-Bukhari and Muslim.) Cf., Zarabozo, *Commentary on the Forty Hadith*, vol. 1, p. 526.

[3] Recorded by Ahmad, al-Tirmidh, al-Nasaa'ee and others. According to al-Albaani, it is *hasan*. See al-Albaani, *Saheeh al-Jaami*, vol. 1, pp. 342-343.

[4] Quoted in Abdul Rahmaan ibn Rajab, *Jaami al-Uloom wa al-Hikm* (Beirut: Muassasat al-Risaalah, 1991), vol. 2, p. 336.

[5] Quoted in ibn Rajab, *Jaami*, vol. 2, p. 336.

> Goodness cannot grow and develop unless one leaves evil, in the same way that a plant cannot develop unless the area around it is thatched. The soul and the deeds are not purified until what negates that is removed. A person cannot be purified unless he abandons what is evil. The soul that does not abandon evil cannot be purified at all for evil pollutes and soils the soul. Ibn Qutaibah said that *dassaaha* ("pollutes it"[1]) means that he has concealed it by [covering it with] lewdness and sins. The immoral person soils his soul; that is, he represses it and hides [what is good in it]. The doer of good, on the other hand, brings out his soul and elevates it. The generous of the Arabs would camp at the higher locations so that they could be seen and noticed while the thieves would stay at the lower portions and valleys.[2]

Avoiding the forbidden deeds is of vital importance in purifying the soul as it is those types of deeds that fill the heart and soul with filth and pollution, while the good deeds fill the heart with goodness and purity. In numerous places, Allah indicates that by avoiding the forbidden, one is avoiding what will soil one's heart and hurt it in its process of purification. For example, Allah says,

قُل لِّلْمُؤْمِنِينَ يَغُضُّوا۟ مِنْ أَبْصَـٰرِهِمْ وَيَحْفَظُوا۟ فُرُوجَهُمْ ۚ ذَٰلِكَ أَزْكَىٰ لَهُمْ ۗ إِنَّ ٱللَّهَ خَبِيرٌۢ بِمَا يَصْنَعُونَ

"Say to the believing men that they should lower their gaze and guard their modesty: that will make for greater purity for them: and Allah is well acquainted with all that they do" (*al-Noor* 30). In fact, after mentioning the great sins of illegal sexual intercourse, slander and marrying a fornicator, Allah states,

---

[1] This is in reference to the verse of the Quran, "And he fails who defiles it (*dassaaha*)" (*al-Shams* 10).

[2] Ibn Taimiyyah, *Tazkiyah*, p. 43-4.

يَٰٓأَيُّهَا ٱلَّذِينَ ءَامَنُواْ لَا تَتَّبِعُواْ خُطُوَٰتِ ٱلشَّيۡطَٰنِۚ وَمَن يَتَّبِعۡ خُطُوَٰتِ
ٱلشَّيۡطَٰنِ فَإِنَّهُۥ يَأۡمُرُ بِٱلۡفَحۡشَآءِ وَٱلۡمُنكَرِۚ وَلَوۡلَا فَضۡلُ ٱللَّهِ
عَلَيۡكُمۡ وَرَحۡمَتُهُۥ مَا زَكَىٰ مِنكُم مِّنۡ أَحَدٍ أَبَدٗا وَلَٰكِنَّ ٱللَّهَ يُزَكِّي
مَن يَشَآءُۗ وَٱللَّهُ سَمِيعٌ عَلِيمٞ

"O you who believe! Follow not Satan's footsteps. If any will follow the footsteps of Satan, he will (but) command what is shameful and wrong. And were it not for the grace and mercy of Allah on you, not one of you would ever have been purified. But Allah does purify whom He pleases. Allah is One Who hears and knows (all things)" (*al-Noor* 21). Ibn al-Qayyim states that Allah's placing of these words after discussing those sins indicates that the process of purification involves remaining away from sinful acts such as those.[1]

In particular, when it comes to avoiding sins, one must pay special attention to avoiding the major sins (*al-kabaair*). Avoiding such sins is one of the keys to being forgiven—and hence purified—from the other lesser sins that one has committed. Allah says,

إِن تَجۡتَنِبُواْ كَبَآئِرَ مَا تُنۡهَوۡنَ عَنۡهُ نُكَفِّرۡ عَنكُمۡ سَيِّـَٔاتِكُمۡ
وَنُدۡخِلۡكُم مُّدۡخَلٗا كَرِيمٗا

"If you avoid the great sins that you have been forbidden, we shall remit your [small] sins for you and we shall enter you through a noble entrance" (*al-Nisaa* 31). Similarly, Allah says,

---

[1] Ibn al-Qayyim, *Ighaathah al-Luhfaan*, vol. 1, p. 55.

ٱلَّذِينَ يَجْتَنِبُونَ كَبَٰٓئِرَ ٱلْإِثْمِ وَٱلْفَوَٰحِشَ إِلَّا ٱللَّمَمَ ۚ إِنَّ رَبَّكَ وَٰسِعُ ٱلْمَغْفِرَةِ ۚ هُوَ أَعْلَمُ بِكُمْ إِذْ أَنشَأَكُم مِّنَ ٱلْأَرْضِ وَإِذْ أَنتُمْ أَجِنَّةٌ فِى بُطُونِ أُمَّهَٰتِكُمْ ۖ فَلَا تُزَكُّوٓا۟ أَنفُسَكُمْ ۖ هُوَ أَعْلَمُ بِمَنِ ٱتَّقَىٰٓ

"Those who avoid great sins and shameful deeds, only (falling into) small faults; verily your Lord is ample in forgiveness. He knows you well when He brings you out of the earth, and when you are hidden in your mothers' wombs. Therefore justify not yourselves: He knows best who it is that guards against evil" (*al-Najm* 32).

A Brief Review of Some Obligatory Deeds and Their Role in the Purification of the Soul

Some people do not seem to understand that Allah obligated specific deeds as a mercy to the believers. By performing the obligatory deeds the person actually comes closer to Allah and becomes a better person. In order to elaborate this aspect further (while still attempting to be brief), some of the deeds of the heart and some of the obligatory deeds shall be highlighted below with an emphasis on their effects on the purification of the soul. The pillars of Islam are discussed below since they form the very foundation of the entire edifice of Islam and the groundwork for the entire system of the purification of the soul. In fact, the Messenger of Allah (peace and blessings of Allah be upon him) said,

بُنِيَ الإِسْلامُ عَلَى خَمْسٍ شَهَادَةِ أَنْ لا إِلَهَ إِلا اللَّهُ وَأَنَّ مُحَمَّدًا رَسُولُ اللَّهِ وَإِقَامِ الصَّلاةِ وَإِيتَاءِ الزَّكَاةِ وَالْحَجِّ الْبَيْتِ وَصَوْمِ رَمَضَانَ

"Islam is built upon five [pillars]: testifying that there is none worthy of worship except Allah and that Muhammad is the Messenger of Allah, establishing the prayers, giving the zakat, making the pilgrimage to the House and fasting the month of Ramadhaan." (Recorded by al-Bukhari and Muslim.)

Love for Allah and Its Effect on Purification of the Soul

Love for Allah is one of the most important obligatory acts of the heart. In fact, ibn Taimiyyah stated that proper love of Allah is the fountainhead of every religious deed.[1] Even though love of Allah is of utmost importance, it is not the type of love that allows one to do any act, claiming that love is the only type of relationship that one must have with Allah. Instead, the proper love must be accompanied with hope in Allah and fear of Allah, in accordance with the verse,

أُوْلَـٰٓئِكَ ٱلَّذِينَ يَدْعُونَ يَبْتَغُونَ إِلَىٰ رَبِّهِمُ ٱلْوَسِيلَةَ أَيُّهُمْ أَقْرَبُ وَيَرْجُونَ رَحْمَتَهُۥ وَيَخَافُونَ عَذَابَهُۥٓ ۚ إِنَّ عَذَابَ رَبِّكَ كَانَ مَحْذُورًا

"Those unto whom they cry seek the way of approach to their Lord, which of them shall be the nearest. They hope for His mercy and they fear His doom. Lo, the punishment of your Lord is to be avoided" (*al-Israa* 57).[2]

Furthermore, this love for Allah, the Beloved, must be accompanied by a love for the acts and people beloved to the Beloved. So if any person claims to love Allah and then dislikes any aspect of Allah's, the Beloved's, religion, which He loves for His

---

[1] Ibn Taimiyyah, *Majmu*, vol. 10, p. 49.

[2] The beliefs of the *ahl al-Sunnah wa al-Jamaa* are the balanced and correct beliefs on the question of the constituent parts of true faith. Other groups have stressed one part and neglected others and, therefore, they have strayed. For example, the group known as the Murjia stressed the hope that one must place in Allah; therefore, evil deeds could be performed with little fear of their consequences. The Khawarij stressed the fear of Allah and belittled hope in Him and belief in His mercy; therefore, to them, anyone who performs a great sin is considered an unbeliever and, as a consequence, his life will become full of despair. And the Sufis stress the love of Allah and downplay the deeds of the person; therefore, among them, one can find many people who claim they love Allah while they perform very few of the deeds praised in the Quran or Sunnah.

slaves, that person does not have the true and proper love of Allah. The greatest sign of this proper love for Allah is obedience to His revelations and His Messenger. In fact, Allah says in the Quran,

قُلْ إِن كُنتُمْ تُحِبُّونَ ٱللَّهَ فَٱتَّبِعُونِى يُحْبِبْكُمُ ٱللَّهُ وَيَغْفِرْ لَكُمْ ذُنُوبَكُمْ ۗ وَٱللَّهُ غَفُورٌ رَّحِيمٌ

"Say [O Muhammad]: If you truly love Allah, follow me and Allah will love you and will forgive your sins. And Allah is forgiving, merciful (*ali-Imraan* 31)." Thus obedience to Allah's commands and to His Messenger is a sign of the true love for Allah because anyone who truly loves Allah wants Allah to love him and, according to this verse, this love only comes about through obedience to His Messenger (which implies obedience to His commands).

If the person has the complete love of Allah, he will be completely humble and submissive to Allah and the pleasure of Allah will be his only desire. Ibn Taimiyyah wrote, "A heart is no good, nor does it have prosperity, pleasure, happiness, goodness, tranquility or peace except by worshipping his Lord, loving Him and turning to Him."[1] Hilmi writes, "Here we see how [ibn Taimiyyah] considered love a dynamic force that spurs the believer to do good and attain happiness."[2] Ibn Taimiyyah also noted, "It is known that love stirs the desires of the heart. Whenever love becomes stronger in the heart, the heart seeks to perform the deeds beloved [by the Beloved]."[3] When the believer reaches the highest degree of love, he does not lose his self or not notice anything else in this world as the Sufis claim but he loves what Allah loves and He dislikes what Allah dislikes. And, furthermore, he will also be willing to face hardships to fulfill the commands of the Beloved. This love of Allah not only stirs the believer to act, it also frees the believer. In Ibn Taimiyyah's words, "Freedom is the freedom of the heart. Worship is the worship of the heart in the same way that richness is the richness of the soul."[4]

---

[1] Ibid., vol. 10, p. 194.
[2] Mustafa Hilmi, *Ibn Taimiyyah wa al-Tasawuf* (Alexandria: Dar al-Dawah, n.d.), p. 496.
[3] Ibn Taimiyyah, *Majmu*, vol. 10, p. 192.
[4] Ibid., vol. 10, p. 186. The last clause is a hadith of the Prophet (peace be upon him).

Love of Allah also makes the person want to get even closer to Allah. As has already been pointed out, the way the person does this is by performing voluntary deeds after performing the obligatory deeds, as is clear in the hadith *qudsi* quoted earlier. The reward for this behavior is something that everyone who loves Allah desires more than anything else imaginable. The reward is a special love from Allah, as Allah mentioned in the same hadith,

وَمَا تَقَرَّبَ إِلَيَّ عَبْدِي بِشَيْءٍ أَحَبَّ إِلَيَّ مِمَّا افْتَرَضْتُهُ عَلَيْهِ وَلاَ يَزَالُ عَبْدِي يَتَقَرَّبُ إِلَيَّ بِالنَّوَافِلِ حَتَّى أُحِبَّهُ فَإِذَا أَحْبَبْتُهُ كُنْتُ سَمْعَهُ الَّذِي يَسْمَعُ بِهِ وَبَصَرَهُ الَّذِي يُبْصِرُ بِهِ وَيَدَهُ الَّتِي يَبْطِشُ بِهَا وَرِجْلَهُ الَّتِي يَمْشِي بِهَا وَلَئِنْ سَأَلَنِي لَأُعْطِيَنَّهُ وَلَئِنِ اسْتَعَاذَنِي لَأُعِيذَنَّهُ

"My servant does not draw near to Me with anything more beloved to Me than the religious duties that I have imposed upon him; and My servant continues to draw near to Me with supererogatory works such that I love him. And when I love him, I am his hearing with which he hears, his seeing with which he sees, his hand with which he strikes, and his leg with which he walks. Were he to ask of Me, I would surely give him; and were he to ask Me for refuge, I would surely grant him it." (Recorded by al-Bukhari.)

This love of Allah does not just bring about pleasure and paradise in the Hereafter, but also in this life; as the person increases his faith, he tastes the sweetness of that faith which is a pleasure in this life that corresponds to the pleasure he will receive in the next.[1] Ibn Taimiyyah once stated, "There is a paradise in this life and the one who does not enter it will not enter the paradise in the next life."[2]

---

[1] Hilmi, p. 197.

[2] Quoted by his student ibn al-Qayyim, *Mudaraj al-Salikeen* (Beirut: Dar al-Kitab al-Arabi, 1973), vol. 1, p. 454.

Patience and Contentment

Two more important actions of the heart are *sabr* (patience) and *ridha* (contentment). According to the Sunni scholars, the concepts of *sabr* and *ridha* should play important roles in the life of the believer. *Sabr* includes keeping one's soul and body attached to performing the obligatory duties and away from the forbidden acts. Beyond that, *ridha* also includes being "pleased" with whatever happens, in the sense that the person knows that whatever occurs in this world is from Allah who rules this world in His infinite wisdom and mercy and that the real goal is not the material possessions of this life but the pleasure of Allah in the Hereafter. In this context, Ali ibn Abu Talib said, "Verily patience is to faith as the head is to the body. If the head is cut off, the body dies." Then he raised his voice and said, "Verily there is no faith for the one who has no patience."[1]

Allah says in the Quran,

وَلَوْ أَنَّهُمْ رَضُوا۟ مَآ ءَاتَىٰهُمُ ٱللَّهُ وَرَسُولُهُۥ وَقَالُوا۟ حَسْبُنَا ٱللَّهُ سَيُؤْتِينَا

ٱللَّهُ مِن فَضْلِهِۦ وَرَسُولُهُۥٓ إِنَّآ إِلَى ٱللَّهِ رَٰغِبُونَ

"(How much more seemly) had they been content with that which Allah and His Messenger had given them and had said: Allah suffices us. Allah will give us of His bounty, and (also) His Messenger. Unto Allah we are suppliants" (*al-Taubah* 59). Ibn Taimiyyah explains this verse by saying that it contains a command to have both *tawakkul* (complete trust and reliance in God) and *ridha*. That is, one must have *tawakkul* before something occurs and then *ridha* after it occurs.

According to ibn Taimiyyah, restraining oneself from sins is a greater test than restraining oneself or being patient during troubled times. For example, ibn Taimiyyah argues that it was much more difficult for Yusuf to be patient when the wife of the Azeez tempted him than it was for him to be patient when his brothers put him in the well. In the latter case, things were out of his hands and he could not do much except accept what was happening to

---

[1] Ibn Taimiyyah, *Majmu*, vol. 10, p. 28.

him but in the other case he had to make the rational choice not to commit a sin with the wife of the Azeez. Ibn Taimiyyah also says that refraining from sins is even a greater type of patience than persevering in performing good deeds. On this point, he quoted an early Sufi, Sahl al-Tustari, who said, "The good deeds are performed by both the pious and the wicked but only the sincere restrain from sins."[1]

The Establishment of the Prayer (*Salaat*) and Its Effect on the Purification of the Soul

The establishment of the prayers is essential for the purification of the soul.[2] Allah says,

قَدْ أَفْلَحَ مَن تَزَكَّىٰ ﴿١٤﴾ وَذَكَرَ ٱسْمَ رَبِّهِۦ فَصَلَّىٰ

"But those will prosper who purify themselves, and remember the name of their Guardian-Lord, and pray" (*al-Ala* 14-15). Al-Raazi notes that the first step on the path of purification is the eradication of false beliefs from one's heart that is followed by knowing and having the correct beliefs about Allah, thus remembering and mentioning Allah properly. This is to be followed by then submitting to and worshipping Allah properly, which is first and foremost found in the prayer.[3] Ibn Abbaas has explained these two verses to mean that one frees oneself from *shirk* (associating partners with Allah), takes God to be only one and one alone and then prays to God alone.[4]

Allah also says,

---

[1] Quoted by Hilmi, p. 503.

[2] Note that in Islam, it is not simply a question of "praying." Instead, it is a matter of "establishing the prayer" (*iqaamat al-salaat*), which includes performing the prayer according to all of the rules and regulations stated in the Shareeah. This author has discussed this point in more detail in *Commentary*, vol. 1, pp. 355-359.

[3] Cf., al-Raazi, vol. 31, pp. 146-147.

[4] Al-Tabari, vol. 15, p. 156 (combining the two comments from ibn Abbaas).

إِنَّمَا تُنذِرُ ٱلَّذِينَ يَخْشَوْنَ رَبَّهُم بِٱلْغَيْبِ وَأَقَامُوا۟ ٱلصَّلَوٰةَ ۚ وَمَن تَزَكَّىٰ فَإِنَّمَا يَتَزَكَّىٰ لِنَفْسِهِۦ ۚ وَإِلَى ٱللَّهِ ٱلْمَصِيرُ

"You can only admonish such as fear their Lord unseen and establish regular prayer. And whoever purifies himself does so for the benefit of his own soul; and the destination (of all) is to Allah" (*Faatir* 18).

A cursory reading of the Quran will demonstrate that all of the previous prophets were also commanded to perform the prayers.[1] Indeed, the prayers are so essential to a person's faith that they are similar to the role of one's beliefs and creed. The Prophet (peace and blessings of Allah be upon him) stated,

إِنَّ بَيْنَ الرَّجُلِ وَبَيْنَ الشِّرْكِ وَالْكُفْرِ تَرْكَ الصَّلاةِ

"Between a person and idolatry and disbelief is the leaving of the prayer." (Recorded by Muslim.) In fact, the believer is identified and characterized by his devotion and attentiveness to the prayer. Note the following verses from the Quran describing the true believers:

وَٱلَّذِينَ يُؤْمِنُونَ بِٱلْءَاخِرَةِ يُؤْمِنُونَ بِهِۦ ۖ وَهُمْ عَلَىٰ صَلَاتِهِمْ يُحَافِظُونَ

"Those who believe in the Hereafter, believe in this (Book), and they are constant in guarding their prayers" (*al-Anaam* 92). In *soorah al-Maarij,* Allah describes those who are of balanced behavior and in particular states those who pray and,

ٱلَّذِينَ هُمْ عَلَىٰ صَلَاتِهِمْ دَآئِمُونَ

"Those who remain steadfast in their prayers" (*al-Maarij* 23).

In the beginning of *soorah al-Muminoon* Allah lists a number of characteristics of the true believers. In that short

[1] Cf., Sulaiman Nadwi, pp. 50-56. Sulaiman Nadwi also quotes from the existing books of the Jews and Christians to show that the movements in the prayers were, in general, common among the different prophets.

passage, two of the verses are directly related to the believers and their prayers. In the second verse, Allah states,

ٱلَّذِينَ هُمْ فِى صَلَاتِهِمْ خَـٰشِعُونَ

"They who are humbly submissive in their prayers" (*al-Muminoon* 2). Just a handful of verses later, Allah again describes the true believers with,

وَٱلَّذِينَ هُمْ عَلَىٰ صَلَوَٰتِهِمْ يُحَافِظُونَ

"And who (strictly) guard their prayers" (*al-Muminoon* 9).

The Prophet (peace and blessings of Allah be upon him) has also described the prayer in its proper time as being the best deed. Al-Bukhari and Muslim record from Abdullah ibn Masood,

قَالَ سَأَلْتُ النَّبِيَّ صَلَّى اللهم عَلَيْهِ وَسَلَّمَ أَيُّ الْعَمَلِ أَحَبُّ إِلَى اللَّهِ قَالَ الصَّلاَةُ عَلَى وَقْتِهَا قَالَ ثُمَّ أَيٌّ قَالَ ثُمَّ بِرُّ الْوَالِدَيْنِ قَالَ ثُمَّ أَيٌّ قَالَ الْجِهَادُ فِي سَبِيلِ اللَّهِ قَالَ حَدَّثَنِي بِهِنَّ وَلَوِ اسْتَزَدْتُهُ لَزَادَنِي

"I asked the Prophet (peace and blessings of Allah be upon him), 'Which deed is most beloved to Allah?' He replied, 'The prayer in its proper time.' Then I asked him which [deed was next]. He said, 'Being righteous towards one parents.' Then I asked him which and he said, 'Jihad for the sake of Allah.' He told me about them and if I had asked him for more, he would have given me more."

Its importance and central role can also be noted in the fact that under no circumstances—except for loss of consciousness—is one excused from performing the prayer in its proper time, even if one can only perform it sitting or by motioning with one's hands and so forth.

Sulaiman Nadwi has given the following comprehensive definition and description of the prayers,

> What is *Salat* (Prayer)? It is the expression of devotedness by the created to his Creator with his whole being, i.e., heart, tongue, feet and hands; it is the remembrance of the Most Merciful and the Most

> Gracious; it is the thanksgiving for His limitless favours; it is the praise and adoration for the eternal beauty of His creation and acknowledgement of His Unity and Greatness; it is the communication of soul with the Beloved Lord; it is the complete obeisance by body and soul to the Master; it is the dedication of one's internal feelings; it is the natural music of one's heart-string; it is the tie of relationship between the Creator and the created and the latter's strong bond of devoutness; it is the comfort for the agitated and uneasy mind; it is the solace for the restless soul; it is the remedy for the hopeless heart; it is the natural internal call of a receptive and sensitive mind; it is the purpose of life and the essence of existence.[1]

The importance of the prayers for the purification of the soul is captured in the following important benefits of the prayers:

(1) The prayer is a source of strength for the believers, as they turn towards the one and only true source of strength in the entire creation. The prayer thereby purifies the soul of many diseases, such as despair and cowardice. This powerful effect of the prayer is alluded to in the verse,

وَٱسْتَعِينُواْ بِٱلصَّبْرِ وَٱلصَّلَوٰةِ ۚ وَإِنَّهَا لَكَبِيرَةٌ إِلَّا عَلَى ٱلْخَـٰشِعِينَ

"Nay, seek (Allah's) help with patient perseverance and prayer: it is indeed hard, except to those who bring a lowly spirit" (*al-Baqarah* 45). In fact, Allah has stated the first portion twice in the Quran, as He has also said,

يَـٰٓأَيُّهَا ٱلَّذِينَ ءَامَنُواْ ٱسْتَعِينُواْ بِٱلصَّبْرِ وَٱلصَّلَوٰةِ ۚ إِنَّ ٱللَّهَ مَعَ

ٱلصَّـٰبِرِينَ

---

[1] Sulaiman Nadwi, pp. 49-50. Although some comments could be made about this passage (for example, the prayer is the comfort for the soul even when the soul is not agitated or uneasy), as a whole, it is a very moving and concise depiction of what occurs in the prayer.

"O you who believe, seek (Allah's) help with patient perseverance and prayer. Certainly, Allah is with those who are patient" (*al-Baqarah* 153).

(2) Besides being a source of strength, the prayer is also a joyous occasion and a chance for the soul to rest as it journeys in this world. It is a time for the soul and mind to completely and absolutely concentrate on the one matter that it knows is the only matter of extreme importance: its relationship with and proper worship of Allah. The soul realizes that in the act of prayer (when performed properly), the person is doing nothing other than getting closer to Allah and partially fulfilling the only purpose for which he was created. Hence, the Prophet (peace and blessings of Allah be upon him) used to tell Bilaal,

يَا بِلاَلُ أَقِمِ الصَّلاَةَ أَرِحْنَا بِهَا

"O Bilaal, make the announcement for the prayer and give us rest by it."[1]

(3) When the prayers are performed in their proper manner and in their respective times, the effects on the person's character and behavior are indeed great, freeing him of many of the diseases of the soul. Allah points out this fact in the following verses,

إِنَّ ٱلْإِنسَٰنَ خُلِقَ هَلُوعًا ۝١٩ إِذَا مَسَّهُ ٱلشَّرُّ جَزُوعًا ۝٢٠ وَإِذَا مَسَّهُ ٱلْخَيْرُ مَنُوعًا ۝٢١ إِلَّا ٱلْمُصَلِّينَ ۝٢٢ ٱلَّذِينَ هُمْ عَلَىٰ صَلَاتِهِمْ دَآئِمُونَ

"Truly man was created very impatient; fretful when evil touches him; and niggardly when good reaches him. Not so those devoted to prayer, those who remain steadfast to their prayer" (*al-Maarij* 19-23).

(4) In another verse, Allah also shows that the prayers should have an obvious and clear effect in keeping the person

---

[1] Recorded by Ahmad and Abu Dawood. According to al-Albaani, it is *sahih*. See al-Albaani, *Saheeh al-Jaami*, vol. 2, p. 1307.

from sinning and defiling his soul with impious deeds, those deeds that bring filth to the soul. Allah says,

إِنَّ ٱلصَّلَوٰةَ تَنْهَىٰ عَنِ ٱلْفَحْشَآءِ وَٱلْمُنكَرِ

"Verily the prayers restrain one from immorality and wrongdoing" (*al-Ankaboot* 45).

(5) When the person does slip and commits acts of filth and sin, the prayer can also purify the soul from those sins. In other words, it has a cleansing effect on the soul. Everyone is bound to make mistakes and commit sins. But these sins need not remain forever on the soul, causing it harm. Instead, there are means to remove them. One of the most important of those means is the performance of good deeds and, in particular, the prayers. The Messenger of Allah (peace and blessings of Allah be upon him) said,

أَرَأَيْتُمْ لَوْ أَنَّ نَهَرًا بِبَابِ أَحَدِكُمْ يَغْتَسِلُ فِيهِ كُلَّ يَوْمٍ خَمْسًا مَا تَقُولُ ذَلِكَ يُبْقِي مِنْ دَرَنِهِ قَالُوا لا يُبْقِي مِنْ دَرَنِهِ شَيْئًا قَالَ فَذَلِكَ مِثْلُ الصَّلَوَاتِ الْخَمْسِ يَمْحُو اللَّهُ بِهِ الْخَطَايَا

"If a person had a stream outside his door and he bathed in it five times a day, do you think he would have any filth left on him?" The people said, "No filth would remain on him whatsoever." The Prophet (peace be upon him) then said, "That is like the five daily prayers: Allah wipes away the sins by them." (Recorded by al-Bukhari and Muslim.) The Messenger of Allah (peace and blessings of Allah be upon him) also said,

مَا مِنِ امْرِئٍ مُسْلِمٍ تَحْضُرُهُ صَلاةٌ مَكْتُوبَةٌ فَيُحْسِنُ وُضُوءَهَا وَخُشُوعَهَا وَرُكُوعَهَا إِلاَّ كَانَتْ كَفَّارَةً لِمَا قَبْلَهَا مِنَ الذُّنُوبِ مَا لَمْ يُؤْتِ كَبِيرَةً وَذَلِكَ الدَّهْرَ كُلَّهُ

"There is no Muslim man who attends the obligatory prayer, while making the ablution, having fear of Allah and performing the bowing all in an excellent manner except that it will be an expiation for him for whatever sins preceded it, as long as he did not perform a major sin. And such is true for the entire year."

(Recorded by Muslim.) Note that this hadith implies that only if the prayer is performed in the proper manner will it be a true source of wiping away one's sins.

(6) One of the greatest diseases afflicting mankind today is heedlessness and forgetfulness—that is, of the more important things in life and the goal of this life itself. Especially in this day and age, one can become so preoccupied and downright exhausted with so many mundane activities that it is easy to forget about Allah. The person forgets what this whole existence is all about and what it means. He forgets that he is a servant of Allah and that there is nothing worth striving for other than that goal. This negligence can be very dangerous for the soul, as the soul forgets what is good for it and what is evil for it. The only remedy for this great disease is the establishment of an act on a regular basis that requires one to remember Allah and, thereby, put everything back in its proper perspective and focus. This is one of the roles and great benefits of the establishment of the five daily prayers. Allah says,

إِنَّنِيٓ أَنَا ٱللَّهُ لَآ إِلَٰهَ إِلَّآ أَنَا۠ فَٱعۡبُدۡنِي وَأَقِمِ ٱلصَّلَوٰةَ لِذِكۡرِيٓ

"Verily, I am Allah: there is no god but I: so serve Me (only), and establish regular prayer for celebrating My remembrance" (*Taha* 14).

(7) Furthermore, these prayers are obligatory upon the person at prescribed times throughout the day. Allah has specifically pointed out this fact in the verse,

إِنَّ ٱلصَّلَوٰةَ كَانَتۡ عَلَى ٱلۡمُؤۡمِنِينَ كِتَٰبٗا مَّوۡقُوتٗا

"Verily, the prayers are enjoined on believers at stated times" (*al-Nisaa* 103). These times are such that in reality a person has either just left being in private conversation with Allah or is just about to enter into such a private conversation.[1] In addition, the believer knows that Allah is fully aware of all of his thoughts and deeds. Thus, the believer should then become shy to disobey Allah after

[1] A hadith recorded by al-Bukhari states, "While the believer is in the prayer, he is in a private conversation with his Lord."

he just met with Him and while realizing that He will stand before him again in a short time.

(8) In addition, in the prayer, the person remembers who he truly is. He is no more than a human being like all of the other humans Allah has created on this earth. It is only by the grace and mercy of Allah that Allah has blessed him with finding the truth and following the Straight Path. He is, in one sense, an equal to all others who are submitting to Allah and performing those same prayers—the only true difference between them being their level of piety. This realization that the person should experience five times a day should help in purifying the soul by removing from it many of the dangerous diseases that strike at the root of its health. In particular, pride, unsanctioned hatred, bigotry and envy towards one fellow Muslims should be removed from his heart as he realizes that they are all working toward the same goal and all trying to serve and worship Allah. In reality, this fact is true for all Muslims as well as all the earlier prophets and their followers. This is a massive community that is all working towards one goal, as Allah has instructed them,

إِنَّ هَٰذِهِۦٓ أُمَّتُكُمۡ أُمَّةٗ وَٰحِدَةٗ وَأَنَا۠ رَبُّكُمۡ فَٱعۡبُدُونِ

"Verily, this community of yours is a single community, and I am your Lord and Cherisher. Therefore serve Me (and no other)" (*al-Anbiyaa* 92).

(9) A commitment to any ideology or program requires self-discipline, a strong will and perseverance. Once again, the importance and ramification of the prayers at regularly stated times are seen. This practice requires the person to overcome laziness and lack of discipline.

(10) As mentioned earlier, the prayer is an act of worship or an end in itself as well as a means to other desirable goals, such as those described above. As for it being a type of end in itself, the Muslim must realize that it is while he is in prayer that he is the closest to Allah. He should feel this fact in his prayer. Allah says in the Quran,

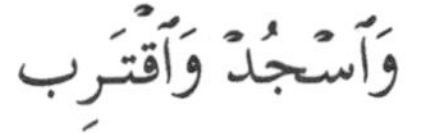

"But prostrate yourself and draw near (unto Allah)" (*al-Alaq* 19). The Prophet (peace be upon him) also said

أَقْرَبُ مَا يَكُونُ الْعَبْدُ مِنْ رَبِّهِ وَهُوَ سَاجِدٌ

"The closest a servant is to his Lord is when he is prostrating." (Recorded by Muslim.)

(11) As for the Hereafter, Allah's forgiveness and pleasure—the final and greatest purifying of the soul—is closely related to the prayers. The Messenger of Allah (peace be upon him) said,

خَمْسُ صَلَوَاتٍ افْتَرَضَهُنَّ اللَّهُ تَعَالَى مَنْ أَحْسَنَ وُضُوءَهُنَّ وَصَلاَّهُنَّ لِوَقْتِهِنَّ وَأَتَمَّ رُكُوعَهُنَّ وَخُشُوعَهُنَّ كَانَ لَهُ عَلَى اللَّهِ عَهْدٌ أَنْ يَغْفِرَ لَهُ وَمَنْ لَمْ يَفْعَلْ فَلَيْسَ لَهُ عَلَى اللَّهِ عَهْدٌ إِنْ شَاءَ غَفَرَ لَهُ وَإِنْ شَاءَ عَذَّبَهُ

"Allah has obligated five prayers. Whoever excellently performs their ablutions, prays them in their proper times, completes their bows and *khushoo'*[1] has a promise from Allah that He will forgive him. And whoever does not do that has no promise from Allah. He may either forgive him or He may punish him."[2]

It must also be noted that the quality of the prayer will also greatly affect the effectiveness of the prayer itself and its role in the purification of the soul. The prayer said without any feeling of the presence of Allah or without any true remembrance of Allah, may have very little effect on the individual. Perhaps simply going through the physical motions of the prayer may have some positive effect on the person praying but there may still be a world of difference between the influence of his prayer on his life

---

[1] *Khushoo'* in the prayer is where the person's heart is attuned to the prayer. This feeling in the heart is then reflected on the body. The person remains still and calm. His gaze is also lowered. Even his voice is affected by this feeling in the heart. For more details on this concept (as well as the difference between it and *khudhoo'*), see Muhammad al-Shaayi, *Al-Furooq al-Laughawiyyah wa Atharahaa fi Tafseer al-Quran al-Kareem* (Riyadh: Maktabah al-Ubaikaan, 1993), pp. 249-254.

[2] Recorded by Malik, Ahmad, Abu Dawood, al-Nasaai and others. According to al-Albaani, it is *sahih*. Al-Albaani, *Saheeh al-Jaami*, vol. 1, p. 616.

compared to that of someone whose heart and soul is attuned to the prayer. Hence, the Prophet (peace be upon him) said,

إِنَّ الرَّجُلَ لَيَنْصَرِفُ وَمَا كُتِبَ لَهُ إِلاَّ عُشْرُ صَلاتِهِ تُسْعُهَا ثُمْنُهَا سُبْعُهَا سُدْسُهَا خُمْسُهَا رُبْعُهَا ثُلُثُهَا نِصْفُهَا

"A person may finish from [the prayer] and all that is recorded for him of his prayer is one-tenth of it, one-ninth, one-eighth, one-seventh, one-sixth, one-fifth, one-fourth, one-third or one-half."[1]

The Zakat and Its Effect on the Purification of the Soul

Another pillar of Islam with important ramifications for the purification of the soul is the paying of the zakat. Zakat is to give up a certain percentage of one's wealth to one of the different categories mentioned by Allah in the Quran.[2] Actually, the word *zakat* comes from the same root as the word *tazkiyah* in *tazkiyah al-nufoos* or "purification of the souls." Its meaning is growth, purity and blessing. According to Karzoon, it is called zakat because it is hoped that it will bring about blessings, purification of the soul and an increase in good deeds.[3] Zakat, therefore, is both an act of worship in itself, pleasing to Allah, and a means of assisting in the purification of the soul.

The concept of being obliged to give up a portion of one's wealth for the sake of God as an act of worship of God is something that one finds in the message of the previous prophets.[4] It can be concluded, therefore, that the nature and ramifications of this type of act are essential for the purification of

---

[1] Recorded by Abu Dawood and Ahmad. According to al-Albaani, it is *sahih*. Al-Albaani, *Saheeh al-Jaami*, vol. 1, p. 335.

[2] Allah has said, "Alms are for the poor and the needy, and those employed to administer the (funds); for those whose hearts are to be reconciled (to the truth); for those in bondage and in debt; in the cause of Allah; and for the wayfarer: (thus is it) ordained by Allah, and Allah is full of knowledge and wisdom" (*al-Taubah* 60).

[3] Karzoon, vol. 1, p. 234.

[4] For details, see Sulaiman Nadwi, pp. 153-155. For a detailed comparison of what is regarded by the Jews as the Law of Moses and the zakat of Islam, see Sulaiman Nadwi, pp. 162-173.

the soul, which was the main purpose for which all of those prophets were sent.

It is perhaps for this reason that zakat is mentioned alongside the prayer in numerous verses of the Quran. In fact, the two are mentioned together in eighty-two places in the Quran. For example, Allah says,

فَإِن تَابُوا۟ وَأَقَامُوا۟ ٱلصَّلَوٰةَ وَءَاتَوُا۟ ٱلزَّكَوٰةَ فَإِخْوَٰنُكُمْ فِى ٱلدِّينِ

"But if they repent, offer prayer and give the zakat, then they are your brethren in religion" (*al-Taubah* 11).

In sum, although prayer is perhaps universally recognized as a means of self-purification, there is no question that the giving of a portion of one's wealth as an act of worship is also an essential step along the path of purification although not everyone may readily recognize this fact. Its important place in the purification of the soul is touched upon by Sulaiman Nadwi who wrote,

> The main cause of spiritual illnesses of human beings is the absence of hope and fear of Allah and lack of love and attachment to Him. Cure to these illnesses is Salat [prayer]. There is also another cause of these illnesses, namely, attachment to worldly possessions, riches and wealth, instead of attachment to Allah. Zakat is the remedy for this second cause of illness.[1]

Although the final form of zakat was not made obligatory until the eighth year after the Hijrah, in numerous revelations Allah made it clear that it must be part of a believer's personality to be willing to give up some of his wealth for the sake of Allah. For example, while the Prophet (peace and blessings of Allah be upon him) was still living in Makkah, Allah revealed the following verses describing the behavior of those who will receive Allah's rewards,

---

[1] Sulaiman Nadwi, p. 179.

وَيُطْعِمُونَ ٱلطَّعَامَ عَلَىٰ حُبِّهِۦ مِسْكِينًا وَيَتِيمًا وَأَسِيرًا ﴿٨﴾ إِنَّمَا نُطْعِمُكُمْ لِوَجْهِ ٱللَّهِ لَا نُرِيدُ مِنكُمْ جَزَآءً وَلَا شُكُورًا ﴿٩﴾ إِنَّا نَخَافُ مِن رَّبِّنَا يَوْمًا عَبُوسًا قَمْطَرِيرًا

"And they feed, for the love of Allah, the indigent, the orphan, and the captive, (saying), 'We feed you for the sake of Allah alone: no reward do we desire from you, nor thanks. We only fear a day of distressful wrath from the side of our Lord." (*al-Dahr* 8-9).

The lessons and important ramifications of zakat with respect to the purification of the soul may be summarized in the following points:

(1) The paying of zakat (as well as the giving of additional charity or *sadaqah*) is a source of great reward from Allah. In other words, Allah is pleased with it, blesses it and multiplies it immensely. Allah says,

مَّثَلُ ٱلَّذِينَ يُنفِقُونَ أَمْوَٰلَهُمْ فِى سَبِيلِ ٱللَّهِ كَمَثَلِ حَبَّةٍ أَنۢبَتَتْ سَبْعَ سَنَابِلَ فِى كُلِّ سُنۢبُلَةٍ مِّا۟ئَةُ حَبَّةٍ ۗ وَٱللَّهُ يُضَٰعِفُ لِمَن يَشَآءُ ۗ وَٱللَّهُ وَٰسِعٌ عَلِيمٌ

"The parable of those who spend their substance for the sake of Allah is that of a grain of corn: it grows seven ears, and each ear has a hundred grains. Allah gives manifold increase to whom He pleases: and Allah cares for all and He knows all things" (*al-Baqarah* 261). Hence, it draws one closer to Allah.

(2) In reality, the payment of zakat should directly help in purifying a person. It also purifies his wealth. Allah said to the Prophet (peace be upon him),

خُذْ مِنْ أَمْوَٰلِهِمْ صَدَقَةً تُطَهِّرُهُمْ وَتُزَكِّيهِم بِهَا

"Take (O Muhammad) alms from their wealth in order to purify them and sanctify them with it" (*al-Taubah* 103). Beyond that, it can purify a believer's soul by cleansing him of the diseases of stinginess and miserliness.

It also purifies the wealth of the person by removing any evil effect from it. The Prophet (peace be upon him) once said,

من أدى زكاة ماله فقد ذهب عنه شره

"Whoever pays the zakat on his wealth will have its evil removed from him."[1]

(3) Anyone who recognizes that wealth is a bounty and blessing that Allah has decreed to bestow upon some and not upon others will realize that wealth is a true trial and test. He will realize that it comes from Allah and, therefore, he should try his best to use it in a way that is a form of thanksgiving, gratitude and worship of Allah. In the Quran, in a beautiful fashion, Allah reminds the believer of this truth. Allah says,

وَءَاتُوهُم مِّن مَّالِ ٱللَّهِ ٱلَّذِىٓ ءَاتَىٰكُمْ

"And give them [your slaves seeking freedom] something out of the wealth which Allah has bestowed upon you" (*al-Noor* 33). Allah also says,

ءَامِنُوا۟ بِٱللَّهِ وَرَسُولِهِۦ وَأَنفِقُوا۟ مِمَّا جَعَلَكُم مُّسْتَخْلَفِينَ فِيهِ

"Believe in Allah and His Messenger and spend from that which He has made you trustees" (*al-Hadeed* 7).

In reality, the wealth that Allah gives a person is a trial while the poverty that a person experiences is also a trial. Sometimes, the test of "having" is much more difficult than the test of "not having." When one is a have-not, one may not have many options available to him save to remain patient and put one's hopes in Allah to make things better. However, when one has wealth, many doors of disobedience to Allah can be opened for him. Hence, this can be a very difficult trial. He may only be successful in such a trial if he has some training that develops

---

[1] Recorded by ibn Khuzaima and al-Tabaraani. According to al-Albaani, it is *hasan*. Cf., Muhammad Naasir al-Deen Al-Albaani, *Saheeh al-Targheeb wa al-Tarheeb*, (Beirut: al-Maktab al-Islaami, 1982), vol. 1, p. 312.

within him the proper discipline and self-control. This training should remind him of where that wealth came from in the first place—from Allah—and what a wonderful bounty it is, reminding him that many people are without that bounty. This will make him realize how important it is for him to use that wealth in a proper manner. This training and development of will power is provided for him in the obligation of zakat.

(4) Zakat is also a strong reminder that wealth is a blessing from Allah. A wealthy person sees around him and throughout the world the kind of misery and destitution that, if Allah willed, he himself could be experiencing. This should develop a very strong feeling of humility and gratitude toward Allah. Perhaps that is part of the meaning behind the verse of the Quran,

إِنَّمَا وَلِيُّكُمُ ٱللَّهُ وَرَسُولُهُۥ وَٱلَّذِينَ ءَامَنُوا۟ ٱلَّذِينَ يُقِيمُونَ ٱلصَّلَوٰةَ

وَيُؤْتُونَ ٱلزَّكَوٰةَ وَهُمْ رَٰكِعُونَ

“Verily, your Protector and Helper is none other than Allah, His Messenger and the believers—those who establish the prayer, give the zakat and bow down [in obedience to Allah]” (*al-Maaidah* 55).[1]

Indeed, the believer should be actively seeking means by which he can thank Allah for the bounties Allah has given him. This feeling should drive him to perform more and more good deeds. The beautiful paradox of this is that if the zakat has this effect on him and he grows more thankful to Allah, Allah will in turn give him ever more blessings in this life and in the Hereafter. Allah says,

وَإِذْ تَأَذَّنَ رَبُّكُمْ لَئِن شَكَرْتُمْ لَأَزِيدَنَّكُمْ وَلَئِن كَفَرْتُمْ إِنَّ

عَذَابِى لَشَدِيدٌ

“And remember! Your Lord caused to be declared (publicly): If you are grateful, I will add more (favors) unto you; but if you

---

[1] Cf., Islahi, p. 268.

show ingratitude, truly My punishment is terrible indeed" (*Ibraaheem* 7).

(5) This act of worship highlights a fact discussed earlier concerning the scope of purification of the soul. Purification does not deal simply with one's interaction with his Lord (if one can somehow compartmentalize that and remove it from all other interactions) but it also deals with one's interaction with the other believers in particular and the rest of humanity in general. Via the zakat, one directly fulfills the needs of others. But it is done as an act of worship of Allah. The basis by which one should interact with others is, once again, the worship of Allah and the attempt to purify oneself. One interacts with others not on some secular basis or some philosophical view of human rights. Instead, one interacts with others based on a much stronger and moving foundation: on the basis of how Allah has instructed one to interact with others. In this way, that interaction actually becomes a form of worship, pleasing to Allah and aiding in the purification of one's soul.

(6) A corollary to the previous point is that one of the beneficial aspects of the importance Allah has placed on the zakat (and charity in general) and one of its many positive effects on the soul is that it develops within the soul a desire to sacrifice and assist others for the sake of Allah. The true believer cultivates in his heart the joy of giving for the sake of Allah, recognizing how pleased Allah is with such a deed. It is not simply a matter of removing the disease of selfishness, the ill amassing of wealth and the harms of egotism from one's heart. It is more than that. It is the replacement of those possible feelings with the feeling that a believer should sacrifice and work for others as a means of getting closer to Allah. This feeling should be so strong that even the one who has nothing or very little will want to sacrifice and give to get closer to Allah. Allah describes such believers when He said,

وَيُؤْثِرُونَ عَلَىٰٓ أَنفُسِهِمْ وَلَوْ كَانَ بِهِمْ خَصَاصَةٌ ۚ وَمَن يُوقَ شُحَّ نَفْسِهِۦ فَأُوْلَـٰٓئِكَ هُمُ ٱلْمُفْلِحُونَ

"They give them preference over themselves, even though poverty was their (own lot). And those saved from the covetousness of their own souls; they are the ones that achieve prosperity" (*al-Hashr* 9). Hence, the feeling of not just thinking about oneself but of going out and doing good for others as an act of worship of Allah is embedded in the heart and soul of the true believer.

Such an attitude was found among the Companions of the Prophet (peace and blessings of Allah be upon him) and the Shareeah explained how even those not blessed with wealth may also share in the experience of giving and develop that attitude in their hearts. Al-Bukhari and Muslim record,

عَلَى كُلِّ مُسْلِمٍ صَدَقَةٌ قِيلَ أَرَأَيْتَ إِنْ لَمْ يَجِدْ قَالَ يَعْتَمِلُ بِيَدَيْهِ فَيَنْفَعُ نَفْسَهُ وَيَتَصَدَّقُ قَالَ قِيلَ أَرَأَيْتَ إِنْ لَمْ يَسْتَطِعْ قَالَ يُعِينُ ذَا الْحَاجَةِ الْمَلْهُوفَ قَالَ قِيلَ لَهُ أَرَأَيْتَ إِنْ لَمْ يَسْتَطِعْ قَالَ يَأْمُرُ بِالْمَعْرُوفِ أَوِ الْخَيْرِ قَالَ أَرَأَيْتَ إِنْ لَمْ يَفْعَلْ قَالَ يُمْسِكُ عَنِ الشَّرِّ فَإِنَّهَا صَدَقَةٌ

"Charity is obligatory upon every Muslim." It was said, "What if someone does not have the means?" He said, "Let him work with his two hands, thus benefiting himself and giving charity." It was then said, "What do you say if he cannot do that?" He answered, "Then he should help one in need." Again it was said to him, "What if he cannot do that?" He replied, "Let him order virtues or goodness." It was said, "What about if he does not do that?" He answered, "He should then abstain from evil, and that will be charity on his behalf."

(7) A great disease that zakat can cure is the insatiable desire for more. This desire is found in virtually all humans and needs to be controlled and resisted. The Messenger of Allah (peace and blessings of Allah be upon him) said,

لَوْ أَنَّ ابْنَ آدَمَ أُعْطِيَ وَادِيًا مَلْئًا مِنْ ذَهَبٍ أَحَبَّ إِلَيْهِ ثَانِيًا وَلَوْ أُعْطِيَ ثَانِيًا أَحَبَّ إِلَيْهِ ثَالِثًا وَلا يَسُدُّ جَوْفَ ابْنِ آدَمَ إِلاَّ التُّرَابُ وَيَتُوبُ اللَّهُ عَلَى مَنْ تَابَ

"If the son of Adam [that is, humans] is given a valley filled with gold, he would love to have a second one. And if he were given two valleys, he would desire a third. Nothing will fill the stomach of the son of Adam except dirt while Allah returns to whoever repents [to Him]." (Recorded by al-Bukhari.) Allah also states mankind's love for wealth in the verse,

وَإِنَّهُۥ لِحُبِّ ٱلْخَيْرِ لَشَدِيدٌ

"And violent is he in his love of wealth" (*al-Aadiyaat* 8).

(8) Another important point related to zakat has to do with the attitude towards wealth in Islam and what is of true value and worth. Islam makes it clear that wealth in itself is neither necessarily good nor evil. Problems occur when the means to attain it and how it is used are abused; however, in itself it is neutral. This is a very important point for the health of the soul. This is because mankind is naturally inclined to loving wealth and wanting to possess at least some wealth. Indeed, Allah says,

زُيِّنَ لِلنَّاسِ حُبُّ ٱلشَّهَوَٰتِ مِنَ ٱلنِّسَآءِ وَٱلْبَنِينَ وَٱلْقَنَٰطِيرِ ٱلْمُقَنطَرَةِ مِنَ ٱلذَّهَبِ وَٱلْفِضَّةِ وَٱلْخَيْلِ ٱلْمُسَوَّمَةِ وَٱلْأَنْعَٰمِ وَٱلْحَرْثِ ۗ ذَٰلِكَ مَتَٰعُ ٱلْحَيَوٰةِ ٱلدُّنْيَا ۖ وَٱللَّهُ عِندَهُۥ حُسْنُ ٱلْمَـَٔابِ

"Fair in the eyes of men is the love of things they covet: women and sons; heaped-up hoards of gold and silver; horses branded (for blood and excellence); and (wealth of) cattle and well-tilled land. Such are the possessions of this world's life; but in nearness to Allah is the best of the goals (to return to)" (*ali-Imraan* 14).

One of the problems with many of the other supposed paths of purification of the soul that were discussed earlier (in particular, Christianity and Buddhism) is that their views of wealth were completely impractical and, most important, not consistent with the natural make-up of humans. Hence, the soul would either have to revolt against a path that it was claiming to recognize as true or would have to continually live with an internal struggle that could lead to other diseases of the soul, such as doubt and misgivings.

(9) Closely related to the previous point, zakat reminds all and sundry that the real goal in life is not the amassing of wealth or becoming rich. Indeed, that is not necessarily even a goal in itself. That is a subgoal only if it can be achieved without

sacrificing the more important aspects of life and only if it can be used in the proper means. Sulaiman Nadwi wrote, "In the sight of the Prophet (peace and blessings of Allah be upon him) poverty and destitution did not mean dishonour or humiliation, neither were riches and wealth equated with honour and dignity. Only virtue and piety were the criteria for reverence and superiority."[1] Indeed, Allah says in the Quran,

إِنَّ أَكْرَمَكُمْ عِندَ ٱللَّهِ أَتْقَىٰكُمْ

"Verily the most honored of you in the sight of Allah is (he who is) the most righteous of you" (*al-Hujuraat* 13). Unfortunately, even Muslim societies today are afflicted with this disease of evaluating a person according to the car he drives, the degree he has and how often he buys new furniture for his house. If a person does not have the finer material things in life, he is worth nothing in the eyes of many Muslims today, even if he is the most pious of all the people.[2]

(10) As a corollary to this last point, the zakat frees oneself the overwhelming desire to "keep up with the Jones," which is so predominant in the world today. When one pays the zakat, it makes him realize that he does not need all of the material goods in this world, in particular he does not necessarily need what everybody is purchasing simply because it is the latest fad. This type of consumption for show and competition with others leads to a great deal of waste. When one is filled with the spirit of zakat, he realizes that such wealth has a much more important purpose and can be much more beneficial for the individual. Instead of buying what others buy in order to keep up with them, the individual realizes that that wealth would be better used if given for charitable contributions for the poor, for jihad,

---

[1] Sulaiman Nadwi, p. 181.

[2] Indeed, some students who came from overseas to the United States are too ashamed to go home if they cannot complete their degrees. They would prefer to stay in the United States by any means and take the most menial of jobs to avoid going home and having to face the shame and dishonor of their families. This author has personally witnessed this for people coming from one of the poorest countries in the world, Bangladesh. In some cases, the person himself found the true Islam and became a dedicated Muslim in the United States but this fact meant nothing to his friends and family back home.

for spreading the faith and so forth. The individual will be happy with that decision for his wealth even if others may look down upon him because he does not have the latest goods that they are all purchasing simply to impress each other.

(11) Zakat is also a reminder that humans are in need of Allah while Allah is not in need of them or their wealth in any way whatsoever. Allah has clearly reminded all of the believers:

هَٰٓأَنتُمۡ هَٰٓؤُلَآءِ تُدۡعَوۡنَ لِتُنفِقُواْ فِي سَبِيلِ ٱللَّهِ فَمِنكُم مَّن يَبۡخَلُۖ وَمَن يَبۡخَلۡ فَإِنَّمَا يَبۡخَلُ عَن نَّفۡسِهِۦۚ وَٱللَّهُ ٱلۡغَنِيُّ وَأَنتُمُ ٱلۡفُقَرَآءُۚ وَإِن تَتَوَلَّوۡاْ يَسۡتَبۡدِلۡ قَوۡمًا غَيۡرَكُمۡ ثُمَّ لَا يَكُونُوٓاْ أَمۡثَٰلَكُم

"Behold, you are those invited to spend (of your substance) for the sake of Allah—but among you are some that are niggardly. Any who are niggardly are so at the expense of their own souls. Allah is free of all wants, and it is you that are needy. If you turn back (from the path), He will substitute in your stead another people; then they would not be like you" (*Muhammad* 38).

(12) Once again, the evil disease of *kibr* (arrogance and pride) is dealt a heavy blow by the actualization and understanding of zakat. First, the fact that Allah requires a person to pay zakat reminds the person that the wealth he has is, in reality, not really his. He is like a caretaker. Furthermore, it reminds him that his "greatness" is not the source of his wealth; instead, the true source of that wealth was actually Allah who, if He had willed, would not have bestowed that wealth on him in the first place. Hence, the believer should become humbled and give the zakat and other charity willfully and happily. He will not become like Qaroon who said,

قَالَ إِنَّمَآ أُوتِيتُهُۥ عَلَىٰ عِلۡمٍ عِندِيٓۚ

"He said, 'This has been given to me because of a certain knowledge which I have'" (*al-Qasas* 78).

(13) Another dangerous disease for the soul is that of stinginess, greed and covetousness. In fact, if one can overcome this tendency in the soul and control it properly, he will have

accomplished a great thing. He will have accomplished something that can definitely set him on the path of true purification and success. Allah says in two places in the Quran,

وَمَن يُوقَ شُحَّ نَفْسِهِۦ فَأُوْلَـٰٓئِكَ هُمُ ٱلْمُفْلِحُونَ

"And those saved from the covetousness of their own souls, they are the ones that achieve prosperity" (*al-Hashr* 9 and *al-Taghaabun* 16).

This disease can be overcome by training oneself to sacrifice, making oneself realize that it is not the material things of this world that one is striving for and making oneself realize that giving up something in this life does not mean the end of the world. One can give and still be just as happy as before giving—indeed, the joy that can come from giving will make the person even happier than if he had not given. The person does not have to live in fear of losing the worldly possessions that are so dear to him—so dear to him because he gives them a weight and importance that is more than they deserve.

However, until someone gives up some of his wealth, he may never realize this fact. If he is always stingy and never willing to give up what he possesses, he may convince himself that this is the only way to behave for he believes that disaster and want will be his plight. Hence, he must be forced at some time to give up some of his wealth so that he will realize that giving up some of one's wealth is not that bad. Indeed, he will realize that it is not bad at all. He will realize that he gave up something for the sake of Allah and, Allah willing, a feeling will overcome him that will make him understand some of the reality related to wealth. It is the obligatory zakat that forces him to take that first step and experience that feeling that he perhaps never imagined could have been the result of sacrificing some of the wealth that he loves so dearly. As this feeling permeates his soul even more deeply when he gives the zakat year after year—and witnesses no loss to his happiness due to giving up some of his wealth—the diseases of miserliness and stinginess will be removed from his heart and he will be on the path of the truly successful.

(14) The institution of zakat not only helps to purify the wealth, it also helps in the purification of the poor recipients of

zakat. It can be instrumental in the removal of the deadly spiritual diseases of envy and hatred from the hearts of the poor toward the rich. When the rich help the poor and give the obligatory zakat and any additional charity that is the result of the spirit developed in them through zakat, this generates love between the rich and the poor. The rich are not leaving the poor behind but they are concerned about them and willing to take care of them as part of their responsibility to Allah.

It is also an opportunity for the poor to give thanks to Allah. The poor receive some wealth that Allah has obligated for them to receive. The commandment of zakat shows that the poor are not despised nor are they to be forgotten. When their cases are sincere, they are to be helped and assisted. Their poverty is not their destined plight necessarily due to their own lack of effort, as the Protestant ethic may lead one to conclude.

Finally, the zakat that the poor person receives is a reminder to the poor that the real distributor of wealth and the real owner of wealth is Allah. Hence, the poor person also has to realize that Allah has decreed for him his current situation and he must react to his situation in a way that is pleasing to Allah. He cannot resort to stealing or violence nor should he curse his situation. Instead, he should be patient, work according to the laws of Allah to improve his situation and realize that there is, Allah willing, some good in the situation he is in even though from a worldly point of view it may look very bleak.

(15) Finally, Islahi makes an interesting point, stating, "Wherever a person invests his money, experience bears witness that his heart too dwells there. Seen in this light it becomes evident that on spending his wealth in the way of God, his heart too will dwell with God since it is with Him that he has done business and his wealth lies with Him."[1]

With respect to zakat, Allah explicitly discusses some matters that must be avoided on the part of the giver. If one does not avoid these matters, the benefits of zakat will be effaced and, hence, the act may have no positive effect on the soul. Although every act may have some negating factors (such as praying only to be seen by others), the negating factors related to zakat and

---

[1] Islahi, p. 250.

charity are very prominent and common. Therefore, it is a must that they be discussed here.

Allah explicitly shows that the act of giving zakat must be free of any show and of any harassing or bothering of the one who receives the charity. Obviously, any act of worship must be done solely for the sake of Allah for it to be acceptable to Allah. This is true for zakat and all other acts of worship. The problem in particular with zakat and charity is that the person may have thought that he is giving away the wealth solely for the sake of Allah but then he ignorantly gives it away or follows it up with such deeds that render the act fruitless. Hence, Allah says in the Quran,

ٱلَّذِينَ يُنفِقُونَ أَمْوَٰلَهُمْ فِى سَبِيلِ ٱللَّهِ ثُمَّ لَا يُتْبِعُونَ مَآ أَنفَقُوا۟ مَنًّا
وَلَآ أَذًى ۙ لَّهُمْ أَجْرُهُمْ عِندَ رَبِّهِمْ وَلَا خَوْفٌ عَلَيْهِمْ وَلَا هُمْ
يَحْزَنُونَ ﴿٢٦٢﴾ ۞ قَوْلٌ مَّعْرُوفٌ وَمَغْفِرَةٌ خَيْرٌ مِّن صَدَقَةٍ يَتْبَعُهَآ
أَذًى ۗ وَٱللَّهُ غَنِىٌّ حَلِيمٌ ﴿٢٦٣﴾ يَٰٓأَيُّهَا ٱلَّذِينَ ءَامَنُوا۟ لَا تُبْطِلُوا۟
صَدَقَٰتِكُم بِٱلْمَنِّ وَٱلْأَذَىٰ كَٱلَّذِى يُنفِقُ مَالَهُۥ رِئَآءَ ٱلنَّاسِ وَلَا
يُؤْمِنُ بِٱللَّهِ وَٱلْيَوْمِ ٱلْءَاخِرِ ۖ فَمَثَلُهُۥ كَمَثَلِ صَفْوَانٍ عَلَيْهِ تُرَابٌ
فَأَصَابَهُۥ وَابِلٌ فَتَرَكَهُۥ صَلْدًا ۖ لَّا يَقْدِرُونَ عَلَىٰ شَىْءٍ مِّمَّا
كَسَبُوا۟ ۗ وَٱللَّهُ لَا يَهْدِى ٱلْقَوْمَ ٱلْكَٰفِرِينَ

"Those who spend their substance in the cause of Allah, and follow not up their gifts with reminders of their generosity or with injury, for them their reward is with their Lord; on them shall be no fear, nor shall they grieve. Kind words and the covering of faults are better than charity followed by injury. Allah is Free of all wants, and He is Most Forbearing. O you who believe! Cancel not your charity by reminders of your generosity or by injury, like those who spend their substance to be seen of men, but believe neither in Allah nor in the Last Day. They are in parable like a hard barren rock, on which is a little soil; on it falls heavy rain, which leaves it (just) a bare stone. They will be able to do nothing with what they have earned. And Allah guides not those who reject faith" (*al-Baqarah* 262-264).

The irony in such an act of harming the one who accepts a person's zakat is that the zakat one is giving is actually a right of the poor person. Allah has given the poor person that right. Hence, the one with wealth is not doing the poor person any favor out of his own choice. Indeed, the poor person is doing the rich person a favor by accepting his zakat. He is accepting from the richer person that payment that will purify the wealthy person's wealth and soul. Hence, the giver should actually be thankful to the poorer person for accepting his zakat.[1] (There have actually been times in the history of Islam where the wealth of the state was so great that nobody was willing to accept other people's zakat. Hence, one should be grateful when he finds somebody who is willing to take his zakat.)

Furthermore, the believer must be willing to give of those things that are beloved to him and those things that are from permissible sources. When paying the zakat or giving charity in general, he should not give away wealth and items that have no meaning or value to him. When doing this, in essence, he is not sacrificing anything and has not really fulfilled the purpose behind these acts. In fact, Allah says,

لَن تَنَالُواْ ٱلْبِرَّ حَتَّىٰ تُنفِقُواْ مِمَّا تُحِبُّونَ ۚ وَمَا تُنفِقُواْ مِن شَىْءٍ

فَإِنَّ ٱللَّهَ بِهِۦ عَلِيمٌ

"By no means shall you attain righteousness unless you give (freely) of that which you love; and whatever you give, of a truth Allah knows it well" (*ali-Imraan* 92). Allah also says,

---

[1] Cf., Karzoon, vol. 1, p. 237.

يَـٰٓأَيُّهَا ٱلَّذِينَ ءَامَنُوٓا۟ أَنفِقُوا۟ مِن طَيِّبَـٰتِ مَا كَسَبْتُمْ وَمِمَّآ أَخْرَجْنَا لَكُم مِّنَ ٱلْأَرْضِ ۖ وَلَا تَيَمَّمُوا۟ ٱلْخَبِيثَ مِنْهُ تُنفِقُونَ وَلَسْتُم بِـَٔاخِذِيهِ إِلَّآ أَن تُغْمِضُوا۟ فِيهِ ۚ وَٱعْلَمُوٓا۟ أَنَّ ٱللَّهَ غَنِىٌّ حَمِيدٌ

"O you who believe! Give of the good things which you have (honorably) earned, and of the fruits of the earth which We have produced for you, and do not even aim at getting anything which is bad, in order that out of it you may give away something, when you yourselves would not receive it except with closed eyes. And know that Allah is free of all wants, and worthy of all praise" (*al-Baqarah* 267).

The Fast (*Siyaam*) of Ramadhaan and Its Effect on the Purification of the Soul

In the Quran, Allah makes it clear that the act of fasting is also another act of worship that was prescribed for the earlier religious communities. Allah has said,

يَـٰٓأَيُّهَا ٱلَّذِينَ ءَامَنُوا۟ كُتِبَ عَلَيْكُمُ ٱلصِّيَامُ كَمَا كُتِبَ عَلَى ٱلَّذِينَ مِن قَبْلِكُمْ لَعَلَّكُمْ تَتَّقُونَ

"O you who believe, fasting has been prescribed for you as it was prescribed for those before you in order for you to attain God-consciousness (*taqwa*)" (*al-Baqara* 183).[1] Fasting is the one act of worship wherein the believer gives up his most basic needs and urges for a lengthy period of time as a form of worship of Allah. In this sense, it is definitely unique and the effects of this practice have been tired directly to the increase of *taqwa* (God-consciousness and fear of Allah).

[1] For a discussion of the fasts of other faiths and the changes brought about by the Islamic Shareeah, see Sulaiman Nadwi, pp. 204-207, 218-222.

The believer gives up his food and drink for an entire month out of a desire and intention to submit to Allah and to do the act that will draw him closer to Allah. The realization and cultivation of obedience to Allah concerning the fast is so precise that even the matter in which the fast is broken is done in accordance to the guidance from Allah. In other words, the believer gives up his food and drink during the daytime as an act of submission and worship and he also breaks his fast as soon as the sun sets as a further act of obedience and submission to Allah. Thus, the breaking of the fast at that exact time is not simply a matter of the person now being free to eat so he eats at that time and does not delay his eating. No, instead, it is another act of obeying the Divine guidance. He breaks his fast at that time in application of the hadith,

لا يَزَالُ النَّاسُ بِخَيْرٍ مَا عَجَّلُوا الْفِطْرَ

"The people will continue to be in a good state as long as they hasten to break the fast." (Recorded by al-Bukhari and Muslim.)

An important conclusion that one gets from the institution of the fast is that the natural inclinations of man—the need for food, drink and sexual intercourse, for example—are not in themselves evil. As was noted earlier, the teachings of Islam are completely consistent with the nature that Allah Himself has given mankind. Hence, these natural wants and desires are not frustrated completely nor denied outright. That would not be practical or achievable given the nature of mankind (and the ascetics throughout history, with their numerous aberrations, have actually demonstrated that fact). At the same time, though, these natural desires cannot be left to run free, as otherwise people will be indulging in their desires regardless of the negative consequences for themselves or for others (as can be witnessed in the world today with its widespread promiscuity, sexually transmitted diseases, alcohol abuse, drug abuse and so forth).

These natural desires are to be harnessed—harnessed in such a way that positive results flow for the soul and even for humanity at large. It is admitted that their harnessing is not always the simplest of tasks. Islahi noted,

> But Islam is a faith in perfect harmony with human nature and these (lusts and passions) are part of that nature, without which the individual and specific demands of man cannot be met. That is why it has not permitted man to put an end to them [completely] but [it] has [been] ordered that they should be tamed and kept on the right track. But it is a patent fact that to keep them under control is a far more difficult task. A headstrong horse if it has to be put an end to needs only a single bullet from a gun. But if it is needed for riding and has to be tamed, an expert horseman with great pains and labour in its training can achieve this end and that too only after facing many dangers.
> The devotional act of fasting has been prescribed by Islam so that the unruly tendencies of the inner self of man, on the one side after attenuation, may come to temperance, and on the other, man's will power may become strong enough to suppress and make them abide by the limits set by God. Due to this dual activity from the point of view of self-purification... this devotional act has a great importance.[1]

The ramifications of the obligatory fast of Ramadhaan for the purification of the soul are numerous. They include the following:

(1) The fast is a source of forgiveness for one's sins. Hence, it removes the effects and stain of these sins from one's heart, leaving the heart pure again. The Prophet (peace be upon him) said,

مَنْ صَامَ رَمَضَانَ إِيمَانًا وَاحْتِسَابًا غُفِرَ لَهُ مَا تَقَدَّمَ مِنْ ذَنْبِهِ

"Whoever fasts the month of Ramadhaan with faith and hoping for its reward (*ihtisaab*) shall have all of his previous sins forgiven for him." (Recorded by al-Bukhari and Muslim.) Al-Khataabi notes that the meaning of *ihtisaab* means with resolve, hoping for its reward while being pleased to perform it without considering it

---

[1] Islahi, p. 272.

something heavy or a hardship. Hence, the true believer for whom the fasting will have its desired effect of removing or effacing his previous sins approaches the fast with a desire and love for it. He does not consider it a burden nor does he participate in it lackadaisically, with some heavy burden on his shoulder, being lazy and complaining until it is time to break the fast.[1]

(2) When one fasts, one should feel that he is performing a deed that is very beloved and special to Allah. This fact, in itself, should remind him of Allah and give his soul the special feeling that overcomes a person as he comes closer to Allah. The Messenger of Allah (peace and blessings of Allah be upon him) said,

كُلُّ عَمَلِ ابْنِ آدَمَ يُضَاعَفُ الْحَسَنَةُ عَشْرُ أَمْثَالِهَا إِلَى سَبْعِمِائَةِ ضِعْفٍ قَالَ اللَّهُ عَزَّ وَجَلَّ إِلاَّ الصَّوْمَ فَإِنَّهُ لِي وَأَنَا أَجْزِي بِهِ يَدَعُ شَهْوَتَهُ وَطَعَامَهُ مِنْ أَجْلِي لِلصَّائِمِ فَرْحَتَانِ فَرْحَةٌ عِنْدَ فِطْرِهِ وَفَرْحَةٌ عِنْدَ لِقَاءِ رَبِّهِ وَلَخُلُوفُ فِيهِ أَطْيَبُ عِنْدَ اللَّهِ مِنْ رِيحِ الْمِسْكِ

"Every deed of the son of Adam is multiplied ten times like it up to seven hundred times. Allah has said, '[That is true] save for the fast. I will reward it [in a special way]. He [the fasting person] leaves his desires and food for My sake.' And for the fasting person is two times of happiness, a time of happiness when he breaks his fast and a time of happiness when he meets his Lord. The change in the breath of his is more pleasing to Allah than the scent of musk." (Recorded by Muslim.)

(3) As was noted earlier, patience or perseverance is one of the most important and healthiest qualities a person can possess and is an important quality found in the purified soul. There is a definite and clear relationship between fasting and patience.[2] Fasting not only strengthens one's quality of patience, it

---

[1] Cf., Karzoon, vol. 1, pp. 254-255.

[2] In fact, there is a hadith which states, "Fasting is half of patience." But this hadith is weak. See Muhammad Naasir al-Deen al-Albaani, *Dhaeef al-Jaami al-Sagheer* (Beirut: al-Maktab al-Islaami, 1988), p. 523. However, some scholars, such as Mujaahid, have interpreted "patience"

actually touches upon all of the branches of patience. Patience is of three types: persevering with respect to continually performing the acts of worship, persevering with respect to refraining from what Allah has prohibited and remaining under control during times of hardship and difficulties. All three of these types are being tested and strengthened through the practice of fasting. While fasting, one adheres to what Allah has obligated, refrains from what he has forbidden of food and drink and also remains patient in the face of the hunger and thirst that he is experiencing.[1]

(4) Fasting is an experience wherein the person leaves his wants and desires for the sake of putting what Allah wants first. This reminds him of his true goal and purpose in life. It is when he experiences these acts that his soul can put matters into proper perspective concerning what he wants out of this life and what is of true importance to him.

(5) When one fasts, his mind is free to think and ponder. This is something that many people notice while fasting. They do not have the energy to do fruitless things and, hence, they take the time to think and ponder. Sulaiman Nadwi aptly described this experience and its benefits when he wrote,

> The starvation and hunger of fasting cools down our hot and excitable bodies, we are freed of the activities of eating and drinking... our hearts and brains are safe from the toxic matters otherwise produced by a full stomach. As a result a kind of peace and tranquility is produced in our feelings and emotions. This condition of having free time, moderation in our physical activities, and peace of heart, mind and emotions is very appropriate to thinking and deliberation, taking stock of our actions, regretting on wrongdoings, and

---

in, "'Seek help with patience and prayer" (*al-Baqarah* 45) as referring to the fast. Cf, ibn Katheer, *Tafseer* (Dar Taibah), vol. 1, p. 251; al-Qurtubi, vol. 1, p. 372.

[1] Cf., Abdul Rahmaan ibn Rajab, *Lataaif al-Maarif feema al-Miwaasim al-Aam min al-Wadhaaif* (Damascus: Daar ibn Katheer, 1996), p. 284.

producing an environment for instilling in us the fear of our accountability to Allah.[1]

(6) The Messenger of Allah (peace and blessings of Allah be upon him) once said,

انْظُرُوا إِلَى مَنْ أَسْفَلَ مِنْكُمْ وَلا تَنْظُرُوا إِلَى مَنْ هُوَ فَوْقَكُمْ فَهُوَ أَجْدَرُ أَنْ لا تَزْدَرُوا نِعْمَةَ اللَّهِ

"Look at those who are lower than you [having less than you] and do not look at those who are above you [having more than you] as otherwise the bounties of Allah upon you would become insignificant to you." (Recorded by Muslim.) In that hadith, the Prophet (peace and blessings of Allah be upon him) has given an instruction that will help one appreciate the numerous benefits that he has received from Allah. The institution of fasting can take the person even further. While fasting, the person does not just view the plight of others, but he can actually begin to feel their plight. Hence, the rich can reflect on what they have been given and give true thanks. Especially in this day and age and in some materially advanced countries, one becomes very much accustomed to easy access to food, drink, clean water, electricity and so on. Since these are readily available, the person starts to take them for granted and does not realize what a great blessing they are and how so many in today's world are actually deprived of these basic needs.

At the end of a third successive verse about the fast, Allah states,

وَلَعَلَّكُمْ تَشْكُرُونَ

"So that perhaps you will be grateful" (*al-Baqarah* 185). Thankfulness and gratitude towards Allah is an essential characteristic of the true believers.[2] People can speak about this

---

[1] Sulaiman Nadwi, p. 228.

[2] In fact, true believers are not simply grateful toward Allah but they are also grateful toward those who do them good in this world. The Messenger of Allah (peace and blessings of Allah be upon him) stated, "Whoever does not show gratitude to the people does not show gratitude to

matter in theoretical terms but there is no substitute for truly feeling the thirst, hunger and exhaustion that others have to go through on a daily basis. Al-Bukhari records that the Messenger of Allah (peace and blessings of Allah be upon him) was the most generous of people and he was even more generous during the month of Ramadhaan.

(7) It is a chance for a person to realize his potential. Concerning the fact that the Lord of Ramadhaan is also the Lord of the other eleven months, ibn Rajab notes that immediately following the command to fast, Allah mentions the prohibition of wrongfully devouring the wealth of the orphans. Ibn Rajab states that this is a clear allusion to the fact that the one who obeyed Allah during the month of Ramadhaan by fasting must also obey Allah during the remainder of the year by abstaining from what is forbidden, such as wrongfully devouring the wealth of orphans.[1]

When this awareness is developed through the fast, the person enters into a state where he is virtually fasting perpetually by avoiding what Allah has forbidden. In fact, ibn Rajab stated, "The entire [life in this] world is a month of fasting for the pious. They abstain therein from the forbidden desires. When death comes to them, the month of their fasting comes to an end and they begin to enjoy the feast of their ending of the fast [via the rewards that Allah bestows on him]."[2]

(8) The purified soul is one that has control over his desires and actions. An important key to such control is the characteristic of *taqwa,* which means that one has a fear of Allah and a recognition of Allah's awareness of his acts. Allah has made it clear that when the fast is performed properly, its result should be an increase in a person's *taqwa*. Allah says,

يَـٰٓأَيُّهَا ٱلَّذِينَ ءَامَنُوا۟ كُتِبَ عَلَيْكُمُ ٱلصِّيَامُ كَمَا كُتِبَ عَلَى
ٱلَّذِينَ مِن قَبْلِكُمْ لَعَلَّكُمْ تَتَّقُونَ

Allah." Recorded by Ahmad and al-Tirmidhi. According to al-Albaani, it is *sahih*. Cf., al-Albaani, *Saheeh al-Jaami*, vol. 2, p. 1114.

[1] Ibn Rajab, *Lataaif*, pp. 292-293.

[2] Quoted in Karzoon, vol. 1, pp. 265-266.

"O you who believe, fasting has been prescribed for you as it was prescribed for those before you so that you may attain *taqwa*" (*al-Baqarah* 183).

The aspects of *taqwa* imply God-consciousness, fear of Allah, realizing Allah's "presence" and having awe and respect for Allah's commands. This is what the fasting person should experience. Throughout the day he is conscious of Allah. He does not eat or drink for one reason and only one reason: Allah has forbidden it at that time and Allah alone knows whether he is truly fulfilling that command. If he can develop this feeling in his heart and mind and carry it over to the rest of his days, he will combat his desires and control his actions. Whenever he considers doing something forbidden, he will remember Allah and he will realize that Allah has forbidden that wrong and he has no reason whatsoever to want to displease Allah. In the same way that he would not want to disobey Allah by eating or drinking during the days that he is fasting, although his need to eat or drink may be stronger than many of his desires that he allows himself to succumb to, he should not be willing to disobey Allah, risking Allah's displeasure and punishment, during the other days of the year.

(9) There is another important facet that one could say is the key to all of this: turning to Allah, realizing one's need for Allah, asking Allah for help and assistance. This is, in fact, what a Muslim does in the month of Ramadhaan. The Muslim should realize during Ramadhaan that the food and drink that he needs for his continual sustenance actually come from Allah. If Allah willed to take away all of the water and food in his area, He has the ability to do so. Therefore, the believer realizes how greatly he is in need of Allah, even for the most mundane and necessary aspects of his life. When the Muslim realizes that fact, he should also realize his great need to have Allah guide him to the straight path and help him to remain firm along that path. When the person realizes this important fact, he turns wholeheartedly with his heart to Allah and begs for Allah's continual help, both with respect to his worldly needs and his spiritual needs.

(10) The Messenger of Allah (peace and blessings of Allah be upon him) said,

مَنْ يَضْمَنْ لِي مَا بَيْنَ لَحْيَيْهِ وَمَا بَيْنَ رِجْلَيْهِ أَضْمَنْ لَهُ الْجَنَّةَ

"For whoever guarantees for me what is between his jawbones and what is between his legs, then I guarantee for him Paradise." (Recorded by al-Bukhari.) This hadith shows that a person's downfall is often rooted in these two sources, his mouth and his private parts. If a person is trained to control these two potential sources of evil, it will be easy for him to control any other sources of evil. On this point, Islahi noted,

> The other blessing of fasting is that it bars to a great extent the main doors of corruption on man. These doors of corruption, as defined in more than one tradition, are his hunger and sex urge. It is due to them that man gets involved in so many troubles and drags others into as many. These are the routes by which Satan attacks man.
>
> Fasting takes best care of these two. While fasting not only eating and drinking are prohibited, but also quarrelling, telling lies, backbiting, indulging in idle talk and gossip, are all at cross purposes with fasting.[1]

(11) Fasting, once again, is a reminder of one's purpose in life. People have to eat and drink to sustain themselves and must procreate to continue the existence of humans. However, that is not what life is all about. These are simply meant to be a means for a greater purpose. Allah says,

وَٱلَّذِينَ كَفَرُواْ يَتَمَتَّعُونَ وَيَأْكُلُونَ كَمَا تَأْكُلُ ٱلْأَنْعَـٰمُ وَٱلنَّارُ مَثْوًى لَّهُمْ

"Those who reject Allah will enjoy (this world) and eat as cattle eat; and the Fire will be their abode" (*Muhammad* 12). The type of behavior described in this verse should never be the life of a believer. A believer is, for example, not simply eating to live but he is eating and living in order to worship Allah properly and to

---

[1] Islahi, pp. 276-277.

get closer to Him. There is a great distance between the one who can recognize this fact and the one who simply eats to live without any real purpose behind his life.[1]

(12) Fasting is an act that demonstrates one's sincerity to Allah. Only Allah is aware if a person truly fasted or not. No one can know if he secretly broke his fast. Therefore, Allah has a special reward for those who fast. This is stated in the following hadith *qudsi,*

يَتْرُكُ طَعَامَهُ وَشَرَابَهُ وَشَهْوَتَهُ مِنْ أَجْلِي الصِّيَامُ لِي وَأَنَا أَجْزِي بِهِ وَالْحَسَنَةُ بِعَشْرِ أَمْثَالِهَا

Allah has said, "He leaves his food, drink and desires because of Me. Fasting is for My sake and I shall reward it [in a special way]. And every good deed shall be rewarded ten-fold." (Recorded by al-Bukhari.) In the Quran, Allah praises those people who are sincere in their worship of Allah, having fear of Him and worshipping Him properly even in private with no human eyes around. In fact, it is these people who truly adhere to the admonitions and it is, in reality, they who are along the path of purification. They are the ones who are truly seeing aright and living in the light of guidance. Allah has said,

وَلَا تَزِرُ وَازِرَةٌ وِزْرَ أُخْرَىٰ ۚ وَإِن تَدْعُ مُثْقَلَةٌ إِلَىٰ حِمْلِهَا لَا يُحْمَلْ مِنْهُ شَيْءٌ وَلَوْ كَانَ ذَا قُرْبَىٰ ۗ إِنَّمَا تُنذِرُ الَّذِينَ يَخْشَوْنَ رَبَّهُم بِالْغَيْبِ وَأَقَامُوا الصَّلَاةَ ۚ وَمَن تَزَكَّىٰ فَإِنَّمَا يَتَزَكَّىٰ لِنَفْسِهِ ۚ وَإِلَى اللَّهِ الْمَصِيرُ ﴿١٨﴾ وَمَا يَسْتَوِي الْأَعْمَىٰ وَالْبَصِيرُ ﴿١٩﴾ وَلَا الظُّلُمَاتُ وَلَا النُّورُ

---

[1] Of course, hedonistic cultures, like perhaps today's modern society, have taken this denigration one step further and live to eat.

"And no bearer of burdens will bear the burden of another. And if a heavily laden soul calls [another] to [carry some of] its load, nothing of it will be carried, even if he should be a close relative. You can only warn those who fear their Lord unseen and establish the prayers. Whoever purifies himself, he purifies himself for his soul and to Allah is the return. Not equal are the blind and the seeing nor the darknesses and the light" (*Faatir* 18-20). Allah also says,

إِنَّ ٱلَّذِينَ يَخْشَوْنَ رَبَّهُم بِٱلْغَيْبِ لَهُم مَّغْفِرَةٌ وَأَجْرٌ كَبِيرٌ

"As for those who fear their Lord [while] unseen, for them is forgiveness and a great reward" (*al-Mulk* 12).[1]

(13) A disease that has spread throughout the world today is "the desire for more." Advertising and other aspects have made humans believe that many things are necessities today that one cannot live without. This puts the human into a rat race wherein he believes that he needs to keep piling up more and more—he has been convinced by Satan or by whoever that this amassing of goods is not a case of extravagance or luxury but it is a matter of basic needs and mere survival. Through the fast, the believer is able to put quite a different perspective on the abundance of goods, including food and drink, that he surrounds himself with. Sulaiman Nadwi noted,

> No doubt the needs and wants of human beings are vast and endless, but it is worth pondering what and how much are his real needs. He has in his heart a hoard of desires, a collection of wishes and self-made needs, but he has to ask himself questions whether it is not possible for him to live without pretty clothes, beautiful houses, delicious food and fast-moving transport... After negating and denying to oneself the

---

[1] There is a difference of opinion among the Quranic commentators as to whether the words *bi-l-ghaib* ("in the unseen") refer to Allah as He is unseen or if it refers to the individuals who have the fear of Allah while not being seen by others. At least with respect to *al-Mulk* 12, ibn Katheer gives only the following interpretation, "Allah speaks about those who fear the standing in front of His Lord while he is alone with Him and out of the view of the people. [Under those circumstances] he refrains from sinning and fulfills the acts of obedience, whereas no one but Allah is seeing him." Ibn Katheer, *Tafseer* (Dar Taibah), vol. 8, p. 179.

> self-made needs, perhaps the vast assemblage of so-called wants will shrink and be confined to a couple of real basic needs, such as food and drink... If all human crimes and sins are listed and if the basic reasons of greed, avarice, destruction and murder are sought, the ultimate link will be found in the excessive desire for pleasure and for these two things, namely food and drink. The real [actually, one] object [of fasting] is that a human being might gradually decrease the multiplicity of his needs and by continuous efforts try to free himself of excessive desire for power and want of food.[1]

When the believer realizes this fact via, for example, the fast of Ramadhaan, he can free himself to concentrate on what is of real importance: not the chasing after the supposed "needs" of this world but the racing forward to earn the pleasure of Allah.

It is interesting to note that the fast of Ramadhaan was not made obligatory until the second year after the Hijrah. Sulaiman Nadwi notes that this may be significant in the fact that during the Makkan stage, in which time the Muslims were very poor and faced starvation on occasion, Allah did not require them to fast. It was only after the obstacles were removed and the material situation of the Muslims began to steadily improve, when worldly luxuries could become available to them, that Allah obliged the Muslims to fast the month of Ramadhaan.[2] If this fact is admitted, it should once again cause one to consider the situation in which many Muslims of today are living. Indeed, the luxuries are there and readily available to them. Unfortunately, many Muslims have succumbed to the diseases of wallowing in these luxuries. This era is perhaps an especially important time to reflect on the importance of the fast and the many lessons it has to offer for the purification of the soul.

It must also be realized that there are some clear indications from the Prophet (peace and blessings of Allah be upon him) that the fast may not have its desired effect in

[1] Sulaiman Nadwi, pp. 207-208.
[2] Sulaiman Nadwi, p. 211.

purifying the soul if it is not performed in the proper manner. In particular, while abstaining from food, drink and sexual intercourse, one is required to make an extra effort to abstain from the other acts that Allah forbids at all times. The Messenger of Allah (peace and blessings of Allah be upon him) said,

مَنْ لَمْ يَدَعْ قَوْلَ الزُّورِ وَالْعَمَلَ بِهِ فَلَيْسَ لِلَّهِ حَاجَةٌ فِي أَنْ يَدَعَ طَعَامَهُ وَشَرَابَهُ

"If one does not give up false speech and acting according to it, then Allah is not in need of him giving up his food and drink." (Recorded by al-Bukhari.) One of the early Muslims said, "The easiest part of fasting is giving up drink and food."

In fact, the fast is meant to be a period of training and development of *taqwa* (God-consciousness). If a person does not abstain from forbidden acts during that time of fasting, then he is actually not receiving or enacting the proper type of training. Hence, the act in itself becomes nothing more than a burden and hardship on the person without any beneficial outcome in this life or, possibly, in the Hereafter. Hence, the Messenger of Allah (peace and blessings of Allah be upon him) also said,

رُبَّ صَائِمٍ لَيْسَ لَهُ مِنْ صِيَامِهِ إِلاَّ الْجُوعُ وَرُبَّ قَائِمٍ لَيْسَ لَهُ مِنْ قِيَامِهِ إِلاَّ السَّهَرُ

"Perhaps the fasting person gets nothing but his fast except hunger. And perhaps the praying person [at night during Ramadhaan] gets nothing from his standing [in prayer] except sleeplessness."[1]

What a contrast is found in the different statements of the Messenger of Allah (peace and blessings of Allah be upon him). In some hadith, there is mention of the great, special reward coming from Allah as believers draw closer to Allah via the fast. Yet, in this hadith, there is a mention of those who get nothing but hunger from the fast. However, as al-Baidhaawi stated, the goal of

---

[1] Recorded by ibn Maajah. According to al-Albaani, it is *sahih*. See al-Albaani, *Saheeh al-Jaami*, vol. 1, p. 656. In a hadith, it is stated that the devils are chained down during the month of Ramadhaan. Thus, if someone still insists on performing forbidden acts during that month, even given the very positive atmosphere and environment to improve his soul, this is a sign that he himself is not truly interested in purifying his soul. It is, therefore, not surprising that he does not receive anything for his fasting save hunger and exhaustion.

fasting is not thirst and hunger. The goal of fasting is the overcoming of one's desires and defeating the base desires of the soul.[1] Ibn al-Qayyim stated this point forcefully when he wrote,

> The purpose of fasting is that the spirit of man was released from the clutches of desires and moderation prevailed in his carnal self, and, through it, he realized the goal of purification and everlasting felicity. It is aimed at curtailing the intensity of desire and lust by means of hunger and thirst, at inducing man to realize how many were there in the world like him who had to go even without a small quantity of food, at making it difficult for the Devil to deceive him, and at restraining his organs from turning towards things in which there was the loss of both worlds. Fasting, thus, is the bridle of the God-fearing, the shield of the crusaders and the discipline of the virtuous.[2]

Jaabir said, "While you are fasting, let your hearing, sight and tongue also abstain from lying and the forbidden. Avoid harming the neighbor. You should have calmness and tranquility on the day of your fast. Do not let the day you fast and the day you break your fast be the same."[3]

This author feels compelled to add a final note of caution. Unfortunately, it is a recognized fact that many people do not leave what is forbidden during the daytime of Ramadhaan. They simply continue in their old ways, even though they may be physically fasting. As for others, as soon as they break their fasts, they go back to their old ways. In the Muslim world today, many spend their whole nights awake, busying themselves with watching soap operas, movies, playing cards, shopping. Many of these people then sleep the whole day until it is time to break the fast. Nowadays, in many parts of the Muslim world, Ramadhaan has become a festival when the stores and shops open all night long and people are partying throughout the night. Instead of

---

[1] Quoted in Ahmad ibn Hajar, *Fath al-Baari* (al-Maktabah al-Salafiyyah, n.d.), vol. 4, p. 117.

[2] Quoted in Abul Hasan Ali Nadwi, *The Four Pillars* (Lucknow, India: Academy of Islamic Research and Publications, 1976), p. 173.

[3] Quoted in ibn Rajab, *Lataaif*, p. 292.

spending this time remembering Allah, praying to Allah, reading the Quran and so forth, they are losing this precious time and for that reason you see no change in them from year to year although they physically fast this month of Ramadhaan. Actually, it is said that one of the signs of the acceptance of one's good deeds is that the person is guided to follow up those good deeds with additional good deeds[1] but many people are not even performing the act properly during the month of Ramadhaan. Hence, everyone has to make an effort to change during the month of Ramadhaan and take advantage of its special blessings and teachings. After Ramadhaan, in order for that fast to be accepted, one should have the intention to continue with the lessons that one learned during the month.

The Pilgrimage (*Hajj*) and Its Effect on the Purification of the Soul

Another of the pillars and essential obligatory practices of Islam is the pilgrimage or Hajj to the House of Allah (Kaabah) in Makkah. It is a very comprehensive and potentially very moving rite. Siddiqi has aptly described the significance of different aspects of the Hajj in the following quote,

> It is rightly said that it [the Hajj] is the perfection of faith since it combines in itself all the distinctive qualities of other obligatory acts. It represents the quality of *salat* [prayer] since a pilgrim offers prayers in the Kaba, the House of the Lord. It encourages spending of material wealth for the sake of the Lord, the chief characteristic of Zakat. When a pilgrim sets out for Hajj, he dissociates himself from his hearth and home, from his dear and near ones to please the Lord. He suffers privation and undertakes the hardship of journey— the lessons we learn from fasting and *itikaf*.[2]

[1] Cf., Saalih al-Fauzaan, *Al-Khutab al-Munbariyyah fi al-Munaasabaat al-Asriyyah* (Beirut: Muassasat al-Risaalah, 1987), vol. 1, p. 104.

[2] *Itikaf* is where one secludes himself in the mosque for personal worship and devotion. Most commonly, this is done at the end of the month of Ramadhaan.

In Hajj one is trained to be completely forgetful of the material comforts and pomp and show of worldly life. One has to sleep on stony ground[1], circumambulate the Kaba, run between Safa and Marwa and spend his night and day wearing only two pieces of unsewn cloth. He is required to avoid the use of oil or scent or any other perfume. He is not even allowed to get his hair cut or trim his beard. In short, he is commanded to abandon everything for the sake of Allah and submit himself before his Lord, the ultimate aim of the life of a Muslim. In fact, physical pilgrimage is a prelude to spiritual pilgrimage to God, when man would bid goodbye to everything of the world and present himself before Him as His humble servant saying: "Here I am before Thee, my Lord, as a slave of Thine."[2]

Allah says about the Hajj,

وَأَذِّن فِي ٱلنَّاسِ بِٱلْحَجِّ يَأْتُوكَ رِجَالًا وَعَلَىٰ كُلِّ ضَامِرٍ يَأْتِينَ مِن كُلِّ فَجٍّ عَمِيقٍ ﴿٢٧﴾ لِّيَشْهَدُوا۟ مَنَٰفِعَ لَهُمْ

"And proclaim the Pilgrimage among men; they will come to you on foot and (mounted) on every kind of camel, lean on account of journeys through deep and distant mountain highways; That they may witness the benefits for them" (*al-Hajj* 27-28). The word "benefits" is in the indefinite, implying all types and numerous forms of benefits. Most notable among these benefits, Karzoon notes, are the purification of the soul, refinement of character, refreshing of one's spirit and the spiritual training that takes place in the most honorable land on this earth.[3]

In addition to the points made above, one may note some of the following effects of Hajj in the purification of one's soul:

(1) There are a number of important historical events that the Hajj commemorates. These events should be a source of

---

[1] This is not a must but it is how many pilgrims spend their nights.

[2] Abdul Hameed Siddiqi, trans., *Sahih Muslim* (Beirut: Dar al-Arabia, n.d.), vol. 2, p. 577. The last statement he made is very close to what the pilgrims chant during the pilgrimage.

[3] Karzoon, vol. 1, pp. 270-271.

reflection as well as inspiration for the believers. These events include but are not restricted to the following few examples:

(a) The Prophet Abraham (peace and blessings of Allah be upon him) left his wife and new son alone in a desolate land, out of sight of any other humans. Allah mentions Abraham's words in the Quran, showing his concern for their material and spiritual well-being and his reliance upon Allah to meet their needs,

رَّبَّنَآ إِنِّىٓ أَسْكَنتُ مِن ذُرِّيَّتِى بِوَادٍ غَيْرِ ذِى زَرْعٍ عِندَ بَيْتِكَ ٱلْمُحَرَّمِ رَبَّنَا لِيُقِيمُوا۟ ٱلصَّلَوٰةَ فَٱجْعَلْ أَفْـِٔدَةً مِّنَ ٱلنَّاسِ تَهْوِىٓ إِلَيْهِمْ وَٱرْزُقْهُم مِّنَ ٱلثَّمَرَٰتِ لَعَلَّهُمْ يَشْكُرُونَ

""O our Lord! I have made some of my offspring to dwell in a valley without cultivation, by Your Sacred House; in order, O our Lord, that they may establish regular prayer. So fill the hearts of some among men with love towards them, and feed them with fruits, so that they may give thanks" (*Ibraaheem* 37).

Al-Bukhari records from ibn Abbaas that the Prophet Abraham (peace and blessings of Allah be upon him) left his wife Hajar and his beloved son alone in that land with no water or other inhabitants. As he walked away, Hajar went after him asking how it was that he was leaving them in that land with no people and no provisions. Abraham did not even look back at her. Finally, she asked if Allah had ordered him to do that and Abraham replied in the affirmative.[1] In another narration in *Sahih al-Bukhari*, Abraham responded that he was leaving them in Allah's care and Hajar responded that she was satisfied with Allah's care. At that time, Hajar responded that Allah, therefore, would not leave them. This demonstrates a true trust in whatever Allah has commanded. Once Hajar knew that Abraham's act was based on a command from Allah, she felt at ease and she immediately recognized that there was good in it. She knew that Allah comes to the aid of the believers. As one approaches Makkah and sees

[1] According to ibn Abbaas, after leaving them a distance, Abraham looked back and made the supplication in the verses quoted above.

the vast desert land all around it, one should keep in mind the faith that Abraham and Hajar had. One should recall how they responded to this command from Allah to inhabit this empty land where there was no sign of any sustenance or provisions. They did that because they believed in Allah and they believed in Allah's promise to help the believers and not to leave their deeds in vain.

(b) Although Hajar had full trust in Allah, she also understood that it is obligatory upon the believers to utilize the permissible means that are available to them in this world. After consuming the little water she had with her, Hajar went back and forth from the top of the hills of al-Safa and al-Marwah to see if she could see anyone who might come to her assistance. She was anxiously looking for water, as she could not bear to watch her young baby suffering and almost dying from thirst. The importance of this event can be seen in the fact that to this day the pilgrims commemorate her actions by retracing her steps, going back and forth between those two hills (al-Safa and al-Marwah).[1] It was at that time that Allah's help came to her. She heard a voice and she asked if it had come to help her. Then she saw the angel with its wing digging the well of Zamzam. This is the same well that pilgrims continue to drink from to this day. Unquestionably, the continued presence of that well should be a very clear reminder for every pilgrim of how Allah blesses the believers and supports them. The angel told her not to be afraid for Allah would not neglect them in that land wherein the House of Allah was built.

(c) Among the most memorable acts of the Hajj is the animal sacrifice that commemorates Abraham's willingness to sacrifice his son as well as his son Ismaaeel's willingness to submit himself to the command of Allah. This event should be very moving with very little need for comment. A father's natural love for his child for whom he had hoped for many years and a young man's natural desire to escape death are obvious to everyone. However, when the love for Allah is very strong in the heart and the belief that there is nothing more important than

[1] Al-Bukhari records that the Prophet (peace and blessings of Allah be upon him) stated that the going back and forth between these two hills during the pilgrimage is in imitation of what Hajar herself did.

worshipping and submitting to Allah is present, the believer is willing to make any and all sacrifices to please Allah. This is one of the clear messages that comes from this incident that is remembered every year at the Hajj and Eid celebrations. This is the type of model that every believer should attempt to emulate. It is this attitude and practice in one's life that every Muslim should be working towards.

(2) In addition to the historical incidents, there are a number of significant aspects of Hajj. For example, one of the greatest ways to remove sins from one's being—and thus aid in the process of purification—is to perform the pilgrimage or Hajj. The Prophet (peace and blessings of Allah be upon him) said,

مَنْ حَجَّ لِلَّهِ فَلَمْ يَرْفُثْ وَلَمْ يَفْسُقْ رَجَعَ كَيَوْمِ وَلَدَتْهُ أُمُّهُ

"Whoever performs the Hajj for the sake of Allah and does not commit any lewdness or evils returns like the day in which his mother gave him birth," that is, without any sins. (Recorded by al-Bukhari and Muslim.) The Prophet (peace and blessings of Allah be upon him) also said,

الْعُمْرَةُ إِلَى الْعُمْرَةِ كَفَّارَةٌ لِمَا بَيْنَهُمَا وَالْحَجُّ الْمَبْرُورُ لَيْسَ لَهُ جَزَاءٌ إِلاَّ الْجَنَّةُ

"One *Umrah*[1] until the next *Umrah* is an expiation for what is between them. And the Hajj that is accepted by Allah and performed properly has no reward other than Paradise." (Recorded by al-Bukhari and Muslim.)

(3) In the Hajj, there is an opportunity for the Muslim to demonstrate his complete submission and obedience to Allah. There are some acts in the Hajj concerning which no human can claim to have a complete understanding of their significance or purpose. However, the Muslim still performs them simply out of the fact that Allah has commanded them and the individual recognizes that his only real purpose in life is to submit to and worship Allah, having full trust in Allah and following everything and anything that Allah may command. Al-Bukhari records that

[1] *Umrah* is sometimes called the "lesser pilgrimage". It contains fewer rites than the Hajj and may be done throughout the year.

when Umar kissed the black stone, he said, "By Allah, I am kissing you while I am fully aware that you are a stone and that you do not bring about benefit or harm. If I had not seen the Messenger of Allah (peace and blessings of Allah be upon him) kissing you, I would not kiss you." In fact, the pilgrim is constantly reminded of this attitude that he is developing in himself by what he chants coming to the Hajj, "O Allah, I am repeatedly at your service." In this chant, the person is committing himself to a continuous and immediate obedience to Allah.[1]

(4) One practical aspect that occurs from the Hajj and that anyone who has performed the Hajj can testify to is that during the Hajj one can see the willingness of other humans to sacrifice for the sake of Allah. While circumambulating the Kaabah, one sees people with no legs or unusable legs pulling themselves around the Kaabah. One can feel the poverty of some of the fellow pilgrims and realize how much and how long they must have sacrificed and saved to make this one Hajj for the sake of Allah. This definitely moves a person and makes him reflect upon his own sacrifices for the sake of Allah. It makes him wonder whether he himself would be willing to make such great sacrifices for the sake of Allah if or when needed.

(5) Furthermore, every believer must realize the relationship between his faith and sacrifice. Sacrifice is an essential aspect of this religion. A true believer should be willing to sacrifice one's time, wealth and even life for the sake of Allah. In addition, the true believer must sacrifice all desires and pleasures that are not consistent with the Quran and Sunnah. In fact, a true believer must sacrifice anything that comes between him and the true worship of Allah alone. Anything that takes a person away from Allah and following his path is detrimental to

---

[1] The pilgrims repeat the chant, "*Labbaika Allaahumma labbaika*..." The word *labbaika* means, "immediate in response to Allah's call and demonstrating one's obedience." It comes from the expression, "the man *labb* in the place," meaning he remained and stayed there. In the chant, the word *labbaika* is repeated to either imply emphasis or a continuous and repeated expression of obedience. Cf., Hamd ibn Muhammad al-Khataabi, *Shan al-Duaa* (Damascus: Daar al-Thaqaafah al-Arabiyyah, 1992), pp. 127-129; Abdul Rahmaan ibn Rajab, *Sharh Hadeeth Labbaika Allaahumma Labbaik* (Makkah: Daar Aalim al-Faraaid, 1417 A.H.), pp. 23-26.

the well-being and spiritual health of a human. Anything that takes that place in the heart that rightfully belongs to Allah can spell disaster for the human. Thus, the person must either control that thing, give it up or be willing to sacrifice it, thus removing it from his life and keeping himself firm on the path to the true worship of Allah.

Islam is not about practicing those aspects of the faith that one finds easy or pleasing—choosing what one wants to apply of Islam and ignoring what one wants to ignore of the teachings of Islam. Islam is, in fact, about submission and sacrifice for Allah alone. This fact should be very clear in the Muslim's mind as every year the Hajj is performed and every year the intended sacrifice of Ismaaeel is commemorated. This sacrifice that is commemorated is not one of blood and flesh. It is the sacrifice by one's heart and soul, demonstrating one's ultimate willingness to submit to Allah and to sacrifice any and all things for the sake of Allah. This is the true believer—his life, his wealth, his ties of kin and friendship, his aspirations, his position in life are all simply matters that he is willing to sacrifice if and whenever called upon by his faith. Allah says in the Quran,

لَن تَنَالُوا۟ ٱلْبِرَّ حَتَّىٰ تُنفِقُوا۟ مِمَّا تُحِبُّونَ ۚ

"By no means shall you attain righteousness unless you give (freely) of that which you love" (*ali-Imraan* 92). Allah also says while describing the true believers who are deserving of His love and pleasure,

إِنَّ ٱللَّهَ ٱشْتَرَىٰ مِنَ ٱلْمُؤْمِنِينَ أَنفُسَهُمْ وَأَمْوَٰلَهُم بِأَنَّ لَهُمُ
ٱلْجَنَّةَ ۚ يُقَٰتِلُونَ فِى سَبِيلِ ٱللَّهِ فَيَقْتُلُونَ وَيُقْتَلُونَ ۖ وَعْدًا عَلَيْهِ
حَقًّا فِى ٱلتَّوْرَىٰةِ وَٱلْإِنجِيلِ وَٱلْقُرْءَانِ ۚ وَمَنْ أَوْفَىٰ بِعَهْدِهِۦ مِنَ ٱللَّهِ ۚ
فَٱسْتَبْشِرُوا۟ بِبَيْعِكُمُ ٱلَّذِى بَايَعْتُم بِهِۦ ۚ وَذَٰلِكَ هُوَ ٱلْفَوْزُ ٱلْعَظِيمُ
﴿١١١﴾ ٱلتَّٰٓئِبُونَ ٱلْعَٰبِدُونَ ٱلْحَٰمِدُونَ ٱلسَّٰٓئِحُونَ

ٱلرَّٰكِعُونَ ٱلسَّٰجِدُونَ ٱلْءَامِرُونَ بِٱلْمَعْرُوفِ وَٱلنَّاهُونَ عَنِ
ٱلْمُنكَرِ وَٱلْحَٰفِظُونَ لِحُدُودِ ٱللَّهِ ۗ وَبَشِّرِ ٱلْمُؤْمِنِينَ

"Allah has purchased from the believers their souls and their wealth. For theirs (in return) is the Garden (of Paradise). They fight for His Cause, and slay and are slain. [This reward is] a promise binding on Him in truth, through the Torah, the Gospel, and the Quran. And who is more faithful to his covenant than Allah? Then rejoice in the bargain that you have concluded. That is the achievement supreme. Those who turn (to Allah) in repentance, serve Him, praise Him, go out for the sake of Allah, and who bow down and prostrate themselves in prayer, enjoin good and forbid evil, and observe the limits set by Allah (these do rejoice). So proclaim the glad tidings to the believers" (*al-Taubah* 111-112).

In another verse, Allah makes it very clear that the love for Allah, His Messenger and striving for His sake must take precedence over any and all other feelings of love. Allah has said,

قُلْ إِن كَانَ ءَابَآؤُكُمْ وَأَبْنَآؤُكُمْ وَإِخْوَٰنُكُمْ وَأَزْوَٰجُكُمْ
وَعَشِيرَتُكُمْ وَأَمْوَٰلٌ ٱقْتَرَفْتُمُوهَا وَتِجَٰرَةٌ تَخْشَوْنَ كَسَادَهَا
وَمَسَٰكِنُ تَرْضَوْنَهَآ أَحَبَّ إِلَيْكُم مِّنَ ٱللَّهِ وَرَسُولِهِۦ وَجِهَادٍ فِى
سَبِيلِهِۦ فَتَرَبَّصُوا۟ حَتَّىٰ يَأْتِىَ ٱللَّهُ بِأَمْرِهِۦ ۗ وَٱللَّهُ لَا يَهْدِى ٱلْقَوْمَ
ٱلْفَٰسِقِينَ

"Say: If your fathers, your sons, your brothers, your wives, your kindred, the wealth that you have gained, the commerce in which you fear a decline, and the dwellings in which you delight are more beloved to you than Allah, His Messenger and striving for His sake, then wait until Allah brings His command (and torment). And Allah guides not the disobedient people" (*al-Taubah* 24).

In fact, in the *soorah* named after the Hajj itself, Allah has described those people who do not fathom this aspect of putting Allah and His religion above everything else and who think that they are free to worship Allah only in those things that are pleasing to them. Allah says,

وَمِنَ ٱلنَّاسِ مَن يَعْبُدُ ٱللَّهَ عَلَىٰ حَرْفٍ فَإِنْ أَصَابَهُۥ خَيْرٌ ٱطْمَأَنَّ بِهِۦ
وَإِنْ أَصَابَتْهُ فِتْنَةٌ ٱنقَلَبَ عَلَىٰ وَجْهِهِۦ خَسِرَ ٱلدُّنْيَا وَٱلْءَاخِرَةَ ذَٰلِكَ
هُوَ ٱلْخُسْرَانُ ٱلْمُبِينُ

"There are among men some who serve Allah, as it were, on the verge: if good befalls them, they are, therewith, well content; but if a trial comes to them, they turn on their faces; they lose both this world and the Hereafter: that is loss for all to see" (*al-Hajj* 11).

It was this attitude of sacrifice that was the way or religion of the Prophet Abraham (peace and blessings of Allah be upon him) and that Muslims recall and contemplate every Hajj season. This is the only true way to be. If anyone follows a way other than that of submission and sacrifice, that is, a way other than that of the Prophet Abraham (peace and blessings of Allah be upon him), he is simply fooling and deceiving himself concerning his own faith. Allah has said,

وَمَن يَرْغَبُ عَن مِّلَّةِ إِبْرَٰهِـۧمَ إِلَّا مَن سَفِهَ نَفْسَهُۥ وَلَقَدِ ٱصْطَفَيْنَٰهُ
فِى ٱلدُّنْيَا وَإِنَّهُۥ فِى ٱلْءَاخِرَةِ لَمِنَ ٱلصَّٰلِحِينَ ﴿١٣٠﴾ إِذْ قَالَ لَهُۥ رَبُّهُۥٓ
أَسْلِمْ قَالَ أَسْلَمْتُ لِرَبِّ ٱلْعَٰلَمِينَ ﴿١٣١﴾ وَوَصَّىٰ بِهَآ إِبْرَٰهِـۧمُ بَنِيهِ

وَيَعْقُوبُ يَٰبَنِيَّ إِنَّ ٱللَّهَ ٱصْطَفَىٰ لَكُمُ ٱلدِّينَ فَلَا تَمُوتُنَّ إِلَّا وَأَنتُم مُّسْلِمُونَ

"And who turns away from the religion of Abraham but such as debase their souls with folly? Him We chose and rendered pure in this world: and he will be in the Hereafter in the ranks of the righteous. Behold! His Lord said to him, 'Submit (to Me).' He said, 'I submit (my will) to the Lord and Cherisher of the Universe.' And this was the Legacy that Abraham left to his sons, and so did Jacob: 'O my sons! Allah has chosen the faith for you; then die not except in the state of submission (to Allah)'" (*al-Baqarah* 130-132).

(6) Selfishness, arrogance, looking down upon others and greed are some of the dangerous diseases that despoil the soul. One must work valiantly to remove any remnants of these diseases. The Hajj should be a helpful step in this process. This is fulfilled via a number of means:

First, in most cases, the Hajj requires a great deal of expenditures (travel, purchasing the animal to be sacrificed and so forth). These are all eagerly spent for the sake of Allah. This helps in purifying the soul from selfishness and greed. It allows the soul to experience the joy of spending some of his wealth directly for the sake of Allah.

Second, as all of the pilgrims gather at one place, in one dress, all submitting to and calling upon their one Lord for forgiveness for the multitude of sins that people commit in this world, the feeling of brotherhood and love should fill the heart of the believer. He should realize that he himself and all the Muslims all only have one purpose in life, are all marching toward one end and they are all the servants of Allah and Allah alone. There is no room for pride and arrogance here. The reality sets in that the only ways by which these different Muslims differ is in their sincerity to Allah and their good deeds. Otherwise, there is no preference nor distinction given to anyone based on nationality, race, wealth or standing in society.

(7) The Day of Arafah, which the Messenger of Allah (peace and blessings of Allah be upon him) described as the

"essence of the Hajj,"[1] should be a very moving experience. On this day, everywhere one looks on the Mount one sees others dressed in the same simple garments, standing and beseeching Allah for forgiveness. It is a moving experience that immediately brings thoughts of the Day of Judgment to one's mind. In one's lifetime, there is probably no other experience that can be such a strong reminder of the day in which the souls will be brought forth from the graves, standing and waiting for the judgment to take place. In fact, the *soorah* named after the Hajj begins with a strong reminder of the resurrection itself. For example, the first couple of verses state,

يَـٰٓأَيُّهَا ٱلنَّاسُ ٱتَّقُوا۟ رَبَّكُمْ ۚ إِنَّ زَلْزَلَةَ ٱلسَّاعَةِ شَىْءٌ عَظِيمٌ ﴿١﴾ يَوْمَ تَرَوْنَهَا تَذْهَلُ كُلُّ مُرْضِعَةٍ عَمَّآ أَرْضَعَتْ وَتَضَعُ كُلُّ ذَاتِ حَمْلٍ حَمْلَهَا وَتَرَى ٱلنَّاسَ سُكَـٰرَىٰ وَمَا هُم بِسُكَـٰرَىٰ وَلَـٰكِنَّ عَذَابَ ٱللَّهِ شَدِيدٌ

"O mankind fear your Lord, for the convulsion of the Hour (of judgment) will be a thing terrible! The day you shall see it, every mother giving suck shall forget her suckling babe, and every pregnant female shall drop her load (unformed): you shall see mankind as in a drunken state, yet not drunk: but dreadful will be the wrath of Allah" (*al-Hajj* 1-2).

(8) Karzoon notes that even the preparation for the journey to the Hajj and the pilgrim's farewells to his family and friends should be a reminder to the believer that he is on a true, lifelong journey for which there is no return. In the same way that he must prepare for the Hajj journey in this life, he must always be prepared for that final journey by having the provisions of *taqwa* (fear of Allah and good deeds), for he knows not when the time of that final journey will occur. Karzoon notes that Allah

---

[1] Literally, the Messenger of Allah (peace and blessings of Allah be upon him) said, "The Hajj is Arafah." Recorded by Ahmad, Abu Dawood, al-Nasaa`ee and others. According to al-Albaani, it is *sahih*. See al-Albaani, *Saheeh al-Jaami*, vol. 1, p. 606.

directs the attention of the believers to the relationship between the journey to Hajj and final journey to the Hereafter in the verse,

ٱلْحَجُّ أَشْهُرٌ مَّعْلُومَٰتٌ ۚ فَمَن فَرَضَ فِيهِنَّ ٱلْحَجَّ فَلَا رَفَثَ وَلَا
فُسُوقَ وَلَا جِدَالَ فِى ٱلْحَجِّ ۗ وَمَا تَفْعَلُوا۟ مِنْ خَيْرٍ يَعْلَمْهُ ٱللَّهُ ۗ
وَتَزَوَّدُوا۟ فَإِنَّ خَيْرَ ٱلزَّادِ ٱلتَّقْوَىٰ ۚ وَٱتَّقُونِ يَٰٓأُو۟لِى ٱلْأَلْبَٰبِ

"For Hajj are the months well-known. If any one undertakes that duty therein, let there be no obscenity, nor wickedness, nor wrangling in the Hajj and whatever good you do, (be sure) Allah knows it. And take a provision (with you) for the journey, but the best of provisions is right conduct (*taqwa*). So fear Me, O you that are wise" (*al-Baqarah* 197).[1] The provision of *taqwa* is the provision that is needed for the journey to Allah in the Hereafter.

(9) Similarly, before the pilgrim enters the inviolable state of Hajj, he performs the *ghusl* (ritual washing of the body) and removes his everyday clothing, putting on the simple garment of Hajj. This should also be a reminder, notes Karzoon, of his final death, in which his body will be washed, he will be clothed in the shroud and placed in his final resting place of this world wherein only his good deeds will remain with him in his grave.[2]

(10) All of the events that one performs at the Hajj and the historical and spiritual significance of the place in which the person performs them—a place where Adam laid the foundation for the first house of worship, a place where Abraham rebuilt that house, leaving his family alone there and a place where the Prophet Muhammad (peace and blessings of Allah be upon him) and his Companions lived the early history of Islam—should have a profound effect on the believer. He should view his own life in the light of the lives of the prophets. He should recognize his own shortcomings and the insignificance of the other aspects of this world that he gives preference to. This should drive the person to repent and ask for forgiveness from his Lord. Indeed, the feelings

---

[1] Karzoon, vol. 1, p. 277.
[2] Karzoon, vol. 1, p. 277.

that should be boiling in his heart at such a place may be those which make his supplications so sincere that Allah will not turn down his pleas. Sulaiman Nadwi noted,

> Sins can be forgiven at any place, no matter where the person is: it is not essential to be at Arafat or Kabah, but because many benefits, blessings, and heartfelt feelings which these Symbols, places and the rites of Hajj produce—which are not found anywhere else—they provide a better environment for asking for forgiveness with sincerity of heart. Because of the honour and reverence in which a Muslim holds these places dear to his heart, the psychological effects produced in him are profound. These are the places where the blessings and mercies of Allah descended on the prophets, where the prophets were showered with Allah's light of guidance, where the Signs of Allah and His prophets are found everywhere, where in the past Allah's devotees have conversed with Him, and where all the pilgrims assemble, pray, cry and lament together for forgiveness. The environment and atmosphere of these places surely help the pilgrims to pray from the bottom of their hearts with the result that the prayers are accepted.[1]

(11) After performing the great act of Hajj, coming closer to Allah and sincerely seeking Allah's forgiveness, the Muslim should become a new person as he returns to his home and to ordinary life. He must return to ordinary life but he need not be his ordinary self; instead, he should be a radically changed person, with a new outlook on life and a belief in a fresh start. Nadwi describes this phenomenon in the following words,

> It is human psychology and an everyday observation that in a person's life there are particular occasions and landmarks which cause important changes in him. On such an occasion, his life becomes divided into two distinct parts: past and future. In some people change

[1] Sulaiman Nadwi, pp. 275-276.

> may be brought about by the change of season. In others change occurs after an important event, such as marriage, having a baby, completion of education, getting employment, some big success... These events produce in them the ability to change and to draw a distinct line between their past and future lives, enabling the direction of their lives to become fixed. In fact the Hajj, in the same way, acts as a landmark between a person's past and future life and provides an opportunity for turning towards change and reform. From this point onward a person ends his previous life, no matter what it has been in the past, and starts his life anew. By presenting himself in these blessed places, by standing and praying where the exalted prophets and Allah's loved ones had stood, by praying in person in the House of Kabah which in the past was the invisible Qibla for his *salats*, by the affirmation of beliefs and the glorification of Allah, by acknowledging the shortcomings of his past life and feeling regret, and by pledging obedience and submission in the future such a great effect is produced that the direction of his life is changed from bad to good and from righteousness to greater righteousness. The old chapter of his life is closed and a new one opened. It could be said that after performing Hajj he is born anew.[1]

Indeed, as noted earlier, the Prophet (peace and blessings of Allah be upon him) did say,

مَنْ حَجَّ لِلَّهِ فَلَمْ يَرْفُثْ وَلَمْ يَفْسُقْ رَجَعَ كَيَوْمِ وَلَدَتْهُ أُمُّهُ

"Whoever performs the Hajj for the sake of Allah and does not commit any lewdness or evils returns like the day in which his mother gave him birth," that is, without any sins. (Recorded by al-Bukhari and Muslim.)

It must be noted, though, that in order for the Hajj to be of maximum benefit to the pilgrim, a number of conditions need

[1] Sulaiman Nadwi, pp. 276-277.

to be met. First, as in all deeds, the act must be done sincerely for the sake of Allah. Allah says,

قُلْ إِنَّ صَلَاتِي وَنُسُكِي وَمَحْيَايَ وَمَمَاتِي لِلَّهِ رَبِّ ٱلْعَٰلَمِينَ ﴿١٦٢﴾ لَا شَرِيكَ لَهُۥ ۖ وَبِذَٰلِكَ أُمِرْتُ وَأَنَا۠ أَوَّلُ ٱلْمُسْلِمِينَ

"Say: 'Truly, my prayer and my service of sacrifice, my life and my death, are (all) for Allah, the Cherisher of the Worlds. No partner has He. This am I commanded, and I am the first of those who bow to His Will'" (*al-Anaam* 162-163). This fact is particularly mentioned here with respect to the Hajj because it can be a source of pride and show, especially in some Muslim countries where the returning pilgrim earns the honorific title of "*hajji*" and is treated as someone special by those around him.

Secondly, the pilgrim must, out of compliance with Allah's command, avoid all forms of *rafath* (any kind of lewd speech and any act, such as sexual intercourse, that violates the Hajj), *fusooq* (sin or disobedience to Allah), *jidaal* (argumentation and disputation leading to hatred and spite) and all acts that harm his Muslim brethren. This in itself can be a great trial and training of patience when one is alongside thousands of other people from different cultures, with different levels of education and understanding, and of different etiquette. Allah says,

ٱلْحَجُّ أَشْهُرٌ مَّعْلُومَٰتٌ ۚ فَمَن فَرَضَ فِيهِنَّ ٱلْحَجَّ فَلَا رَفَثَ وَلَا فُسُوقَ وَلَا جِدَالَ فِي ٱلْحَجِّ ۗ وَمَا تَفْعَلُوا۟ مِنْ خَيْرٍ يَعْلَمْهُ ٱللَّهُ ۗ وَتَزَوَّدُوا۟ فَإِنَّ خَيْرَ ٱلزَّادِ ٱلتَّقْوَىٰ ۚ وَٱتَّقُونِ يَٰٓأُو۟لِى ٱلْأَلْبَٰبِ

"For Hajj are the months well-known. If any one undertakes that duty therein, let there be no obscenity, nor wickedness, nor wrangling in the Hajj and whatever good you do, (be sure) Allah knows it. And take a provision (with you) for the journey, but the best of provisions is right conduct. So fear Me, O you that are wise" (*al-Baqarah* 197).

Further Purifying of One's Soul and Getting Even Closer to Allah by Performing the Voluntary Deeds

If a person fulfills only the obligatory acts in their proper fashion, he should be able to reach a certain level of spiritual purification. Maybe this is part of what is meant by the hadith wherein the Bedouin is asking the Prophet (peace and blessings of Allah be upon him) about Islam. The following part of the conversation was heard by the companion Talhah ibn Ubaidullah:

فَقَالَ رَسُولُ اللَّهِ صَلَّى اللَّهم عَلَيْهِ وَسَلَّمَ خَمْسُ صَلَوَاتٍ فِي الْيَوْمِ وَاللَّيْلَةِ فَقَالَ هَلْ عَلَيَّ غَيْرُهَا قَالَ لا إِلاَّ أَنْ تَطَوَّعَ قَالَ رَسُولُ اللَّهِ صَلَّى اللَّهم عَلَيْهِ وَسَلَّمَ وَصِيَامُ رَمَضَانَ قَالَ هَلْ عَلَيَّ غَيْرُهُ قَالَ لا إِلاَّ أَنْ تَطَوَّعَ قَالَ وَذَكَرَ لَهُ رَسُولُ اللَّهِ صَلَّى اللَّهم عَلَيْهِ وَسَلَّمَ الزَّكَاةَ قَالَ هَلْ عَلَيَّ غَيْرُهَا قَالَ لا إِلاَّ أَنْ تَطَوَّعَ قَالَ فَأَدْبَرَ الرَّجُلُ وَهُوَ يَقُولُ وَاللَّهِ لا أَزِيدُ عَلَى هَذَا وَلا أَنْقُصُ قَالَ رَسُولُ اللَّهِ صَلَّى اللَّهم عَلَيْهِ وَسَلَّمَ أَفْلَحَ إِنْ صَدَقَ

The Messenger of Allah (peace and blessings of Allah be upon him) said, "Five prayers during the day and night." He [the Bedouin] said, "Is there any other [prayer] upon me?" He replied, "No, unless you do so voluntarily." The Messenger of Allah (peace and blessings of Allah be upon him) then said, "And fast Ramadhaan." He asked, "Is there any other [fast] upon you?" He replied, "No, unless you do so voluntarily." The Messenger of Allah (peace and blessings of Allah be upon him) then mentioned the zakat to him and he said, "Is there any other [charity] upon me?" He said, "No, unless you do so voluntarily." The man turned away saying, "By Allah, I shall neither add anything to that nor shall I decrease anything from it." The Messenger of Allah (peace and blessings of Allah be upon him) then said, "He will be successful if he is telling the truth." (Recorded by al-Bukhari and Muslim.)

Ibn Taimiyyah noted,

> The path [can be broken into] two paths. [First,] there is the path of the pious, the Companions of the Right.[1] This is the path of fulfilling the obligatory deeds and abstaining from the forbidden deeds, both the esoteric and external of those categories. Second is the path of *al-muqarabeen al-saabiqeen* [those who outstripped others and were brought near to Allah] who perform the obligatory and recommended deeds to the best of their abilities and refrain from the disliked and forbidden deeds. As the Prophet (peace and blessings of Allah be upon him) said, "What I have forbidden you, stay away from. What I have ordered you [to do], do as much of it as you can." [Recorded by al-Bukhari and Muslim.][2]

However, most likely, the process of purification will not stop at the obligatory deeds alone. The feeling and love for more purifying acts will flow and the believer will seek other righteous deeds that will bring him even closer to Allah. Hence, the third step in the purification of one's soul is the performance of the voluntary deeds after one has attended to the deeds that are obligatory upon him.

The voluntary deeds include all of the deeds that are not strictly obligated and which have some sign that they are praiseworthy acts. These deeds are also at different levels of virtue. Some virtuous deeds were greatly emphasized by the Prophet (peace be upon him) while others were not so emphasized. In other words, some voluntary deeds are much more virtuous than others. The more virtuous a voluntary deed, the closer it takes a person to Allah.

In referring to the very important hadith *qudsi* referred to herein more than once, in which the Allah has stated,

وَمَا تَقَرَّبَ إِلَيَّ عَبْدِي بِشَيْءٍ أَحَبَّ إِلَيَّ مِمَّا افْتَرَضْتُ عَلَيْهِ وَمَا يَزَالُ عَبْدِي يَتَقَرَّبُ إِلَيَّ بِالنَّوَافِلِ حَتَّى أُحِبَّهُ

---

[1] For a description of the "Companions of the Right," see, for example, *al-Waaqiah* 27-40.

[2] Ibn Taimiyyah, *Majmoo*, vol. 10, p. 463.

"My servant does not draw near to Me with anything more beloved to Me than the religious duties that I have imposed upon him; and My servant continues to draw near to Me with supererogatory works such that I love him,"[1] Fareed states that one can understand from this hadith that if a person is lacking in his performance of the obligatory deeds—in the sense that he does not perform them and is complacent with respect to them[2]—but he performs many voluntary deeds, that will not lead him to becoming a beloved of Allah. One only comes closer to Allah by performing voluntary deeds after the person fulfills the obligatory deeds. This is the path of purification according to the *ahl al-Sunnah*.[3] In fact, as ibn Hubairah pointed out, something can only be "extra" if the necessary or obligatory portions are fulfilled.[4]

Finally, it is very important to note—and it is a great blessing from Allah—that this path is not a path that necessarily takes a long amount of time or requires that the person pass through certain stages. A person can become one of the purified and devoted servants of Allah very quickly by sincerity and devotion to Allah. This true sincerity and devotion may come after he performs only a few deeds. Indeed, from the outset, he may perform those deeds that are obligatory upon him and he becomes beloved to Allah. Then he continues on that path, with Allah guiding him to what is good and proper. This will be a sign that he is continuing as one of Allah's *auliyaa* (devoted servants). Again, this "easy path" is part of the great mercy and blessings of Allah. [5]

---

[1] Recorded by al-Bukhari.

[2] This portion between the dashes is not from Ahmad Fareed but it must be added. This is because a person's shortcoming with respect to his obligatory deeds is made up by his voluntary deeds, unless, of course, he simply does not perform them or is not keen on performing them. Allah knows best.

[3] Fareed, *Tazkiyah*, p. 24.

[4] Quoted in Fareed, *Tazkiyah*, p. 24.

[5] Cf., Ibraaheem Hilaal, introduction to Muhammad ibn Ali al-Shaukaani, *Qatr al-Wali ala Hadeeth al-Wali* (Beirut: Daar Ihyaa al-Turaath al-Arabi, n.d.), p. 149.

The Importance of Voluntary Deeds

A conclusion from the hadith *qudsi* above is that some believers move even closer to Allah by not only fulfilling the obligatory duties but by additionally performing the voluntary deeds (and these are numerous). When a person performs the obligatory deeds, he demonstrates his willingness to submit to Allah. In addition, he is doing what he needs to do to protect himself from Allah's punishment. However, if on top of those deeds he also performs voluntary deeds, this demonstrates his sincerity to Allah and his true willingness to please Allah. This is no longer a matter of fulfilling a command from Allah or rescuing oneself from punishment. Now one is doing the acts to get even closer and become more beloved to Allah.[1]

Ibn Hajar points out that, in general, a person becomes beloved to another by doing more than the minimum or doing more than what is simply required. If a person, for example, returns money to another person and he also gives him some presents in addition, he is usually more beloved to the other person than the one who simply returned the money. The same aspect is true with respect to Allah, in a manner, of course, that is befitting of Allah and free of any imperfections.[2]

The performance of voluntary deeds also includes staying away from the disliked acts. In other words, the devoted believers exert themselves to come even closer to their beloved Lord by performing more deeds of obedience for His sake and staying away from the acts that are simply reprehensible. In other words, they, by no means, stop at the "legal definition" of a disliked act (which implies that there is no sin in the act). They go beyond that and see in a disliked act a deed which, by refraining from it for the

---

[1] Al-Nawawi states that the meaning of Allah loving someone is that Allah wants good for that person. He and others have made similar statements because they are not willing to accept the fact that Allah could have love for someone, as love implies some emotions that are befitting humans but not befitting Allah. There is no need for such interpretations. Allah loves His *auliyaa*. That is a true love but it is also a love that is becoming of Allah and it does not have the deficiencies that a human love has. Cf., Yahya al-Nawawi, *Sharh Matin al-Arbaeen al-Nawawiya* (Jeddah: Daar al-Mujtama, 1986) p. 143.

[2] Ibn Hajar, *Fath* (al-Maktaba al-Tijaariyyah), vol. 13, p. 145.

sake of Allah, they can draw themselves even closer to their Beloved Allah.

This last point deserves some emphasis. Unfortunately, too many people consider the "legal" definition of *makrooh* (a disliked act), which states that it is an act that the person will be rewarded for avoiding and will not be punished for committing, and they then consider it permissible and of no harm to engage in such actions. Again, the pious Muslim must look beyond such a legal definition and consider the act from another point of view: what is the value of that act in Allah's sight. When looked at from this angle, the nature of the disliked acts, although they are not forbidden, radically changes. The person who is seeking the love of Allah can place no value in such acts and can receive no joy or benefit from performing them. Therefore, he does his best to remain away from them although, according to the jurists, they are not strictly forbidden.

Furthermore, when a person involves himself in the disliked deeds, he may very easily fall into committing the forbidden acts. The case is different with those people who avoid even the disliked deeds. If these people should slip, as all humans are apt to do, then, most likely, they will simply slip into the disliked deeds and not fall all the way to those deeds that are greatly hated by Allah.

Another important aspect of the voluntary deeds that, unfortunately, some people tend to forget or neglect is that they make up for the shortcomings of the obligatory deeds that the person performs. It can be argued that very few Muslims, if any, perform the prayer in the manner that they are supposed to perform it. Many Muslims move about while praying, fidgeting with their clothing, looking here and there. And, more importantly, for many of them, their hearts are not attuned to the prayers. Satan comes to them and makes them think about almost everything except what they should be concentrating on in their prayers. Again, this is the case with many Muslims, even with some who are righteous. But the difference between the righteous and the lackadaisical Muslims is that the righteous make up for such shortcomings by performing voluntary prayers (or deeds in general) that take them closer to Allah. In another hadith of the Prophet (peace be upon him), it is clear that this principle is true for all of the actions that a person performs. Abu Hurairah reported that the Messenger of Allah (peace and blessings of Allah be upon him) said,

إِنَّ أَوَّلَ مَا يُحَاسَبُ بِهِ الْعَبْدُ يَوْمَ الْقِيَامَةِ مِنْ عَمَلِهِ صَلاتُهُ فَإِنْ صَلُحَتْ فَقَدْ أَفْلَحَ وَأَنْجَحَ وَإِنْ فَسَدَتْ فَقَدْ خَابَ وَخَسِرَ فَإِنِ انْتَقَصَ مِنْ فَرِيضَتِهِ شَيْءٌ قَالَ الرَّبُّ عَزَّ وَجَلَّ انْظُرُوا هَلْ لِعَبْدِي مِنْ تَطَوُّعٍ فَيُكَمَّلَ بِهَا مَا انْتَقَصَ مِنَ الْفَرِيضَةِ ثُمَّ يَكُونُ سَائِرُ عَمَلِهِ عَلَى ذَلِكَ

"The first deeds for which the slave of Allah will be held accountable on the Day of Judgment will be his prayers. If they are in order, he will have prospered and been successful. But if they are wanting, he will have failed and been a loser. If there is some shortcoming in his obligatory prayers, the Lord will say, 'See if My slave has any voluntary prayers with which may be completed that which was wanting in his obligatory prayers.' Then the rest of his deeds will be judged in like fashion."[1]

Therefore, it is no wonder that such people who perform the voluntary deeds (which includes staying away from the disliked deeds) receive a special love from Allah in both this life and in the Hereafter. Allah says about such a servant in the hadith *qudsi* quoted earlier,

وَمَا يَزَالُ عَبْدِي يَتَقَرَّبُ إِلَيَّ بِالنَّوَافِلِ حَتَّى أُحِبَّهُ فَإِذَا أَحْبَبْتُهُ كُنْتُ سَمْعَهُ الَّذِي يَسْمَعُ بِهِ وَبَصَرَهُ الَّذِي يُبْصِرُ بِهِ وَيَدَهُ الَّتِي يَبْطِشُ بِهَا وَرِجْلَهُ الَّتِي يَمْشِي بِهَا وَإِنْ سَأَلَنِي لَأُعْطِيَنَّهُ وَلَئِنِ اسْتَعَاذَنِي لَأُعِيذَنَّهُ

"My servant continues to draw near to Me with supererogatory works such that I love him. And when I love him, I am his hearing with which he hears, his seeing with which he sees, his hand with which he strikes, and his leg with which he walks. Were he to ask

[1]Recorded by al-Tirmidhi and others. According to al-Albaani, it is *sahih*. See al-Albaani, *Saheeh al-Jaami*, vol. 1, p. 405.

of Me, I would surely give him; and were he to ask Me for refuge, I would surely grant him it." (Recorded by al-Bukhari.)

In this hadith, Allah describes those persons who have earned His love. This makes this a most important hadith. This is the goal of the true believers: to purify oneself by worshipping Allah properly and, thereby, gain the love, mercy, pleasure and forgiveness of Allah. In other words, the goal is to become a *wali* (a true devoted servant) of Allah. As discussed in a previous chapter, this is the greatest achievement. Indeed, this is the achievement that no one could ever take from a person. Anyone, by Allah's leave, may destroy whatever another person possesses and prizes of this world but no one can ever touch his religion (which is first and foremost in his heart) and his relationship to Allah.

This love of Allah leads to all the good in the heavens and the earth. As noted earlier, the Messenger of Allah (peace be upon him) said,

إِنَّ اللَّهَ إِذَا أَحَبَّ عَبْدًا دَعَا جِبْرِيلَ فَقَالَ إِنِّي أُحِبُّ فُلاَنًا فَأَحِبَّهُ قَالَ فَيُحِبُّهُ جِبْرِيلُ ثُمَّ يُنَادِي فِي السَّمَاءِ فَيَقُولُ إِنَّ اللَّهَ يُحِبُّ فُلاَنًا فَأَحِبُّوهُ فَيُحِبُّهُ أَهْلُ السَّمَاءِ قَالَ ثُمَّ يُوضَعُ لَهُ الْقَبُولُ فِي الأَرْضِ

"If Allah loves a slave, He announces to Gabriel, 'Verily Allah loves so and so, so love him.' Then Gabriel loves him and he announces to the inhabitants of the heavens, 'Verily Allah loves so and so, so love him.' Then the inhabitants of the heavens love him. And then he is granted the acceptance of the people on earth." (Recorded by al-Bukhari and Muslim.)

Allah Himself will never take this special relationship and love away from the person as long as that person is sincere to Allah. Indeed, in His ever abundant mercy to His creatures, He turns to them whenever they turn to Him. This is made clear in another hadith *qudsi* in which Allah says,

أَنَا عِنْدَ ظَنِّ عَبْدِي بِي وَأَنَا مَعَهُ إِذَا ذَكَرَنِي فَإِنْ ذَكَرَنِي فِي نَفْسِهِ ذَكَرْتُهُ فِي نَفْسِي
وَإِنْ ذَكَرَنِي فِي مَلَإٍ ذَكَرْتُهُ فِي مَلَإٍ خَيْرٍ مِنْهُمْ وَإِنْ تَقَرَّبَ إِلَيَّ بِشِبْرٍ تَقَرَّبْتُ إِلَيْهِ
ذِرَاعًا وَإِنْ تَقَرَّبَ إِلَيَّ ذِرَاعًا تَقَرَّبْتُ إِلَيْهِ بَاعًا وَإِنْ أَتَانِي يَمْشِي أَتَيْتُهُ هَرْوَلَةً

"I am as My servant expects Me to be. I am with him when he makes mention of Me. If he makes mention of Me to himself, I make mention of him to Myself. And if he makes mention of Me in an assembly, I make mention of him in an assembly better than it. And if he draws near to Me a hand's span, I draw near to him a forearm's length. And if he draws near to Me a forearm's length, I draw near to him an arm's length. And if he comes to Me walking, I go to him at speed." (Recorded by al-Bukhari and Muslim.)

When a believer gets to that state, then all the minor things of this life become irrelevant. Any harm that should come to him, any worldly disaster or the like thereof, will not mean anything to him as long as he knows that by his actions he is pleasing Allah.

Many unbelievers of today are fond of saying, "As long as I have my health I cannot complain," but to the true believer even his health is not of everlasting importance. Indeed, to him, his health is simply an important resource and blessing from Allah to be used for the sake of Allah.[1] But if his health and everything else of this world is taken from him and he is left in a most miserable condition, he will still have happiness as long as he knows that the deeds that he is performing are those that Allah wants him to perform.[2]

---

[1] Of course, given that it is such an important need for the one who wants to strive and work for the sake of Allah, it becomes obligatory upon that believer to preserve his health as this will help him become a stronger worker for the sake of Allah.

[2] The essence of this point is demonstrated in the Prophet's supplication to Allah, "O Allah, give us certainty [in faith] such that it would make the hardships of this world easy upon us... And do not make our trials related to our religion..." [Recorded by al-Tirmidhi. According to al-Albaani, it is *hasan*. See al-Albaani, *Saheeh Sunan al-Tirmidhi*, vol. 3, p. 168.] The greatest harm that could come to any Muslim is the type of trial that could affect his relationship with Allah and because of his own shortcomings make him a weaker Muslim. The Prophet (peace and blessings of Allah be upon him) has instructed, by example, that the Muslim should ask Allah to keep him safe from such a trial. And the first part of the supplication demonstrates that the person with a firm faith will be able to face any trial related to this world.

This puts the believer on a completely different level from the rest of humanity who are not blessed with the knowledge of their Lord and Creator. This level comes when the person tastes the sweetness of faith, when he comes to realize and experience the real meaning of "There is no one worthy of worship except Allah." This sweetness of faith is a type of paradise in this world, as ibn Taimiyyah once said, "There is a paradise in this world and the one who does not enter it will not enter the paradise in the next world."[1] This paradise is that which is achieved by performing the obligatory deeds followed by the voluntary deeds, all done for the sake of Allah and according to the revelation from Allah.

Allah's Mercy as Exhibited in the Voluntary Deeds

Allah, the Creator and Fashioner of humans, has obligated certain deeds. Those are deeds that are needed by all humans for the purification of their souls. Beyond those deeds, though, Allah has left the door wide open for individuals to concentrate on those deeds that they are most inclined to. For example, some people are dedicated to the voluntary prayers. They receive great increases in their faith and benefit from them. They feel sorrow whenever they miss those prayers. Hence, they tend to them to the best of their ability. Those voluntary prayers— in addition to the general obligatory deeds— may be the way that they get closer to Allah. It may be the key to their entering Paradise. Others may be attracted to fasting, charity or the pilgrimage.

There are yet others who are more inclined to doing good toward others. They perform the obligatory deeds and then beyond that they spend their time tending to others' needs. Those good voluntary deeds bring them closer to Allah and more beloved to Him. Yet others are attracted to voluntary jihad, teaching the religion, calling non-Muslims to Islam and so forth. When these people tend to those matters, they become the key by which they come closer to Allah and enter Paradise. Someone else might do a

---

[1] Quoted in Muhammad ibn al-Qayyim, *al-Waabil al-Sayyib min al-Kalim al-Tayyib* (Beirut: Daar al-Bihaar, 1986), p. 73.

little of all of the different types of voluntary deeds and that is what makes him beloved to Allah.[1]

This reality is all by the mercy of Allah. Beyond the obligatory deeds, people are free to pursue those good voluntary deeds that they are most attracted to. There are so many areas of voluntary deeds that it seems inconceivable that a person could not find some voluntary deed or deeds that he would like to perform in order to get closer to Allah. Allah's path to paradise is wide enough to accommodate all of those different leanings. However, this is all dependent on the individual first fulfilling, in general, the obligatory deeds. If the person does not do that, then he may not be on the straight path at all.

The Mistake of Excelling in Voluntary Deeds while Ignoring Many Obligatory Deeds

Al-Maaz speaks about those whose voluntary deeds preoccupy them such that they do not perform the obligatory deeds properly. For example, one misses the prayer in congregation, in particular the Fajr Prayer, because he spent the night in *tahajjud* or one is busy calling the others to the straight path while he forgets his obligation to himself and to his family.[2] This is a way by which one is deceived by Satan into ignoring more important duties on the pretext that one is involved in doing good deeds. Satan gets the person involved in less important matters and the person himself does not even realize how he has succumbed to a plot of Satan. In fact, he may be very happy with himself and the numerous wonderful acts that he is performing. This fact in itself emphasizes the importance of knowledge and a deep insight into the religion. There are priorities in the religion itself as set by Allah or demonstrated by the Prophet (peace and blessings of Allah be upon him). If one ignores these priorities, one is in danger of swerving off of the Straight Path.

One always has to put in front of himself the fact that the first steps or the true path is first and foremost in fulfilling the

---

[1] Cf., quote in Fareed (pp. 30-31) from Muhammad ibn al-Qayyim, *Tareeq al-Hijratain*, p. 179.
[2] Al-Maaz, p. 115.

different obligations. This is clear in the hadith *qudsi* that has already been quoted a number of times. Indeed, it is said, "If the obligatory deeds preoccupy one from performing the voluntary deeds, he is excused. But if the voluntary deeds preoccupy one from performing the obligatory deeds, then he is deceived."[1]

At the same time, though, it must be noted that everybody is going to have some shortcoming in his obligatory deeds. Hence, the point being made in this section does not mean that one has to perfect the obligatory deeds before moving on to any voluntary deeds. Two points must be considered. First, the person should see where he is very lacking in any of the obligatory deeds and try to discover if the reason for his weakness is his over-involvement in particular voluntary acts. If he finds that to be the case, he must curtail his voluntary act in order to shore up his obligatory acts. Second, some people intentionally or willingly ignore the obligatory deeds (maybe because they do not like them or do not feel inclined to them) and simply concentrate on voluntary deeds still trying to tell themselves that they are somehow becoming very pleasing to Allah while acting in that manner. In this case, Satan has duped the person. The individual has to wake up to what is occurring, correct his ways and do his best to fulfill the deeds that Allah or His Messenger (peace and blessings of Allah be upon him) have declared obligatory.

Purification of the Soul and the Avoidance of Doubtful Matters

An additional step in the process of purifying one's soul is the avoidance of doubtful or questionable matters. By avoiding such doubtful matters, one can be certain that his practice and faith are protected and innocent. There is no question that such an approach is very healthy for the soul and the heart.

This step is based on many well-known hadith of the Prophet (peace and blessings of Allah be upon him). Indeed, there is ample evidence showing that the truly pious person must stay away from those things that are simply disliked (that is, not

[1] Quoted in Fareed, *Tazkiyah*, p. 23.

strictly forbidden) as well as those matters that are simply doubtful. The Prophet (peace be upon him) said,

اجعلوا بينكم وبين الحرام سترة من الحلال

"Place between you and the forbidden acts a covering [or barrier] of permissible acts."[1] The Messenger of Allah (peace be upon him) also stated,

دَعْ مَا يَرِيْبُكَ إِلَى مَا لاَ يَرِيْبُكَ

"Leave what makes you doubt for what does not make you doubt."[2] In a very comprehensive statement, the Messenger of Allah (peace and blessings of Allah be upon him) also said,

إِنَّ الْحَلالَ بَيِّنٌ وَإِنَّ الْحَرَامَ بَيِّنٌ وَبَيْنَهُمَا أُمُوْرٌ مُشْتَبِهَاتٌ لا يَعْلَمُهُنَّ كَثِيرٌ مِنَ النَّاسِ فَمَنِ اتَّقَى الشُّبُهَاتِ فَقَدْ اسْتَبْرَأَ لِدِينِهِ وَعِرْضِهِ وَمَنْ وَقَعَ فِي الشُّبُهَاتِ وَقَعَ فِي الْحَرَامِ كَالرَّاعِي يَرْعَى حَوْلَ الْحِمَى يُوشِكُ أَنْ يَرْتَعَ فِيهِ أَلاَ وَإِنَّ لِكُلِّ مَلِكٍ حِمًى أَلا وَإِنَّ حِمَى اللَّهِ مَحَارِمُهُ أَلا وَإِنَّ فِي الْجَسَدِ مُضْغَةً إِذَا صَلَحَتْ صَلَحَ الْجَسَدُ كُلُّهُ وَإِذَا فَسَدَتْ فَسَدَ الْجَسَدُ كُلُّهُ أَلا وَهِيَ الْقَلْبُ

"That which is lawful is clear and that which is unlawful is clear and between the two of them are doubtful [or ambiguous] matters about which not many people are knowledgeable. Thus, he who avoids these doubtful matters certainly clears himself in regard to his religion and his honor. But he who falls into the doubtful matters falls into that which is unlawful like the shepherd who pastures around a sanctuary, all but grazing therein. Verily every king has a sanctuary and Allah's sanctuary is His prohibitions. In the body there is a morsel of flesh which, if it be sound, all the body is sound and which, if it be diseased, all of the

---

[1] Recorded by ibn Hibbaan. Al-Albaani declared it *sahih*. See Muhammad Naasir al-Deen al-Albaani, *Silsilat al-Ahadeeth al-Saheehah* (Damascus: al-Maktab al-Islaami, 1979), vol. 2, p. 594-596.

[2] Recorded by Ahmad, al-Tirmidhi and ibn Hibbaan. According to al-Albaani, it is *sahih*. Cf., al-Albaani, *Saheeh al-Jaami*, vol. 1, p. 637.

body is diseased. This part of the body is the heart." (Recorded by al-Bukhari and Muslim.)

Purification of the Soul and Avoidance of Over-Indulgence in Non-Beneficial, Permissible Acts

This author could not come across any evidence that indicates that permissible acts are harmful to one's spiritual purification[1], although one would come to that conclusion upon reading some books related to this topic. Indeed, as al-Tiraiqi noted, "Allah has permitted for us all of the pure matters of sustenance. This includes everything in which there is benefit or pleasure that is void of any harm to the body or mind."[2]

That having been said, an over indulgence in such permissible acts can be detrimental. This is an opportunity cost type of issue. One has limited time and energy and one should always be aware of what one is missing while doing something else. The astute person will not allow himself to lose much of his precious time and energy on non-beneficial acts. In fact, this can be reckoned as yet another one of the plots of Satan.

Of course, the discussion here does not extend to extravagance or indulging in luxuries. Those are clearly disliked by Allah, implying a distancing from Allah. Allah has said, for example,

يَٰبَنِيٓ ءَادَمَ خُذُواْ زِينَتَكُمۡ عِندَ كُلِّ مَسۡجِدٖ وَكُلُواْ وَٱشۡرَبُواْ وَلَا تُسۡرِفُوٓاْۚ إِنَّهُۥ لَا يُحِبُّ ٱلۡمُسۡرِفِينَ

---

[1] If the acts were truly harmful in some fashion, they should be at least regarded as "reprehensible" (*makrooh*) in the Shareeah. The fact that they, in their essence, are not considered as such is a sign that they are actually not harmful. Over-indulging in such acts can have a different ruling than committing the act itself (say, on a one-time or non-often basis). Allah knows best.

[2] Abdullah ibn Muhammad al-Tiraiqi, *Al-Israaf: Diraasah Fiqhiyyah Muqaaranah bain al-Madhaahib al-Arbaah* (published by its author, 1992), p. 151. The reader interested in more details on extravagance should consult this work as it is a comprehensive work on all conceivable forms of extravagance.

"O children of Adam, wear your clothing at every mosque, and eat and drink, but be not excessive. Indeed, He likes not those who commit excess" (*al-Araaf* 31). The goal is to be neither extravagant nor miserly but to spend on what deserves to be spent on according to the law of Allah. Hence, Allah says while describing His true servants,

وَٱلَّذِينَ إِذَآ أَنفَقُواْ لَمْ يُسْرِفُواْ وَلَمْ يَقْتُرُواْ وَكَانَ بَيْنَ ذَٰلِكَ قَوَامًا

"And [they are] those who, when they spend, do so not excessively or sparingly but are ever between that, [justly] moderate" (*al-Furqaan* 67).

Summary of the Process

The process of spiritual purification is actually something "simple" in the sense that it is available and within the means of all humans who are willing to dedicate themselves to this purpose. There are no mysteries or secret teachings. There are no special individuals who alone can teach this path. The path has been clearly espoused by the Quran and the example of the Prophet (peace and blessings of Allah be upon him), as well as the way of his Companions. There are no special exercises or rituals that require one to virtually injure oneself or do damage to the natural feelings of the soul.

No, indeed, the path is simply one of purifying one's beliefs by turning to the Quran and Sunnah and allowing them to explain what is true and what one must believe in. This step is simply a matter of accepting what the revelation states and having the intention to internalize those beliefs, such that their effects are seen on the person himself. As the person is learning more about the proper beliefs, he is also doing his best to fulfill the obligatory duties of which he is knowledgeable. While meeting those obligatory duties, he turns his attention to the vast arena known as voluntary deeds. In this field, he is now free to choose any or many of the various deeds that are pleasing to Allah.

Whichever he chooses, they are means by which he gets closer and closer to Allah, resulting in a special love from Allah and a truly purified soul.

Chapter 6
Means and Measures to Help One Along the Path of Purification

The previous chapter dealt with the basic outline of the process of purification of the soul. It is admitted that it is much easier to identify that process than it is to make oneself walk along that path. Therefore, in this chapter specific means and measures that in general should help one follow the path of purification are detailed. In essence, these "means and measures" simply fall into one of the steps described in the process of purification (that is, they fall into the category of either obligatory or recommended acts). However, within those steps, there are some acts that seem most prominent in bringing about additional benefit for the purification of the soul. Hence, they are specifically highlighted in this chapter.

Turning to Allah and Praying for His Help

A first and essential step is a sincere turning to Allah and seeking Allah's help. Like all and any form of guidance, true guidance can only come from Allah and true spiritual purification is also from Allah alone. In fact, it is a great blessing from Allah. It can only come as a grace and bounty from Allah. Allah says,

يَـٰٓأَيُّهَا ٱلَّذِينَ ءَامَنُوا۟ لَا تَتَّبِعُوا۟ خُطُوَٰتِ ٱلشَّيْطَـٰنِ ۚ وَمَن يَتَّبِعْ خُطُوَٰتِ

ٱلشَّيْطَـٰنِ فَإِنَّهُۥ يَأْمُرُ بِٱلْفَحْشَآءِ وَٱلْمُنكَرِ ۚ وَلَوْلَا فَضْلُ ٱللَّهِ

عَلَيْكُمْ وَرَحْمَتُهُۥ مَا زَكَىٰ مِنكُم مِّنْ أَحَدٍ أَبَدًا وَلَٰكِنَّ ٱللَّهَ يُزَكِّي مَن يَشَآءُ ۗ وَٱللَّهُ سَمِيعٌ عَلِيمٌ

"O you who believe! Follow not Satan's footsteps. If any will follow the footsteps of Satan, he will (but) command what is shameful and wrong: and were it not for the grace and mercy of Allah on you, not one of you would ever have been pure. Allah does purify whom He pleases. And Allah is One Who hears and knows (all things)" (*al-Noor* 21). Everyone must recognize the fact that this great act of self-purification comes from Allah. Allah grants it to whomever He wills, according to His Wisdom and Justice. But in any case, He is the true source of this purification. Hence, everyone must turn to Him and seek His purification and guidance to this noble path.

Turning to Allah and praying to Him is an act that is actually another one of the obligatory acts and it is an act that is pleasing to Allah. When supplicating, the individual turns to Allah and, in so doing, he is admitting his own weakness while affirming Allah's ability to respond to His call and Allah's ability to fulfil His own will. Hence, the act of supplication is in itself an act of worship and a step in the purification of the soul. Thus, the Prophet (peace and blessings of Allah be upon him) said,

الدُّعَاءُ هُوَ الْعِبَادَةُ

"Supplication is the [essence of] worship."[1]

The Messenger of Allah (peace and blessings of Allah be upon him) also stated,

مَنْ لَمْ يَسْأَلِ اللَّهَ يَغْضَبْ عَلَيْهِ

"Whoever does not ask of Allah, He is angry with him."[2] And Allah Himself says,

---

[1] Recorded by Ahmad, al-Nasaa`ee, Abu Dawood, al-Tirmidhi and others. According to al-Albaani, it is *sahih*. See al-Albaani, *Saheeh al-Jaami*, vol. 1, p. 641.

[2] Recorded by al-Tirmidhi. According to al-Albaani, it is *hasan*. Cf., al-Albaani, *Saheeh Sunan al-Tirmidhi*, vol. 3, p. 138.

وَقَالَ رَبُّكُمُ ٱدْعُونِىٓ أَسْتَجِبْ لَكُمْ ۚ إِنَّ ٱلَّذِينَ يَسْتَكْبِرُونَ عَنْ عِبَادَتِى سَيَدْخُلُونَ جَهَنَّمَ دَاخِرِينَ

"And your Lord says: 'Call on Me; I will answer your (prayer).' But those who are too arrogant to serve Me will surely find themselves in Hell, in humiliation" (*Ghaafir* 60). Thus, when supplicating to Allah, one is demonstrating his want and desire to worship Allah as well as his lack of arrogance and pride that keep people from humbly submitting to Allah..

Hence, nothing but good should be expected from supplicating to Allah. Indeed, the Messenger of Allah (peace and blessings of Allah be upon him) said,

مَا مِنْ مُسْلِمٍ يَدْعُو بِدَعْوَةٍ لَيْسَ فِيهَا إِثْمٌ وَلاَ قَطِيعَةُ رَحِمٍ إِلاَّ أَعْطَاهُ اللَّهُ بِهَا إِحْدَى ثَلاَثٍ إِمَّا أَنْ تُعَجَّلَ لَهُ دَعْوَتُهُ وَإِمَّا أَنْ يَدَّخِرَهَا لَهُ فِي الْآخِرَةِ وَإِمَّا أَنْ يَصْرِفَ عَنْهُ مِنَ السُّوءِ مِثْلَهَا

"There is no Muslim who supplicates Allah with a supplication that does not contain anything sinful or asks for the ties of kinship to be broken save that Allah gives him one of three things: either He will give him what he asks for soon, or He will delay it for him for the Hereafter or He will keep a similar evil away from him."[1]

In fact, the true believer is always desiring of having Allah's guidance at all times, never having to rely on himself. This is true for all times but it is especially true for times of anxiety, weakness, stress and confusion along the path. Hence, the

---

[1] Recorded by Ahmad, Abu Yala, al-Haakim and others. According to al-Shaukaani, its chain is good. Al-Haithami stated that the chain of Ahmad, Abu Yala and one chain of al-Bazzaar contains narrators of the two *Sahihs* of al-Bukhari and Muslim, save for Ali ibn Ali al-Rifaai who is, though, a trustworthy narrator. Al-Haakim called the hadith *sahih* and al-Dhahabi approved of his conclusion. See Muhammad ibn Ali al-Shaukaani, *Qatr al-Wali ala Hadeeth al-Wali* (Beirut: Daar Ihyaa al-Turaath al-Arabi, n.d.), p. 441; Ahmad al-Banna, *Al-Fath al-Rabbaani li-Tarteeb Musnad al-Imaam Ahmad ibn Hanbal al-Shaibaani* (Cairo: Dar al-Hadeeth, n.d.), vol. 14, p. 266.

Prophet (peace and blessings of Allah be upon him) taught a supplication for the believers during time of grief, distress and anxiety. The Messenger of Allah (peace and blessings of Allah be upon him) said,

دَعَوَاتُ الْمَكْرُوبِ اللَّهُمَّ رَحْمَتَكَ أَرْجُو فَلا تَكِلْنِي إِلَى نَفْسِي طَرْفَةَ عَيْنٍ وَأَصْلِحْ لِي شَأْنِي كُلَّهُ لا إِلَهَ إِلاَّ أَنْتَ

"The supplication of the worried (and grieved) is, 'O Allah, Your mercy do I hope for. Do not leave me to rely on myself even for the [time of the] blinking of an eye. Make all my affairs good. There is no God except You.'"[1]

With particular regards to the purification of the soul, the Prophet (peace and blessings of Allah be upon him) set the example for all believers by praying to Allah for Allah to purify his soul. Indeed, in a lengthy supplication, the Prophet (peace and blessings of Allah be upon him) covered a number of items, all of which are central to the spiritual purification and growth. Muslim records the following hadith on the authority of the Companion Zaid ibn Arqam:

كَانَ رَسُولُ اللَّهِ صَلَّى اللَّهم عَلَيْهِ وَسَلَّمَ يَقُولُ اللَّهُمَّ إِنِّي أَعُوذُ بِكَ مِنَ الْعَجْزِ وَالْكَسَلِ وَالْجُبْنِ وَالْبُخْلِ وَالْهَرَمِ وَعَذَابِ الْقَبْرِ اللَّهُمَّ آتِ نَفْسِي تَقْوَاهَا وَزَكِّهَا أَنْتَ خَيْرُ مَنْ زَكَّاهَا أَنْتَ وَلِيُّهَا وَمَوْلاهَا اللَّهُمَّ إِنِّي أَعُوذُ بِكَ مِنْ عِلْمٍ لا يَنْفَعُ وَمِنْ قَلْبٍ لا يَخْشَعُ وَمِنْ نَفْسٍ لا تَشْبَعُ وَمِنْ دَعْوَةٍ لا يُسْتَجَابُ لَهَا

The Prophet (peace and blessings of Allah be upon him) used to say, "O Allah, I seek refuge in you from being incapable, lazy, cowardly, miserly, senile and [I also seek refuge in You from] the punishment in the grave. O Allah, give my soul its *taqwa* ['God-consciousness'] and purify it. You are the best to purify it. You are its guardian and protector. O Allah, I seek refuge in You from knowledge that is not benefiting, a heart that is not fearing, a soul

---

[1] Recorded by Ahmad and Abu Dawood. According to al-Albaani, it is *hasan*. See al-Albaani, *Saheeh al-Jaami*, vol. 1, p. 638.

that cannot be satisfied and a supplication that is not responded to."

In reality, turning to Allah and supplicating for guidance and help is necessary as an initial step as well as for every step along the path. Islahi wrote,

> [Another] essential is seeking and praying for God's help constantly. Anyone looking to the service and worship of God is tried for his sincerity of purpose at every step. And only those who can measure upto it who are blessed with the grace and help of God, and for want of them, the strongest persons are unable to stand their ground in face of the hurdles of the path. That is why it is imperative that all those treading this path must, in all humility, keep praying to God, at every step, for His Help. The part of the opening Surah of the Quran (Al-Fatihah), "Thee alone we worship and it is Thy Help we seek" has been intended for this purpose and is a reminder to the servant of God that the resolve of God's worship and service to Him cannot be translated into action without His help.[1]

In addition to what Islahi noted, the guidance to the Straight Path and the ability to remain along the Straight Path also requires Allah's help and grace. Hence, immediately after stating, "You alone do we worship and in You alone do we seek help," the believer states, "Guide us to the Straight Path..."

For this supplication to be really effective and answered by Allah, one should follow it up with, at the very least, a sincere intention to perform righteous deeds and to obey Allah. This was the practice of the prophets—they would supplicate and at the same time they would excel in performing the good deeds. The two go hand in hand and work to support one another. For example, Allah says while describing Zakariya, his wife and John,

---

[1] Islahi, p. x.

إِنَّهُمْ كَانُوا۟ يُسَٰرِعُونَ فِى ٱلْخَيْرَٰتِ وَيَدْعُونَنَا رَغَبًا وَرَهَبًا ۖ وَكَانُوا۟ لَنَا خَٰشِعِينَ

"These (three) were ever quick in emulation in good works; they used to call on Us with love and reverence, and humble themselves before Us" (*al-Anbiyaa* 90).

Sound and Beneficial Knowledge[1]

In the various verses quoted earlier concerning the role of the Prophet (peace and blessings of Allah be upon him) in purifying the people (such as the verse from *soorah al-Jumuah*), this role of his is always tied into the fact that he was also sent to teach the Book and the "Wisdom" (or Sunnah). This is a clear sign that the knowledge of these two sources is directly related to and necessary for the goal of purifying the soul.

In the previous section, the importance of supplicating to God for guidance and aid in purifying one's soul was discussed. Allah responds to the supplication of the sincere seeker by giving him the guidance that he needs to follow the path. That guidance consists of faith in the heart as well as the knowledge of the details of the path itself. But this knowledge is bestowed upon the person via his sincere supplication that is followed by the acts needed to reach the goal of the supplication itself. Allah then blesses him by making those acts easy for him. In other words, the individual asks for guidance and knowledge and then he must pursue those obvious steps that will provide him that knowledge.

The Messenger of Allah (peace and blessings of Allah be upon him) said,

طَلَبُ الْعِلْمِ فَرِيضَةٌ عَلَى كُلِّ مُسْلِمٍ

---

[1] Obviously, there is a direct and obvious connection between the first three topics discussed here (sound and beneficial knowledge, reading and pondering over the Quran and studying the hadith and life of the Prophet). In order to highlight certain facets of each of these closely related topics, they are each dealt with separately.

"Seeking knowledge is an obligation upon every Muslim."[1] This hadith demonstrates that knowledge has to be "sought" and it also proves that the seeking of knowledge is one of the obligatory acts that like other obligatory acts, as discussed earlier, takes one closer to Allah. Al-Raaghib al-Asfahaani stated, "Knowledge and acts of worship are purifying agents for the soul. Their effects are like the effect of water in cleaning the body."[2]

Karzoon defines the beneficial knowledge that helps to bring about purification as the knowledge "that brings one closer to Allah, increasing one's fear of Him and driving one to perform good deeds. First and foremost this is made up by knowledge of the Shareeah. Then comes the other branches of knowledge that drive a person to reflect upon the creation and recognize the power of Allah and the amazing aspects of His creation."[3]

Indeed, without proper knowledge a person will not know how to behave. In other words, he will not know what deeds he should perform and what deeds he should refrain from. This points to the fact that knowledge must precede action and deeds. One must know that what he is doing is correct and pleasing to Allah before he performs the deeds.[4] Without this, his intention behind the act cannot be certain and definitively for a good cause.

---

[1] Recorded by al-Baihaqi and numerous others. According to al-Albaani, it is *sahih*. See al-Albaani, *Saheeh al-Jaami*, vol. 2, p. 727. Knowledge is of two types: knowledge which is obligatory upon every individual and knowledge which is obligatory upon the community as a whole. Concerning the first type, every Muslim must know what to believe in (in general), how to pray, how to fast and so forth. Everyone has to know these things because everyone has to perform these acts. It is required for a Muslim to seek this type of knowledge. If he has the ability to do so but he does not do so, he is sinful. Knowledge which is obligatory upon the community as a whole would include more detailed knowledge concerning those matters which not everyone is required to know as well as knowledge of matters that do not concern every individual in the community. Cf., Mustafa al-Bugha and Muhyi al-Deen Mistu, *al-Waafi fi Sharh al-Arbaeen al-Nawawiya* (Damascus: Muassasat Uloom al-Quran, 1984), p. 299. [This footnote was taken from the author's *Commentary on the Forty Hadith of al-Nawawi*, vol. 3, p. 1330.]

[2] Quoted in Karzoon, vol. 1, p. 200.

[3] Karzoon, vol. 1, p. 183. The topic of contemplation and reflection shall be dealt with later. Hence, the emphasis in this particular section is on the knowledge of the religion itself.

[4] Abu Zahrah writes about Abu Hanifah, "Abu Hanifah was of the view that a righteous act must be built upon sound understanding. The good person, in his view, was not one who simply performed good deeds. Instead, in his view, the good person is the one who knows what is good and what is evil. [Thereupon he] intends to do the good based on the knowledge that

Even the testimony of faith must be preceded by the knowledge of its basic and essential meaning. Knowledge is considered one of the "prerequisites" of the testimony of faith.[1] In fact, the very act of seeking forgiveness must be preceded by the knowledge that Allah and Allah alone forgives sins. Allah says,

فَٱعْلَمْ أَنَّهُۥ لَآ إِلَٰهَ إِلَّا ٱللَّهُ وَٱسْتَغْفِرْ لِذَنۢبِكَ وَلِلْمُؤْمِنِينَ وَٱلْمُؤْمِنَٰتِ

"Know, therefore, that there is no god but Allah, and ask forgiveness for your fault, and for the men and women who believe" (*Muhammad* 19). In his *Sahih,* al-Bukhari has quoted this verse to highlight the importance of knowledge and the fact that it must precede action.

When sound and beneficial knowledge are obtained with the proper intention and, therefore, implemented in the proper way, the effect on the soul is profound. It is clearly stated by Allah in the Quran,

إِنَّمَا يَخْشَى ٱللَّهَ مِنْ عِبَادِهِ ٱلْعُلَمَٰٓؤُا۟

"It is only those who have knowledge among His slaves who fear Allah" (*Faatir* 28). In other words, such true knowledge leads to a proper form of fear of Allah and it is only those with that true knowledge who have that correct fear of Allah.

The Prophet (peace and blessings of Allah be upon him) also said about himself,

مَا بَالُ أَقْوَامٍ يَتَنَزَّهُونَ عَنِ الشَّيْءِ أَصْنَعُهُ فَوَاللَّهِ إِنِّي أَعْلَمُهُمْ بِاللَّهِ وَأَشَدُّهُمْ لَهُ خَشْيَةً

"What is wrong with some people who abstain from something that I do? By Allah, I am certainly the most knowledgeable of Allah and I have the greatest fear of Him." (Recorded by al-

---

distinguishes the two categories and he avoids the evil understanding its vileness. [This is similar to the case of] the just person who is not going to be truly just without first knowing what injustice is. Instead, the truly just person is the one who recognizes injustice and its evil results as well as recognizes justice and its goal. Hence, he intends what is just due to what it entails of an honorable goal and a good result." Muhammad Abu Zahrah, *Abu Haneefah: Hayaatuhu, Asruhu, Araauhu wa Fiqhuhu* (Daar al-Fikr al-Arabi, n.d.), p. 183.

[1] Numerous works discuss the "conditions or prerequisites" of the statement of faith. One may consult, for example, Zarabozo, *Commentary*, vol. 1, pp. 337-346.

Bukhari.) The two, being most knowledgeable about Allah and having the greatest fear of Him, should go hand in hand. One's in-depth knowledge of Allah should then keep the person from disobeying Him and displeasing Him.

In another verse, Allah displays the difference between people of true knowledge and those lacking in knowledge by picturing the beloved and righteous deeds that the well-grounded in knowledge strive to perform. Allah says,

أَمَّنْ هُوَ قَـٰنِتٌ ءَانَآءَ ٱلَّيْلِ سَاجِدًا وَقَآئِمًا يَحْذَرُ ٱلْأَخِرَةَ وَيَرْجُواْ رَحْمَةَ رَبِّهِۦ ۗ قُلْ هَلْ يَسْتَوِى ٱلَّذِينَ يَعْلَمُونَ وَٱلَّذِينَ لَا يَعْلَمُونَ ۗ إِنَّمَا يَتَذَكَّرُ أُوْلُواْ ٱلْأَلْبَـٰبِ

"Is one who worships devoutly during the hours of the night prostrating himself or standing (in adoration), who takes heed of the Hereafter, and who places his hope in the mercy of his Lord, (like one who does not)? Say: 'Are those equal, those who know and those who do not know?' It is those who are endued with understanding that receive admonition" (*al-Zumar* 9). The clear message in the verse is that these acts of devotion, the fear of the Hereafter and the hope in Allah are all the result of their beneficial knowledge that clearly distinguishes them from those who do not possess such knowledge.

Al-Shaukaani noted the relationship between purification and knowledge in the incident concerning ibn Umm Maktoom. Ibn Umm Maktoom was the blind man who came to the Prophet (peace and blessings of Allah be upon him) to ask him about the faith but the Prophet (peace and blessings of Allah be upon him) was busy with some nobles from the Quraish, so he frowned and turned away. Concerning ibn Umm Maktoom, Allah says,

وَمَا يُدْرِيكَ لَعَلَّهُۥ يَزَّكَّىٰٓ

"But what could tell you but that perchance he might grow (in spiritual understanding)?" (*Abasa* 3). Al-Shaukaani states that he was attempting to purify himself via his questioning and getting the true knowledge of the faith.[1]

Allah also says in the Quran,

وَلَكِنْ كُونُوا رَبَّانِيِّينَ بِمَا كُنْتُمْ تَعْلَمُونَ الْكِتَابَ وَبِمَا كُنْتُمْ تَدْرُسُونَ

"[The prophet would say:] Be you *rabbaaniyyeen* (pious scholars) because of what you know of the Book and because of what you have studied" (*ali-Imraan* 79).[2] Al-Shaukaani notes that this means that when one has the correct knowledge, it is expected of him that he should become a pious person due to that knowledge that he has.[3] Indeed, there is really no excuse for such a person to be anything other than a pious, righteous and purified soul.

The Prophet (peace and blessings of Allah be upon him) has even shown that the efforts required to obtain knowledge are, in the long-run when accompanied by the appropriate conditions, going to help the person along the path to Paradise, the final abode of the purified souls. The Prophet (peace and blessings of Allah be upon him) said,

مَنْ سَلَكَ طَرِيقًا يَلْتَمِسُ فِيهِ عِلْمًا سَهَّلَ اللَّهُ لَهُ بِهِ طَرِيقًا إِلَى الْجَنَّةِ

"Whoever follows a path in order to seek knowledge thereby, Allah will make easy for him, due to it, a path to Paradise." (Recorded by Muslim.) Paradise is the abode for those souls that have been purified; hence, the seeking of knowledge must be a very important aid in the purification of the soul.

In sum, the importance of beneficial knowledge for spiritual purification can be summarized in the following points[4]:

(1) By beneficial knowledge, the Muslim learns the correct Islamic beliefs and he continues to grow and add to his knowledge of these matters. The importance of purifying one's beliefs was discussed earlier. The point to be noted here is that

---

[1] Al-Shaukaani, *Fath al-Qadeer*, vol. 5, p. 382.

[2] Note that the above Arabic text and translation of the verse is based on the reading of ibn Katheer, Naafi and Abu Amr. See Ahmad Mukhtaar Umar and Abd al-Aal Saalim Mukram, *Mujam al-Qiraa`aat al-Quraaniyyah* (Intishaaraat Uswah, 1991), vol. 2, p. 46.

[3] Al-Shaukaani, *Fath al-Qadeer*, vol. 1, p. 355.

[4] Somewhat similar points and a different discussion may be found in Karzoon, vol. 1, pp. 197-201.

there is a big difference between one who knows those beliefs in a very vague and general manner and one who knows those beliefs in a detailed, effective manner. The more one knows about the various articles of faith, the greater will be the effect on his soul. For example, the levels of the fear of Allah, the love for Allah and the hope in Allah vary greatly even among believers. However, the more knowledge one has about Allah, the greater will be these aspects of faith and the greater will be their impact for the purification of the soul. As discussed earlier, without a doubt the proper beliefs are the most important starting point on the road to purification of the soul and increasing one's knowledge of those articles of faith are important in moving one along that path of purification.

(2) Via beneficial knowledge, the Muslim is able to identify the righteous deeds. He will be able to know what is permissible and what is forbidden. As noted earlier, faith must be followed up by deeds. However, those deeds must be the correct deeds and they must also be performed in correct manner. A person cannot be certain about either of these two matters unless he has knowledge. In addition, the knowledgeable person will be able to recognize, given his circumstances, what are the best deeds for him to perform, the deeds that are most pleasing to Allah given his time and place. Satan will not be able to fool him into performing acts that are not very beneficial for him. Only the one who is truly knowledgeable knows and understands this aspect.

Furthermore, it must be understood that sound knowledge is one of the most important keys in recognizing the correct path of purification and distinguishing it from all the stray paths. This fact is known and recognized by all those charlatans who attempt to steer their followers from the Straight Path. Hence, ibn al-Jauzi noted, "You should know that the greatest entryway by which Iblis [Satan] enters upon the people is via ignorance. He can safely enter upon the ignorant person while he has to enter upon the knowledgeable like a thief. In fact, Iblis has deceived many among the worshippers due to their lack of knowledge as most of them are preoccupied with acts of worship and cannot judge matters based on knowledge."[1]

---

[1] Quoted from ibn al-Jauzi's *Talbees Iblees* by al-Abdul Lateef, p. 78.

Many spiritual leaders (and Islamic "groups" for that matter) are known for insisting that their followers not read or study any other works. They are to listen to their group's teachers, shaikhs or leaders only. They must have complete faith and trust in their leaders.[1] It is even claimed that the students and followers are not in a position to read and that by reading even the Quran and hadith they may easily be misled. The students then have no means of knowing when they are being rightly guided or misguided by their shaikhs and teachers. Indeed, they can then be easily misled. In fact, one cannot truly recognize the mistakes or innovations of one's teacher until one learns from other teachers and scholars as well.

(3) Closely related to the previous point is the fact that sound knowledge can protect a person from being duped into being misguided or falling into one of the traps of Satan. Virtually every believer is continually exposed to plots to deceive him. Satan and his armies do not rest in their battle to mislead mankind. One of their greatest weapons is the casting of doubts and misunderstandings into the minds of the believer. These doubts shake the faith of the person. When this happens, his resolve and application of his faith is not as strong as it should or could be. In general, though, these doubts are easily dispelled by sound knowledge—turning to the Quran, hadith and statements of the scholars to discover the truths in such matters. But if a person is not trained in attaining such knowledge, perhaps not even knowing where to turn to for such sound knowledge and refutation of false claims, his doubts may linger until his faith is diminished and has virtually no influence over his life.

(4) Seeking and getting knowledge is both an act of worship in itself as well as a means to further purify one's soul. (In this way, it is like the ritual acts of worship that are both ends in themselves as well as means to other goals.) The act of seeking knowledge itself is a potential means of receiving forgiveness and

---

[1] In fact, some statements this author has heard from those who claim to be on the path of purification are simply astonishing. One can find statements that are completely inconsistent with the teachings and message of the Quran and Sunnah. But if the student or novice does not have a good background in the Quran or Sunnah or is not even allowed to read the Quran and Sunnah, he will never be able to recognize that fact.

mercy from Allah while it, in turn, has an effect upon the person that leads to even more benefits. The Messenger of Allah (peace and blessings of Allah be upon him) said,

وَمَنْ سَلَكَ طَرِيقًا يَلْتَمِسُ فِيهِ عِلْمًا سَهَّلَ اللَّهُ لَهُ بِهِ طَرِيقًا إِلَى الْجَنَّةِ وَمَا اجْتَمَعَ قَوْمٌ فِي بَيْتٍ مِنْ بُيُوتِ اللَّهِ يَتْلُونَ كِتَابَ اللَّهِ وَيَتَدَارَسُونَهُ بَيْنَهُمْ إِلاَّ نَزَلَتْ عَلَيْهِمُ السَّكِينَةُ وَغَشِيَتْهُمُ الرَّحْمَةُ وَحَفَّتْهُمُ الْمَلاَئِكَةُ وَذَكَرَهُمُ اللَّهُ فِيمَنْ عِنْدَهُ وَمَنْ بَطَّأَ بِهِ عَمَلُهُ لَمْ يُسْرِعْ بِهِ نَسَبُهُ

"Whoever follows a path in order to seek knowledge thereby, Allah will make easy for him, due to it, a path to Paradise. No people gather together in a house of the houses of Allah, reciting the Book of Allah and studying it among themselves, except that tranquillity is descended upon them, mercy covers them, the angels surround them and Allah makes mention of them to those in His presence. Whoever is slowed by his deeds will not be hastened forward by his lineage." (Recorded by Muslim.)

In addition, though, the act of seeking knowledge has its own important results. Umar ibn al-Khataab is reported to have said, "A man leaves from his house having sins similar in size to the Mount of Tuhaama. But when he hears some knowledge, he becomes fearful and repents. He returns to his home afterwards with no sins. Thus you should never abandon attending the gatherings of the scholars."[1]

(5) According to ibn Taimiyyah, knowledge can have a great effect on the psychological and physiological well-being of the soul. Ibn al-Qayyim narrated that once ibn Taimiyyah was ill and a doctor told him that his long hours of academic research and discussions were adding to his illness. Ibn Taimiyyah stated that he could not remain silent in the face of that statement and he debated the doctor on his own grounds. He told the doctor, "Isn't it the case that when the soul becomes happy and pleased, its innate natural health is then strengthened and it can repel diseases?" The doctor affirmed what he said. Ibn Taimiyyah then

---

[1] Quoted in Karzoon, vol. 1, p. 199.

told him, "My soul is very pleased by knowledge and its health is then strengthened and I find true relaxation." The doctor then said, "This is beyond our remedies."[1]

There is a great benefit to having such a strong appreciation for knowledge. When one truly appreciates knowledge, he receives a great pleasure whenever he is able to gain new knowledge. Such a person continually desires more knowledge, thus knowing more about Allah and getting even closer to Him. In other words, there is something special about the pursuance of knowledge in that it has its own driving force that drives the person to learn even more and more and get even closer and closer to Allah. The Messenger of Allah (peace and blessings of Allah be upon him) alluded to this positive aspect of knowledge while also mentioning worldly allurements that can have the same effect but in a negative manner. The Prophet (peace and blessings of Allah be upon him) said,

منهومان لا يشبعان طالب العلم وطالب الدنيا

"There are two strong likings that can never be satisfied: The seeking after knowledge and the seeking after this world."[2]

Lastly, there are two very important issues in the relationship between knowledge and the purification of the soul: first is sincerity in obtaining knowledge and the second is application of that knowledge by living according to its ramifications. In obtaining knowledge, the person must be very clear to himself with respect to his intention. Although this point is true for all acts of worship, it is especially important with respect to obtaining knowledge, as it is an area in which it is easy for a person to fail and stray. Failing in this area is very dangerous because it can actually lead to a person distancing himself from Allah instead of coming closer to Allah. When a person attains some level of knowledge while his intention is not completely pure, his knowledge can become a source of evil. It can make him

---

[1] Muhammad ibn al-Qayyim, *Raudhah al-Muhibeen wa Nuzhah al-Mushtaaqeen* (Aleppo, Syria: Daar al-Wa'ee, n.d.), p. 71.

[2] Recorded by al-Bazaar and others. According to al-Albaani, it is *sahih*. Cf. al-Albaani, *Saheeh al-Jaami*, vol. 2, p. 1125.

very arrogant and, instead of using this knowledge to bring himself and others to the Straight Path, he simply starts to criticize and attack others, many times defaming them in the process. Thus, he ends up simply piling up sins for himself.[1]

Hence, the Prophet (peace and blessings of Allah be upon him) specifically spoke about the intention behind seeking knowledge. The Prophet (peace and blessings of Allah be upon him) said,

مَنْ طَلَبَ الْعِلْمَ لِيُمَارِيَ بِهِ السُّفَهَاءَ أَوْ لِيُبَاهِيَ بِهِ الْعُلَمَاءَ أَوْ لِيَصْرِفَ وُجُوهَ النَّاسِ إِلَيْهِ فَهُوَ فِي النَّارِ

"Whoever learns knowledge to defeat in debate the ignorant, to compete with it among the scholars or to have the people's faces turn to him shall be in the Fire."[2] The Messenger of Allah (peace and blessings of Allah be upon him) also said,

مَنْ تَعَلَّمَ عِلْمًا مِمَّا يُبْتَغَى بِهِ وَجْهُ اللَّهِ عَزَّ وَجَلَّ لا يَتَعَلَّمُهُ إِلاَّ لِيُصِيبَ بِهِ عَرَضًا مِنَ الدُّنْيَا لَمْ يَجِدْ عَرْفَ الْجَنَّةِ يَوْمَ الْقِيَامَةِ

"Whoever learns some knowledge by which the Face of Allah is sought yet he does not learn it save to get a portion of this world, then he will not even experience the scent of Paradise on the Day of Resurrection."[3]

Second, after striving and working to attain knowledge, one must strive again and, perhaps, even harder to then put that knowledge into practice under the appropriate and feasible circumstances. Knowledge does not benefit anyone without applying it properly; indeed, it can even be a proof against the

---

[1] Similarly, one person may pray with a sincere intention while another prays simply to be seen by the people. The act is one and the same but in the former case it leads to Allah's pleasure while in the latter it leads only to sins.

[2] Recorded by ibn Maajah. According to al-Albaani, it is *sahih*. Cf., al-Albaani, *Saheeh al-Jaami*, vol. 2, p. 1060.

[3] Recorded by Ahmad, Abu Dawood and ibn Maajah. According to al-Albani, it is *sahih*. Cf., Albaani, *Saheeh al-Jaami*, vol. 2, p. 1060.

person on the Day of Judgment. The Prophet (peace and blessings of Allah be upon him) said about the Quran, for example,

الْقُرْآنُ حُجَّةٌ لَكَ أَوْ عَلَيْكَ كُلُّ النَّاسِ يَغْدُو فَبَايِعٌ نَفْسَهُ فَمُعْتِقُهَا أَوْ مُوبِقُهَا

"The Quran is either an argument for or against you. And everyone goes out in the morning and sells himself, either freeing or destroying himself." (Recorded by Muslim.) In a very moving hadith, touching on much more than just applying one's knowledge, the Messenger of Allah (peace and blessings of Allah be upon him) said,

لا تَزُولُ قَدَمَا عَبْدٍ يَوْمَ الْقِيَامَةِ حَتَّى يُسْأَلَ عَنْ أَرْبَعٍ عَنْ عُمُرِهِ فِيمَا أَفْنَاهُ وَعَنْ جَسَدِهِ فِيمَا أَبْلاهُ وَعَنْ مَالِهِ مِنْ أَيْنَ اكْتَسَبَهُ وَفِيمَا وَضَعَهُ وَعَنْ عِلْمِهِ مَاذَا عَمِلَ فِيهِ

"On the Day of Resurrection, the two feet of the servant will not move until he is asked about four matters: about his life and how he spent it, about his body and how he used it up, about his wealth and how he earned it and where he used it, and about his knowledge and what actions he did in accord with it."[1]

While discussing the reading of the Quran, the first source of true knowledge and the next topic to be discussed, Saalih al-Fauzaan notes, "If we stop at reciting and pondering over the Quran [or attaining any other knowledge] and we leave its application, then, in reality, we are stopping at the beginning of the path. We would not have achieved anything. Our efforts would go without any benefit. This is because we exhausted ourselves in the cause and we abandon its fruit, as the fruit is the acting in accord with the Quran."[2]

---

[1] Recorded by al-Daarimi. Al-Tirmidhi has virtually the same. Graded *sahih* by al-Albaani. Cf., al-Albaani, *Saheeh al-Jaami*, vol. 2, p. 1221.

[2] Saalih al-Fauzaan, *Muhaadharaat fi al-Aqeedah wa al-Dawah* (Riyadh: Daar al-Aasimah, 1415 A.H.), vol. 2, p. 302.

Comments on the Current Situation

Before moving from this issue of beneficial knowledge, this author feels compelled to comment on some of the phenomena currently existing among Muslim communities. These phenomena have a direct and clear influence upon the purification of individuals and communities as a whole. For example, it is very sad that in a Muslim community of three or four thousand, one can find only a handful who are qualified to give the Friday *khutbah* or who even know the basics of how to prepare a lecture on an Islamic topic. This is true even with respect to those who have memorized much of the Quran—may Allah reward them for their efforts in memorizing the Quran. On the other hand, tens, if not hundreds, could discuss in detail computers, engineering, politics and even sports or entertainment.[1]

The ramifications of this phenomenon are much greater than people seem to realize. The people of knowledge are not just people to be turned to when a problem or issue arises. Instead, these people—or a good number of them—are needed for the community as a whole. They are needed to be good examples for the others, to advise them when they are confused and to correct

---

[1] It is often argued that computer science, medicine and so forth are also obligations upon the Muslim nation as a whole and if a person studies them with the intent of benefiting the Muslims, he will be rewarded. At one level, there certainly seems to be nothing wrong with this argument. However, a few comments must be made concerning this type of argument. First, there is a question of priority and where the greater need exists today. Although there may be some need for that "secular" knowledge for the Muslim nation as a whole, one must ask whether or not that need is already being met with numerous Muslims excelling in computers, engineering and other important areas. Concerning the Muslim communities living in the West, there is no question that there are more than enough Muslims in most of these fields while at the same time there are very few Muslims who are specialized in Islamic sciences. Even among those Muslims who are "active" and attend meetings and lectures in the mosques, one is hard-pressed to find those who are capable of giving good lectures on Islamic topics and inspiring others via his knowledge of the Quran and Sunnah while, in many places, one is not hard-pressed to find many who could speak about other matters. Second, even if someone undertook those studies with the intention of benefiting the Muslims, there is also the question of how much the Muslim nation is truly benefiting from these studies, especially among those Muslims who have taken their knowledge and used it to get jobs and to live in the West. Besides financial benefit that may be spread via donations, for example, to other Muslims or Islamic projects, the benefit is very limited. A scholar of Islam who can lead, inspire, teach and guide the Muslims is of much greater benefit in this era when there are so few Muslims of that caliber.

them when they are doing wrong. In many mosques today, one can hear complaints about poor participation. One of the reasons for that is that there are very few people who can inspire the others with their knowledge and piety, bringing them to the mosque and inspiring to learn and practice their faith. There may be many who can excite others about computers, engineering and other topics, because they have some interesting information about those fields that the others may not have. But if everyone only has a very limited knowledge of Islam and its various sciences, it is not surprising that the people are not inspired or excited to learn more.

One of the points related to purification of the soul that is noted by many a writer, and that shall be discussed later here, is the importance of being in the company of pious, knowledgeable people. However, if those pious and knowledgeable people are so small in number, their ability to associate with the masses will be limited. What that leaves for the rest of the people is friends and associates like themselves, having a limited knowledge of the religion and not able to guide anyone else. Indeed, when they get together, if any religious topic should happen to come up, it becomes the blind leading the blind, with opinions being offered that may make the people stray far from the Straight Path.

It seems clear, Allah knows best, that this phenomenon will get worse before it gets better. Most Muslims today are primarily concerned with their child's secular education. They are primarily concerned with their child's ability to earn a living in the future. It is as if they believe that the provisions only come from a bachelor's degree and not from Allah. It is certainly true that one must follow the "worldly causes" to meet one's needs in this world. However, there are two matters to be greatly concerned with here. First, one must be wary of putting a complete reliance upon these worldly causes. There are numerous unemployed Ph.D.'s in this country and throughout the world. Even if one takes all of the "worldly" steps, in the end, it is actually Allah alone who provides. Second, one must also be wary of allowing those goals to dominate one's life, such that one either turns away from the knowledge of the religion or rarely seeks it. Allah's words should provide a clear warning concerning this type of behavior,

فَأَعْرِضْ عَن مَّن تَوَلَّىٰ عَن ذِكْرِنَا وَلَمْ يُرِدْ إِلَّا ٱلْحَيَوٰةَ ٱلدُّنْيَا ﴿٢٩﴾ ذَٰلِكَ مَبْلَغُهُم مِّنَ ٱلْعِلْمِ إِنَّ رَبَّكَ هُوَ أَعْلَمُ بِمَن ضَلَّ عَن سَبِيلِهِۦ وَهُوَ أَعْلَمُ بِمَنِ ٱهْتَدَىٰ

"Therefore shun those who turn away from Our Message and desire nothing but the life of this world. That is what they could reach of knowledge. Verily your Lord knows best those who stray from His Path, and He knows best those who receive guidance" (*al-Najm* 29-30). Every Muslim—parent or otherwise—must realize that there are things in life that are much more important and enriching than wealth, cars, houses, fine clothing and things of that nature. But these greater things are only the result of true faith and understanding of the religion.

This situation is especially disheartening for those living in the West because to get true Islamic knowledge takes even greater effort in those environments. The parents have to be even stronger in their will to ensure that their children get a strong and sound foundation of Islamic knowledge. What is going to happen to all of these children in the future? If a new problem that requires an Islamic answer arises, where will they find the answer to that problem? Can they turn to someone of deep Islamic knowledge? What if there is nobody around? The result may be that they end up doing something completely wrong according to the religion because they had no means of knowing and no one was available to guide them. Indeed, if *al-maseeh al-dajjaal* (the anti-Christ) appeared in their times, would they be able to recognize him or would they become one of his followers? Who will Allah hold responsible for that? Maybe Allah will hold the parents of that generation responsible, those who did not care enough to ensure that their children had a sound grounding in the religion and those who did not bother to note that the number of youth seriously studying Islam was shrinking.

Probably, most everyone notices how many great and leading scholars pass away almost every year. This should be a cause for reflection and action. Who is there to take the place of those scholars and where are the parents encouraging their gifted children to follow in their paths? One should keep in mind the words of the Messenger of Allah (peace and blessings of Allah be upon him),

إِنَّ اللَّهَ لا يَقْبِضُ الْعِلْمَ انْتِزَاعًا يَنْتَزِعُهُ مِنَ الْعِبَادِ وَلَكِنْ يَقْبِضُ الْعِلْمَ بِقَبْضِ الْعُلَمَاءِ حَتَّى إِذَا لَمْ يُبْقِ عَالِمًا اتَّخَذَ النَّاسُ رُءُوسًا جُهَّالاً فَسُئِلُوا فَأَفْتَوْا بِغَيْرِ عِلْمٍ فَضَلُّوا وَأَضَلُّوا

"Verily, Allah does not seize the knowledge by removing it from the servants. Instead, He removes the knowledge by removing the scholars until no scholar is left. The people [then] take as their leaders ignorant people. They are asked and they give responses without knowledge. They are misguided and they misguide others." (Recorded by al-Bukhari and Muslim.)

It is not the case that it is obligatory upon everyone to train their children to be *mujtahids* (in-depth scholars). However, the in-depth knowledge of the religion is a *fardh kifaayah* (a communal obligation). Although many of the Muslims in the West today actually grew up in the Muslim world, there are still not enough well-educated Muslims to meet the needs of the Muslims communities. If that is true today, one can only expect that situation to get worse over time as more and more of the Muslim youth grow up only in the West and only exposed to secular education and materialistic propaganda.

This is a dilemma that all Muslims must be concerned about. Hence, proper Islamic knowledge is not simply a matter for the individual's purification. Instead—like so many issues related to the individual's purification—it is something that the Muslim community as a whole is in need of greatly.[1]

---

[1] Another point concerning the Muslim community as a whole and, in particular, Muslim countries, is that Muslims must be very wary of having only the poorer students sifted into Islamic studies. This is something that has occurred in the Muslim world, especially since the colonial days wherein Islamic studies was not considered as prestigious as other studies. The positions of the Islamic studies in society must be enhanced. The better students should be given more alluring scholarships to study in those areas. With scientific, technological and medical breakthroughs every day, many new issues are occurring, many are the problems that

Reciting and Pondering over the Quran

The first key to the sound and beneficial knowledge that was just discussed is the reading and study of the revelation from Allah: the Book and the Sunnah. In the verses in which Allah mentions that the Prophet (peace and blessings of Allah be upon him) was sent to purify the servants, they clearly mention that he was given the Book and the *Hikmah* (the Sunnah). These are the keys to the door of purification and true knowledge. Ibn Taimiyyah stated, "Knowledge is that which is built upon evidence. The beneficial part of it is what was brought by the Prophet (peace and blessings of Allah be upon him)."[1] He also stated, "Goodness, happiness, completeness and righteousness are all captured in two matters: beneficial knowledge and righteous deeds. And Allah has sent Muhammad with the best of them: the guidance (*al-huda*) and the religion of truth (*deen al-haqq*)."[2]

The Messenger of Allah (peace and blessings of Allah be upon him) said,

خَيْرُكُمْ مَنْ تَعَلَّمَ الْقُرْآنَ وَعَلَّمَهُ

"The best among you is whoever learns the Quran and teaches it." (Recorded by al-Bukhari.) The Prophet's words, "The best among you," obviously, are in reference to the most pious and most devout worshipper of Allah. Hence, this hadith sheds important light on the question of purification of the soul. Allah Himself describes the Quran in the following verse,

---

Muslims are facing now that many of the scholars of the past never faced. The Muslim community needs the best and most capable thinkers to discuss and solve these issues in the light of the teachings of the Quran and Sunnah. Again, much of this attitude in the Muslim world was the result of the previous few generations' defeat at the hands of the colonialists and the influence of secular minded Muslims who were devastated by such defeats. It is now time for the Muslims of this generation who are suffering due to the mistakes of the past generations to have the courage to steer their own children into learning about Islam and specializing in its various fields.

[1] Ibn Taimiyyah, *Majmoo*, vol. 13, p. 136.

[2] Ibid., vol. 19, pp. 169-70.

شَهْرُ رَمَضَانَ ٱلَّذِىٓ أُنزِلَ فِيهِ ٱلْقُرْءَانُ هُدًى لِّلنَّاسِ وَبَيِّنَـٰتٍ مِّنَ ٱلْهُدَىٰ وَٱلْفُرْقَانِ ۚ

"Ramadan is the (month) in which was sent down the Quran as a guide to mankind, also clear (signs) for guidance and judgment (between right and wrong)" (*al-Baqarah* 185). The Quran is guidance for all of mankind, in that it clearly points the way to the straight path whether humans wish to benefit from it or not. However, it is not simply guidance for mankind but it is the detailed, explained guidance that suffices for the soul's purification. It is also the *furqaan* (criterion) that clearly distinguishes the truth from falsehood and what is beneficial and good from what is harmful and evil or, in other words, the path of purification from the path of misguidance. Hence, it must be the first source for anyone trying to find the path and way of purification.

In another verse, Allah calls what He revealed to the Prophet (peace and blessings of Allah be upon him) a *rooh*. Allah says,

وَكَذَٰلِكَ أَوْحَيْنَآ إِلَيْكَ رُوحًا مِّنْ أَمْرِنَا ۚ مَا كُنتَ تَدْرِى مَا ٱلْكِتَـٰبُ وَلَا ٱلْإِيمَـٰنُ وَلَـٰكِن جَعَلْنَـٰهُ نُورًا نَّهْدِى بِهِۦ مَن نَّشَآءُ مِنْ عِبَادِنَا ۚ وَإِنَّكَ لَتَهْدِىٓ إِلَىٰ صِرَٰطٍ مُّسْتَقِيمٍ ﴿٥٢﴾ صِرَٰطِ ٱللَّهِ ٱلَّذِى لَهُۥ مَا فِى ٱلسَّمَـٰوَٰتِ وَمَا فِى ٱلْأَرْضِ ۗ أَلَآ إِلَى ٱللَّهِ تَصِيرُ ٱلْأُمُورُ

"And thus have We, by Our command, sent inspiration to you. You knew not (before) what was revelation, and what was faith. But We have made the (Quran) a Light, wherewith We guide such of Our servants as We will. And verily you do guide (men) to the Straight Way, the Way of Allah, to Whom belongs whatever is in the heavens and whatever is on earth. Behold (how) all affairs tend towards Allah" (*al-Shoora* 52-53). Saalih al-Fauzaan noted,

It is a *rooh* for the hearts. The *rooh* of the hearts is more specific than the *rooh* for the physical body. Allah has called it a *rooh* because it brings life to the hearts. When this Quran permeates the heart, it gives it life and enlightens it. It then knows its Lord and worships Allah upon guidance. It also fears Him, is aware of Him, loves Him, and extols Him. This is because this Quran is a *rooh* that moves the hearts like the *rooh* moves the bodies and forms. Similarly, the *rooh* enters the body and moves it and gives it life and the Quran as well when it enters the hearts gives them life and moves them with the fear of Allah and love for Him. But if the hearts are void of the Quran, they die in the same way that if the body is void of the *rooh* it also dies. In reality, there are two types of deaths and two types of lives. As for the two deaths, they are the death of the body and the death of the heart. As for the two lives, they are the life of the body and the life of the heart. But there is a life in the bodies of the believers, the disbelievers, the pious and the impious. In fact, there is the same biological life for humans and animals with no distinguishing feature between them. The distinguishing feature is found in the life of the heart. This is not obtained except by the believing, pious servants of Allah. As for the disbelievers and the animals, they are missing the life of the hearts even though they may possess a life of the physical body.[1]

Allah has also described the Quran as a healing. Allah says,

يَـٰٓأَيُّهَا ٱلنَّاسُ قَدْ جَآءَتْكُم مَّوْعِظَةٌ مِّن رَّبِّكُمْ وَشِفَآءٌ لِّمَا فِى ٱلصُّدُورِ وَهُدًى وَرَحْمَةٌ لِّلْمُؤْمِنِينَ

"O mankind! There has come to you a direction from your Lord and a healing for the (diseases) in your hearts, and for those who

[1] al-Fauzaan, *Muhaadharaat*, vol. 2, pp. 291-292.

believe, a Guidance and a Mercy" (*Yoonus* 57). It is first and foremost a healing and a cure for the many diseases that are found in the souls of mankind. It purifies the soul from all sorts of filth that humans bring upon themselves—the filth of pride, arrogance, envy, desire for power and to lord over others and so forth. Ibn Taimiyyah stated,

> The Quran is a healing for what is in the chests and for whoever has the diseases of doubts and lusts in his heart... The Quran removes those diseases that bring about evil desires until the heart becomes sound, thereby making its intentions sound. It then returns to its natural state in which it was created like a body returns to its natural healthy state. The heart is fed with faith and the Quran that purify it and support it like a body is fed with what makes it grow and strengthens it. The growth and purification of the heart is like the growth of the body.[1]

However, an essential point related to the Quran that is, at least in practice, sometimes forgotten by many Muslims is that the Quran is not meant just to be read or memorized. But, instead, it is meant to be pondered over, studied and understood. Without this effort, one will not be able to derive its guidance and thereby worship Allah in the proper manner. As Allah says in the Quran,

كِتَـٰبٌ أَنزَلْنَـٰهُ إِلَيْكَ مُبَـٰرَكٌ لِّيَدَّبَّرُوٓا۟ ءَايَـٰتِهِۦ وَلِيَتَذَكَّرَ أُو۟لُوا۟ ٱلْأَلْبَـٰبِ

"(Here is) a book which We have sent down unto you, full of blessings, that they may meditate on its signs, and that men of understanding may receive admonition" (*Saad* 29). This verse, though, also mentions that the Quran is blessed. One receives blessings via it by pondering over it, by learning it and by applying it.

---

[1] Ibn Taimiyyah, *Majmoo*, vol. 10, pp. 95-6.

The Messenger of Allah (peace and blessings of Allah be upon him) also said,

اقْرَءُوا الْقُرْآنَ مَا ائْتَلَفَتْ عَلَيْهِ قُلُوبُكُمْ فَإِذَا اخْتَلَفْتُمْ فَقُومُوا عَنْهُ

"Recite the Quran as long as your hearts are inclined to it. When they differ from it, then get up [and remove yourselves] from [reciting] it." (Recorded by al-Bukhari and Muslim.) Ibn Katheer has stated that in this hadith, the Messenger of Allah (peace and blessings of Allah be upon him) has instructed this Nation to recite the Quran as long as their hearts are attune to the recitation, thinking and pondering over its meaning. They are not to be reciting it while they are preoccupied or bored with its reading. In those cases, they will not be achieving the goal of its reading. Hence, they should discontinue reading under conditions like that.[1]

Finally, one should always keep in mind the following truth:[2] The Quran and the Sunnah of the Messenger of Allah (peace be upon him) are not just a matter of laws and regulations but, more importantly, they are the guidance to the means by which a human approaches Allah. For example, the Quran is not simply a book of laws— of dos and don'ts— but it is foremost a book of *tarbiyyah* or a book that develops and allows people to grow spiritually and morally. In the following verse, Allah describes the Quran as a *mauidhah*,

هَٰذَا بَيَانٌ لِّلنَّاسِ وَهُدًى وَمَوْعِظَةٌ لِّلْمُتَّقِينَ

"Here is a plain statement to men, a guidance and admonition (*mauidhah*) to those who fear Allah" (*ali-Imraan* 138). Lane gives the following definition for the word *mauidhah*,

> He exhorted him, admonished him, or warned him; he put him in fear; he exhorted him to obedience; commanded him to obey; he gave him good advice, or

---

[1] Ismaaeel ibn Katheer, *Kitaab Fadhaail al-Quraan* (Cairo: Maktabah ibn Taimiyyah, 1416 A.H.), p. 269.

[2] The following passage is taken in greatly abridged form from the author's *How to Approach and Understand the Quran* (Boulder, CO: Al-Basheer Company for Publications and Translations, 1999), p. 127-134.

> counsel; and reminded him of the results of affairs; he reminded him by informing him of that which should make the heart tender; he reminded him of that which should soften his heart by the mention of reward and punishment.[1]

So, *mauidhah* involves warning the person about the consequences of his actions. It includes reminding him of what his wrong actions will lead him to. It also includes, as the English expression states, "putting the fear of God in him" as well as making his heart soft and submissive to the truth.

Hence, the Quran is a book that is meant to reform the individual, either changing him if he were void of guidance or improving him if he already was walking along its straight path. It brings him from the death of *jaahiliya* (ignorance) to the life of Islam— such that in his heart and mind he sees things in the light of Allah's guidance and he acts accordingly. The Quran way of living is the true life for a human, a life which is different from that of one in ignorance just as life is different from death. Allah says in the Quran,

أَوَمَن كَانَ مَيْتًا فَأَحْيَيْنَٰهُ وَجَعَلْنَا لَهُۥ نُورًا يَمْشِى بِهِۦ فِى ٱلنَّاسِ كَمَن مَّثَلُهُۥ فِى ٱلظُّلُمَٰتِ لَيْسَ بِخَارِجٍ مِّنْهَا ۚ كَذَٰلِكَ زُيِّنَ لِلْكَٰفِرِينَ مَا كَانُوا۟ يَعْمَلُونَ

"Can he who was dead to whom We gave life, and a light whereby he can walk among men, be like him who is in the depths of darkness, from which he can never come out? Thus to those without faith their own deeds seem pleasing" (*al-Anaam* 122). The disbelievers are in such darkness that they cannot even recognize the evil of their ways, thinking that their path is very beautiful. And,

---

[1] Lane, vol. 2, p. 2953.

إِنْ هُوَ إِلَّا ذِكْرٌ وَقُرْءَانٌ مُّبِينٌ ﴿٦٩﴾ لِّيُنذِرَ مَن كَانَ حَيًّا وَيَحِقَّ ٱلْقَوْلُ عَلَى ٱلْكَٰفِرِينَ

"This is no less than a message and a Quran making things clear: that it may give admonition to any (who are) alive, and that the word may be proved true against those who reject (truth)" (*Ya Seen* 69-70).

In other words, the Quran is not just giving the human the knowledge (*ilm*) of what is correct but is also imbibing him with the feeling of fear, love and responsibility to Allah (*taqwa*) that will drive him to do what is proper and correct. In fact, after almost every law stated in the Quran, Allah closes the relevant verses with the remembrance of Allah, promises of reward for those who stay within His limits and promises of punishment for those who wish not to abide by His commands. This is one way by which the Quran gives both knowledge and *taqwa* to the individual.

The importance of giving both *ilm* (knowledge) and *taqwa* (fear of Allah and God-consciousness) cannot be overemphasized. If a person simply has the knowledge of what is right without anything in his soul driving him to perform that right deed, all of that knowledge will be of no avail or benefit to him. This can clearly be seen in Western societies, for example. How many people in the West know very well the dangers and harmful effects of smoking, drinking, drugs and so on, but, at the same time, how many of these same people have the will and drive to refrain from these acts that they know are so harmful to them?[1]

One must not forget the effect that the Quran has upon the health of the soul and, in turn, its readiness to move forward along the path of purification. Al-Fauzaan noted that when one reads the Quran, with one's heart fully in attendance and while pondering over its meaning, it removes worries, pains and evil

---

[1] This ends the portion taken from the author's *How to Approach and Understand the Quran*. Note that in the previous section of this work on knowledge there was a discussion of the current situation. For the author's view of the current situation with respect to how the Quran is approached, see *How to Approach and Understand the Quran*, pp. 55-116.

thoughts in the heart. These are all replaced with a tranquil feeling of spiritual happiness and an increase in faith that is difficult to put in words. Allah says,

إِنَّمَا ٱلْمُؤْمِنُونَ ٱلَّذِينَ إِذَا ذُكِرَ ٱللَّهُ وَجِلَتْ قُلُوبُهُمْ وَإِذَا تُلِيَتْ
عَلَيْهِمْ ءَايَٰتُهُۥ زَادَتْهُمْ إِيمَٰنًا وَعَلَىٰ رَبِّهِمْ يَتَوَكَّلُونَ

"For believers are those who when Allah is mentioned feel a tremor in their hearts, and when they hear His Signs rehearsed, find their faith strengthened, and put (all) their trust in their Lord" (*al-Anfaal* 2).[1] Actually, reading and studying the Quran is a part of remembering Allah Who also has said,

ٱلَّذِينَ ءَامَنُوا۟ وَتَطْمَئِنُّ قُلُوبُهُم بِذِكْرِ ٱللَّهِ ۗ أَلَا بِذِكْرِ ٱللَّهِ تَطْمَئِنُّ
ٱلْقُلُوبُ

"Those who believe, and whose hearts find satisfaction in the remembrance of Allah: for without doubt in the remembrance of Allah do hearts find satisfaction" (*al-Rad* 28).

Al-Fauzaan also argues that it is due to man's own turning away from the Quran that they have encountered the difficulties and stresses that they face in life, thus causing harm to their soul. In support of his argument, al-Fauzaan quotes the following verses,

فَهَلْ عَسَيْتُمْ إِن تَوَلَّيْتُمْ أَن تُفْسِدُوا۟ فِى ٱلْأَرْضِ وَتُقَطِّعُوٓا۟ أَرْحَامَكُمْ
﴿٢٢﴾ أُو۟لَٰٓئِكَ ٱلَّذِينَ لَعَنَهُمُ ٱللَّهُ فَأَصَمَّهُمْ وَأَعْمَىٰٓ أَبْصَٰرَهُمْ ﴿٢٣﴾
أَفَلَا يَتَدَبَّرُونَ ٱلْقُرْءَانَ أَمْ عَلَىٰ قُلُوبٍ أَقْفَالُهَآ ﴿٢٤﴾ إِنَّ ٱلَّذِينَ
ٱرْتَدُّوا۟ عَلَىٰٓ أَدْبَٰرِهِم مِّنۢ بَعْدِ مَا تَبَيَّنَ لَهُمُ ٱلْهُدَى ۙ ٱلشَّيْطَٰنُ

[1] Al-Fauzaan, *Muhaadharaat*, vol. 2, p. 301.

سَوَّلَ لَهُمْ وَأَمْلَىٰ لَهُمْ ﴿٢٥﴾ ذَٰلِكَ بِأَنَّهُمْ قَالُوا۟ لِلَّذِينَ كَرِهُوا۟ مَا نَزَّلَ ٱللَّهُ سَنُطِيعُكُمْ فِى بَعْضِ ٱلْأَمْرِ ۖ وَٱللَّهُ يَعْلَمُ إِسْرَارَهُمْ

"Then, is it to be expected of you [people], if you were put in authority, that you will do mischief in the land and break your ties of kith and kin. Such are the men whom Allah has cursed for He has made them deaf and blinded their sight. Do they not then earnestly seek to understand the Quran, or are their hearts locked up by them? Those who turn back as apostates after guidance was clearly shown to them, Satan has instigated them and buoyed them up with false hopes. This, because they said to those who hate what Allah has revealed, 'We will obey you in part of (this) matter'; but Allah knows their (inner) secrets" (*Muhammad* 22-26). Al-Fauzaan commented,

> If they had pondered over the Quran all of those diseases and evil occurrences would not have existed; they would have kept the ties of kin and have ties with those whom Allah ordered them to have ties with and would have obeyed Allah and His Messenger. However, when they turned away from the Quran and did not ponder over its meanings, they were tried by all of those hardships. They were tried by cutting off the ties of kin, deserving the curses and falling into apostasy. All of that was because they did not ponder over the Quran. When a person turns away from the Quran, his heart becomes hardened and diseased. In the end, there is a covering over it such that guidance and light cannot reach it. This is its punishment--and refuge is sought in Allah alone [from such punishment]. This is all due to a lack of pondering over the Quran.[1]

[1] Al-Fauzaan, *Muhaadharaat*, vol. 2, p. 301-2.

Reading and Studying the Hadith and Life of the Prophet (peace and blessings of Allah be upon him)

Of course, studying the hadith of the Prophet (peace and blessings of Allah be upon him) should go hand in hand with reading and studying the Quran. They are the two forms of revelation and true sources of guidance for the Muslim Nation. But studying the hadith and life of the Prophet (peace and blessings of Allah be upon him) is being highlighted here for specific reasons.

First, almost everyone has a copy of the Quran yet there are many Muslims who do not possess any collection of hadith. This is very sad because the hadith are nothing but an extension and application of the guidance of the Quran. Indeed, one's understanding of the Quran cannot be complete unless he sees how the Quran's teachings were implemented and further expounded by the Prophet (peace and blessings of Allah be upon him). This was one of the vital roles of the Prophet (peace and blessings of Allah be upon him) vis-à-vis the Quran. Hence, everyone needs to be reminded that in addition to reading the Quran, one should also dedicate some time to studying the hadith and biography of the Prophet (peace and blessings of Allah be upon him).

Second, many people are affected by the hadith and life of the Prophet (peace and blessings of Allah be upon him) differently than they are affected by reading the Quran. The Prophet's life and example take the teachings of the Quran from a theoretical abstract level to a very practical, easily visible level. One is virtually seeing the teachings of the Quran being put into practice when studying the life and behavior of the Prophet (peace and blessings of Allah be upon him).

Third, the life of the Prophet (peace and blessings of Allah be upon him) and his sayings are definitely a source of inspiration. For many reasons, the statements of the Prophet (peace and blessings of Allah be upon him) are more practical, simpler and easier to read than the verses of the Quran.

Perhaps the most obvious reason for studying the life and sayings of the Prophet (peace and blessings of Allah be upon him) is that his example is the prime example for anyone seeking to purify his soul. Al-Qahtaani noted,

> All facets of his life are lessons in the purification of the soul, [including] his faith, *tauheed*, patience, stating of the truth, calmness, generosity, jihad, prayers, pilgrimage, abstinence from this world, character, behavior, manners, dignity, keeping of ties with relatives, ordering the good and eradicating evil. In all things big and small he was the model and the example. The one who purifies his soul by following him is the happiest in this life and successful on the Day of Resurrection.[1]

In addition, studying the life of the Prophet (peace and blessings of Allah be upon him) and his numerous sacrifices for the sake of Allah should develop a stronger appreciation and love for the Prophet (peace and blessings of Allah be upon him) himself. This should translate into a great desire to emulate this wonderful man. This feeling in the heart assists in the process of purification by turning the believer's attention more and more toward the example *par excellence* of a purified soul.

Studying the Prophet's life also shows how much he exerted himself in his worship of Allah. One will learn how he and his Companions raced to attain Allah's pleasure. In the light of the example of the Prophet (peace and blessings of Allah be upon him) and his Companions, the individual can look at his own efforts, sacrifices and his own use of time and wealth. He can compare that to the Prophet (peace and blessings of Allah be upon him) and his Companions. This is an important humbling step as it shows the great potential that humans can achieve. This is of extreme importance in contemporary times wherein a Muslim may be satisfied by comparing himself to the weaker Muslims around him. One may be easily deceived or fooled by comparing himself to people who are fairly inactive or even disobedient to Allah. The Prophet (peace and blessings of Allah be upon him) and the Companions were all mere human beings but they have set the standard and the goal for others to emulate. However, one

---

[1] Al-Qahtaani, p. 21.

cannot truly appreciate or even know those standards without making the effort to learn about the Prophet (peace and blessings of Allah be upon him) and his Companions.

In addition, the Prophet's life should play a similar role for the Muslims that the stories of the previous prophets played for the Prophet (peace and blessings of Allah be upon him) himself. Allah tells the Prophet (peace and blessings of Allah be upon him),

وَكُلًّا نَّقُصُّ عَلَيْكَ مِنْ أَنۢبَآءِ ٱلرُّسُلِ مَا نُثَبِّتُ بِهِۦ فُؤَادَكَ ۚ وَجَآءَكَ فِى هَٰذِهِ ٱلْحَقُّ وَمَوْعِظَةٌ وَذِكْرَىٰ لِلْمُؤْمِنِينَ

"All that We relate to you of the stories of the messengers, with it We make firm your heart: in them there comes to you the truth, as well as an exhortation and a message of remembrance to those who believe" (*Hood* 120). The Prophet's example and the many ways by which Allah supported him and his followers should bring solace to the heart of the believer. It should strengthen his resolve and his belief in the ultimate triumph of this religion. Allah will never allow the righteous deeds of the true believers to go to waste.

Finally, an in-depth understanding of the chronology of events in the Prophet's life as well as the chronology of the revelation of the Quran allows one to have an understanding of the different "sociologic laws" (*sunan*) of Allah. In the past few decades, Muslims have had to face a number of trials and tribulations. This has led to confusion, weakness of purpose and even extremism. However, going back to the life of the Prophet (peace and blessings of Allah be upon him) will demonstrate that the hardships that the Prophet (peace and blessings of Allah be upon him) and his earliest companions faced were much greater than what most Muslims today are facing. Going back to his life will also make the person realize that it is part of the Way of Allah that he puts the believers to tests and trials. This is, in fact, how they demonstrate their true faith and loyalty to Allah.

For example, it was when the Muslims were a very small and weak band in Makkah, being persecuted by the disbelievers, that Allah revealed the verses,

أَحَسِبَ ٱلنَّاسُ أَن يُتْرَكُوٓاْ أَن يَقُولُوٓاْ ءَامَنَّا وَهُمْ لَا يُفْتَنُونَ ﴿٢﴾ وَلَقَدْ فَتَنَّا ٱلَّذِينَ مِن قَبْلِهِمْ فَلَيَعْلَمَنَّ ٱللَّهُ ٱلَّذِينَ صَدَقُواْ وَلَيَعْلَمَنَّ ٱلْكَٰذِبِينَ

"Do men think that they will be left alone on saying, 'We believe,' and that they will not be put to trials? We did try those before them, and Allah will certainly know [and show] those who are true from those who are false" (*al-Ankaboot* 2-3).

During that time Companions like Bilaal and the family of Yaasir were being severely tortured by the disbelievers, to the point that Yaasir's wife Sumayyah became the first martyr for the sake of Allah. It was during this time that Khabbaab ibn al-Aratt and others went to the Prophet (peace and blessings of Allah be upon him) and pleaded with him to ask Allah to give them help, support and victory. The Prophet (peace and blessings of Allah be upon him) responded with words that every Muslim today should consider dearly,

كَانَ الرَّجُلُ فِيمَنْ قَبْلَكُمْ يُحفَرُ لَهُ فِي الأَرْضِ فَيُجعَلُ فِيهِ فَيجاءُ بِالْمِنْشارِ فَيوضَعُ عَلَى رَأْسِهِ فَيُشَقُّ بِاثْنَتَيْنِ وَمَا يَصُدُّهُ ذَلِكَ عَنْ دِينِهِ وَيُمْشَطُ بِأَمْشَاطِ الْحَدِيدِ مَا دُونَ لَحْمِهِ مِنْ عَظْمٍ أَوْ عَصَبٍ وَمَا يَصُدُّهُ ذَلِكَ عَنْ دِينِهِ وَاللَّهِ لَيُتِمَّنَّ هَذَا الأَمْرَ حَتَّى يَسِيرَ الرَّاكِبُ مِنْ صَنْعَاءَ إِلَى حَضْرَمَوْتَ لا يَخَافُ إِلاَّ اللَّهَ أَوِ الذِّئْبَ عَلَى غَنَمِهِ وَلَكِنَّكُمْ تَسْتَعْجِلُونَ

"Among those before you a [believing] man would be put in a ditch that was dug for him, and a saw would be put over his head and he would be cut into two pieces; yet that [torture] would not make him give up his religion. His body would be combed with iron combs that would remove his flesh from the bones or nerves, yet that would not make him abandon his religion. By Allah, this religion will prevail to the point that a traveler from Sana to

Hadhramaut will fear none but Allah or a wolf as regards his sheep. But you people are hasty." (Recorded by al-Bukhari.)

One should also recall that it was during those difficult times that the Quraish, who had the upper hand but who could recognize the threat of the true religion of Allah, tried to convince the Prophet (peace and blessings of Allah be upon him) to compromise. If the Prophet (peace and blessings of Allah be upon him) would only compromise and recognize the validity of what they worshipped, things could have come to a peaceful conclusion and the suffering would have come to an end. But the goal of the true believer is not simply the end of suffering—not if it comes at the price of the truth and Allah's faith. Hence, it was during those times that Allah revealed to the Prophet (peace and blessings of Allah be upon him) the *soorah* that should be a clear reminder to all believers that they are on a path different from all of the disbelievers on this earth. It was during those difficult times that Allah revealed the *soorah*,

قُلْ يَـٰٓأَيُّهَا ٱلْكَـٰفِرُونَ ﴿١﴾ لَآ أَعْبُدُ مَا تَعْبُدُونَ ﴿٢﴾ وَلَآ أَنتُمْ عَـٰبِدُونَ مَآ أَعْبُدُ ﴿٣﴾ وَلَآ أَنَا۠ عَابِدٌ مَّا عَبَدتُّمْ ﴿٤﴾ وَلَآ أَنتُمْ عَـٰبِدُونَ مَآ أَعْبُدُ ﴿٥﴾ لَكُمْ دِينُكُمْ وَلِىَ دِينِ

"Say: O disbelievers! I do not worship what you worship nor are you worshipping what I worship. And I will not be a worshipper of what you worship nor will you be worshippers of what I worship. For you is your religion and for me is my religion." (*al-Kaafiroon* 1-6).[1]

In fact, all of that suffering and persecution was part of the plan of Allah to develop a strong Muslim community that would put Allah above everything else. Had Allah willed, Allah could have given the Prophet (peace and blessings of Allah be upon him) dominance from the first day of his mission. But that is not how Allah decreed it based on His infinite knowledge. Those Muslims who live in relative luxury today and who scream

[1] Cf., ibn Katheer, *Tafseer* (Daar Taibah), vol. 8, p. 507.

and flee from their religion the first moment a trial comes to them should go back to study the life of the Prophet (peace and blessings of Allah be upon him) and his Companions in Makkah. The Prophet's life is a vivid lesson that Allah tries and tests all believers and it is through these tests that one truly exhibits his love for Allah and his dedication to Allah's religion.

On the other hand, a great danger to the purification of one's soul is the practice of going to an extreme (*al-ghulu*). The Prophet (peace and blessings of Allah be upon him) gave many warnings about extremism. That concept is also very relevant with respect to studying the life of the Prophet (peace and blessings of Allah be upon him). The extremists of today who resort to violence and terror against innocent people and even other Muslims must also take a lesson from the life of the Prophet (peace and blessings of Allah be upon him). There is no extremist today who has more of a love and jealousy for the religion of Allah than the Prophet (peace and blessings of Allah be upon him) had. But the Prophet (peace and blessings of Allah be upon him) never went beyond the limits of the law of Allah. No matter how difficult the times, the believer must have trust in Allah that by following the commands of the Shareeah the best result will come about—in both this world and in the Hereafter. This was the way of the Prophet (peace and blessings of Allah be upon him) and his Companions and it must be the way of everyone who wishes to purify his soul.

The Proper Remembrance of Allah (*al-Dhikr*)

Dhikr or the proper remembrance of Allah is beyond doubt one of the greatest and most important acts a person can perform. In a relevant passage in which Allah commands the making of *dhikr* as well as indicates it benefits, Allah says,

يَـٰٓأَيُّهَا ٱلَّذِينَ ءَامَنُوا۟ ٱذْكُرُوا۟ ٱللَّهَ ذِكْرًا كَثِيرًا ﴿٤١﴾ وَسَبِّحُوهُ بُكْرَةً وَأَصِيلًا ﴿٤٢﴾ هُوَ ٱلَّذِى يُصَلِّى عَلَيْكُمْ وَمَلَـٰٓئِكَتُهُۥ لِيُخْرِجَكُم مِّنَ ٱلظُّلُمَـٰتِ إِلَى ٱلنُّورِ ۚ وَكَانَ بِٱلْمُؤْمِنِينَ رَحِيمًا

"O you who believe! Make remembrance of Allah often and extol Him morning and evening. He it is [then] Who sends blessings on you, as do His angels, that He may bring you out from the depths of darkness into light: and He is Full of Mercy to the believers" (*al-Ahzaab* 41-43).

In another verse, Allah shows that there is an important relationship between *dhikr* and true success, which is the same success that is enjoyed by the one who purifies his soul. Allah has said,

وَٱذْكُرُوا۟ ٱللَّهَ كَثِيرًا لَّعَلَّكُمْ تُفْلِحُونَ

"Remember Allah often (and without stint) that you may prosper" (*al-Jumuah* 10).

Allah also says about *dhikr*,

وَلَذِكْرُ ٱللَّهِ أَكْبَرُ ۗ وَٱللَّهُ

"And the remembrance of Allah is greater" (*al-Ankaboot* 45). One interpretation of this verse is that the remembrance of Allah is greater than any other act of worship.[1] In fact, the Messenger of Allah (peace and blessings of Allah be upon him) stated,

أَلاَ أُخْبِرُكُمْ بِخَيْرِ أَعْمَالِكُمْ وَأَرْفَعِهَا فِي دَرَجَاتِكُمْ وَأَزْكَاهَا عِنْدَ مَلِيكِكُمْ وَخَيْرٍ لَكُمْ مِنْ إِعْطَاءِ الذَّهَبِ وَالْوَرِقِ وَخَيْرٍ لَكُمْ مِنْ أَنْ تَلْقَوْا عَدُوَّكُمْ فَتَضْرِبُوا أَعْنَاقَهُمْ وَيَضْرِبُوا أَعْنَاقَكُمْ قَالُوا بَلَى قَالَ ذِكْرُ اللَّهِ تَعَالَى

"Shall I inform you of the best of your deeds, the one that raises you most in rank, most purifying to your Lord, which is better for

[1] Cf., Sadeeq ibn Hasan al-Qatooji al-Bukhari, vol. 10, pp. 198-199.

you than giving gold and silver and better for you than meeting your enemy and striking their necks and them striking your necks?" They said, "Certainly, [tell us]." He said, "It is the remembrance of Allah, the Exalted."[1]

And Allah directly related the purification of the soul with remembrance of Allah when He said,

قَدْ أَفْلَحَ مَن تَزَكَّىٰ ﴿١٤﴾ وَذَكَرَ ٱسْمَ رَبِّهِۦ فَصَلَّىٰ

"But those will prosper who purify themselves, and remember the name of their Guardian-Lord, and perform the prayer" (*al-Ala* 14-15).

Even an elementary understanding of what *dhikr* truly implies will allow one to understand why *dhikr* is of such great importance. First it should be noted that when people think of *dhikr*, they think of it in a very narrow sense. However, when the scholars discuss the term *dhikr*, they show that in reality it is *the* remembrance or conscious thought about Allah that should exist behind every righteous deed that a person performs. In that sense, *dhikr* is definitely of utmost importance. This understanding of the concept of *dhikr* is clear in the statements of many scholars. For example, Saeed ibn Jubair said, "*Dhikr* is obedience to Allah. Whoever obeys Allah has in fact remembered Him. Whoever does not obey Him is not one who is remembering Him, even if he says *tasbeeh*[2] and recites the Book a lot."[3] Ibn Taimiyyah also stated, "Every statement made by the tongue and conceived by the heart which takes one closer to Allah, including learning knowledge, teaching it, ordering good and eradicating evil, is a form of *dhikr* of Allah."[4]

Actually, after attaining knowledge (the step previously discussed in this chapter), one must have the *dhikr*—the

---

[1] Recorded by Ahmad, al-Tirmidhi, ibn Maajah and Malik. According to al-Albaani, its chain is *sahih*. See Muhammad Naasir al-Deen al-Albaani, footnotes to Muhammad al-Tabreezi, *Mishkat al-Masaabeeh* (Beirut: al-Maktab al-Islaami, 1985), vol. 2, p. 702. See Muhammad al-Shaukaani, *Tuhfah al-Dhaakireen* (Beirut: Daar al-Kutub al-Ilmiyah, 1988), p. 14.

[2] The statement, "*Subhaanallaah* (exalted and perfect is Allah)."

[3] Quoted in al-Husain al-Baghawi, *Sharh al-Sunnah* (Beirut: al-Maktab al-Islaami, 1983), vol. 5, p. 10. Also quoted in Karzoon, vol. 1, p. 309.

[4] Ibn Taimiyyah, *Majmoo*, vol. 10, p. 661.

remembrance or the cognizance—that will make him aware of Allah and that will be the driving force behind his putting that knowledge into actual practice. This is what is expected from the proper *dhikr,* as is clear from the statement of Saeed ibn Jubair quoted above. In other words, *dhikr* should remind the person of his purpose in life, returning him back to the path of purification that he is supposed to follow.

The opposite of remembrance is heedlessness and neglect. The correct *dhikr* cannot be but with awareness and cognizance. This is almost like the proverbial light going on above one's head wherein he sees and remembers what he is supposed to do. This is a key to righteous deeds while its opposite leads to evil. This is why al-Muhaasabi said, "Awareness is the foundation of every good just as negligence is the foundation of every evil."[1]

In all frankness, without remembrance one may as well be dead because during times of neglect, one is not remembering his purpose and therefore he is not doing a useful act. Hence, the hadith of the Prophet (peace and blessings of Allah be upon him),

مَثَلُ الَّذِي يَذْكُرُ رَبَّهُ وَالَّذِي لا يَذْكُرُ رَبَّهُ مَثَلُ الْحَيِّ وَالْمَيِّتِ

"The similitude of the one who remembers his Lord and the one who does not remember his Lord is like the similitude of death and life." (Recorded by al-Bukhari and Muslim.) This real life that the Prophet (peace and blessings of Allah be upon him) is referring to is the life of the purified person who remembers Allah and recognizes his purpose in life. He does not wander about aimlessly not recalling why he is even existing.

As such, remembrance of Allah is like blood and nourishment for the heart, without which it would die. *Dhikr* keeps the heart nourished and healthy. When one is in a state of remembrance of Allah it is very difficult for him to sin or fail to perform the obligatory deeds. Indeed, if the remembrance is truly strong, it is difficult for the person to do something that is simply disliked by Allah. This is because he is remembering Allah. And who is Allah? If he remembers Allah intently, by Allah's names and attributes, he will be very cautious about any movement or

[1] Quoted in Karzoon, vol. 1, p. 309.

statement he makes. The *dhikr of Allah* is not simply statements that one makes when getting up, going out, eating and so forth. But they are reminders of Allah, putting the thought of Allah back into one's heart. This brings with it peace and tranquility to the true believers—and with that peace and tranquility they have no desire to do anything which is displeasing to Allah. Allah says,

قُلْ إِنَّ ٱللَّهَ يُضِلُّ مَن يَشَآءُ وَيَهْدِىٓ إِلَيْهِ مَنْ أَنَابَ ﴿٢٧﴾ ٱلَّذِينَ ءَامَنُوا۟ وَتَطْمَئِنُّ قُلُوبُهُم بِذِكْرِ ٱللَّهِ ۗ أَلَا بِذِكْرِ ٱللَّهِ تَطْمَئِنُّ ٱلْقُلُوبُ

"Say, 'Truly Allah leaves, to stray, whom He will; but He guides to Himself those who turn to Him in penitence. Those who believe, and whose hearts find satisfaction in the remembrance of Allah: for without doubt in the remembrance of Allah do hearts find satisfaction" (*al-Rad* 28).

There are two distinct modes of *dhikr* or remembrance of Allah. One is a constant and continuous form of *dhikr* wherein the person is always mindful of Allah as he goes about his daily routine and affairs. This form of *dhikr*, though, is developed and assisted by the more formal form of *dhikr* wherein a person remembers Allah at specific times via the means of specific words that have come from the Prophet (peace and blessings of Allah be upon him). In fact, the most important of these formal means is the prayer itself. Allah says,

وَأَقِمِ ٱلصَّلَوٰةَ لِذِكْرِىٓ

"Establish the prayer for My remembrance" (*Taha* 14).

Before concluding this section on *dhikr*, some other points need to be mentioned. First, when it comes to those words of remembrance that are specific for certain times and occasions, as taught by the Prophet (peace and blessings of Allah be upon him), one must do one's best to adhere to the exact wording taught by the Prophet (peace and blessings of Allah be upon him). Allah alone knows the full wisdom and significance of these words of *dhikr*.[1] Hence, any deviation from what has been specified should

---

[1] Cf., ibn Hajar, *Fath*, vol. 11, p. 116.

be avoided.[1] This point was taught and emphasized by the Prophet (peace and blessings of Allah be upon him) himself as can be seen in the following hadith from *Sahih al-Bukhari*:

قَالَ <الْبَرَاءُ> قَالَ لِي رَسُولُ اللَّهِ صَلَّى اللَّهم عَلَيْهِ وَسَلَّمَ إِذَا أَتَيْتَ مَضْجَعَكَ فَتَوَضَّأْ وَضُوءَكَ لِلصَّلَاةِ ثُمَّ اضْطَجِعْ عَلَى شِقِّكَ الْأَيْمَنِ وَقُلِ اللَّهُمَّ أَسْلَمْتُ نَفْسِي إِلَيْكَ وَفَوَّضْتُ أَمْرِي إِلَيْكَ وَأَلْجَأْتُ ظَهْرِي إِلَيْكَ رَهْبَةً وَرَغْبَةً إِلَيْكَ لَا مَلْجَأَ وَلَا مَنْجَا مِنْكَ إِلَّا إِلَيْكَ آمَنْتُ بِكِتَابِكَ الَّذِي أَنْزَلْتَ وَبِنَبِيِّكَ الَّذِي أَرْسَلْتَ فَإِنْ مُتَّ مُتَّ عَلَى الْفِطْرَةِ فَاجْعَلْهُنَّ آخِرَ مَا تَقُولُ فَقُلْتُ أَسْتَذْكِرُهُنَّ وَبِرَسُولِكَ الَّذِي أَرْسَلْتَ قَالَ لَا وَبِنَبِيِّكَ الَّذِي أَرْسَلْتَ

[Al-Baraa] said, "The Messenger of Allah (peace and blessings of Allah be upon him) said to me, 'When you come to your bed, you should make ablution like the ablution for the prayer and then lie on your right said. [Then] say, "O Allah, I have submitted my soul to You and have entrusted my affairs to You. I also rely upon You, with hope and fear in You. There is no escape or refuge from You except to You. I have believed in Your book that You revealed and Your prophet that You sent." If you then die [during that night], you would die upon your natural disposition [*fitrah*]. And make those the last words you state.' I then repeated them back to him and while doing so, I said, '[I believe in] Your messenger that You sent.' He then said to me, 'No, [it is] Your prophet that You sent.'"[2]

---

[1] The exception to this would be wherein one cannot remember exactly the words of the specific supplication.

[2] Two other important incidents from the Companions are the following: Abdullah ibn Masood heard about a group of people who would gather in the mosque after the Sunset Prayer. One of them would say, "Declare Allah's greatness [by saying *Allaahu akbar*]so many times, declare Allah's perfection so many times, praise Allah so many times." In other words, there were making *dhikr* in congregation and in a way that was not taught by the Prophet (peace and blessings of Allah be upon him). Ibn Masood went to them and told them, "You have wrongfully brought an innovation. Or have you more surpassed the Companions of Muhammad in knowledge?" They sought Allah's forgiveness and ibn Masood told them, "You must follow the path and stick to it. If you were to go to the right or to the left, you would stray far away." [This reported was recorded by al-Daarimi and ibn Widhaah in *al-Bidah*. According to Salmaan, it is

Another very important point that must be stated here is that all of the words of remembrance that have come from the Prophet (peace and blessings of Allah be upon him) are complete sentences with an understandable meaning to them. For example, the Prophet (peace and blessings of Allah be upon him) taught expressions like, "*al-hamdulilaah* (all praise be to Allah)," "*laa ilaaha illa-llaah* (there is none worthy of worship except Allah)". There is no report whatsoever of the Prophet (peace and blessings of Allah be upon him) ever simply repeating the word Allah or one of the names of Allah and considering that repetition as a form of *dhikr*. Similarly, there is no report of the Prophet (peace and blessings of Allah be upon him) ever saying only the pronoun, "*huwa* (he)," and considering that as a type of *dhikr* that is pleasing to Allah or that somehow brings one closer to Allah. Although this fact is very clear to anyone familiar with the Sunnah of the Prophet (peace and blessings of Allah be upon him), there are many who espouse the practice of repeating those words alone—without full sentences as in the *dhikr* of the Prophet (peace and blessings of Allah be upon him)—and they claim that such is the best way to make *dhikr*, the way of those who truly know Allah—claiming apparently that the Prophet (peace and blessings of Allah be upon him) himself did not know Allah.[1]

---

sahih due to its numerous chains. See Mashhoor Hasan Salmaan, footnotes to Jalaal al-Deen al-Suyooti, *Al-Amr bi-l-Itibaa wa al-Nahi an al-Ibtidaa* (al-Damaam, Saudi Arabia: Daar ibn al-Qayyim, 1995), pp. 83-84.] In another incident, the Companion ibn Umar heard someone sneeze and say, "All praise be to Allah and blessings be upon the Messenger of Allah." Ibn Umar objected to this and said, "From where does one say, 'All praise be to Allah and blessings be upon the Messenger of Allah'? That is not how the Messenger of Allah (peace and blessings of Allah be upon him) taught us. He taught us to say [only], 'All praise be to Allah under all circumstances.'" (This was recorded by al-Tirmidhi and al-Haakim. According to al-Hilaali, it is *hasan*. See Saleem al-Hilaali, *Sahih Kitaab al-Adhkaar wa Dhaeefuhu* (Madinah: Maktabah al-Ghurabaa al-Athariyyah, 1997), vol. 2, pp. 671-672.)

[1] For a lengthier discussion of this obvious but unfortunately abused issue, see Al-Ameen al-Haaj Muhammad Ahmad, *Al-Tareeq ila Wilaayah Allaah* (Jeddah: Daar al-Matbooaat al-Hadeethah, 1989), pp. 117-119. Also, Ibn Taimiyyah has a lengthy refutation of those who only say Allah or just *huwa*, see *ibn Taymiyyah's Essay*, pp. 181-196.

Should One Make *Dhikr* with One's Tongue Although the Heart is Not Truly Present?

Although at first when the word *dhikr* is mentioned it is usually thought of as a mentioning by the tongue, al-Qurtubi states that the original meaning of the word *dhikr* implies an alertness or realization in the heart. In other words, mentioning something by the tongue is called *dhikr* only because it is supposed to be an indication that the thing mentioned is being thought of in the mind and heart.[1] In fact, al-Nawawi said, "The purpose of dhikr is the presence of the heart. This must be the goal of the one making remembrance and he must be keen to achieve that, to ponder over what he is stating and recognize its meaning."[2]

Hence, the important question arises as to whether one should continue to make *dhikr* although one's heart is not present and whether or not such an act would still be pleasing to Allah. This is a question that has been answered differently by different people.

Karzoon and al-Ramly, for example, argue that making *dhikr* while the heart is not present is better than remaining silent, this is because one is using one's bodily part in an act of obedience to Allah. They say that at the very least the person is keeping his tongue from doing something forbidden, such as backbiting. Hence, *dhikr,* even with heedlessness, protects the tongue from destructive acts. Furthermore, it is possible that the heart may be affected with some form of feeling at one time or another while making *dhikr* in such a manner. Indeed, one may even move to a state where he is completely cognizant and considering what he is saying. They also argue that if the tongue stops making *dhikr,* then the heart will become even more heedless than when the tongue makes *dhikr.*[3]

---

[1] Al-Qurtubi, *al-Jaami*, vol. 2, p. 171.

[2] Quoted in Karzoon, vol. 1, p. 309.

[3] Cf., Karzoon, vol. 1, p. 320; Muhammad Shoomaan al-Ramli, *Al-Mushawwiq ila Dhikrilaahi Taala* (Al-Damaam, Saudi Arabia: Daar ibn al-Qayyim, 1421 A.H.), p. 21.

The above view is a view that has been held by many of the scholars throughout the history of Islam.[1] Ibn al-Qayyim, for example, wrote, "Mentioning the name of Allah with heedlessness in any case is better than a complete forgetfulness. Whenever the tongues abandon the mentioning of Allah—who is their beloved—it becomes occupied with mentioning what is hated and despised to Him."[2] Ibn Taimiyyah also noted, "*Dhikr* can be with the tongue of the person. His heart will have some portion of that as the bodily parts do not move save by the intention of the heart. However, heedlessness may dominate his act. In any case, that speech is better than its non-existence and Allah loves it and has ordered it."[3]

On the other hand, al-Maraaghi wrote,

> *Dhikr* by the tongue only without remembrance in the heart and noting the meaning of the statement does not produce any benefit. How many supplications and words of remembrance of Allah do we see people repeating in the hundreds or thousands yet they do not benefit them in knowing Allah and realizing Allah's watchful presence over them? This is the case because such has become a customary act for those people, accompanied by other objectionable customary acts. Therefore, it is obligatory to combine together the remembrance in the heart with the mentioning by the tongue.[4]

Dhiyaa al-Deen al-Izzi also argues that *dhikr* without the presence of the heart and without the feeling of humility and submission to Allah can have detrimental results. First, such *dhikr* produces hardness in the heart that can then lead to clear misguidance. Allah says,

---

[1] Cf., al-Ramli, *Al-Mushawwiq*, pp. 14-22.
[2] Ibn al-Qayyim, *Madaarij al-Saalikeen*, vol. 3, p. 45.
[3] Ahmad ibn Taimiyyah, *al-Istiqaamah* (Maktabah al-Tauiyah al-Islaamiyyah li-Ihyaa al-Turaath al-Islaami, n.d.), vol. 2, p. 17.
[4] Ahmad Mustafa al-Maraaghi, *Tafseer al-Maraaghi* (Beirut: Daar Ihyaa al-Turaath al-Arabi, n.d.), vol. 9, p. 156.

فَوَيْلٌ لِّلْقَـٰسِيَةِ قُلُوبُهُم مِّن ذِكْرِ ٱللَّهِ ۚ أُو۟لَـٰٓئِكَ فِى ضَلَـٰلٍ مُّبِينٍ

"Woe to those hearts which are hardened of the remembrance of Allah. They are in manifest error" (*al-Zumar* 22). It also develops an estrangement in the soul from the acts of worship. Finally, it opens the door to acting for the sake of show and leads to hypocrisy in the heart, as Allah says about the hypocrites,

إِنَّ ٱلْمُنَـٰفِقِينَ يُخَـٰدِعُونَ ٱللَّهَ وَهُوَ خَـٰدِعُهُمْ وَإِذَا قَامُوٓا۟ إِلَى ٱلصَّلَوٰةِ

قَامُوا۟ كُسَالَىٰ يُرَآءُونَ ٱلنَّاسَ وَلَا يَذْكُرُونَ ٱللَّهَ إِلَّا قَلِيلًا

"The hypocrites, they think they are over-reaching Allah but He will over-reach them. When they stand up to prayer, they stand without earnestness, to be seen of men, but little do they hold Allah in remembrance" (*al-Nisaa* 142). Those who remember Allah by their tongues only, while not understanding or pondering over what they say, do not have any real fear of Allah or humility towards Him in their hearts at that time. Therefore, the result is the opposite of what should be hoped for. It is, thus, clearly harmful for the individual. Since they are being heedless and forgetful of Allah by definition (since their *dhikr* is not present in the heart and mind), hardness instead of calmness descends into his heart. Instead of remembering Allah, they are thinking of their wealth, children, wife, work and so forth while Allah has not placed "two hearts" in the chests of anyone.[1]

Although the phenomenon al-Maraaghi described is certainly true, al-Izzi's arguments are not completely convincing. Perhaps the correct response to this question, Allah knows best, deals with the intention of the person. The Messenger of Allah (peace and blessings of Allah be upon him) said,

إِنَّمَا الأَعْمَالُ بِالنِّيَّاتِ وَإِنَّمَا لِكُلِّ امْرِئٍ مَا نَوَى

"Surely, all actions are but driven by intentions and, verily, every man shall have but that which he intended." (Recorded by al-

---

[1] Dhiyaa al-Deen al-Izzi, *Silat al-Insaan bi-laah min Wajhah Nadhar al-Quraan al-Kareem wa al-Sunnah al-Nabawiyyah* (Riyadh: Maktabah al-Ubaikaan, 1997), pp. 137-138.

Bukhari and Muslim.) The person who is making *dhikr* without giving it any true thought and without even realizing what he is saying may be similar to the person who after washing his hands automatically, without any conscious intention, starts to perform the acts of the ablution. He completes the ablution without even realizing what he was doing because so often after washing his hands he makes ablution. Such an ablution, without any intention, is not a valid ablution. Similarly, if a person makes *dhikr* after the prayer, for example, but it is simply a matter of his tongue moving on to something that he customarily does at that time without his heart being present and a true intention behind that act, the person may receive nothing for that act of *dhikr*. On the other hand, if a person consciously intends and wants to make *dhikr* and starts on that process but while making that *dhikr* his heart wanders and he is not truly cognizant of what he is saying, then, perhaps, in that case he will be rewarded for his act due to his good intention and because at the very least he has set his tongue on a deed that is better than remaining silent and better than doing sinful acts.

In sum, there are different levels of proper *dhikr*. However, if done with the proper intention, Allah willing, all of them will bring about benefit and assist the person in his process of purification. These levels include: (1) simply stating the words of remembrance without the heart being truly attentive; (2) stating the words of remembrance with the heart realizing what one is saying; (3) stating the words of remembrance with the heart not simply realizing what is being stated but also contemplating over the meaning and ramification of that statement; (4) stating the words of remembrance, contemplation in the heart accompanied by a strong feeling of the greatness of Allah and a deep understanding of what one is saying, in turn leading to living one's life in the shade of what one has remembered and contemplated.

Contemplation and Reflection[1]

Aamir ibn Abd Qais stated, "I heard more than one, two or three of the Companions of the Prophet (peace and blessings of Allah be upon him) say, 'The lamp of the faith or the light of the faith is *al-tafakkur* (contemplation and reflection).'"[2]

In the hustle and bustle of the modern world, contemplation and reflection is one important tool of purification (and an act of worship in itself) that is often neglected. Indeed, it seems as though Satan and his troops have a major plan for the humans of the Twenty-First Century: keep them so busy and preoccupied that they have no time to reflect upon what they are truly here for, what they should be doing and what their priorities should be. Nowadays, in a world in which technology is supposed to make things easier for people, people are flooded with information, most of it useless, trivial or simply time-consuming. Furthermore, in order to keep up with the pace of life, many have to work overtime or take on two or three jobs as everything is looked upon as a necessity of life: everyone has to have a cell phone, a newspaper delivered, internet access, cable TV, at least two cars and so forth. All of these cost money and, for the majority of people, they cannot be obtained save through sweating more and more hours at work. Then when the person finally has some free time, he only has the mental and physical energy to seek entertainment, relaxation and fun. And the modern world is ready to fill that desire and need in so many various ways that

---

[1] "Contemplation and Reflection" are used for the Arabic word *tafakkur*. See Badri, p. xiv, concerning the difficulty of capturing the meaning of *tafakkur* in English. Note that in addition to Allah commanding and praising contemplation and reflection, Allah has also strongly censured the *ghafileen* (those who are heedless, who do not benefit from lessons and what has occurred around them). Note, for example, the following verses: "Those who rest not their hope on their meeting with Us, but are pleased and satisfied with the life of the present, and those who heed not Our signs, their abode is the Fire because of the (evil) they earned" (*Yoonus* 7-8); "This because they love the life of this world better than the Hereafter: and Allah will not guide those who reject faith. Those are they whose hearts, ears, and eyes Allah has sealed up, and they are heedless. Without doubt, in the Hereafter they will perish" (*al-Nahl* 107-109).

[2] Quoted in ibn Katheer, *Tafseer* (Daar Taibah), vol. 2, p. 185. One of the most important forms of contemplation and reflection is contemplating over the verses of the Quran and the statements of the Prophet (peace and blessings of Allah be upon him). Both of those points have been discussed or alluded to earlier.

once again the person feels exhausted and has no mental energy left to simply contemplate and think. As Yassine described it, "[Y]ou are scattered by a thousand preoccupations, forever distracted, often depressed, and rarely in the proper state of mind."[1]

One of the greatest blessings that Allah has bestowed upon humans is the human mind and its ability to reflect and understand. When a person uses that mind in the proper way and according to its potential he should be led directly to the truth of God's oneness and a strong desire to worship the one God. On the other hand, if a person uses his mind simply to ponder over more ways to enjoy himself in useless pursuits and lusts, he will not have benefited from this great blessing and he will have wasted something that could have greatly helped in saving his very soul. In this way, his action becomes even more foolish than those creatures that have not been granted this blessing. Hence, Allah says,

وَلَقَدْ ذَرَأْنَا لِجَهَنَّمَ كَثِيرًا مِّنَ ٱلْجِنِّ وَٱلْإِنسِ لَهُمْ قُلُوبٌ لَّا
يَفْقَهُونَ بِهَا وَلَهُمْ أَعْيُنٌ لَّا يُبْصِرُونَ بِهَا وَلَهُمْ ءَاذَانٌ لَّا يَسْمَعُونَ
بِهَآ أُوْلَٰٓئِكَ كَٱلْأَنْعَٰمِ بَلْ هُمْ أَضَلُّ أُوْلَٰٓئِكَ هُمُ ٱلْغَٰفِلُونَ

"Many are the jinn and men We have made for Hell. They have hearts wherewith they understand not, eyes wherewith they see not, and ears wherewith they hear not. They are like cattle, nay more misguided: for they are heedless" (*al-Araaf* 179).

One very important type of contemplation is the reflecting on nature and this creation. In fact, there are numerous verses in the Quran in which Allah exhorts mankind to ponder over different aspects of this creation.[2] For example, Allah says,

---

[1] Yassine, p. xxvii.

[2] These include *al-Ankaboot* 20, *al-Ghaashiyyah* 17-20, *al-Talaaq* 5-7 and *Fussilat* 53.

إِنَّ فِي خَلْقِ ٱلسَّمَٰوَٰتِ وَٱلْأَرْضِ وَٱخْتِلَٰفِ ٱلَّيْلِ وَٱلنَّهَارِ لَأَيَٰتٍ لِّأُوْلِى ٱلْأَلْبَٰبِ ﴿١٩٠﴾ ٱلَّذِينَ يَذْكُرُونَ ٱللَّهَ قِيَٰمًا وَقُعُودًا وَعَلَىٰ جُنُوبِهِمْ وَيَتَفَكَّرُونَ فِي خَلْقِ ٱلسَّمَٰوَٰتِ وَٱلْأَرْضِ رَبَّنَا مَا خَلَقْتَ هَٰذَا بَٰطِلًا سُبْحَٰنَكَ فَقِنَا عَذَابَ ٱلنَّارِ

"Behold! In the creation of the heavens and the earth, and the alternation of night and day, there are indeed signs for men of understanding. [Such are] those who remember Allah, standing, sitting, and lying down on their sides, and contemplate the (wonders of) creation in the heavens and the earth, (with the thought): 'Our Lord! Not for naught have You created (all) this! Exalted be You! Give us salvation from the penalty of the Fire" (*ali-Imraan* 190-191). In this verse, Allah clearly ties contemplating the creation with remembrance of Allah and the conclusion that it is unacceptable to believe that Allah created this creation in vain and without a noble purpose. The Messenger of Allah (peace and blessings of Allah be upon him) would recite these verses often late at night (as Muslim records). In fact, the Messenger of Allah (peace and blessings of Allah be upon him) once said about these verses,

ويل لمن قرأها و لم يتفكر فيها

"Woe to the one who reads it and does not contemplate over it."[1]

Hence, the issue is not simply a matter of appreciating the beauty and excellence of the creation. This is something that even the disbelievers do. Unfortunately for them, though, as with so many aspects of this world, the disbelievers cannot seem to go beyond the "tip of the iceberg" to see the reality and importance

[1] Recorded by ibn Hibbaan. Its authenticity is discussed and confirmed by al-Albaani in Muhammad Naasir al-Deen al-Albaani, *Silsilat al-Ahaadeeth al-Saheehah* (Damascus: al-Maktab al-Islaami, 1979), vol. 1, pp. 106ff.

that lies beyond it.[1] The believer, on the other hand, uses that contemplation and appreciation of creation to bring him closer to Allah, remembering Allah through all of these sights and loving Allah more due to His great ability and attributes that led to this amazing creation.

As is well known, faith increases and decreases. Every Muslim should seek those means that are helpful in increasing one's faith. One of the greatest benefits of the proper form of contemplation is that it increases the faith in one's heart. It increases one's certainty that this existence definitely has a creator—it is impossible, for example, that this creation was the result of a random collision of molecules. It also increases one's appreciation for that Creator, as this creation has miraculous aspects in it that only the most wise and powerful could have created. In fact, Allah says,

وَتَرَى ٱلْجِبَالَ تَحْسَبُهَا جَامِدَةً وَهِىَ تَمُرُّ مَرَّ ٱلسَّحَابِ ۚ صُنْعَ ٱللَّهِ
ٱلَّذِىٓ أَتْقَنَ كُلَّ شَىْءٍ ۚ إِنَّهُۥ خَبِيرٌۢ بِمَا تَفْعَلُونَ

"You see the mountains and think them firmly fixed: but they shall pass away as the clouds pass away. (Such is) the artistry of Allah, Who disposes of all things in perfect order. He is well acquainted with all that you do" (*al-Naml* 88).

Beyond that, as one reflects upon the world around him, one also comes to the realization, under the guidance of the Quran, that all objects, the animate beings and even the inanimate, are engaged in a worship of Allah. One begins to appreciate the meaning of Allah's words,

تُسَبِّحُ لَهُ ٱلسَّمَٰوَٰتُ ٱلسَّبْعُ وَٱلْأَرْضُ وَمَن فِيهِنَّ ۚ وَإِن مِّن شَىْءٍ إِلَّا
يُسَبِّحُ بِحَمْدِهِۦ وَلَٰكِن لَّا تَفْقَهُونَ تَسْبِيحَهُمْ ۗ

[1] As Allah says about them, "They know but the outer (things) in the life of this world: but of the Hereafter they are heedless" (*al-Room* 7). In other words, they are heedless of what all the lessons of the different aspects of this creation point to.

"The seven heavens and the earth, and all beings therein, declare His glory: there is not a thing but celebrates His praise; and yet you understand not how they declare His glory" (*al-Israa* 44), and,

أَلَمْ تَرَ أَنَّ ٱللَّهَ يُسَبِّحُ لَهُۥ مَن فِى ٱلسَّمَٰوَٰتِ وَٱلْأَرْضِ وَٱلطَّيْرُ صَٰٓفَّٰتٍ ۖ

كُلٌّ قَدْ عَلِمَ صَلَاتَهُۥ وَتَسْبِيحَهُۥ ۗ وَٱللَّهُ عَلِيمٌۢ بِمَا يَفْعَلُونَ

"Do you not see that it is Allah Whose praises all beings in the heavens and on earth do celebrate, and the birds (of the air) with wings outspread? Each one knows its own (mode of) prayer and praise. And Allah knows well all that they do" (*al-Noor* 41).

An astounding result of this realization is that when the person truly obeys Allah, he is overcome with the feeling that he and all the forces of this creation are acting as one in worshipping the one and only true God and Creator.[1]

At this same time, contemplation makes one realize how weak he truly is and how greatly he is dependent upon his Creator for everything, from the clean air he breathes to the clean water he drinks to, most importantly, the guidance he has received to live properly in this world and receive Allah's pleasure in the Hereafter. This should cleanse the soul from arrogance and thinking that he has accomplished everything on his own. Indeed, he should realize that he cannot accomplish anything on his own as there is so much of this creation that is well beyond any God-given control of the humans. This realization brings true knowledge to the person that in turn should lead to a true fear of Allah. Hence, Allah says,

أَلَمْ تَرَ أَنَّ ٱللَّهَ أَنزَلَ مِنَ ٱلسَّمَآءِ مَآءً فَأَخْرَجْنَا بِهِۦ ثَمَرَٰتٍ مُّخْتَلِفًا

أَلْوَٰنُهَا ۚ وَمِنَ ٱلْجِبَالِ جُدَدٌۢ بِيضٌ وَحُمْرٌ مُّخْتَلِفٌ أَلْوَٰنُهَا وَغَرَابِيبُ

---

[1] For an excellent discussion of the worship of Allah by the inanimate objects of creation, see Fareed al-Tooni, *Uboodiyyah al-Kaainaat li-Rabb al-Alaameen* (Jeddah: Maktabah al-Dhiyaa, 1992), pp. 283-337.

سُودٌ ﴿٢٧﴾ وَمِنَ ٱلنَّاسِ وَٱلدَّوَآبِّ وَٱلۡأَنۡعَٰمِ مُخۡتَلِفٌ أَلۡوَٰنُهُۥ

كَذَٰلِكَۗ إِنَّمَا يَخۡشَى ٱللَّهَ مِنۡ عِبَادِهِ ٱلۡعُلَمَٰٓؤُاْۗ إِنَّ ٱللَّهَ عَزِيزٌ غَفُورٌ

"Do you not see that Allah sends down rain from the sky? With it We then bring out produce of various colors. And in the mountains are tracts white and red, of various shades of color, and black intense in hue. And so among men and crawling creatures and cattle, are they of various colors. Those truly fear Allah, among His Servants, who have knowledge: for Allah is Exalted in Might, Oft-Forgiving" (*Faatir* 27-28). Bishr al-Haafi said, "If the people were to reflect upon the greatness of Allah, they would not disobey Him."[1]

Indeed, contemplation and reflection is not limited to the wonderful facets of nature or even the positive events in life. One should also reflect upon unpleasant experiences that have occurred to one's self or to others. Badri notes, "In fact, witnessing terrifying scenes or undergoing personal hardships can lead one to contemplate and learn lessons probably in a more effective manner than when one is prompted by a placid appreciation of the beauty, size and precision of a building."[2]

In addition, one should reflect upon the various peoples who were destroyed by Allah due to their disobedience and sinning ways. Reflecting on matters like this can also be very moving and very awakening to the soul. In numerous places in the Quran, Allah reminds the believers of what happened to such people and instructs them to reflect on such realities. For example, Allah says,

---

[1] Quoted in ibn Katheer, *Tafseer* (Daar Taibah), vol. 2, p. 185.

[2] Badri, p. 35. This fact once again demonstrates that there is no pure evil that is to be attributed to Allah. Even the destruction of a people or the hardships one faces should have numerous positive results when reflected upon in the proper manner. Another very important topic of contemplation and reflection is one's own weaknesses and shortcomings. That is part of what is discussed in this chapter under the heading "Taking Account of One's Deeds, Behavior and Character."

قَدْ خَلَتْ مِن قَبْلِكُمْ سُنَنٌ فَسِيرُوا۟ فِى ٱلْأَرْضِ فَٱنظُرُوا۟ كَيْفَ كَانَ عَـٰقِبَةُ ٱلْمُكَذِّبِينَ ﴿١٣٧﴾ هَـٰذَا بَيَانٌ لِّلنَّاسِ وَهُدًى وَمَوْعِظَةٌ لِّلْمُتَّقِينَ

"Many were the ways of life that have passed away before you: travel through the earth, and see what was the end of those who rejected Truth. Here is a plain statement to men, a guidance and instruction to those who fear Allah" (*ali-Imraan* 137-138). Indeed, those who do not wake up to those signs—those who do not reflect, ponder and learn from these lessons—are the ones who have a blindness the like of which is more harmful than any other type of blindness.[1] Allah says,

فَكَأَيِّن مِّن قَرْيَةٍ أَهْلَكْنَـٰهَا وَهِىَ ظَالِمَةٌ فَهِىَ خَاوِيَةٌ عَلَىٰ عُرُوشِهَا وَبِئْرٍ مُّعَطَّلَةٍ وَقَصْرٍ مَّشِيدٍ ﴿٤٥﴾ أَفَلَمْ يَسِيرُوا۟ فِى ٱلْأَرْضِ فَتَكُونَ لَهُمْ قُلُوبٌ يَعْقِلُونَ بِهَآ أَوْ ءَاذَانٌ يَسْمَعُونَ بِهَا ۖ فَإِنَّهَا لَا تَعْمَى ٱلْأَبْصَـٰرُ وَلَـٰكِن تَعْمَى ٱلْقُلُوبُ ٱلَّتِى فِى ٱلصُّدُورِ

"And how many a city did We destroy while it was committing wrong—so it is (now) fallen into ruin—and [how many] an abandoned well and [how many] a lofty palace? So have they not traveled through the earth and have hearts by which to reason and ears by which to hear? For indeed, it is not eyes that are blinded

---

[1] Many modern scientists are cold-hearted archaeologists, dead to the realities of faith. They dig through the ruins of ancient civilizations, some whose lands were mysteriously deserted. Yet many of them never reflect or understand anything of deep significance from what they are studying. On the other hand, while the Messenger of Allah (peace and blessings of Allah be upon him) was passing through the land in which the people of Thamood were destroyed, he said, "Do not enter upon those who were destroyed unless you are crying. If you are not crying, do not go upon them lest you be afflicted with what they were afflicted with." (Recorded by al-Bukhari and Muslim.)

but blinded are the hearts which are within the breasts" (*al-Hajj* 45-46).

Another important aspect that the individual should reflect upon is what will occur to him after his death. He should remember and contemplate death, the grave, the resurrection and the Hereafter. The Messenger of Allah (peace and blessings of Allah be upon him) said,

أَلا إِنِّي قَدْ كُنْتُ نَهَيْتُكُمْ عَنْ ثَلاثٍ ثُمَّ بَدَا لِي فِيهِنَّ نَهَيْتُكُمْ عَنْ زِيَارَةِ الْقُبُورِ ثُمَّ بَدَا لِي أَنَّهَا تُرِقُّ الْقَلْبَ وَتُدْمِعُ الْعَيْنَ وَتُذَكِّرُ الآخِرَةَ فَزُورُوهَا

"I used to forbid you three things and then their matters were made clear to me. I prohibited you from visiting the graves and then it was made clear to me that [such visiting] softens the heart, makes the eyes tear and reminds one of the Hereafter. Therefore, visit them."[1] Contemplating over these matters increases one's belief in the Hereafter. In addition, it drives one to prepare for that day by performing good deeds and abstaining from sinful acts with the full realization that one's death may come at any moment, as one sees youthful people dying around him every day.[2]

This contemplation over death should also remind the person of the very important words of the Prophet (peace and blessings of Allah be upon him) that should drive him to keep striving, keep learning about his faith and keep trying to improve himself, not leaving any crack open for him to slip through. The Messenger of Allah (peace and blessings of Allah be upon him) said,

إِنَّ الْعَبْدَ لَيَعْمَلُ فِيمَا يَرَى النَّاسُ عَمَلَ أَهْلِ الْجَنَّةِ وَإِنَّهُ لَمِنْ أَهْلِ النَّارِ وَيَعْمَلُ فِيمَا يَرَى النَّاسُ عَمَلَ أَهْلِ النَّارِ وَهُوَ مِنْ أَهْلِ الْجَنَّةِ وَإِنَّمَا الأَعْمَالُ بِخَوَاتِيمِهَا

---

[1] Recorded by Ahmad and others. According to al-Arnaaoot, et al., it is *sahih* due to its supporting evidence. See Shuaib al-Arnaaoot, et al., *Musnad al-Imaam Ahmad* (Beirut: Muassasah al-Risaalah, 1998), vol. 21, pp. 141-3.

[2] Cf., al-Maaz, p. 106.

"A person does deeds that the people see as being the deeds of the people of Paradise but he is from the inhabitants of Hell. And one does deeds that the people see as the acts of the people of Hell while he is from the people of Paradise. The deeds are according to what seals them [that is, what the person is performing at the end of his life]." (Recorded by al-Bukhari.)

In addition, it should remind him that this world is passing and it is passing quickly. All of the things that he is enjoying in this world will soon come to an end. The person should reflect upon what this reality should mean for him. In fact, the Prophet (peace and blessings of Allah be upon him) encouraged the Muslims to think about this aspect a great deal, as he said,

أَكْثِرُوا ذِكْرَ هَاذِمِ اللَّذَّاتِ المَوْتُ فَإِنَّهُ لَمْ يَذْكُرُهُ أَحدٌ فِي ضيقٍ منَ العيشِ إلاَّ وسَّعهُ عليهِ ولا ذكرهُ في سَعةٍ إلا ضيَّقها عليه

"Increase your remembrance of the destroyer of pleasures: death. No one thinks about it during times of straitened circumstances except that it makes it easier upon him. And no one thinks about it during times of ease except that it constrains it upon him."[1] In other words, even during times of ease this reflection brings him back to the reality that he is not going to live forever with these worldly possessions and pleasures. The most important matter is to work for the long-run goal that one faces at the time of death.

In addition, there are many aspects of this life that, upon reflection, can serve as great reminders of one's final return to Allah. For example, virtually every day a person's lies down to sleep. When he sleeps, he enters into a different realm, a realm that is very close to what occurs to the person after he is put into the grave.[2] This is a nightly reminder to the person. He is

---

[1] Recorded by al-Baihaqi, ibn Hibbaan and al-Bazaar. According to al-Albaani, it is *hasan*. See al-Albaani, *Saheeh al-Jaami*, vol. 1, p. 264.

[2] Allah states (*al-Anaam* 60) that the soul is taken during sleep and Allah returns it only to the one who is going to continue living. Furthermore, upon going to bed the Prophet's invocation was, "In Your name my Lord do I lay myself on my side and by You I rise. If You keep my soul, then show it mercy. If You return it [to live longer], then protect it in the manner that You protect Your righteous servants." (Recorded by al-Bukhari.) Upon rising, one says, for example,

suspended in such a fashion that he can no longer perform any good deeds. Any deeds are now beyond his control. This is what every human goes through virtually every night, yet very few ever ponder over this daily event.

Note that contemplation not only has the positive ramifications discussed above, in addition it is a tool in blocking off the development of evil inclinations. Every believer is sometimes afflicted with thoughts of an evil nature, many times spurred on by Satan. The believer who constantly contemplates and reflects can easily deflect those thoughts and prevent them from developing into a harmful act or belief. Badri describes this aspect in the following passage:

> While internal cognitive activity is the key to every good and proper action, it is also the source of all disobedience, whether implied or overt. A meditative heart, which contemplates the grace of God and is mindful of the Hereafter, can easily detect the evil notions that pass through the mind as a result of the great sensitivity that the mind has acquired from long contemplation and continued remembrance. As soon as an evil notion passes through the mind, good sense detects it, confines it, and defuses its effect, just as a sound immune system in the body detects the intrusion of germs and antigens, which it then besieges and destroys with specialized cells and antibodies. The psyche or soul of those who are constantly contemplating the grace of God is like a protected fortress: whenever evil notions try to enter, the acute perception acquired through contemplation and remembrance quickly attacks and destroys them. The Quran states: "Those who fear God, when an evil thought from Satan assaults them, bring God to mind and, lo, they see clearly" [*al-Araaf* 201].[1]

"All praise be to Allah who gave us life after He had given us death and to Him is the return." (Recorded by al-Bukhari.)

[1] Badri, p. 28.

A very important point to note concerning the proper form of contemplation and reflection is that the goal is in no way some kind of "mystical experience" wherein one "feels" that he has experienced or witnessed the reality. This type of goal has been the mistake of many, including Sufis as well as non-believers, who are seeking any kind of "experience" through contemplation, chanting and so forth. Islamic contemplation is a "rational" form of contemplation, as Badri describes,

> Islamic contemplation is based on the progression from meditating on the creation to its Creator.[1] It is a smooth rational movement, since the Islamic faith is uncorrupted by any association of creatures or objects with the Almighty or any polytheistic deviations...
> As for practicing Muslims, their contemplation is a spiritual practice in which all their cognitive and spiritual faculties are activated in pursuit of the true cognizance of the Almighty. It is not an irrational or emotional endeavor to cure a disorder, nor a painful exercise in which the body is tortured by standing for several days on one leg... Islamic contemplation is a form of worship that binds the heart with the mind, the rational with the emotional, and the sensible with the passionate, so that sober contemplators may be in a better spiritual state in which their prayers, God willing, will be more acceptable. Irrational and highly emotional responses are frowned upon in Islamic contemplation, and altered states of consciousness are not, as previously mentioned, an end in themselves. Likewise, the occasional paranormal experiences that may occur as a result of very deep meditation, and which are so valued by Eastern and Western mystics to the extent that they are prepared to discard reasoning or tolerate severe bodily pain to secure them, are neither sought nor are they objects of excitement in true Islamic contemplation. Furthermore, since many

---

[1] What Badri means by "to its Creator" is that one strongly recognizes the existence and the greatness of the Creator via witnessing the creation, as Badri himself makes clear later in his work (p. 67).

> worshippers of Satan can produce paranormal performances, genuine Muslim worshippers and meditators view such phenomena with suspicion.[1]

In the process of contemplation and reflection, though, one must ponder over any of the various aspects of the creation and not try to imagine or conceive what the Creator is like. This is another mistake made by many, although the Prophet (peace and blessings of Allah be upon him) clearly stated,

لا تفكروا في الله وتفكروا في خلق الله

"Do not contemplate about Allah but contemplate about Allah's creation."[2] In reality, it is virtually impossible for a human to ponder over the essence of the Divine Being Allah since there is nothing similar to Allah that a human could possibly be familiar with. One may, though, contemplate upon His attributes and how those attributes are manifested in this creation.

Perhaps an excellent quote to end this section on contemplation and reflection is the statement of Abu Sulaimaan al-Daaraani who said, "When I leave from my house, my sight does not fall upon anything save that I see in it a blessing from Allah upon me as well as a lesson in it for me."[3] In other words, one should take every advantage to learn and benefit from what occurs to him. One need not run off to some secluded place to reflect and contemplate, what is around him on a daily basis should provide ample lessons for him to reflect upon.[4]

---

[1] Badri, pp. 49-50. Badri also discusses how contemplation is advocated by non-Muslims and the goals that they are trying to achieve.

[2] This hadith is recorded by Abu Nuaim in *al-Hilyah*. It has been recorded with various texts by other compilers. Al-Albaani concluded that it is *hasan* due to corroborating reports. See Muhammad Naasir al-Deen al-Albaani, *Silsilat al-Ahaadeeth al-Saheehah* (Kuwait: al-Daar al-Salafiyyah, 1983), vol. 4, pp. 395-397.

[3] Quoted in ibn Katheer, *Tafseer* (Daar Taibah), vol. 2, p. 185.

[4] The effectiveness and results of one's own contemplation and reflection are influenced by a number of factors. Badri discusses nine such factors, including depth of faith, depth and length of concentration and so forth. The interested reader should consult Badri, pp. 78-91.

Realizing the True Nature of This Worldly Existence

One of the greatest realizations that comes from studying the Quran as well as personal contemplation and reflection concerns the fleeting nature of this life. There is no escaping the fact that everyone shall taste death. It is inevitable. And when it comes, one has to leave behind all of the material goods and wealth of this transient existence.

This worldly life is referred to in Arabic as *al-hayaat al-dunya*. Linguistically, *dunya* comes from a root meaning both closeness and something despicable or lowly. This world is called *dunya* for two reasons: First, at the present time, it is closer (*adnaa*) to the humans than the Hereafter. Second, it is despicable or abased (*daneeah*) in comparison to the Hereafter.[1]

It is only those who are deceived by the glitter they see around them who become engrossed in this world and desire it till their deaths. When a person realizes the true nature of this world, as taught in the Quran and Sunnah, it becomes very easy for him to become "detached" from this world and to deal with it in the proper way.

The importance of this "detachment" can be seen in the numerous verses of the Quran in which Allah explains to mankind the reality of this worldly life and warns them about being overcome by its glitter. Note the following verses:

ٱعْلَمُوٓا۟ أَنَّمَا ٱلْحَيَوٰةُ ٱلدُّنْيَا لَعِبٌ وَلَهْوٌ وَزِينَةٌ وَتَفَاخُرٌۢ بَيْنَكُمْ
وَتَكَاثُرٌ فِى ٱلْأَمْوَٰلِ وَٱلْأَوْلَٰدِ ۖ كَمَثَلِ غَيْثٍ أَعْجَبَ ٱلْكُفَّارَ نَبَاتُهُۥ
ثُمَّ يَهِيجُ فَتَرَىٰهُ مُصْفَرًّا ثُمَّ يَكُونُ حُطَٰمًا ۖ وَفِى ٱلْءَاخِرَةِ عَذَابٌ شَدِيدٌ
وَمَغْفِرَةٌ مِّنَ ٱللَّهِ وَرِضْوَٰنٌ ۚ وَمَا ٱلْحَيَوٰةُ ٱلدُّنْيَآ إِلَّا مَتَٰعُ ٱلْغُرُورِ

"Know that the life of this world is but amusement and diversion and adornment and boasting to one another and competition in

[1] Cf., Muhammad ibn Uthaimeen, *Sharh Riyaadh al-Saaliheen* (Riyadh: Daar al-Watn, 1995), vol. 6, pp. 6-7.

increase of wealth and children. [In reality, it is] like the example of a rain whose [resulting] plant growth pleases the disbelievers.[1] When it dries, you see it turn yellow, and then it becomes [scattered] debris. And in the Hereafter is severe punishment and forgiveness from Allah and approval. And what is the worldly life except the enjoyment of delusion" (*al-Hadeed* 20). The fleeting pleasures and diversions of this worldly life mean nothing when one realizes that in the end it is with Allah wherein lies one's punishment or reward. That final return is the reality of utmost importance.

وَمَا ٱلْحَيَوٰةُ ٱلدُّنْيَآ إِلَّا لَعِبٌ وَلَهْوٌ ۖ وَلَلدَّارُ ٱلْءَاخِرَةُ خَيْرٌ لِّلَّذِينَ يَتَّقُونَ ۗ

أَفَلَا تَعْقِلُونَ

"And the worldly life is not but amusement and diversion. But the home of the Hereafter is best for those who fear Allah. So will you not then reason?" (*al-Anaam* 32).

وَمَا هَٰذِهِ ٱلْحَيَوٰةُ ٱلدُّنْيَآ إِلَّا لَهْوٌ وَلَعِبٌ ۚ وَإِنَّ ٱلدَّارَ ٱلْءَاخِرَةَ لَهِىَ

ٱلْحَيَوَانُ ۚ لَوْ كَانُوا۟ يَعْلَمُونَ

"And this worldly life is not but diversion and amusement. And, indeed, the home of the Hereafter, that is the [true and eternal] life, if only they knew" (*al-Ankaboot* 64).

وَٱضْرِبْ لَهُم مَّثَلَ ٱلْحَيَوٰةِ ٱلدُّنْيَا كَمَآءٍ أَنزَلْنَٰهُ مِنَ ٱلسَّمَآءِ

فَٱخْتَلَطَ بِهِۦ نَبَاتُ ٱلْأَرْضِ فَأَصْبَحَ هَشِيمًا تَذْرُوهُ ٱلرِّيَٰحُ ۗ وَكَانَ

---

[1] The word, *al-kuffaar*, could be understood to mean, "tillers, farmers". However, some commentators prefer to understand it to mean, "unbelievers." This is because it is the unbelievers, in general, who are most pleased with this world. In fact, this is truly the only world that many of them are living for. Cf., Muhammad al-Ramli, *Mathal al-Hayaat al-Dunyaa fi al-Kitaab wa al-Sunnah wa Kalaam al-Ulamaa* (al-Khobar, Saudi Arabia: Daar ibn Affaan, 1995), p. 13.

ٱللَّهُ عَلَىٰ كُلِّ شَىْءٍ مُّقْتَدِرًا ﴿٤٥﴾ ٱلْمَالُ وَٱلْبَنُونَ زِينَةُ ٱلْحَيَوٰةِ ٱلدُّنْيَا

وَٱلْبَٰقِيَٰتُ ٱلصَّٰلِحَٰتُ خَيْرٌ عِندَ رَبِّكَ ثَوَابًا وَخَيْرٌ أَمَلًا

"And present to them the example of the life of this world: [It is] like rain which We send down from the sky, and the vegetation of the earth mingles with it and [then] it becomes dry remnants, scattered by the winds. And Allah is ever perfect in ability over all things. Wealth and children are [but] adornment of the worldly life. But the enduring good deeds are better with your Lord and better for [one's] hope" (*al-Kahf* 45-46).

The Prophet (peace and blessings of Allah be upon him) also give clear warnings and lessons concerning this worldly life. For example, Muslim records a hadith that states that the Prophet (peace be upon him) passed by a dead goat which had either very small ears or mutilated ears. The Prophet (peace be upon him) took it and said to his Companions, "Which of you would like to have this for one *dirham*?" They said, "We do not desire it. What would we use it for?" The Prophet again said, "Would you like to have it for your own [free]?" They said, "By Allah, even if it were alive, we would find it defective, since it has small ears; what do you think now that it is dead?" The Messenger of Allah (peace be upon him) then told them,

فَوَاللَّهِ لَلدُّنْيَا أَهْوَنُ عَلَى اللَّهِ مِنْ هَذَا عَلَيْكُمْ

"By Allah, the world is more insignificant to Allah than this [dead goat] is to you."

In another hadith, the Messenger of Allah (peace be upon him) said,

لَوْ كَانَتِ الدُّنْيَا تَعْدِلُ عِنْدَ اللَّهِ جَنَاحَ بَعُوضَةٍ مَا سَقَى كَافِرًا مِنْهَا شَرْبَةَ مَاءٍ

"If this worldly life were equivalent in Allah's sight to even a wing of a mosquito, He would not have given a disbeliever even a drink of water in it."[1] An unbeliever is an enemy to Allah and the enemy should not be given anything of real value. But the unbeliever is given plenty of this world, implying that a world void of faith and good deeds is of no real value whatsoever.

In another hadith, the Messenger of Allah (peace and blessings of Allah be upon him) made it very clear what of this world has any true meaning and importance to it. He stated,

أَلا إِنَّ الدُّنْيَا مَلْعُونَةٌ مَلْعُونٌ مَا فِيهَا إِلاَّ ذِكْرُ اللَّهِ وَمَا وَالاهُ وَعَالِمٌ أَوْ مُتَعَلِّمٌ

"Certainly, this world is accursed and everything in it is accursed save for the remembrance of Allah, what He likes, the scholar and the student."[2]

Even though this is what the Quran and what the Prophet (peace and blessings of Allah be upon him) say about the goods of this worldly life, it is these things that play a strong role in most people's lives. For many people, their goals are almost completely limited to the things of this life and they can hardly raise their vision above them to consider and work for the Hereafter instead.

It is not a coincidence that some of the most moving early verses of the Quran were reminders of how people are with respect to this world. The disbelievers at the time of the Prophet (peace and blessings of Allah be upon him) were preoccupied with worldly things like the people today. Hence, Allah said to them,

أَلْهَىٰكُمُ ٱلتَّكَاثُرُ ﴿١﴾ حَتَّىٰ زُرْتُمُ ٱلْمَقَابِرَ

"The mutual rivalry for piling up (the good things of this world) diverts you (from the more serious things), until you visit the graves" (*al-Takaathur* 1-2). Allah also said,

وَيْلٌ لِّكُلِّ هُمَزَةٍ لُّمَزَةٍ ﴿١﴾ ٱلَّذِى جَمَعَ مَالًا وَعَدَّدَهُۥ ﴿٢﴾ يَحْسَبُ أَنَّ مَالَهُۥٓ أَخْلَدَهُۥ

---

[1] Recorded by al-Tirmidhi and others. According to al-Albaani, it is *sahih*. See al-Albaani, *Saheeh al-Jaami*, vol. 2, p. 937.

[2] Recorded by al-Tirmidhi and ibn Maajah. According to al-Albaani, it is *hasan*. See Muhammad Naasir al-Deen al-Albaani, footnotes to al-Tabreezi, vol. 3, p. 1431.

"Woe to every (kind of) scandal-monger and backbiter, who piles up wealth and (continuously) counts it, thinking that his wealth would make him last for ever" (*al-Humazah* 1-3).

However, Allah reminds everyone,

مَا عِندَكُمْ يَنفَدُ وَمَا عِندَ ٱللَّهِ بَاقٍ

"What is with you must vanish: what is with Allah will endure" (*al-Nahl* 96). When one considers the true nature of this passing world, as is pointed out in this verse, one is automatically reminded of death and what he has prepared for the Hereafter. Karzoon notes that the more one gets engrossed in this world and more one has wealth, influence and power, the more he is in need of remembering death even more in order that this world not become a great trial for him that he cannot overcome.[1] In fact, the Messenger of Allah (peace and blessings of Allah be upon him) put everything in a stark and clear perspective when he stated,

إِنَّ مَطْعَمَ ابْنِ آدَمَ ضُرِبَ لِلدُّنْيَا مَثَلاً بِمَا خَرَجَ مِنِ ابْنِ آدَمَ وَإِنْ قَزَّحَهُ وَمَلَّحَهُ فَانْظُرْ مَا يَصِيْرُ إِلَيْهِ

"The food of humans strikes a parable of this worldly life: From what comes out of humans [as waste], even after they had seasoned it and added salt to it [and made it very tasty], look at what it ends up as."[2] In other words, even though humans work very hard to make the food taste excellent, the food finally results in something that is very disgusting and distasteful. The same is true for this world and all of its glitter. It will all end in destruction and waste.[3]

When one thinks of what occurs to him at and after death—his soul leaving his body, his body being washed by others as he has no ability to do it himself, his body being placed in a grave surrounded by worms and creatures, his wealth being distributed among others and so forth—one can recall with pity

---

[1] Karzoon, vol. 1, p. 463.

[2] Recorded by ibn Hibbaan. According to al-Albaani, it is *hasan*. See al-Albaani, *Saheeh al-Jaami*, vol. 1, pp. 437-438.

[3] Cf., al-Ramli, *Mathal*, pp. 42-3.

how much effort he has put into this life and how little he has earned for the Hereafter. There is no question that one needs to live and work in this world but one must always keep in mind what are the long-term and true goals. One takes only what he needs from this world while working for the Hereafter. This puts everything in the proper perspective that Allah has summarized in one verse:

وَٱبْتَغِ فِيمَآ ءَاتَىٰكَ ٱللَّهُ ٱلدَّارَ ٱلْءَاخِرَةَ ۖ وَلَا تَنسَ نَصِيبَكَ مِنَ ٱلدُّنْيَا ۖ وَأَحْسِن كَمَآ أَحْسَنَ ٱللَّهُ إِلَيْكَ ۖ وَلَا تَبْغِ ٱلْفَسَادَ فِى ٱلْأَرْضِ ۖ إِنَّ ٱللَّهَ لَا يُحِبُّ ٱلْمُفْسِدِينَ

""But seek, with the (wealth) which Allah has bestowed on you, the home of the Hereafter. But do not forget your portion in this world. Do good as Allah has been good to you, and seek not (occasions for) mischief in the land. Allah loves not those who do mischief" (*al-Qasas* 77). The Prophet (peace and blessings of Allah be upon him) also beautifully expressed this balance when he stated,

كُنْ فِي الدُّنْيَا كَأَنَّكَ غَرِيبٌ أَوْ عَابِرُ سَبِيلٍ

"Be in the world as if you were a stranger or a traveler along a path." (Recorded by al-Bukhari.)

Striving Against Any Evil Inclinations of the Soul

Allah says,

وَجَٰهِدُوا۟ فِى ٱللَّهِ حَقَّ جِهَادِهِۦ ۚ

"And strive for the sake of Allah as you ought to strive" (*al-Hajj* 78). Al-Raazi has quoted the great *mujaahid* and scholar Abdullah ibn al-Mubaarak as interpreting, "strive as you ought to strive" as meaning, "Struggling against the soul and desires."[1]

[1] Al-Raazi, vol. 23, p. 72.

The Messenger of Allah (peace and blessings of Allah be upon him) said,

الْمُجَاهِدُ مَنْ جَاهَدَ نَفْسَهُ

"The [true] *mujaahid*[1] is the one who strives against his own soul."[2] As was noted earlier, the soul is not necessarily inherently evil. However, the soul has both propensities in it: it can turn toward good and it can turn toward evil. Hence, the individual has to work to extinguish or greatly weaken the evil propensities. This is a type of struggle and, hence, it is a kind of jihad.

In fact, there are various types of jihad. Unfortunately, many times people go to extremes by stressing one at the expense of others. For example, there are many in this world today, given the current plight of the Muslims, who stress jihad against the disbelievers. At the same time, they fail to recognize the importance of jihad against any evil inclinations in the soul, which probably lie at the root of the matter leading to the current plight of the Muslims. On the other hand, some stress jihad against the soul and ignore, downplay or deny the validity of any other form of jihad.

Although both of these extremes are to be avoided, the overall importance of "victory" in the jihad against the soul needs to be emphasized. When one encounters the enemies on the physical battlefield, the most that can happen to a person is that he loses his life. His enemy cannot pry the faith from the believer's heart. His enemy can only put an end to the believer's worldly life. But if the believer loses his life while having faith and fighting for the sake of Allah, that is not a bad thing whatsoever. His worldly life may come to an end but he has gained an everlasting victory and happiness. On the other hand, if the believer loses in the battle against evil inclinations in one's soul, he will harm his own soul. In fact, if he does not strive against any of the evil inclinations in his soul, the result can be everlasting misery and punishment in the Hereafter. In other words, instead

---

[1] *Mujaahid* means the one who makes jihad.

[2] Recorded by al-Tirmidhi and ibn Hibbaan. According to al-Albaani, it is *sahih*. See al-Albaani, *Saheeh al-Jaami*, vol. 2, p. 1133.

of purifying his soul, his soul will be completely soiled and corrupted, leading to Allah's displeasure.

In essence, what is meant by "jihad against any evil inclination in the soul" is that sometimes the soul may desire or long after something that is harmful for the soul itself. Allah has described this occurrence in a couple of places in the Quran. For example, concerning the son of Adam who killed his brother and was the first to commit murder, Allah says,

فَطَوَّعَتْ لَهُۥ نَفْسُهُۥ قَتْلَ أَخِيهِ فَقَتَلَهُۥ فَأَصْبَحَ مِنَ ٱلْخَٰسِرِينَ

"The (selfish) soul of the other led him to the murder of his brother: he murdered him, and became (himself) one of the lost ones" (*al-Maaidah* 30).[1] Allah also clearly points out the importance of forbidding one's soul from following such vain desires when they occur. For example, Allah says,

وَأَمَّا مَنْ خَافَ مَقَامَ رَبِّهِۦ وَنَهَى ٱلنَّفْسَ عَنِ ٱلْهَوَىٰ ۝٤٠ فَإِنَّ ٱلْجَنَّةَ هِىَ ٱلْمَأْوَىٰ

"And for such as had entertained the fear of standing before their Lord's (tribunal) and had restrained (their) soul from lower desires, their abode will be the Garden" (*al-Naaziaat* 40-41).

Ibn Hazm once stated a very precise golden rule concerning this matter. He said, "There are two things that if you do them you will attain the good of this world and the Hereafter... [They are] that you bear what you dislike if it is beloved to Allah and you leave what you like if it is disliked by Allah."[2] Not always, especially as one is beginning along the path of purification, are the acts of worship pleasing and easy upon the soul. Similarly, refraining from what Allah dislikes may also not be that easy in the early stages of one's spiritual growth. However, the person must always keep in mind that the key to his purification and the key to his reaching his goal is to do what is pleasing to Allah and

[1] Other similar verses include *Yoosuf* 18 and *Taha* 96.

[2] Quoted in al-Bilaali, pp. 128-129.

to refrain from what is displeasing to Allah, regardless of whether the soul is ready and easily accepting of that.

Therefore, whenever one's soul prompts a Muslim to perform an evil deed, he should first recognize in his mind that such is an evil deed. Unfortunately, though, when an inclination to sin exists in the soul, Satan will try to pounce on this opportunity to urge the person to perform that harmful act. If the person has evil friends, they may also encourage him to do such evil. Now the individual himself must decide what to do. He has contradictory pressures within his own being. He may give in to his soul's temporary lust and longing and do something that he knows is not correct and not beneficial. On the other hand, he may strive against this feeling or lust. He may restrain himself, correctly convincing himself that to forego that act is better than to perform it. This restraint is a type of patience and striving, patience in the face of what the soul is longing for and striving against its harmful demands.

But there is more to it than refraining oneself from chasing after lusts and desires. One also has to "move" one's soul and oneself. That is, one has to strive against being complacent and lazy. Today, no specific individual has a guarantee of Paradise. Hence, every individual should fear that he could lose whatever good he has attained and could even lose his faith altogether. Therefore, he must always strive to maintain his faith, improve himself, and perform as many good deeds as he can. In fact, he should not even be content if he remains stationary. He should hope for improvement in every day of his life. In fact, the early scholar Sulaimaan al-Daaraani stated, "If a person's day is just like yesterday, then he has a shortcoming."[1]

In particular, he must push himself to perform the obligatory duties, from the prayer five times a day to the obligations he has towards all others. Given all the temptations, constraints and struggles a person faces, this is indeed a true form of striving in every sense of the word. The individual cannot afford to be lackadaisical since he never knows when the angel of death may come to him.

---

[1] Quoted in al-Bilaaali, p. 64.

The main weapon in this battle is patience. Patience has many aspects to it. Patience has been defined by ibn al-Qayyim as, "confirming the demands of the [intelligent and rational] mind and faith against the urges of desires and lusts."[1] One of the most important forms of patience is the patience and perseverance that is required on a daily basis to make oneself perform the obligatory duties. It also includes patience in the sense of restraining oneself from committing sinful acts. Hence, the quality of patience is definitely a must for the purified soul. Indeed, it is one of the true signs of a purified soul and it is one of the aspects concerning which Allah tests mankind. Allah has said,

وَلَنَبْلُوَنَّكُمْ حَتَّىٰ نَعْلَمَ ٱلْمُجَٰهِدِينَ مِنكُمْ وَٱلصَّٰبِرِينَ وَنَبْلُوَا۟ أَخْبَارَكُمْ

"We shall try you until We show who are the *mujahideen* among you and who are the patient. And We shall test your facts [to display your true nature]" (*Muhammad* 31).

In fact, one of the greatest benefits of jihad is that it is both an act of patience as well as an act that develops further patience. The Prophet (peace and blessings of Allah be upon him) has stated,

حُجِبَتِ النَّارُ بِالشَّهَوَاتِ وَحُجِبَتِ الْجَنَّةُ بِالْمَكَارِهِ

"The Hell-fire has been covered in lusts while Paradise is covered in hardships." (Recorded by al-Bukhari.) Paradise is not obtained simply through play, rest and relaxation while merely stating with one's tongue that one is a believer. Indeed, when one claims to be a believer, Allah will put that person to the test to demonstrate, prove and increase his faith. Allah says,

---

[1] Muhammad ibn al-Qayyim, *Iddah al-Saabireen wa Dhakheerah al-Shaakireen* (Beirut: Daar al-Kutub al-Ilmiyyah, 1983), p. 16.

أَحَسِبَ ٱلنَّاسُ أَن يُتْرَكُوٓا۟ أَن يَقُولُوٓا۟ ءَامَنَّا وَهُمْ لَا يُفْتَنُونَ ۝٢ وَلَقَدْ فَتَنَّا ٱلَّذِينَ مِن قَبْلِهِمْ ۖ فَلَيَعْلَمَنَّ ٱللَّهُ ٱلَّذِينَ صَدَقُوا۟ وَلَيَعْلَمَنَّ ٱلْكَٰذِبِينَ

"Do men think that they will be left alone on saying, 'We believe,' and that they will not be tested? We did test those before them, and Allah will certainly know those who are true from those who are false" (*al-Ankaboot* 2-3). The demonstration of one's faith and its increase is achieved through sacrifice, patience and jihad.

A very important aspect in the jihad against the evil inclinations of the soul is the repelling of any evil thoughts that pop into one's mind. Evil ideas occur to everybody. The important thing is to stamp them out as soon as they appear and not to allow them to grow and flourish until the person himself begins to desire or intend to do that evil act. When caught in their early moments, there is no sin upon the person for what occurred in his mind. A hadith, recorded by al-Bukhari and Muslim, states,

إِنَّ اللَّهَ تَجَاوَزَ عَنْ أُمَّتِي مَا حَدَّثَتْ بِهِ أَنْفُسَهَا مَا لَمْ تَعْمَلْ أَوْ تَتَكَلَّمْ

"Verily, Allah has overlooked for [the members of] my nation what their souls think about as long as they do not act on it or speak about it." As one allows the evil thoughts to persist, the stronger they become and the more difficult they are to overcome and defeat. If the individual allows them to grow until they become true wants and intentions, then he may commit a sin depending upon the entire situation and what he does afterwards.[1]

An additional aid in struggling against the soul is to specifically seek refuge with Allah from any evil inclination in the soul. Actually, the believer should do this every morning, every evening and upon going to bed. The Prophet (peace be upon him)

---

[1] For a more detailed discussion of this point, see Zarabozo, *Commentary on the Forty Hadith of al-Nawawi*, vol. 3, pp. 1354ff.

told his dear Companion Abu Bakr (may Allah be pleased with him),

قُلِ اللَّهُمَّ فَاطِرَ السَّمَوَاتِ وَالأَرْضِ عَالِمَ الْغَيْبِ وَالشَّهَادَةِ رَبَّ كُلِّ شَيْءٍ وَمَلِيكَهُ أَشْهَدُ أَنْ لا إِلَهَ إِلاَّ أَنْتَ أَعُوذُ بِكَ مِنْ شَرِّ نَفْسِي وَشَرِّ الشَّيْطَانِ وَشِرْكِهِ وَأَنْ أَقْتَرِفَ عَلَى نَفْسِي سُوْءً أَوْ أَجُرَّهُ إِلَى مُسْلِمٍ قَالَ قُلْهَا إِذَا أَصْبَحْتَ وَإِذَا أَمْسَيْتَ وَإِذَا أَخَذْتَ مَضْجَعَكَ

"Say: O Allah, creator of the heavens and the earth, knower of the unseen and seen, Lord of everything and its Sovereign, I bear witness that there is none worthy of worship except You. I seek refuge in You from the evil in my soul and from the evil of Satan and his ascribing of partners to Allah. [I also seek refuge from] acquiring any evil for myself or bringing such upon any Muslim." Then the Prophet (peace be upon him) said, "Say that when you are in the early morning, late afternoon and when you take to your bed."[1]

As noted earlier, the soul is not necessarily inherently evil, although some writers may give that impression. Dealing with the soul is a case of developing its natural good qualities and suppressing any evil qualities that may have crept into it. This struggle with the soul is not an impossible task. It is something that Allah requires from every human and it is well within the means of every human if he so chooses that path. The following verse makes it clear that this obligation—this struggle against the soul which is so often pictured or conceived of as some insurmountable task—is within the means of mankind without even any unbearable hardship. Allah has said,

وَجَٰهِدُوا۟ فِى ٱللَّهِ حَقَّ جِهَادِهِۦ ۚ هُوَ ٱجْتَبَىٰكُمْ وَمَا جَعَلَ عَلَيْكُمْ فِى ٱلدِّينِ مِنْ حَرَجٍ ۚ

[1] Recorded by Ahmad and Abu Dawood. According to al-Hilaali, this hadith is *sahih*. See Saleem al-Hilaali, *Sahih Kitaab al-Adhkaar wa Dhaeefuhu* (Madinah: Maktabah al-Ghurabaa al-Athariyyah, 1997), vol. 1, pp. 223-224.

"And strive in His cause as you ought to strive. He has chosen you, and has imposed no difficulties on you in religion" (*al-Hajj* 78).

Perhaps one of the greatest foundations that can assist one in striving against any evil desires or inclinations in his soul is having a noble and supreme purpose. That is, if one keeps in mind his goal in life, setting that goal in front of him, he will recognize those acts that veer him away from that goal. He will realize what is more important and he will in most cases—Allah willing—not give in to any temporary temptations.

Jihad in All of Its Other Forms

Allah says,

وَٱلَّذِينَ جَٰهَدُوا۟ فِينَا لَنَهْدِيَنَّهُمْ سُبُلَنَا ۚ وَإِنَّ ٱللَّهَ لَمَعَ ٱلْمُحْسِنِينَ

"And those who strive for Our (Cause), We will certainly guide them to Our Paths: for verily Allah is with those who do right" (*al-Ankaboot* 69). Commenting on this verse, ibn al-Qayyim wrote,

> Allah has connected guidance with jihad. The people who have the most complete guidance are those who make the greatest jihad. The forms of jihad which are most obligatory upon a person are the jihad against the soul, jihad against desires, jihad against Satan and jihad against [being overcome by this] worldly life. Whoever strives against these four for the sake of Allah, Allah guides him to the paths that are pleasing to Him, leading to His Paradise. Whoever abandons the jihad would lose a corresponding portion of guidance based on how much jihad he failed to perform... One cannot fight the external enemy unless one fights these internal enemies. Whoever is given victory over them will be given victory over his [external] enemy.[1]

Jihad can be used in a very comprehensive sense that embodies all forms of sacrificing and standing up for the sake of

[1] Muhammad ibn al-Qayyim, *al-Fawaaid* (Beirut: Daar al-Nafaais, 1984), p. 78.

Allah.[1] It includes fighting against the disbelievers with one's life or wealth, struggling against heresies and sins by one's pen or speech, ordering good and eradicating evil, speaking the truth to an unjust ruler and so on. All of these acts fall under the most general usage of the term jihad and all of them can be beneficial in purifying the soul.

Karzoon points out that Allah states that success (*falaah*) is directly related to purifying the soul, as in the verse,

قَدْ أَفْلَحَ مَن زَكَّىٰهَا

"Truly he succeeds that purifies it [that is, the soul]" (*al-Shams* 9). At the same time, though, Allah also states that that same success is also directly related to striving for the sake of Allah in its various forms. For example, Allah says,

يَـٰٓأَيُّهَا ٱلَّذِينَ ءَامَنُوا۟ ٱتَّقُوا۟ ٱللَّهَ وَٱبْتَغُوٓا۟ إِلَيْهِ ٱلْوَسِيلَةَ وَجَـٰهِدُوا۟

فِى سَبِيلِهِۦ لَعَلَّكُمْ تُفْلِحُونَ

"O you who believe! Do your duty to Allah, seek the means of approach unto Him, and strive with might and main in His cause that you may prosper [that is, attain *falaah*]" (*al-Maaidah* 35). Enjoining virtue and eradicating vice is also a form of jihad. Concerning that act, Allah has said,

وَلْتَكُن مِّنكُمْ أُمَّةٌ يَدْعُونَ إِلَى ٱلْخَيْرِ وَيَأْمُرُونَ بِٱلْمَعْرُوفِ

وَيَنْهَوْنَ عَنِ ٱلْمُنكَرِ ۚ وَأُو۟لَـٰٓئِكَ هُمُ ٱلْمُفْلِحُونَ

"Let there arise out of you a band of people inviting to all that is good, enjoining what is right, and forbidding what is wrong: they are the ones to attain felicity (*falaah*)" (*ali-Imraan* 104).

---

[1] The technical definition of jihad and its first meaning in the texts of the Quran and Sunnah is the fighting against the disbelievers to make the word of Allah supreme. As noted above, here it is being used in a much more general sense, which would include striving against the wrongdoers (by ordering good and eradicating evil) and striving against the hypocrites and so forth.

Hence, this makes it clear that jihad in all of its various forms is actually part and parcel of the process of purification of the soul as it is one of the means of success and prosperity which can only be achieved through the purification of the soul.[1] Given this fact, it is not surprising that the Messenger of Allah (peace and blessings of Allah be upon him) said,

رَأْسُ الأَمْرِ الإِسْلاَمُ وَعَمُودُهُ الصَّلاَةُ وَذِرْوَةُ سَنَامِهِ الْجِهَادُ

"The head of the matter is Islam. Its pillar is prayer. And its apex is jihad."[2]

Jihad frees the soul from the love and attachment to this world, which is one of the greatest roadblocks to the complete purification of the soul. By participating in jihad, by risking one's life, wealth or even love of the people (by advising them to do what is right and offering them sincere comments), one begins to truly feel and experience the true purpose of this life. One begins to truly realize that he is meant to be a servant of Allah, living for the Hereafter and not living for the petty things of this world. He is willing to please Allah alone and his ultimate loyalty is only to Allah—no matter what sacrifices that reality may entail. When one is willing to do that, he has taken part in the exchange by the true believers that Allah describes in the Quran,

إِنَّ ٱللَّهَ ٱشْتَرَىٰ مِنَ ٱلْمُؤْمِنِينَ أَنفُسَهُمْ وَأَمْوَٰلَهُم بِأَنَّ لَهُمُ ٱلْجَنَّةَ ۚ يُقَٰتِلُونَ فِى سَبِيلِ ٱللَّهِ فَيَقْتُلُونَ وَيُقْتَلُونَ ۖ وَعْدًا عَلَيْهِ حَقًّا فِى ٱلتَّوْرَىٰةِ وَٱلْإِنجِيلِ وَٱلْقُرْءَانِ ۚ وَمَنْ أَوْفَىٰ بِعَهْدِهِۦ مِنَ ٱللَّهِ ۚ فَٱسْتَبْشِرُوا۟ بِبَيْعِكُمُ ٱلَّذِى بَايَعْتُم بِهِۦ ۚ وَذَٰلِكَ هُوَ ٱلْفَوْزُ ٱلْعَظِيمُ

---

[1] Karzoon, vol. 1, p. 285.

[2] Recorded by Ahmad, al-Tirmidhi and others. According to al-Albaani, it is *sahih*. See al-Albaani, *Saheeh Sunan al-Tirmidhi*, vol. 2, pp. 328-329. As is well known, there are numerous verses of the Quran and hadith that demonstrate the importance and virtues of jihad.

﴿١١١﴾ ٱلتَّٰٓئِبُونَ ٱلْعَٰبِدُونَ ٱلْحَٰمِدُونَ ٱلسَّٰٓئِحُونَ ٱلرَّٰكِعُونَ ٱلسَّٰجِدُونَ ٱلْءَامِرُونَ بِٱلْمَعْرُوفِ وَٱلنَّاهُونَ عَنِ ٱلْمُنكَرِ وَٱلْحَٰفِظُونَ لِحُدُودِ ٱللَّهِ ۗ وَبَشِّرِ ٱلْمُؤْمِنِينَ

"Allah has purchased of the believers their souls and their wealth. For them (in return) is the Garden (of Paradise). They fight for His Cause, and slay and are slain. [This reward is] a promise binding on Him in truth, through the Torah, the Gospel, and the Quran. And who is more faithful to his covenant than Allah? Then rejoice in the bargain that you have concluded. It is the achievement supreme. Those that turn (to Allah) in repentance, serve Him, praise Him, go about for the sake of Allah, bow down and prostrate themselves in prayer, enjoin good and forbid evil, and observe the limits set by Allah, (these do rejoice). So proclaim the glad tidings to the believers" (*al-Taubah* 111-112). (It should be noted that in the second verse above, Allah describes those who have made that trade with Allah with the attributes of those who have truly purified their souls. These characteristics also demonstrate that these believers are not simply making jihad against the disbelievers but that they are in fact making jihad according to its most comprehensive usage.)

It is the individual himself in the process of self-purification who is the real recipient of the benefits of jihad. Allah says,

وَمَن جَٰهَدَ فَإِنَّمَا يُجَٰهِدُ لِنَفْسِهِۦٓ ۚ إِنَّ ٱللَّهَ لَغَنِىٌّ عَنِ ٱلْعَٰلَمِينَ

"And if any do strive, they do so for their own souls: for Allah is free of all needs from all creation" (*al-Ankaboot* 6); and, again, as was stated at the beginning of this section, Allah clearly promises,

وَٱلَّذِينَ جَٰهَدُوا۟ فِينَا لَنَهْدِيَنَّهُمْ سُبُلَنَا ۚ وَإِنَّ ٱللَّهَ لَمَعَ ٱلْمُحْسِنِينَ

"And those who strive for Our (Cause), We will certainly guide them to Our Paths: for verily Allah is with those who do right" (*al-Ankaboot* 69).

Having Righteous Companions, Friends and Spouses

Allah says,

وَٱصۡبِرۡ نَفۡسَكَ مَعَ ٱلَّذِينَ يَدۡعُونَ رَبَّهُم بِٱلۡغَدَوٰةِ وَٱلۡعَشِيِّ يُرِيدُونَ
وَجۡهَهُۥۖ وَلَا تَعۡدُ عَيۡنَاكَ عَنۡهُمۡ تُرِيدُ زِينَةَ ٱلۡحَيَوٰةِ ٱلدُّنۡيَاۖ وَلَا تُطِعۡ
مَنۡ أَغۡفَلۡنَا قَلۡبَهُۥ عَن ذِكۡرِنَا وَٱتَّبَعَ هَوَىٰهُ وَكَانَ أَمۡرُهُۥ فُرُطٗا ﴿٢٨﴾
وَقُلِ ٱلۡحَقُّ مِن رَّبِّكُمۡۖ فَمَن شَآءَ فَلۡيُؤۡمِن وَمَن شَآءَ فَلۡيَكۡفُرۡۚ

"And keep your soul content with those who call on their Lord morning and evening, seeking His Face; and let not your eyes pass beyond them, seeking the pomp and glitter of this life; nor obey any whose heart We have permitted to neglect the remembrance of Us, one who follows his own desires, whose case has gone beyond all bounds. Say, 'The Truth is from your Lord.' Let him who will, believe, and let him who will, reject (it)" (*al-Kahf* 28-29).

Allah also says,

يَٰٓأَيُّهَا ٱلَّذِينَ ءَامَنُواْ ٱتَّقُواْ ٱللَّهَ وَكُونُواْ مَعَ ٱلصَّٰدِقِينَ

"O you who believe! Fear Allah and be with those who are true (in word and deed)" (*al-Taubah* 119).

In addition, in a moving and telling example, Allah presents the story of the Messenger Moses (peace and blessings of Allah be upon him). When Allah ordered him to go to Pharaoh, he requested Allah to send with him Aaron as a supporter, helper and one who can work with him to worship Allah and strive together with him for the sake of Allah. Allah says,

ٱذۡهَبۡ إِلَىٰ فِرۡعَوۡنَ إِنَّهُۥ طَغَىٰ ﴿٢٤﴾ قَالَ رَبِّ ٱشۡرَحۡ لِى صَدۡرِى ﴿٢٥﴾
وَيَسِّرۡ لِىٓ أَمۡرِى ﴿٢٦﴾ وَٱحۡلُلۡ عُقۡدَةٗ مِّن لِّسَانِى ﴿٢٧﴾ يَفۡقَهُواْ قَوۡلِى

وَٱجْعَل لِّي وَزِيرًا مِّنْ أَهْلِي ﴿٢٩﴾ هَـٰرُونَ أَخِي ﴿٣٠﴾ ٱشْدُدْ بِهِۦٓ أَزْرِي ﴿٣١﴾ وَأَشْرِكْهُ فِيٓ أَمْرِي ﴿٣٢﴾ كَيْ نُسَبِّحَكَ كَثِيرًا ﴿٣٣﴾ وَنَذْكُرَكَ كَثِيرًا ﴿٣٤﴾ إِنَّكَ كُنتَ بِنَا بَصِيرًا ﴿٣٥﴾ قَالَ قَدْ أُوتِيتَ سُؤْلَكَ يَـٰمُوسَىٰ

"Go to Pharaoh, for he has indeed transgressed all bounds. (Moses) said, 'O my Lord! Expand me my chest, ease my task for me and remove the impediment from my speech so they may understand what I say. And give me an assistant from my family, Aaron, my brother. Add to my strength through him, and make him share my task. That we may extol You without stint and remember You without stint. For You are He that is (ever) watching us.' (Allah) said, 'Granted is your prayer, O Moses'" (*Taha* 24-34).

The Prophet (peace and blessings of Allah be upon him) said,

عَلَيْكُمْ بِالْجَمَاعَةِ وَإِيَّاكُمْ وَالْفُرْقَةَ فَإِنَّ الشَّيْطَانَ مَعَ الْوَاحِدِ وَهُوَ مِنَ الِاثْنَيْنِ أَبْعَدُ

"Stick to the congregation and avoid separation. Certainly, Satan is with the one [by himself] while he is further away from the two."[1]

The Messenger of Allah (peace and blessings of Allah be upon him) also said,

الرَّجُلُ عَلَى دِينِ خَلِيلِهِ فَلْيَنْظُرْ أَحَدُكُمْ مَنْ يُخَالِلُ

"A person is on the religion of his close friend (*khaleel*). Therefore, you should look to see [that is, be careful about] who you take as a close friend."[2] To be one's *khaleel* implies the greatest form of

[1] Recorded by al-Tirmidhi and others. According to al-Albaani, it is *sahih*. Cf., al-Albaani, *Saheeh Sunan al-Tirmidhi*, vol. 2, p. 232.
[2] Recorded by Ahmad, Abu Dawood and al-Tirmidhi. According to al-Albaani, it is *sahih*. See al-Albaani, *Saheeh al-Jaami*, vol. 2, p. 1114.

friendship and closeness. In a situation of that nature, there is no question that there will be a direct effect of each friend upon the other. Hence, it is of extreme importance for the purification of the soul that one take only pious people as their closest and most intimate friends. In this hadith, the Prophet (peace and blessings of Allah be upon him) has clearly indicated that, regardless of whether one realizes it or wishes to admit it, one is following the same way of life and religion as his intimate and closest friend.

The Prophet (peace and blessings of Allah be upon him) also said,

مَثَلُ الْجَلِيسِ الصَّالِحِ وَالْجَلِيسِ السَّوْءِ كَمَثَلِ صَاحِبِ الْمِسْكِ وَكِيرِ الْحَدَّادِ لا يَعْدَمُكَ مِنْ صَاحِبِ الْمِسْكِ إِمَّا تَشْتَرِيهِ أَوْ تَجِدُ رِيحَهُ وَكِيرُ الْحَدَّادِ يُحْرِقُ بَدَنَكَ أَوْ ثَوْبَكَ أَوْ تَجِدُ مِنْهُ رِيحًا خَبِيثَةً

"The example of a good companion [who sits with you] in comparison with a bad companion is like that of the perfume seller and the blacksmith. From the first, you would either buy musk or enjoy its good smell. However, the blacksmith will either burn your clothes or your house or you will get a bad smell from him." (Recorded by al-Bukhari.)

The Messenger of Allah (peace and blessings of Allah be upon him) also gave further advice on this topic when he said,

لا تُصَاحِبْ إِلاَّ مُؤْمِنًا وَلا يَأْكُلْ طَعَامَكَ إِلاَّ تَقِيٌّ

"You should not accompany save a believer and no one but a pious person should eat your food."[1]

Another hadith demonstrates the importance and the benefit of being in the midst of sincere worshippers of Allah. In the famous hadith of the person who killed one hundred people and wanted to repent, the most knowledgeable person told him that the door to repentance was still open to him. Then he told him,

---

[1] Recorded by Ahmad, Abu Dawood, al-Tirmidhi, ibn Hibbaan and al-Haakim. According to al-Albaani, it is *hasan*. See al-Albaani, *Saheeh al-Jaami*, vol. 2, p. 1226.

انْطَلِقْ إِلَى أَرْضِ كَذَا وَكَذَا فَإِنَّ بِهَا أُنَاسًا يَعْبُدُونَ اللَّهَ فَاعْبُدِ اللَّهَ مَعَهُمْ وَلا تَرْجِعْ إِلَى أَرْضِكَ فَإِنَّهَا أَرْضُ سَوْءٍ

"Go to such and such land as therein are people who worship Allah and you should worship Allah with them. Do not go back to your land for it is an evil place." (Recorded with this wording by Muslim.)

The benefits of having pious friends and companions are numerous. They include the following:

(1) When one intentionally seeks pious friends and companions for the sake of Allah, he is on the path to attaining Allah's love in return. Due to this effort on his part, Allah willing, he will be in Allah's shade on a day in which there is no shade save Allah's. The Messenger of Allah (peace and blessings of Allah be upon him) said,

سَبْعَةٌ يُظِلُّهُمُ اللَّهُ فِي ظِلِّهِ يَوْمَ لا ظِلَّ إِلاَّ ظِلُّهُ.. رَجُلانِ تَحَابَّا فِي اللَّهِ اجْتَمَعَا عَلَيْهِ وَتَفَرَّقَا عَلَيْهِ

"Seven will be shaded by Allah on a day in which there is no shade save His shade... Two men who loved each other for the sake of Allah, coming together on that basis and parting from one another on that basis." (Recorded by al-Bukhari and Muslim.) Muslim also records the following hadith:

قَالَ رَسُولُ اللَّهِ صَلَّى اللَّهم عَلَيْهِ وَسَلَّمَ إِنَّ اللَّهَ يَقُولُ يَوْمَ الْقِيَامَةِ أَيْنَ الْمُتَحَابُّونَ بِجَلالِي الْيَوْمَ أُظِلُّهُمْ فِي ظِلِّي يَوْمَ لا ظِلَّ إِلاَّ ظِلِّي

The Messenger of Allah (peace and blessings of Allah be upon him) said, "Allah will say on the Day of Resurrection, 'Where are the people who loved each other for My greatness. Today, I shall shade them in My shade, a day in which there is no shade save My shade.'"

(2) Pious friends can be a continual source of advice, guidance and strength. Al-Bilaali noted, "A man by himself is weak but with his brethren he is strong. It is difficult for a man by

himself to overcome this soul that drives one to evil without support from his brethren."[1] It is common for a person to go through periods of weakness or confusion. It is at times like these when the true friends for the sake of Allah are most needed. When one is in a state of weakness with respect to his faith, it is his pious friends who can remind him of the reality of his situation and pull him out of his plight. They can remind him via verses of the Quran and hadith of the Prophet (peace and blessings of Allah be upon him), such that his faith may be rejuvenated and he sets his course back on the right path. In fact, sometimes all the person needs to get over his weakness is a simple reminder of something from the Quran and hadith but if he does not have pious or knowledgeable people around him, he may have no one who is able to offer him that simple reminder.

At other times, the proper intention is there but a person is simply confused as to what to do. One may be confused as to what course of action one should follow when making *dawah* or trying to apply his religion. This is especially possible in this day and age when there are so many opinions being expressed as to "which" Islam one should follow. Perhaps one's righteous friends have already gone through such a stage in their lives. Hence, they may be able to advise him in such a way that he will see clearly what path he must follow.

(3) It is very possible that one does not notice his own shortcomings. He may think, for example, that he is calling others to the path of Allah in the best of manners while, in fact, he is driving people away from the Straight Path. He may also think that he is attending the mosque on a regular basis while others may notice how often he is actually absent from the mosque. It is in matters like these that one truly benefits from having pious companions who sincerely care about each other for the sake of Allah. It is these friends who can notice one's shortcomings and attempt to correct them, in a way that is beneficial and not simply embarrassing. Indeed, this is part of the goals of the Islamic brotherhood. The Messenger of Allah (peace and blessings of Allah be upon him) said,

---

[1] Al-Bilaali, p. 76.

الْمُؤْمِنُ مِرْآةُ الْمُؤْمِنِ وَالْمُؤْمِنُ أَخُو الْمُؤْمِنِ يَكُفُّ عَلَيْهِ ضَيْعَتَهُ وَيَحُوطُهُ مِنْ وَرَائِهِ

"The believer is the believer's mirror and the believer is the believer's brother. He guards him against loss and protects him when he is absent."[1] (Note that this is the nature of a true friend for the sake of Allah. Many people think that friendship implies overlooking the faults of one's friend. That is not the Islamic form of friendship. Indeed, a friend of that nature simply watches his friend as he moves closer to the Hell-fire. The true believer and the true friend for the sake of Allah could not do that. Instead, he will take whatever steps he can to improve his friend, help him purify his soul and bring him closer to Allah by convincing him to give up any deed which is improper.)

(4) A very important role that pious people play is that of being an excellent example for others. This was the role that the Prophet (peace and blessings of Allah be upon him) played for his people as a whole[2] and it is a role that the pious must fulfill for others. For some people, reading about excellent examples of the past is not sufficient as they think their situation is different from those of the past. Hence, an example living under the current circumstances is what is needed. Without such an example, some find it difficult to excel or push themselves unless they see a true example in front of them. Otherwise, they will just go with the flow. They do not have the will power to push themselves above and beyond what others are doing, thus in a way separating themselves from the others. Therefore, if everybody else is involved in forbidden acts or not taking their religion very seriously, then they do the same. However, if there is a person or group of people who are setting an example for others, they see the good that they should be doing and by their example they are encouraged to strive for that level of goodness. The mere presence of these good examples reminds the others that they need not be complacent and lackadaisical about their faith like so many others.

---

[1] Recorded by Abu Dawood. According to al-Albaani, it is *hasan*. Cf., al-Albaani, *Saheeh al-Jaami*, vol. 2, p. 1130.

[2] Allah says, "You have indeed in the Messenger of Allah a beautiful pattern (of conduct) for anyone whose hope is in Allah and the Final Day, and who engages much in the praise of Allah" (*al-Ahzaab* 21).

Instead, they can work to improve themselves, attain a great deal of knowledge concerning the faith, for example, and bring themselves closer to Allah.

(5) The good example brings the teachings of Islam from an abstract and theoretical level to a visible, practical and more understandable level. This aspect is extremely important in general but it is even more important for those who grew up in non-Muslim environments, void of Islamic character, etiquette and behavior.[1] One can read about proper Islamic character (including, for example, remaining patient, controlling one's anger, how to treat one's guests), but until one actually sees it in action, he may never completely understand how such is to be fulfilled. If he cannot completely understand the concept, it is difficult to imagine that he will ever be able to implement it properly in his own life.

(6) Associating with the pious can give one the proper perspective and put some balance in one's life. In this day and age, even in the mosques, much of the conversation centers around computer technology, secular politics, the Internet, sports, fashion and other worldly matters that can make one forget one's overall purpose in life. Without a doubt, in this age of information and media, there are many topics to preoccupy one's time today. Some balance is definitely needed. People must be reminded of Allah. People must also be reminded that it is not for this world that a Muslim is living. People also need to be reminded that it is the Quran and the Sunnah that deserve much of their time. One's pious friends may be the only beacon of light and example reminding oneself that there are other things in life that are more important than those many things that the masses consume their time in.

A hadith clearly summarizes the importance of associating with the pious. The Messenger of Allah (peace and blessings of

---

[1] In fact, after embracing Islam some Muslims hardly change their behavior or manners. This author has noticed that this usually occurs in those environments in which the person embraces Islam among other converts who have also never had the ability to change their ways under the influence of a good example or who continue to live and associate extensively with the non-Muslim population.

Allah be upon him) was once asked, "Who is the best of those whom we sit with?" He replied,

من ذكركم الله رؤيته وزاد في علمكم منطقه وذكركم في الآخرة عمله

"He whose sight reminds you of Allah, he whose speech increases your knowledge and he whose actions remind you of the Hereafter."[1]

This topic also highlights the importance of belonging to a good community and being close to a mosque, especially when living in a non-Muslim environment with the influence of disbelief all around. In fact, when it comes to the issue of associating with good Muslims, the first question one would probably ask is: Where can such pious companions be found?[2] The most obvious answer should be the mosque and those institutions dedicating to spreading the word of Allah. Even in this case, one must approach other Muslims with the correct intention. For example, one should not interact with them for any type of worldly benefit. Such an intention must be cleared from his heart.

---

1 Recorded by Abu Yala. According to al-Haithami, all of its narrators save Mubaarak ibn Hasaan, who could be considered trustworthy, are from the narrators of the *Sahib* collections. In general, Mubaarak's hadith are not considered strong enough to be accepted in and of themselves. According to al-Darweesh, this hadith has supporting evidence in Abdullah ibn al-Mubaarak's *Zuhd* with a *sahib* chain. Cf., al-Haithami, *Bughyah*, vol. 10, p. 389. Also see Abdullah Muhammad al-Darweesh, footnotes to Noor al-Deen Ali al-Haithami, *[Bughyah al-Raaid fi Tahqeeq] Majma al-Zawaaid wa Manba al-Fawaaid* (Beirut: Daar al-Fikr, 1992), vol. 10, p. 80.

2 There are a number of points that should be kept in mind here. Ibn al-Jauzi, who died in 597 A.H., noted that in his time it was very difficult to find true and sincere companions and friends—most of them were simply out for worldly benefit and if they did not achieve their goals, they would become the greatest of enemies and most envious of people. Karzoon noted that this does not mean that one gives up trying to find the good, pious companions. One continues to seek such good companions because they are very helpful in the process of purifying one's soul. Then Karzoon quotes al-Ghazaali noting a very important point: When seeking good companions one should not expect the companion to be perfect. Indeed, the person who is seeking good companions himself is not perfect. It is sufficient if a person's good outweighs his sins and if the benefit of being with him is greater than the harm. If one does not take this type of approach, one will be forced to abandon everyone as everyone has some evils to him. Furthermore, one should approach his friends with good thoughts about them and mercy, not with hatred and waiting to pounce on the first mistake that they make. Cf., Karzoon, vol. 1, pp. 422-423.

One should come close to the pious Muslims only in order to find pious companions who can help him come closer to Allah. If this proper intention is there, Allah will bless the relationship and make it strong and beneficial for all parties, even perhaps in this worldly life.

In sum, having righteous companions and friends can be very helpful on the road to purifying one's soul. At the same time, though, not having righteous companions or finding only a few righteous friends should never be used as an excuse for not standing up for the truth and adhering to the straight path. One of the early scholars stated, "You must follow the path of truth and do not be saddened by the fact that there are very few on that path. Stay away from the path of falsehood and do not be deceived by the large numbers of those who are to be destroyed."[1] Indeed, while along the straight path, one should realize that he has countless virtuous companions who have treaded the same path, including the prophets, the sincere, the pious and the martyrs. The individual should reflect upon their lives and actions as if he were their close friend living among them. This can strengthen a person's resolve and make his heart firm upon the truth. This is, in fact, one of the goals behind the stories found in the Quran, as Allah says,

وَكُلًّا نَّقُصُّ عَلَيْكَ مِنْ أَنۢبَآءِ ٱلرُّسُلِ مَا نُثَبِّتُ بِهِۦ فُؤَادَكَ ۚ

"All that We relate to you of the stories of the messengers, with it We make firm your heart" (*Hood* 120). In the Hereafter, Allah willing, he will meet up with those righteous companions although they may not be present with him today.

It should also be noted that the friendship that is for the sake of Allah and based on the tenets of faith will be the only true and eternal friendship. Allah says,

ٱلْأَخِلَّآءُ يَوْمَئِذٍۭ بَعْضُهُمْ لِبَعْضٍ عَدُوٌّ إِلَّا ٱلْمُتَّقِينَ

"Friends on that Day will be foes one to another except the righteous" (*al-Zukhruf* 67). On the other hand, those who chose friends for worldly reasons even if those friends were following a

---

[1] Quoted in ibn al-Qayyim, *Madaarij*, vol. 1, p. 21.

path of falsehood will be very upset about the friends that they did choose instead of the Prophet (peace and blessings of Allah be upon him) and the true believers. Allah says,

وَيَوْمَ يَعَضُّ ٱلظَّالِمُ عَلَىٰ يَدَيْهِ يَقُولُ يَٰلَيْتَنِى ٱتَّخَذْتُ مَعَ ٱلرَّسُولِ سَبِيلًا ﴿٢٧﴾ يَٰوَيْلَتَىٰ لَيْتَنِى لَمْ أَتَّخِذْ فُلَانًا خَلِيلًا ﴿٢٨﴾ لَّقَدْ أَضَلَّنِى عَنِ ٱلذِّكْرِ بَعْدَ إِذْ جَآءَنِى ۗ وَكَانَ ٱلشَّيْطَٰنُ لِلْإِنسَٰنِ خَذُولًا

"The Day that the wrongdoer will bite at his hands, he will say, 'Oh! Would that I had taken a (straight) path with the Messenger! Ah! Woe is me! Would that I had never taken such a one for a friend! He did lead me astray from the message (of Allah) after it had come to me! Ah! Satan is but a traitor to man" (*al-Furqaan* 27-29).

Before concluding this section, it may be important to note that this concept of mixing only with the pious people is often misunderstood by those who seek spiritual purification. Al-Maaz perceptively notes that attempting to mix and be with pious people does not mean that one should cut oneself off from the rest of society. This would imply failing to perform many obligatory deeds, including ordering good and eradicating evil. What this concept means is that one should do his best to spend most of his time with pious people and try to benefit from them. When among not so pious people, he should try to influence them in the best way and remind them of Allah while they are being forgetful of Him.[1] Indeed, there is even a hadith from the Prophet (peace and blessings of Allah be upon him) which states,

الْمُؤْمِنُ الَّذِي يُخَالِطُ النَّاسَ وَيَصْبِرُ عَلَى أَذَاهُمْ أَعْظَمُ أَجْرًا مِنَ الْمُؤْمِنِ الَّذِي لا يُخَالِطُ النَّاسَ وَلا يَصْبِرُ عَلَى أَذَاهُمْ

"The believer who mixes with the people and is patient with respect to their harmful acts has a greater reward[2] than the

---

[1] Cf., al-Maaz, p. 114.
[2] Other narrations of this hadith state, "is better than the believer who..."

believer who does not mix with the people and does not have patience over their harmful acts."[1] At the same time, while in the midst of not so pious people, one should always be aware of their state and not allow them to become an influence in one's life. Therefore, in reality, one must judge himself to see how much and how badly one is being affected by others and adjust his own interaction with them accordingly.

A Pious Spouse

Besides seeking pious companions and friends, marriage is also a very important step on the road to purifying the soul.[2] The Messenger of Allah (peace and blessings of Allah be upon him) stated,

إذا تزوج العبد فقد استكمل نصف الدين فليتق الله في النصف الباقي

[1] Recorded, with this wording, by ibn Maajah. According to al-Albaani, it is *sahih*. See al-Albaani, *Saheeh al-Jaami*, vol. 2, p. 1129.

[2] Given the past Christian and Sufi views, some may find it strange to consider marriage an important step for purification of the soul. [For example, al-Ghazaali, a Sufi-oriented writer, wrote, "You should know that the student (*mureed*) at the beginning of his journey should not occupy himself with getting married. This preoccupies the person from advancing along the path and leads the person to take comfort and find delight with the spouse. Whoever finds comfort and delight with anyone other than Allah has become preoccupied from Allah. One should not be deceived by the Messenger of Allah's numerous marriages, since all of this world could not preoccupy him from Allah." Al-Ghazaali, *Ihyaa*, vol. 3, p. 101. Note that al-Ghazaali does make an allowance for those who cannot control their sexual desires. See Karzoon's critique of al-Ghazaali's views in Karzoon, vol. 2, pp. 746-750.] The fact is that marriage helps the person control one's desires that are naturally found within him. Instead of an internal struggle wherein the "pious" person supposedly fights off those natural desires, those desires are fulfilled in a way that is wholesome and good for the individual and for society as a whole. Hence, the Messenger of Allah (peace and blessings of Allah be upon him) encouraged marriage. He stated, "O young people, whoever among you has the means to get married should get married as it lowers the gaze and protects one's chastity. Whoever does not have such means should fast for it is a protection." (Recorded by al-Bukhari and Muslim.) In fact, marriage was the practice of the Prophet Muhammad (peace and blessings of Allah be upon him) as well as the previous prophets, who were the most purified of all of mankind. Allah says, "We did send messengers before you, and appointed for them wives and children" (*al-Rad* 38).

"When the person gets married, he has completed half of his faith, so let him beware of Allah concerning the remaining half."[1] Commenting on this and another similar hadith, Karzoon noted that marriage fulfills a number of goals in Islam. In particular, it helps the person refrain from some of the greatest sins and lewd acts. When the goal is accomplished through marriage, all that remains is for the spouses to assist each other in developing the positive characteristics and virtuous manners of Islam, which represents the second portion of one's faith.[2]

In fact, one's most intimate companion and the person with whom one spends most of his time will be his spouse. It is therefore of extreme importance that one choose one's spouse wisely, on the basis of the proper criteria and with a pious intention. The Prophet (peace and blessings of Allah be upon him) himself said,

تُنْكَحُ الْمَرْأَةُ لِأَرْبَعٍ لِمَالِهَا وَلِحَسَبِهَا وَجَمَالِهَا وَلِدِينِهَا فَاظْفَرْ بِذَاتِ الدِّينِ تَرِبَتْ يَدَاكَ

"A woman is married for four reasons: for her wealth, for her lineage, for her beauty or for her religion. Get the one who is religious and may your hands cling to dust[3]." (Recorded by al-Bukhari and Muslim.) Furthermore, the Prophet (peace and blessings of Allah be upon him) has given clear advice to the guardian of the woman that he must first take into consideration the piety and character of a perspective groom for otherwise there may be dire consequences for the society as a whole. The Prophet (peace and blessings of Allah be upon him) said,

---

[1] Recorded by al-Baihaqi in *Shaab al-Imaan*. According to al-Albaani, it is *hasan*. See al-Albaani, *Saheeh al-Jaami*, vol. 1, pp. 136-137. Karzoon also quotes another narration recorded by al-Tabaraani and al-Haakim which al-Albaani declares weak. It states, "Whoever Allah provides a pious wife has been helped concerning half of his faith. So let him beware of Allah concerning the remaining half." See Muhammad Naasir al-Deen al-Albaani, *Dhaeef al-Jaami* p. 807.

[2] Karzoon, vol. 1, p. 432.

[3] The expression "May your hands cling to dust" is many times an imprecation, meaning "may you not achieve any good." Here, however, it used to mean, "may you be successful and prosperous."

إِذَا خَطَبَ إِلَيْكُمْ مَنْ تَرْضَوْنَ دِينَهُ وَخُلُقَهُ فَزَوِّجُوهُ إِلاَّ تَفْعَلُوا تَكُنْ فِتْنَةٌ فِي الْأَرْضِ وَفَسَادٌ عَرِيضٌ

"If someone whose religion and character is pleasing to you proposes to you, you should marry [the one under your care] to him. If you do not do so, there will be trials on the earth and widespread immorality."[1]

In fact, a pious spouse is definitely one of the greatest blessings that a Muslim can receive in this life. Such a spouse can help the person improve his own religion and enjoy peace and happiness in this life. Hence, the Prophet (peace and blessings of Allah be upon him) stated,

قلبٌ شاكرٌ ولسانٌ ذاكرٌ وزوجةٌ صالحةٌ تُعينكَ على أمرِ دُنياك ودينِكَ خيرُ ما أكتنز الناسُ

"A thankful heart, a tongue that mentions [Allah] and a pious wife to help you in the affairs of your world and your religion are better than what the people are treasuring and hoarding."[2]

The desired goals of marriage should result when the intent was sincere and the spouse was chosen based on piety and character. Allah has described this kind of marriage in the verse,

وَمِنْ ءَايَـٰتِهِۦٓ أَنْ خَلَقَ لَكُم مِّنْ أَنفُسِكُمْ أَزْوَٰجًا لِّتَسْكُنُوٓا۟ إِلَيْهَا وَجَعَلَ بَيْنَكُم مَّوَدَّةً وَرَحْمَةً ۚ إِنَّ فِى ذَٰلِكَ لَـَٔايَـٰتٍ لِّقَوْمٍ يَتَفَكَّرُونَ

"And among His Signs is this, that He created for you wives from among yourselves, that you may find repose in them, and He has put between you affection and mercy. Verily, in that are indeed Signs for a people who reflect" (*al-Room* 21).

---

[1] Recorded by al-Tirmidhi. According to al-Albaani, it is *hasan*. See al-Albaani, *Saheeh Sunan al-Tirmidhi*, vol. 1, pp. 314-315.

[2] Recorded by al-Baihaqi. According to al-Albani, it is *sahih*. See al-Albani, *Saheeh al-Jaami*, vol. 2, p. 812.

On the other hand, if a person is simply overcome by one's desire for beauty, youth or wealth in a spouse, the choice that is made may have disastrous long-term effects on the purification of the soul. Choosing a spouse who is not pious simply due to being overcome by those other criteria can damage a person's faith in numerous ways. For example, it is not uncommon to see a person who is single attending the mosque on a regular basis but after marrying someone who is not very pious, he discontinues this practice due to his wife's request and his desire to win his wife's love. Had he chosen a pious wife who had a good understanding of the faith, his wife would have supported him and encouraged him to attend the prayers in the mosque. Thus, she would have further contributed to his spiritual purification, as well as to her own by encouraging what is good and pleasing to Allah.

Attending the Mosque

Allah says,

إِنَّمَا يَعْمُرُ مَسَـٰجِدَ ٱللَّهِ مَنْ ءَامَنَ بِٱللَّهِ وَٱلْيَوْمِ ٱلْـَٔاخِرِ وَأَقَامَ ٱلصَّلَوٰةَ وَءَاتَى ٱلزَّكَوٰةَ وَلَمْ يَخْشَ إِلَّا ٱللَّهَ فَعَسَىٰٓ أُو۟لَـٰٓئِكَ أَن يَكُونُوا۟ مِنَ ٱلْمُهْتَدِينَ

"The mosques of Allah shall be visited and maintained by such as believe in Allah and the Last Day, establish regular prayers, and practice regular charity, and fear none (at all) except Allah. It is they who are expected to be on true guidance" (*al-Taubah* 18). In other words, it is expected and required of those of true faith—those on the path of purification—that they attend the mosques.[1]

[1] Of course, attending the mosque refers to attending the mosque on a daily basis to perform the obligatory, daily prayers. It is definitely not a reference to attending the mosque only once a week for the Friday Prayer. Indeed, one should not expect that just one hour a week would be able to protect him from the negative influences that one is possibly bombarded with throughout every day of the week. Again, this aspect takes on even greater significance the more non-Islamic one's society and surroundings are.

This important act has a number of beneficial facets to it, in particular for those who are living in non-Muslim environments. One may note the following:

(1) There are greater rewards and blessings in the prayer that is said in congregation. This great disparity between the virtues of a prayer said outside of the mosque and one said in congregation has been explained by the Prophet (peace and blessings of Allah be upon him) when he said,

صَلاةُ الرَّجُلِ فِي الْجَمَاعَةِ تُضَعَّفُ عَلَى صَلاتِهِ فِي بَيْتِهِ وَفِي سُوقِهِ خَمْسًا وَعِشْرِينَ ضِعْفًا وَذَلِكَ أَنَّهُ إِذَا تَوَضَّأَ فَأَحْسَنَ الْوُضُوءَ ثُمَّ خَرَجَ إِلَى الْمَسْجِدِ لا يُخْرِجُهُ إِلاَّ الصَّلاةُ لَمْ يَخْطُ خَطْوَةً إِلاَّ رُفِعَتْ لَهُ بِهَا دَرَجَةٌ وَحُطَّ عَنْهُ بِهَا خَطِيئَةٌ فَإِذَا صَلَّى لَمْ تَزَلِ الْمَلائِكَةُ تُصَلِّي عَلَيْهِ مَا دَامَ فِي مُصَلاهُ اللَّهُمَّ صَلِّ عَلَيْهِ اللَّهُمَّ ارْحَمْهُ وَلا يَزَالُ أَحَدُكُمْ فِي صَلاةٍ مَا انْتَظَرَ الصَّلاةَ

"Prayer of a man said in congregation is twenty-seven times better than his prayer in his house or his market. And that is if he makes ablution and does it well, then he goes to the mosque solely for the sake of prayer, then he does not take a step except that his rank is increased, and a sin is removed from him. And when he prays, the angels do not stop praying for him, saying, 'Allah, bless him, O Allah, have mercy on him.' And one of you is always in prayer while he is waiting for the prayer." (Recorded by al-Bukhari.) Indeed, if the benefits mentioned in this hadith were the only benefits accruing to one praying in the mosque, it would be enough to demonstrate the role and importance of attending the mosque for the purification of one's soul. Of great importance is that with every step he takes, a sin is removed from him and while he is in his place of prayer, the wonderful angels are praying on his behalf.

(2) Upon attending the mosques, one gets into contact with other active and dedicated Muslims, people who sacrifice their time to come to the mosque to get closer to Allah. These can be—and should be—the most dedicated of the Muslim community. By attending the mosque and getting to know people

of such caliber, one can get inspired and moved by their example and dedication. Their actions and their words should remind oneself of one's true purpose and goal in one's life. This is, of course, of extreme importance when one is living in a non-Muslim environment and is surrounded by a non-Islamic culture and non-Muslims. Constant interaction with such a disbelieving, materialistic or secular environment can make one fall to their level which does not place a great importance on worshipping God. Hence, the example and practical reminder that one finds in the attendees of the mosque is of extreme importance to set one's sights on the right path. Even if one does not have the means to attend the mosque five times a day, interaction with such good examples even once or twice a day should have a strong effect on the individual and should counterbalance some of the negative and non-Islamic influences in his life.

(3) By attending the mosque and becoming a true member of the Muslim community, one increases the feeling of brotherhood and support that are essential components of a true Muslim community. This makes it easier for the Muslims to know and support each other financially and morally. In addition, many people, if not most, are "social creatures" and desire a sense of belonging. This feeling of belonging helps to further reinforce their own confidence and good feeling about what they are doing in their lives. They do not then feel alone and feel like they are battling a struggle all on their own. They know that when things get difficult along their desired path, there are people who have the same goal and purpose who would be willing to help and strengthen the individual's will.

Indeed, if the person does not attend the mosque on a regular basis or, in other words, come together with others to establish the ever important prayer, he leaves himself open to all forms of attack which he may not have the strength to counter on his own. The Messenger of Allah (peace and blessings of Allah be upon him) said,

مَا مِنْ ثَلاثَةٍ فِي قَرْيَةٍ وَلا بَدْوٍ لا تُقَامُ فِيهِمُ الصَّلاةُ إِلاَّ قَدِ اسْتَحْوَذَ عَلَيْهِمُ الشَّيْطَانُ فَعَلَيْكُمْ بِالْجَمَاعَةِ فَإِنَّمَا يَأْكُلُ الذِّئْبُ الْقَاصِيَةَ

"There are not three persons in a city or desert except that they must establish the prayer, otherwise they are overcome by Satan. Stick to the congregational [prayer] for the wolf eats the sheep that is remote from the pack."[1]

(4) Attending the mosque can also be quite helpful for solving the questions, doubts and confusions that may come to one's mind and cause some unrest or uncertainty in one's soul. Among the individuals who attend the mosque, there should be some who have knowledge, insight and experience. They have passed through many stages that others have not yet experienced. Hence, they can answer with ease the kinds of questions or concerns that occur to others, especially those who are still young in their process of spiritual purification.

(5) By attending the mosque, one also sets a good example for others, especially but not exclusively the other members of one's family. In this way, it becomes yet another source of reward and Allah's good pleasure. Again, if one were living in a very non-Islamic environment, the setting of such an example may be of great importance and may influence many who otherwise would not have seriously considered attending the mosque regularly.

(6) Finally, in the previous chapter there was a discussion of the importance of prayer for the purification of the soul. In general, the quality of their prayers said in the mosque is much greater than the quality of their prayers said in their homes. If a mosque has a pious Imam who understands the requirements of the prayer, he will perform the prayer in a manner that will encourage the worshippers to concentrate on their prayers. Indeed, when praying in a mosque, the entire ambience of the mosque reminds the person of why he is there and what he is doing there. When praying alone in one's house, many do not tend to these aspects. While praying at home, one often hurries one's prayers because the prayers come in the middle of something. However, when intentionally going out to the mosque for the prayer, the prayer and its proper importance is the goal.

---

[1] Recorded by Abu Dawud, al-Nasaai and others. According to al-Albaani, it is *hasan*. See al-Albaani, *Saheeh al-Jaami*, vol. 2, p. 994. Al-Saaib, the subnarrator, explained that "congregation" in this hadith refers to the congregational prayer.

Hence, the prayer gets the time and attention that it deserves and needs. When this occurs, it is more likely that a prayer of that nature will have the desired effects of the prayers (discussed earlier) upon the individual.

Taking Account of One's Deeds, Behavior and Character

Allah says,

ٱقْتَرَبَ لِلنَّاسِ حِسَابُهُمْ وَهُمْ فِي غَفْلَةٍ مُّعْرِضُونَ

"[The time of] their reckoning is getting close while they are in heedlessness, turned away" (*al-Anbiyaa* 1). In this verse, Allah gives a clear reminder that the final reckoning and accounting is coming close. People should not be heedless of this fact. Instead, they must prepare for that reckoning. One of the most important ways of preparing for that reckoning which is ever getting closer is by evaluating one's own deeds and taking an honest account of one's acts before it is too late.

In fact, numerous authors who have written about purification of the soul emphasize this concept of taking account of one's deeds. This is where a person reflects upon the deeds that he has performed in the past (either that day, that week, that month, that year or in his entire lifetime), is currently performing and plans to perform in the future. Allah says,

يَٰٓأَيُّهَا ٱلَّذِينَ ءَامَنُوا۟ ٱتَّقُوا۟ ٱللَّهَ وَلْتَنظُرْ نَفْسٌ مَّا قَدَّمَتْ لِغَدٍ

وَٱتَّقُوا۟ ٱللَّهَ إِنَّ ٱللَّهَ خَبِيرٌۢ بِمَا تَعْمَلُونَ

"O you who believe! Fear Allah, and let every soul look to what (provision) he has sent forth for the morrow. Yea, fear Allah, for Allah is well-acquainted with (all) that you do" (*al-Hashr* 18). While commenting on this verse, ibn Katheer wrote, "You must take account of yourself before you are held accountable and look at what you have stored for yourself of good deeds for the day of your return and when you are presented to your Lord... And know that He knows all of your deeds and affairs and not a secret of yours will be hidden."[1]

Allah also says,

بَلِ ٱلْإِنسَٰنُ عَلَىٰ نَفْسِهِۦ بَصِيرَةٌ ﴿١٤﴾ وَلَوْ أَلْقَىٰ مَعَاذِيرَهُۥ

"Nay, man will be evidence against himself even though he were to put up his excuses" (*al-Qiyaamah* 14-15). Karzoon notes that this verse implies that humans will be or are well aware of their sins and transgressions. Even if they make excuses for themselves on the Day of Judgment, that will be of no avail to them. This, therefore, implies the necessity of reckoning one's own soul and uncovering its shortcomings before it is too late and there is nothing one can do about it.[2]

The caliph Umar ibn al-Khattaab is famous for his statement, "Reckon yourselves before you are to be reckoned. Weigh yourselves[3] before you are to be weighed. Certainly, it is easier upon you to reckon yourself today than it will be tomorrow. Beautify yourself for the greatest appearance [before your Lord], the day you shall be presented [for judgment] and not a secret of yours shall be hidden."[4]

Many people conceive of taking account of one's deeds as something that one does only after he has performed some acts. Actually, the process should commence even before a person commits an act (although this is difficult when overcome by emotions or desires at the time of an act). At that time, he should consider the act itself and why he is going to do the act. If he finds that his intentions are good and the act is righteous or permissible, then he should continue and perform the act. If he finds that his intention is not proper although the act is righteous, he must first change his intention before embarking upon the act. Finally, if he feels his intention is good but the act is neither righteous nor permissible, he must refrain from performing the act, as his supposed "good intention" cannot justify doing something that is not sanctioned by the Shareeah.

---

[1] Ibn Katheer, *Tafseer* (Daar Taibah), vol. 8, p. 77.
[2] Karzoon, vol. 1, p. 338.
[3] That is, weight the strength and goodness of your deeds before your deeds are weighed.
[4] Recorded by Ahmad in *al-Zuhd* and by al-Tirmidhi.

Even while performing the act itself there must be some level of self-criticism and evaluation of one's deed. One may begin a deed with a proper intention but in the midst of the deed, his intention may change. The classic example is that of a person performing a voluntary prayer in the mosque. At first, his intention may be sound and proper. However, during the prayer he notices certain people around him, perhaps people he wants to impress, so he tries to make his prayer even better than he would do so otherwise. This is where the importance of taking account of one's deeds even while performing the deed itself becomes of extreme importance. At that time, he must stop his evil intention, regroup himself and proceed along the proper path of performing that act for Allah's sake alone.

The process of taking account of one's deeds and reckoning oneself continues after the performance of deeds. At this point, taking account of one's deeds should encompass all of the following matters:

(1) The Muslim should think about the various obligatory acts that he is required to perform. First, he should think about whether or not he fulfilled what is obligatory upon him. If he did not, then he has obviously committed a sin and he must decide to rectify his behavior or make up for his past mistakes. Secondly, though, he should also consider the quality of his acts. In other words, he should consider whether he or not he performed them in the best manner or if he simply, for example, did the minimum to get them out of the way.

(2) The believer should consider each and every sin that he has committed. This includes the major sins as well as the minor sins. This also includes any sin that he committed openly as well as any sin he committed privately. It also includes the sins of the outward deeds as well as the sins found in the heart, such as the acts of envy and hatred. He should realize that unless he repents or otherwise effaces the effects of each sin, he may be held accountable for each transgression. Allah has said,

وَذَرُواْ ظَـٰهِرَ ٱلْإِثْـمِ وَبَاطِنَهُۥٓ ۚ إِنَّ ٱلَّذِينَ يَكْسِبُونَ ٱلْإِثْـمَ سَيُجْزَوْنَ

بِمَا كَانُواْ يَقْتَرِفُونَ

"Avoid all sin, open or secret. Those who earn sin will get due recompense for that which they used to commit" (*al-Anaam* 120). In fact, it is one of the signs of the true believers that he takes every sin that he commits very seriously and he fears that Allah may be displeased with him due to that sin. The Companion Abdullah ibn Masood said, "The believer views his sins as if he were sitting at the base of a mountain and it was about to collapse upon him. [On the other hand,] the wicked person views his sins as if they were like a fly that landed upon his nose and he just motions it away like that." (Recorded by al-Bukhari.)

(3) The believer should also ask himself the very important question, "Why?" In other words, he should ask himself, "Why did I do that?" "Why did I say that?" "Why did I listen to that?" "Why did I watch that?" With respect to good deeds, he should ask himself, "Did I do that act purely for the sake of Allah, for show, simply out of fear of what people would say if I did not do it or simply to get close to someone for some worldly benefit?" He should also ask himself, "Did I do such and such deed simply out of spite, envy or anger?" "Did I do such and such deed because I am, in reality, giving preference to this life over the Hereafter?"

Taking account of one's intentions is one of the most significant and necessary facets of reckoning oneself before one is being held to account by Allah. Even if the deed is a proper deed according to the outward signs of the Shareeah, the internal intention may ruin any reward or benefit from that deed. Indeed, the internal intention can make what looks like a pious deed a source of extreme punishment in the Hereafter. Hence, it is a must that one ask himself these types of questions concerning the various deeds that he performs.

(4) The believer should also consider the important opportunities that he missed and ask himself why he has allowed himself to miss those important opportunities. Every day, a believer has many opportunities and much time to use in getting closer to Allah, yet how many of those opportunities and how much of that time does one usually spend in matters that take one closer to Allah? He should be constantly aware of—and he can become more aware of that fact if he repeatedly takes account of his deeds—how much time and energy he spends on things that

are truly beneficial. He must also remind himself that he shall be asked about all of these aspects. The Messenger of Allah (peace and blessings of Allah be upon him) stated,

لا تَزُولُ قَدَمَا عَبْدٍ يَوْمَ الْقِيَامَةِ حَتَّى يُسْأَلَ عَنْ عُمُرِهِ فِيمَا أَفْنَاهُ وَعَنْ عِلْمِهِ فِيمَ فَعَلَ وَعَنْ مَالِهِ مِنْ أَيْنَ اكْتَسَبَهُ وَفِيمَ أَنْفَقَهُ وَعَنْ جِسْمِهِ فِيمَ أَبْلاه

"The servant's two feet will not move away on the Day of Resurrection until he is asked about his life and how he spent it, about his knowledge and how he acted upon it, about his wealth and how he earned and spent it, and about his body and how he used it."[1] The one who does not resort to self-inspection and taking account of his deeds may learn to regret his failure in this regard. The day will come when he will wish that he could make up for all of those lost opportunities. Allah describes the cry of those who only realize the golden opportunities that they are missing when it is too late,

أَن تَقُولَ نَفْسٌ يَٰحَسْرَتَىٰ عَلَىٰ مَا فَرَّطتُ فِى جَنۢبِ ٱللَّهِ وَإِن كُنتُ لَمِنَ ٱلسَّٰخِرِينَ ﴿٥٦﴾ أَوْ تَقُولَ لَوْ أَنَّ ٱللَّهَ هَدَىٰنِى لَكُنتُ مِنَ ٱلْمُتَّقِينَ ﴿٥٧﴾ أَوْ تَقُولَ حِينَ تَرَى ٱلْعَذَابَ لَوْ أَنَّ لِى كَرَّةً فَأَكُونَ مِنَ ٱلْمُحْسِنِينَ

"Lest the soul should (then) say, 'Ah! Woe is me in that I neglected (my duty) towards Allah, and was but among those who mocked!' Or (lest) it should say, 'If only Allah had guided me, I should certainly have been among the righteous!' Or (lest) it should say when it (actually) sees the punishment, 'If only I had another chance, I should certainly be among those who do good'" (*al-Zumar* 56-58).

[1] Recorded by al-Tirmidhi. According to al-Albaani, it is *hasan*. See al-Albaani, *Saheeh al-Jaami*, vol. 2, pp. 1220-1221.

(5) Finally, the believer should take account of himself with respect to the bounties that Allah has given him and how he has used those bounties. First, he should reflect upon how many bounties Allah has actually given him. When he does that, after a short time of reflection, he will quickly realize that there is no way he can actually encompass all of the various bounties that Allah has bestowed upon him. In fact, Allah has reminded humans of this reality, saying,

وَإِن تَعُدُّوا۟ نِعْمَتَ ٱللَّهِ لَا تُحْصُوهَآ

"But if you [were to try to] count the favors of Allah, never will you be able to number them" (*Ibraaheem* 34). However, the issue is much more than simply recognizing the numerous bounties that Allah has bestowed upon the believer. Beyond that, one should realize that he shall be asked about all of these bounties that he has received. Allah says,

ثُمَّ لَتُسْـَٔلُنَّ يَوْمَئِذٍ عَنِ ٱلنَّعِيمِ

"Then shall you be questioned that day about the joy (you indulged in)" (*al-Takaathur* 8). Hence, the person must reflect and try to recognize the various bounties he receives, he must be thankful to Allah for them as Allah gave them all to him as a grace and bounty and, finally, he must use them in the proper way that Allah has sanctioned. These three aspects the believer must consider and account for while dealing with the numerous bounties from Allah.

The more seriously one takes this concept of self-examination and reckoning of one's deeds, the more often he will perform this type of act and the more intense will be his self-examination. There are a number of factors that may assist a person in taking this concept more seriously. The first is a strong recognition and feeling that Allah is aware of and watching every act that a person performs and every thought that a person has. The more that one is aware of this fact, the more he takes even the most obscure or trivial of his deeds seriously. The person realizes that Allah knows and records even those small deeds that others may not notice or that he himself may sometimes forget. When a person realizes this, he will be anxious to recount and think about what he has done. He will try not to neglect any of his deeds and he will think about all of them. He will judge everything that he has done, down to the most seemingly insignificant of deeds. Even for those types of deeds, he will seek Allah's forgiveness and attempt to rectify his acts.

Second, remembering the Day of Judgment and being questioned on that day about one's deeds further assists in the self-reckoning of one's deeds. On the Day of Judgment, all of one's deeds shall be presented in a recording. Allah describes the reaction of those who were not concerned or careful about the deeds that they performed in this world:

وَوُضِعَ ٱلْكِتَـٰبُ فَتَرَى ٱلْمُجْرِمِينَ مُشْفِقِينَ مِمَّا فِيهِ وَيَقُولُونَ

يَـٰوَيْلَتَنَا مَالِ هَـٰذَا ٱلْكِتَـٰبِ لَا يُغَادِرُ صَغِيرَةً وَلَا كَبِيرَةً إِلَّآ أَحْصَىٰهَا ۚ

وَوَجَدُوا۟ مَا عَمِلُوا۟ حَاضِرًا ۗ وَلَا يَظْلِمُ رَبُّكَ أَحَدًا

"And the book (of deeds) will be placed (before you); and you will see the sinful in great terror because of what is (recorded) therein. They will say, 'Ah! Woe to us! What a book is this! It leaves out nothing small or great, but takes account thereof!' They will find all that they did placed before them and not one will your Lord treat with injustice" (*al-Kahf* 49). Those who will be successful on that day are those who are mindful of their deeds, think about what they have done, examine themselves, correct themselves and change their ways. Allah has very beautifully alluded to the importance of this approach to life when He stated,

يَوْمَ يَبْعَثُهُمُ ٱللَّهُ جَمِيعًا فَيُنَبِّئُهُم بِمَا عَمِلُوٓا۟ ۚ أَحْصَىٰهُ ٱللَّهُ وَنَسُوهُ ۚ وَٱللَّهُ

عَلَىٰ كُلِّ شَىْءٍ شَهِيدٌ

"On the day that Allah will raise them all up (again) and show them the truth (and meaning) of their conduct. Allah has reckoned its (value), though they may have forgotten it, for Allah is witness to all things" (*al-Mujaadilah* 6). Every human should recall that on that day his excuses will be fruitless and his own limbs will be witnesses against him. Allah says,

ٱلْيَوْمَ نَخْتِمُ عَلَىٰٓ أَفْوَٰهِهِمْ وَتُكَلِّمُنَآ أَيْدِيهِمْ وَتَشْهَدُ أَرْجُلُهُم بِمَا كَانُوا۟ يَكْسِبُونَ

"That day shall We set a seal on their mouths. But their hands will speak to Us, and their feet bear witness, to all that they did" (*Ya Seen* 65).

When a person is sincere in this matter and truly reflects upon his own sins and shortcomings, he becomes more worried about his own shortcomings than the shortcomings of others. Indeed, when a person recognizes the sins that he himself performs, the poor quality of his own acts of worship, and his own lack of knowledge, he will definitely spend more time in reforming himself than speaking at length about the mistakes and errors of anyone else.[1]

In addition, thinking about his own mistakes will make him more humble, removing the diseases of pride and arrogance from his heart as he recognizes that he himself has room for improvement. In fact, the Messenger of Allah (peace and blessings of Allah be upon him) even stated,

لو لم تكونوا تذنبون خشيت عليكم أكثر من ذلك العجب

[1] It is amazing that in this day and age there are many who are concerned about the statements of others such that if anyone has the slightest error (or what they have proclaimed to be an error), they immediately declare said person a deviant and off the straight path. Although it is extremely important to correct mistakes and fight against heresies, one must be careful and make sure that in the same process one is not committing sins. For example, if one has the confidence and knowledge to be involved in criticism, it is very important that at the same time he avoids piling up sins for himself, sins like having evil suspicions concerning his brothers, falsifying and distorting statements, passing on malicious reports without verifying the truth of those reports, backbiting and slander.

"If you were not to commit sins, I would fear something even greater [and more harmful] for you than that: conceit and vanity (*al-ajab*)."[1]

On the other hand, the one who does not consider this issue and does not review the acts that he has performed may be fooled by Satan into thinking that his acts are overall good and he himself is a great person while in fact his deeds may be very bad when taken as a whole. In addition, his soul may deceive him into thinking that he is doing enough to attain Allah's pleasure while in reality he is not. A few moments of sincere self-introspection could possibly be enough to make that fact clear to the person.

It is when the person truly recognizes his sins and shortcomings—and how harmful they can be for his well-being and his relationship to Allah—that he becomes prepared for a most important step in the process of purification: the step of repenting to Allah. This process will, Allah willing, save oneself from one of the most dangerous plots of Satan. This is where Satan convinces the servant to delay his repentance and to delay his changing of his ways by relying upon Allah's great mercy and his mere statement of asking for forgiveness. This is indeed a great threat as it could possibly, and probably many times does, keep a person from ever repenting from his sins. In the end, he dies while he continues to amass sins and never takes the steps to remove those sins.

There is no question that every believer should have good expectations and hopes in Allah, hoping for His mercy and forgiveness. In reality, though, some people go to an extreme by relying on the fact that Allah is merciful while neglecting the fact that Allah is stern in punishment for those who continue to transgress and are not concerned with repenting. Allah reminds all humans that He is both forgiving as well as severe in punishment. Allah says,

---

[1] Recorded by al-Uqaili and others. Graded *hasan* by al-Albaani. See Muhammad Naasir al-Deen al-Albaani, *Silsilat al-Ahaadeeth al-Saheehah* (Damascus: al-Maktab al-Islaami, 1979), vol. 2, pp. 263-265.

نَبِّئْ عِبَادِىٓ أَنِّىٓ أَنَا ٱلْغَفُورُ ٱلرَّحِيمُ ﴿٤٩﴾ وَأَنَّ عَذَابِى هُوَ ٱلْعَذَابُ ٱلْأَلِيمُ

"Tell My servants that I am indeed the Oft-Forgiving, Most Merciful, and that My punishment will be indeed the most grievous penalty" (*al-Hijr* 49-50). Allah also states,

إِنَّ رَبَّكَ لَسَرِيعُ ٱلْعِقَابِ وَإِنَّهُۥ لَغَفُورٌ رَّحِيمٌ

"Your Lord is quick in retribution, but He is also Oft-Forgiving, Most Merciful" (*al-Araaf* 167). One should, therefore, hope for Allah's forgiveness by following the steps that will most likely bring about his promised forgiveness. The most important act in this regard is sincerely repenting to Allah, which should flow from a true accounting of one's deeds.

(After repenting, the step of accounting oneself becomes important again as one then has to inspect his actions to verify that he has remained true to his act of repentance. For that reason, ibn al-Qayyim describes the act of repentance as being enveloped in between two acts of reckoning one's own soul.[1])

Repentance

Even if one tries his best to follow all of the steps and means that help one purify his soul, the nature of man is such that, in general, he is bound to falter every now and then. In fact, the Prophet (peace and blessings of Allah be upon him) said,

كُلُّ بَنِي آدَمَ خَطَّاءٌ وَخَيْرُ الْخَطَّائِينَ التَّوَّابُونَ

"All humans continually commit sins. The best of those who continually commit sins are those who repent often."[2]

When a person falters and sins, though, that is not the end of the matter. As long as he has not reached the moment of

---

[1] Ibn al-Qayyim, *Madaarij*, vol. 1, p. 170.

[2] Recorded by Ahmad, al-Tirmidhi, ibn Maajah and al-Haakim. According to al-Albaani, it is *hasan*. See al-Albaani, *Saheeh al-Jaami*, vol. 2, p. 831.

death, the door to repentance will remain open to him. He need not despair—as long as he brings himself to account and repents to Allah for the sins and transgressions he has committed. Allah clearly states,

قُلْ يَـٰعِبَادِىَ ٱلَّذِينَ أَسْرَفُوا۟ عَلَىٰٓ أَنفُسِهِمْ لَا تَقْنَطُوا۟ مِن رَّحْمَةِ ٱللَّهِ ۚ
إِنَّ ٱللَّهَ يَغْفِرُ ٱلذُّنُوبَ جَمِيعًا ۚ إِنَّهُۥ هُوَ ٱلْغَفُورُ ٱلرَّحِيمُ

"Say: O My servants who have transgressed against their souls, despair not of the mercy of Allah for Allah forgives all sins, He is Oft-Forgiving, Most Merciful" (*al-Zumar* 53). Indeed, Allah calls upon all believers to sincerely repent to Him so that He may forgive their sins and grant them the greatest blessing of paradise and bounties in the Hereafter. Allah says,

يَـٰٓأَيُّهَا ٱلَّذِينَ ءَامَنُوا۟ تُوبُوٓا۟ إِلَى ٱللَّهِ تَوْبَةً نَّصُوحًا عَسَىٰ رَبُّكُمْ أَن
يُكَفِّرَ عَنكُمْ سَيِّـَٔاتِكُمْ وَيُدْخِلَكُمْ جَنَّـٰتٍ تَجْرِى مِن تَحْتِهَا ٱلْأَنْهَـٰرُ
يَوْمَ لَا يُخْزِى ٱللَّهُ ٱلنَّبِىَّ وَٱلَّذِينَ ءَامَنُوا۟ مَعَهُۥ ۖ نُورُهُمْ يَسْعَىٰ بَيْنَ
أَيْدِيهِمْ وَبِأَيْمَـٰنِهِمْ يَقُولُونَ رَبَّنَآ أَتْمِمْ لَنَا نُورَنَا وَٱغْفِرْ لَنَآ ۖ إِنَّكَ
عَلَىٰ كُلِّ شَىْءٍ قَدِيرٌ

"O you who believe! Turn to Allah with sincere repentance in the hope that your Lord will remove from you your evil and admit you to gardens beneath which rivers flow; the Day that Allah will not permit the Prophet and those who believe with him to be humiliated. Their light will run forward before them and by their right hands, while they say, 'Our Lord! Perfect our light for us, and grant us forgiveness for You have power over all things'" (*Al-Tahreem* 8).

The true repentance includes (1) stopping oneself from the sin that one is committing, (2) feeling remorse and (3) having the sincere intention to never again return to performing that sin.[1] In essence, it is a true return to serving Allah, as is the human's purpose in this life. Without these components, the individual has not truly or completed repented to Allah.

Ibn Taimiyyah writes that *taubah* is of two types: obligatory or recommended. The obligatory *taubah* is obligatory on responsible slaves of Allah. This type of *taubah* is repenting from not performing the obligatory deeds or from performing forbidden deeds. The recommended *taubah* is repenting from not performing recommended acts or from performing disliked deeds. The person who performs the first type of *taubah* is from the pious while the person who performs both of them is from those special people who are closest to Allah. If a person does not perform either of them, he is either an unbeliever or an evildoer.[2]

In one passage, ibn Taimiyyah points out that *taubah* is not just from the performance of evil deeds, as, he says, "many ignorant people think". These people think that repentance is just from the evil deeds of the person but, he writes, it is more important to repent from the lack of performing the good deeds. "Most people do not do what Allah has ordered them to do from the 'statements' and actions of the heart or the 'statements' and actions of the body. They may not know what they are ordered to do or they may know it yet they don't follow it. They are, therefore, either misguided because of their lack of beneficial knowledge or they are those who have earned the anger of Allah because of their refusal to follow the truth after they have known it."[3]

Parallel to the discussion presented earlier concerning the greater importance of the deeds of the heart, ibn Taimiyyah perceptively pointed out that it is more important to make *taubah* from wrong beliefs than it is to repent from evil desires. He explains his reasoning behind this argument by stating,

> If someone does not perform an obligatory deed or does perform an evil deed, while he believes in its obligation

[1] If the sin also involved the rights of other humans, one must, if possible, also rectify the wrong that he has done.

[2] Ibn Taimiyyah, "Risaalah fi al-Taubah," *Jaami al-Rasaail* (Cairo: Maktaba ibn Taimiyyah, 1984), vol. 1, p. 227.

[3] Ibn Taimiyyah, "Risaalah fi al-Taubah," vol. 1, p. 228.

[for the former] or its evil [for the latter], then that belief will urge him on to do the obligatory deed and will keep him from the evil deed. There will not be something constantly urging him or keeping him from doing such deeds. In fact, the urging and preventing forces will be fighting each other. This means that sometimes one will overtake the other and vice-versa and his soul will be watching over him. Sometimes he will perform the obligatory deed and sometimes he will not perform it. And sometimes he will perform the evil deed and sometimes he will not perform it. This is the case with many evildoing Muslims who sometimes fulfill rights and other times do not and who sometimes do evil deeds and other times do not because the desires are contradicting in his heart [that is, the desire to do good and the desire to do evil are both in his heart and are competing against each other] since he has in his heart the foundation of faith that orders him to do good and keeps him from evil. But at the same time he has desires and lusts that call him to the opposite of that.

But if the person performs deeds that he [wrongfully] believes are obligatory or he leaves deeds believing they are forbidden, then the driving forces to leave or perform the deed will be constant in his heart and that is much more serious than the first case [mentioned in the paragraph above]. This person must make *tauba* to correct his beliefs first and to find the truth. And this can be much more difficult than the first case if there is nothing driving him to leave his false beliefs- as the person in the first case has something urging him to leave his evil deeds...[1]

---

[1] Ibn Taimiyyah, "Risaalah fi al-Taubah," vol. 1, pp. 237-238. This is similar to the argument that states that there is "no *taubah* for the people of innovations." For more on that point, see Jamaal al-Din Zarabozo, "Islam and Innovations I: The Meaning of *Bida*," *Al-Basheer* (Vol. 1, No. 4, Nov.-Dec. 1987), p. 20.

This last point is a very important point that people who are working for *dawah* or the message of Islam today must keep in mind, especially when it comes to reforming the Muslims. Many of the sins committed by Muslims are due to their believing that the sins are minor or are not really sins, such as some people who take interest from the banks or those women who do not dress properly according to Islamic law. Hence, they must first be convinced of their wrong beliefs concerning those sins and then they will be able, from within themselves, to change their deeds. Or, in the words of ibn Taimiyyah, they must make *taubah* from their incorrect beliefs first and this will lead them to correct their deeds.

In reality, every time someone commits a sin, he is actually distancing himself from Allah—as is clearly implied in the hadith quoted earlier stating that one draws closer to Allah by fulfilling the obligatory deeds and then the voluntary deeds. If that is the case, the believer should immediately seek to remove the negative effect of any sin. This is accomplished by not persisting in sin but by returning to Allah, repenting to Him and seeking His forgiveness. Indeed, it is truly heart moving how in the same set of verses, Allah speaks about the believers committing *faahishah* (shameful acts) and harming their own souls and yet describing them as the inhabitants of paradise. Their key is that they stop their sin and earnestly seek Allah's forgiveness. Allah says,

وَٱلَّذِينَ إِذَا فَعَلُواْ فَٰحِشَةً أَوْ ظَلَمُوٓاْ أَنفُسَهُمْ ذَكَرُواْ ٱللَّهَ
فَٱسْتَغْفَرُواْ لِذُنُوبِهِمْ وَمَن يَغْفِرُ ٱلذُّنُوبَ إِلَّا ٱللَّهُ وَلَمْ يُصِرُّواْ عَلَىٰ
مَا فَعَلُواْ وَهُمْ يَعْلَمُونَ ﴿١٣٥﴾ أُوْلَٰٓئِكَ جَزَآؤُهُم مَّغْفِرَةٌ مِّن رَّبِّهِمْ
وَجَنَّٰتٌ تَجْرِى مِن تَحْتِهَا ٱلْأَنْهَٰرُ خَٰلِدِينَ فِيهَا ۚ وَنِعْمَ أَجْرُ
ٱلْعَٰمِلِينَ

"And those who having done something to be ashamed of or wronged their own souls earnestly bring Allah to mind and ask for forgiveness for their sins—and who can forgive sins except Allah? And are never obstinate in persisting knowingly in (the wrong) they have done. For such the reward is forgiveness from their Lord, and gardens with rivers flowing underneath, an eternal dwelling. How excellent a recompense for those who work (and strive)" (*ali-Imraan* 135-136).

Indeed, Allah is very pleased with the servant whenever he repents. By repenting, the servant demonstrates his belief that Allah is compassionate, forgiving and merciful. He is also showing his awareness that, deep in his soul, he does not wish to displease Allah or to move away from what pleases Allah. The Messenger of Allah (peace and blessings of Allah be upon him) stated,

لَلّهُ أَشَدُّ فَرَحًا بِتَوْبَةِ عَبْدِهِ الْمُؤْمِنِ مِنْ رَجُلٍ فِي أَرْضٍ دَوِّيَّةٍ مَهْلِكَةٍ مَعَهُ رَاحِلَتُهُ عَلَيْهَا طَعَامُهُ وَشَرَابُهُ فَنَامَ فَاسْتَيْقَظَ وَقَدْ ذَهَبَتْ فَطَلَبَهَا حَتَّى أَدْرَكَهُ الْعَطَشُ ثُمَّ قَالَ أَرْجِعُ إِلَى مَكَانِيَ الَّذِي كُنْتُ فِيهِ فَأَنَامُ حَتَّى أَمُوتَ فَوَضَعَ رَأْسَهُ عَلَى سَاعِدِهِ لِيَمُوتَ فَاسْتَيْقَظَ وَعِنْدَهُ رَاحِلَتُهُ وَعَلَيْهَا زَادُهُ وَطَعَامُهُ وَشَرَابُهُ فَاللَّهُ أَشَدُّ فَرَحًا بِتَوْبَةِ الْعَبْدِ الْمُؤْمِنِ مِنْ هَذَا بِرَاحِلَتِهِ

"Allah is more delighted by the repentance of His believing servant than [the delight of the following person]: A person in a waterless desert having his food and drink upon his camel who sleeps and wakes to find his provisions having been lost. He searches for them until he is about to be overtaken by thirst. He says to himself, 'I shall return to the place where I was and I shall sleep until I die.' He put his head upon his pillow ready to die. Then he awakes to find his camel and his provisions, food and drink with him. Allah is more delighted with the repentance of the believing servant than that [person] is with [finding] his provision." (Recorded by Muslim.) Allah's great pleasure is a very special reward for the repentant. Indeed, when the believer realizes this fact and keeps this is mind, the drive to repent from all of his sins and shortcomings becomes very strong in his heart.

The importance of repentance for the purification of the soul cannot be overstated. It is the final pouring out of the human towards his Lord to remove all remaining blemishes and impurities from the soul, such that the soul is ready to be entered into Allah's paradise. No matter how pious a soul is, there will undoubtedly be shortcomings with respect to the rights of his Lord. These shortcomings, many of which were already touched upon while discussing contemplation since there is a strong relationship between such contemplation and the move to repent, include the following:

(a) A person's acts of worship and obedience to Allah will many times (if not almost always) fall short of his maximum potential. Indeed, being overly pleased and satisfied with one's act of worship is very dangerous for the soul. In fact, those who are truly aware of their relationship with Allah are even more earnest in their seeking of Allah's forgiveness after they complete an act of worship. They understand that they have some shortcoming in their act of worship, such as not being completely attuned to their prayers. The Prophet (peace and blessings of Allah be upon him) taught all believers to ask for Allah's forgiveness three times as soon as one had finished the obligatory prayers. This practice is reflective of this fact that one can find shortcomings even in his acts of worship.

(b) The believer will never be able to thank Allah completely for all of the bounties that Allah has bestowed on him, no matter how obedient he is to Allah. For example, how can an individual completely thank Allah for Allah's bounty giving him life in the first place? Hence, the individual must repent to Allah for this inability to thank Him completely or sufficiently.

(c) There may even be some portion of "acting for the sake of show" (*riyaa*) in some of an individual's deeds. If this is the case, then he definitely must repent to Allah for that aspect.

Hence, even the pious must always seek to repent to Allah and ask for His forgiveness. Ibn Taimiyyah wrote,

> The servant is always between a blessing from Allah that requires his thanks and a sin that requires the seeking of forgiveness. Both of these circumstances, by necessity, are always with the servant. He is constantly moving among the blessings and bounties of Allah and he is always sinful and in need of repentance and

> asking for forgiveness. For that reason, the chief of all humans and the leader of the pious, Muhammad (peace and blessings of Allah be upon him), would seek forgiveness in all situations.[1]

The Prophet (peace and blessings of Allah be upon him) himself used to repent to Allah and seek His forgiveness more than one hundred times a day (as recorded by Muslim).

Besides removing the sins from a person, sincere repentance plays other important roles in purifying the soul. For example, it aids the person in truly humbling himself before his Lord. As the believer recognizes his weaknesses and sins, he realizes that he has no rescue except to turn to Allah humbly, seeking Allah's forgiveness for his errors. This brings him closer to Allah, even though what led him to this particular stage was a sin that he had committed (such is the mercy and grace of Allah). As he considers more of his sins (through taking himself to account for his deeds) and sincerely repents from them, he realizes how far he has strayed and his heart sincerely and humbly tries to submit completely to Allah in the proper way given his abilities.

In her Master's thesis, Naseer notes that repenting to Allah generates in the soul a new potential and freshness to follow the path of purification. In other words, there is a change that occurs in the very soul of the person, since he feels remorse for the sin he did and he has committed himself to not repeating that act. He is, indeed, now filled with the feeling of love from Allah and a new closeness to Him that spurs him on further. He can experience the joy behind Allah's words,

إِنَّ ٱللَّهَ يُحِبُّ ٱلتَّوَّٰبِينَ وَيُحِبُّ ٱلْمُتَطَهِّرِينَ

"Allah loves those who repent to Him constantly and He loves those who keep themselves pure and clean" (*al-Baqarah* 222). He should feel a true feeling of happiness in returning to Allah since he knows that Allah is happy with his sincere repentance. This, in

[1] Ibn Taimiyyah, *Majmoo*, vol. 10, p. 88.

turn, should lead to a great change in his own character and behavior, keeping him moving along the path of purification.[1]

Repentance is a door that is always open for the person to rectify his ways. No matter how evil a person has become and no matter how many sins he has committed, there is no excuse for him not to mend his ways and to try to purify his soul. A powerful reminder of this fact is Allah's words while mentioning those who burned the believers alive in the incident discussed in *soorah al-Burooj*. Allah says about them,

إِنَّ ٱلَّذِينَ فَتَنُوا۟ ٱلْمُؤْمِنِينَ وَٱلْمُؤْمِنَٰتِ ثُمَّ لَمْ يَتُوبُوا۟ فَلَهُمْ عَذَابُ
جَهَنَّمَ وَلَهُمْ عَذَابُ ٱلْحَرِيقِ

"Those who persecuted the believers, men and women, and do not turn in repentance will have the penalty of Hell: they will have the penalty of the Burning Fire" (*al-Burooj* 10). Obviously, then, the door to repentance will be open to any sinner and he need not despair.

Thus, once the person sets himself on the right path, Allah willing, he need not allow what he did in the past to prevent him from getting closer to Allah by performing pious deeds. Some scholars even argue that his state after repenting should be even better than his state beforehand, as he has experienced the sin, realized how wrong it was, turned wholeheartedly to Allah and has vowed to change his ways. As long as one does change and mend his ways, he need not look back at his sins as necessarily evil in the long-run for his spiritual purification. He may have learned a great lesson from that act and it may have helped him reform himself in a way that would not have been possible without his experiencing a need to repent, while that repentance further uplifted his soul via the joy of returning back to one's Lord.

---

[1] Cf., Amaal bint Saalih Naseer, *Al-Taubah fi Dhau al-Quraan al-Kareem* (Jeddah: Daar al-Andalus al-Khudhraa, 1998), p. 515.

Summary

There are many facets that can help a person in his path of self-purification. A number of them have been discussed in this chapter. It is not necessarily the case that one progress from one mean to another in some kind of orderly succession. But they are all tied together. However, in some ways, there is a need to build upon one in order to firmly and completely take advantage of some other means.

A brief summary of the various steps may be beneficial at this point. They are:

(1) Turning to and praying to Allah for help and guidance: This step usually takes place before the attaining of knowledge. One should seek guidance from Allah concerning all matters but especially to know the path that leads to His pleasure.

(2) Taking the steps to attain sound and beneficial knowledge: Allah willing, knowledge will be given to the person by Allah as a result of his sincere supplication and his taking the steps to attain that knowledge. In particular, though, the relevant knowledge concerning spiritual purification cannot be found in detail unless one studies both the Quran and the hadith of the Messenger of Allah (peace and blessings of Allah be upon him).

(3) Proper *dhikr* (remembrance of Allah): After the knowledge comes *dhikr* which, in essence, means keeping that awareness and knowledge alive and at a conscious level. Without this awareness, there is no hope in one actually applying or benefiting from what one has learned.

(4) Contemplation and reflection: Contemplation moves one to a stronger and greater level of faith. It builds upon and strengthens the *dhikr*. It also assists the individual in developing a more mature understanding of the knowledge he has received. It also helps him in tying that knowledge into everything that is happening around him, in turn enhancing his intensity of *dhikr*.

(5) Realizing the true nature of this worldly existence: This can really be considered a result of contemplation or a further development in one's spiritual progression. It refers to a deeper understanding that the life of the Hereafter is the only real life and that this worldly life is not the life that one has been created to live for or seek after with all of one's means and

abilities. The realizing of the true importance or lack thereof of this worldly life assists in repelling the strong temptations found in this world.

(6) Striving against any evil inclinations in the soul: "Striving against the soul" (*jihaad al-nafs*) becomes much easier after the above steps have been taken. The soul may always present some temptations, diseases or weaknesses. One must strive but it is very possible and plausible given the right tools to overcome any weakness that the soul may possess.

(7) Jihad in all of its various other forms: The other forms of jihad further develop the character and the strength of the individual. He removes everything that is standing in between him and his goal, sacrificing anything else for his goal of pleasing his Beloved Allah.

(8) Having righteous companions, friends and spouses: This is to give one further strength and support. The goal of being surrounded by pious companions is that they keep that *dhikr* alive. Such companions also advise each other, give strength to each other when they become weak and encourage each other to do the correct deeds. In addition, they can offer each other knowledge and guidance, especially during troubling or confusing times.

(9) Attending the mosques: Attending the mosques strengthens the ties with other righteous Muslims, helps improve one's prayers (which in itself is a key to spiritual purification), allows one to gain access to sources of knowledge, provides a place for being reminded of one's purpose in life and provides a place to witness pious examples which encourage one to strive harder for spiritual purification.

(10) Taking account of one's deeds, behavior and character: This is the refinement process that no program can be successful without. One must constantly go over the different steps that one has taken and the different actions that one has performed to see where there are faults and what must be improved. One must never be negligent of this practice as otherwise one may be falling into a deep abyss and never even realize what is occurring. Without realizing what is occurring, it is difficult to imagine that the person will be able to do anything about it.

(11) Repentance: Shortcomings are always there. When the person opens his soul to Allah and pleads for Allah's forgiveness and mercy, Allah will overlook his mistakes and fortify him with a new strength, new knowledge and so forth, so that he can move along the path of getting even closer to Allah.

Chapter 7
Impediments and Dangers to One's Spiritual Purification

Obviously, anyone serious about his path of purification will want to know what some of the impediments, dangers and pitfalls are along the path. It probably goes without saying that many of the impediments are simply the opposite of the acts that were discussed in the previous chapter. That having been said, they still need to be discussed in detail as negative factors. For example, the ways in which they affect a person need to be noted. Similarly, some of the most important means by which they can be overcome should also be noted. Furthermore, by identifying the negative factors, one can monitor them closely and restrict their effects as much as possible. For this reason, the Quran and Sunnah have identified them and explained them in some detail.

As a general introduction concerning negative factors that can fill one's soul, ibn al-Qayyim derived some important points from the following statement of the Messenger of Allah (peace and blessings of Allah be upon him):

لَأَنْ يَمْتَلِئَ جَوْفُ رَجُلٍ قَيْحًا يَرِيهِ خَيْرٌ مِنْ أَنْ يَمْتَلِئَ شِعْرًا

"It is better for a person's stomach to be filled with puss than for [him] to be filled with poetry." (Recorded by al-Bukhari and Muslim.) Ibn al-Qayyim noted,

> [In this hadith, the Messenger of Allah (peace and blessings of Allah be upon him)] explained that the stomach (*jauf*) can be filled with poetry. Similarly then it could possibly be filled with misconceptions, doubts, imagination and assumptions for which there is no reality, knowledge that is not beneficial, stories, jokes and the like. [The true harm is that] if the *jauf* is filled

> with things of that nature, then when the realities of the Quran and knowledge come to it—and these are what perfect it and bring it happiness—they find no free space therein and no acceptance. Hence, they are repelled and forced out to some other place. Similarly, if sincere advice is given to a heart that is filled with its opposite, there is nothing therein to execute it, for it neither accepts it or not does the advice penetrate it.[1]

Hence, one has to work to remove these kinds of impediments in order to make room for all of the positive means discussed in the previous chapter. If those positive means meet no resistance via negative factors, they are free to work and be as effective as possible. However, if someone has a number of positive factors in combination with a number of negative factors, they may constantly be canceling each other, leaving the individual with virtually no improvement. If the negative factors greatly outweigh or outnumber the positive factors, the individual may find himself slipping spiritually and may not understand why given that he has fulfilled some of the beneficial aspects. They key, therefore, is to explicitly recognize the beneficial means and maximize their use while explicitly recognizing the negative factors and do one's best to remove them from his life.

Desires, Lusts and Passions (*Ahwaa* and *Shahawaat*)

Allah says,

وَأَمَّا مَنْ خَافَ مَقَامَ رَبِّهِۦ وَنَهَى ٱلنَّفْسَ عَنِ ٱلْهَوَىٰ ﴿٤٠﴾ فَإِنَّ ٱلْجَنَّةَ هِىَ ٱلْمَأْوَىٰ

"But as for he who feared standing before their Lord's (tribunal) and prevented the soul from lower desires, then indeed Paradise will be his refuge" (*al-Naaziaat* 40-41). In addition, the Prophet (peace and blessings of Allah be upon him) made a statement that clearly demonstrates the dangers of desires and lusts—he made it

---

[1] Quoted from Ibn al-Qayyim by al-Bilaali, p. 41.

clear that these can lead one directly to Hell. Al-Bukhari records that the Messenger of Allah (peace and blessings of Allah be upon him) said,

حُجِبَتِ النَّارُ بِالشَّهَوَاتِ وَحُجِبَتِ الْجَنَّةُ بِالْمَكَارِهِ

"Hell is covered in desires while Paradise is covered in hardships."

It can be argued that the most important impediments to spiritual purification are (1) desires and (2) *shubahaat* (uncertainty, doubts and misconceptions), the first two to be discussed here. Ibn al-Qayyim noted that the desires lead to one's wants and goals being distorted or ruined. In other words, when one is overcome by harmful desires, one's goals and wants become things that are not beneficial. This causes the person to commit sins. On the other hand, uncertainty, doubts and misconceptions lead one's knowledge and beliefs to be distorted or ruined.[1] In other words, one cannot see and understand clearly when his vision is fogged by such doubts of what is certainly true or by misconceptions which further make the person question what is true. This causes the person to follow innovations. This can also cause the person to overindulge in this worldly life because he lacks the conviction concerning the reality of the Hereafter, its rewards and punishments.

Al-Qurtubi quotes ibn Masood as saying, "You are living in a time in which the desires are steered [and controlled] by truth. There will come a time in which the truth will be steered [and controlled] by the desires. We seek refuge in Allah from that time."[2] Ibn Taimiyyah once noted that the root of deviation from the straight path lies in either giving preference to one's own deductions and conclusions over the text of the Quran and Sunnah or in following one's desires rather than the Command of Allah.[3]

Furthermore, a very dangerous facet concerning desires is that they can afflict a person even after he has attained knowledge.

---

[1] Muhammad ibn al-Qayyim, *Ighaathah al-Luhfaan min Masaayid al-Shaitaan* (Makkah: al-Maktabah al-Tijaariyyah, n.d.), p. 15.

[2] Al-Qurtubi, vol. 19, p. 208.

[3] Cf., *Ibn Taymiyyah's Essay*, pp. 71-72.

In fact, Sayyid Qutb noted, "Ignorance is easy to cure. However, desires after knowledge are a destructive force in the soul that needs a long-term, difficult jihad to cure."[1]

To make matters even worse is that the desires and lusts in the soul are of numerous varieties. Perhaps if one can control one or some of them, he may not be able to control the others. There are, for example, the desires for power, prestige, authority over others due to piety or knowledge, praise, respect and awe, wealth, sexual pleasures and so forth.

Some of these are actually quite natural to the human being. For example, the innate desire for wealth and sexual pleasure aids in establishing civilizations on earth as well as propagating the species. However, in order for them not to have a negative effect, they must be nurtured and restrained according to the teachings of the Quran and Sunnah. If they are allowed to grow and develop in a way that is not consistent with the Quran and Sunnah, they go beyond their natural usefulness and become very harmful, in the same way that food is beneficial and a necessity for the body but overeating and bad nutrition become very dangerous for one's health.

In fact, the effect of desires and lusts on the soul can even be debilitating. The soul's happiness and unhappiness become completely tied to those things he desires, such that the person is only happy when he fulfills his desires and he is discontent if he cannot fulfill them. This is, in reality, a true form of slavery—a slavery to something other than Allah. Ibn Taimiyyah wrote,

> If he attains it [that is, what he desires], he is pleased and if he is unable to attain it, he becomes discontented. Such a person is the *'abd* [slave] of what he desires of these matters and he is a slave of it, since slavery and servitude are in reality the enslavement and servitude of the heart. Thus, for whatever enslaves the heart and puts it under its servitude, the heart is then a slave of that object. This is why it is said, "The slave [human] is free as long as he is content [with what

[1] Sayyid Qutb, vol. 6, p. 3818.

Allah has given him] and the free one is a slave as long as he desires."[1]

What ibn Taimiyyah stated above is echoed in the following verse of the Quran that describes how evil one's plight can become. One truly can become enslaved to what he is desiring such that desire becomes the controlling factor in his life. If anything is a controlling factor in a person's life, it takes on the role of his god and lord. Thus, Allah has said,

أَفَرَءَيْتَ مَنِ ٱتَّخَذَ إِلَٰهَهُۥ هَوَىٰهُ وَأَضَلَّهُ ٱللَّهُ عَلَىٰ عِلْمٍ وَخَتَمَ عَلَىٰ
سَمْعِهِۦ وَقَلْبِهِۦ وَجَعَلَ عَلَىٰ بَصَرِهِۦ غِشَٰوَةً فَمَن يَهْدِيهِ مِنۢ بَعْدِ ٱللَّهِ ۚ
أَفَلَا تَذَكَّرُونَ

"Have you seen he who has taken as his god his [own] desire, and Allah has sent him astray due to knowledge [that Allah has concerning him] and has set a seal upon his hearing and his heart and put over his vision a veil? So who will guide him after Allah? Will you not then be reminded" (*al-Jaathiyah* 23).

There is no question that the force and influence of desires and lusts can be very great. Indeed, to repel them undoubtedly takes effort and a strong resolve. Obviously, the steps that were mentioned in Chapter 6 are all matters that will help one become strong enough to overcome these desires. However, an additional point is for the person to seriously think about the end result of his pursuing and satisfying unlawful desires. Even if he should get some fleeting pleasure from such acts in this life, in the Hereafter, the results of satisfying such forbidden pleasures can be nothing but evil—unless Allah forgives him out of His mercy. Even in this life, the results of seeking those pleasures can be disastrous as one's family, well-being, honor and respect may be completely destroyed due to one's inability to overcome desires that bring about nothing but evil to one's soul.[2]

---

[1] Cf., *Ibn Taymiyyah's Essay*, pp. 100-101.

[2] In an Islamic state there are other aspects that aid one in curbing the satisfaction of one's illegal desires. For example, the punishments for fornication, adultery, homosexuality and

Ignorance, Doubts and Misconceptions

Ignorance, doubts, uncertainty and misconceptions are all grouped together here because they all flow from the same root: a lack of true knowledge. In other words, it is actually ignorance that leads one to have doubts, uncertainty and misconceptions. Thus, ignorance is extremely dangerous in a two-fold way. First, it is due to ignorance that people perform acts that are wrong and displeasing to Allah.[1] Second, it is also due to ignorance that people have doubts which in turn lead to a lack of conviction and lack of resolve—without conviction and resolve it cannot be expected that a person would make these sacrifices needed to truly purify his soul. For these reasons, knowledge is stressed in Islam and is an important step along the path of purification, as discussed in the previous chapter.

There are numerous verses in the Quran which highlight the dangers of allowing oneself to remain ignorant—that is, refusing to give the tools given by Allah to understand and comprehend reality and truth. For example, Allah says about those in the Hell-fire,

وَقَالُوا۟ لَوْ كُنَّا نَسْمَعُ أَوْ نَعْقِلُ مَا كُنَّا فِىٓ أَصْحَـٰبِ ٱلسَّعِيرِ

"And they will say, 'If only we had been listening or reasoning, we would not be among the companions of the Blaze" (*al-Mulk* 10);

---

drinking alcohol are all deterrents keeping one from satisfying those lusts. In fact, when it comes to the purification of the soul, the Shareeah has made use of all possible means to assist the individual, including the use of force, state intervention and the law. Although, in general, such means are not available to most Muslim communities today, the communities should use any means available to them to further support the goal of spiritual purification. This would include the ordering of good and eradicating of evil within the community and the mosque. It may even include boycotting those who commit sins if the strict conditions for such a boycott are satisfied.

[1] In a hadith recorded by al-Bukhari and Muslim concerning the removal of the scholars, the Messenger of Allah (peace and blessings of Allah be upon him) stated that afterwards will come ignorant people who will lead themselves astray as well as lead others astray.

أَرَءَيْتَ مَنِ ٱتَّخَذَ إِلَـٰهَهُۥ هَوَىٰهُ أَفَأَنتَ تَكُونُ عَلَيْهِ وَكِيلًا ﴿٤٣﴾ أَمْ تَحْسَبُ أَنَّ أَكْثَرَهُمْ يَسْمَعُونَ أَوْ يَعْقِلُونَ ۚ إِنْ هُمْ إِلَّا كَٱلْأَنْعَـٰمِ ۖ بَلْ هُمْ أَضَلُّ سَبِيلًا

"Do you see such a one as takes for his god his own passion (or impulse)? Are you [possibly] a disposer of affairs for him? Or do you think that most of them actually listen or understand? They are only like cattle. Nay, they are worse astray in [their] path" (*al-Furqaan* 43-44).[1]

Ibn al-Jauzi perceptively wrote, "The first means by which Iblis deceives mankind is by blocking their means to knowledge. This is because knowledge is a light. If he can extinguish their lamps, he can knock them into darkness by any means he wills."[2] With respect to the topic of this book, ignorance causes a person to be ignorant of the very path of purification and, in addition, it causes some people to believe that they are on a path of purification while in fact they are not.

Of course, there are a number of causes for ignorance. One of the greatest causes is the unwillingness of the individual to spend the time and energy it takes to attain knowledge. Nowadays, a relatively small number of Muslims do serious reading. Most are content with hearing a lecture every now and then—unaware of the fact that general lectures never contain the detailed type of information that one needs to truly understand most topics. Even the conferences, where one could interact with people of knowledge, are mere social events for the vast majority. Until someone is really ready to learn his faith, it is not surprising that he will be lost and wandering, not sure of what he should be doing and not feeling the inspiration and guidance that comes from truly delving into the Quran, Sunnah and writings of the respected scholars.

---

[1] For a discussion of a number of verses touching upon the question of ignorance, see Muhammad ibn Saeed ibn Rislaan, *Dham al-Jahil wa Bayaan Qabeeh Athaarihi* (Cairo: Daar al-Uloom al-Islaamiyyah, n.d.), pp. 21-80.

[2] Abdul Rahmaan Ibn al-Jauzi, *Talbees Iblees* (Beirut: Daar al-Qalam, n.d.), p. 310.

As alluded to in the opening paragraph of this section, a great danger that results from ignorance is uncertainty and doubt. Many times, inactivity and lack of sacrifice are not because people do not believe. Instead, it is because they lack the level of certainty (based on knowledge) that will allow them to truly sacrifice—knowing Allah's promise of success and pleasure is true. With certainty, a person develops a confidence, passion and exuberance that allows him to plunge deeply into the work that he does. It also allows him to sacrifice because he is certain that his sacrifice is for the right cause and that it will not go unnoticed by Allah, his Beloved. Note in the following verse how Allah mentions being free of doubt as a characteristic of the true believers who are willing to sacrifice for Allah's sake:

إِنَّمَا ٱلْمُؤْمِنُونَ ٱلَّذِينَ ءَامَنُوا۟ بِٱللَّهِ وَرَسُولِهِۦ ثُمَّ لَمْ يَرْتَابُوا۟ وَجَٰهَدُوا۟ بِأَمْوَٰلِهِمْ وَأَنفُسِهِمْ فِى سَبِيلِ ٱللَّهِ ۚ أُو۟لَٰٓئِكَ هُمُ ٱلصَّٰدِقُونَ

"Only those are believers who have believed in Allah and His Messenger, and have never since doubted, but have striven with their belongings and their persons in the cause of Allah: such are the sincere ones" (*al-Hujuraat* 15).

Innovations and Heresies

Allah has said,

ٱلْيَوْمَ أَكْمَلْتُ لَكُمْ دِينَكُمْ وَأَتْمَمْتُ عَلَيْكُمْ نِعْمَتِى وَرَضِيتُ لَكُمُ ٱلْإِسْلَٰمَ دِينًا ۚ

"This day have I perfected for you your religion and have completed My blessings upon you and have chosen for you Islam as a religion" (*al-Maaidah* 3). This verse shows that there is nothing to be added to this religion; it is already complete and perfect and it cannot be improved upon, perfected or completed in any way. Indeed, if in anyone's practice he attempts to add or delete anything from it, his own practice will then be deficient and contrary to the complete and perfect faith laid down by the Prophet (peace and blessings of Allah be upon him).

There is no question that heresies and innovations lead people away from the path of Allah—the only true path of spiritual purification. The Prophet (peace and blessings of Allah be upon him) made this point very clear when he would state at the beginning of his speeches,

شَرُّ الأُمُورِ مُحْدَثَاتُهَا وَكُلُّ بِدْعَةٍ ضَلاَلَةٌ

"The worst actions are the invented ones. And every innovation is a going astray (Ar., *dhalaalah*[1])." (Recorded by Muslim.) In other narrations he would say,

وَكُلُّ ضَلاَلَةٍ فِي النَّارِ

"And every going astray is in the hell fire." (Recorded by al-Nasaai.) Furthermore, the Prophet (peace and blessings of Allah be upon him) also made it clear that heretical acts will never be accepted by Allah. He stated,

مَنْ أَحْدَثَ فِي أَمْرِنَا هَذَا مَا لَيْسَ مِنْهُ فَهُوَ رَدٌّ

"Whoever introduces anything into this affair of ours that does not belong to it will have it rejected." (Recorded by al-Bukhari and Muslim.)

Hence, by following innovations one is following a path that is, by definition, taking him away from the path of purification to a path that leads one to Hell. Thus, anyone sincerely interested in purifying his soul must take great pains to make sure that his beliefs and actions are free of any heresies or innovations. If he finds that he has some heretical beliefs or is practicing some innovations, he must leave them immediately, as

[1] The word *dhalaalah* means, "Erring, straying, or going astray; deviating from the right way or course, or from that which is right; missing or losing the right way." E. W. Lane, vol. 2, p. 1798.

they will never be pleasing to Allah and they are taking him away from his ultimate goal of worshipping Allah in the proper manner.

Therefore, heresies and innovations are extremely dangerous for the health and well-being of one's faith and spiritual purification. One reason that they can be extremely dangerous is that they are usually presented as the truth that one must follow to achieve salvation and purification. In other words, people are seduced into following heresies by the false claim that they are true. Given this belief, the followers then are willing to fight tooth and nail to support and implement their heresies. They believe that they are definitely on the right path and they refuse to give up the wrong they are following. This is why Sufiyaan al-Thauri once said, "Innovations are more beloved to Satan than sins because one may repent from sins but one does not repent from innovations."[1] Their innovations have blinded them from the truth. It is then very difficult for them to open their eyes, see how far they were from the straight path, repent and come back to the true way of spiritual purification.

In fact, when one considers the negative effects of heresies, one realizes how amazing it is that many who claim to be the most interested in purification of the soul are the same people who seem to be the less interested in ensuring that the path they are following is free of innovations and heresies. It is also amazing that many are upset by any attempt to remove innovations and heresies from the mosque or Muslim community. At the very least, innovations and heresies are an affront to the Messenger of Allah (peace and blessings of Allah be upon him). In essence, accepting innovations and heresies implies a dissatisfaction with what the Prophet (peace and blessings of Allah be upon him) practiced and preached. It is as if what the Prophet (peace and blessings of Allah be upon him) did was not sufficient and that there must be some better way of getting closer to Allah and pleasing Him. This attitude could not be further from the truth. As was stated earlier, the Prophet (peace and blessings of Allah be upon him) is *the* example; he was the most knowledgeable and most fearful of Allah. If anyone tries to please Allah or purify his soul by any means that are not consistent with

[1] Quoted in al-Suyooti, *al-Amr*, pp. 66-67.

what the Prophet (peace and blessings of Allah be upon him) brought, he will simply be taking himself astray, displeasing Allah and certainly not purifying his soul.

In particular, with respect to the purification of the soul, heresies and innovations may be broken into two major categories:[1]

(1) Heresies wherein someone adds something to what is sanctioned by Allah or His Messenger (peace and blessings of Allah be upon him) and goes to an extreme in the religion. This type of heresy was exhibited by many who claimed to be on the path of purification, hence deviating from that path either a small or large amount. This category would include the special meetings or forms of *dhikr,* ways of breathing and contemplation and so forth that one finds among many mystical orders.

(2) Heresies wherein one abandons part of what is commanded by Allah or His Messenger (peace and blessings of Allah be upon him). This type is also exhibited by those who claim to be on the path of purification, as they abandon the obligatory prayers, obligatory fasts and so forth in order to occupy themselves with other deeds of a lesser status or of a heretical nature.

Thc only true way to free oneself completely from all forms of innovations and heresies is by trying to be as exacting as possible in one's following of the Messenger of Allah (peace and blessings of Allah be upon him) and his Companions. In one's outward actions, inward feelings, beliefs, character, esoteric aspects as well as law one should try to pattern oneself as closely as possible to what the Prophet (peace and blessings of Allah be upon him) taught. This is the only surefire way to protect oneself from any and all forms of innovation that clearly and unquestionably make one stray from the true path of purification. In order to achieve this, one should turn sincerely to Allah and ask for His guidance while doing one's utmost to learn the true path of the Prophet (peace and blessings of Allah be upon him) by studying the Quran and the Sunnah.

---

[1] Cf., Karzoon, vol. 2, p. 563.

The Harmful Effects of Sins

Sins are of varying degrees. One thing, though, is certain: every sin is potentially dangerous and harmful for the soul. The "smaller" sins in particular can be extremely dangerous because many have a tendency to downplay small sins and regard them as insignificant. Hence, the Prophet (peace and blessings of Allah be upon him) specifically warned all believers about those "insignificant" sins. He stated,

إِيَّاكُمْ وَمُحَقَّرَاتِ الذُّنُوبِ كَقَوْمٍ نَزَلُوا فِي بَطْنِ وَادٍ فَجَاءَ ذَا بِعُودٍ وَجَاءَ ذَا بِعُودٍ حَتَّى أَنْضَجُوا خُبْزَتَهُمْ وَإِنَّ مُحَقَّرَاتِ الذُّنُوبِ مَتَى يُؤْخَذْ بِهَا صَاحِبُهَا تُهْلِكْهُ

"Be aware of the paltriest of sins. They are like a people who stop in a valley and one of them comes with one stick of wood and another with one more until their bread is well cooked [due to the intensity of the fire]. When the person is taken due to his paltry sins, they destroy him."[1] In other words, a person's small sins keep building up like twigs on a fire. After some time, even though each of the twigs is quite small in and of itself, the fire is big and can burn with great intensity.

The Companions of the Prophet (peace and blessings of Allah be upon him) greatly appreciated the danger of small sins. The Companions who were taught directly by the Prophet (peace and blessings of Allah be upon him) were very cautious concerning deeds that later people, including the people today, would consider very insignificant and not worth worrying about. In fact, Anas, the young Companion of the Prophet (peace and blessings of Allah be upon him), said to those who came after the Companions, "You do some acts that are smaller in your eyes than a strand of hair. However, during the time of the Prophet (peace and blessings of Allah be upon him) we would use to reckon those same deeds as being among the destructive sins." (Recorded by al-Bukhari.)

One of the keys to overcoming this incorrect approach towards sins and small sins in particular is to consider the effect

---

[1] Recorded Ahmad, al-Tabaraani and al-Baihaqi. According to al-Albaani, it is *sahih*. See al-Albaani, *Saheeh al-Jaami*, vol. 1, pp. 522-523.

that such sins has on one's relationship with Allah. Any forbidden act, no matter how small, implies some amount of Allah's displeasure. In other words, Allah hates all sins and the true believer should also hate whatever Allah hates. When one keeps this fact in mind, his motivation toward the small sins change. Even if they are small sins, he will not want to perform them because he knows whom those deeds are displeasing to. Hence, Bilaal ibn Saad said, "Do not look at the smallness of the sin but look at who you have disobeyed."[1]

In reality, the true believer should always be fearful concerning his sins, regardless of whether they are major or minor. Abdullah ibn Masood said, "A believer perceives his sins as if he were sitting at the bottom of a mountain and he fears that it were to crush upon him. On the other hand, the evildoer sees his sins as if they are a fly that is upon his noise and he can just motion like that [to get rid of them and their harm]." (Recorded by al-Bukhari.)

In sum, it is very important that the individual recognize sin—both major and minor—as a barrier to his soul's purification. The avoidance of sin should be something that is developed within the soul via the purification of one's beliefs. The avoidance of sin should not only comprise avoiding a specific act. In addition to avoiding the act, there should be a feeling in the heart that the act itself deserves to be avoided due to its overriding evil and harm that it can cause to the soul. When this belief system is developed within the soul, it becomes much easier for the person to refrain from sins because he believes that they are bad. This belief greatly weakens any desire in his soul to perform that sin. For example, many people may be naturally averse to eating flesh that they find dead and mangled by the side of the road due to a car accident. This feeling may keep them from consuming that flesh. However, that is not the goal and overriding benefit of purification of the soul. Instead, the person will have a strong belief that consuming something of that nature will be bad for his soul because it will distance him from Allah who had prohibited that meat. Hence, the driving force in this person to refrain from that meat is much greater and stronger than the driving force in

[1] Ibn al-Qayyim, *al-Jawaab al-Kaafi*, p. 62.

the person who feels some natural dislike for eating something of that nature. If the latter person is somehow tempted to eat that meat by some means, say someone offers him some money to do so, he may overcome his natural dislike for it and he will consume it. On the other hand, the one who avoids that meat due to his belief that it is bad for his whole being and bad for his relationship to Allah will not be so easily tempted or coerced into doing that act. Such is the case with all of the acts that Allah has forbidden, such as the taking of interest, fornication and so forth. If the strong belief is there that the act is harmful to what is of real importance for the person, his worship of Allah, he will refrain from that act no matter how strong the pressure or desire may build up in his soul. Indeed, perhaps very little or no desire will build up in his soul as he will recognize that act as a disgusting deed that he will want no part of, since he understands how evil it may be for his soul and overall well-being.

There is one group of sins that need to be pointed out explicitly here: the "sins" of the heart. In the same way that the actions of the heart are among the most important of all obligatory acts, the sins of the heart (what are commonly referred to as the diseases of the heart) are from among the horrendous sins. One reason they are so horrendous is that they are not simply one act in and of themselves; instead, they spark many other acts of disobedience to Allah. In other words, being present in the heart allows them to steer the individual to numerous acts that are displeasing to Allah.

It would be beneficial here to explicitly speak about *kibr* ("arrogance, pride"), one of the most important of these "sins" of the heart. *Kibr* can be found in the heart in different degrees; however, there is no question that no matter how much is found, it is very dangerous for the individual. Indeed, the Messenger of Allah (peace and blessings of Allah be upon him) said,

لا يَدْخُلُ الْجَنَّةَ مَنْ كَانَ فِي قَلْبِهِ مِثْقَالُ ذَرَّةٍ مِنْ كِبْرٍ

"Whoever has a grain's weight of *kibr* in his heart shall not enter Paradise."[1] (Recorded by Muslim.)

The danger that *kibr* poses is that it sets up a barrier between the individual and his following or accepting the truth. For example, in some cases of *kibr*, a person will not accept the truth if it comes from others or people he does not like instead of himself or people he likes. The Prophet (peace and blessings of Allah be upon him) defined *kibr* in this fashion when he said,

الْكِبْرُ بَطَرُ الْحَقِّ وَغَمْطُ النَّاسِ

"*Kibr* is to refuse [and reject] the truth and to have disdain for the people." (Recorded by Muslim.)

Actually, one of the first sins ever committed, the act of disobedience by Satan himself, was built upon the disease of *kibr*. Allah states that He ordered the angels and all with them to bow down to Adam. However, as Allah says,

وَإِذْ قُلْنَا لِلْمَلَٰٓئِكَةِ ٱسْجُدُوا۟ لِءَادَمَ فَسَجَدُوٓا۟ إِلَّآ إِبْلِيسَ أَبَىٰ وَٱسْتَكْبَرَ وَكَانَ مِنَ ٱلْكَٰفِرِينَ

"And behold, We said to the angels, 'Bow down to Adam,' and they bowed down—but not so Iblis. He refused and was arrogant. He was of the disbelievers" (*al-Baqarah* 34).

This shows that the evil of *kibr* can be so great that it can be the main reason for a person refusing to embrace Islam and submit himself to Allah; in other words, it is *kibr* that earns many people an eternal punishment in the Hell-fire. No matter how many proofs and signs are given showing that Islam is the truth and all other ways of life are false, out of arrogance and pride many refuse to accept the truth and submit to the revelation that has come from Allah. Such people are actually not even deserving

[1] This is a hadith that is often misunderstood. It does not mean that even the slightest amount of *kibr* is equivalent to disbelief. Instead, it means that the person who has even the slightest amount of *kibr* will not enter Paradise with those who enter Paradise without any punishment in the Hereafter.

of Allah's guidance and showing them the Straight Path. On this point, one should pay heed to the following verses of the Quran:

وَمَن يَسْتَنكِفْ عَنْ عِبَادَتِهِۦ وَيَسْتَكْبِرْ فَسَيَحْشُرُهُمْ إِلَيْهِ جَمِيعًا ﴿١٧٢﴾ فَأَمَّا ٱلَّذِينَ ءَامَنُوا۟ وَعَمِلُوا۟ ٱلصَّٰلِحَٰتِ فَيُوَفِّيهِمْ أُجُورَهُمْ وَيَزِيدُهُم مِّن فَضْلِهِۦ ۖ وَأَمَّا ٱلَّذِينَ ٱسْتَنكَفُوا۟ وَٱسْتَكْبَرُوا۟ فَيُعَذِّبُهُمْ عَذَابًا أَلِيمًا وَلَا يَجِدُونَ لَهُم مِّن دُونِ ٱللَّهِ وَلِيًّا وَلَا نَصِيرًا

"Those who disdain His worship and are arrogant, He will gather them all together unto Himself to (answer). But to those who believe and do deeds of righteousness, He will give their (due) rewards, and more, out of His bounty. But those who are disdainful and arrogant, He will punish with a grievous penalty; They will not find, besides Allah, any to protect or help them" (*al-Nisaa* 172-173);

سَأَصْرِفُ عَنْ ءَايَٰتِىَ ٱلَّذِينَ يَتَكَبَّرُونَ فِى ٱلْأَرْضِ بِغَيْرِ ٱلْحَقِّ وَإِن يَرَوْا۟ كُلَّ ءَايَةٍ لَّا يُؤْمِنُوا۟ بِهَا وَإِن يَرَوْا۟ سَبِيلَ ٱلرُّشْدِ لَا يَتَّخِذُوهُ سَبِيلًا وَإِن يَرَوْا۟ سَبِيلَ ٱلْغَىِّ يَتَّخِذُوهُ سَبِيلًا ۚ ذَٰلِكَ بِأَنَّهُمْ كَذَّبُوا۟ بِـَٔايَٰتِنَا وَكَانُوا۟ عَنْهَا غَٰفِلِينَ

"Those who behave arrogantly on the earth in defiance of right, them will I turn away from My Signs: even if they see all the Signs, they will not believe in them. And if they see the way of right conduct, they will not adopt it as the way. But if they see the way of error, that is the way they will adopt—for they have rejected Our Signs and [arrogantly] failed to take warning from them" (*al-Araaf* 146).

In many ways, this disease of the heart is truly the antithesis of faith. Once one realizes who Allah is and believes in Him, humility and the will to submit should fill one's heart. The believer recognizes Allah's greatness as well as Allah's bounties upon him. Given that, there is no room in his heart for any kind of arrogance before Allah. When the believer reaches that state, he could reject or object to anything that has come from Allah simply on the basis of what his own arrogant soul has concocted. His way of life would be filled only with "listening and submitting."

Given the grave dangers of *kibr*, the believer must strive to completely eradicate this disease from his heart, leaving not even a trace of it leftover. If he does not do so and he allows *kibr* to remain or grow in his heart, he will never satisfactorily purify his soul with such a disease in his heart.

Of course, the greatest sins that one can commit are those of disbelief (*kufr*) and idolatry (*shirk*). Disbelief and idolatry are such impurities and foul acts that they cannot be removed by expiating good deeds, the supplications of other believers, the supplications of the angels or the hardships that one faces in this world. Numerous Quranic verses are related to the eternal punishment resulting from *shirk* and *kufr*, some quoted earlier. In addition to those quoted earlier, one should particularly note the following verses:

وَمَن يَرْتَدِدْ مِنكُمْ عَن دِينِهِۦ فَيَمُتْ وَهُوَ كَافِرٌ فَأُو۟لَـٰٓئِكَ حَبِطَتْ أَعْمَـٰلُهُمْ فِى ٱلدُّنْيَا وَٱلْـَٔاخِرَةِ ۖ وَأُو۟لَـٰٓئِكَ أَصْحَـٰبُ ٱلنَّارِ ۖ هُمْ فِيهَا خَـٰلِدُونَ

"And if any of you apostate from their faith and die in unbelief, their works will be rendered fruitless in this life and in the Hereafter; they will be companions of the Fire and will abide therein" (*al-Baqarah* 217);

إِنَّ ٱلَّذِينَ كَفَرُوا۟ وَمَاتُوا۟ وَهُمْ كُفَّارٌ أُو۟لَـٰٓئِكَ عَلَيْهِمْ لَعْنَةُ ٱللَّهِ وَٱلْمَلَـٰٓئِكَةِ وَٱلنَّاسِ أَجْمَعِينَ ﴿١٦١﴾ خَـٰلِدِينَ فِيهَا ۖ لَا يُخَفَّفُ عَنْهُمُ ٱلْعَذَابُ وَلَا هُمْ يُنظَرُونَ

"Those who reject faith, and die rejecting it, on them is Allah's curse, and the curse of angels, and of all mankind; They will abide therein: their penalty will not be lightened, nor will respite be their (lot)" (*al-Baqarah* 161-162).

Allah is definitely the Most Merciful. Every aspect of mercy that one witnesses in this world is but a small reflection of His total mercy. Yet even though His mercy and compassion is so great, there is still an important key that one needs before receiving His mercy. That key is the avoidance of *shirk*. No matter how many sins a person may commit, at all costs he must avoid ever falling into disbelief and idolatry. The Prophet (peace and blessings of Allah be upon him) has quoted Allah as saying,

يَا ابْنَ آدَمَ إِنَّكَ لَوْ أَتَيْتَنِي بِقُرَابِ الْأَرْضِ خَطَايَا ثُمَّ لَقِيتَنِي لا تُشْرِكُ بِي شَيْئًا لَأَتَيْتُكَ بِقُرَابِهَا مَغْفِرَةً

"O son of Adam, if you were to come to Me with sins that are close to filling the Earth and you would then meet Me without ascribing any partners with Me, I would certainly [also] bring to you forgiveness close to filling it [the Earth]."[1]

Actually, every human knows that he does commit sins and that he is in need of Allah's forgiveness. Therefore, at the very least, the person must make sure that he stays within the fold of Islam. Once he leaves that fold, he has lost any and all sense of purification of the soul. His soul is completely soiled and rotten. He is not deserving of any form of forgiveness. He does not deserve to even smell the beautiful scent of Paradise in the Hereafter; therefore, he will remain in the Hell-fire forever. Hence,

[1] Recorded by al-Tirmidhi. It is *hasan* due to its supporting evidence. See the discussion in Zarabozo, *Commentary*, vol. 3, pp. 1580-1584.

the first obligation upon any human is to free himself from all forms of idolatry and first purify his heart with the minimum of *tauheed*. After that, he should also work on himself to avoid all types of sins, both major and minor.

Being Overcome by This World and its Glitter

There has already been a discussion of the role of realizing the true place of this world. In this section, there will only be a discussion of the negative aspects of being overcome by this world and its glitter.

Undoubtedly, the pleasures of this life can make one forget about Allah and one's true purpose in life. Allah has reminded the believers of such a fact through His command,

يَٰٓأَيُّهَا ٱلَّذِينَ ءَامَنُواْ لَا تُلۡهِكُمۡ أَمۡوَٰلُكُمۡ وَلَآ أَوۡلَٰدُكُمۡ عَن ذِكۡرِ ٱللَّهِۚ وَمَن يَفۡعَلۡ ذَٰلِكَ فَأُوْلَٰٓئِكَ هُمُ ٱلۡخَٰسِرُونَ

"O you who believe! Let not your riches or your children divert you from the remembrance of Allah. If any act thus, the loss is their own" (*al-Munaafiqoon* 9).

It is important to note that Islam does not prohibit efforts to provide for one's sustenance and living in this world.[1] Instead, it guides the human to the proper way of supporting himself and living in this world. It guides the human to the proper balance between this life and the Hereafter. It is natural for humans to find the good things of this life attractive and alluring. However, the believer knows with full conviction that there is something much better and more important than all that this world has to offer. Furthermore, he knows exactly what are the keys to the more important rewards. Allah has said,

---

[1] There has been a discussion among the scholars as to which of the following conditions is considered the best state for the servant of Allah: being poor, being rich or having only sufficient means. The interested reader should consult Al-Ameen Ahmad, pp. 132-144.

زُيِّنَ لِلنَّاسِ حُبُّ ٱلشَّهَوَٰتِ مِنَ ٱلنِّسَآءِ وَٱلْبَنِينَ وَٱلْقَنَٰطِيرِ
ٱلْمُقَنطَرَةِ مِنَ ٱلذَّهَبِ وَٱلْفِضَّةِ وَٱلْخَيْلِ ٱلْمُسَوَّمَةِ وَٱلْأَنْعَٰمِ
وَٱلْحَرْثِ ۗ ذَٰلِكَ مَتَٰعُ ٱلْحَيَوٰةِ ٱلدُّنْيَا ۖ وَٱللَّهُ عِندَهُۥ حُسْنُ ٱلْمَـَٔابِ
﴿١٤﴾ ۞ قُلْ أَؤُنَبِّئُكُم بِخَيْرٍ مِّن ذَٰلِكُمْ ۚ لِلَّذِينَ ٱتَّقَوْا۟ عِندَ رَبِّهِمْ
جَنَّٰتٌ تَجْرِى مِن تَحْتِهَا ٱلْأَنْهَٰرُ خَٰلِدِينَ فِيهَا وَأَزْوَٰجٌ مُّطَهَّرَةٌ
وَرِضْوَٰنٌ مِّنَ ٱللَّهِ ۗ وَٱللَّهُ بَصِيرٌۢ بِٱلْعِبَادِ

"Fair in the eyes of men is the love of things they covet: women and sons; heaped-up hoards of gold and silver; horses branded (for blood and excellence); and (wealth of) cattle and well-tilled land. Such are the possessions of this world's life; but in nearness to Allah is the best of the goals (to return to). Say: Shall I inform you of things far better than those? For the righteous are gardens in nearness to their Lord, with rivers flowing beneath; therein is their eternal home; with companions pure (and holy) and the good pleasure of Allah. In Allah's sight are (all) His servants" (*ali-Imraan* 14-15).

When the individual has a proper perspective on this world, he then does not seek after the goods of this world at any expense. Indeed, he also does not become selfish and greedy with respect to the goods of this world, as he has this full realization that there are other things that are more important.

The key behind the proper balance is for the individual not to make the goods of this world his utmost goal. He should benefit from what is available to him in this world by using it in a way that will fulfill his needs in this life while at the same time benefiting him in the Hereafter. In other words, his ultimate goal must always be the Hereafter and Allah's pleasure. The worldly needs and pleasures never penetrate his heart such that they become prominent therein and become his main preoccupation and goal.

Allah says,

مَن كَانَ يُرِيدُ ٱلْحَيَوٰةَ ٱلدُّنْيَا وَزِينَتَهَا نُوَفِّ إِلَيْهِمْ أَعْمَٰلَهُمْ فِيهَا وَهُمْ فِيهَا لَا يُبْخَسُونَ ﴿١٥﴾ أُوْلَٰٓئِكَ ٱلَّذِينَ لَيْسَ لَهُمْ فِى ٱلْءَاخِرَةِ إِلَّا ٱلنَّارُ ۖ وَحَبِطَ مَا صَنَعُوا۟ فِيهَا وَبَٰطِلٌ مَّا كَانُوا۟ يَعْمَلُونَ

"Those who desire the life of this world and its glitter, to them We shall pay (the price of) their deeds therein, without diminution. They are those for whom there is nothing in the Hereafter but the Fire: vain are the designs they frame therein, and void are the deeds that they do" (*Hood* 15-16).

Similarly, in yet another set of verses, Allah says,

مَّن كَانَ يُرِيدُ ٱلْعَاجِلَةَ عَجَّلْنَا لَهُۥ فِيهَا مَا نَشَآءُ لِمَن نُّرِيدُ ثُمَّ جَعَلْنَا لَهُۥ جَهَنَّمَ يَصْلَىٰهَا مَذْمُومًا مَّدْحُورًا ﴿١٨﴾ وَمَنْ أَرَادَ ٱلْءَاخِرَةَ وَسَعَىٰ لَهَا سَعْيَهَا وَهُوَ مُؤْمِنٌ فَأُوْلَٰٓئِكَ كَانَ سَعْيُهُم مَّشْكُورًا

"Whoever desires the immediate [worldly gratifications], We hasten for him from it what We will to whom We please. Then We have made for him Hell, [in] which he will burn, censured and banished. But whoever desires the Hereafter and exerts the effort due to it while he is a believer, it is those whose effort is appreciated" (*al-Israa* 18-20).

In numerous verses of the Quran, Allah warns about being overcome and deceived by the passing enjoyments of this worldly life. For example, Allah says,

يَٰٓأَيُّهَا ٱلنَّاسُ إِنَّ وَعْدَ ٱللَّهِ حَقٌّ ۖ فَلَا تَغُرَّنَّكُمُ ٱلْحَيَوٰةُ ٱلدُّنْيَا ۖ وَلَا يَغُرَّنَّكُم بِٱللَّهِ ٱلْغَرُورُ

"O mankind, indeed, the promise of Allah is true, so let not the worldly life deceive you and be not deceived about Allah by the Deceiver [Satan]" (*Faatir* 5). Allah has also said,

قَدْ أَفْلَحَ مَن تَزَكَّىٰ ﴿١٤﴾ وَذَكَرَ ٱسْمَ رَبِّهِۦ فَصَلَّىٰ ﴿١٥﴾ بَلْ تُؤْثِرُونَ ٱلْحَيَوٰةَ ٱلدُّنْيَا ﴿١٦﴾ وَٱلْـَٔاخِرَةُ خَيْرٌ وَأَبْقَىٰٓ ﴿١٧﴾ إِنَّ هَٰذَا لَفِى ٱلصُّحُفِ ٱلْأُولَىٰ ﴿١٨﴾ صُحُفِ إِبْرَٰهِيمَ وَمُوسَىٰ

"But those will prosper who purify themselves and extol the name of their Guardian-Lord, and (lift their hearts) in prayer. Nay (behold), you prefer the life of this world. But the Hereafter is better and more enduring. And this is in the Books of the earliest (revelations), the Books of Abraham and Moses" (*al-Ala* 14-19). In the following set of verses Allah gives a very strong warning:

فَأَمَّا مَن طَغَىٰ ﴿٣٧﴾ وَءَاثَرَ ٱلْحَيَوٰةَ ٱلدُّنْيَا ﴿٣٨﴾ فَإِنَّ ٱلْجَحِيمَ هِىَ ٱلْمَأْوَىٰ

"Then, for such as had transgressed all bounds, and had preferred the life of this world, the abode will be Hell-Fire" (*al-Naaziaat* 37-39).

There is, therefore, no question that the relentless pursuit and goal of wealth and worldly prestige is extremely damaging to one's soul. In fact, the Messenger of Allah (peace and blessings of Allah be upon him) said,

مَا ذِئْبَانِ جَائِعَانِ أُرْسِلاَ فِي غَنَمٍ بِأَفْسَدَ لَهَا مِنْ حِرْصِ الْمَرْءِ عَلَى الْمَالِ وَالشَّرَفِ لِدِينِهِ

"Two hungry wolves set upon sheep are not more destructive to them than a person's coveting wealth and honor is to his faith."[1]

---

[1] Recorded by Ahmad, al-Tirmidhi and others. According to al-Albaani, it is *sahih*. See al-Albaani, *Saheeh al-Jaami*, vol. 2, p. 983.

The believer must also realize that there is no escape from death. At the same time, though, he cannot cling to the things of this life. Hence, he must concentrate on what is of lasting benefit for his soul rather than of immediate but short-term pleasure. In fact, the alert soul would never want to be from those whom Allah has described in the Quran:

أُوْلَـٰٓئِكَ ٱلَّذِينَ ٱشْتَرَوُاْ ٱلْحَيَوٰةَ ٱلدُّنْيَا بِٱلْأَخِرَةِ فَلَا يُخَفَّفُ عَنْهُمُ ٱلْعَذَابُ وَلَا هُمْ يُنصَرُونَ

"These are the people who buy the life of this world at the price of the Hereafter: their penalty shall not be lightened nor shall they be helped" (*al-Baqarah* 86).

When the human is deceived and allured by this world and its glitter his entire purpose and goal changes. He is no longer very interested in purifying his soul. He becomes interested only in amassing what he can of this life and enjoying every moment in this world. In fact, the more a person is overcome by this world and desires this world, the less and less he will be able to follow along the path of self-purification. Indeed, his heart will become diseased with those ills that take one far from the path of purification, such as the diseases of greed, envy and fear of losing what one possesses. This, in turn, drives him to many deeds that further soil his soul, such as cutting off familial and brotherly relations due to unwillingness to sacrifice for others and a drive to have everything for one's own pleasure. Such a person becomes truly diseased and wretched, as the Messenger of Allah (peace and blessings of Allah be upon him) noted,

تَعِسَ عَبْدُ الدِّينَارِ وَعَبْدُ الدِّرْهَمِ وَعَبْدُ الْخَمِيصَةِ إِنْ أُعْطِيَ رَضِيَ وَإِنْ لَمْ يُعْطَ سَخِطَ تَعِسَ وَانْتَكَسَ وَإِذَا شِيكَ فَلا انْتَقَشَ طُوبَى لِعَبْدٍ آخِذٍ بِعِنَانِ فَرَسِهِ فِي سَبِيلِ اللَّهِ أَشْعَثَ رَأْسُهُ مُغْبَرَّةٍ قَدَمَاهُ إِنْ كَانَ فِي الْحِرَاسَةِ كَانَ فِي الْحِرَاسَةِ وَإِنْ كَانَ فِي السَّاقَةِ كَانَ فِي السَّاقَةِ إِنِ اسْتَأْذَنَ لَمْ يُؤْذَنْ لَهُ وَإِنْ شَفَعَ لَمْ يُشَفَّعْ

"May the slave of *dinars, dirhams, qateefah* and *khameesah*[1] perish as he is pleased if these things are given to him and if not, he is displeased. But glad tidings be for him who holds the reins of his horse to strive for the sake of Allah with his hair unkempt and his feet covered with dust. [He is such a person that] if he is appointed in the vanguard, he is perfectly satisfied with his post of guarding and if he is appointed in the rear guard, he accepts his post with satisfaction. [He is so simple and unambitious with respect to worldly wealth that] if he asks for permission, he is not granted it, and if he intercedes, his intercession is not accepted." (Recorded by al-Bukhari.)

It is important that every Muslim realize that if Allah grants a person much wealth or many of the sought after aspects of this world, this in no way means that Allah is pleased with him or is blessing him. Indeed, such bounties are all a trial for him and may be the greatest source of his destruction in the Hereafter. The important question is not what one is given of this world but how one behaves with respect to what one is or is not given. Allah says,

فَأَمَّا ٱلْإِنسَٰنُ إِذَا مَا ٱبْتَلَىٰهُ رَبُّهُۥ فَأَكْرَمَهُۥ وَنَعَّمَهُۥ فَيَقُولُ رَبِّىٓ أَكْرَمَنِ ﴿١٥﴾ وَأَمَّآ إِذَا مَا ٱبْتَلَىٰهُ فَقَدَرَ عَلَيْهِ رِزْقَهُۥ فَيَقُولُ رَبِّىٓ أَهَٰنَنِ ﴿١٦﴾ كَلَّا

"Now, as for man, when his Lord tries him, giving him honor and gifts, then he says, (puffed up), 'My Lord has honored me.' But when He tries him, restricting his subsistence for him, then he says (in despair), 'My Lord has humiliated me!' Nay, nay!" (*al-Fajr* 15-17). The Messenger of Allah (peace and blessings of Allah be upon him) said,

إِنَّ لِكُلِّ أُمَّةٍ فِتْنَةً وَفِتْنَةُ أُمَّتِي الْمَالُ

[1] These four are different forms of money and expensive clothing.

"For every Nation there is a [specific] trial and the trial for my Nation is that of wealth."[1] Indeed, the wealth that one receives is a great trial and not everyone is able to handle such a trial. In other words, for some people, it would be best not to have wealth as the wealth will just cause them harm.

The epidemic of being overcome by the glitter of this world has even spread to Third World or poorer Muslim countries. What is occurring nowadays, with all of the international means of communication and all the time that people spend on those means, be they television, the Internet and so forth, is that people are seeing more and more how others live, in particular the "rich and famous". Of course, the media rarely gives a true portrayal of life. Those in Muslim lands are particularly duped into thinking that the lifestyles of the people of the West are very grand. Hence, they begin to yearn after those things with a very strong craving.[2]

---

[1] Recorded by al-Tirmidhi and al-Haakim. According to al-Albaani, it is *sahih*. See al-Albaani, *Saheeh al-Jaami*, vol. 1, p. 430.

[2] An example of international media and how it creates a longing for the glitter of this world can be seen in MTV, a television station devoted to musical videos and programming directed toward the youth. MTV has just celebrated its twentieth year and many in the West even debated its impact. By 1993, it was found in seventy-one countries and available to 210 million households worldwide. By 2001, it was available to 25 million Middle East TV households. Furthermore, MTV India was voted the most popular music channel in Pakistan. Richard J. Barnet and John Cavanaugh stated that MTV "may be the most influential educator of young children on five continents." They also said, "The performances and the ads merge to create a mood of longing—for someone to love, for something exciting to happen, for an end to loneliness, and for things to buy—a record, a ticket to a rock concert, a T-shirt, a Thunderbird. The advertising is all the more effective because it is not acknowledged as such ... All across the planet, people are using the same electronic devices to watch or to listen to the same commercially produced songs and stories." [Quoted in David C. Korten, *When Corporations Rule the World* (West Hartford, CN and San Francisco: Kumarian Press Inc. and Berrett-Koehler Publishers, Inc., 1995), pp. 153-154.] In addition to that, the United States government is trying to use international MTV stations as propaganda tools for increasing the acceptance of Western policies among the important and growing 15-30 age group. Reuters noted, "Rushing to shift perceptions of the United States in the Islamic world, Washington and Hollywood are not brainstorming about how the entertainment business might help convey a wider—and more positive—range of perceptions about America. And no demo is more crucial to the future of Islamic-Western relations than the 15-30 age group. That's where MTV comes in. The potential to intersperse messages between programming segments—as with the 'Rock the Vote' campaign, for example—makes the music cable channel an obvious vehicle. And a top priority for MTV is to give young people a way to express their views via local MTV channels around the world, whether through man-on-the street interviews or interactive shows. Such efforts were

When one ponders over the effects of today's media, it can remind one of the story of Qaaroon of the Tribe Israel. Allah describes his situation and the masses' response to his wealth in the following passage:

إِنَّ قَـٰرُونَ كَانَ مِن قَوْمِ مُوسَىٰ فَبَغَىٰ عَلَيْهِمْ ۖ وَءَاتَيْنَـٰهُ مِنَ ٱلْكُنُوزِ
مَآ إِنَّ مَفَاتِحَهُۥ لَتَنُوٓأُ بِٱلْعُصْبَةِ أُو۟لِى ٱلْقُوَّةِ إِذْ قَالَ لَهُۥ قَوْمُهُۥ لَا
تَفْرَحْ ۖ إِنَّ ٱللَّهَ لَا يُحِبُّ ٱلْفَرِحِينَ ﴿٧٦﴾ وَٱبْتَغِ فِيمَآ ءَاتَىٰكَ ٱللَّهُ ٱلدَّارَ
ٱلْـَٔاخِرَةَ ۖ وَلَا تَنسَ نَصِيبَكَ مِنَ ٱلدُّنْيَا ۖ وَأَحْسِن كَمَآ أَحْسَنَ ٱللَّهُ إِلَيْكَ ۖ
وَلَا تَبْغِ ٱلْفَسَادَ فِى ٱلْأَرْضِ ۖ إِنَّ ٱللَّهَ لَا يُحِبُّ ٱلْمُفْسِدِينَ ﴿٧٧﴾ قَالَ
إِنَّمَآ أُوتِيتُهُۥ عَلَىٰ عِلْمٍ عِندِىٓ ۚ أَوَلَمْ يَعْلَمْ أَنَّ ٱللَّهَ قَدْ أَهْلَكَ مِن
قَبْلِهِۦ مِنَ ٱلْقُرُونِ مَنْ هُوَ أَشَدُّ مِنْهُ قُوَّةً وَأَكْثَرُ جَمْعًا ۚ وَلَا يُسْـَٔلُ
عَن ذُنُوبِهِمُ ٱلْمُجْرِمُونَ ﴿٧٨﴾ فَخَرَجَ عَلَىٰ قَوْمِهِۦ فِى زِينَتِهِۦ ۖ قَالَ
ٱلَّذِينَ يُرِيدُونَ ٱلْحَيَوٰةَ ٱلدُّنْيَا يَـٰلَيْتَ لَنَا مِثْلَ مَآ أُوتِىَ قَـٰرُونُ إِنَّهُۥ
لَذُو حَظٍّ عَظِيمٍ ﴿٧٩﴾ وَقَالَ ٱلَّذِينَ أُوتُوا۟ ٱلْعِلْمَ وَيْلَكُمْ ثَوَابُ ٱللَّهِ
خَيْرٌ لِّمَنْ ءَامَنَ وَعَمِلَ صَـٰلِحًا وَلَا يُلَقَّىٰهَآ إِلَّا ٱلصَّـٰبِرُونَ ﴿٨٠﴾
فَخَسَفْنَا بِهِۦ وَبِدَارِهِ ٱلْأَرْضَ فَمَا كَانَ لَهُۥ مِن فِئَةٍ يَنصُرُونَهُۥ

---

underway before the attacks [of September 11], but the events of September 11 brought a new sense of urgency... What such efforts on the part of MTV and other U.S. outlets abroad will cost is anyone's guess. But signs are that, spurred by Washington, money will be spent." Quoted from "U.S. wants its MTV to get message out in Arab world," CNN.com, Nov. 19, 2001.

مِن دُونِ ٱللَّهِ وَمَا كَانَ مِنَ ٱلْمُنتَصِرِينَ ﴿٨١﴾ وَأَصْبَحَ ٱلَّذِينَ تَمَنَّوْا۟
مَكَانَهُۥ بِٱلْأَمْسِ يَقُولُونَ وَيْكَأَنَّ ٱللَّهَ يَبْسُطُ ٱلرِّزْقَ لِمَن يَشَآءُ
مِنْ عِبَادِهِۦ وَيَقْدِرُ ۖ لَوْلَآ أَن مَّنَّ ٱللَّهُ عَلَيْنَا لَخَسَفَ بِنَا ۖ وَيْكَأَنَّهُۥ لَا
يُفْلِحُ ٱلْكَٰفِرُونَ

"Indeed, Qaaroon was from the people of Moses, but he tyrannized them. And We gave him of treasures whose keys would burden a band of strong men; thereupon his people said to him, 'Do not exult. Indeed, Allah does not like the exultant. But seek through that which Allah has given you the home of the Hereafter and [yet] do not forget your share of this world. And do goodness as Allah has been good to you. And desire not corruption in the land. Indeed, Allah does not like corrupters.' He said, 'I was only given it because of knowledge I have.' Did he not know that Allah had destroyed before him of generations those who were greater than him in power and greater in accumulation [of wealth]? But the criminals, about their sins, will not be asked. So he came out before his people in his adornment. Those who desired the worldly life said, 'Oh, would that we had like what was given to Qaaroon. Indeed, he is one of great fortune.' But those who had been given knowledge said, 'Woe to you! The reward of Allah is better for he who believes and does righteousness. And none are granted it save those who are patient.' And We cause the earth to swallow him and his home. And there was for him no company to aid him other than Allah, nor was he of those who [could] defend themselves. And those who had wished for his position the previous day began to say, 'Oh, how Allah extends provision to whom He wills of His servants and restricts it! If not that Allah had conferred favor on us, He would have caused it to swallow us. Oh how the disbelievers do not succeed'" (*al-Qasas* 76-82). This is the Quranic message and it is as if it were directly included in the Quran for today's age. This is what happens—and this is exactly what the people of the media and advertising understand so well. People see something and they want it, even though beforehand they would have never even conceived of it. Only those who were strong in faith were able to realize that it is not these things that we should be striving for. But if a person is not strong in faith, and has grown up on the media of the West, his will may succumb and his desires for the goods of this world may overtake him.

This point was actually noted by ibn Taimiyyah centuries ago when he wrote, "How many are there who do not desire good or evil until they see someone else—especially if they are a similar colleague—perform said act and then they also do it? People are like flocks of sand grouses by nature driven to resemble and imitate one another."[1] (This point also emphasizes the importance of good companions and being in a good environment, a topic discussed below.)

Perhaps reflection upon a hadith and continual remembrance of this hadith will help bridle a person's desire for this life and bring an end to his being overcome by what it contains. Al-Bukhari and Muslim recorded on the authority of Anas ibn Maalik that the Messenger of Allah (peace and blessings of Allah be upon him) said,

يَقُولُ اللَّهُ تَبَارَكَ وَتَعَالَى لِأَهْوَنِ أَهْلِ النَّارِ عَذَابًا لَوْ كَانَتْ لَكَ الدُّنْيَا وَمَا فِيهَا أَكُنْتَ مُفْتَدِيًا بِهَا فَيَقُولُ نَعَمْ فَيَقُولُ قَدْ أَرَدْتُ مِنْكَ أَهْوَنَ مِنْ هَذَا وَأَنْتَ فِي صُلْبِ آدَمَ أَنْ لا تُشْرِكَ فَأَبَيْتَ إِلاَّ الشِّرْكَ

"Allah will say to the one who has the lightest punishment in Hell, 'If you had the world and all that it contained, would you offer it as a ransom [to get you out of your present state]?' He will say, 'Yes.' Then [Allah] will say, 'I asked you for something much easier than that while you were in the loins of Adam: not to associate any partner [with Me]. But you refused and insisted on associating partners [with Me].'"

---

[1] Ibn Taimiyyah, *Majmoo*, vol. 28, pp. 149-150.

Evil Companions, Environment and Surroundings

Allah says,

وَٱصْبِرْ نَفْسَكَ مَعَ ٱلَّذِينَ يَدْعُونَ رَبَّهُم بِٱلْغَدَوٰةِ وَٱلْعَشِيِّ يُرِيدُونَ
وَجْهَهُۥ ۖ وَلَا تَعْدُ عَيْنَاكَ عَنْهُمْ تُرِيدُ زِينَةَ ٱلْحَيَوٰةِ ٱلدُّنْيَا ۖ وَلَا تُطِعْ
مَنْ أَغْفَلْنَا قَلْبَهُۥ عَن ذِكْرِنَا وَٱتَّبَعَ هَوَىٰهُ وَكَانَ أَمْرُهُۥ فُرُطًا ﴿٢٨﴾
وَقُلِ ٱلْحَقُّ مِن رَّبِّكُمْ ۖ فَمَن شَآءَ فَلْيُؤْمِن وَمَن شَآءَ فَلْيَكْفُرْ ۚ

"And keep your soul content with those who call on their Lord morning and evening, seeking His Face; and let not your eyes pass beyond them, seeking the pomp and glitter of this Life; nor obey any whose heart We have permitted to neglect the remembrance of Us, one who follows his own desires, whose case has gone beyond all bounds. Say, 'The Truth is from your Lord.' Let him who will, believe, and let him who will, reject (it)" (*al-Kahf* 28-29).

Karzoon notes that a person's companion does influence him, even if only after some time. Whoever thinks that he is not affected by an evil friend is probably mistaken. Such a friend makes the person incline towards sins and causes him not to object to some wrong in his presence. This acceptance increases in the heart until the person himself actually begins to participate in the sinful acts.[1]

In fact, there is no question that, at the very least, when continually being in the company of sinful companions one may sooner or later commit sins by failing to order what is good and eradicate what is evil and accepting the sin. At first, one may tell his friend that such and such is a sin that he should stop. After a number of attempts to stop the sin, one may decide just to accept his friend's behavior and consider the sin something not harmful or not reprehensible. The friendship of the evil friend becomes the most important object. This is very dangerous for a person's soul

---

[1] Karzoon, vol. 1, p. 407.

and it may lead to him being cursed by Allah. Allah says about the Tribes of Israel,

لُعِنَ ٱلَّذِينَ كَفَرُوا۟ مِنۢ بَنِىٓ إِسْرَٰٓءِيلَ عَلَىٰ لِسَانِ دَاوُۥدَ وَعِيسَى ٱبْنِ مَرْيَمَ ۚ ذَٰلِكَ بِمَا عَصَوا۟ وَّكَانُوا۟ يَعْتَدُونَ ﴿٧٨﴾ كَانُوا۟ لَا يَتَنَاهَوْنَ عَن مُّنكَرٍ فَعَلُوهُ ۚ لَبِئْسَ مَا كَانُوا۟ يَفْعَلُونَ

"Curses were pronounced on those among the Children of Israel who rejected faith, by the tongue of David and of Jesus the son of Mary, because they disobeyed and persisted in excesses. Nor did they forbid one another the iniquities which they committed: evil indeed were the deeds which they did" (*al-Maaidah* 78-79).[1]

One of the negative effects of evil friends is that often they give their friends ideas that they would have never thought of on their own. Unfortunately, the process usually does not stop there. In addition to coming up with evil ideas, the evil friend will also often encourage and assist his friends to do those evil acts.[2] For example, this author knows of some Muslim youth who never considered consuming alcohol or engaging with the opposite sex until close friends, many times from the same "Islamic school," encouraged them and prodded them, hurling them with insults and snide remarks, until they also participated in such activities.

A sad occurrence in the modern age is the fact that the media is playing that same type of role that evil friends play. More and more, the media is presenting and discussing things that

---

[1] This truly becomes a sin when one has the ability to eradicate the evil but does not do so or when one begins to accept the sins of his friend as if there were nothing wrong with it. However, if one tries to correct the wrong without any response but is in a situation where he is forced to associated with such a person—while appreciating the friend's good deeds but still hating his sinful deeds—then he is not committing a sin, Allah willing.

[2] This kind of behavior is often found among children. It is sometimes the case that a specific child is overall well-behaved and not of evil intent. However, when mixing with specific friends, those friends give him evil ideas and urge him on. It is when the normally well-behaved child is with and urged on by those friends that he does mischievous and evil acts.

perhaps no one would have ever considered—but after hearing about such things, perhaps on the news or some fictional program, a person may find desires becoming inflamed and he cannot stop thinking about doing those things. The end result for many is that they fulfill those desires or fantasies that they only even considered after having come across them in the media. Hence, in the same way that an evil friend should be avoided, these forms of media that propagate or present illicit behavior should also be avoided and removed from one's household.

In general, it is the Muslim himself who allows himself to associate with evil friends. Similarly, it is the Muslim himself who allows the different form of media to be in his house. The Muslim must realize what he is doing and what may be the negative ramifications of this seemingly benign behavior. He must realize that Allah may hold him to account for who he spends his time with and what he allows into his presence or house. The Muslim should always keep in mind the important advice of the Prophet (peace and blessings of Allah be upon him) when he said,

لا تُصَاحِبْ إِلاَّ مُؤْمِنًا وَلا يَأْكُلْ طَعَامَكَ إِلاَّ تَقِيٌّ

"You should not accompany save a believer and no one but a pious person should eat your food."[1] Indeed, the following passage from the Quran should set the guiding principle for a Muslim's interaction with others—be they Muslims or non-Muslims. The principle is that if anyone is offensive to Allah and His faith, be it via mockery or invitation to sin, he must be reminded of the truth and his speech is to be shunned and avoided. Allah says,

وَإِذَا رَأَيْتَ ٱلَّذِينَ يَخُوضُونَ فِىٓ ءَايَـٰتِنَا فَأَعْرِضْ عَنْهُمْ حَتَّىٰ يَخُوضُوا۟

فِى حَدِيثٍ غَيْرِهِۦ ۚ وَإِمَّا يُنسِيَنَّكَ ٱلشَّيْطَـٰنُ فَلَا تَقْعُدْ بَعْدَ

ٱلذِّكْرَىٰ مَعَ ٱلْقَوْمِ ٱلظَّـٰلِمِينَ ﴿٦٨﴾ وَمَا عَلَى ٱلَّذِينَ يَتَّقُونَ

[1] Recorded by Ahmad, Abu Dawood, al-Tirmidhi, ibn Hibbaan and al-Haakim. According to al-Albaani, it is *hasan*. See al-Albaani, *Saheeh al-Jaami*, vol. 2, p. 1226.

مِنْ حِسَابِهِم مِّن شَيْءٍ وَلَٰكِن ذِكْرَىٰ لَعَلَّهُمْ يَتَّقُونَ ﴿٦٩﴾
وَذَرِ ٱلَّذِينَ ٱتَّخَذُوا۟ دِينَهُمْ لَعِبًا وَلَهْوًا وَغَرَّتْهُمُ ٱلْحَيَوٰةُ ٱلدُّنْيَا ۚ
وَذَكِّرْ بِهِۦٓ أَن تُبْسَلَ نَفْسٌۢ بِمَا كَسَبَتْ لَيْسَ لَهَا مِن دُونِ
ٱللَّهِ وَلِىٌّ وَلَا شَفِيعٌ وَإِن تَعْدِلْ كُلَّ عَدْلٍ لَّا يُؤْخَذْ مِنْهَآ ۗ أُو۟لَٰٓئِكَ
ٱلَّذِينَ أُبْسِلُوا۟ بِمَا كَسَبُوا۟ ۖ لَهُمْ شَرَابٌ مِّنْ حَمِيمٍ وَعَذَابٌ أَلِيمٌۢ بِمَا
كَانُوا۟ يَكْفُرُونَ

"And when you see those who engage in [offensive] discourse concerning Our verses, then turn away from them until they enter into another conversation. And if Satan should cause you to forget, then do not remain after remembrance with the wrongdoing people. And those who fear Allah are not held accountable for those [disbelievers and wrongdoers] at all, but only for a reminder—that perhaps they will fear Him. And leave those who take their religion as amusement and diversion and whom the worldly life has deluded. But remind with it [that is, with the Quran], lest a soul be given up to destruction for what it earned. It will have other than Allah no protector and no intercessor. And if it should offer every compensation, such would not be taken from it. Those are the ones who are given to destruction for what they have earned. For them will be a drink of scalding water and a painful punishment because they used to disbelieve" (*al-Anaam* 68-70).

A Muslim should keep in mind that one of the basic teachings of the religion of Islam is that a true believer should be different from disbelievers and sinners. He should be different both outwardly and inwardly—in his looks, behavior, aspirations and even psyche.[1] If they influence him negatively, he should avoid

[1] This is a point that ibn Taimiyyah proves with a great deal of evidence in his work *Iqtidhaa al-Siraat al-Mustaqeem Mukhaalafah Ashaab al-Jaheem*. The essence of that work can be found

contact with them unless absolute necessary. In fact, if he cannot avoid their influences and they are actually harming his faith, he should even make *hijrah* (emigration) from them and their land.[1] The hadith mentioned earlier while discussing the concept of repentance sheds light on the fact that a person's surrounding may be harmful for him and he should then seek a better land with a better people. In that hadith, the scholar told the person who had killed one hundred people,

انْطَلِقْ إِلَى أَرْضِ كَذَا وَكَذَا فَإِنَّ بِهَا أُنَاسًا يَعْبُدُونَ اللَّهَ فَاعْبُدِ اللَّهَ مَعَهُمْ وَلا تَرْجِعْ إِلَى أَرْضِكَ فَإِنَّهَا أَرْضُ سَوْءٍ

"Go to such and such land and therein are people who worship Allah. So worship Allah with them and do not return to your land for it is a land of evil." (Recorded by Muslim.)

Bad Parenting

A very particular case of evil companions and environment is where bad parenting is involved. The Messenger of Allah (peace and blessings of Allah be upon him) said,

---

in Muhammad Umar Memon, *Ibn Taimiya's Struggle Against Popular Religion* (The Hague: Mouton & Co., 1976), *passim*.

[1] Cf., al-Ashqar, *Minhaaj Tazkiyah*, p. 35. It would be hoped that one could emigrate to a "Muslim" land. It must be realized, though, that there is actually a strange paradox existing in the world today. This is the contrast between the Muslim minorities living in non-Muslim societies with those Muslims living in what is called a "Muslim country or culture." The former group recognizes the evil around them much more easily because they know that most of it comes from a non-Islamic source. Many members of the latter group assume that everything must be acceptable because Muslim masses and, to some extent, even Muslim leaders are participating in that culture. However, everything must be judged according to the Quran and Sunnah. Especially in this day and age, there are a lot of non-Islamic practices passing as "Muslim practice or culture" in the Muslim worlds. One has to strive to recognize that fact and not be sucked into the practices and innovations that have spread so widely. This stance may require courage as one has to struggle against his brethren Muslims as opposed to standing out and being different from the disbelievers, which every Muslim can fathom.

مَا مِنْ مَوْلُودٍ إِلَّا يُولَدُ عَلَى الْفِطْرَةِ فَأَبَوَاهُ يُهَوِّدَانِهِ أَوْ يُنَصِّرَانِهِ أَوْ يُمَجِّسَانِهِ كَمَا تُنْتَجُ الْبَهِيمَةُ بَهِيمَةً جَمْعَاءَ هَلْ تُحِسُّونَ فِيهَا مِنْ جَدْعَاءَ ثُمَّ يَقُولُ أَبُو هُرَيْرَةَ رَضِي اللَّهم عَنْهم (فِطْرَةَ اللَّهِ الَّتِي فَطَرَ النَّاسَ عَلَيْهَا) الآيَةَ

"Every child is born on the *fitrah* [the natural disposition in which humans are created]. Then his parents convert him to Judaism, Christianity or Magianism. Just like an animal giving birth to a perfect baby animal, do you find it mutilated at all?" Then Abu Hurairah read the verse, "Allah's *fitrah* upon which He has created mankind. [Let there be no change in the creation or religion of Allah, that is the straight religion]" (*al-Room* 30). (Recorded by al-Bukhari and Muslim.) This hadith shows how parents can even drive their offspring to disbelief.

However, there is another more compelling aspect that the author would like to touch upon here. This is where the parents may be dedicated Muslims but due to their bad parenting they have a detrimental effect on the purification of their children. For example, when it comes to raising children, some Muslim parents allow their emotions and compassion to overrule their common sense and their responsibility to train and teach their child. The child often becomes spoiled, having no sense of responsibility, purpose or sacrifice. Indeed, such children usually do not even have respect for others, in particular the elders and scholars. For such children and "young adults", life is nothing but enjoyment and getting their way. And this approach even lasts until the child is well into their college years. In fact, even by the time they get married, they have yet to understand what are responsibilities, work and sacrifice for others. (When they have children, the weakness of their own upbringing is simply magnified and most likely passed on to the next generation.) Such children are without any serious preparation for a serious life. They are left without truly realizing their goal and purpose in life.

It is difficult to determine whether this phenomenon is a result of the Muslim parents naively being extremely nice and seemingly merciful to their children or if it is an instance of the Muslim parents not taking upon their shoulders their responsibility in bringing up their children in a proper way such that they know their purpose in life and they work for that purpose. In any case, every Muslim parent must realize that it is his responsibility to teach and train his child such that the child understands what it means to be a Muslim. This is the most important facet that a parent can give his child. This is much more important than luxurious living. Furthermore, in this way, the parent will be meeting his responsibility before meeting Allah in the Hereafter. The Prophet (peace and blessings of Allah be upon him) reminded all believers,

أَلا كُلُّكُمْ رَاعٍ وَكُلُّكُمْ مَسْئُولٌ عَنْ رَعِيَّتِهِ فَالأَمِيرُ الَّذِي عَلَى النَّاسِ رَاعٍ وَهُوَ مَسْئُولٌ عَنْ رَعِيَّتِهِ وَالرَّجُلُ رَاعٍ عَلَى أَهْلِ بَيْتِهِ وَهُوَ مَسْئُولٌ عَنْهُمْ وَالْمَرْأَةُ رَاعِيَةٌ عَلَى بَيْتِ بَعْلِهَا وَوَلَدِهِ وَهِيَ مَسْئُولَةٌ عَنْهُمْ وَالْعَبْدُ رَاعٍ عَلَى مَالِ سَيِّدِهِ وَهُوَ مَسْئُولٌ عَنْهُ أَلا فَكُلُّكُمْ رَاعٍ وَكُلُّكُمْ مَسْئُولٌ عَنْ رَعِيَّتِهِ

"All of you are 'shepherds' [that is, people in positions of responsibility] and you will all be asked about your 'flock'. The leader over the people is a 'shepherd' and he is responsibility for his ward. The man is a 'shepherd' for the members of his household and he will be asked about them. The woman is a 'shepherdess' over the house and children of her husband and she will be asked about them. The slave is a 'shepherd' over the wealth of his owner and he will be asked about it. Certainly, all of you are 'shepherds' and you will all be asked about your ward." (Recorded by al-Bukhari and Muslim.)

There is yet another devastating effect that comes about via one's parents: being a bad example and leading one's child astray. It is natural for every person to respect and love his parents, as well as his grandparents, uncles, aunts and others of his family. This respect is often demonstrated by following their ways and customs. It is also demonstrated by an unwillingness to say that one's parents or near relatives are in the wrong or, even worse, that one's relatives are doing things that may take them to the Hell-fire. These natural aspects develop in the person a desire and willingness to follow the same path as his parents or, at the very least, to be silent in the face of their vices. This is dangerous when the parents' way is not the correct way. The attitude that may be developed in the child is an attitude that Allah has warned about on a number of occasions. For example, it is mentioned in the following verse,

وَإِذَا قِيلَ لَهُمْ تَعَالَوْا۟ إِلَىٰ مَآ أَنزَلَ ٱللَّهُ وَإِلَى ٱلرَّسُولِ قَالُوا۟ حَسْبُنَا مَا وَجَدْنَا عَلَيْهِ ءَابَآءَنَآ ۚ أَوَلَوْ كَانَ ءَابَآؤُهُمْ لَا يَعْلَمُونَ شَيْـًۭٔا وَلَا يَهْتَدُونَ ﴿١٠٤﴾ يَـٰٓأَيُّهَا ٱلَّذِينَ ءَامَنُوا۟ عَلَيْكُمْ أَنفُسَكُمْ ۖ لَا يَضُرُّكُم مَّن ضَلَّ إِذَا ٱهْتَدَيْتُمْ ۚ إِلَى ٱللَّهِ مَرْجِعُكُمْ جَمِيعًۭا فَيُنَبِّئُكُم بِمَا كُنتُمْ تَعْمَلُونَ

"When it is said to them, 'Come to what Allah has revealed and come to the Messenger,' they say, 'Enough for us are the ways we found our fathers following.' What! Even though their fathers were void of knowledge and guidance? O you who believe! Guard your own souls: if you follow (right) guidance, no hurt can come to you from those who stray. The goal of you all is to Allah: it is He that will show you the truth of all that you do" (*al-Maaidah* 104-105).[1]

[1] A classic example of parents' customs leading the children to fall into what is forbidden is the issue of the wife mixing with her in-laws. This is an evil custom that is found throughout the Muslim world. The custom exists even through the Prophet's statement is clear and very threatening. The Prophet (peace and blessings of Allah be upon him) said, "Be aware of entering upon women." A man asked, "What about the in-law [such as the brother-in-law]?" The Messenger of Allah (peace and blessings of Allah be upon him) replied, "The in-law is death." (Recorded by al-Bukhari and Muslim.) Often the son knows that this custom is wrong but out of reverence for his parents, he simply acquiesces to their evil custom. Unfortunately, the son usually forces his wife to also acquiesce. Hence, the son is committing wrong due to the behavior of the parents and his unwillingness to displease them (even if it means he has to displease Allah) and, on top of that, he forces his wife to also commit a sin.

Satan and His Soldiers

Allah has said in the Quran,

إِنَّ ٱلشَّيْطَٰنَ لَكُمْ عَدُوٌّ فَٱتَّخِذُوهُ عَدُوًّا ۚ إِنَّمَا يَدْعُوا۟ حِزْبَهُۥ لِيَكُونُوا۟ مِنْ أَصْحَٰبِ ٱلسَّعِيرِ

"Verily Satan is an enemy to you. So treat him as an enemy. He only invites his adherents that they may become companions of the Blazing Fire" (*Faatir* 6). In Allah's infinite wisdom, Allah created this enemy of humans. The enmity between Satan and humans goes back to the first human ever, Adam (peace and blessings of Allah be upon him). The source of this enmity was, in reality, the arrogance and envy of Satan—arrogance and envy being two of the greatest sources of intense hatred. Thus, Satan has set as his goal the eternal damnation of all members of mankind.

But Allah clearly warned mankind about Satan, leaving no real excuse for anyone to follow in his footsteps. Allah has said, for example,

أَلَمْ أَعْهَدْ إِلَيْكُمْ يَٰبَنِىٓ ءَادَمَ أَن لَّا تَعْبُدُوا۟ ٱلشَّيْطَٰنَ ۖ إِنَّهُۥ لَكُمْ عَدُوٌّ مُّبِينٌ ﴿٦٠﴾ وَأَنِ ٱعْبُدُونِى ۚ هَٰذَا صِرَٰطٌ مُّسْتَقِيمٌ ﴿٦١﴾ وَلَقَدْ أَضَلَّ مِنكُمْ جِبِلًّا كَثِيرًا ۖ أَفَلَمْ تَكُونُوا۟ تَعْقِلُونَ

"Did I not enjoin on you, O Children of Adam, that you should not worship Satan for that he was to you an enemy avowed? And that you should worship Me, (for that) this was the Straight Way? But he did lead astray a great multitude of you. Did you not, then, understand?" (*Yaaseen* 60-62).

In the following verse, Allah discusses the following of Satan in the context of the purification of the soul. Allah says,

يَـٰٓأَيُّهَا ٱلَّذِينَ ءَامَنُوا۟ لَا تَتَّبِعُوا۟ خُطُوَٰتِ ٱلشَّيْطَـٰنِ ۚ وَمَن يَتَّبِعْ خُطُوَٰتِ ٱلشَّيْطَـٰنِ فَإِنَّهُۥ يَأْمُرُ بِٱلْفَحْشَآءِ وَٱلْمُنكَرِ ۚ وَلَوْلَا فَضْلُ ٱللَّهِ عَلَيْكُمْ وَرَحْمَتُهُۥ مَا زَكَىٰ مِنكُم مِّنْ أَحَدٍ أَبَدًا وَلَـٰكِنَّ ٱللَّهَ يُزَكِّى مَن يَشَآءُ ۗ وَٱللَّهُ سَمِيعٌ عَلِيمٌ

"O you who believe! Follow not Satan's footsteps. If any will follow the footsteps of Satan, he will (but) command what is shameful and wrong. And were it not for the grace and mercy of Allah on you, not one of you would ever have been purified. But Allah does purify whom He pleases. And Allah is One Who hears and knows (all things)" (*al-Noor* 21).

In fact, in numerous places in the Quran, Allah has warned mankind about Satan and his evil. There is a very important aspect that ibn al-Qayyim notes concerning Satan and his ability to lead people away from the path of purification. Indeed, his discussion sheds light directly upon why those who claim to be on the path of purification seem to be the furthest from the true path of purification, making claims and statements that clearly contradict the Quran and Sunnah. Ibn al-Qayyim noted,

> The followers of the path [meaning the mystics and Sufis] of later times were not as concerned with him [that is, Satan] as they were with mentioning the soul (*nafs*), its shortcomings and diseases. They discussed the [latter] aspect in great detail and barely touched upon [the former]. Whoever studies the Quran and Sunnah will find that those texts are more concerned with mentioning Satan and battling against him than they are with mentioning the soul. The blameworthy soul is mentioned in "the soul is a persistent enjoiner of evil" [*Yusoof* 53]. The reproaching soul is mentioned only in "And I swear by the reproaching soul" [*al-Qiyaamah* 2]. The blameworthy soul is also referred to

> in "and prevented the soul from [unlawful] inclination" [*al-Naaziaat* 40]. On the other hand, Satan is mentioned in a number of places. A whole *soorah* is dedicated to [warning about] him. The Lord's warnings to His slaves concerning him are much greater than His warnings concerning the soul. This is how it must be for the evil and harm of the soul springs from his [Satan's] whispering. This is his medium, the place of his evil and the place of his obedience. Allah has ordered the taking of refuge from him upon reading the Quran and at other times. This is due to the great need of seeking refuge from him. [On the other hand, Allah] did not order the seeking of refuge from the soul in any place. Seeking of refuge from the evil in the soul is only mentioned in the opening of a speech wherein one says, "We seek refuge in Allah from the evils of our souls."[1]

Al-Ghazaali wrote that it is obligatory to protect oneself from the secret whispering of Satan. Since this can only be done via knowing his means and modes of operation, it is then obligatory to study and learn these matters.[2] This is based on the fiqh principle that if an obligatory matter cannot be accomplished save via a specific mean, that mean also becomes obligatory.

One must be aware of Satan's techniques. For example, Allah says about Satan deceiving and misleading Adam and Eve,

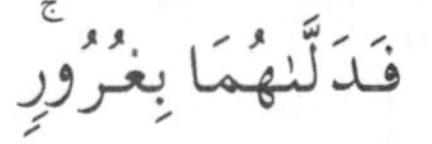

---

[1] Ibn al-Qayyim, *Ighaathah*, p. 100. There are actually a couple of hadith in which one seeks refuge from the evil in the soul. One such hadith was presented earlier.

[2] Al-Ghazaali, *Ihyaa*, vol. 3, p. 30. The varying goals and means of Satan are discussed in numerous places including al-Ashqar, *The World of the Jinn*, 72-129; ibn al-Qayyim, *Madaarij*, vol. 1, pp. 244-249. In short, Satan's goals include driving people to (1) committing ***kufr*** and ***shirk*** (disbelief and idolatry), (2) believing in heresies and committing innovations, (3) committing major sins, (4) committing minor sins. If he cannot accomplish any of those goals, he will try to prevent people from performing good deeds or will keep them busy with simply permissible, non-meritorious acts. Indeed, he will even try to keep a person busy with a good deed while making him ignore an even more important good deed.

"So he made them fall step by step through deception" (*al-Araaf* 22). The word *dallaahuma* in this verse implies that Satan tries to fulfill his plan through steps, in the same way that a person lowers the bucket turn by turn into a well. Satan either starts by prompting someone to commit blasphemy and idolatry and then when he is not successful he takes the individual to lesser evils or he starts by prompting him to do a minor sin and when successful prompts him to perform greater sins.[1] In either way, one must be very wary of the plots and machinations of this avowed enemy.

Actually, Satan has many means by which he attempts to achieve his goals.[2] These means include encouraging people to go to extremes, making people fail to perform their responsibilities through false hopes and dreams (especially concerning Allah's forgiveness), making people procrastinate and become lazy and so forth.

However, perhaps Satan's greatest scheme by which he deceives many is that of making what is evil look good and beneficial. Ibn Taimiyyah made a very perceptive point,

> The desire [in one's soul] by itself is not sufficient to make a person commit a sin unless it is accompanied by ignorance. Otherwise, if the one having that desire knows definitively that such an act will harm more than benefit him, he will naturally turn away from that act... Therefore, the greatest travesty that comes from Satan is not simply via the soul [and making it desire something]. Instead, Satan makes the sinful act seem very alluring and appealing, ordering the person to perform it and mentioning to him all of the good things that it entails.[3]

In fact, this is the means by which Satan was able to deceive the parents of mankind. Allah has spoken about that incident and, thereby, warned about this trick of Satan in the following verses,

---

[1] Cf., al-Raazi, vol. 13, p. 52.

[2] Cf., al-Ashqar, *The World of the Jinn*, pp. 96-127. Also see Karzoon, vol. 2, pp. 668f, for other machinations of Satan.

[3] Ibn Taimiyyah, *Majmoo*, vol. 14, pp. 289-290.

فَوَسْوَسَ لَهُمَا ٱلشَّيْطَـٰنُ لِيُبْدِىَ لَهُمَا مَا وُۥرِىَ عَنْهُمَا مِن سَوْءَ
ٰتِهِمَا وَقَالَ مَا نَهَىٰكُمَا رَبُّكُمَا عَنْ هَـٰذِهِ ٱلشَّجَرَةِ إِلَّآ أَن تَكُونَا
مَلَكَيْنِ أَوْ تَكُونَا مِنَ ٱلْخَـٰلِدِينَ ﴿٢٠﴾ وَقَاسَمَهُمَآ إِنِّى لَكُمَا لَمِنَ
ٱلنَّـٰصِحِينَ

"Then Satan began to whisper suggestions to them, in order to reveal to them their shame that was hidden from them (before). He said, 'Your Lord only forbade you this tree, lest you should become angels or such beings as live forever.' And he swore to them both that he was from the sincere advisers" (*al-Araaf* 20-21). Indeed, Satan is continuing to play that trick on mankind today. For example, sexual licentiousness and immorality are being spread in the name of "human rights," "art," "culture" and "modern civilization." Those who oppose such "freedoms" are termed "religious extremists," "uncivilized" and "backwards."

Before concluding this section on Satan, this author feels it a must to discuss one of the main ways by which Satan has deceived many today. This is the belief that "there are many paths and they all lead to God."

Many Hindus, for example, believe that all humans are on different paths on the same mountain, leading to the final destination. Similarly, many Liberal Jews take this approach, "There are many roads and they all lead to God." Many Christians who are dissatisfied with what they call "organized religion" have also come to this conclusion, that whoever is "good" is a child of God and God will bless them all with Paradise in the Hereafter. It is due to this mindset that many people do not even care about how historically or rationally unjustifiable their religion is. It is also because of this that many Muslims do not bother to note how close they are to the true path of the Prophet Muhammad (peace and blessings of Allah be upon him).

It is not necessarily the case that those who have fallen for this false belief are disinterested in purifying their souls. On the contrary, their "disinterest" may simply be because they have been convinced that they do not have to follow a certain path to purify their souls and that whether they follow one path or the other is all the same. Unfortunately for them, in reality, they simply end up following whatever matches their desires. The path they follow may not be pleasing to Allah but Satan has convinced them that it is.

The truth is that once the Prophet (peace and blessings of Allah be upon him) has come and people become aware of his teaching, there is only one path open to mankind to attain Allah's pleasure. In fact, the Prophet (peace and blessings of Allah be upon him) himself said,

وَالَّذِي نَفْسُ مُحَمَّدٍ بِيَدِهِ لا يَسْمَعُ بِي أَحَدٌ مِنْ هَذِهِ الأُمَّةِ يَهُودِيٌّ وَلا نَصْرَانِيٌّ ثُمَّ يَمُوتُ وَلَمْ يُؤْمِنْ بِالَّذِي أُرْسِلْتُ بِهِ إِلاَّ كَانَ مِنْ أَصْحَابِ النَّارِ

"By the One in whose hand is the soul of Muhammad, anyone of this community [that I have been sent to] who hears of me, whether he be a Jew or Christian, and dies without believing in that with which I have been sent will be from the companions of the Fire." (Recorded by Muslim.)

As noted earlier, that path is very wide and can accommodate all humans who want to walk on it. The path is wide enough to encompass all sorts of special characteristics, specialties and so forth. But it is one path and only one path. Anything that goes against the principles of that path will be rejected by Allah and will not bring the person any closer to Allah.

Finally, the only way to completely protect oneself from Satan, one's avowed enemy who will try to bring about any form of evil to the individual that he can, is by sincerely desiring and working to become a true slave and servant of Allah. When one puts one's utmost efforts towards that goal, Allah will help him and he will be among those whom Satan cannot influence. Allah has said about His sincere servants, for example,

قَالَ رَبِّ بِمَآ أَغْوَيْتَنِى لَأُزَيِّنَنَّ لَهُمْ فِى ٱلْأَرْضِ وَلَأُغْوِيَنَّهُمْ أَجْمَعِينَ ﴿٣٩﴾ إِلَّا عِبَادَكَ مِنْهُمُ ٱلْمُخْلَصِينَ ﴿٤٠﴾ قَالَ هَٰذَا

صِرَٰطٌ عَلَيَّ مُسۡتَقِيمٌ ﴿٤١﴾ إِنَّ عِبَادِي لَيۡسَ لَكَ عَلَيۡهِمۡ سُلۡطَٰنٌ إِلَّا

مَنِ ٱتَّبَعَكَ مِنَ ٱلۡغَاوِينَ

"(Iblis) said, 'O my Lord! Because You have put me in the wrong, I will make (wrong) fair-seeming to them on the earth, and I will put them all in the wrong, except Your servants among them, sincere and purified (by Your grace).' (Allah) said, 'This (way of My sincere servants) is indeed a way that leads straight to Me. For over My servants no authority shall you have, except such as put themselves in the wrong and follow you'" (*Al-Hijr* 39-42).

The Enemies of Allah: Those Who Have Earned His Wrath and Those Who Have Gone Astray

Besides Satan and the devils, one must be very cautious concerning those humans whose efforts are also for Satan—even those who may even claim a godly purpose and life. This category includes all of the disbelievers in the world who hate to see the Muslims stick to their faith or establish their true religion in any part of the world

In every prayer, the Muslim repeats the words from the Quran,

ٱهۡدِنَا ٱلصِّرَٰطَ ٱلۡمُسۡتَقِيمَ ﴿٦﴾ صِرَٰطَ ٱلَّذِينَ أَنۡعَمۡتَ عَلَيۡهِمۡ غَيۡرِ

ٱلۡمَغۡضُوبِ عَلَيۡهِمۡ وَلَا ٱلضَّآلِّينَ

"Guide us to the Straight Path, the path of whose whom You have blessed, and not the path of those whose portion is wrath nor of those who have gone astray" (*al-Faatihah* 6-7). In this prayer, the believer is requesting Allah to guide him to the Straight Path, which is none other than the path of spiritual purification. In these verses, Allah has made it clear that that path is different from the path of those people who have earned Allah's anger and those people who have gone astray. In a hadith recorded by al-Tirmidhi, the Prophet (peace and blessings of Allah be upon him) explained that those who have earned Allah's anger refers (first and foremost) to the Jews while those who have gone astray refers (first and foremost) to the Christians.[1]

In numerous verses of the Quran, Allah warns the believers about the Jews and the Christians. He warns them about the fact that their ways are not the true ways and no Muslim should fall into the trap of following their false ways, even if they may be displeased by this fact. Their ways are based on desires and ignorance while the way of Allah is that of knowledge and light. Allah says,

وَلَن تَرْضَىٰ عَنكَ ٱلْيَهُودُ وَلَا ٱلنَّصَٰرَىٰ حَتَّىٰ تَتَّبِعَ مِلَّتَهُمْ ۗ قُلْ
إِنَّ هُدَى ٱللَّهِ هُوَ ٱلْهُدَىٰ ۗ وَلَئِنِ ٱتَّبَعْتَ أَهْوَآءَهُم بَعْدَ ٱلَّذِى
جَآءَكَ مِنَ ٱلْعِلْمِ ۙ مَا لَكَ مِنَ ٱللَّهِ مِن وَلِىٍّ وَلَا نَصِيرٍ

"And never will the Jews and the Christians approve of you until you follow their religion. Say: 'Indeed the guidance of Allah is the [only] guidance.' If you were to follow their desires after what has come to you of knowledge, you would have against Allah no protector or helper" (*al-Baqarah* 120). Allah also says,

وَلَئِنْ أَتَيْتَ ٱلَّذِينَ أُوتُوا۟ ٱلْكِتَٰبَ بِكُلِّ ءَايَةٍ مَّا تَبِعُوا۟ قِبْلَتَكَ ۚ وَمَآ
أَنتَ بِتَابِعٍ قِبْلَتَهُمْ ۚ وَمَا بَعْضُهُم بِتَابِعٍ قِبْلَةَ بَعْضٍ ۚ وَلَئِنِ ٱتَّبَعْتَ
أَهْوَآءَهُم مِّنۢ بَعْدِ مَا جَآءَكَ مِنَ ٱلْعِلْمِ ۙ إِنَّكَ إِذًا لَّمِنَ ٱلظَّٰلِمِينَ

"And if you brought to those who were given the Scripture every sign, they would not follow your *qiblah*. Nor will you be a follower of their *qiblah*. Nor would they be followers of one another's *qiblah*. So if you were to follow their desires after what has come to you of knowledge, indeed, you would then be among the wrongdoers" (*al-Baqarah* 145). In yet another verse, Allah says,

---

[1] According to al-Albaani, this hadith is *sahih*. See al-Albaani, *Saheeh Sunan al-Tirmidhi*, vol. 3, p. 20.

وَدُّوا۟ لَوْ تَكْفُرُونَ كَمَا كَفَرُوا۟ فَتَكُونُونَ سَوَآءً

"They but wish that you should reject faith, as they do, and thus be on the same footing (as they)" (*al-Nisaa* 89).

The Muslim must realize that his very goal, purpose and way in life is fundamentally different from everyone else in the world today. For example, today, in particular, those who have previous scriptures are, for the most part, secularized in their thinking, especially about social and political issues. The Muslim's life, on the other hand, is supposed to be based completely on the guidance that has come from Allah. No human opinion or view can ever take the place of what Allah or His Messenger (peace and blessings of Allah be upon him) have stated.

In reality, non-Muslims are either of bad intentions or they are ignorant of the final revelation that has come from Allah via the Prophet Muhammad (peace and blessings of Allah be upon him). Therefore, when it comes to spiritual knowledge, worship and belief in God, ethics and morals, they have virtually nothing—if anything at all—to offer the Muslim. Indeed, they can only harm the Muslim.

Since most non-Muslims do not understand Islam at all—and perhaps view it within the light of their own faiths that have been modernized—even those who seem sympathetic to Muslims want something from Muslims that is no more than an abandonment of Islam. Allah will judge such people who think themselves sincere and just. However, that does not change what the Muslim's attitude must be today: he must stick to his religion no matter how much these people strive, no matter how good their intentions are made to look and no matter how many wonderful sounding slogans they may give.

In other words, in what they see as the best approach for Muslims, they want to see Islam changed. This is in reality nothing more than them taking the Muslim away from the path of purification. Even if one claims that their intentions are good but they are simply ignorant, the end result is the same for the Muslim: they are working to distort the path of purification. The result is clearly one: The Muslim must remain on the Straight Path and ignore any suggestions to do otherwise.

Of course, there is yet another group of non-Muslims who have nothing but a clear hatred for Islam. Among this group there are even those who have a hatred for anything truly moral. Their views of Islam are totally biased and their goal is simply to destroy Islam. These types of people do not need much comment because their hatred is clear and any perceptive Muslim would not give their statements much consideration.

Summary

In this chapter, the major impediments and dangers to one's spiritual purification were covered. The different topics may be summarized as follows:

(1) Desires, lusts and passions: These are the urges that occur in the soul and drive a person to commit an act that he knows is displeasing to Allah. Unless one works to control and overcome these desires, they can be disastrous for his effort of purification. Indeed, they can even completely overcome the person and become the "god" which he starts to worship.

(2) Ignorance, doubts and misconceptions: It is via ignorance that one does not know what the correct path is. When a person does not realize his own ignorance, he acts thinking that what he is doing is correct while it may actually be very harmful. In addition, ignorance can also lead to doubts and uncertainty. Doubts and uncertainty in turn affect a person's resolve and willingness to sacrifice to remain upon the path of purification.

(3) Innovations and heresies: These are of extreme danger for the purification of the soul. In essence, they can lead a person down an errant path while he believes that he is following nothing but the truth. It is only by sound knowledge and by following the way of the Prophet (peace and blessings of Allah be upon him) closely that one can avoid falling into this major pitfall.

(4) Sins: One gets closer to Allah by acts of obedience and one distances himself from Allah by sins and acts of disobedience. No matter whether the sin is a major or minor one, it signifies, at least to some extent, a step back in one's journey of spiritual purification.

(5) Being overcome by this world and its glitter: One of the greatest dangers, especially in this day and age, is to be overcome with all of the "pleasures and excitement" that this world has to offer. This worldly life can make one lose one's focus. Instead of concentrating on the Hereafter, one begins to work to accumulate the goods of this world. The situation can be so bad that the individual sacrifices the Hereafter for this life. This would sound a crushing defeat for the soul's purification process.

(6) Evil companions, environment and surroundings: One's surroundings and one's friends can greatly influence an individual. For example, at the very least, evil friends may suggest deeds and ideas that are displeasing to Allah and harmful to the soul. Beyond that, they may further encourage and even help the person perform acts that are clearly disliked by Allah. Such friends and environments can clearly be a hindrance in one's path of purification.

(7) Satan and his soldiers: When Allah created man, He had already created an enemy that was going to test his will and his devotion to Allah. When mankind gives into Satan, Satan's only goal is to drag him into the Hell-fire. To protect himself on the path of purification, the believer must always be aware of Satan and his ways of operating.

(8) The enemies of Allah (those who have earned His wrath and those who have gone astray): These are the people who have either knowingly or unknowingly gone away from the path of purification. One must always be wary of them as they will either intentionally try to drive a person away from the Straight Path or they may inadvertently misadvise a Muslim causing him to swerve from the Straight Path.

Chapter 8
The Path and Goal of Purification of the Sufis vis-à-vis the Way of the Sunnah

As was noted in the introduction, historically and contemporarily speaking, the Sufis claim to follow the path of purification. It was also noted that this book is certainly not meant to be a critique of Sufism. However, since Sufis claim to be those who know best about purification of the soul[1], this work would be incomplete without some comparison between the path of purification as clearly defined in the Quran and Sunnah vis-à-vis the path of purification espoused in the various works of Sufi leaders and "shaikhs". For brevity's sake only the following points that were discussed earlier in the light of the Quran and Sunnah will be discussed:

(1) The path and goal of purification of the soul;

---

[1] It is strange how "purified" Sufis openly speak about the great blessings and unveilings they receive. They imply or explicitly state that they have moved along the stages to the level of being purified souls, with all of reality open to them, while Allah has clearly warned in the Quran, "Have you seen those who claim purity for themselves? Nay, but Allah does purify whom He pleases" (*al-Nisaa* 49). If others were to make the same types of claim that some Sufis make (having seen Allah and all truths revealed to them, sitting in the presence of the prophets and so forth), they would probably be branded hypocrites or grave sinners due to their boasting. Yet for some inexplicable reason, such behavior and statements are generally accepted from this group who claims to know the mysteries of purification. Another amazing aspect is how quickly and "arrogantly" some of them claim that they meet with Allah or received direct revelation or inspiration from Allah, although they have no real proof to back up their claims. At the very least, before making such claims, they should fear the warning contained in the verse, "Who can be more wicked than one who invents a lie against Allah, or said, 'I have received inspiration,' when he has received none, or (again) who says, 'I can reveal the like of what Allah has revealed?' If you could but see how the wicked (do fare) in the flood of confusion at death! The angels stretch forth their hands, (saying), 'Yield up your souls: this day shall you receive your reward, a penalty of shame, for that you used to tell lies against Allah, and scornfully reject His Signs'" (*al-Anaam* 93).

(2) The concept of love of Allah among the Sufis, being one of the obligatory acts of the heart discussed earlier;

(3) The attitude of the Sufis toward attaining knowledge of the Quran and Sunnah, discussed earlier as an important means to aid one in the purification of the soul;

(4) The Sufi concept of repentance, also discussed earlier as an important means to aid one in the purification of the soul.

Before beginning this discourse an important point needs to be made. Like all heretical groups, not all Sufis are the same.[1] Indeed, not everyone who has even a leaning toward Sufism is the same. Some are much more steeped in heretical beliefs and practices than others. However, by definition and their own admission, there must be something in Sufism that is distinct and separate from what all other scholars recognize to be the clear and manifest teachings of the Quran and Sunnah. Hence, by definition, there must be something new—that is, an innovation according to the Shareeah—in their beliefs, way or practice. Therefore, the important point to keep in mind is that once a person starts following a heresy or innovation, no matter how small, it becomes easier for him to start following a greater and worse heresy. This is a very dangerous path that can lead one to pure *kufr* and falling out of the fold of Islam.[2] The only real way to save oneself from such a danger is to avoid all heresies and innovations, no matter how "small" they seem to be. Indeed, this

---

[1] Mahmood Al-Qaasim has convincingly argued that all Sufi groups have, in essence, the same beliefs and the same goals. [See Mahmood al-Qaasim, *Al-Kashf an Haqeeqah al-Soofiyah li-Awal Marrah fi al-Tareekh* (Amman, Jordan: al-Maktabah al-Islaamiyah, 1413 A.H.), pp. 9-308.] However, even if that is the case, it does not mean that everyone who is influenced by Sufism is knowledgeable of the actual teachings and goal of the Sufi group that he is in contact with. Furthermore, even some of those who have been considered within the fold of the *ahl al-sunnah wa al-jamaah* and non-extremist Sufis had, upon closer inspection, many teachings that clearly violated the principle of *tauheed* or Islamic monotheism. One example of this nature is Abu al-Qasim al-Junaid whose thoughts are studied in detail in David Ludwig Martin, "Al-Fana' (Mystical Annihilation of the Soul) and Al-Baqa' (Subsistence of the Soul) in the Work of Abu al-Qasim al-Junayd al-Baghdadi" (Ph.D. dissertation, University of California at Los Angeles, 1984), *passim*.

[2] One of the ways of Satan is to lead people into greater and greater sins. What starts out as something small is made bigger and bigger over time. For more on this point and its relation to innovations, see Saeed al-Ghaamdi, *Haqeeqat al-Bidah wa Ahkaamuhu* (Riyadh: Maktabah al-Rushd, 1992), vol. 1, pp. 79-86.

in itself is an important aspect of following the path of the purification of the soul.

The Path and Goal of Purification According to Sufism

The Path of Purification

Unfortunately, the essential instruction of Islam, that the way of self-purification or *tazkiyah* is by following the way of the Sunnah, seems to have been lost on some Muslims. They, therefore, turned to other paths for self-purification. In essence, over time, self-purification became the claimed monopoly of the groups known as the Sufi *tariqah*s or orders. This stronghold was reinforced by support given to the Sufis by the very influential Abu Haamid al-Ghazaali, the author of *Revival of the Religious Sciences* or *Ihyaa Uloom al-Deen*. He declared that the path of the Sufis was the best path for the purification of mankind—almost as if there was no such thing as the Sunnah of the Prophet (peace be upon him) and the path of his noble Companions and their followers as a means of purification. Concerning the Sufis, al-Ghazaali wrote,

> I learnt with certainty that it is above all the mystics [Sufis] who walk on the road of God; their life is the best life, their method the soundest method, their character the purest character; indeed, were the intellect of the intellectuals and the learning of the learned and the scholarship of the scholars, who are versed in the profundities of revealed truth, brought together in the attempt to improve the life and character of the mystics, they would find no way of doing so.[1]

Historically, what has been known as Sufism passed through three distinct stages. The original Sufis—that is, those who later people called Sufis although they were known simply as

---

[1] Montgomery Watt, *The Faith of Practice of al-Ghazali* (Chicago: Kazi Publications, 1982), p. 60.

"worshippers"—were basically pious people, some having great knowledge of the Quran and Sunnah, who stressed the Islamic concepts of *ibaadah* (worship) and *zuhd* (impartiality to the things of this world) as found in the Sunnah of the Prophet (peace be upon him). Their attitude was in response to what they viewed as an over indulgence in worldly luxuries as the Islamic state grew and became richer. Over time, though, this simple stress on some basic concepts led to an entire edifice of a specific terminology (some Islamically correct, some not) used by spiritual leaders to propagate the essential teachings of this outlook. Finally, in its third stage, partially due to foreign influences, the movement began to develop its own philosophy and practices—such as the goal of personal incarnation and recognition of monism—which are alien to the Quran and Sunnah.[1] The result was that the Sunnah was disregarded as *the* way of *tazkiyah* in favor of the innovations that the Sufis invented.

The next obvious question then is: What is the path of purification that is prescribed by the Sufis and how does that differ, if at all, from the way taught by the Quran and the Sunnah?[2]

The path to become a *wali* (a "saint" or devoted servant from the elite of devoted servants) of Allah is a lengthy and arduous journey for the Sufis. A person must pass from state to state. He must exert himself and go through specific spiritual exercises and routines before he can get to the exalted state of being a Sufi *wali*. Mention was made earlier of the importance of understanding the goal and understanding the true beliefs. Herein is a classic example of how the Sufis were misled.

In one approach, perhaps an approach that is much closer to the Sunnah than that espoused by other Sufis, that path starts with fulfilling obligatory deeds. However, in the second level, when the "student" moves on, al-Ghazzaali recommends that he only perform the obligatory deeds and not perform the voluntary

---

[1] For a somewhat similar discussion, see Ihsaan Ilaahi Dhaheer, *al-Tasawwuf: Al-Mansha wa al-Masaadir* (Lahore, Pakistan: Idaarah Tarjumaan al-Sunnah, 1986), pp. 40-48.

[2] Due to space limitations, this topic cannot be dealt with in great detail. However, the interested reader may consult the different sources that are quoted throughout this section.

deeds as there are more important matters to tend to.[1] There are, in fact, many different levels or stages that a disciple must go through, each in its proper turn.

The path of the Sufis and its various stages entail many aspects that are not to be found in the Quran and Sunnah. These include a type of *zuhd* (renunciation of the world) that is not found in the Quran or Sunnah.[2] One is also expected to practice a kind of monasticism where one retires from the relations of this world, even if one has a wife and children.[3] Then they also have their own special forms of *dhikr*[4] and rhythmic chanting[5], listening

---

[1] Abu Haamid Muhammad al-Ghazzaali, *Ihyaa Uloom al-Deen* (Beirut: Daar al-Marifah, n.d.), vol. 2, pp. 19-20.

[2] For example, Sahl ibn Abdullah al-Tustari favored near starvation as a part of *zuhd*. He even was opposed to those who ate only with the intention of making themselves strong enough to perform the obligatory deeds. He stated that not being able to perform the obligatory deeds because one has not eaten enough is better than being able to perform the deeds with a full stomach. He argued that the prayer of a near starving person made sitting is better than the prayer performed standing. Ibn al-Jauzi responds by saying that when one eats to make oneself strong enough to perform the obligatory deeds, that act of eating is a form of worship in itself. See ibn al-Jauzi, *Talbees Iblees*, p. 204; Ibraheem Hilaal, Introduction to al-Shaukaani, *Qatr*, pp. 154-155; Fareed, *Tazkiyah*, pp. 37-41. Furthermore, although it is confirmed that the Prophet (peace be upon him) ate meat and did not say that it was spiritually harmful, some Sufis stated, "Eating just a quarter's amount of meat deadens the heart for forty days." Quoted in ibn al-Jauzi, *Talbees*, p. 203; Hilaal, p. 156.

[3] This retirement and monasticism is considered a must at the beginning of the rites of passage. (See Hilaal, p. 157.) Al-Qushairi said, "The servant cannot completely get close to Allah unless he gets away from the creation." [See Abdul Kareem al-Qushairi, *Al-Risaalah al-Qushairiyyah* (Muhammad Ali Sabeeh, 1957), p. 42.] On the other hand, al-Shaukaani pointed out that if he interacts with the people in the proper way (such as teaching them or ordering good and eradicating evil), he gets closer to Allah by his interaction with the creation. (See al-Shaukaani, *Qatr*, pp. 417-418.)

[4] A common form of their *dhikr* is simply to repeat Allah's name over and over again or simply to say, "He, He," over and over again. This is not the type of *dhikr* that was taught by the Prophet (peace be upon him). As noted earlier, every expression of *dhikr* taught by the Prophet (peace be upon him) was a complete sentence with an understandable meaning. For example, one repeats, "Allah is greatest," "All praise be to Allah," "There is none worthy of worship except Allah" and so forth. See Fareed, *Tazkiyah*, pp. 35-37.

[5] Much of their *dhikr* is more akin to chanting than it is to *dhikr*. Al-Sahuwaardi said, "Our purpose is not to make mention of Allah but to make all of the heart concentrate on one matter in order for it to be ready for what appears to it." (Quoted in Hilaal, p. 173.) Ibn Taimiyyah quoted a similar passage from one of them who also said that it makes no difference what the person is chanting at that time, whether it be the name of Allah or even some idol. (Quoted in Hilaal, p. 173.) For more about their *dhikr*, see M. al-Qaasim, pp. 338-341.

to songs and music as well as dancing.[1] After all of these, one finally "witnesses" Allah. This, for them, is the essence of being a *wali* and the goal of this creation.[2]

A typical or common view of the path of *tazkiyah* among the Sufis is a seven-step approach. These seven steps are the following:

(1) Search. This involves the desire to seek the inward self and it involves "many years of effort to detach the soul from worldly desires and to cleanse the spirit from mundane passions."

(2) Love: Here, "the seeker realizes the hardships of purifying the heart and spirit in pursuit of the 'divine union.'"

(3) Knowledge: Here the seeker begins to learn the inward, intuitive knowledge.

(4) Detachment: "This is the period that the seeker should relinquish all dependence 'upon others and upon the world' and put his total trust on God."

(5) Divine Oneness or Unification: "This station teaches the Oneness and Unity of Divine Essence beyond all the multiplicities and varieties and this state 'dissolves the sense of thou and I, of this or that, of here and there, of now and then, and realized all in God and God in all.'"

(6) Wonder: This comprises a stage wherein the person becomes confused and tries to get beyond self-consciousness, losing a sense of time and space.

(7) Extinction: In this stage, "'the lower self dies and the higher soul is unified with the one reality, the Godhead, as drops unify with the ocean, a state of final union.' In this state, the triumphant seeker realizes 'the God within by knowing himself.'"[3]

---

[1] Like many modern-day Christians, Sufis considered singing and dancing as a way of getting closer to Allah. These actions stir the emotions, which they claim is simply another way of expressing one's love for God. In fact, for many of them, listening to the Quran does not have as much of an effect on them as the music and singing that they prefer. See Hilaal, pp. 161-166; Fareed, *Tazkiyah*, pp. 32-35,

[2] Cf., Hilaal, pp. 149-181.

[3] The above is from Hossein Manoochehri, "Towards an Explanation of the Islamic Ideal of Human Perfection (With Emphasis on the Doctrine of Inner Jihad)" (Ph.D. dissertation, University of Kansas, 1988), pp. 205-207. Manoochehri states that the stages may not always be exactly the same and in this order but the general view and approach is the same among the different Sufi orders.

The Goal of the Path of Purification

As discussed in detail earlier, the goal of *tazkiyah* (purification) according to the Quran and Sunnah is to become as complete a servant of Allah as one can be. The goal of *tazkiyah* among the Sufis is completely different. It is not the worship of Allah that is their goal. Manoochehri notes, "Almost all Sufi branches, although different on the stages of mystical journey... focus on the concept of Unity (*Tawhid*)... to develop their theory of union of man with God as the ultimate goal of a Sufi's mystical journey."[1]

Hence, the goals of the Sufis are the witnessing of Allah in this life, getting knowledge directly from Allah (which makes them no longer in need of the Quran and Sunnah[2]), the supposed temporary unifying with Allah or the complete loss of one's humanity in the realization that everything is Allah.[3] The goal for many others is to recognize that all of this creation is simply an illusory manifestation of Allah and that everything and everyone is "part" of Allah or is Allah. (This is also part of the concept known as *wahdat al-wujud* or monism.) In fact, in Sufi works such as Sanoosi's *Salsabil* and the Qaadiri Sufi work *al-Fuyoodhaat al-Rabbaaniyyah*, they clarify the stages that a "seeker" is to go through, very similar to the seven stages described above. For example, the fourth stage is that of the "tranquil soul" where one is in journey with God and is living in the mystery of the heart. The fifth stage is that of the "contented soul" wherein one is journeying within God and is residing within the mystery of the mystery. The ultimate goal

---

[1] Manoochehri, p. 214.

[2] The early Sufi Abu Yazeed al-Bustaami said, "Those poor people [referring to the scholars of hadith, *fiqh*, *tafseer* and so forth]. They take their knowledge from the dead on the authority of the dead while we take our knowledge directly from the Living who does not die." (Quoted in ibn al-Jauzi, *Talbees*, p. 320.) The knowledge from the "dead on the authority of the dead" is the knowledge of the Quran, hadith and fiqh that has been passed on from the Prophet (peace be upon him) and his Companions. That type of knowledge is not what al-Bustaami and his likes are interested in.

[3] This last concept is known as *wahdat al-wujood* (pantheism or monism). It is believed in by a number of Sufis, especially the more extreme among them. It is a *kufr* (blasphemy) that is worse than the *kufr* of the Christians. The Christians claimed that Jesus and God form one unity while these Sufis claim that all of creation is nothing but Allah Himself. For more on this concept, see Mahmood al-Qaasim, pp. 105-262 and 703-712.

is the seventh stage or that of "the perfected soul" wherein one is journeying into God, witnessing the world of plurality and oneness, living in God and the complete essence of God (*dhaat al-kull*).[1]

A Critique of the Goal and the Path of Sufism

Obviously the goal of the Sufis cannot be claimed to be the same as the goal of life as stated in the Quran. The Quran never encourages the Muslims to become one with Allah. As was made abundantly clear earlier, the Quran orders the Muslims to worship Allah by believing in Him, submitting to Him and obeying His commands. Allah says,

وَمَا خَلَقْتُ ٱلْجِنَّ وَٱلْإِنسَ إِلَّا لِيَعْبُدُونِ

"I have only created jinn and men, that they may worship Me" (*al-Dhaariyaat* 56). And, furthermore, the Quran repeatedly stresses the difference between the Creator and the created. There is no one and nothing similar to Allah. Allah has said, for example,

قُلْ هُوَ ٱللَّهُ أَحَدٌ ۝١ ٱللَّهُ ٱلصَّمَدُ ۝٢ لَمْ يَلِدْ وَلَمْ يُولَدْ ۝٣ وَلَمْ يَكُن لَّهُۥ كُفُوًا أَحَدٌۢ

"Say: He is Allah, the One, the Unique, He begets not nor was He begotten, and there is none like unto Him" (*al-Ikhlaas* 1-4).

The Sufi path and the goal that al-Ghazaali claimed no one could ever improve upon is, in general, a heretical path that is not related to the way of the Prophet (peace and blessings of Allah be upon him). Therefore, it will not lead to one becoming a beloved of Allah or a true *wali* as has been expressed in this hadith.

In critiquing their approach, ibn Taimiyyah notes that what the Sufis call different "stages" are not stages that the person progresses or moves through but, in fact, every believer should possess all of them at all times. He wrote, "Everyone, the elite and

[1] Cf., J. Spencer Trimingham, *The Sufi Orders in Islam* (New York: Oxford University Press, 1998), pp. 152-154; Manoochehri, p. 210.

the commoners, must fulfill these [acts] and leaving them is not praiseworthy under any circumstances even if the person has moved on to a higher state."[1] On the other hand, the Sufi al-Hujwiri wrote, "It is not permissible that he [any person] should **quit** 'his' station without fulfilling the obligations thereof. Thus, the first 'station' is repentance (*tauba*), then comes conversion (*inabat*), then renunciation (*zuhd*), then trust in God (*tawakkul*), and so on; it is not permissible that anyone should pretend to conversion without repentance, or to renunciation without conversion, or to trust in God without renunciation."[2] Actually, repentance should go hand in hand with putting one's trust and reliance in Allah. In fact, one turns to Allah to help him and guide him to repent.

Even more astonishing is that the Sufis even talk about a point wherein the person has gone beyond the "states". The same al-Hujwiri wrote,

> They do not refer these expressions to "knowledge" (*ilm*) or to "state" (*hal*), but apply them solely to the degree of perfection attained by the saints who have become free from the pains of mortification and have escaped from the prison of "stations" and the vicissitude of "states", and whose search has ended in discovery, so that they have seen all things visible, and have heard all things audible, and have discovered all the secrets of the heart...[3]

Some of the Sufis explicitly declare the goal to be "knowing Allah" or knowledge about Allah (*marifah*). Therefore, they do not require worship or acting in accord with the Shareeah once one has achieved the reality of the knowledge. They even say that the actions prescribed in the Shareeah were not obligatory upon the prophets but they performed them only to convey the message and to lead the people. Some Sufis base this claim on a gross misinterpretation of the verse,

---

[1] Ibn Taimiyyah, *Majmoo*, vol. 10, p. 16.

[2] Ali Bin Uthman al-Hujwiri, *Kashf al-Mahjub* (Lahore: Islamic Book Foundation, 1982), p. 181. Note that al-Hujwiri is considered a "non-extreme" Sufi.

[3] Al-Hujwiri, p. 243.

وَٱعْبُدْ رَبَّكَ حَتَّىٰ يَأْتِيَكَ ٱلْيَقِينُ

"And worship Allah until the certainty comes to you" (*al-Hijr* 99). They claim that they have certainty and, hence, the Shareeah commands are no longer obligatory upon them. However, in this verse, certainty does not mean certainty of knowledge but it means death.[1]

The widely accepted Abu Haamid al-Ghazaali wrote that *al-mukaashifah* ("unveiling" of Allah) refers to "a light that appears in the heart when it is purified and cleansed of all base qualities." It is a result and goal of the process of *tazkiyah* according to the Sufi al-Ghazzaali. He then says that this light opens to the person many realities, including all of Allah's attributes and qualities. This light gives the person the knowledge of prophecy and how the angel brought the revelation to the Messenger of Allah (peace be upon him). All of the dominions of the heavens and the earth will become clear and exposed to the person who has experienced this unveiling.[2]

If a person's goal is simply to witness the reality of Allah or to realize that everything is actually only Allah, once he has achieved that goal, what is the purpose of continuing to perform deeds or acts of worship of Allah? Many Sufis themselves answered this question. They claimed that they were no longer obliged to pray or perform any of the acts of worship because they had already reached their goal. Furthermore, all the forbidden becomes permissible because the purpose of the forbidden is to help the person reach his goal.[3]

For the pantheistic or monistic Sufis, the question then becomes: When a person comes to the realization that everything is Allah, what is the purpose of good deeds or acts of worship? Everything is Allah and Allah is entirely perfect and good. Thus,

---

[1] Cf., ibn Katheer, *Tafseer* (Dar Taibah), vol. 4, p. 553. For more on this point and a refutation of the Sufis, see al-Kurdi, p. 169

[2] See Abu Haamid Muhammad al-Ghazzaali, *Ihyaa Uloom al-Deen* (Beirut: Daar al-Marifah, n.d), vol. 1, pp. 19-20.

[3] For comments from Sufis on that matter, see ibn Taimiyyah, *Majmoo*, vol. 11, p. 403.

there is then no such thing as evil or sin. Hence, ibn Arabi[1], one of the most extreme of the pantheists and monists, once said in well-known lines of poetry,

"The Lord is reality and the slave is [the same] reality
Woe to me, then who is the one who is responsible for doing deeds?
If you say, 'The slave,' but he is the Lord
And if you say, 'The Lord,' then who can burden him with responsibility?"[2]

Ibn Taimiyyah described the ludicrous conclusions that result from such beliefs. Ibn Taimiyyah noted,

> The knowledgeable *shaikh* Kamaal al-Deen al-Maraaghi, the *shaikh* of his time, narrated to me when he came and it reached him what [the Sufis] say about *tauheed*: I read some of what they say of al-Afeef al-Tilimisaani [the leading Sufi of his time] and I found him in

[1] Muhiyy al-Deen Ibn Arabi (560-638 A.H.) is a rather controversial figure in Islam. Many authors like to refer to him as, "the greatest Shaikh." Like the lines of poetry upcoming in the text, his words are filled with clear and blatant *kufr* (blasphemies). Some people claim that he was writing at an esoteric level that only those who are deeply ingrained in the Sufi tradition can understand. If, as these people claim, ibn Arabi was presenting the same truths that are clearly and understandably presented in the Quran, hadith, statements of the Companions and thousands of scholars, there was no need for him to resort to such esoteric and confusing language. He could have stated them clearly, leading to no confusion while making his point understandable. In fact, the Prophet (peace be upon him) and his Companions never spoke words that were clearly *kufr* while apparently having some hidden meaning to them. Again, if he were supposedly presenting those same Islamic truths, he should be considered a poor writer who had no conception of how to present his material in a clear fashion while the Quran and the Prophet (peace be upon him) were able to present such information clearly. However, if ibn Arabi was teaching ideas that contradict the Quran and Sunnah—which was more likely the case as it is very difficult to try to reconcile his writings with the Quran and Sunnah—then his writings should be condemned for the pure *kufr* and blasphemies they contain. This much more logical approach has been the approach of many great scholars throughout the history of Islam. One could consult numerous works for further information about ibn Arabi including: Burhaan al-Deen al-Buqaaee, *Masra al-Tasawwuf au Tanbeeh al-Ghabi ila Takfeer ibn Arabi* (Daar al-Taqwa, n.d.), *passim*; Kamaal Isa, *Nadharaat fi Mutaqidaat ibn Arabi* (Jeddah: Daar al-Mujtama, 1986), *passim*; Abdul Qaadir al-Sanadi, *Kitaab ibn Arabi al-Soofi fi Meezaan al-Bahth wa al-Tahqeeq* (Buraida, Saudi Arabia: Daar al-Bukhaari, 1991), vol. 2, *passim*; Kamaal Aoon, *Kitaab al-Fatoohaat al-Makkiyyah wa ma Waraahu min Ayaad Khafiyyah* (Tanta, Egypt: Daar al-Basheer, 1989), *passim*.

[2] Quoted in Fareed, *Tazkiyah*, p. 50.

> contradiction with the Quran and Sunnah. When I mentioned that to him, he said, "The Quran does not contain *tauheed*. In fact, all of it is *shirk*. Whoever follows the Quran will not achieve *tauheed*." I said to him, "In your people's opinion, what is the difference between [having sexual intercourse with] a wife, a non-related woman and a sister. Or are they all the same?" He said, "The people who are veiled [from the truth] believe that they are forbidden [that is, to have sexual intercourse with a non-related woman or one's sister]. They are forbidden for them. But for us, they are not forbidden."[1]

These errant results are all the byproduct of an errant path and an errant goal of purification. After making some of the above points, Fareed concluded,

> We have presented this clear *kufr*— and quoting *kufr* is not in itself *kufr*— so that it may be made clear to our brethren how innovated methodologies take their followers away and where the path of misguidance leads its adherents. [We also presented it] to demonstrate the purity of the way of the *salaf*[2] and how their path is the path of safety and success in this life as it is also the path to Paradise, for it is the path of the prophets and those who followed in their footsteps.[3]

One final note concerning the path and goal of purification among the Sufis deals with the issue of the "scope of purification." It was noted earlier that the purification of the soul encompasses every aspect of one's life, including one's role in the family and society. Every act, no matter how "mundane," should be within the limits set by Allah's revelation. This is the behavior of the purified soul according to the Quran and Sunnah. Islahi contrasts that with the Sufi approach to this question:

---

[1] Ibn Taimiyyah, *Majmoo*, vol. 2, pp. 244-245. Ibn Taimiyyah then goes on to refute such blasphemous beliefs.

[2] The *salaf* are the pious early generations of Islam.

[3] Fareed, *Tazkiyah*, p. 51.

> In mysticism purification and development of self are confined to a very limited sphere of man's life. But in the Quran and the Sunnah it pervades and penetrates every aspect of our lives—not only individual but the collective life as well. The discussion in the second part of this [Islahi's] book will bring to light the fact that just as it is essential for the purification and development of self that man's relations with God be based on certain definite bases and without which self-purification is inconceivable, his relations with the society, the government and the mankind as a whole on certain definite bases are just as essential, and without them, self-culture is similarly inconceivable. In other words, we can also say that for purification and development of self, one's prayer, communion with God, his austere piety and extreme simplicity of style, dress and habits are not enough; to me, it is essential for him, from the Islamic point of view, to be devoted to the service of the society and to be a duty-conscious citizen of his state in its Islamic sense.[1]

The Sufi Attitude Toward Knowledge of the Quran and Sunnah

Previously in this work, the attaining of knowledge was mentioned as an important means of helping oneself along the path of purification. If Satan can somewhere keep a person from turning to the true sources of knowledge—the Quran and Sunnah—it can be easy for Satan to mislead the person, since he will be a person not able to recognize true guidance. In fact, any time one is told by someone who is supposedly an "Imam" or "shaikh," "Do not read, do not study, just listen to me...," a warning signal should immediately go off.[2] A common expression

---

[1] Islahi, pp. xi-xii.

[2] Idrees notes that the only way the Sufis can have people accept their supposed sources of knowledge is if they drive the people away from the Quran and Sunnah. See Idrees Muhammad Idrees, *Madhaahir al-Inhiraafaat al-Aqadiyyah ind al-Soofiyyah wa Atharuhaa al-Sayi ala al-Ummah al-Islaamiyyah* (Riyadh: Maktabah al-Rushd, 1998), vol. 1, p. 83.

is, "Knowledge is power," and although there is some problem with that expression the fact is that the best way to keep others under one's control and keep them blind to what is good for them is to keep them from obtaining knowledge. Hence, the person of knowledge becomes the greatest enemy to those who want to steer people away from the truth.[1]

Even though there are numerous verses and hadith explaining the virtues of seeking knowledge, one can find a general dislike among Sufis for true knowledge or what the Quran describes as *ilm*.[2] In fact, when speaking in a positive sense, Sufis rarely use the term *ilm*. Ibn al-Qayyim noted that they developed *marifah* or cognition. Islahi concludes that they use this new term because the old term, *ilm*, became inseparably associated with the Quran, Sunnah and the Shareeah. To them, this is not the "true" and "superior" knowledge. Hence, they coined a new term to refer to their supposed superior branch of knowledge.[3]

Since they claim to have their own sources of knowledge, such as directly from Allah via "unveiling,"[4] they do not stress the study of the Quran and Sunnah, especially beyond the first stages of initiation into the order. In fact, al-Ghazaali makes it very clear that true knowledge does not come via study and that is why the

---

[1] Indeed, the Sufi ibn Arabi stated in *al-Fatoohaat al-Makkiyyah* that the greatest and strongest enemies of the true "knowers of Allah" who get their knowledge directly from Allah—he is referring to Sufis and mystics like himself—are those who are the scholars of the written and recorded knowledge (meaning the Quran and Sunnah). He likens those scholars to the Pharaoh vis-à-vis the messengers. Cf., Idrees, vol. 1, p. 103.

[2] Even moderate Sufis such as al-Haruwi consider knowledge (*ilm*) to be a curtain preventing one from the true cognition. Cf., ibn al-Qayyim, *Madaarij*, vol. 3, p. 165.

[3] Cf., Islahi, pp. 43-44, fn. 1.

[4] Other sources of their supposed knowledge include meeting in visions, dreams and seances with the prophets and "saints" after their deaths, meeting with Khidhr and so forth. Hence, they claim to be receiving knowledge directly from Allah and the prophets without any intermediaries whatsoever. For example, in the famous and widely accepted work by al-Sulami, *Tabaqaat al-Soofiyyah*, the author recounts the following story: Ibraaheem ibn Adham's father was one of the kings of Khurasaan. One day he went out hunting with his father and he heard a call or a voice without seeing anyone. The voice said, "O Ibraaheem, was it for this that I created you and is this what I have ordered you?" Afterwards the voice said, "This is not why I created you nor what I ordered you." So then Ibraaheem left all of his possessions and lived in the deserts, valleys and forests seeking guidance. He then met the Prophet Dawood who taught him Allah's greatest name. After that, he met Khidhr who told him, "The one who taught you Allah's greatest name was my brother Dawood." Cf., Idrees, vol. 1, pp. 83ff.

Sufis, he says, do not stress the study of *ilm*.[1] He says that through spiritual exercises and struggle, effacing the blameworthy attributes and turning all of one's attention toward Allah, one receives that special light in his heart that makes all matters clear to him, as described earlier. He says that such was the way by which the prophets received their knowledge. So, he says, one should free one's mind from all other thoughts and not think about reading the Quran, studying its commentary or recording hadith. Instead, one should strive to have the patience needed to be able to concentrate on Allah and nothing else, while one's tongue is busy saying, "Allah, Allah..." Then he will receive the mercy and guidance that was bestowed upon the prophets and saints.[2]

In fact, it is not surprising that Sufis downplay the knowledge of the Quran and Sunnah. This is because their goal is to experience something which, they claim, is above the normal senses and beyond the limits of being proven. It is this level of knowledge that only the "elite" can appreciate. As Islahi noted,

> The true cognition which is the share of the selected few among the elite is beyond the reach of intellect, reasoning, proof and evidence. Those elevated to this position of cognition observe the truths and the facts instead of trying to perceive them through reason. They are then above the limits and restrictions of

---

[1] The Prophet (peace and blessings of Allah be upon him) clearly stated, "Knowledge is through learning." (Recorded by al-Bukhari in *mualaq* form.) Even though, the Prophet (peace and blessings of Allah be upon him) said that, al-Ghazaali argues in *Ihyaa Uloom al-Deen* about the *muaamalaat* (practical matters) rather than the knowledge of the unveiling (*ilm al-mukaashafah*) because, he said, "One is not allowed to write [that latter knowledge] down in books although it is the real purpose of the seeker." *Ihyaa*, vol. 1, pp. 10-11. It is interesting to note that the Quran is the speech of Allah and it was written down during the lifetime of the Prophet (peace and blessings of Allah be upon him), under his supervision. Similarly, the Prophet's speech is inspiration from Allah and the process of its recording also took place during the lifetime of the Prophet (peace and blessings of Allah be upon him). Although al-Ghazaali was well-aware of these true sources of knowledge and the fact that they were written down, he believes that what they have is so special and blessed that its ruling goes above and beyond what is permissible for the Quran and Sunnah, claiming that this special knowledge cannot be written about although it is the real purpose of the seeker. This directly implies that, in their boldness, they claim to have something superior to the Quran and Sunnah.

[2] Cf., Idrees, vol. 1, p. 90.

> knowledge and get lost in the person of the real Witnessed One.[1]

In other words, they, like the Christians, seek to avoid any questioning of their falsehood by claiming that it is a "mystery" beyond the means of a commoner to understand. If one cannot understand it, it is simply because he is ignorant and not of the elite. This is a very clever but completely fallacious argument. Every Muslim should and must realize that the Quran and Sunnah came for the complete guidance of mankind. If anything cannot be substantiated in any way via the Quran or in the actual experience of the Prophet (peace and blessings of Allah be upon him), it must not be a means to Allah but can, in reality, only be a means to Satan.

The reality, again, is that the Quran and the Sunnah are the essential sources of guidance. As soon as one ignores them, even to a small extent, or takes other sources in preference to them, one is bound to stray. In fact, as al-Abdul Lateef noted, it is this turning away from what the Prophet (peace and blessings of Allah be upon him) brought that lies at the root of the innovations and misguidance that one especially finds among the later day Sufis.[2] When one is straying, it is virtually impossible for the end result to be the purification of his soul, as the Sufis claim is their end result. Paradise, therefore, will also not be the final destination. Instead, it is as the Prophet has said,

شَرُّ الأُمُورِ مُحْدَثَاتُهَا وَكُلُّ بِدْعَةٍ ضَلالَةٌ

"The worst actions are the invented ones. And every innovation is a going astray (Ar., *dhalaalah*[3])." (Recorded by Muslim.) In other narrations he would say,

---

[1] Islahi, p. 49. Islahi has a lengthy and detailed refutation of the Sufi concept of knowledge. See Islahi, pp. 41-70.

[2] Al-Abdul Lateef, p. 18. He goes on to quote ibn Taimiyyah who noted that the innovations and heresies related to *sulook* (or following of the path of purification) are more than those heresies related to beliefs.

[3] The word *dhalaalah* means, "Erring, straying, or going astray; deviating from the right way or course, or from that which is right; missing or losing the right way." E. W. Lane, vol. 2, p. 1798.

وَكُلُّ ضَلَالَةٍ فِي النَّارِ

"And every going astray is in the hell fire." (Recorded by al-Nasaai.)

The Sufi Concept of Love of Allah

The love of Allah was discussed earlier as one of the obligatory acts of the heart. As an obligatory act, it has a leading role in the purification of the soul according to the Quran and Sunnah. However, in order for that role to be fulfilled properly, the concept of love must be understood and applied in the proper manner.

Sufis also emphasize the importance of the love of Allah. Al-Hujwiri writes about the concept of love (*mahabba*) for Allah[1] throughout his *Kashf al-Mahjub* but the following passage is representative of much of what he says on the topic.

> Master Abu l-Qasim Qushayri writes, "Love is the effacement of the lover's attributes and the establishment of the Beloved's essence,"[2] i.e. since the Beloved is subsistent (*baqi*) and the lover is annihilated (*fani*) the jealousy of love requires that the lover should make the subsistence of the Beloved absolute by negating himself, and he cannot negate his own attributes except by affirming the essence of the Beloved. No lover can stand by his own attributes, for in that case he would not need the Beloved's beauty; but when he knows that his life depends on the Beloved's beauty, he necessarily seeks to annihilate his own attributes, which

---

[1] He also writes about *ishq*, which is a separate and important category for the Sufis. *Ishq* is an excessive type of emotional love but this word is never found in the Quran or Sunnah to describe the relationship between Allah and the slaves of Allah; hence, it is best to avoid this type of terminology.

[2] Note how the Sufis concentrate on the aspect of essence of the self and the Beloved while forgetting the direct aspect of love as described in the Quran: love for Allah leading to submitting to His commands and prohibitions.

> veil him from his Beloved; and thus in love for his Friend he becomes an enemy to himself.[1]

And al-Kalabadhi wrote,

> One of the great Sufis said, "Love is a pleasure, and with God there is no pleasure: for the stations of reality are astonishment, surrender and bewilderment. The love of man for God is a reverence indwelling in his heart, and not countenancing the love of any other than God. The love of God for man is, that He afflicts him, and so renders him improper for any but Him. This is the sense of God's words: 'And I have chosen thee for Myself'." By the words "renders him improper for any but Him" he means, that there remains no part over in him wherewith he may attend to other things, or pay heed to material conditions.[2]

Perhaps it goes without saying that there is no source in the Quran or Sunnah in the belief that the soul must be negated and so on. Indeed, all of the Companions, and, in fact, the Prophet (peace be upon him) himself, were all well aware at all times of who they were, what their relationship was to Allah and how to act according to this relationship. This is the essence of worship that the Sufi masters, in their path of *tazkiya,* have neglected and therefore their teachings, goals and results are, for the most part, misguided.

One of the criticisms that ibn Taimiyyah makes of the Sufi view of love of Allah is that they love Allah without any will on their part. According to them, they submerge themselves in the will of Allah and lose their sense of self. Therefore, ibn Taimiyyah states, "They think that a human acts without any will, desire or love. This is an errant conception of faith, religion and the Hereafter."[3]

---

[1] al-Hujwiri, p. 311.
[2] Abu Bakr al-Kalabadhi, *The Doctrine of the Sufis*, A. J. Arberry, trans. (Cambridge: Cambridge University Press, 1989), pp. 102-3.
[3] Ibn Taimiyyah, *Majmoo*, vol. 10, p. 694.

In opposition to the Sufis also,[1] Ibn Taimiyyah saw a direct connection between loving Allah and sacrificing for His cause. Ibn Taimiyyah quoted the Quranic verse,

قُلْ إِن كَانَ ءَابَآؤُكُمْ وَأَبْنَآؤُكُمْ وَإِخْوَٰنُكُمْ وَأَزْوَٰجُكُمْ
وَعَشِيرَتُكُمْ وَأَمْوَٰلٌ ٱقْتَرَفْتُمُوهَا وَتِجَٰرَةٌ تَخْشَوْنَ كَسَادَهَا
وَمَسَٰكِنُ تَرْضَوْنَهَآ أَحَبَّ إِلَيْكُم مِّنَ ٱللَّهِ وَرَسُولِهِۦ وَجِهَادٍ فِى
سَبِيلِهِۦ فَتَرَبَّصُوا۟ حَتَّىٰ يَأْتِىَ ٱللَّهُ بِأَمْرِهِۦ ۗ وَٱللَّهُ لَا يَهْدِى ٱلْقَوْمَ
ٱلْفَٰسِقِينَ

"Say: If your fathers, and your sons, and your brethren, and your wives, and your tribe, and the wealth you have acquired, and merchandise for which you fear that there will be no sale, and dwellings you desire are dearer to you than Allah and His Messenger and jihad in His way, then wait till Allah brings His command to pass" (*al-Taubah* 24). This means that the true believer loves Allah, His Messenger and jihad in His way more than his own wealth or relatives of this world.[2] It is the love of Allah that drives the believer to face any hardship in order to please Allah, his beloved. Ibn Taimiyyah even defines jihad as "exerting one's abilities to achieve what Allah loves and to defend against what Allah dislikes."[3]

The Sufi Concept of Repentance

Al-Hujwiri gave the moderate Sufi view of repentance when he wrote,

---

[1] In general, the Sufis (in particular the later Sufis) were not fond of jihad since they saw in it a kind of displeasure with what Allah decreed for them. See Muhammad al-Abduh and Taariq Abdul Haleem, *al-Soofiyyah: Nashatuha wa Tatauraha* (al-Kuwait: Dar al-Arqam, 1986), pp. 92-95.
[2] Ibn Taimiyyah, *Majmoo*, vol. 10, p. 751.
[3] Ibid., vol. 10, pp. 193-194.

Tauba has three stations, viz., *tauba* through fear of divine punishment; *inabat,* through desire of Divine reward; and *aubat,* for the sake of keeping the Divine command. *Tauba* is the station of the mass of believers, and implies repentance from great sins; and *inabat* is the station of the saints and favorites of God; and *awbat* is the station of the prophets and apostles. *Tauba* is to return from great sins to obedience; *inabat* is to return from minor sins to love; and *awbat* is to return from one's self to God... Moses, while his attributes were subsistent, said, "I repent towards Thee" but the Prophet [Muhammad], while his attributes were annihilated[1], said, "I cannot tell Thy praise." Inasmuch as it behooves the penitent not to remember his own selfhood,[2] how should he remember his sin?... As regards the elect, it is impossible that they should repent of sin. Do not you perceive that all the world feel regret for having lost the vision of God? Moses desired that vision and repented, because he asked for it with his own volition, for in love personal volition is a taint. The people thought he had renounced the vision of God, but what he really renounced was his personal volition. As regards those who love God, they repent not only of the imperfection of a station below the station to which they have attained, but also of being conscious of any "station" or "state" whatsoever.... Ordinary men shall be questioned concerning their outward behavior, but the elect shall be questioned concerning the real nature of their conduct... Abu Hafs Haddad says: "Man has no part in repentance, because repentance is from God to Man, not from Man to God..." The repentance of fear is caused by revelation of God's majesty, while the repentance of shame is caused by vision of God's beauty.

[1] It is not established that the Prophet's attributes were ever annihilated at any time in his life.
[2] This is a constant teaching of the Sufis that, in fact, has no basis in the Quran or Sunnah.

> Those who feel shame are intoxicated, and those who feel fear are sober.[1]

Perhaps the above passage does not need much comment. It is a mixture of truth and concepts that have no relation to the Quran and Sunnah, such as, man has to lose his own selfhood, the Prophet (peace be upon him) was in a state where his senses were annihilated, ordinary men shall be questioned for their outward deeds only and so on. Al-Kalabadhi was a much earlier writer and therefore his writing is not filled with as many deviations as al-Hujwiri, although he does have some interesting quotes. On repentance, he quoted Ruwaym who said, "The meaning of repentance is that thou shouldst repent from repentance."[2]

Ibn Taimiyyah defines *taubah* as repenting from what one is returning from to what one is returning to. That is, it is returning from committing wrong by returning to Allah. In his essay on *taubah,* ibn Taimiyyah began with twenty-seven passages from the Quran and eleven hadith of the Prophet (peace be upon him).[3] He stated that the slave of Allah is *always* (that is, it is not just a state that one passes through) in need of repenting to Allah and asking for His forgiveness and that everyone must make *taubah* in one form or another, including even the prophets from Adam to Noah to Moses to Muhammad (peace and blessings of Allah be upon them all). The Messenger of Allah (peace be upon him), the leaders of the Muslims, constantly asked Allah to forgive him.[4] No stronger proof for the fact that one never gets beyond a level of having to repent can be found other than that the Messenger of Allah (peace and blessings of Allah be upon him) was ordered to ask for forgiveness after he was made successful in his struggle against the disbelievers and the religion was made dominant. At that time, Allah revealed

---

[1] al-Hujwiri, pp. 295-299.

[2] Al-Kalabadhi, p. 83. This is the kind of statement that many mystics make. At first it sounds like some philosophical truth has been uncovered—and it strikes directly at the heart and emotions. However, upon closer inspection, one will then realize that the statement actually is completely illogical and unacceptable. When one repents from repenting, he is performing another act of repentance. It is not possible to repent by repenting.

[3] Ibn Taimiyyah, "Risaalah fi al-Taubah," vol. 1, pp. 219-226.

[4] Ibn Taimiyyah, *al-Tuhfa*, p. 64.

the following command to the Messenger of Allah (peace and blessings of Allah be upon him),

إِذَا جَآءَ نَصْرُ ٱللَّهِ وَٱلْفَتْحُ ۝١ وَرَأَيْتَ ٱلنَّاسَ يَدْخُلُونَ فِى دِينِ ٱللَّهِ أَفْوَاجًا ۝٢ فَسَبِّحْ بِحَمْدِ رَبِّكَ وَٱسْتَغْفِرْهُ ۚ إِنَّهُۥ كَانَ تَوَّابًۢا

"When Allah's succor and the triumph comes, and you see mankind entering the religion of Allah in troops, then hymn the praises of your Lord and seek forgiveness of Him. Lo, He is ever ready to show mercy" (*al-Nasr* 1-3).

Conclusions Concerning the Sufi Path of Purification vis-à-vis the Way of the Sunnah

The way of purification of the Quran and Sunnah is perfect and complete. It cannot be improved upon. Any straying from it will mean a movement away from the Straight Path and away from what one's goal should be. The conclusion concerning Sufism is that if it possesses anything that is good and sound, that thing must have already been captured in the Quran and Sunnah itself. If it contains any path or teachings that are outside of the Quran and Sunnah, then that path or teachings must be condemned as not being able to purify one's soul. Hence, the concept of Sufism is either superfluous (unnecessary) or misleading (misguidance). In other words, one need only stick to the Quran, the Sunnah and what can be derived from those two sources. When one does that, he can rest assured that he is on the Straight Path, the path of purification of the soul. The person will be fulfilling his purpose in life, pleasing his Lord and in the Hereafter he will be from those whom Allah is pleased with, residing in the Paradise that Allah has promised to the true believers and workers of righteousness.

This is exactly what ibn Taimiyyah concluded when he stated,

> The *sulook* (that is, the proper way of behavior in totality) is the path that Allah and His Messenger ordered with regards to beliefs, worship and behavior.

> All of that is made clear in the Book and the Sunnah. Its place is like that of food without which a Believer cannot dispense. Hence, all of the Companions leaned *sulook* from the indications of the Book and the Sunnah and what was conveyed from the Messenger... Concerning *sulook* there are some issues concerning which the scholars may have differed but one can find in the Book and the Sunnah [relevant] texts that indicate what is correct concerning those [disputed issues], which are understood by most of the 'travelers.' Thus, the issues of *sulook* are from the same category as the issues of beliefs which are all explicitly stated in the Book and the Sunnah."[1]

Since all these matters are covered in the Quran and Sunnah, there is no need to look elsewhere for them.

Finally, it should be noted that the way of purification according to the Quran and Sunnah is the true and balanced approach. It avoids the extremes that the Sufis fell into—and it also avoids the extremes that some of the jurists unfortunately fell into throughout the years, which was to stress the outward deeds without regard to what was really occurring in the heart. This mistake on the part of jurists in the past or similar mistakes on the part of any callers to Islam today does not justify one fleeing from them and heading towards the opposite extreme. What it does justify is a correction in the calling to Islam and in the example that is set. The correction must be done so that people may see the true Islam and not be driven by the mistakes of the callers to Islam to an incorrect but more spiritual version of Islam. On this point, ibn Taimiyyah noted,

> Many of those who went deeply into fiqh deviated from the matters of obedience and worship in the heart, matters such as purity towards Allah, putting one's trust and reliance in Him, love for Him, fear and Him and the like. And many of the faqirs and Sufis deviated when it came to the Shareeah acts of obedience. Once they received the oneness in the heart and recognizing

[1] Ibn Taimiyyah, *Majmoo*, vol. 19, pp. 273-274.

of God, they would not ask about what Allah has obligated for them concerning prayers and other matters of the faith, such as reciting the Quran, words of remembrance and supplications. Indeed, they would not be concerned even if they do what Allah had forbidden them or performed heretical acts of worship like monasticism and so forth. Indeed, they would rather sit for sessions of singing and chanting than listening to the Quran.[1]

Ibn al-Qayyim also wrote,

> There are two types of worship of Allah [obligatory] upon the servant: The inward or esoteric form of worship and the outward form of worship. Hence, there is a type of worship obligatory on the heart. But there is also a type of worship upon the tongue and physical limbs. One must fulfil the outward forms of worship while at the same time freeing oneself from any inward form of worship that does not draw one closer to his Lord and for which there is no reward and no acceptance of his deed. When those concerned about the hearts saw the path of those others [meaning the jurists], they diverted from their path to direct their attention to the worship of the hearts. In essence, they cancelled the worship of the physical limbs. They claimed that the true purpose was the rectifying of the heart by its true service, while the limbs were simply followers. These two groups [the jurists and the Sufis] vehemently opposed each other. Those [Sufis] never turned their attention to the worship of the limbs and, thereby, the worship of their hearts was also destroyed and ruined. On the other hand, the others [the jurists] never turned their attention to the worship of the hearts and, therefore, the worship of their limbs and physical acts were destroyed and ruined. The true believers, the ones who truly are aware of Allah and His commands fulfill for Him the reality of esoteric and

[1] Ibn Taimiyyah, *Majmoo*, vol. 20, pp. 72-73.

> external worship. They present their hearts in service and they make their limbs follow that lead. Hence, the commander [the heart] and his soldiers [the physical limbs] stand in serving the Worshipped. This is the true essence of servitude [*uboodiyyah*].[1]

The proper and balanced approach is clear in Allah's words that are stated in the midst of discussing which foods (a clearly outward act) are permissible and which are not,

وَذَرُواْ ظَـٰهِرَ ٱلۡإِثۡمِ وَبَاطِنَهُۥٓۚ إِنَّ ٱلَّذِينَ يَكۡسِبُونَ ٱلۡإِثۡمَ سَيُجۡزَوۡنَ بِمَا كَانُواْ يَقۡتَرِفُونَ

"Eschew all sin, open or secret: those who earn sin will get due recompense for their earnings" (*al-Anaam* 120). In the next verse, Allah prohibits the eating of any animal upon which Allah's name was not mentioned and then reminds the believers:

أَوَمَن كَانَ مَيۡتٗا فَأَحۡيَيۡنَـٰهُ وَجَعَلۡنَا لَهُۥ نُورٗا يَمۡشِي بِهِۦ فِي ٱلنَّاسِ كَمَن مَّثَلُهُۥ فِي ٱلظُّلُمَـٰتِ لَيۡسَ بِخَارِجٖ مِّنۡهَاۚ كَذَٰلِكَ زُيِّنَ لِلۡكَـٰفِرِينَ مَا كَانُواْ يَعۡمَلُونَ

"Can he who was dead, to whom We gave life and a light whereby he can walk among men, be like him who is in the depths of darkness, from which he can never come? Thus to those without faith their own deeds seem pleasing" (*al-Anaam* 122).

---

[1] Quoted from Ibn al-Qayyim, *Badaai al-Fawaaid* by al-Abdul Lateef, pp. 27-28.

Chapter 9
The Results and Benefits of the Proper Purification of the Soul

As noted earlier, the true importance of purification of the soul for the individual and for society actually lies in the benefits and results of purifying the soul. It would be virtually impossible to try to discuss all of the goodness that comes to the one who has purified his soul. This would imply discussing all of the blessings that Allah bestows on His devoted servants in this world, in the grave, on the Day of Judgment and in Paradise. Such a discussion goes well beyond what one is even capable of discussing. Hence, in this chapter only a select and small portion of the great blessings and rewards that come to the purified soul will be discussed.

From the outset, though, the following point from Karzoon should be noted, "[The fruits of purification of the soul] are perpetual fruits for every times. The servant finds their taste, experiences their sweetness and moves about in its pleasures. Every time the person increases in the steps of purification, those fruits likewise increase."[1] Ibn al-Qayyim further stated,

> Do not consider that Allah's words, "Indeed, the righteous will be in pleasure and indeed the wicked will be in Hell-fire" [*al-Infitaar* 13-14] are restricted only to the pleasures and hell of the Hereafter alone. Actually, it applies to their [humans'] three stages, that is, the life in this world, the life in *al-barzakh* [after death and before resurrection] and the life in the permanent abode [after resurrection]. Those [purified souls] are in pleasure while the others are in a hell. Isn't pleasure only the pleasure of the heart and

[1] Karzoon, vol. 2, p. 753.

> punishment only the punishment of the heart? What punishment can be harsher than fear, worry, anxiety and uneasiness [faced by those whose souls are not purified]? [What can be harsher than] its turning away from Allah and the abode of the Hereafter, its clinging on to something other than Allah and its being disconnected from Allah?[1]

Karzoon also states that whoever strives to purify and improve his soul until he reaches the level of *ihsaan* shall achieve the happiness of this life and that of the Hereafter. This is the true happiness that differs greatly from the supposed and distorted happiness that people of this world always seek. Their yearnings and desperate search for happiness—the wrong type of happiness—simply increases their unhappiness and misery. It is true, he notes, that at first the achieving of this true happiness may involve some hardship and striving on the part of the individual. However, as he continues along its path, he will taste the true sweetness of this faith and he will experience the worth of his struggle.[2]

The Benefits of Purification of the Soul for the Individual in This Life

In the final analysis, the purification of the soul is only for the benefit of the human himself. It does not help or benefit Allah in the least. As quoted earlier, Allah clearly states,

وَمَن تَزَكَّىٰ فَإِنَّمَا يَتَزَكَّىٰ لِنَفْسِهِۦ وَإِلَى ٱللَّهِ ٱلْمَصِيرُ

"And whoever purifies himself does so for the benefit of his own soul; and the destination (of all) is to Allah" (*Faatir* 18).

---

[1] Muhammad ibn al-Qayyim, *Al-Jawaab al-Kaafi liman Sa`ala an al-Dawaa al-Shaafi* (Beirut: Dar al-Kutub al-Ilmiyyah, 1983), p. 88-89. Unfortunately, this author could not find any Quranic commentator who explicitly supports ibn al-Qayyim's interpretation of *al-Infitaar* given above, especially considering that the next verse reads, "They will [enter to] burn therein on the Day of Recompense" (*al-Infitaar* 15). Allah knows best.

[2] Karzoon, pp. 754-755.

Indeed, there are numerous verses of this nature that demonstrate that whenever any believer follows the truth, improves himself and does what is right, he is in reality only helping himself and benefiting his own soul. For example, in another verse, Allah says,

إِنَّآ أَنزَلْنَا عَلَيْكَ ٱلْكِتَـٰبَ لِلنَّاسِ بِٱلْحَقِّ ۖ فَمَنِ ٱهْتَدَىٰ فَلِنَفْسِهِۦ ۖ وَمَن ضَلَّ فَإِنَّمَا يَضِلُّ عَلَيْهَا ۖ وَمَآ أَنتَ عَلَيْهِم بِوَكِيلٍ

"Verily We have revealed the book to you in truth, for (instructing) mankind. He, then, who receives guidance benefits his own soul. But he who strays injures his own soul. Nor are you [O Muhammad] set over them to dispose of their affairs" (*al-Zumar* 41; see also, for example, *al-Anaam* 104 and *Fussilat* 46). Allah also says,

مَّنِ ٱهْتَدَىٰ فَإِنَّمَا يَهْتَدِى لِنَفْسِهِۦ ۖ وَمَن ضَلَّ فَإِنَّمَا يَضِلُّ عَلَيْهَا ۚ وَلَا تَزِرُ وَازِرَةٌ وِزْرَ أُخْرَىٰ ۗ وَمَا كُنَّا مُعَذِّبِينَ حَتَّىٰ نَبْعَثَ رَسُولًا

"Who receives guidance, receives it for his own benefit. Who goes astray does so to his own loss. No bearer of burdens can bear the burden of another nor would We visit with Our wrath until We had sent a messenger (to give warning)" (*al-Israa* 15).

When the person stands in front of Allah on the Day of Judgement, he will be standing alone. He will not be standing with his spiritual guide (*shaikh*), leader (*imaam*) or even with his Nation (*ummah*) as a whole. Hence, it is a must for every soul to find the means to purify himself, such that when he meets Allah, Allah will enter him among His devoted servants and into His paradise. As Allah has said,

وَمَن يَأْتِهِۦ مُؤْمِنًا قَدْ عَمِلَ ٱلصَّٰلِحَٰتِ فَأُو۟لَٰٓئِكَ لَهُمُ ٱلدَّرَجَٰتُ
ٱلْعُلَىٰ ﴿٧٥﴾ جَنَّٰتُ عَدْنٍ تَجْرِى مِن تَحْتِهَا ٱلْأَنْهَٰرُ خَٰلِدِينَ فِيهَا ۚ
وَذَٰلِكَ جَزَآءُ مَن تَزَكَّىٰ

"But such as come to Him as believers who have worked righteous deeds, for them are ranks exalted, Gardens of Eternity, beneath which flow rivers. They will dwell therein forever. Such is the reward of those who purify themselves (from evil)" (*Taha* 75-76).

In the following verse, a number of benefits are described for those who purify their souls. This verse is a reference to such people because it is only those people who truly follow and benefit from the revelation and reminder that Allah has sent. Allah says,

يَٰٓأَيُّهَا ٱلنَّاسُ قَدْ جَآءَتْكُم مَّوْعِظَةٌ مِّن رَّبِّكُمْ وَشِفَآءٌ لِّمَا فِى
ٱلصُّدُورِ وَهُدًى وَرَحْمَةٌ لِّلْمُؤْمِنِينَ ﴿٥٧﴾ قُلْ بِفَضْلِ ٱللَّهِ
وَبِرَحْمَتِهِۦ فَبِذَٰلِكَ فَلْيَفْرَحُوا۟ هُوَ خَيْرٌ مِّمَّا يَجْمَعُونَ

"O mankind, there has come to you admonition from your Lord and healing for what is in the breasts and guidance and mercy for the believers. Say, 'In the bounty of Allah and in His mercy—in that let them rejoice; it is better than what they accumulate'" (*Yoonus* 57-58). The benefits that accrue to the one who has purified his soul include understanding the admonition from his Lord, having a healing for the diseases in the heart as well as a guidance and mercy. This is the bounty of Allah that He has bestowed on the true believers and it is much more rewarding and pleasing than everything that anyone could amass in this worldly life.

Indeed, the one who purifies his soul by following Allah's guidance will never have to grieve or sorrow. On the other hand, the one who turns away from purifying his soul by turning away from the revelation that Allah revealed will be barred from all of those blessings. Allah describes that person's life and his experience on the Day of Resurrection in the following passage,

فَإِمَّا يَأْتِيَنَّكُم مِّنِّى هُدًى فَمَنِ ٱتَّبَعَ هُدَاىَ فَلَا يَضِلُّ وَلَا
يَشْقَىٰ ﴿١٢٣﴾ وَمَنْ أَعْرَضَ عَن ذِكْرِى فَإِنَّ لَهُۥ مَعِيشَةً ضَنكًا
وَنَحْشُرُهُۥ يَوْمَ ٱلْقِيَٰمَةِ أَعْمَىٰ ﴿١٢٤﴾ قَالَ رَبِّ لِمَ حَشَرْتَنِىٓ أَعْمَىٰ
وَقَدْ كُنتُ بَصِيرًا ﴿١٢٥﴾ قَالَ كَذَٰلِكَ أَتَتْكَ ءَايَٰتُنَا فَنَسِيتَهَا
وَكَذَٰلِكَ ٱلْيَوْمَ تُنسَىٰ ﴿١٢٦﴾ وَكَذَٰلِكَ نَجْزِى مَنْ أَسْرَفَ وَلَمْ
يُؤْمِنۢ بِـَٔايَٰتِ رَبِّهِۦ وَلَعَذَابُ ٱلْءَاخِرَةِ أَشَدُّ وَأَبْقَىٰٓ

"But if, as is sure, there comes to you guidance from Me, whosoever follows My guidance, will not lose his way, nor fall into misery. But whosoever turns away from My Message, verily for him is a life narrowed down, and We shall raise him up blind on the Day of Judgment. He will say, 'O my Lord! Why have You raised me up blind, while I had sight (before)?' (Allah) will say, 'Thus did you, when Our Signs came to you, disregard them, so will you, this day, be disregarded'" (*Taha* 123-127).

All of the Benefits of *Taqwa*, *Ihsaan*, Patience and Sincerity

The purpose or goal of this book has not been to describe the characteristics of the purified soul.[1] However, *taqwa*[2], patience and sincerity are certainly some of the most important attributes

---

[1] Another work available in English, *Purification of the Soul* is, in fact, more of a description of those characteristics that a purified soul would possess. Cf., Ibn Rajab al-Hanbali, ibn al-Qayyim al-Jawziyya [sic] and Abu Hamid al-Ghazali, *The Purification of the Soul* (London: Al-Firdous Ltd. 1993), *passim*.

[2] *Taqwa* may be defined as a type of correct fear of Allah and God-consciousness.

of the purified soul.[1] What this implies is that the person who truly purifies his soul will receive those blessings and rewards that Allah gives to a believer due to those characteristics. For the sake of brevity, only a small number of examples will be given.

Due to a believer's patience and *taqwa*, Allah protects him from any long-run harm resulting from the evil plots of the disbelievers and enemies of Allah. Allah says,

إِن تَمْسَسْكُمْ حَسَنَةٌ تَسُؤْهُمْ وَإِن تُصِبْكُمْ سَيِّئَةٌ يَفْرَحُوا۟ بِهَا ۖ وَإِن تَصْبِرُوا۟ وَتَتَّقُوا۟ لَا يَضُرُّكُمْ كَيْدُهُمْ شَيْـًٔا ۗ إِنَّ ٱللَّهَ بِمَا يَعْمَلُونَ مُحِيطٌ

"If anything that is good befalls you, it grieves them. But if some misfortune overtakes you, they rejoice at it. But if you are constant and do right, not the least harm will their cunning do to you, for Allah compasses round about all that they do" (*ali-Imraan* 120).

Allah will also save the person of *taqwa* from the blazing Fire in the Hereafter. Allah says,

---

[1] In fact, Saleem al-Hilaali (pp. 19-20) equates *taqwa* with *tazkiyah al-nafs*. After quoting some verses concerning *taqwa*, he states that the reader may ask what is the relevance of those texts to purification of the soul. He replies, "O servant of Allah, don't you see that *taqwa* of Allah is exactly, step by step and inch by inch, the same as purification of the soul" His proof includes *al-Shams* verses 7-10 in which Allah says, "And by the soul and He who proportioned it and inspired it [with discernment of] its wickedness and its righteousness (*taqwa*), He has succeeded who purifies it and he has failed who instills it [with corruption]." He says that this is an explicit text showing that a person purifies his soul by *taqwa*. He also quotes *al-Najm* 32 and *al-Lail* 18 as further evidence. Admittedly, there is no question that *taqwa* is a key—if not the key—characteristic of purification of the soul. At the same time, though, it seems accepted by virtually all other writers that there is some difference between the two terms. Furthermore, al-Hilaali later quotes texts about having good character and then poses a similar question to that above and says (p. 23), "Isn't the purification of the soul but by having noble character, adhering to reforming one's character, clinging to its benchmarks and calling people to improving it." In sum, it seems that al-Hilaali's intention was not to be very precise as to the exact definition of purification of the soul. See Saleem ibn Eid al-Hilaali, *Manhaj al-Anbiyaa fi Tazkiyah al-Nufoos* (Al-Khobar, Saudi Arabia: Daar ibn Affaan, 1992), pp. 19-20 and 23.

فَأَنذَرْتُكُمْ نَارًا تَلَظَّىٰ ﴿١٤﴾ لَا يَصْلَىٰهَآ إِلَّا ٱلْأَشْقَى ﴿١٥﴾ ٱلَّذِى
كَذَّبَ وَتَوَلَّىٰ ﴿١٦﴾ وَسَيُجَنَّبُهَا ٱلْأَتْقَى ﴿١٧﴾ ٱلَّذِى يُؤْتِى مَالَهُۥ
يَتَزَكَّىٰ ﴿١٨﴾ وَمَا لِأَحَدٍ عِندَهُۥ مِن نِّعْمَةٍ تُجْزَىٰٓ ﴿١٩﴾ إِلَّا ٱبْتِغَآءَ
وَجْهِ رَبِّهِ ٱلْأَعْلَىٰ ﴿٢٠﴾ وَلَسَوْفَ يَرْضَىٰ ﴿٢١﴾

"So I have warned you of a Fire which is blazing. None will [enter to] burn therein except the most wretched one who had denied and turned away. But the *atqaa* (righteous one with *taqwa*) will avoid it—he who gives from his wealth to purify himself and not [giving] for anyone who has [done him] a favor to be rewarded but only seeking the Countenance of his Lord, Most High. And he is going to be satisfied" (*al-Lail* 14-17).

As a result of one's sincerity to Allah, Allah may protect the person from evil and lewd acts. This is what Allah did with His Prophet Joseph due to his sincerity. Allah says,

كَذَٰلِكَ لِنَصْرِفَ عَنْهُ ٱلسُّوٓءَ وَٱلْفَحْشَآءَ ۚ إِنَّهُۥ مِنْ عِبَادِنَا
ٱلْمُخْلَصِينَ

"Thus (did We order) that We might turn away from him (all) evil and shameful deeds for he was one of Our servants, sincere and purified" (*Yoosuf* 24).

A Special Love and Closeness with Allah

Allah says,

مَا تَقَرَّبَ إِلَيَّ عَبْدِي بِشَيْءٍ أَحَبَّ إِلَيَّ مِمَّا افْتَرَضْتُ عَلَيْهِ وَمَا يَزَالُ عَبْدِي يَتَقَرَّبُ
إِلَيَّ بِالنَّوَافِلِ حَتَّى أُحِبَّهُ فَإِذَا أَحْبَبْتُهُ كُنْتُ سَمْعَهُ الَّذِي يَسْمَعُ بِهِ وَبَصَرَهُ الَّذِي يُبْصِرُ
بِهِ وَيَدَهُ الَّتِي يَبْطِشُ بِهَا وَرِجْلَهُ الَّتِي يَمْشِي بِهَا وَإِنْ سَأَلَنِي لَأُعْطِيَنَّهُ وَلَئِنِ اسْتَعَاذَنِي

لَأُعِيذَنَّهُ وَمَا تَرَدَّدْتُ عَنْ شَيْءٍ أَنَا فَاعِلُهُ تَرَدُّدِي عَنْ نَفْسِ الْمُؤْمِنِ يَكْرَهُ الْمَوْتَ وَأَنَا أَكْرَهُ مَسَاءَتَهُ

"My servant does not draw near to Me with anything more loved by Me than the religious duties I have imposed upon him. And My servant continues to draw near to Me with supererogatory works so that I shall love him. When I love him, I am his hearing with which he hears, his seeing with which he sees, his hand with which he strikes, and his leg with which he walks. Were he to ask [something] of Me, I would surely give it to him; and were he to ask Me for refuge, I would surely grant him it." (Recorded by al-Bukhari.)

The love referred to in this hadith is a special love that is the result of following the purification process of performing the obligatory deeds followed by performing voluntary deeds. Allah then bestows upon such a person a special love for doing deeds that were not obligated of him. The slave is doing more than what is required of him simply to please Allah more. Therefore, this is a different type of love. The one who performs the obligatory deeds is beloved to Allah. There is no question about that. But the one who goes beyond and purifies his soul further via the voluntary deeds is even more beloved to Allah and gets the special love from Allah that is described herein. Hence, there are two types of love that come about due to two different causes. But it should not be forgotten that the first cause is a prerequisite for the second type of love. In other words, if a person does not perform the obligatory deeds, he will not receive the first or second type of love, even if he performs numerous voluntary deeds.[1]

---

[1] Al-Shaukaani, *Qatr*, pp. 419-421.

True Contentment, Peace and Honor in This Life

Allah has stated,

مَنْ عَمِلَ صَـٰلِحًا مِّن ذَكَرٍ أَوْ أُنثَىٰ وَهُوَ مُؤْمِنٌ فَلَنُحْيِيَنَّهُۥ حَيَوٰةً طَيِّبَةً وَلَنَجْزِيَنَّهُمْ أَجْرَهُم بِأَحْسَنِ مَا كَانُوا۟ يَعْمَلُونَ

"Whoever does righteous deeds—whether male or female—while a believer, We shall certainly give them a good life and We will certainly grant them their rewards in accordance to the best of what they used to perform" (*al-Nahl* 97). In his commentary to this verse, ibn Katheer notes that this means that whoever performs the righteous deeds, which are acts of obedience in accord with the Quran and Sunnah, will be given a good life in this world and in the Hereafter he will receive rewards according to the best of what he used to perform. He stated that "the good life" implies all forms of contentment and tranquility. Such has been reported from Ali, ibn Abbaas, Ikrimah and Wahb ibn Munnabih. It is also recorded from ibn Abbaas that it means happiness. Al-Dhuhaak states that it refers to lawful provisions and worship in this life.[1]

As noted previously, every Muslim must realize that true success and happiness do not lie in the possessing of wealth, power, status, fine cars and houses and all of the allurements of this world. In fact, those worldly possessions are not even the things that actually make a person rich in a true sense. The Prophet (peace and blessings of Allah be upon him) explained this fact most succinctly when he stated,

لَيْسَ الْغِنَى عَنْ كَثْرَةِ الْعَرَضِ وَلَكِنَّ الْغِنَى غِنَى النَّفْسِ

"True richness is not via much property and belongings but true richness is in self-contentment." (Recorded by al-Bukhari and Muslim.)

Indeed, there is no real benefit to any worldly possessions if one's soul is uneasy, depressed, extremely doubtful about its

---

[1] Ibn Katheer, *Tafseer*, vol. 4, p. 601.

own future, full of anxiety and always desiring for more when it can never be content with what it has. In general though, this is what happens to human beings; they are always filled with anxiety, concerned about losing what they have while always yearning for more. The Messenger of Allah (peace and blessings of Allah be upon him) pointed out this general fact of mankind when he said,

لَوْ أَنَّ لِابْنِ آدَمَ وَادِيًا مِنْ ذَهَبٍ أَحَبَّ أَنْ يَكُونَ لَهُ وَادِيَانِ

"If the human had one valley of gold, he would love to have two valleys worth." (Recorded by al-Bukhari.)

In fact, it is due to this misconception as to wherein lies the true happiness of this life that many are of the false impression that it is impossible to "enjoy" or be happy in both the life of this world as well as that of the Hereafter.[1] In reality, though, by concentrating one's intention on the Hereafter, the matters of this world become much "easier" and less tense. Allah thereby increases one's happiness in this world. In a very important hadith for this day and age, the Messenger of Allah (peace and blessings of Allah be upon him) said,

مَنْ كَانَتِ الآخِرَةُ هَمَّهُ جَعَلَ اللَّهُ غِنَاهُ فِي قَلْبِهِ وَجَمَعَ لَهُ شَمْلَهُ وَأَتَتْهُ الدُّنْيَا وَهِيَ رَاغِمَةٌ وَمَنْ كَانَتِ الدُّنْيَا هَمَّهُ جَعَلَ اللَّهُ فَقْرَهُ بَيْنَ عَيْنَيْهِ وَفَرَّقَ عَلَيْهِ شَمْلَهُ وَلَمْ يَأْتِهِ مِنَ الدُّنْيَا إِلاَّ مَا قُدِّرَ لَهُ

"If a person's main concern is the Hereafter, Allah puts his richness in his heart, makes his affairs together for him and gives to him the world while it is not desirable to him. And if a person's main concern is this world, Allah will put his poverty in front of his eyes, make his affairs disunited and will not give him of this world save what has been decreed for him."[2]

The real rest and the real happiness can only come to those whom Allah blesses with such a blessing and which is

---

[1] Cf., al-Bilaali, pp. 127ff.

[2] Recorded by al-Tirmidhi and ibn Maajah. According to al-Albaani, it is *sahih*. See al-Albaani, *Saheeh al-Jaami*, vol. 2, pp. 1110-1111.

received when one purifies one's soul and worships Allah alone with a true and complete form of worship. When a person accomplishes these matters, he becomes overcome with a joy that never leaves him and that is difficult to put into words.

Ibn Taimiyyah attempted to express the joy that he felt from his faith in Allah and the deeds he performed. He once said, "In this world there is a Paradise that whoever does not enter it will not enter the Paradise in the Hereafter." He also said, "What can my enemies do to me? Certainly, my paradise and garden are in my chest."[1] In fact, ibn al-Qayyim, ibn Taimiyyah's closest student who would visit him often in the citadel prison, stated,

> Allah knows that I have never seen anyone having a better life than him. [This was true] even though he was in straitened circumstances and not living in luxuries and comforts. On the contrary, he was on the opposite extreme. Even though he faced imprisonment, torture and threats, he still had the most pleasurable life among the people, with the most relaxed feelings, strongest in heart and happiest of all of them. The experiencing of joy could be seen on his face. Whenever we were very fearful, feeling bad expectations and felt the earth constricting upon us, we would come to him and we only needed to see him and listen to his words that all of those emotions would leave us. Instead, we would be filled with rest, strength, certainty and tranquility. Exalted be the One who allows His servant to witness His Paradise before he meets Him.[2]

Of course, such a beautiful feeling from one's faith was not restricted to ibn Taimiyyah. Ibn al-Qayyim quotes another devout

---

[1] Quoted in Ibn al-Qayyim, *al-Waabil al-Sayyib*, p. 73.

[2] Ibn al-Qayyim, *al-Waabil al-Sayyib*, p. 73. Of course, ibn Taimiyyah was not a Companion of the Prophet (peace and blessings of Allah be upon him) nor was he even a student of the Companions. Indeed, he lived some eight centuries after the Prophet (peace and blessings of Allah be upon him). In fact, in many ways, ibn Taimiyyah lived in an environment not very much different from the lives of many Muslims today. His devotion to the Quran, the Sunnah and the acts of purification of the soul, by the grace and mercy of Allah, allowed him to reach the stage which his close student ibn al-Qayyim described above.

Muslim as saying, "If the kings and the children of the kings knew what [felicity] we are in, they would fight us over it with their swords." Yet another stated, "The inhabitants of this world are miserable. They leave this world and they do not taste the most wonderful aspect that it contains." When asked what that was, he replied, "Love for Allah, knowing Him and remembering Him." Ibn al-Qayyim also quoted another who said, "There comes some times in which I say, 'If the people of Paradise are in a state like this, they are enjoying a good life.'"[1]

On the other hand, Allah says,

وَقَدۡ خَابَ مَن دَسَّىٰهَا

"And he fails who corrupts (*khaab*) it" (*al-Shams* 10). The Arabic word *al-khaibah* has many aspects to it, including:

(1) weakness in one's soul, as the soul does not have the strength and courage to follow what it knows is the truth;
(2) hesitation and confusion as every time it wants to do good, the soul drags it back down and fights it;
(3) true psychological humiliation as he is worshipping something that has no benefit to it and it is not worthy of a human being to be worshipping something of that nature;
(4) cowardice and stinginess as his soul knows that he is disobeying his Lord and he cannot look forward to anything positive; hence, he has to hang on to his life and everything that he possesses in the strongest fashion;
(5) loss of modesty and dignity as his soul drives him to be shameless acts to the point that he accepts them, supports them and loses all shame concerning them.

---

[1] See ibn al-Qayyim, *al-Waabil al-Sayyib*, pp. 73. Ibn al-Qayyim also quoted ibn Taimiyyah as saying, "If you do not find any sweetness and relaxation in your heart from a [good] deed, then you should suspect your heart. Verily, Allah is grateful. That is, He must reward the doer of a deed for his deed in this world by a sweetness he finds in his heart, a stronger feeling of relaxation and a joy in his eyes. If the person does not find these things, it means that something has entered upon his deed [and made it not correct and purely for Allah's sake]." See ibn al-Qayyim, *Madaarij*, vol. 2, p. 68.

This is all part of the reality that happens to him in this world. And that is all much less than the disgrace that he will face in the Hereafter.[1]

When one has purified his soul, it means that he has fulfilled the true meaning of *tauheed* or taking no one as a God other than Allah. This gives the believer an honor and a dignity that no other people could possibly comprehend. When a person finally comes upon the realization of the meaning of *tauheed,* it fills his heart with a feeling of true importance and recognition of his purpose in life. Hence, his life becomes an honorable one with an honorable purpose.[2] All of the desires and lusts should then be expelled from his heart as they are no longer befitting someone of that nature.

Furthermore, when one truly lives in the shade of *tauheed,* it means that he is not submitting to or bowing down to anyone other than Allah. Indeed, when a human bows down and grovels to anything other than Allah, he is truly disgracing himself. This is because nothing is deserving of such submissiveness except Allah. Hence, those who bend their lives out of shape trying to seek the lowly pleasures and prestige of this world and those who live their lives bowing down to other humans or false gods are, in reality, doing nothing but debasing themselves. They are performing acts that are not becoming a human in any way, shape or form. When the believer looks around him and sees everyone bowing down to false forms of worship and chasing useless matters, he feels very happy that Allah has guided him to Islam and this path of *tauheed.* This is, in fact, another aspect of the honor that purification of the soul brings to his heart.

In fact, in a number of passages in the Quran Allah makes it very clear that true nobility and honor belong only to Allah. In turn, He bestows it only upon His true believers. For example, Allah has said,

---

[1] For a similar discussion, see al-Bilaali, p. 33.

[2] This is true no matter how debased or despised he was before. Umar ibn al-Khattaab is quoted as saying, "We were the most despised people and then Allah honored us by Islam. Whenever we seek honor via something other than that which Allah honored us by, Allah will make us despised [again]." Recorded by al-Haakim and ibn Abi Shaibah.

مَن كَانَ يُرِيدُ ٱلْعِزَّةَ فَلِلَّهِ ٱلْعِزَّةُ جَمِيعًا

"If any do seek honor and glory, [know that] to Allah belong all glory and power" (*Faatir* 10). Allah also said,

وَلِلَّهِ ٱلْعِزَّةُ وَلِرَسُولِهِۦ وَلِلْمُؤْمِنِينَ وَلَٰكِنَّ ٱلْمُنَٰفِقِينَ لَا يَعْلَمُونَ

"Honor belongs to Allah and His Messenger, and to the Believers; but the hypocrites know not" (*al-Munaafiqoon* 8).

Furthermore, in the following verses, Allah makes it clear that many are seeking honor and dignity but they cannot achieve or find it because, simply put, they are seeking it from the wrong places. Some seek it by ignoring the tenets of the faith and trying to make friendships with disbelievers, thinking that such will somehow bring them some honor and distinction. Allah has said about them,

ٱلَّذِينَ يَتَّخِذُونَ ٱلْكَٰفِرِينَ أَوْلِيَآءَ مِن دُونِ ٱلْمُؤْمِنِينَ أَيَبْتَغُونَ عِندَهُمُ ٱلْعِزَّةَ فَإِنَّ ٱلْعِزَّةَ لِلَّهِ جَمِيعًا

"To those who take for friends unbelievers rather than believers [should be said]: Is it honor they seek among them? Nay all honor is with Allah" (*al-Nisaa* 139). Others seek it by worshipping their false gods. Concerning them Allah has said,

وَٱتَّخَذُوا۟ مِن دُونِ ٱللَّهِ ءَالِهَةً لِّيَكُونُوا۟ لَهُمْ عِزًّا ﴿٨١﴾ كَلَّا سَيَكْفُرُونَ بِعِبَادَتِهِمْ وَيَكُونُونَ عَلَيْهِمْ ضِدًّا

"And they have taken (for worship) gods other than Allah, to give them power and glory! Instead, they shall reject their worship, and become adversaries against them" (*Maryam* 81-82).

The Results of Purification of the Soul for the Muslim Nation (*Ummah*) and Society

In Chapter 3 there was a discussion of the importance of purification of the soul for the Muslim Nation as a whole. That discussion demonstrated that the purification of the soul is not a matter concerning individuals alone. Actually, it is a necessity for the Muslim nation as a whole. In this chapter, some of the benefits and results of that purification for the Muslim nation will be briefly discussed.

The prosperity and well-being of the society is going to be the result of the purification of the souls by the individuals of that society. When they consciously work to purify their own souls as well as the souls of those around them, the benefits and fruits of those efforts will be seen throughout the society as a whole. In particular, Allah will support them, give them victory and establish them in the land. When they believe, Allah then showers them with His blessings in various forms, as the following verse demonstrates:

وَلَوْ أَنَّ أَهْلَ ٱلْقُرَىٰٓ ءَامَنُوا۟ وَٱتَّقَوْا۟ لَفَتَحْنَا عَلَيْهِم بَرَكَـٰتٍ مِّنَ

ٱلسَّمَآءِ وَٱلْأَرْضِ وَلَـٰكِن كَذَّبُوا۟ فَأَخَذْنَـٰهُم بِمَا كَانُوا۟ يَكْسِبُونَ

"If the people of the towns had but believed and feared Allah, We should indeed have opened out to them (all kinds of) blessings from heaven and earth; but they rejected (the truth), and We brought them to task for their misdeeds" (*al-Araaf* 96).

Karzoon discusses many of the blessings and benefits that flow to any society that adheres to Islam (being of purified souls).[1] These include the following that spring directly from the basic teachings of Islam that such individuals are applying in their lives[2]:

---

[1] Cf., Karzoon, vol. 2, pp. 805-826.

[2] Of course, it is not necessary that everyone in the society be of purified souls. Indeed, there were hypocrites living in Madinah at the time of the Prophet (peace and blessings of Allah be upon him) yet that did not keep that community from enjoying the many blessings referred to above. The important aspect is that those of purified souls are the leaders and that the word of

(1) True brotherhood and love among the members of society: The Messenger of Allah (peace and blessings of Allah be upon him) said,

لا يُؤْمِنُ أَحَدُكُمْ حَتَّى يُحِبَّ لأخيهِ مَا يُحِبُّ لِنَفْسِهِ

"None of you truly believes until he loves for his brother what he loves for himself." (Recorded by al-Bukhari and Muslim.) In reality, it is only in a truly Islamic society wherein one can find a blessing of this nature. This is because the behavior of the purified souls is driven by their desire to please Allah. Indeed, when one truly understands the concept of faith, one realizes that he should love solely for the sake of Allah. In other words, he loves whatever Allah loves, which includes first and foremost the religion itself and the other believers. Hence, the believers love one another for the sake of Allah. This is a beneficial type of love that goes beyond mere expressions to actual care and concern for one another. It extends to a level where one tries to keep anything harmful from coming to his brothers and sisters. In fact, the Messenger of Allah (peace and blessings of Allah be upon him) gave a clear example of the behavior of the believers and how such behavior is pleasing to Allah. In a hadith recorded by al-Bukhari and Muslim on the authority of Abu Hurairah, the Messenger of Allah (peace and blessings of Allah be upon him) said,

مَرَّ رَجُلٌ بِغُصْنِ شَجَرَةٍ عَلَى ظَهْرِ طَرِيقٍ فَقَالَ وَاللَّهِ لَأُنَحِّيَنَّ هَذَا عَنِ الْمُسْلِمِينَ لا يُؤْذِيهِمْ فَأُدْخِلَ الْجَنَّةَ

"A person passed by a branch along the road and he said, 'By Allah, I shall certainly remove this from the Muslims so it will not harm them.' Thus he was entered into Paradise." (This wording is from Muslim.) In other words, from the most trivial matters to the most important matters, each individual believer is looking after the welfare of his fellow brethren and society as a whole. No worldly gain is the motive here, only the pleasure of Allah.

Allah is the main criterion for behavior and law. Hence, two very important factors work in such a society: the force of the law and the moral reliability of the majority of its people.

In fact, the true Muslims—those who are along the path of spiritual purification—have been described by the Prophet (peace and blessings of Allah be upon him) in the following hadith:

الْمُسْلِمُ مَنْ سَلِمَ الْمُسْلِمُونَ مِنْ لِسَانِهِ وَيَدِهِ

"The Muslim is the one from whose tongue and hand the Muslims are safe." (Recorded by al-Bukhari and Muslim.)

The spiritually purified people, therefore, seek not to harm others and they seek to protect others from harm. Indeed, they should be free of lowly, selfish motivations and ulterior motives, so therefore they can extend a true brotherhood and love to all the members of society. They would not seek to take advantage of each other. When they become purified in their souls, their actions also become pure and sincere. A true believer would never seek to harm, cheat or take advantage of anyone else. This righteous behavior then creates a special bond between the members of society.

This is, in fact, what occurred among the Companions. Allah has described how greatly they were changed due to their faith and how Allah brought their hearts together. Allah says,

وَٱذْكُرُواْ نِعْمَتَ ٱللَّهِ عَلَيْكُمْ إِذْ كُنتُمْ أَعْدَآءً فَأَلَّفَ بَيْنَ قُلُوبِكُمْ فَأَصْبَحْتُم بِنِعْمَتِهِۦٓ إِخْوَٰنًا وَكُنتُمْ عَلَىٰ شَفَا حُفْرَةٍ مِّنَ ٱلنَّارِ فَأَنقَذَكُم مِّنْهَا

"Remember [with gratitude] Allah's favor on you for you were enemies and He joined your hearts in love, so that by His Grace, you became brethren; and you were on the brink of the pit of Fire, and He saved you from it. Thus does Allah make His Signs clear to you that you may be guided" (*ali-Imraan* 103). Allah also makes it clear that this type of coming together of the hearts, that is the result of true faith, is something that cannot be achieved by the worldly alliances, friendships and means of drawing each other close to one another. Allah clearly states,

وَأَلَّفَ بَيْنَ قُلُوبِهِمْ ۚ لَوْ أَنفَقْتَ مَا فِي الْأَرْضِ جَمِيعًا مَّا أَلَّفْتَ
بَيْنَ قُلُوبِهِمْ وَلَٰكِنَّ اللَّهَ أَلَّفَ بَيْنَهُمْ ۚ إِنَّهُ عَزِيزٌ حَكِيمٌ

"And (moreover) He has put affection between their hearts: not if you had spent all that is in the earth could you have produced that affection. But Allah has done it: for He is Exalted in might, Wise" (*al-Anfaal* 63).

(2) Economic security, mutual assistance, support and compassion: Allah has ordered the believers,

وَتَعَاوَنُوا عَلَى الْبِرِّ وَالتَّقْوَىٰ ۖ وَلَا تَعَاوَنُوا عَلَى الْإِثْمِ وَالْعُدْوَانِ ۚ
وَاتَّقُوا اللَّهَ ۖ إِنَّ اللَّهَ شَدِيدُ الْعِقَابِ

"Help one another in righteousness and piety, but help not one another in sin and rancor: fear Allah for Allah is strict in punishment" (*al-Maaidah* 2).

As noted above, the behavior of the purified souls is driven by their desire to please Allah. Hence, they deal with each other in a very pure sense without any ulterior motives. Indeed, they give freely and sacrifice for each other because they know that their reward lies with Allah. When this belief is strong in a person's heart, he is able to sacrifice for his fellow human beings even when he himself is in need. Allah describes the believers among the Ansar ("Helpers") in Madinah in the following verse,

وَالَّذِينَ تَبَوَّءُوا الدَّارَ وَالْإِيمَانَ مِن قَبْلِهِمْ يُحِبُّونَ مَنْ هَاجَرَ إِلَيْهِمْ
وَلَا يَجِدُونَ فِي صُدُورِهِمْ حَاجَةً مِّمَّا أُوتُوا وَيُؤْثِرُونَ عَلَىٰ
أَنفُسِهِمْ وَلَوْ كَانَ بِهِمْ خَصَاصَةٌ ۚ وَمَن يُوقَ شُحَّ نَفْسِهِ فَأُولَٰئِكَ
هُمُ الْمُفْلِحُونَ

"But those who, before them, had homes (in Madinah) and had adopted the faith, show their affection to such as came to them for refuge, and entertain no desire in their hearts for things given to the (latter), but give them preference over themselves, even though poverty was their (own lot). And those saved from the covetousness of their own souls, they are the ones who achieve success" (*al-Hashr* 9).

Although such is a description of the Companions of the Prophet (peace and blessings of Allah be upon him), it sets a noble example and a goal for all believers who come afterwards. In fact, in another verse Allah again gives a description of those who are truly with the Prophet Muhammad (peace and blessings of Allah be upon him),

مُّحَمَّدٌ رَّسُولُ ٱللَّهِ ۚ وَٱلَّذِينَ مَعَهُۥٓ أَشِدَّآءُ عَلَى ٱلْكُفَّارِ رُحَمَآءُ بَيْنَهُمْ

"Muhammad is the Messenger of Allah; and those who are with him are strong against unbelievers, (but) compassionate among each other" (*al-Fath* 29).

Finally, the Prophet (peace and blessings of Allah be upon him) himself gave the following description of how the purified souls and true believers are supposed to be. He stated,

مَثَلُ الْمُؤْمِنِينَ فِي تَوَادِّهِمْ وَتَرَاحُمِهِمْ وَتَعَاطُفِهِمْ مَثَلُ الْجَسَدِ إِذَا اشْتَكَى مِنْهُ عُضْوٌ تَدَاعَى لَهُ سَائِرُ الْجَسَدِ بِالسَّهَرِ وَالْحُمَّى

"The parable of the believers with respect to their love, mercy and compassion for one another is like that of the body: if one of its limbs is hurting, the remainder of the body is afflicted by sleeplessness and fever." (Recorded by Muslim; al-Bukhari has something similar.)

(3) Security and freedom from excessive criminal behavior: In a society in which the souls are purified and the people are morally conscious and responsible, there is a minimum recourse to criminal activity.[1] If the state is also morally responsible and having the will to implement laws of a strong

---

[1] Every society is bound to have some criminal behavior. Even during the time of the Prophet (peace and blessings of Allah be upon him), there were some who committed adultery, drank alcohol and so forth. However, such acts would be minimized and their effects mitigated if the majority of society were not involved in them and worked to remove them from their midst.

moral nature, the society can become virtually free of excessive criminal behavior and the people live with a true feeling of security and peace. They need not fear when they leave their homes; they need not fear if their children are out of their sight in a crowded marketplace and so forth. This was a reality during the time of the Rightly Guided caliphs and it can be a reality again, Allah willing, if the masses and the rulers return to the process of spiritual purification.[1]

(3) Honor and being established in the land: Allah says,

وَعَدَ ٱللَّهُ ٱلَّذِينَ ءَامَنُوا۟ مِنكُمْ وَعَمِلُوا۟ ٱلصَّٰلِحَٰتِ لَيَسْتَخْلِفَنَّهُمْ فِى ٱلْأَرْضِ كَمَا ٱسْتَخْلَفَ ٱلَّذِينَ مِن قَبْلِهِمْ وَلَيُمَكِّنَنَّ لَهُمْ دِينَهُمُ ٱلَّذِى ٱرْتَضَىٰ لَهُمْ وَلَيُبَدِّلَنَّهُم مِّنۢ بَعْدِ خَوْفِهِمْ أَمْنًا ۚ يَعْبُدُونَنِى لَا يُشْرِكُونَ بِى شَيْـًٔا ۚ وَمَن كَفَرَ بَعْدَ ذَٰلِكَ فَأُو۟لَٰٓئِكَ هُمُ ٱلْفَٰسِقُونَ

"Allah has promised to those among you who believe and work righteous deeds that He will, of a surety, grant them in the land inheritance (of power) as He granted it to those before them; that He will establish in authority their religion, the one which He has chosen for them; and that He will change (their state), after the fear in which they (lived), to one of security and peace. They will worship Me (alone) and not associate anything with Me. If any do reject faith after this, they are rebellious and wicked" (*al-Noor* 55). This aspect was discussed earlier. This is a result for both the individual and the Muslim community as a whole.

---

[1] Of course, there are many factors involved that Islam establishes which further lead to this beneficial result. For example, in Islam there is a strong emphasis on the family as the basic foundation of society. This family, in turn, develops the youth in such a way that they are God-fearing, respectful of others and aware of their responsibility towards others. Furthermore, Allah has blessed this Nation by revealing the penal laws known as the *hudood*, which act as further restraints on people's behavior out of fear of punishment and humiliation.

Allah's Pleasure and Paradise in the Hereafter and True Happiness in All Stages of Life

Allah's pleasure and one's happiness in the Hereafter are the greatest and most important results of purifying one's soul. The life of the Hereafter is the only real life to be sought after. Yet that real life will only be granted to those who can raise themselves above the lowly desires of this worldly life by seeking Allah's pleasure instead. In other words, it will be for those who have purified their souls, thus pleasing Allah and deserving His blessed reward of Paradise in the Hereafter. Allah reminds all of mankind of this fact when He says,

وَمَا هَٰذِهِ ٱلْحَيَوٰةُ ٱلدُّنْيَآ إِلَّا لَهْوٌ وَلَعِبٌ وَإِنَّ ٱلدَّارَ ٱلْءَاخِرَةَ لَهِىَ ٱلْحَيَوَانُ لَوْ كَانُوا۟ يَعْلَمُونَ

"What is the life of this world but amusement and play? But verily the home in the Hereafter, that is life indeed, if they but knew" (*al-Ankaboot* 64). Allah has also said,

تِلْكَ ٱلدَّارُ ٱلْءَاخِرَةُ نَجْعَلُهَا لِلَّذِينَ لَا يُرِيدُونَ عُلُوًّا فِى ٱلْأَرْضِ وَلَا فَسَادًا وَٱلْعَٰقِبَةُ لِلْمُتَّقِينَ

"That abode of the Hereafter We shall give to those who intend not high-handedness or mischief on earth: and the end is (best) for the righteous" (*al-Qasas* 83).

In fact, the one who purifies himself will experience happiness in all stages of his life. As was noted earlier, he experiences true happiness in this life while others are seeking imaginary or mirage-type happiness. At the time of his death, also, his soul will flow freely from his body surrounded by a beautiful smell as he begins to experience the first taste of the pleasures of the Hereafter. The angels come to him and give him glad tidings of the things to come. Allah has beautifully described what will occur in the following verse,

إِنَّ ٱلَّذِينَ قَالُوا۟ رَبُّنَا ٱللَّهُ ثُمَّ ٱسْتَقَـٰمُوا۟ تَتَنَزَّلُ عَلَيْهِمُ ٱلْمَلَـٰٓئِكَةُ أَلَّا تَخَافُوا۟ وَلَا تَحْزَنُوا۟ وَأَبْشِرُوا۟ بِٱلْجَنَّةِ ٱلَّتِى كُنتُمْ تُوعَدُونَ ﴿٣٠﴾ نَحْنُ أَوْلِيَآؤُكُمْ فِى ٱلْحَيَوٰةِ ٱلدُّنْيَا وَفِى ٱلْـَٔاخِرَةِ ۖ وَلَكُمْ فِيهَا مَا تَشْتَهِىٓ أَنفُسُكُمْ وَلَكُمْ فِيهَا مَا تَدَّعُونَ ﴿٣١﴾ نُزُلًا مِّنْ غَفُورٍ رَّحِيمٍ

"In the case of those who say, 'Our Lord is Allah,' and, further stand straight and steadfast, the angels descend on them (from time to time): 'Fear not nor grieve! But receive the glad tidings of the garden (of bliss) that you were promised. We are your protectors in this life and in the Hereafter: therein shall you have all that your souls shall desire; therein shall you have all that you ask for! A hospitable gift from One Oft-Forgiving, Most Merciful!'" (*Fussilat* 30-32; also see *Yoonus* 62-64).

In the grave, also, he will experience happiness as his grave is expanded for him and he can see his seat in Paradise while the disbeliever's grave is constricted upon him as he is viewing his seat in the Hell-fire.

On the Day of Resurrection the difference between those who purified their souls and those who refused to do so will be great. Note how Allah describes the events of that Day. Allah has said,

يَـٰٓأَيُّهَا ٱلنَّاسُ ٱتَّقُوا۟ رَبَّكُمْ ۚ إِنَّ زَلْزَلَةَ ٱلسَّاعَةِ شَىْءٌ عَظِيمٌ ﴿١﴾ يَوْمَ تَرَوْنَهَا تَذْهَلُ كُلُّ مُرْضِعَةٍ عَمَّآ أَرْضَعَتْ وَتَضَعُ كُلُّ ذَاتِ حَمْلٍ حَمْلَهَا وَتَرَى ٱلنَّاسَ سُكَـٰرَىٰ وَمَا هُم بِسُكَـٰرَىٰ وَلَـٰكِنَّ عَذَابَ ٱللَّهِ شَدِيدٌ

"O mankind, fear your Lord! For the convulsion of the Hour (of Judgment) will be a thing terrible! The Day you shall see it, every mother giving suck shall forget her suckling babe, and every pregnant female shall drop her load (unformed): you shall see mankind as in a drunken riot, yet not drunk: but dreadful will be the Wrath of Allah" (*al-Hajj* 1-2); Allah also says,

فَإِذَا نُقِرَ فِي ٱلنَّاقُورِ ﴿٨﴾ فَذَٰلِكَ يَوْمَئِذٍ يَوْمٌ عَسِيرٌ ﴿٩﴾ عَلَى ٱلْكَٰفِرِينَ غَيْرُ يَسِيرٍ

"Finally, when the Trumpet is sounded, that will be—that Day—a Day of distress, far from easy for those who disbelieve" (*al-Muddaththir* 8-10). On the other hand, Allah describes the believers on that day—those who purified their souls—with the following beautiful words,

إِنَّ ٱلَّذِينَ سَبَقَتْ لَهُم مِّنَّا ٱلْحُسْنَىٰٓ أُو۟لَٰٓئِكَ عَنْهَا مُبْعَدُونَ ﴿١٠١﴾ لَا يَسْمَعُونَ حَسِيسَهَا ۖ وَهُمْ فِي مَا ٱشْتَهَتْ أَنفُسُهُمْ خَٰلِدُونَ ﴿١٠٢﴾ لَا يَحْزُنُهُمُ ٱلْفَزَعُ ٱلْأَكْبَرُ وَتَتَلَقَّىٰهُمُ ٱلْمَلَٰٓئِكَةُ هَٰذَا يَوْمُكُمُ ٱلَّذِي كُنتُمْ تُوعَدُونَ

"Those for whom the good (record) from Us has gone before will be removed far therefrom. Not the slightest sound will they hear of Hell. They shall dwell in what their souls desired. The Great Terror will bring them no grief: but the angels will meet them (with mutual greetings): 'This is your Day, (the Day) that you were promised'" (*al-Anbiyaa* 101-103); and Allah says,

وَيُنَجِّي ٱللَّهُ ٱلَّذِينَ ٱتَّقَوْا۟ بِمَفَازَتِهِمْ لَا يَمَسُّهُمُ ٱلسُّوٓءُ وَلَا هُمْ يَحْزَنُونَ

"But Allah will deliver the righteous to their place of salvation: no evil shall touch them, nor shall they grieve" (*al-Zumar* 61).

In fact, Allah will further purify the purified soul of all or any of his remaining sins such that he will then be in a state where he is allowed to enter into Paradise. This is a special blessing that only comes to those who sought to purify themselves with belief and good deeds in this life. As Allah has stated (in more than one place) about the disbelievers,

إِنَّ ٱلَّذِينَ يَشْتَرُونَ بِعَهْدِ ٱللَّهِ وَأَيْمَـٰنِهِمْ ثَمَنًا قَلِيلًا أُو۟لَـٰٓئِكَ لَا خَلَـٰقَ لَهُمْ فِى ٱلْـَٔاخِرَةِ وَلَا يُكَلِّمُهُمُ ٱللَّهُ وَلَا يَنظُرُ إِلَيْهِمْ يَوْمَ ٱلْقِيَـٰمَةِ وَلَا يُزَكِّيهِمْ وَلَهُمْ عَذَابٌ أَلِيمٌ

"As for those who sell the faith they owe to Allah and their own plighted word for a small price, they shall have no portion in the Hereafter, nor will Allah (deign to) speak to them or look at them on the Day of Judgment, nor will He purify them (of sin). They shall have a grievous Penalty" (*ali-Imraan* 77).

On the other hand, the purified souls will be saved all of the discomforts of the Day of Resurrection until they are granted entrance into Paradise:

يَـٰٓأَيَّتُهَا ٱلنَّفْسُ ٱلْمُطْمَئِنَّةُ ﴿٢٧﴾ ٱرْجِعِىٓ إِلَىٰ رَبِّكِ رَاضِيَةً مَّرْضِيَّةً ﴿٢٨﴾ فَٱدْخُلِى فِى عِبَـٰدِى ﴿٢٩﴾ وَٱدْخُلِى جَنَّتِى

"(To the righteous soul will be said:) 'O soul in (complete) rest and satisfaction! Come back to your Lord, well pleased (yourself), and well-pleasing unto Him! Enter, then, among My servants. Yea, enter My Heaven'" (*al-Fajr* 27-30);

وَسِيقَ ٱلَّذِينَ ٱتَّقَوْا۟ رَبَّهُمْ إِلَى ٱلْجَنَّةِ زُمَرًا حَتَّىٰٓ إِذَا جَآءُوهَا وَفُتِحَتْ أَبْوَٰبُهَا وَقَالَ لَهُمْ خَزَنَتُهَا سَلَـٰمٌ عَلَيْكُمْ طِبْتُمْ

فَٱدْخُلُوهَا خَـٰلِدِينَ ﴿٧٣﴾ وَقَالُوا۟ ٱلْحَمْدُ لِلَّهِ ٱلَّذِى صَدَقَنَا وَعْدَهُۥ
وَأَوْرَثَنَا ٱلْأَرْضَ نَتَبَوَّأُ مِنَ ٱلْجَنَّةِ حَيْثُ نَشَآءُ ۖ فَنِعْمَ أَجْرُ ٱلْعَـٰمِلِينَ

"And those who feared their Lord will be led to the Garden in crowds: until behold, they arrive there; its gates will be opened; and its keepers will say, 'Peace be upon you! You have done well! Enter here, to dwell therein.' They will say, 'Praise be to Allah, Who has truly fulfilled His promise to us, and has given us (this) land in heritage: we can dwell in the Garden as we will: how excellent a reward for those who work (righteousness)'" (*al-Zumar* 73-74).

In reality, above and beyond all of that is that they shall receive Allah's good pleasure. Allah says,

وَعَدَ ٱللَّهُ ٱلْمُؤْمِنِينَ وَٱلْمُؤْمِنَـٰتِ جَنَّـٰتٍ تَجْرِى مِن تَحْتِهَا ٱلْأَنْهَـٰرُ
خَـٰلِدِينَ فِيهَا وَمَسَـٰكِنَ طَيِّبَةً فِى جَنَّـٰتِ عَدْنٍ ۚ وَرِضْوَٰنٌ مِّنَ ٱللَّهِ
أَكْبَرُ ۚ ذَٰلِكَ هُوَ ٱلْفَوْزُ ٱلْعَظِيمُ

"Allah has promised to the believers—men and women—gardens under which rivers flow, to dwell therein, and beautiful mansions in gardens of everlasting bliss. But the greatest bliss is the good pleasure of Allah: that is the supreme felicity" (*al-Taubah* 72).

Finally, there comes the greatest reward of all for those who purified themselves in this life via true faith, good deeds and *ihsaan*: the opportunity to see Allah. Allah has said,

لِّلَّذِينَ أَحْسَنُوا۟ ٱلْحُسْنَىٰ وَزِيَادَةٌ ۖ وَلَا يَرْهَقُ وُجُوهَهُمْ قَتَرٌ وَلَا ذِلَّةٌ ۚ
أُو۟لَـٰٓئِكَ أَصْحَـٰبُ ٱلْجَنَّةِ ۖ هُمْ فِيهَا خَـٰلِدُونَ

"To those who do right is a goodly (reward), yea, more (than in measure)! No darkness or shame shall cover their faces! They are Companions of the Garden; they will abide therein (forever)" (*Yoonus* 26). In a hadith recorded by Muslim, the Messenger of

Allah (peace and blessings of Allah be upon him) explained the "more" (*ziyaadah)* as being blessed with the ability to see Allah.

Summary

The main point of this chapter can virtually be summed up in one sentence: All of the true goodness and blessings come to those who purify their souls—by the grace and mercy of Allah.

Conclusions: The Individual's Decision

In Allah's mercy, Allah sent the Prophet Muhammad (peace and blessings of Allah be upon him), His final prophet, with a clear book and a clear message. In Allah's final revelation, Allah has made it very clear that the path of purification is open to anyone who sincerely desires it and turns to Allah for guidance. However, the individual must make that choice. Indeed, the burden is upon the individual to make that choice. But once that individual makes that choice, the guidance is there for him and the path is not an overburdening one. Note the following verses of the Quran in which Allah makes these points concerning individual responsibility and the clear guidance in front of the individual crystal clear:

Allah says,

يَـٰٓأَيُّهَا ٱلَّذِينَ ءَامَنُواْ عَلَيْكُمْ أَنفُسَكُمْ ۖ لَا يَضُرُّكُم مَّن ضَلَّ إِذَا ٱهْتَدَيْتُمْ ۚ إِلَى ٱللَّهِ مَرْجِعُكُمْ جَمِيعًا فَيُنَبِّئُكُم بِمَا كُنتُمْ تَعْمَلُونَ

"O you who believe! Guard your own souls: if you follow (right) guidance, no hurt can come to you from those who stray. The goal of you all is to Allah: it is He that will show you the truth of all that you do" (*al-Maaidah* 105).

وَنَفْسٍ وَمَا سَوَّىٰهَا ﴿٧﴾ فَأَلْهَمَهَا فُجُورَهَا وَتَقْوَىٰهَا ﴿٨﴾ قَدْ أَفْلَحَ مَن زَكَّىٰهَا ﴿٩﴾ وَقَدْ خَابَ مَن دَسَّىٰهَا

"By the Soul, and the proportion and order given to it; And its enlightenment as to its wrong and its right; Truly he succeeds that purifies it, And he fails that corrupts it" (*al-Shams* 7-10).

أَلَمْ نَجْعَل لَّهُۥ عَيْنَيْنِ ۝٨ وَلِسَانًا وَشَفَتَيْنِ ۝٩ وَهَدَيْنَٰهُ ٱلنَّجْدَيْنِ

"Have We not made for him a pair of eyes? And a tongue, and a pair of lips? And shown him the two highways [of good and evil]?" (*al-Balad* 8-10).

إِنَّا هَدَيْنَٰهُ ٱلسَّبِيلَ إِمَّا شَاكِرًا وَإِمَّا كَفُورًا

"We showed him the Way: whether he be grateful or very ungrateful (rests on his will)" (*al-Insaan* 3).

لَا يُكَلِّفُ ٱللَّهُ نَفْسًا إِلَّا وُسْعَهَا ۚ لَهَا مَا كَسَبَتْ وَعَلَيْهَا مَا ٱكْتَسَبَتْ ۗ

"On no soul does Allah place a burden greater than it can bear. It gets every good that it earns, and it suffers every ill that it earns" (*al-Baqarah* 286).

In reality, no one (other than God, of course) can enter upon a person's individual decision as to whether to follow the path of purification or not. The enemies of Islam cannot interfere between a person and his own soul. Even Satan cannot overpower or mislead a person if he truly turns to Allah as his only lord and guardian and Allah then guides him. The individual is free then to use his will and intelligence to decide to follow the path of purification. Indeed, this is probably the gravest question that he faces in his worldly existence. The decision is truly his and he has no one else to blame if he makes an improper choice, leading to eternal damnation in the Hereafter.

All of these points demonstrate that if a person claims that it is not within him to turn to God, do good deeds, refrain from evil and purify himself, he is simply being untruthful. Allah has created every soul upon the true path of life and Allah has given guidance to all of mankind.[1] It is the individual's own decision as to what path he wishes to follow. If he chooses a path of evil that leads him to the Hell-fire, he cannot blame anyone else for his decision but his own soul, which he himself has turned his back on by not purifying it.

The only hope for purification and salvation is to purify oneself. When one does that, Allah will accept the person and be pleased with him. The Messenger of Allah (peace and blessings of Allah be upon him) stated,

أَيُّهَا النَّاسُ إِنَّ اللَّهَ طَيِّبٌ لا يَقْبَلُ إِلاَّ طَيِّبًا

"O People! Verily Allah is good and pure and He does not accept but what is good." (Recorded by Muslim.) Whenever a person makes his soul more wholesome and pure, he draws himself closer to Allah. However, if he refuses to do that, Allah will not accept his soul and will not enter him into His Paradise.

The final result of spiritual purification is something worth sacrificing for. Although the path is within one's means, this does not mean that it will not require sacrifice and effort on the part of the individual. However, the person must realize the worth of his goal and this will give him the resolve to sacrifice for the sake of that goal. It will give him more than just resolve, it will drive him to plant his steps carefully and to take advantage of the great opportunities available to him, always wary of any setbacks or impediments along the way. The Messenger of Allah (peace and blessings of Allah be upon him) said,

مَنْ خَافَ أَدْلَجَ وَمَنْ أَدْلَجَ بَلَغَ الْمَنْزِلَ أَلاَ إِنَّ سِلْعَةَ اللَّهِ غَالِيَةٌ أَلاَ إِنَّ سِلْعَةَ اللَّهِ الْجَنَّةُ

---

[1] There is a difference of opinion concerning what will occur to those people who never heard the true teachings of the Prophet Muhammad (peace and blessings of Allah be upon him). The strongest opinion seems to be that Allah will give them a special trial on the Day of Judgment. Allah alone knows best. For a detailed discussion of this question, see Muwafaq Ahmad Shukri, *Ahl al-Fitrah wa man fi Hukmihim* (Damascus: Daar ibn Katheer, 1988), *passim*.

"He who fears sets out at nightfall. And whoever sets out at nightfall reaches his destination. Certainly, God's commodity is very dear. And God's commodity is [none other than] Paradise."[1]

There are many points that one must be conscious about concerning his goal to purify himself. Purification of the soul, it can be argued, is a "natural goal" deeply rooted in the soul and common to virtually all humans. Humans all over the world are looking for ways to purify themselves and free themselves from guilt, evil and filth. Unfortunately, Satan and his troops seem to be well aware of this fact. They also know, like Satan told Adam about the tree, that people can easily be duped into following a certain path if that path is consistent with what they desire and if it can be made to look as if it will achieve good in the end.

Hence, like how one views those who sell medical potions, the individual must be very careful about what path he chooses to follow in his quest to purify his soul. Not all paths lead to God and not all paths lead to spiritual purification. Indeed, there is only one path that truly leads to spiritual purification and God's good pleasure. And that is the path taught and practiced by the Messenger of Allah Muhammad (peace and blessings of Allah be upon him), as found in the Quran and Sunnah.

Thus, as one journeys through life, many people may appear claiming to have the key to well-being, happiness, salvation and purification. They may go by many names (Guru, spiritual healer, doctor, psychologists, Shaikh, Maulana, Father, brother, and even just "friend"). When bombarded with such various approaches, one must always remember that he will meet Allah alone without any help from such people. Hence, there are two key questions that the individual must ask himself, including:

(1) "What is my true purpose and goal in this creation? Is what they are calling me to consistent with that purpose and goal or not?"

(2) "Is the thing that they are calling me to consistent with what the Prophet (peace and blessings of Allah be upon him) brought, practiced and imparted to his Companions?"

---

[1] Recorded by al-Tirmidhi. According to al-Albaani, it is *sahih*. Cf., al-Albaani, *Saheeh al-Jaami*, vol. 2, p. 1069.

If the individual guides himself by these basic yet essential questions, he will be able to protect himself from straying from the true path of purification.

He will then be able to keep himself along the true path of purification, the path of purification espoused by the Quran and Sunnah. He will live a happy life along that path as it is the balanced path consistent with his true nature, avoiding all of the extremes found in the various paths one confronts in this world, from materialism and this worldly concentration to monasticism and denying what the soul naturally requires. He will be happy because he will have certainty that he is on the correct path. Furthermore, his life will be balanced when it comes to the actions of the heart or internal actions vis-à-vis the external actions. The needs of his soul will be met as well as the needs of his physical body, neither will be sacrificed for the happiness of the other. Everything will be in balance and successful by sticking to both the wording and the meaning of the texts of the Quran and Sunnah, sacrificing neither of them.

This is Allah's promise. Allah says,

يَـٰٓأَيُّهَا ٱلَّذِينَ ءَامَنُوا۟ ٱسْتَجِيبُوا۟ لِلَّهِ وَلِلرَّسُولِ إِذَا دَعَاكُمْ لِمَا يُحْيِيكُمْ

"O you who believe! Respond to Allah and His Messenger when He calls you to that which will give you life" (*al-Anfaal* 24). It is the real life—the only life that is worthy of living—that Allah and His Messenger are calling each and every individual to. It is the real life and salvation for the heart as it frees it from being enslaved to desires, lusts and doubts. It is the real life for the mind and it rescues it from ignorance, doubt and confusion. It is the real life for the human himself as it frees him from servitude and slavery to other humans and ideologies. It frees him to worship and serve Allah alone, the ultimate goal that his own self recognizes and yearns for. This is the source of his honor and dignity, the purpose for which he has been created. In the end, it is the real life of eternal bliss and happiness, in Paradise, being pleased with the Lord and the Lord being pleased with the servant.

Summary

One can sum up the concept of purification of the soul as being wherein a person recognizes his purpose and goal in life. He then focuses on that purpose. He realizes that this concept means that he must worship Allah alone and worship Him in the proper way. The first aspect means that he attempts to put Allah first in his heart, well above everything else, and has a sincere intention to act sincerely for the sake of Allah. The individual must recognize that any time his action is not sincere and pure for the sake of Allah then that act is not helping him to achieve his overall purpose and goal—indeed, it may be very damaging for his overall goal. The second aspect means that he worships Allah according to the guidance of the revelation from Allah (the Quran and the Sunnah). This also implies that any time his act of worship is not correct according to the Quran and Sunnah, it will not benefit him. These two points are beautifully captured in the verse at the end of *soorah al-Kahf* (which many Muslims read every Friday and which serves as an important reminder to light one's entire week between the two Fridays),

فَمَن كَانَ يَرْجُوا۟ لِقَآءَ رَبِّهِۦ فَلْيَعْمَلْ عَمَلًا صَـٰلِحًا وَلَا يُشْرِكْ
بِعِبَادَةِ رَبِّهِۦٓ أَحَدًۢا

"Whoever hopes to meet his Lord, let him work righteousness, and, in the worship of his Lord, admit no one as partner" (*al-Kahf* 110).

As for the process of purification, it starts with the correction of one's beliefs. This includes properly understanding the articles of faith and believing in them with a complete certainty, thus allowing them to have the proper effect on one's life. This is further fortified and enhanced by the performance of the obligatory deeds and the avoiding of the forbidden acts. These two, in themselves, help increase a person's faith (*imaan*), thus having further repercussions in one's life and behavior. In order to purify oneself even further, this step is further enhanced and strengthened by the performance of the recommended deeds and the avoidance of the disliked acts. By following these three steps sincerely and faithfully, the soul will truly become purified and in a state ready to meet Allah wherein Allah will be pleased with the individual and the individual will be pleased to meet Allah.

To help the individual along his journey of spiritual purification, there are certain means that he should pay attention to—some of them obligatory in themselves. In addition, he must be aware of and avoid obvious impediments and pitfalls, including following a path that is claimed to be the path of purification while in reality it is not based on the Quran and Sunnah.

The end result of this process will be blessings from Allah in both this life and the Hereafter. The purified soul will then return to Allah with Allah being pleased with him and he being pleased with what he finds with Allah.

Bibliography

al-Abduh, Muhammad [محمد العبده] and Taariq Abdul Haleem [طارق عبد الحليم]. *al-Soofiyyah: Nashatuha wa Tatauraha* [الصوفية نشأتها وتطورها]. al-Kuwait: Dar al-Arqam. 1986.

al-Abdul Lateef, Abdul Azeez [عبد العزيز العبد اللطيف]. *Maalim fi al-Sulook wa Tazkiyah al-Nufoos* [معالم في السلوك وتزكية النفوس]. Riyadh: Daar al-Watan. 1414 A.H.

Abdul Raheem, Al-Sayyid [السيد عبد الرحيم], footnotes to Ali al-Maawardi [علي الماوردي]. *al-Nukat wa al-Uyoon Tafseer al-Maawardi* [النكت والعيون تفسير الماوردي]. Beirut: Daar al-Kutub al-Ilmiyah. 1992.

Abu Hayyaan, Muhammad ibn Yoosuf [محمد بن يوسف أبو حيان]. *Al-Bahr al-Muheet fi al-Tafseer* [البحر المحيط في التفسير]. Makkah: al-Maktabah al-Tijaariyyah. n.d.

Abu Zahrah, Muhammad [محمد أبو زهرة]. *Abu Haneefah: Hayaatuhu, Asruhu, Araauhu wa Fiqhuhu* [أبو حنيفة حياته وعصره وأراءه وفقهه]. Daar al-Fikr al-Arabi. n.d.

Ahmad, Al-Ameen al-Haaj Muhammad [الأمين الحاج محمد أحمد]. *Al-Tareeq ila Wilaayah Allaah* [الطريق إلى ولاية الله]. Jeddah: Daar al-Matbooaat al-Hadeethah. 1989.

Ahmad, Qazi Ashfaq. *Words that Moved the World: How to Study the Quran.* Leicester, United Kingdom: The Islamic Foundation. 1999.

al-Albani, Muhammad Nasir al-Din [محمد ناصر الدين الألباني]. *Dhaeef al-Jaami al-Sagheer* [ضعيف الجامع الصغير]. Beirut: al-Maktab al-Islaami. 1988.

-----*Khutbah al-Haajah* [خطبة الحاجة]. Damascus: al-Maktab al-Islaami. 1400 A.H.

-----*Saheeh al-Jaami al-Sagheer* [صحيح الجامع الصغير]. Beirut: al-Maktab al-Islaami. 1986.

-----*Saheeh Sunan Abi Dawood* [صحيح سنن أبي داود]. Riyadh Maktab al-Tarbiyah al-Arabi li-Duwal al-Khaleej. 1989.

-----*Saheeh Sunan al-Tirmidhi* [صحيح سنن الترمذي]. Riyadh: Maktab al-Tarbiyyah al-Arabi li-Duwal al-Khaleej. 1988.

-----*Saheeh al-Targheeb wa al-Tarheeb* [صحيح الترغيب و الترهيب]. Beirut: al-Maktab al-Islaami. 1982.

-----*Silsilat al-Ahadeeth al-Saheehah* [سلسلة الأحاديث الصحيحة]. Damascus: al-Maktab al-Islaami. 1979. Vol. 2.

-----*Silsilat al-Ahadeeth al-Saheehah* [سلسلة الأحاديث الصحيحة]. Kuwait: al-Daar al-Salafiyyah. 1983. Vol. 4

-----Footnotes to Muhammad al-Tabreezi [محمد التبريزي]. *Mishkat al-Masaabeeh* [مشكاة المصابيح]. Beirut: al-Maktab al-Islaami. 1985.

al-Aloosi, Mahmood [محمود الألوسي]. *Rooh al-Maani fi Tafseer al-Quran wa al-Saba al-Mathaani* [روح المعاني في تفسير القرآن العظيم والسبع المثاني]. Cairo: Maktabah Daar al-Turaath. n.d.

Aoon, Kamaal [كمال عون]. *Kitaab al-Fatoohaat al-Makkiyyah wa ma Waraahu min Ayaad Khafiyyah* [كتاب الفتوحات المكية و ما وراءه من أياد خفية]. Tanta, Egypt: Daar al-Basheer. 1989.

al-Arnaaoot, Shuaib [شعيب الأرناؤوط], et al. *Musnad al-Imaam Ahmad* [مسند الإمام أحمد]. Beirut: Muassasat al-Risaalah. 1996.

Asad, Muhammad. *The Message of the Quran*. Gibraltar: Dar al-Andalus. 1980.

al-Asfahaani, Al-Raaghib [الراغب الأصفهاني]. *Mufradaat Alfaadh al-Quraan* [مفردات ألفاظ القرآن]. Damascus: Daar al-Qalam. 1997.

al-Ashqar, Umar [عمر الأشقر]. *Minhaaj Tazkiyah al-Nafs fi al-Islaam* [منهاج تزكية النفس في الإسلام]. Amman, Jordan: Daar al-Nafaais. 1992.

-----*The World of the Jinn and Devils*. Boulder: Al-Basheer Company for Publications and Translations. 1998.

Azami, M. Mustafa. *Quranic Text—Recording and Collection: A Comparative Study with the Old and New Testaments*. Forthcoming.

Badri, Malik. *Contemplation: An Islamic Psychospiritual Study*. Herndon, VA: IIIT. 2000.

al-Baghawi, al-Husain [الحسين البغوي]. *Sharh al-Sunnah* [شرح السنة]. Beirut: al-Maktab al-Islaami. 1983.

-----*Tafseer al-Baghawi: Maalim al-Tanzeel* [تفسير البغوي: معالم التنزيل]. Riyadh: Daar Taiba. 1409 A.H.

al-Banna, Ahmad [أحمد البنا]. *Al-Fath al-Rabbaani li-Tarteeb Musnad al-Imaam Ahmad ibn Hanbal al-Shaibaani* [الفتح الرباني لترتيب مسند الإمام أحمد بن حنبل الشيباني]. Cairo: Dar al-Hadeeth. n.d.

Al-Bilaali, Abdul Hameed. *Manhaj al-Taabieen fi Tarbiyah al-Nufoos*. Kuwait: Maktabah al-Manaar al-Islaamiyyah. 1997.

al-Bugha, Mustafa [مصطفي البغى] and Muhyi al-Deen Mistu [محي الدين مستو]. *al-Waafi fi Sharh al-Arbaeen al-Nawawiya* [الوفي في شرح الأربعين النووية]. Damascus: Muassasat Uloom al-Quran. 1984.

al-Bukhaari, Sideeq ibn Hasan [صديق بن احسن الخباري]. *Fath al-Bayaan fi Maqaasid al-Quraan* [فتح البيان في مقاصد القرآن]. Beirut: al-Maktabah al-Ariyyah. 1992.

al-Buqaaee, Burhaan al-Deen [برهان الدين البقاعي]. *Masra al-Tasawwuf au Tanbeeh al-Ghabi ila Takfeer ibn Arabi* [مصرع التصوف أو تنبيه الغبي إلى تكفير ابن عربي]. Daar al-Taqwa. n.d.

al-Darweesh, Abdullah Muhammad [عبد الله محمد الرويش]. Footnotes to Noor al-Deen Ali al-Haithami. *[Bughyah al-Raaid fi Tahqeeq] Majma al-Zawaaid wa Manba al-Fawaaid* [بغية الزائد في تحقيق مجمع الزوائد ومنبع الفوائد]. Beirut: Daar al-Fikr. 1992.

al-Dhahabi, Muhammad [محمد الذهبي]. *Meezaan al-Itidaal fi Naqd al-Rijaal* [ميزان الاعتدال في نقد الرجال]. Beirut: Daar al-Marifah, n.d.

Dhaheer, Ihsaan Ilaahi [إحسان إلهى ظهير]. *al-Tasawwuf: Al-Mansha wa al-Masaadir* [التصوف: المنشأ والمصادر]. Lahore, Pakistan: Idaarah Tarjumaan al-Sunnah. 1986.

Douglas, Elmer H., (translator) and Ibrahim M. Abu-Rabi (editor). *The Mystical Teachings of al-Shadhili Including His Life, Prayers, Letters and Followers: A Translation from the Arabic of ibn al-Sabbagh's* Durrat al-Asrar wa Tuhfat al-Abrar. Albany, NY: State University of New York Press. 1993.

Encyclopædia Britannica. Computer Software Version.

al-Fairoozabaadi, Muhammad [محمد الفيروزابادي]. *Basaair Dhawi al-Tamyeez fi Lataaif al-Kitaab al-Azeez* [بصائر ذوى التمييز في لطائف الكتاب العزيز]. Beirut: al-Maktabah al-Ilmiyyah. n.d.

Fareed, Ahmad [أحمد فريد]. *Al-Tazkiyah bain Ahl al-Sunnah wa al-Soofiyyah* [التزكية بين أهل السنة والصوفية]. No publication information given.

-----*al-Thamaraat al-Zakiyyah fi al-Aqaaid al-Salafiyyah* [الثمرات الزكية في العقائد السلفية]. Maktabah al-Tauiyyah al-Islaamiyyah. 1409 A.H.

al-Fauzaan, Saalih [صالح الفوزان]. *Al-Khutab al-Munbariyyah fi al-Munaasabaat al-Asriyyah* [الخطب المنبرية في المناسبات العصرية]. Beirut: Muassasat al-Risaalah. 1987.

-----*Muhaadharaat fi al-Aqeedah wa al-Dawah* [محاضرات في العقيدة والدعوة]. Riyadh: Daar al-Aasimah. 1415 A.H.

Funk, Robert W., Roy W. Hoover and the Jesus Seminar. *The Five Gospels: What did Jesus Really Say?* New York: MacMillan Publishing Company. 1993.

al-Ghaamdi, Saeed [سعيد الغامدي]. *Haqeeqat al-Bidah wa Ahkaamuhu* [حقيقة البدعة وأحكامه]. Riyadh: Maktabah al-Rushd. 1992.

Ghaushah, Abdullah [عبـــد الله غوشـــة]. *Al-Jihaad Tareeq al-Nasr* [الجهاد طريق النصر]. Wizaarah al-Auqaaf. 1976.

Al-Ghazaali, Muhammad ibnMuhammad [محمد بن محمد الغزالي]. *Ihyaa Uloom al-Deen* [إحياء علوم الديـــن]. No publication information given.

-----*Ihyaa Uloom al-Deen* [إحياء علوم الدين]. Beirut: Daar al-Marifah. n.d.

al-Haithami, Noor al-Deen Ali [نور الدين على الهيثمي]. [*Bughyah al-Raaid fi Tahqeeq*] *Majma al-Zawaaid wa Manba al-Fawaaid* [بغية الزائد في تحقيق مجمع الزوائد ومنبع الفوائد]. Beirut: Daar al-Fikr. 1992.

-----*Kashf al-Astaar an Zawaaid al-Bazzaar ala al-Kutub al-Sittah* [كشـــف الأستار عن زوائد البزار]. Beirut: Muassasah al-Risaalah. 1984.

-----*Kitaab Majma al-Bahrain fi Zawaaid al-Mujamain* [مجمع البحرين فـــي زوائد معجمين]. Riyadh: Maktabah al-Rushd. 2000.

Hannah, Barbara. *Jung: His Life and Work.* Wilmette, IL: Chiron Publications. 1999.

Hasan, Suhaib. *The Journey of the Soul.* London: Al-Quran Society. 1995.

Hilaal, Ibraaheem [إبراهيم هلال]. Introduction to Muhammad ibn Ali al-Shaukaani [الشوكاني]. *Qatr al-Wali ala Hadeeth al-Wali* [قطر الولي على حديث الولي]. Beirut: Daar Ihyaa al-Turaath al-Arabi. n.d.

al-Hilaali, Saleem [سليم الـــهلالي]. *Manhaj al-Anbiyaa fi Tazkiyah al-Nufoos* [منهج الأنبياء في تزكية النفـــوس]. Al-Khobar, Saudi Arabia: Daar ibn Affaan. 1992.

-----*Sahih Kitaab al-Adhkaar wa Dhaeefuhu* [صحيح كتاب الأذكار وضعيفه]. Madinah: Maktabah al-Ghurabaa al-Athariyyah. 1997.

Hilmi, Mustafa [مصطفى حلمي]. *Ibn Taimiyyah wa al-Tasawwuf* [ابن تيمية والتصوف]. Alexandria: Dar al-Dawah. n.d.

Hofmann, Murad Wilfried. *Islam the Alternative.* Beltsville, MD: Amana Publications. 1992.

-----*Journay to Islam: Diary of a German Diplomat 1951-2000.* Leicester, United Kingdom: The Islamic Foundation. 2001.

al-Hujwiri, Ali Bin Uthman. *Kashf al-Mahjub.* Lahore: Islamic Book Foundation. 1982.

Hunt, Morton. *The Story of Psychology.* New York: Anchor Books. 1994.

Ibn Abi al-Izz. *Commentary on the Creed of At-Tahawi by ibn Abi al-Izz*. Riyadh: Al-Imam Muhammad ibn Saud Islamic University. 2000.

ibn Atiyyah, Abdul Haqq [عبد الحق بن عطية]. *al-Muharrar al-Wajeez fi Tafseer al-Kitaab al-Azeez* [المحرر الوجيز في تفسير الكتاب العزيز]. Beirut: Daar al-Kutub al-Ilmiyyah. 1993.

ibn Hajar, Ahmad [أحمد بن حجر]. *Fath al-Baari bi-Sharh Saheeh al-Bukhaari* [فتح الباري بشرح صحيح البخاري]. Makkah: al-Maktabah al-Tijaariyah. 1993.

-----*Fath al-Baari bi-Sharh Saheeh al-Bukhaari* [فتح الباري بشرح صحيح البخاري]. al-Maktabah al-Salafiyyah. n.d.

-----*Tahdheeb al-Tahdheeb* [تهذيب التهذيب]. Beirut: Muassasah al-Risaalah. 1996.

ibn Hasan, Uthmaan ibn Ali [عثمان بن علي بن الحسن]. *Manhaj al-Istidlaal ala Masaail al-Itiqaad ind Ahl al-Sunnah wa al-Jamaah* [منهج الاستدلال على مسائل الاعتقاد]. Riyadh: Maktabah al-Rushd. 1992.

ibn Hazm al-Andalusi, Ali [علي بن حزم]. *Al-Akhlaaq wa al-Seer fi Mudaawaah al-Nufoos* [الأخلاق والسير في مداواة النفوس]. Shariqah, UAE: Daar al-Fath. 1993.

----- *In Pursuit of Virtue*. London: Ta Ha Publishers. 1998.

ibn Hubairah, al-Wazeer [الوزير ابن هبيرة]. *Al-Ifsaah an Maana al-Sihaah* [الإفصاح عن معانى الصحاح]. Riyadh: Daar al-Watn. 1996.

ibn al-Jauzi, Abdul Rahmaan [عبد الرحمن بن الجوزي]. *Talbees Iblees* [تلبيس إبليس]. Beirut. Daar al-Qalam. N.d.

-----*Zaad al-Maseer fi Ilm al-Tafseer* [زاد المسير في علم التفسير]. Beirut: Daar al-Fikr. 1987.

ibn Katheer, Ismaaeel [إسماعيل ابن كثير]. *Kitaab Fadhaail al-Quraan* [كتاب فضائل القرآن]. Cairo: Maktabah ibn Taimiyyah. 1416 A.H.

-----*Tafseer al-Quraan al-Adheem* [تفسير القرآن العظيم]. Kuwait: Jamiyyah Ihyaa al-Turaath al-Islaami. 1991.

-----*Tafseer al-Quraan al-Adheem* [تفسير القرآن العظيم]. Riyadh: Dar Taibah. 1999.

Ibn al-Mandhoor, Muhammad [محمد ابن المنذور]. *Lisaan al-Arab* [لسان العرب]. Beirut: Daar Saadir. n.d.

ibn al-Qayyim, Muhammad [محمد بن القيم]. *al-Fawaaid* [الفوائد]. Beirut: Daar al-Nafaais. 1984.

-----*Iddah al-Saabireen wa Dhakheerah al-Shaakireen* [عدة الصابرين وذكيرة الشاكرين]. Beirut: Daar al-Kutub al-Ilmiyyah. 1983.

-----*Ighaathah al-Luhfaan min Masaayid al-Shaitaan* [[إغاثة اللحفان من مصايد الشيطان]]. Beirut: Daar al-Fikr. N.d.

-----*Ighaathah al-Luhfaan min Masaayid al-Shaitaan* [إغاثة اللحفان من مصايد الشيطان]. Makkah: al-Maktabah al-Tijaariyyah. n.d.

-----*Al-Jawaab al-Kaafi liman Sa`ala an al-Dawaa al-Shaafi* [الجواب الكافي لمن سأل عن الدواء الشافي]. Beirut: Daar al-Nadwah al-Hadeethah. 1405 A.H.

-----*Al-Jawaab al-Kaafi liman Sa`ala an al-Dawaa al-Shaafi* [الجواب الكافي لمن سأل عن الدواء الشافي]. Beirut: Dar al-Kutub al-Ilmiyyah. 1983.

-----*Miftaah Daar al-Saadah* [مفتاح دار السعادة]. Beirut: Daar al-Fikr. n.d.

-----*Mudaarij al-Saalikeen bain Manaazil Iyyaaka Nabudu wa Iyyaaka Nastaeen* [مدارج السالكين بين منازل إياك نعبد وإياك نستعين]. Beirut: Daar al-Kitaab al-Arabi. n.d.

-----*Raudhah al-Muhibeen wa Nuzhah al-Mushtaaqeen* [روضة المحبين ونزهة المشتقين]. Aleppo, Syria: Daar al-Wa'ee. n.d.

-----*al-Rooh fi al-Kalaam ala Arwaah al-Amwaat wa al-Ahyaa* [الروح في الكلام على أرواح الأموات والأحياء]. Riyadh: Daar ibn Taimiyyah. 1992.

-----*al-Waabil al-Sayyib min al-Kalim al-Tayyib* [الوابل الصيب من الكلم الطيب]. Beirut: Daar al-Bihaar. 1986.

ibn Rajab, Abdul Rahmaan [عبد الرحمن بن رجب]. *Jaami al-Uloom wa al-Hikm* [جامع العلوم والحكم]. Beirut: Muassasat al-Risaalah. 1991.

-----*Lataaif al-Maarif feema al-Miwaasim al-Aam min al-Wadhaaif* [لطائف المعارف فيما المواسم العام من الوظائف]. Damascus: Daar ibn Katheer. 1996.

-----*Sharh Hadeeth Labbaika Allaahumma Labbaik* [شرح حديث لبيك اللهم لبيك]. Makkah: Daar Aalim al-Faraaid. 1417 A.H.

Ibn Rajab al-Hanbali, ibn al-Qayyim al-Jawziyya [sic] and Abu Hamid al-Ghazali. *The Purification of the Soul*. London: Al-Firdous Ltd. 1993.

ibn Rislaan, Muhammad ibn Saeed [محمد بن سعيد بن رسلان]. *Dham al-Jahil wa Bayaan Qabeeh Athaarihi* [ذم الجهل وبيان قبيح أثاره]. Cairo: Daar al-Uloom al-Islaamiyyah. n.d.

ibn Taimiyyah, Ahmad [أحمد بن تيمية]. *Ibn Taymiyyah's Essay on Servitude*. Birmingham, United Kingdom: al-Hidaayah Publishing and Distribution. 1999.

-----*al-Istiqaamah* [الاستقامة]. Maktabah al-Tauiyah al-Islaamiyyah li-Ihyaa al-Turaath al-Islaami, n.d.

-----*Majmoo Fatawaa Shaikh al-Islaam ibn Taimiya* [مجموع فتــاوى شــيخ الإسلام بن تيميــة]. Collected by Abdul Rahmaan Qaasim and his son Muhammad. No publication information given.

----- *Majmooah al-Fataawa* [مجمــوع الفتـــاوي]. Riyadh: Maktabah al-Ubaikaan. 1997.

-----"Risaalah fi al-Taubah [رسالة في التوبـــة]," *Jaami al-Rasaail* [جامع الرسائل]. Cairo: Maktaba ibn Taimiyyah. 1984.

----- *Tazkiyah al-Nafs* [تزكية النفس]. Riyadh: Daar al-Muslim. 1994.

ibn Uthaimeen, Muhammad [محمد بن عثيمين]. *Sharh Riyaadh al-Saaliheen* [شرح رياض الصالحين]. Riyadh: Daar al-Want. 1995.

Idrees, Idrees Muhammad [إدريس محمد إدريس]. *Madhaahir al-Inhiraafaat al-Aqadiyyah ind al-Soofiyyah wa Atharuhaa al-Sayi ala al-Ummah al-Islaamiyyah* [مظاهر الانحرافات العقدية عند الصوفية وآثارها السيء على الأمة الإسلامية]. Riyadh: Maktabah al-Rushd. 1998.

Isa, Kamaal [كمال عيســـى]. *Nadharaat fi Mutaqidaat ibn Arabi* [نظران في معتقدات ابن عربي]. Jeddah: Daar al-Mujtama. 1986.

Islahi, Amin Ahsan. *How to Attain True Piety and Righteousness*. Safat, Kuwait: Islamic Book Publishers. 1982.

-----*Self-Purification and Development*. Delhi: Adam Publishers and Distributors. 2000.

al-Izzi, Dhiyaa al-Deen [ضياء الديـــن العـــزي]. *Silat al-Insaan bi-laah min Wajhah Nadhar al-Quraan al-Kareem wa al-Sunnah al-Nabawiyyah* [صلة الإنسان بالله من وجهة نضر القرآن والسنة النبويـــة]. Riyadh: Maktabah al-Ubaikaan. 1997.

Jameelah, Maryam. *Islam Versus the West*. Lahore, Pakistan: Muhammad Yusuf Khan. 1971.

al-Kalabadhi, Abu Bakr. *The Doctrine of the Sufis*. A. J. Arberry, trans. Cambridge: Cambridge University Press. 1989.

al-Kanadi, Abu Bilal Mustafa. *Mysteries of the Soul Expounded*. Jeddah: Abul-Qasim Publishing IIouse. 1994.

Karzoon, Anas [أنس كـــرزون]. *Manhaj al-Islaam fi Tazkiyah al-Nafs* [منهج الإسلام في تزكية النفس]. Jeddah: Daar Noor al-Maktabaat. 1997.

Khan, Muhammad Muhsin. *The Translation of the Meanings of Sahih al-Bukhari*. Riyadh: Darussalam Publishers and Distributors. 1997.

al-Khataabi, Hamad ibn Muhammad [حمد بن محمد الخطـــابي]. *Shan al-Duaa* [شأن الدعـــاء]. Damascus: Daar al-Thaqaafah al-Arabiyyah. 1992.

King James Version [of the Bible]. *PC Study Bible*. New Reference Library Computer Software.

Korten, David C. *When Corporations Rule the World*. West Hartford, CN and San Francisco: Kumarian Press Inc. and Berrett-Koehler Publishers, Inc. 1995.

al-Kurdi, Fauz bint Abdul Lateef [فوز بنت عبد اللطيف الكردي]. *Tahqeeq al-Uboodiyyah bi-Marifah al-Asmaa wa al-Sifaat* [تحقيق العبودية بمعرفة الأسماء والصفات]. Riyadh: Daar Taibah. 1421 A.H.

Lane, E.W. *Arabic-English Lexicon*. Cambridge, England: The Islamic Texts Society. 1984.

Larousse Dictionary of Beliefs and Religions. Edinburgh: Larousse. 1995.

Ludwig, Theodore. *The Sacred Paths of the East*. Upper Saddle River, NJ: Prentice-Hall. 2001.

al-Maaz, Nabeel Haamid [نبيل حامد المعلز]. *Al-Tazkiyah: Dharooratuhaa, Wasaailuhaa, Mawaaniuhaa* [التزكية: ضرورتها، وسائلها، موانعها]. Cairo: Daar al-Tauzee wa al-Nashr al-Islaami. 1998.

Manoochehri, Hossein. "Towards an Explanation of the Islamic Ideal of Human Perfection (With Emphasis on the Doctrine of Inner Jihad)." Ph.D. dissertation. University of Kansas. 1988.

Maroof, Bashaar [بشار معروف] and Shuaib al-Arnaaoot [شعيب الأرناؤوط]. *Tahreer Taqreeb al-Tahdheeb li-l-Haafidh Ahmad ibn Ali ibn Hajar al-Asqalaani* [تحرير تقريب التهذيب لحافظ أحمد بن على ابن حجر العسقلاني]. Beirut: Muassasah al-Risaalah. 1997.

Martin, David Ludwig. "Al-Fana' (Mystical Annihilation of the Soul) and Al-Baqa' (Subsistence of the Soul) in the Work of Abu al-Qasim al-Junayd al-Baghdadi." Ph.D. dissertation. University of California at Los Angeles. 1984.

Maudoodi, Abul Ala. *The Meaning of the Quran*. Lahore, Pakistan: Islamic Publications, Ltd. 1981.

al-Meedaani, Abdul Rahman Habankah [عبد الرحمن حبنكة الميداني]. *al-Akhlaaq al-Islaamiyyah* [الأخلاق الإسلامية]. Beirut: Daar al-Qalam. n.d.

Memon, Muhammad Umar. *Ibn Taimiya's Struggle Against Popular Religion*. The Hague: Mouton & Co. 1976.

al-Mizi, Yusuf [يوسف المزي]. *Tahdheeb al-Kamaal fi Asmaa al-Rijaal* [تهذيب الكمال في أسماء الرجال]. Beirut: Muassasah al-Risaalah. 1992.

al-Maraaghi, Ahmad Mustafa [أحمد مصطفى المراغي]. *Tafseer al-Maraaghi* [تفسير المراغي]. Beirut: Daar Ihyaa al-Turaath al-Arabi. n.d.

Murad, Khurram. *In the Early Hours: Reflections on Spiritual and Self Development*. Markfield, United Kingdom: Revival Publications. 2000.

al-Mutairi, Abdul Rahmaan. *Religious Extremism in the Lives of Contemporary Muslims.* Denver, CO: Al-Basheer Company for Publications and Translations. 2001.

Nadwi, Abul Hasan Ali. *The Four Pillars of Islam.* Lucknow, India: Academy of Islamic Research and Publications. 1976.

Nadwi, Sulaiman. *Worship in Islam.* Karachi: Darul Ishaat. 1994.

Naseer, Amaal bint Saalih [آمال بنت صالح نصير]. *Al-Taubah fi Dhau al-Quraan al-Kareem* [التوبة في ضوء القرآن الكريم]. Jeddah: Daar al-Andalus al-Khudhraa. 1998.

Naumsook, Abdullah Mustafa [عبد الله مصطفى نومسوك]. *Al-Boodhiyyah: Tareekhuhaa wa Aqaaiduhaa wa Alaaqah al-Soofiyyah biha* [البوذية: تاريخها وعقائدها وعلاقة الصوفية بها]. Riyadh: Adhwa al-Salaf. 1999.

al-Nawawi, Yahya [يحيى النووي]. *Sharh Matin al-Arbaeen al-Nawawiya* [شرح متن الأربعين النووية]. Jeddah: Daar al-Mujtama. 1986.

-----*Sharh Saheeh Muslim* [شرح صحيح مسلم]. Beirut: Daar al-Fikr, n.d.

New International Version [of the Bible]. *PC Study Bible.* New Reference Library Computer Software.

New King James Version [of the Bible]. *PC Study Bible.* New Reference Library Computer Software.

Peck, M. Scott. *Denial of the Soul: Spiritual and Medical Perspectives on Euthanasia and Morality.* New York: Harmony Books. 1997.

----- *People of the Lie: The Hope for Healing Evil.* New York: Touchstone Books. 1983.

al-Qaari, Abdul Azeez. "*Aqeeda* First... If they but Knew." *Al-Basheer.* March-April 1989. Vol. 2. No. 6.

al-Qaari, Ali ibn al-Sultaan [على بن سلطان القارئ]. *Mirqaat al-Mafaateeh Sharh Mishkaat al-Masaabeeh* [مرقاة المفاتيح شرح مشكاة المصابيح]. Multaan, Pakistan: Maktabah Hapaaniyah. n.d.

al-Qaasim, Mahmood [محمود القاسم]. *Al-Kashf an Haqeeqah al-Soofiyah li-Awal Marrah fi al-Tareekh* [الكشف عن حقيقة الصوفية لأول مرة في التأريخ]. Amman, Jordan: al-Maktabah al-Islaamiyah. 1413 A.H.

al-Qaasimi, Jamaal al-Deen [جمال الدين القاسمي]. *Mahaasin al-Taweel* [محاسن التأويل]. Cairo: Dar Ihyaa al-Kutub al-Arabi. n.d.

al-Qahtaani, Muhammad ibn Saeed [محمد بن سعيد القحطاني]. Introduction to Ahmad ibn Taimiyyah. *Tazkiyah al-Nafs* [تزكية النفس]. Riyadh: Daar al-Muslim. 1994.

al-Qaradhaawi, Yoosuf [يوسف الفرضاوي]. *al-Sabr fi al-Quraan* [الصبر في القرآن]. Beirut: Muassasah al-Risaalah. 1985.

al-Qasim, Abdul Malik. *Silent Moments: The Description of Before & After Death Aspects.* Riyadh: Darussalam. 1999.

al-Qurtubi, Abu Abdillaah Muhammad [أبو عبد الله محمد القرطبي]. *Al-Jaami li-Ahkaam al-Quraan* [الجامع لأحكام القرآن]. Beirut: Daar Ihyaa al-Turaath al-Arabi. 1966.

al-Qushairi, Abdul Kareem [عبد الكريم القشيري]. *Al-Risaalah al-Qushairiyyah* [الرسالة القشيرية]. Muhammad Ali Sabeeh. 1957.

Qutb, Muhammad [محمد قطب]. *Diraasaat fi Nafs al-Isnaaniyyah* [دراسات في نفس الإنسانية]. Beirut: Dar al-Shurooq. 1983.

Qutb, Sayyid [سيد قطب]. *Fi Dhilaal al-Quraan* [في ظلال القرآن]. Beirut: Daar al-Shurroq. 1981.

al-Raazi, al-Fakhar [الفخر الرازي]. *Al-Tafseer al-Kabeer* [التفسير الكبير]. Beirut: Daar Ihyaa al-Turaath al-Arabi. n.d.

al-Ramli, Muhammad Shoomaan [محمد الرملي]. *Mathal al-Hayaat al-Dunyaa fi al-Kitaab wa al-Sunnah wa Kalaam al-Ulamaa* [مثل الحياة الدنيا في الكتاب والسنة وكلام العلماء]. al-Khobar, Saudi Arabia: Daar ibn Affaan. 1995.

-----*Al-Mushawwiq ila Dhikrilaahi Taala* [المشوق إلى ذكر الله تعالى]. Al-Damaam, Saudi Arabia: Daar ibn al-Qayyim. 1421 A.H.

Rasheed, Maadoon [معدون رشيد]. *Qadhaayaa al-Lahu wa al-Tarfeeh bain al-Haajah al-Nafsiyyah wa al-Dhawaabit al-Shariyyah* [قضايا اللهو والترفيه بين الحاجة النفسية والضوابط الشرعية]. Riyadh: Dar Taibah. 1998.

Salmaan, Mashhoor Hasan [مشهور حسن سلمان]. Footnotes to Jalaal al-Deen al-Suyooti [جلال الدين السيوطي]. *Al-Amr bi-l-Itibaa wa al-Nahi an al-Ibtidaa* [الأمر بالاتباع والنهي عن الابتداع]. Al-Damaam, Saudi Arabia: Daar ibn al-Qayyim. 1995.

al-Sanadi, Abdul Qaadir [عبد القادر السندي]. *Kitaab ibn Arabi al-Soofi fi Meezaan al-Bahth wa al-Tahqeeq* [كتاب ابن عربي الصوفي في ميزان البحث والتحقيق]. Buraida, Saudi Arabia: Daar al-Bukhaari. 1991.

Shaakir, Ahmad [أحمد شاكر]. Footnotes to Ahmad ibn Hanbal. *Al-Musnad* [المسند]. Cairo: Daar al-Hadeeth. 1995.

al-Shaatibi, Ibraaheem [إبراهيم الشاطبي]. *Al-Muwaafaqaat fi Usool al-Shareeah* [الموافقات في أصول الشريعة]. Beirut: Daar al-Marafah. n.d.

al-Shaayi, Muhammad [محمد الشايع]. *Al-Furooq al-Laughawiyyah wa Atharahaa fi Tafseer al-Quran al-Kareem* [الفروق اللغوي وأثرها في تفسير القرآن الكريم]. Riyadh: Maktabah al-Ubaikaan. 1993.

Shahak, Israel. *Jewish History, Jewish Religion: The Weight of Three Thousand Years*. London: Pluto Press. 1997.

Shames, Laurence. *The Hunger for More: Searching for Values in an Age of Greed*. New York: Times Books. 1989.

al-Shaukaani, Muhammad ibn Ali [محمد بن علي الشوكاني]. *Fath al-Qadeer al-Jaami bain Fanna al-Riwaayah wa al-Diraayah min Ilm al-Tafseer* [فتح القدير الجامع بين الرواية والدراية من علم التفسير]. Egypt: Mustafa al-Baabi and sons. 1964.

-----*Tuhfah al-Dhaakireen* [تحفة الذاكرين]. Beirut: Daar al-Kutub al-Ilmiyah. 1988.

-----*Qatr al-Wali ala Hadeeth al-Wali* [قطر الولي على حديث الولي]. Beirut: Daar Ihyaa al-Turaath al-Arabi. n.d.

Shukri, Muwafaq Ahmad [موفق أحمد شكري]. *Ahl al-Fitrah wa man fi Hukmihim* [أهل الفترة ومن في حكمهم]. Damascus: Daar ibn Katheer. 1988.

Siddiqi, Abdul Hameed, trans. *Sahih Muslim*. Beirut: Dar al-Arabia. n.d.

Suhrawardi, Shahab-ud-Din. *The Awarif-ul-Maarif*. Lahore, Pakistan: Sh. Muhammad Ashraf. 1991.

al-Suyooti, Jalaal al-Deen [جلال الدين السيوطي]. *al-Durr fi al-Tafseer al-Mathoor* [الدر في التفسير المأثور]. Beirut: Daar al-Kutub al-Ilmiyyah. 1990.

al-Tabari, Muhammad ibn Jareer [محمد بن جرير الطبري]. *Jaami al-Bayaan an Taweel Aayi al-Quraan* [جامع البيان عن تأويل آي القرآن]. Beirut: Daar al-Fikr. 1988.

al-Tiraiqi, Abdullah ibn Muhammad [عبد الله بن محمد الطريقي]. *Al-Israaf: Diraasah Fiqhiyyah Muqaaranah bain al-Madhaahib al-Arbaah* [الإسراف: دراسة فقهية مقارنة بين المذاهب الأربعة]. Published by its author. 1992.

al-Tooni, Fareed [فريد التوني]. *Uboodiyyah al-Kaainaat li-Rabb al-Alaameen* [عبودية الكائنات لرب العالمين]. Jeddah: Maktabah al-Dhiyaa. 1992.

Trimingham, J. Spencer. *The Sufi Orders in Islam*. New York: Oxford University Press. 1998.

Umar, Ahmad Mukhtaar [أحمد مختار عمر], and Abd al-Aal Saalim Mukram [عبد العال سالم مكرم]. *Mujam al-Qiraa`aat al-Quraaniyyah* [معجم القراءات القرآنية]. Intishaaraat Uswah. 1991.

"U.S. wants its MTV to get message out in Arab world." CNN.com. Nov. 19, 2001.

Uthmaan, Ali Ahmad [علـى أحمـد عثمـان]. *Tazkiyah al-Nafs wa Makaanatuhaa fi al-Islaam* [تزكية النفس ومكانتها في الإسلام]. 1416 A.H.

Watt, Montgomery. *The Faith of Practice of al-Ghazali.* Chicago: Kazi Publications. 1982.

Webster's Encyclopedic Unabridged Dictionary of the English Language. New York: Portland House. 1989.

Wizaarah al-Auqaaf wa al-Shuoon al-Islaamiyyah [Ministry of Endowments and Islamic Affairs]. *al-Mausooah al-Fiqhiyyah* [الموسوعة الفقهية]. Kuwait: Wizaarah al-Auqaaf wa al-Shuoon al-Islaamiyyah. 1988.

Yassine, Abdessalam. *Winning the Modern World for Islam.* Iowa City, IA: Justice and Spirituality Publishing, Inc. 2000.

al-Zajjaaj, Ibraaheem [إبراهيم الزجاج]. *Maani Al-Quran wa Iraabuhu* [معاني القرآن وإعرابه]. Beirut: Aalim al-Kitaab. 1988.

Zarabozo, Jamaal. *Commentary on the Forty Hadith of al-Nawawi*. Boulder, CO: al-Basheer Company for Publications and Translations. 1998.

-----*How to Approach and Understand the Quran.* Boulder, CO: Al-Basheer Company for Publications and Translations. 1999.

-----"Islam and Innovations I: The Meaning of *Bida,*" *Al-Basheer.* Vol. 1, No. 4. Nov.-Dec. 1987.

Quranic Verses Cited

General Index